VISUAL QUICKSTART GUIDE

QuarkXPress 6

FOR MACINTOSH AND WINDOWS

Elaine Weinmann
Peter Lourekas

 **Peachpit Press**

For Alicia

Visual QuickStart Guide
QuarkXPress 6 for Macintosh and Windows
Elaine Weinmann and Peter Lourekas

Peachpit Press
1249 Eighth Street
Berkeley, CA 94710
510/524-2178
800/283-9444
510/524-2221 (fax)

Find us on the World Wide Web at: www.peachpit.com

Visual QuickStart Guide is a trademark of Peachpit Press,
a division of Pearson Education

Cover design: The Visual Group
Interior design and illustrations: Elaine Weinmann and
    Peter Lourekas

Colophon
This book was created with QuarkXPress 5 on a Power
Macintosh G4 dual 500 and a Power Macintosh G4 450. The pri-
mary fonts used are New Baskerville, Gill Sans, Franklin Gothic,
Caflisch Script, Officina, and Futura from Adobe Systems Inc.

Permissions
Definitions on page vi from *The Oxford Encyclopedic English
Dictionary,* 1991, edited by Joyce M. Hawkins and Robert Allen,
reprinted by permission of Oxford University Press.

Notice of Rights

Notice of Liability

ISBN 0-321-20548-0

9 8 7 6 5 4

Printed and bound in the United States of America

Our thanks to

Nancy Aldrich-Ruenzel, publisher of Peachpit Press

Cary Norsworthy, editor

Marjorie Baer, managing editor

Victor Gavenda, technical editor

Gary-Paul Prince, publicist

Keasley Jones, associate publisher

Lisa Brazieal, production editor

And the rest of the terrific staff at *Peachpit Press*

Glen Turpin, communications manager at Quark Inc., *Tim Banister*, product manager, and the beta team, who answered our technical questions

Cyndie Shaffstall, at *thepowerxchange.com*, for supplying us with information about Quark XTensions

Nathan Olson, freelance writer, for helping us revise this edition

Jeff Seaver, freelance writer and illustrator, for helping us revise this edition

Rebecca Pepper, copy editor

Steve Rath, indexer

quark[1] /kwɑːk/ *n. Physics* any of a group of (originally three) postulated components of elementary particles Quarks are held to carry a charge one-third or two-thirds that of the proton Many predictions of this theory have been corroborated by experiments but free quarks have yet to be observed. In a sense, quark theory recapitulates at a deeper level efforts earlier this century to explain all atomic properties in terms of electrons, protons, and neutrons [coined by M Gell-Mann, 1964, from phrase 'Three quarks for Muster Mark!' in James Joyce's *Finnegans Wake* (1939)]

quark[2] /kwɑːk/ *n.* a type of low-fat curd cheese.

From The Oxford Encyclopedic English Dictionary, 1991, Oxford University Press

Table of Contents

Note! New or substantially changed features are listed in **boldface.** In addition to the changes we have noted, there are dozens and dozens of new sidebars, introductory paragraphs, and other improvements throughout the book—more than we could note.

Chapter 1: **The Basics**

Chapter 2: **Startup**

Chapter 5: **Text Flow**

Chapter 6: **Formats**

Chapter 8: **Tables and Tabs**

Chapter 9: **Pictures**

Chapter 11: **Pictures and Text**

Chapter 12: **Lines**

Chapter 20: **Libraries**

Chapter 23: **Preferences**

The Basics 1

"Beauty! I've starved myself since you forgot about me. Now at least I shall die in peace…"
"Live!" cried Beauty. "And let us marry. How could I live without you, my dearest Beast?"

1 *A text box with a frame*

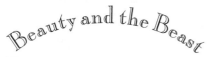

2 *Text on a path*

3 *A picture in a picture box (with a delicate .5-point frame)*

4 *A picture in a box without a frame*

What is QuarkXPress?

QuarkXPress is a page layout application. A page layout application is a central gathering place for text, pictures, lines, and tables, all of which together make up a page or series of pages. QuarkXPress can be used to produce anything from a tiny hang tag for a line of apparel to a multiple-volume encyclopedia. A finished layout can be output on a home laser printer (newsletter, party invitation, etc.), output on a high-end imagesetter for final printing by a commercial printer (book, magazine, brochure, etc.), or exported for online viewing.

This chapter is a reference guide to the basic QuarkXPress features. In the remaining chapters you'll learn how to actually build pages and page elements.

The QuarkXPress building blocks

■ To place text on a page, you must type or import text into a rectangular or irregularly shaped **text box 1** or along the edge of a Bézier **text path 2**.

Similarly, to place a picture on a page, you must first create a container for it, whether it's a simple rectangular or intricate Bézier **picture box.** Then you can import a picture into it. If you want the border of a text or picture box to print, you must apply a frame to it **3**–**4**.

Lines can be straight or curved and function as decorative elements. **Tables** hold a checkerboard of cells, which can contain text or pictures.

■ A text box, text path, picture box, table, or line is called an **item.** The picture or text a box contains is called its **contents.**

A picture or text box can also be rendered contentless, after which it functions strictly as a colored shape.

■ Tool selection appears as a step in most of the instructions in this book. To create an item, for example, you'll use an item creation tool, such as the Line tool or the Rectangle Text Box tool.

To move a whole item or a group of items across a page, you'll use the **Item** tool 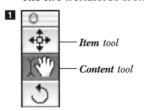, since you'll be working with the overall container.

To copy/paste, delete, or restyle text or a picture after it's input or imported, you'll use the **Content** tool, since you'll be working with the contents of, not the outside of, the container.

For some tasks the Item and Content tools are interchangeable. For example, the Content tool can be used to reshape or resize items, or to select multiple items, and the Item tool can be used to import a picture.

■ An item or its contents must be selected before either one can be modified ■–■.

■ The readouts on the Measurements palette vary depending on which tool and which kind of item are selected. The left side of the palette displays information pertaining to an item—a picture box, text box, text path, table, or line—if that item and the Item or Content tool are selected (■, next page). Item information includes dimensions and location on the page.

If an item is selected with the Content tool, the right side of the Measurements palette displays content information about that item (e.g., picture size, font, type style) (■, next page). If a line and the Item or Content tool are selected, the right side of the Measurements palette displays line style and width information. The palette is blank when no items are selected (■, next page).

The two workhorse tools

— *Item* tool
— *Content* tool

■ *A picture box that **isn't selected***

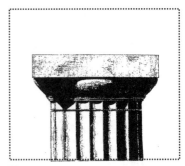

■ *Eight handles display when a box is selected.*

X:	3p	W:	18p	◿	0°
Y:	4p	H:	16p	Cols:	1

1 *The Measurements palette when the* **Item** *tool and a* **text box** *are selected*

Item information   *Content information*

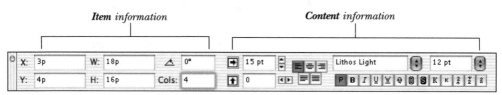

X:	3p	W:	18p	◿	0°	➡	15 pt		Lithos Light		12 pt	
Y:	4p	H:	16p	Cols:	4	⬆	0		P B *I* U ...			

2 *The Measurements palette when the* **Content** *tool and* **text** *are selected*

3 *The Measurements palette is* **blank** *when* **no** *items are selected. Select an item to make the palette light up.*

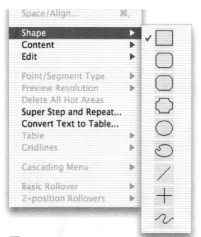

4 *Using the Item > **Shape** submenu, you can convert one shape into another, such as a box into a line or a standard box into a Bézier box.*

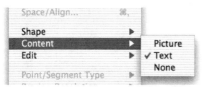

5 *Using the Item > **Content** submenu, you can change a text box into a picture box, or vice versa, or make any box contentless. You can change the content of a table cell, too.*

If it's not one thing, it's another

Our first encounter with QuarkXPress was in 1988 (ancient history in the software world), and we were impressed with its precision but frustrated by the inflexibility of its parent/child architecture. New items were drawn inside—and constrained by—existing items.

Now QuarkXPress is as flexible as it originally was brittle. Not only can you place an item anywhere, you can turn just about anything (text box, text path, picture box, or line) into something else **4**–**5**. If you're brand new to QuarkXPress (or are chronically indecisive), simply ignore this aspect of QuarkXPress for the moment. But just to whet your appetite, these are a few of the easy conversions you can make:

- Change a text box into a picture box, a line into a box or a text path, and vice versa.
- Make a text box, picture box, or table cell contentless—capable only of being recolored or resized (the contents of either kind of box are deleted during the conversion).
- Change a standard box into a Bézier box or Bézier line, or vice versa.
- Change a text character into a picture box.
- Convert a text box into a table; convert a table into a text box or a group of items.

Pet Living

The Magazine for Pet Lovers

December 2002

A transparent text box on top of a picture box

SPECIAL HOLIDAY ISSUE
Kibble Snacks for Kwanzaa

Helping Your Pet Cope with Holiday Depression

Cat Treats for Chanukah

Type on a Bézier path

A Bézier picture box with a frame

A line

Decorating the Doghouse

Schnauzer Strudel

PLUS

Cake Decorations

The Best Pet Gifts

*The QuarkXPress building blocks: **Picture boxes, text boxes, text paths, lines** (and tables, not illustrated).*

What's an HTML text box?

When we refer to HTML text boxes throughout the book, we mean text boxes in Web layouts for which the Convert to Graphic on Export box is *unchecked* in the Item > Modify dialog box.

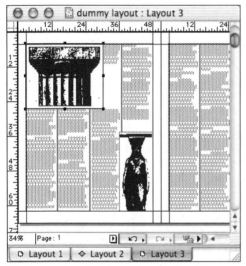

1 *This is a QuarkXPress **project window.** There are three **layouts** in this project, as indicated by the three tabs at the bottom of the project window. Only one layout can be displayed at a time.*

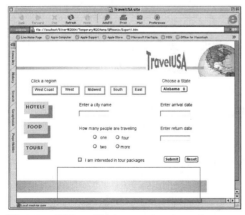

2 *A QuarkXPress Web layout, viewed in a **browser***

Projects and layouts 6.0!

Just as a welcome innovation freed QuarkXPress users from the confines of constraining boxes over a decade ago, version 6 introduces an equally significant innovation: projects and multiple layouts. What were previously called "documents" are now called "projects."* Each project, in turn, can hold one or more "layouts" **1**. Each layout has its own Layout Properties settings (width, height, margin guides, column guides, etc.) and its own output medium (print or Web). Text can even be synchronized across multiple layouts, making it easy to standardize content between print and Web work (see Chapter 21).

We offer a more thorough introduction to this new substructure in the next chapter, and throughout the book we discuss the many repercussions it has on the day-to-day operations of the program.

Print layouts and Web layouts

As you learn how to create print layouts, starting with the next chapter, *Startup,* bear in mind that most, but not all, of the features that are used to create print layouts are also available for creating Web layouts (text features that aren't available for Web layouts are listed on page 136). The Web features of QuarkXPress **2** are covered in Chapter 19.

You can build a Web page in QuarkXPress using editable HTML text; rasterized text; pictures; tables; interactive elements, such as image maps and rollovers; buttons; and forms with text entry fields and check boxes. When your Web layout is finished, you can preview it using whichever browser is currently installed in your operating system. In a print layout you can create boxes, lines, text paths, and tables; in a Web layout, you can create all of the above, plus forms and form controls.

*The words "file" and "project" are interchangeable.

The QuarkXPress screen in Mac OS X

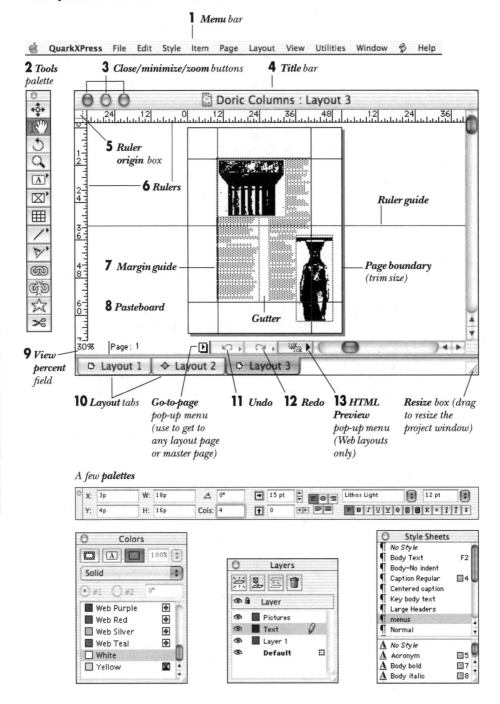

1 *Menu bar*

2 *Tools palette*

3 *Close/minimize/zoom buttons*

4 *Title bar*

5 *Ruler origin box*

6 *Rulers*

Ruler guide

7 *Margin guide*

Page boundary (trim size)

8 *Pasteboard*

Gutter

9 *View percent field*

10 *Layout tabs*

Go-to-page pop-up menu (use to get to any layout page or master page)

11 *Undo*

12 *Redo*

13 *HTML Preview pop-up menu (Web layouts only)*

Resize box (drag to resize the project window)

A few **palettes**

Key to the QuarkXPress screen in Mac OS X

1 *Menu bar*
Press any menu name to access a list of commands. XTensions are also accessed via the menu bar.

2 *Tools palette*
Most of the palettes are opened from the Window menu: Tools (and Web Tools), Measurements, Page Layout, Style Sheets, Colors, Trap Information, Lists, Layers, Profile Information, Synchronized Text, Hyperlinks, Index, Sequences, and Placeholders. Many of the commands found under the menu bar can be accessed more quickly from the Measurements palette. Palettes that are open when you quit QuarkXPress will reopen when the application is relaunched.

3 *Close/minimize/zoom buttons* 6.0!
To close a file or a palette, click its close (red) button. Click the minimize (yellow) button to stow it in the Dock. Click the zoom (green) button to enlarge a window or the Page Layout palette to maximum size.

4 *Title bar*
The name of the project and the currently displayed layout are displayed on the project title bar. Drag the bar to move the project window.

5 *Ruler origin box*
Drag from the ruler origin box to reposition the intersection of the horizontal and vertical rulers, also known as the zero point. Click the ruler origin box again to reset the zero point to the upper left corner of the page. Each layout can have a different ruler origin position.

6 *Rulers*
You can choose inches, inches decimal, picas, points, millimeters, centimeters, ciceros, or agates as the default measurement increment for rulers and entry fields. In a Web layout, you can also choose pixels. Choose View > Show Rulers or Hide Rulers. Non-printing guides, which are dragged from the vertical and horizontal rulers, are used for aligning and positioning objects.

7 *Margin guides*
Margin guides don't print. Choose View > Show Guides or Hide Guides.

8 *Pasteboard*
This functions as a scratchboard for creating items or as a holding area for storing items for later use. Web layouts don't have a pasteboard.

9 *View percent field*
The zoom level of a layout is displayed, and can be modified, in this field.

10 *Layout tabs* 6.0!
Display a layout by clicking its tab. Print layouts have a ⬦ icon; Web layouts have a ⬦ icon.

11 *Undo* 6.0!
Click to undo the last undoable edit, or choose from the pop-up menu.

12 *Redo* 6.0!
Click to redo the last redoable edit, or choose from the pop-up menu.

13 *HTML Preview* (*Web layouts only*)
Click this button to display the current Web layout in the default browser, or choose from the pop-up menu to display the layout in one of the currently installed browsers.

QuarkXPress Screen: Mac OS X

The QuarkXPress screen in Windows

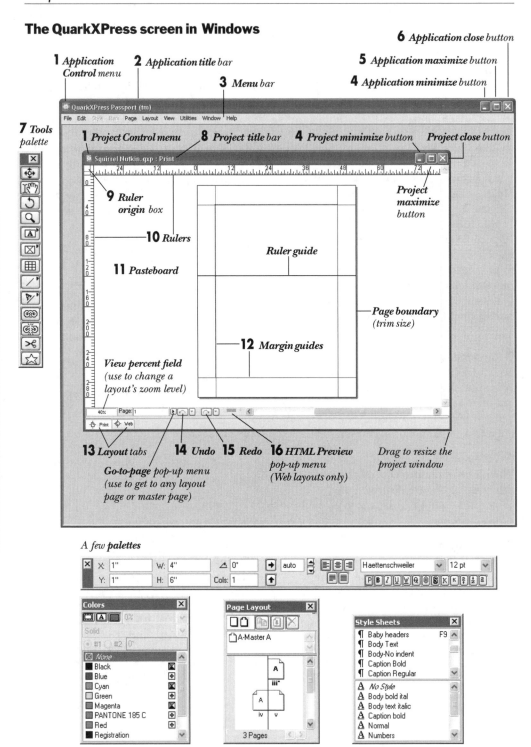

1 *Application Control* menu **2** *Application title* bar

3 *Menu* bar

6 *Application close* button
5 *Application maximize* button
4 *Application minimize* button

7 *Tools palette*

1 *Project Control menu* **8** *Project title* bar **4** *Project mimimize* button *Project close* button

9 *Ruler origin* box

Project maximize button

10 *Rulers*

Ruler guide

11 *Pasteboard*

Page boundary (trim size)

12 *Margin guides*

View percent field (use to change a layout's zoom level)

13 *Layout tabs* **14** *Undo* **15** *Redo* **16** *HTML Preview pop-up menu (Web layouts only)* *Drag to resize the project window*

Go-to-page pop-up menu (use to get to any layout page or master page)

A few **palettes**

X: 1"   W: 4"   ⊿ 0°   → auto   Haettenschweiler   12 pt
Y: 1"   H: 6"   Cols: 1   ↑   P B I U W Q O S K K

Colors
0%
Solid
#1 ○ #2 0°
None
Black
Blue
Cyan
Green
Magenta
PANTONE 185 C
Red
Registration

Page Layout
A-Master A

A
iii"

A
iv v

3 Pages

Style Sheets
¶ Baby headers   F9
¶ Body Text
¶ Body-No indent
¶ Caption Bold
¶ Caption Regular
A No Style
A Body bold ital
A Body text italic
A Caption bold
A Normal
A Numbers

Key to the QuarkXPress screen in Windows

1 *Application (or project) Control menu*
The application Control menu commands are Restore, Move, Size, Minimize, Maximize, and Close. The project Control menu commands are Restore, Move, Size, Minimize, Maximize, Close, and Next.

2 *Application title bar*
The application title bar contains the name of the application. If a project is maximized, the project name appears in the application title bar.

3 *Menu bar*
Press any menu name to access commands.

4 *Application (or project) minimize button*
Click the application minimize button to shrink the application to an icon on the Taskbar; click the icon to restore the application window to its previous size.

Click the project minimize button to shrink the project to an icon at the bottom left corner of the application window. Click the icon to restore the project window to its previous size.

5 *Application (or project) maximize/ restore button*
Click the application or project restore button to restore a window to its previous size. When a window is at its restored size, the restore button turns into a maximize button. Click the maximize button to enlarge the window.

6 *Close buttons*
To close the application, a project, a dialog box, or a palette, click its close button.

7 *Tools palette*
Most of the palettes are opened from the Window menu: Tools (and Web Tools), Measurements, Page Layout, Style Sheets, Colors, Trap Information, Lists, Layers, Profile Information, Hyperlinks, Index, Synchronized Text, Sequences, and Placeholders.

8 *Project title bar*
The name of the project and the currently displayed layout are shown on the title bar. Drag the title bar to move the layout within the application window (this won't work if the project window is maximized).

9 *Ruler origin box*
Drag from the ruler origin box to reposition the intersection of the horizontal and vertical rulers (the "zero point"). Click the ruler origin box again to reset the zero point to the upper left corner of the page. Each layout can have a different ruler origin position.

10 *Rulers*
You can choose inches, inches decimal, picas, points, millimeters, centimeters, ciceros, or agates as the default measurement increment for rulers and entry fields. In a Web layout, you can also choose pixels. Choose View > Show Rulers or Hide Rulers. Non-printing guides, which are dragged from the vertical and horizontal rulers, are used for aligning and positioning objects.

11 *Pasteboard*
This functions as a scratchboard for creating items or as a holding area for storing items for later use. Web layouts don't have a pasteboard.

12 *Margin guides*
Margin don't print. Choose View > Show Guides or Hide Guides.

13 *Layout tabs* **6.0!**
Display a layout by clicking its tab. Print layouts have a ⊞ icon; Web layouts have a ⊕ icon.

14 *Undo* **6.0!**
Click to undo the last undoable edit, or choose from the pop-up menu.

15 *Redo* **6.0!**
Click to redo the last redoable edit, or choose from the pop-up menu.

16 *HTML Preview* (*Web layouts only*)
Click this button to display the current Web layout in the default browser, or choose from the pop-up menu to display the layout in one of the currently installed browsers.

QuarkXPress Screen: Windows

The QuarkXPress menus in Mac OS X

QuarkXPress

About QuarkXPress™...	
Preferences...	⌥⇧⌘Y
Services	▶
Hide QuarkXPress	⌘H
Hide Others	⌥⌘H
Show All	
Quit QuarkXPress	⌘Q

6.0! *The Preferences command is on this menu.*

File

New	▶
Open	▶
Close	⌘W
Save	⌘S
Save as...	⌥⌘S
Revert to Saved	
Get Text...	⌘E
Save Text...	⌥⌘E
Append...	⌥⌘A
Export	▶
Save Page as EPS...	⌥⇧⌘S
Collect for Output...	
Page Setup...	⌥⌘P
Print...	⌘P

Edit

Undo Text Box Change	⌘Z
Redo Text Box Change	⇧⌘Z
Cut	⌘X
Copy	⌘C
Paste	⌘V
Paste In place	⌥⇧⌘V
Clear	
Select All	⌘A
Show Clipboard	
Find/Change	⌘F
Style Sheets...	⇧F11
Colors...	⇧F12
H&Js...	⌥⌘J
Lists...	
Dashes & Stripes...	
Print Styles...	
Tagging Rules...	
Hyperlinks...	
Jabberwocky Sets...	
Underline Styles...	
Menus...	
Meta Tags...	
CSS Font Families...	
Cascading Menus...	

Style

Font	▶
Size	▶
Type Style	▶
Color	▶
Shade	▶
Horizontal/Vertical Scale...	
Track...	
Baseline Shift...	
Character...	⇧⌘D
Character Style Sheet	▶
Text to Box	
Alignment	▶
Leading...	⇧⌘E
Formats...	⇧⌘F
Tabs...	⇧⌘T
Rules...	⇧⌘N
Paragraph Style Sheet	▶
Flip Horizontal	
Flip Vertical	
Synchronize Text...	
Unsynchronize Text...	
Hyperlink	▶
Anchor	▶
Underline Styles	▶

Text *selected*

Style

Line Style	▶
Arrowheads	▶
Width	▶
Color	▶
Shade	▶
Hyperlink	▶
Anchor	▶

Line *selected*

Style

Color	▶
Shade	▶
Negative	⇧⌘-
Contrast...	⇧⌘C
Halftone...	⇧⌘H
Flip Horizontal	
Flip Vertical	
Center Picture	⇧⌘M
Fit Picture To Box	⇧⌘F
Fit Picture To Box (Proportionally)	⌥⇧⌘F
Fit Box To Picture	
Hyperlink	▶
Anchor	▶

Picture *selected*

Item

Modify...	⌘M
Frame...	⌘B
Runaround...	⌘T
Clipping...	⌥⌘T
Duplicate	⌘D
Step and Repeat...	⌥⌘D
Delete	⌘K
Group	⌘G
Ungroup	⌘U
Constrain	
Lock	F6
Merge	▶
Split	▶
Send to Back	⇧F5
Bring to Front	F5
Space/Align...	⌘,
Shape	▶
Content	▶
Edit	▶
Point/Segment Type	▶
Preview Resolution	▶
Delete All Hot Areas	
Super Step and Repeat...	
Convert Text to Table...	
Table	▶
Gridlines	▶
Cascading Menu	▶
Basic Rollover	▶
2-position Rollovers	▶

Page

Insert...	
Delete...	
Move...	
Master Guides...	
Section...	
Previous	
Next	
First	
Last	
Go to...	⌘J
Display	▶
Preview HTML	▶

Layout

New...	
Duplicate...	
Delete	
Layout Properties...	
Previous	
Next	
First	
Last	
Go to	▶

View

Fit in Window	⌘0
50%	
75%	
Actual Size	⌘1
200%	
Thumbnails	⇧F6
Hide Guides	F7
Show Baseline Grid	⌥F7
✓ Snap to Guides	⇧F7
Show Rulers	⌘R
Hide Invisibles	⌘I
Hide Visual Indicators	
Show Tagged Content	
Hide Full Res Previews	

Utilities

Check Spelling	▶
Auxiliary Dictionary...	
Edit Auxiliary...	
Suggested Hyphenation...	⌥⇧⌘H
Hyphenation Exceptions...	
Usage...	
XTensions Manager...	
Component Status...	
PPD Manager...	
Profile Manager...	
Guide Manager...	
Build Index...	
Jabber	
Tracking Edit...	
Kerning Table Edit...	
Remove Manual Kerning	
Line Check	▶
Convert Old Underlines	

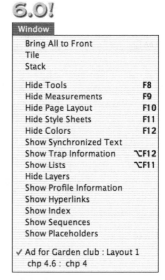

Window

Bring All to Front	
Tile	
Stack	
Hide Tools	F8
Hide Measurements	F9
Hide Page Layout	F10
Hide Style Sheets	F11
Hide Colors	F12
Show Synchronized Text	
Show Trap Information	⌥F12
Show Lists	⌥F11
Hide Layers	
Show Profile Information	
Show Hyperlinks	
Show Index	
Show Sequences	
Show Placeholders	
✓ Ad for Garden club : Layout 1	
chp 4.6 : chp 4	

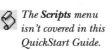

*The **Scripts** menu isn't covered in this QuickStart Guide.*

Help

Help Topics

The Menus in Mac OS X

The QuarkXPress menus in Windows

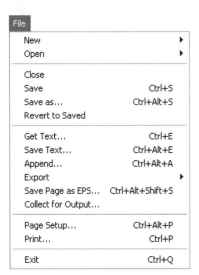

File

New	▶
Open	▶
Close	
Save	Ctrl+S
Save as...	Ctrl+Alt+S
Revert to Saved	
Get Text...	Ctrl+E
Save Text...	Ctrl+Alt+E
Append...	Ctrl+Alt+A
Export	▶
Save Page as EPS...	Ctrl+Alt+Shift+S
Collect for Output...	
Page Setup...	Ctrl+Alt+P
Print...	Ctrl+P
Exit	Ctrl+Q

Edit

Undo Text Box Change	Ctrl+Z
Redo Text Box Change	Ctrl+Y
Cut	Ctrl+X
Copy	Ctrl+C
Paste	Ctrl+V
Paste In Place	Ctrl+Alt+Shift+V
Paste Special...	
Delete	
Select All	Ctrl+A
Links...	
Object	
Insert Object...	
Show Clipboard	
Find/Change	Ctrl+F
Preferences...	Ctrl+Alt+Shift+Y
Style Sheets...	Shift+F11
Colors...	Shift+F12
H&Js...	Ctrl+Shift+F11
Lists...	
Dashes & Stripes...	
Print Styles...	
Tagging Rules...	
Hyperlinks...	
Jabberwocky Sets...	
Underline Styles...	
Menus...	
Meta Tags...	
CSS Font Families...	
Cascading Menus...	

Style

Font	▶
Size	▶
Type Style	▶
Color	▶
Shade	▶
Horizontal/Vertical Scale...	
Track...	
Baseline Shift...	
Character...	Ctrl+Shift+D
Character Style Sheet	▶
Text to Box	
Alignment	▶
Leading...	Ctrl+Shift+E
Formats...	Ctrl+Shift+F
Tabs...	Ctrl+Shift+T
Rules...	Ctrl+Shift+N
Paragraph Style Sheet	▶
Flip Horizontal	
Flip Vertical	
Synchronize Text...	
Unsynchronize Text...	
Hyperlink	▶
Anchor	▶
Underline Styles	▶

Text *selected*

Style

Line Style	▶
Arrowheads	▶
Width	▶
Color	▶
Shade	▶
Hyperlink	▶
Anchor	▶

Line *selected*

Style

Color	▶
Shade	▶
Negative	Ctrl+Shift+-
Contrast...	Ctrl+Shift+O
Halftone...	Ctrl+Shift+H
Flip Horizontal	
Flip Vertical	
Center Picture	Ctrl+Shift+M
Fit Picture To Box	Ctrl+Shift+F
Fit Picture To Box (Proportionally)	Ctrl+Alt+Shift+F
Fit Box To Picture	
Hyperlink	▶
Anchor	▶

Picture *selected*

Item

Modify...	Ctrl+M
Frame...	Ctrl+B
Runaround...	Ctrl+T
Clipping...	Ctrl+Alt+T
Duplicate	Ctrl+D
Step and Repeat...	Ctrl+Alt+D
Delete	Ctrl+K
Group	Ctrl+G
Ungroup	Ctrl+U
Constrain	
Lock	F6
Merge	▶
Split	▶
Send Backward	Ctrl+Shift+F5
Send to Back	Shift+F5
Bring Forward	Ctrl+F5
Bring to Front	F5
Space/Align...	Ctrl+,
Shape	▶
Content	▶
Edit	▶
Point/SegmentType	▶
Preview Resolution	▶
Delete All Hot Areas	
Super Step and Repeat...	
Convert Text to Table...	
Table	▶
Gridlines	▶
Cascading Menu	▶
Basic Rollover	▶
2-position Rollovers	▶

View

Fit in Window	Ctrl+0
50%	
75%	
✔ Actual Size	Ctrl+1
200%	
Thumbnails	Shift+F6
Hide Guides	F7
Show Baseline Grid	Ctrl+F7
✔ Snap to Guides	Shift+F7
Hide Rulers	Ctrl+R
Show Invisibles	Ctrl+I
Hide Visual Indicators	
Hide full-res previews.	

Page

Insert...	
Delete...	
Move...	
Master Guides...	
Section...	
Previous	
Next	
First	
Last	
Go to...	Ctrl+J
Display	▶
Preview HTML	▶

Utilities

Check Spelling	▶
Auxiliary Dictionary...	
Edit Auxiliary...	
Suggested Hyphenation...	Ctrl+H
Hyphenation Exceptions...	
Usage...	
XTensions Manager...	
Component Status...	
PPD Manager...	
Use German (Reformed)	
Profile Manager...	
Show Tagged Content	
Guide Manager...	
Build Index...	
Jabber	
Tracking Edit...	
Kerning Table Edit...	
Remove Manual Kerning	
Line Check	▶
Convert Old Underlines	

Layout

New...	
Duplicate...	
Delete	
Layout Properties...	
Previous	
Next	
First	
Last	
Go to	▶

Window

Cascade	
Tile Horizontally	
Tile Vertically	
Arrange Icons	
Close All	
Hide Tools	F8
Hide Measurements	F9
Hide Page Layout	F4
Hide Style Sheets	F11
Hide Colors	F12
Show Synchronized Text	
Show Trap Information	Ctrl+F12
Show Lists	Ctrl+F11
Show Layers	
Show Profile Information	
Hide Hyperlinks	
Show Index	
Show Sequences	
Show Placeholders	
✔ 1 Squirrel Nutkin.qxp : Print	
2 Import tests.qxp : Printsly web	

Help

Contents	F1
Search...	
Index...	
About QuarkXPress(tm)...	

Dialog boxes

Dialog boxes are like fill-in forms with multiple choices. The various methods of indicating one's choices are shown in the illustrations on this page and the next. Numbers can be typed into fields in any of the measurement units that are used in QuarkXPress. Click OK or press Return/ Enter to exit a dialog box and implement the indicated changes.

A dialog box can be opened from a menu or via its assigned keyboard shortcut. A dialog box will open when any menu item that has an ellipsis (…) is chosen.

TIP In any dialog box, you can press Tab to highlight the next field or press Shift-Tab to highlight the previous field.

TIP For some dialog boxes, you can use the Cmd-Z/Ctrl-Z shortcut while the dialog box is open to restore the last-used values.

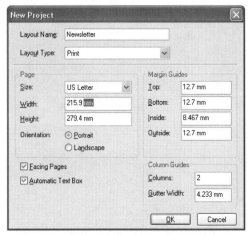

*In Windows, if you press **Alt** plus the letter on the keyboard that corresponds to an **underlined letter** in a dialog box, that field will become highlighted. For example, in the dialog box illustrated above, pressing Alt-W would cause the Width field to become highlighted.*

*To **move** a dialog box, drag its title bar.*

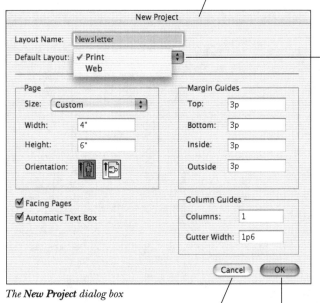

*In Mac OS X, click a double arrowhead to open a **pop-up menu**; in Windows, it's a single downward-pointing arrowhead.*

*The **New Project** dialog box*

*Click **Cancel** (or press **Esc**) to exit a box with no changes taking effect.*

*Click **OK** or press **Return/Enter** on the keyboard to exit a box and accept the new settings. You can press Return/Enter for any highlighted button, such as Save.*

It's all a blank

If the currently selected text or items have different values, the corresponding field will be blank. For example, if highlighted text contains both 8 pt. and 12 pt. leading, the Leading field will be blank, as in the Leading field in the illustration below.

Dialog box panes

In many dialog boxes, such as Modify and Paragraph Attributes **1**, related panes are housed under one roof (one-stop shopping!). In most cases, you'll see a series of tabs lined up across the top; simply click a tab to display that pane. In the Preferences dialog box, click a category on the list on the left side to switch between panes.

Tab availability will vary depending on what type of item or items are selected. If you were to select a text box, for example, and choose Item > Modify, you could then change the Vertical Alignment for the box in the Text pane, click the Frame tab, choose frame specifications, click the Box tab, add a background color, and so on. Or with Item > Modify open for a picture, you could change settings in the Box, Picture, Frame, Runaround, Clipping, and OPI tabs.

*Click a **tab** to display a pane.*

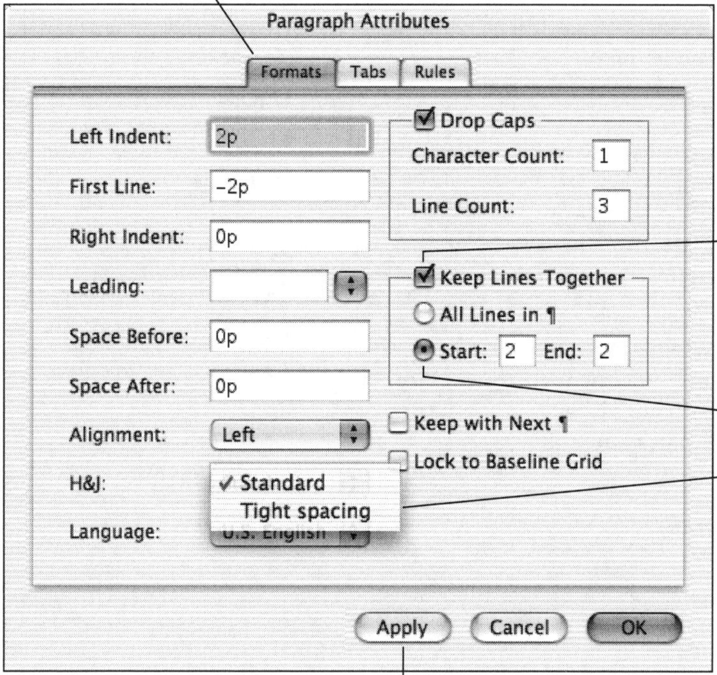

Paragraph Attributes

| Formats | Tabs | Rules |

Left Indent: `2p`

First Line: `-2p`

Right Indent: `0p`

Leading: [ ] [⇕]

Space Before: `0p`

Space After: `0p`

Alignment: [Left ⇕]

H&J:

Language:

✓ Standard
  Tight spacing

☑ Drop Caps
Character Count: `1`
Line Count: `3`

☑ Keep Lines Together
○ All Lines in ¶
● Start: `2` End: `2`

☐ Keep with Next ¶
☐ Lock to Baseline Grid

(Apply) (Cancel) (OK)

*A **check box** option can be clicked on or off.*

*Only one **radio** button can be on at a time in a related group.*

*Press/click to choose from a **pop-up** menu.*

*Click **Apply** (or press **Cmd-A** in Mac OS X) to preview modifications in the layout with the dialog box open. Press **Tab** to execute a change while a dialog box is open.*

The QuarkXPress palettes*

The Tools palette

The Tools palette contains 30 tools, which are used for item creation and editing.

- To open the Tools palette, choose Window > Show Tools (F8).

- Choose a visible tool by clicking on it; choose a hidden tool from a pop-out menu.

- The default Tools palette is pictured at right. To move a tool from a pop-out menu to its own slot on the palette, hold down Control/Ctrl as you choose the tool. Control-click/Ctrl-click a tool to restore it to its default pop-out menu.

- Hold down Option/Alt and choose any item creation or linking tool to keep it selected. To deselect a tool, click another tool.

- To set preferences for a tool, double-click the tool, then click Modify (see page 425).

- To access the Item tool while the Content tool is chosen, hold down Cmd/Ctrl.

- To restore the default Tools palette, choose QuarkXPress (Edit, in Windows) > Preferences > Print Layout or Web Layout > Tools, click Default Tool Palette, then click OK.

- If Show Tool Tips is checked in QuarkXPress (Edit, in Windows) > Preferences > Application > Interactive, you can rest the pointer on any visible tool or palette button and its name will appear on the screen.

 The palettes open from the Window menu.

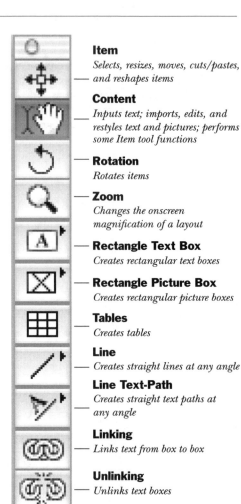

Item
Selects, resizes, moves, cuts/pastes, and reshapes items

Content
Inputs text; imports, edits, and restyles text and pictures; performs some Item tool functions

Rotation
Rotates items

Zoom
Changes the onscreen magnification of a layout

Rectangle Text Box
Creates rectangular text boxes

Rectangle Picture Box
Creates rectangular picture boxes

Tables
Creates tables

Line
Creates straight lines at any angle

Line Text-Path
Creates straight text paths at any angle

Linking
Links text from box to box

Unlinking
Unlinks text boxes

Starburst
Creates star-shaped picture boxes

Scissors
Cuts lines, paths, and boxes

Tools on the default pop-out menus

Text Box tools

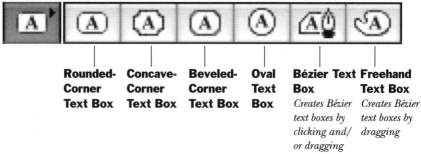

Rounded-Corner Text Box

Concave-Corner Text Box

Beveled-Corner Text Box

Oval Text Box

Bézier Text Box
Creates Bézier text boxes by clicking and/ or dragging

Freehand Text Box
Creates Bézier text boxes by dragging

Picture Box tools

Rounded-Corner Picture Box

Concave-Corner Picture Box

Beveled-Corner Picture Box

Oval Picture Box

Bézier Picture Box
Creates picture boxes by clicking and/or dragging

Freehand Picture Box
Creates Bézier picture boxes by dragging

Line tools

Bézier Line
Creates open paths by clicking and/or dragging

Orthogonal Line
Creates straight vertical or horizontal lines

Freehand Line
Creates freehand lines by dragging

Text-Path tools

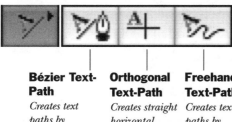

Bézier Text-Path
Creates text paths by clicking and/or dragging

Orthogonal Text-Path
Creates straight horizontal or vertical text paths

Freehand Text-Path
Creates text paths by dragging

Rectangle Image Map

Form Box

Text Field

Button

Image Button

Pop-up Menu

List Box

Radio Button

Check Box

Rollover Linking

Rollover Unlinking

The **Web Tools** *palette (see Chapter 19)*

Tools Palette

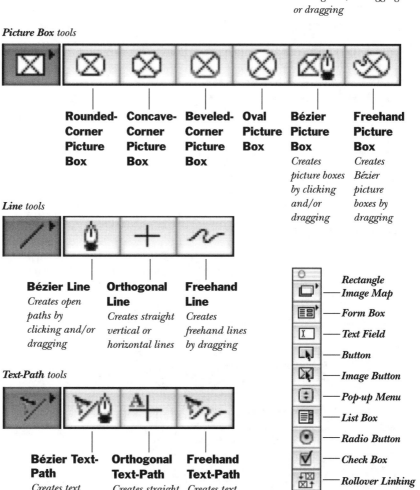

17

The Measurements palette

The Measurements palette contains some of the same commands and options that are available under the menus. The options on the Measurements palette change depending on what kind of item and which tool are selected in your layout. The palette is blank when nothing is selected.

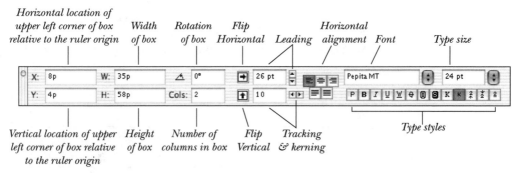

*The Measurements palette with the **Content** tool and a **text box** selected*

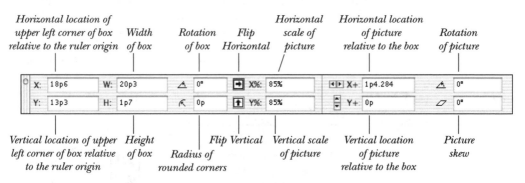

*The Measurements palette with the **Content** tool and a **picture box** selected*

Measurements palette shortcuts	
Show/hide the palette	F9
Highlight the first field	Cmd-Option-M/Ctrl-Alt-M
Highlight the Font field	Cmd-Option-Shift-M/ Ctrl-Alt-Shift-M
Highlight the next field	Tab
Highlight the previous field	Shift-Tab
Exit the palette without applying changes	Esc

Measurements Palette

Horizontal position of
the line's left endpoint
(based on the line mode) · Angle of
rotation · Line mode · Line width · Line style · Arrowheads

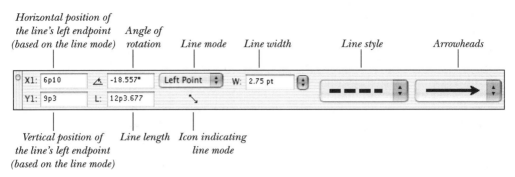

Vertical position of
the line's left endpoint
(based on the line mode) · Line length · Icon indicating
line mode

*The Measurements palette with the **Content** tool and a straight **line** selected*

(Point conversion buttons)

Horizontal position
of Bézier bounding
box relative to
the ruler origin · Width of
Bézier item · Rotation of
Bézier item · Symmetrical
point · Smooth point · Horizontal
position of
selected point · Angle of
diamond-
shaped curve
handle · Angle of
square-shaped
curve handle

Corner
point

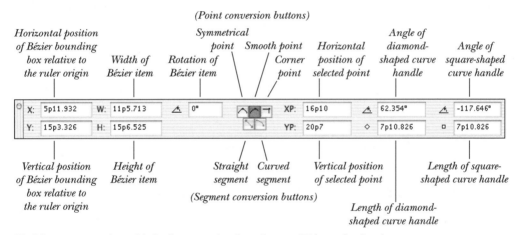

Vertical position
of Bézier bounding
box relative to
the ruler origin · Height of
Bézier item · Straight
segment · Curved
segment · Vertical position
of selected point · Length of square-
shaped curve handle

(Segment conversion buttons)

Length of diamond-
shaped curve handle

*The Measurements palette with the **Content** tool and a point on a **Bézier path** selected*

Align with text ascent

Horizontal position of guide

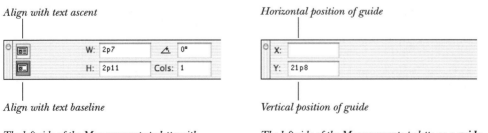

Align with text baseline

Vertical position of guide

*The left side of the Measurements palette with
the **Content** tool and an **anchored box** selected*

*The left side of the Measurements palette as a **guide**
is being dragged downward from the horizontal ruler*

The Page Layout palette

The Page Layout palette lets you rearrange, insert, and delete layout pages; move through a layout; create and modify master pages; apply master pages to layout pages; and renumber sections of a layout. Display a layout page by double-clicking its icon or by clicking its number.

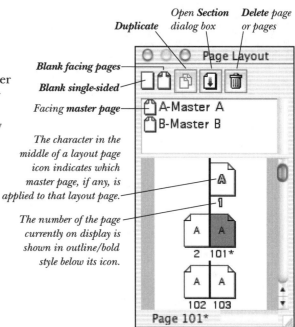

Open Section dialog box

Delete page or pages

Duplicate

Blank facing pages

Blank single-sided

Facing master page

The character in the middle of a layout page icon indicates which master page, if any, is applied to that layout page.

The number of the page currently on display is shown in outline/bold style below its icon.

The Style Sheets palette

The Style Sheets palette lets you apply style sheets, which are sets of character and paragraph specifications.

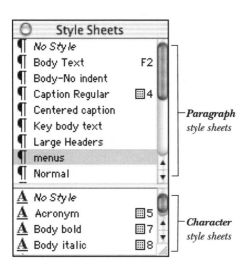

Paragraph style sheets

Character style sheets

The Colors palette

The Colors palette lets you apply process, spot, and Web-safe solid colors and blends to selected items.

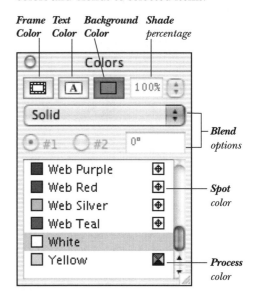

Frame Color   *Text Color*   *Background Color*   *Shade percentage*

Blend options

Spot color

Process color

Page Layout, Style Sheets, Colors Palettes

The Synchronized Text palette 6.0!

Text passages that are stored on the Synchronized Text palette can be added, via the palette, to one or more print and/or Web layouts within the same project. All instances of the text update automatically any time an instance of that text is edited in any layout in the project. An entry can consist of anything from a word or phrase to a series of paragraphs.

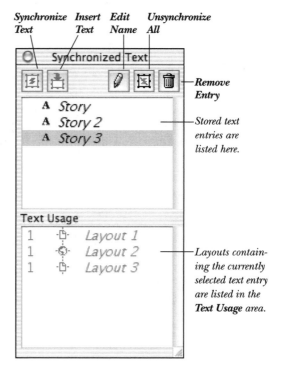

Synchronize Text   *Insert Text*   *Edit Name*   *Unsynchronize All*

Remove Entry

Stored text entries are listed here.

Layouts containing the currently selected text entry are listed in the Text Usage area.

The Trap Information palette

The Trap Information palette lets you assign trapping specifications to individual objects.

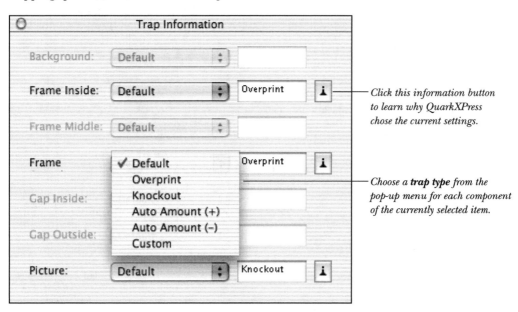

Click this information button to learn why QuarkXPress chose the current settings.

*Choose a **trap type** from the pop-up menu for each component of the currently selected item.*

Synchronized Text, Trap Information Palettes

The Lists palette

The Lists palette lets you build a table of contents or an alphabetized list of headings for the current layout or for multiple chapter files in a book.

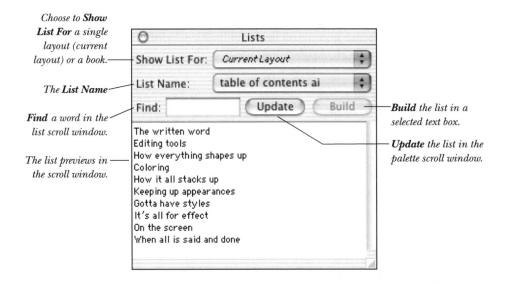

*Choose to **Show List For** a single layout (current layout) or a book.*

*The **List Name***

***Find** a word in the list scroll window.*

The list previews in the scroll window.

***Build** the list in a selected text box.*

***Update** the list in the palette scroll window.*

The Layers palette

The Layers palette lets you organize objects in a layout according to their front-to-back stacking order. Using this palette, you can create new layers, move an item to a different layer, merge two or more layers together, restack layers, delete layers, lock/unlock layers, and make layers temporarily invisible or nonprintable.

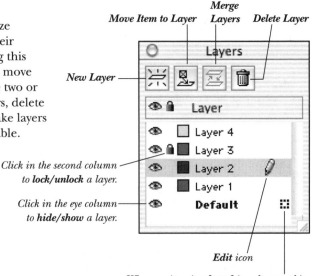

Move Item to Layer *Merge Layers* *Delete Layer*

New Layer

*Click in the second column to **lock/unlock** a layer.*

*Click in the eye column to **hide/show** a layer.*

***Edit** icon*

*When an item is **selected** in a layout, this indicator shows which layer the object is on.*

The Profile Information palette

The Profile Information palette lets you display the current characteristics of a selected picture and change its color profile or rendering intent for color management.

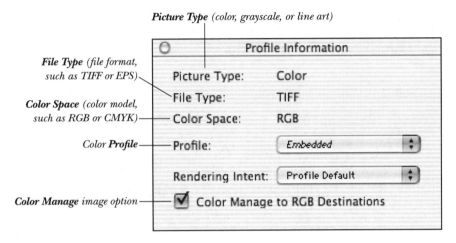

Picture Type (color, grayscale, or line art)

File Type (file format, such as TIFF or EPS)

Color Space (color model, such as RGB or CMYK)

Color Profile

Color Manage image option

The Hyperlinks palette

Hyperlinks ("links" for short) are the graphic devices that Web designers use to help users navigate between Web pages. Links range from simple underlined words to image maps and rollovers. In QuarkXPress, the Hyperlinks palette is used to assign a link to highlighted text, an image map area, a picture box, or other selected item. Links are interactive only when viewed in a browser. Links can also be assigned to text in a print layout and then exported as a PDF file.

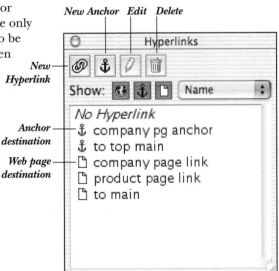

New Anchor Edit Delete

New Hyperlink

Anchor destination

Web page destination

The Index palette

It takes several steps to construct an index. First, individual entries are marked in a layout. Second, the Index palette is used to assign formatting specifications for how each entry will appear in the index, such as its style and level of indentation. And finally, the Utilities > Build Index command is chosen with a text box selected.

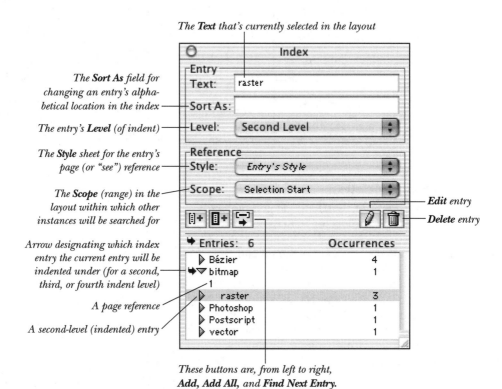

*The **Text** that's currently selected in the layout*

*The **Sort As** field for changing an entry's alphabetical location in the index*

*The entry's **Level** (of indent)*

*The **Style** sheet for the entry's page (or "see") reference*

*The **Scope** (range) in the layout within which other instances will be searched for*

Arrow designating which index entry the current entry will be indented under (for a second, third, or fourth indent level)

A page reference

A second-level (indented) entry

Edit entry

Delete entry

*These buttons are, from left to right, **Add**, **Add All**, and **Find Next Entry**.*

Index Palette

The XML Workspace palette

XML is a system that allows text and picture content to be categorized in order to provide greater flexibility when outputting to the Web or print. First each basic element within XML (e.g., each field of text or data) is assigned its own name and given a hierarchical relationship to other elements in the XML file. Then the contents (items or paragraphs) of a QuarkXPress file are tagged to various XML elements. This is done by dragging item boxes onto elements on the XML Tree on the XML Workspace palette, which displays when an XML file is created or opened. This palette is also used to define and view XML elements and their content, and also to preview the actual code in the XML file.

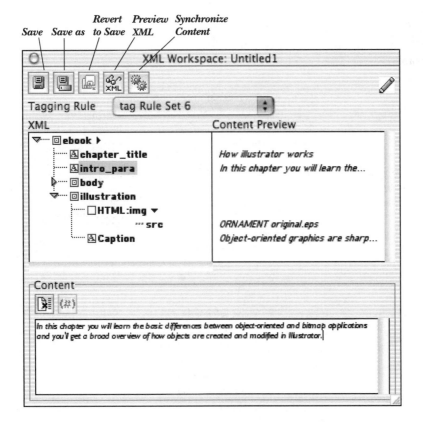

The Placeholders palette

In QuarkXPress, placeholders are used for styling and placing XML element content. First a QuarkXPress template is created, and blank text boxes and style sheets are created in the template. Next, an XML file is opened via the Placeholders palette; the hierarchical outline of the XML elements (as defined in a DTD) is displayed on the palette. Element names are then dragged from the Placeholders palette into each text box in the QuarkXPress template, and each placeholder name in the template is styled via a style sheet.

Next, an XML file with matching elements is opened using the Placeholders palette. Each XML element will be matched up with a placeholder of the same name, and the XML content acquires style sheet attributes from that placeholder. To preview the XML content that will be substituted for the placeholders in the template, the Toggle Placeholders/Content button is clicked. Finally, to make the imported XML content permanent, the Convert placeholders to Text button is clicked. For more information about placeholders, see the QuarkXPress documentation (it isn't discussed elsewhere in this book).

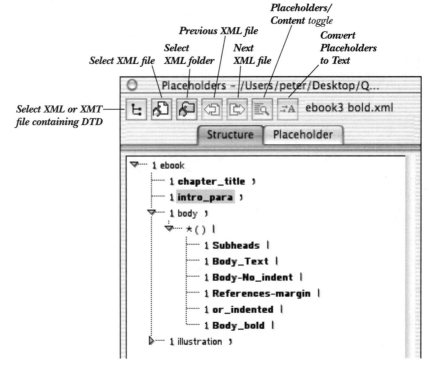

The Sequences palette

The Sequences palette lets you make a list of items in a QuarkXPress layout, known as a sequence. If a sequence is dragged from the Sequences palette onto the topmost element on the XML Workspace palette, the content from those items is tagged automatically to the appropriate XML elements.

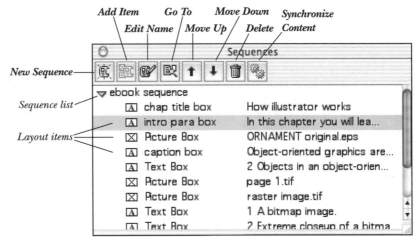

The Find/Change palette

The Find/Change palette lets you search for and replace text characters, fonts, point sizes, type styles, colors, or all of the above. The palette can also be used to apply or remove paragraph or character style sheets from text. The Find/Change palette is opened from the Edit menu.

*The text, style sheets, and attributes to be searched for are entered or chosen in the **Find What** area.*

*The text, style sheets, and attributes to be changed to are entered or chosen in the **Change To** area.*

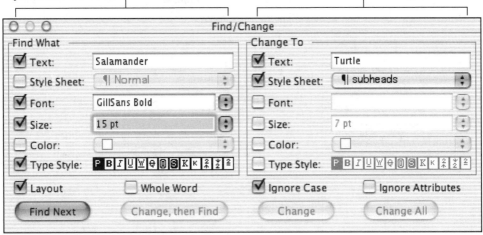

*This is the Find/Change palette when **Ignore Attributes** is **unchecked**.*

Sequences, Find/Change Palettes

A library

Libraries aren't palettes, per se. They're separate user-created files that are used for storing any type of individual items, combinations of items, or groups of items, including picture boxes (with or without pictures), text boxes (with or without text), lines, text paths, and tables.

To add an item to a library, simply drag it into the palette. To retrieve an item (or group) from a library, drag it from the library into your project window; a copy of the item will appear in your layout. You can create an unlimited number of library palettes, and more than one library palette can be open at a time.

*Once a **label** has been assigned to the items in a library, you can display them selectively by label category via this pop-up menu.*

Library items display as thumbnails.

A book palette

A book is a collection of individual chapter files in which style sheets, colors, H&Js (settings for hyphenation and justification), lists, and dashes & stripes (line and frame styles) are synchronized. Each book has its own palette that is used to add, delete, print, and change the order of chapters.

The Status column on the palette shows whether a chapter is Available, Modified, Missing, or Open on your computer. If a user name is listed, it means that another person on your network has that chapter open on their computer.

*The **Synchronize Book** button synchronizes style sheets, colors, H&Js, lists, and dashes & stripes between the master file and chapter files.*

Move Chapter Down

Print Chapter

Remove Chapter

Move Chapter Up

Add Chapter

*The **master** file from which all the style sheets, colors, etc. are derived*

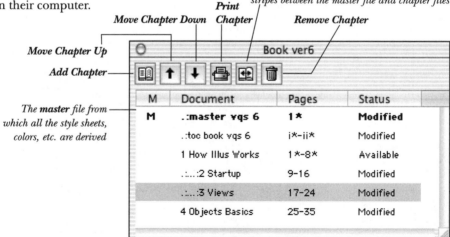

M	Document	Pages	Status
M	.:master vqs 6	1*	Modified
	.:toc book vqs 6	i*–ii*	Modified
	1 How Illus Works	1*–8*	Available
	.:...:2 Startup	9–16	Modified
	.:...:3 Views	17–24	Modified
	4 Objects Basics	25–35	Modified

shopping for XTensions

Some XTensions are sold individually, whereas others are sold in a bundle, such as XPert Tools Pro. Luckily, most XTensions are available in a demo version so you can try them out before shelling out beans.

For a directory of XTensions, visit the Quark Web site: **www.quark.com/products/xtensions,** then click XTensions Catalog. You can conduct a search or download the PDF catalog. For a list of domestic and international distributors, click Where to Buy. You'll also find a link on that page for downloading free XTensions, as well as XTension betas, demos, and updaters (to get there directly, go to **www.quark.com/support/downloads**). Make sure whatever you download is 6.0-compatible!

If you prefer to shop from an assortment of developers via one distributor, one option is to go to **www.thepowerxchange.com** (click QuarkXPress on their home page).

Ask whichever manufacturer or distributor you purchase your XTensions from what their upgrade policy is and what technical support they offer, if any.

And while you're at it, check out this site for QuarkXPress tips and resources (even XTensions info): **www.xpressobar.com** (no relation to Quark, Inc.).

In Mac OS X, hold down Option and choose QuarkXPress > About QuarkXPress™; in Windows, hold down Alt and choose Help > About QuarkXPress™. The **QuarkXPress™ Environment** dialog box opens, displaying a list of installed XTensions, your program serial number, and other information about the program.

---

*To whet your appetite, we're giving you a taste of what's out there in XTensionland, with an emphasis on relatively inexpensive XTensions that are more likely to be of interest to individual QuarkXPress users than to output service providers. We didn't do any comparison shopping.

XTending XPress with XTensions

What's an XTension?

QuarkXPress doesn't do everything. In fact, one of its strengths is that third-party developers have written hundreds of add-on software modules for the program, called XTensions, that extend or enhance its features. XTensions perform a variety of tasks, from simple object alignment to catalog databasing, and they range in price from petty cash to hundreds of dollars.

A small sampling of XTensions are mentioned in this book.* Some XTensions are available for Mac OS X only, and some are available for both platforms. Make sure whatever XTensions you buy are optimized for QuarkXPress version 6 (at the time of this writing, we couldn't verify availability). To get info about an XTension that's already installed, choose Utilities > XTensions Manager, click the XTension name, then click About.

Where should I install them?

In order to use an XTension, it has to be installed in the XTension folder inside the QuarkXPress application folder. Some XTensions ship with an installer that will do the job for you; others must be copied manually into the XTension folder. If an installer places an XTension in the QuarkXPress folder but not in the XTension folder, make sure to drag it into the XTension folder yourself.

Once an XTension has been correctly installed on your hard drive, you can use the XTensions Manager feature within the application to enable or disable it (see pages 427–428). In order to use a newly enabled XTension, you must re-launch QuarkXPress. In QuarkXPress (Edit, in Windows) > Preferences > Application > XTensions Manager, you can choose whether or not the XTensions Manager will open automatically when the program is launched.

XTensions

Measurement units

Most values in palettes and dialog boxes display in the current default horizontal or vertical measurement units. To change the default units for future Web or print layouts, close all projects; to change the units for just the currently displayed layout, leave it open. Choose QuarkXPress (Edit, in Windows) > Preferences. Under Print Layout or Web Layout (or Default Print Layout or Default Web Layout), click Measurements, then for Horizontal and/or Vertical, choose Inches, Inches Decimal, Picas, Points, Millimeters, Centimeters, Ciceros, or Agates. For a Web layout, you can also choose Pixels ■. A different unit can be chosen for each layout in a project ■–■. With a layout displayed, you can also Control-click/Right-click either ruler and choose from the Measure submenu.

To enter a value in a non-default unit, you must use the proper abbreviation (see the sidebar). For example, you can use "pt" or "p" for points, but not "pts". Agates, in case you're wondering, are used for measuring vertical column lengths in classified ads.

Picas and points

A pica is the standard unit of measure used in the graphic arts industry. Six picas equals 1 inch; 1 pica equals 12 points. Picas and points can be combined in the same entry field. For example, to indicate 4 picas and 6 points, you would enter "4p6."

Regardless of the current units, points are always used to measure type sizes, leading, rule widths, frame widths, and line widths.

Using math in a field

To add, enter + after the current number, then the amount you want to add; to subtract, enter -, then the value you want to subtract; to multiply, enter *, then the multiplier; and to divide, enter /, then the divisor. To divide 38 by 3, for example, you would enter "38/3". In each case, press Return/Enter to execute the math.

Abbreviations

Inches	in *or* "
Inches Decimal	in *or* " with a decimal
Picas	p
Points	pt *or* p followed by a number (as in "p6")
Millimeters	mm
Centimeters	cm
Ciceros	c
Agates	ag
quarter of a millimiter	q
Pixels	px*

In a print layout, pixels can't be chosen as the default unit, but "px" can be used when entering values.

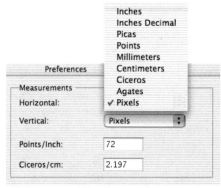

■ **Measurement** *units available for a Web layout*

■ *Enter a value in any measurement unit used in QuarkXPress.*

■ *When Return/Enter is pressed, the value is converted into the currently chosen default measurement units.*

Preferences (a sneak preview)

Preferences are the default settings that can be chosen either for an individual layout or for the application as a whole. The Preferences dialog box is discussed in detail in Chapter 23, and some preferences are discussed in individual chapters when they pertain to a particular task. You'll learn gradually which preferences affect whole projects and which preferences affect individual layouts.

Preferences are chosen in QuarkXPress (Edit, in Windows) > Preferences. Click a name on the left side of the dialog box to display that pane. Here's an example of the way we've notated it: QuarkXPress (Edit, in Windows) > Preferences > Application > Interactive.

In the shaded box below you'll see a partial listing of preferences, just to give you an idea of some of the available options.

Think creatively

To create a second de facto Rectangle Text Box tool or Rectangle Picture Box tool, change the Corner Radius to zero for one of the tools that you rarely use, such as the Beveled-Corner Text Box tool or Beveled-Corner Picture Box tool. For this "new" tool, you can apply special default settings, such as a frame in a particular width, or turn Runaround on or off.

Note: If you add, delete, or edit style sheets (including the Normal style sheet), colors, hyphenation exceptions, H&Js (settings for hyphenation and justification), or an auxiliary dictionary when no projects are open, those specifications will become the defaults for future projects. The same holds true for any Default Print Layout or Default Web Layout preferences that are changed while no projects are open, such as measurement units, Auto Page Insertion, or Auto Picture Import on or off.

A partial listing of preferences

Margin, ruler, or grid Guide Colors

Preview resolution for imported pictures

Scrolling speed

Smart Quotes options

Drag and Drop Text on or off

Pasteboard Width

Auto Save and Auto Backup options

Auto Library Save on or off

Save Document Position on or off

Show XTensions Manager options

Measurement Units for rulers, dialog boxes, and the Measurements palette

Auto Page Insertion options

Guides in front or behind

Auto Picture Import options

Keep or delete Master Page Items

Live Refresh on or off

Baseline Grid increment

Hyphenation method

Auto Kern Above value

Flex Space Width

Ligatures options

Text inset, runaround, line width, etc.

Trapping options

Tool preferences, such as style, width, color, shade, and Runaround settings for the Line or Text-Path tools; background color, angle, frame, and Runaround settings for the Picture Box or Bézier tools; background color, number of columns, frame, and Runaround for the Text Box tools; and the Zoom percentage for each click of the Zoom tool.

Context menus

Many commands and features can be accessed using context menus **1**–**3**, thus eliminating the need to trek all the way over to a menu or even to a palette. The choices on a context menu will vary depending on whether the pointer is over the pasteboard, the rulers, a blank area, or a picture box, text box, contentless box, text path, line, table, or palette.

In Mac OS X, you have a choice of two preference settings for context menus. Choose QuarkXPress > Preferences, then click Interactive below Application on the left side of the dialog box. If you click Control Key Activates: Contextual Menu, then all you have to do to open a context menu is Control-click. If you click Control Key Activates: Zoom instead, you'll need to Control-Shift-click to access context menus. In Windows, it's simpler: Just Right-click (you don't need to choose a Preferences setting).

1 *This context menu appears if you Control-click/Right-click a line with the Item tool.*

2 *This context menu appears if you Control-click/Right-click a picture with the Item tool.*

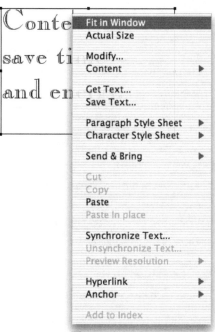

3 *This context menu appears if you Control-click/Right-click a text box with the Content tool.*

Startup 2

1 *Click the application icon on the Dock to launch or switch back to QuarkXPress.*

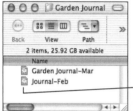

2 *Or double-click any QuarkXPress **file icon** to launch the application and open that file simultaneously.*

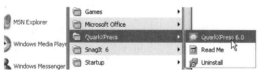

3 *Click **QuarkXPress 6.0** on the **Start** menu.*

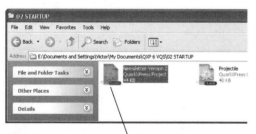

4 *Or double-click any QuarkXPress **file** icon to launch the application and open that file simultaneously.*

5 *You can choose any open application from the **Taskbar**.*

Getting started
To launch QuarkXPress in Mac OS X:

Click the QuarkXPress application icon on the Dock **1**. If you haven't yet placed the application icon there, drag the application file icon 🌼 from the QuarkXPress folder to the Dock.

or

Open the QuarkXPress folder in the Finder, then double-click the QuarkXPress application icon.

or

Double-click any existing QuarkXPress file icon on the Finder desktop (the program will launch automatically)**2**.

TIP If you activate the Finder desktop by clicking on it—whether intentionally or not—and you want to get back into QuarkXPress, click in any open QuarkXPress project window or click the application icon on the Dock.

To launch QuarkXPress in Windows:

In Windows 2000 or Windows XP, click the Start button on the Taskbar, choose All Programs, choose QuarkXPress, then click QuarkXPress 6.0 **3**.

or

In Windows Explorer, double-click a QuarkXPress file icon. The application will launch and that file will be maximized onscreen **4**.

TIP Once QuarkXPress is running, you can choose it (or any other open application) from the Taskbar at the bottom of the screen **5**.

Launch QuarkXPress

33

6.0! Projects and layouts

In QuarkXPress version 6, you will need to acquaint yourself with a whole new substructure: projects and layouts. The entity that is saved, and that is identified by an icon on the Desktop, is called a **project.** Each project, in turn, holds one or more **layouts.** Layouts hold the "actual" page elements, such as text, lines, tables, and pictures. Each layout has its own Layout Properties settings, which include the page width, height, margin guides, column guides, and layout type (print or Web).

Physically, what you'll see onscreen is a project window and, inside the window, the currently displayed layout. To switch between multiple layouts in a project, click a layout tab at the bottom of the project window **1**. Only one layout can be displayed at a time.

When a new project is created, it automatically contains a default layout. You can create additional layouts either by choosing Layout > New **2** or by choosing Layout > Duplicate (more about this later). When you duplicate a layout, its style sheets, master page items, and layout properties also appear in the duplicate. Each project can hold up to 25 layouts, and each layout can contain up to 2,000 pages. You can also delete any layout from a project; a minimum of one layout must remain.

Not only can print and Web layouts be contained within the same project, you can even switch the layout type for any existing layout from print to Web, or vice versa, via Layout > Layout Properties. Each layout type has its own features and parameters. In Chapter 21, we'll show you how to synchronize text across multiple layouts so you can standardize content more easily between your print work and Web work.

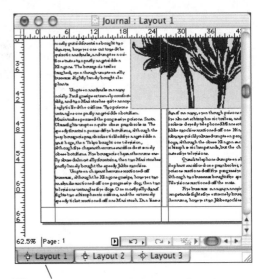

1 *Use the **layout tabs** at the bottom of the project window to switch between layouts.*

2 *Use commands on the **Layout** menu to create, delete, reconfigure, or navigate between layouts within a project.*

Projects and Layouts

Learning the lingo

Quark, Inc. is using new terminology, and we're following suit:

What were previously called documents are now called **projects** or **files.**

Projects contain up to 25 layout spaces. We'll refer to layout spaces as **layouts.**

One layout at a time can be displayed in the **project window.**

The Document Layout palette is now called the Page Layout palette, and document pages are called layout pages.

To make it easier to remember which features apply to whole projects and which features apply just to individual layouts, we've created the handy chart below. Refer to it as often as you need to until you get your bearings.

6.0!

TIP If you undo a project-level command, such as H&Js, the undo will affect the whole project. If you undo a layout-specific command, such as a text edit, the undo will affect only that layout.

TIP To combine multiple QuarkXPress 4 or 5 documents into one QuarkXPress 6 project, start by creating a project, and inside that project, add a layout for each of the documents that you want to convert. Open one of the old documents and the new project and choose View > Thumbnails for both. Resize the windows, if need be, then drag pages from the old document into a layout. Repeat for the other old documents.

QuarkXPress features that apply to whole projects	**QuarkXPress features that apply to individual layouts**
Application Preferences	Print Layout and Web Layout Preferences
Style sheets	Zoom levels
Colors	Layers
H&Js	Layout Properties, including page dimensions, margin guides, column guides, and layout type
Dashes & Stripes	
Save command	Master pages
Print Styles	Check Spelling
Nonmatching Preferences alert dialog box (see page 45)	Find/Change
	Indexing
Web layouts only:	Hyphenation Exceptions
Cascading menus	Collect for Output command
Meta tags	Export command for PDF or for HTML
Menus	
	Print layouts only:
	Kerning/tracking
	Trapping
	Print command

Project and Layout Features Compared

Every new project automatically contains one layout. The parameters for that layout are specified in the New Project dialog box (formerly known as the New Document or New Web Document dialog box).

To create a project:

1. Launch QuarkXPress (instructions on page 33), then choose File > New > Project (Cmd-N/Ctrl-N). (*Don't* choose File > Open—that command opens only existing, already saved files.)

Change any of the following settings (press Tab to move from one field to the next):

2. Leave the default name for the layout as is, or enter a new Layout Name.

   6.0!

3. From the Layout Type pop-up menu (**1**, next page), choose Print. The dialog box will display options for print layouts. (For Web layouts, see pages 323–324. The layout type can be changed at any time.)

   6.0!

4. Choose a preset size from the Size pop-up menu.
   or
   Enter numbers in the Width and Height fields to create a custom-size layout. (This is the layout size, not the paper size, and it can be changed later.) You can enter values in any measurement unit used in QuarkXPress (see page 30).

5. *Optional:* Click the unselected Orientation icon/button to swap the layout's width and height values.

6. Change any of the Margin Guides. If you check Facing Pages, the Left and

Predefined layouts

You can avoid having to reenter New Project values using the **XPert PageSets** XTension, which is part of the XPert Pro Tools toolkit from a lowly apprentice production, inc. This XTension allows you to create layout styles, called pagesets, that contain page dimensions, margins, columns, and other specifications. Any pagesets you create will appear on, and can be chosen from, a menu in the New Project dialog box.

Right Margin Guides fields will convert to Inside and Outside and layout pages will be arranged in pairs.

7. Change the number of Columns. If the number of columns is greater than 1, change the Gutter Width. Try 1p or 1p6.

8. *Optional:* Check Automatic Text Box to have a text box appear automatically within the margin guides on master page A and on every layout page with which master page A is associated (see Chapter 14). This is used for multipage layouts.

9. Double-check that you're satisfied with the current settings. Your choices aren't irrevocable, but it's easier to change them now than it is to fix them later. Click OK. A new project window will appear on your screen.

TIP The last settings used in the New Project dialog box will reappear the next time it's opened.

*Choose a preset **Page Size** or enter a number between 0.112" and 48"
in the **Width** and **Height** fields. A4 Letter is 210 mm x 297 mm,
B5 Letter is 182 mm x 257 mm, and Tabloid is 11" x 17". Numbers
can be entered in any measurement unit used in QuarkXPress.*

1 *Choose **Layout*** **6.0!**
*Type: **Print**. To
create Web layouts,
see page 323.*

*Click the Portrait
or Landscape
Orientation
icon/button.*

*Margin guides** don't
print. The **Left** and
Right fields convert
to **Inside** and
Outside when Facing
Pages is checked.*

*For **Columns** (guides),
enter a number
between 1 and 30.*

*If the number of
columns is greater
than 1, enter a
Gutter Width
between 3 and 288
points (4").*

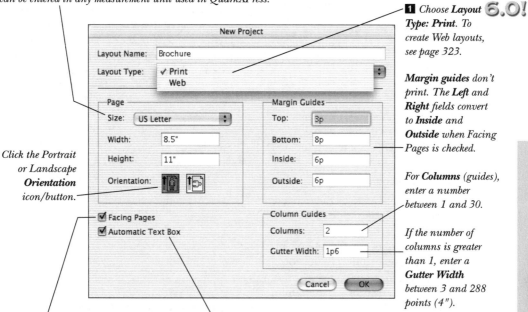

*With **Facing Pages** checked, layout page 1
will appear by itself on the right-hand side
and any additional pages will be stacked
below it in pairs. The Facing Pages format
is used for books, magazines, and the like.*

*With **Automatic Text Box** checked, a text box containing the number of columns and gutter width
specified in the Column Guides fields will appear
on the default master page A and on any layout
pages that are associated with that master.*

Create a Project

Margin   Column   Gutter

First of all he said
to himself: "That
buzzing-noise
means something,
You don't get a
buzzing-noise like
that, just buzzing
and buzzing, with-
out its meaning
something. If
there's a buzzing-

noise, somebody's
making a buzzing-
noise, and the only
reason for making
a buzzing-noise
that I know of is
because you're a
bee.
    Then he thought
another long time,
and said: "And the

only reason for
being a bee that I
know of is making
honey."
    And then he got
up, and said: "And
the only reason for
making honey is so
I can eat it." So he
began to climb the
tree.   *A.A. Milne*

Saving files

If your file has never been saved, ever, these are the instructions for you. To resave an already saved file, see page 40.

6.0! **To save an unsaved file:**

1. Choose File > Save (Cmd-S/Ctrl-S).

2. Type a name for the file. The Save As/ File Name field will become highlighted automatically **1**.

3. In Mac OS X, choose Type: Project. In Windows, choose Save as type: Project (*.qxp). To create a template, see page 41.

4. Choose a location for the file:

   In Mac OS X: Navigate to the desired folder or drive, making sure that location appears on the Where pop-up menu at the top of the dialog box **2**. *Optional:* To create a new folder for the file in the location you've chosen, click New Folder, enter a name, then click Create.

Faster save

If you tend to Save or Save As over and over to the same folder, you can make that folder appear automatically as the location for saving by choosing it in QuarkXPress (Edit, in Windows) > Preferences > Application > **Default Path** (see page 415). While you're at it, you can also choose a default path for the Open, Get Text, or Get Picture dialog box. Every little bit helps.

1 *Type a* **name** *for the new project.*

2 *For* **Where,** *make sure the name of the drive or folder into which you've chosen to save the file appears here.*

Leave the **Version** *setting on* **6.0**—*unless you need to save to an earlier version.*

For a non-template project, choose **Type: Project.**

Mac OS X only: Check **Include Preview** *to save a thumbnail of the first page of the first layout in the project for display in the Open dialog box.*

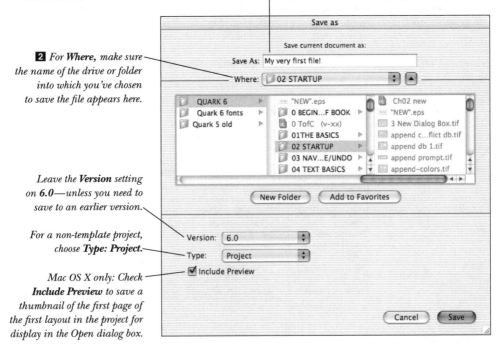

Save an Unsaved File

1 *Make sure the name of the drive or folder into which you've chosen to save the file appears in the **Save in** field.*

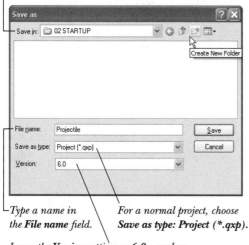

*Type a name in the **File name** field.*

*For a normal project, choose **Save as type: Project (*.qxp).***

*Leave the **Version** setting as **6.0**—unless you have a particular reason to change it.*

In Windows: Use the Up One Level button and the Folder List arrow to navigate to the desired location. Make sure the drive or folder into which you have chosen to save the file appears in the Save in field **1**. *Optional:* To create a new folder for the file in the location you've chosen, click the Create New Folder button, and type a name for the new folder; double-click the new folder to open it.

5. *Optional in Mac OS X:* Check Include Preview to have a thumbnail of the first page of the first layout in the project display when you reopen the file using File > Open **2**. If you forget to check Include Preview here, you can add the preview later using Save As (see page 40).

6. Click Save.

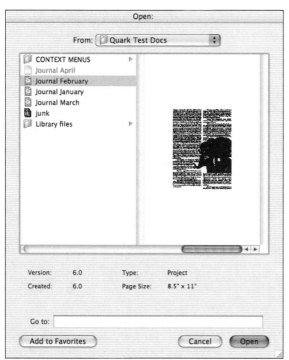

2 *In Mac OS X: In order to see a preview in the **Open** dialog box, a file has to be saved with **Include Preview** checked.*

Save frequently! We save almost every time we make a change—it's like an automatic reflex. *Note:* In addition to manual saving, you may also want to use the Auto Save feature (see the sidebar).

To resave a file:

Choose File > Save (Cmd-S/Ctrl-S) or Control-click/Right-click a blank area in any layout and choose Save. The Save command will be dimmed if no modifications were made to the file since it was last saved.

The Save As command creates a copy of a whole project under a different name. Now that you can create multiple variations of a layout within the same project, we use Save As less. Occasionally, if we have a corrupted file (e.g., it won't let us save), we'll try a Save As on it—sometimes that does the trick. This command is also used for saving a project for QuarkXPress version 5.0.

To save a new version of a file:

1. Open the file to be duplicated.

2. Choose File > Save As (Cmd-Option-S/Ctrl-Alt-S).

3. Change the name in the Save As field (Mac OS X)**1**/File name field (Win) **2**.

4. *Optional in Mac OS X:* Check Include Preview to have a thumbnail of the first page of the first layout display in the Open dialog box.

5. *Optional:* To downsave the file, choose Version: 5.0 (see the sidebar on page 45).

6. Choose a location in which to save the duplicate file.

7. Click Save. The new version of the file will remain open; the original version of the file will close.

TIP If you don't change the file name in the Save as dialog box, a warning prompt will appear when you click Save. Click Replace to save over the original file, or click Cancel.

Auto Save or Auto Backup?

Auto Save is like power or system failure insurance—when you reboot, you'll be able to rescue the last mini-saved version of your file. The **Auto Backup** feature creates multiple backups of a file. Both features are discussed on page 413.

1 *In Mac OS X, enter a different **name** for the duplicate file or alter the existing name, then click **Save**.*

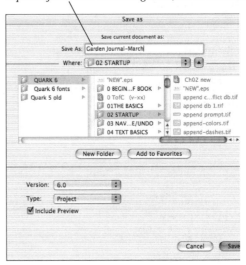

2 *In Windows, type a different **File name** for the duplicate file or modify the existing name, then click **Save**.*

Resave; Save New Version

Lock it another way

In Mac OS X, to prevent any type of file from being saved over, highlight its icon in the Finder, choose File > **Get Info** > General (Cmd-I), then check **Locked**. If you check **Stationery Pad** instead, a copy of the file will open when you try to open it and the original will remain closed.

To do the same thing in Windows, select a file in Windows Explorer, Right-click its icon so the contextual menu appears, choose **Properties**, make sure the **Read-only** attribute is checked, then click OK to close the Properties dialog box.

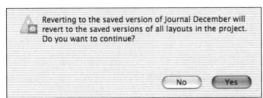

1 *If you choose File > **Revert to Saved**, this prompt will appear. Click Yes to restore the last saved version of the file.*

A template is a version of a project that you use as a boilerplate to spawn versions from. It can contain master page items, style sheets, custom colors, H&J settings, etc.—any items or layout specifications.

To create a template:

1. Choose File > Save As (Cmd-Option-S/ Ctrl-Alt-S).

2. In Mac OS X, choose Type: Project Template. In Windows, choose Save as type: Project Template (*.qpt).

3. Enter a name for the template (include the word "template" in the name, if you like), choose a location for the template, then click Save.

   To create a normal project using the template, open the template file, choose File > Save (the Save As dialog box will open automatically), enter a name for the non-template version, then click Save.

TIP To edit the template itself, open it, edit it, choose File > Save, reenter the template's *exact* same name, choose its *current* location, click Save, then click Replace/Yes when the prompt appears.

The Revert to Saved command, which restores the last-saved version of a file, isn't going to be of much help unless you invoke the Save command frequently as you work. We save our files constantly, especially before performing any complicated maneuvers, such as rearranging pages, creating a book, or reshaping a Bézier item— anything we'd hate to have to do again!

To revert to the last saved version:

1. Choose File > Revert to Saved.

2. When the alert prompt appears, click Yes **1** (it was an OK button in previous application versions).

TIP Choose Revert to Saved with Option/Alt held down to revert the file to its last Auto-Saved version (see page 413).

Create a Template; Open a File

6.0! Working with layouts

Every new project automatically contains a default layout. You can add more layouts to any project, up to a total of 25. To do this, you can either add an empty layout using the New Layout dialog box, or you can duplicate an existing layout, complete with all its contents (for the latter, follow the instructions on the next page).

To add a layout to a project:

1. With a project open **1**, choose Layout > New.
   or
   Control-click/Right-click a layout tab and choose New.

   The New Layout dialog box opens **2**. (It looks just like the New Project dialog box.)

2. *Optional:* Change the Layout Name.

3. From the Layout Type pop-up menu, you can choose Print or Web as the output medium for the layout. Options in the dialog box will change depending on what type of layout you choose. For now, choose Print.

4. Choose Page, Margin Guides, Facing Pages, Automatic Text Box, and Column Guides values and options, as per our instructions on page 36.

5. Click OK. A tab for the new layout will appear after the last tab at the bottom of the project window **3** (regardless of which layout was showing when you created the new one), and the new layout will be displayed in the project window.

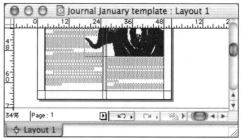

1 *The original project, which contains one layout*

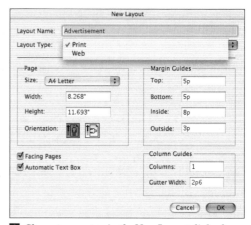

2 *Choose parameters in the **New Layout** dialog box.*

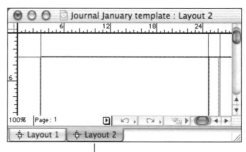

3 *Layout 2 is added to the project.*

Add Layout

No can do

If you reduce a layout's width and/or height values and you get an alert prompt indicating the existing page items won't fit within the new dimensions **1**, click Cancel, drag any page items that would extend beyond the new dimensions toward the **upper left** corner of the page, then choose the Duplicate command again.

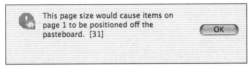

1 *This prompt will appear if the current page items won't fit within the new page dimensions you chose.*

Project name   Name of currently displayed layout

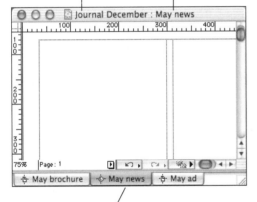

2 *Click a layout tab at the bottom of the project window.*

If you duplicate a layout, all the master and layout page items, style sheets, and other layout elements from the original layout will also show up in the duplicate— the whole kit and caboodle.

To duplicate a layout: 6.0!

1. Display the layout you want to duplicate (click its tab), and display a layout page—not a master page.

2. Choose Layout > Duplicate.
   or
   Control-click/Right-click a layout tab and choose Duplicate.

3. Change any Page settings, if desired, in the Duplicate Layout dialog box, then click OK.

TIP Any synchronized text in the original layout will be synchronized with text in the duplicate layout (see Chapter 21).

TIP To change the layout properties (layout name, page dimensions, margin guides, column guides, layout type, etc.) of an existing layout, see page 36.

Only one layout can be displayed at a time in the project window.

To switch between layouts: 6.0!

Click a layout tab at the bottom of the project window **2**. Print layout tabs have a ⊹ icon; Web layout tabs have a ⊹ icon. The name of the currently displayed layout appears next to the project name in the title bar at the top of the project window.

Each project must contain a minimum of one layout; a project can't be layout-free.

To delete a layout: 6.0!

1. Display the layout you want to delete, then choose Layout > Delete.
   or
   Control-click/Right-click a layout tab and choose Delete.

2. When the alert dialog box appears, click Yes. You can't undo the deletion.

Duplicate, Delete Layout; Switch Layouts

Opening files

To open a QuarkXPress project from within the application:

1. Choose File > Open (Cmd-O/Ctrl-O).

2. Locate and click a file name, then click Open **1**–**2**.

   or

   Double-click a file name. The number of QuarkXPress projects that can be open at a time is limited only by available memory.

   Note: Be sure to read "Things that may happen when a file is opened," starting on the following page.

   TIP In Windows, choose Details from the View menu to see the file's storage size, type, and date last modified. If you're going to reopen a recently opened and saved file, instead of going all the way back to the Open dialog box, you can reopen it from the File menu. Books can't be reopened this way.

To reopen a recently opened and saved file:

Choose from a list of recently opened files on the File > Open submenu or at the bottom of the Open menu **3**. The location of the list will depend on the current File List Location setting in File List preferences (see page 415).

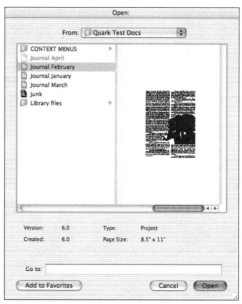

1 *The* **Open** *dialog box in* **Mac OS X**

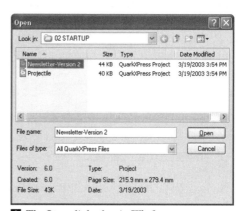

2 *The* **Open** *dialog box in* **Windows**

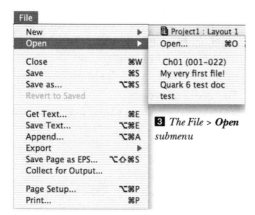

3 *The File >* **Open** *submenu*

Downsaving

If you downsave a QuarkXPress 6.0 file to version 5.0, some layout elements that were created using 6.0 features will revert back to their 5.0 equivalents. You won't see these changes until you close and then reopen the file.

As an example, if you try to downsave a project that contains multiple layouts, an alert dialog box will appear. If you click Yes, a folder will be created, and inside it will be a separate print or Web file for each layout. **6.0!**

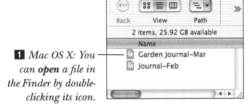

1 *Mac OS X: You can* **open** *a file in the Finder by double-clicking its icon.*

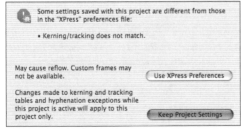

2 *Windows Explorer: Double-click the file you want to open.*

3 *The* **XPress Preferences** *prompt*

To open a QuarkXPress file from the Finder/Windows Explorer:

In Mac OS X: Double-click a QuarkXPress file icon **1** or drag a QuarkXPress file icon over the application icon on the Dock.

In Windows Explorer: Double-click a QuarkXPress file icon **2** or drag a QuarkXPress file over the program shortcut on the Desktop.

If QuarkXPress hasn't yet been launched, it will launch now.

To convert a file from a previous version of QuarkXPress to 6.0:

1. Open the file using File > Open—not by double-clicking its icon in the Finder.

2. Immediately after the file opens and you've responded to the XPress Preferences prompt, choose File > Save.

3. Choose 6.0 from the Version pop-up menu, click Save, then click Replace. The file will be converted into a project containing one layout.

Things that may happen when a file is opened

Non-matching preferences prompt

Kerning and tracking table settings and hyphenation exceptions are stored in individual projects and in the QuarkXPress folder in a file called XPress Preferences. If, upon opening a file, the project settings don't match the XPress Preferences settings, a prompt will appear **3**. Click **Use XPress Preferences** (or press Cmd-./Alt-U) to apply the preferences currently resident on that machine to all the layouts in the project (the text may reflow!), or click **Keep Project Settings** (Return/Enter) to preserve all the current preferences for each layout in the project.

(Continued on the following page)

Fonts are missing

If you open a file that uses fonts that aren't installed or aren't currently available in your system (perhaps the font is temporarily deactivated), a prompt will appear:

1. Click List Fonts to see a list of missing fonts . *Note:* If you click Continue and the missing fonts subsequently become available, they will display properly.

2. To replace a missing font, click a font name ❷. An asterisk in the Replacement Fonts column indicates that that font has *not* been replaced.

3. Click Replace.

4. In the Replacement Font dialog box, choose a font from the pop-up menu ❸.

5. Click OK. *Beware!* All instances of the font will be replaced, including any use of the font in a style sheet.

6. Repeat steps 2–5 for any other missing fonts you want to replace. If you change your mind after choosing a replacement font, click the replacement font, then click Reset.

7. Click OK.

Profiles are missing

This is a giant leap ahead, but we'll be brief. "Profiles" is short for Quark Color Management System profiles, which the program uses to achieve color matching among various devices. If a profile that's been assigned to your file is missing when you try to open it (or print it), the missing profiles prompt will appear ❹. You can either click Continue to open the file without replacing the missing profile (the simplest solution for now) or click List Profiles to proceed ahead to the Missing profiles dialog box (❶, next page). Profiles are assigned to input and output devices as well as to individual pictures. Read more about profiles on pages 432–438.

❶ *If the **missing fonts** prompt appears, click **List Fonts** to open the Missing Fonts dialog box, or click **Continue** to open the file without replacing the missing fonts.*

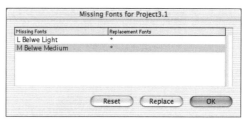

❷ *In the **Missing Fonts** dialog box, click a font name, click **Replace**...*

❸ *...then choose a **replacement font** from the pop-up menu.*

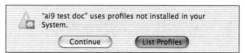

❹ *If the **missing profiles** prompt appears, click **List Profiles** to substitute profiles, or click **Continue** to open the file without replacing the missing profiles.*

Missing Fonts; Missing Profiles

What about modified pictures? 6.0!

If **Auto Picture Import: On** is chosen in QuarkXPress (Edit, in Windows) > Preferences > General, then modified pictures (pictures that are imported into QuarkXPress and subsequently opened and resaved in another application) are updated *automatically* when a project is reopened; no action is required on your part. If Verify is chosen, a prompt will appear (click Yes). If Auto Picture Import: Off is chosen, no prompt will appear but you can use Utilities > Usage to update the pictures after opening the file (see page 180).

1 *In the* **Missing profiles** *dialog box, click a profile name, click* **Replace**, *choose a replacement profile, click OK, then click OK again.*

2 *This prompt will appear if, when you open a file, any original picture files for the project are* **missing** *or were* **modified**.

3 *In Utilities >* **Usage** *> Pictures, double-click a missing picture file name. Then, in the Find dialog box, locate and click the picture file name, then click Open.*

Pictures are missing 6.0!

If your file contains pictures that were moved or renamed since it was last opened and Auto Picture Import: Verify is chosen in QuarkXPress (Edit, in Windows) > Preferences > Print Layout or Web Layout > General, yet another alert dialog box will open **2**. Click Yes to proceed, and then to update the picture/file link(s), choose Utilities > Usage, click the Pictures tab, double-click the name of a missing picture **3**, locate and click the picture file name in the Find dialog box, then click Open (or click OK). Repeat for any other missing pictures. Click Done when you're done. See pages 179–180.

If a prompt appears that indicates an XTension is missing, the project contains a PCX, JPEG, PhotoCD, PNG, PDF, or LZW TIFF picture for which an import XTension filter must be enabled (see below).

Note: If additional missing (not modified) pictures are located in the same folder as the first missing picture, you'll get a prompt indicating that you can update them all at once.

XTensions Manager

In addition to the prompts that may appear when a file is opened, the XTensions Manager may open when the application is launched. To use the XTensions Manager, see page 427.

To specify whether the XTensions Manager should open automatically when the application is launched, go to QuarkXPress (Edit, in Windows) > Preferences > Application > XTensions Manager. Click Show XTensions Manager at Startup: Always to have the XTensions Manager appear with every launch; or click When: "XTension" folder changes to have the Manager open only if an XTension was added to or removed from the XTension folder; or click When: Error loading XTension occurs to have it open only if an error occurs when XTensions are loaded.

6.0! Changing layout properties

The Layout Properties dialog box replaces the Document Setup dialog box from QuarkXPress 5, and new controls have been added, such as the ability to change a layout's type or name.

To change a layout's dimensions or type:

1. Display the layout whose properties you want to change, then choose Layout > Layout Properties.
   or
   Control-click/Right-click a layout tab and choose Layout Properties.

2. Do any of the following **1**:

   Change the Layout Name.

   Choose Layout Type: Print or Web. *Note:* If you change the Layout Type, items that are found only in the current type (such as form controls in a Web layout or tabs, kerning, tracking, or H&Js in a print layout) may be altered.

   Choose a preset Page Size.

   Change the Width and/or Height values (see the sidebar on page 43).

   Click the unselected page Orientation icon/button.

   To convert a single-sided layout to a facing-pages layout, check Facing Pages (to learn more about facing pages, see page 243). Converting a facing-pages layout into a single-sided layout is more complicated, because it involves deleting master pages, which we cover in Chapter 14.

3. Click OK. If you changed the layout's type, an alert dialog box will appear **2**. Click Yes to continue.

   Any text box that fits exactly within the margin guides (such as the automatic text box) will resize automatically to fit within the new margins.

Show/hide guides

Press **F7** to show/hide guides. With guides hidden, margin guides, ruler guides, column guides, the X in empty picture boxes, and the edges of any unselected boxes that don't have a frame will disappear from view. Show guides to position objects; hide them to judge the overall compositional balance of a page.

Column and margin guides are modified via the **Master Guides** dialog box, which can be opened from the Page menu only when a master page is currently displayed (see page 243).

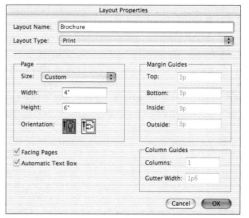

1 *Change a layout name, output type, dimensions, and other parameters in the **Layout Properties** dialog box.*

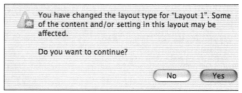

2 *This prompt will appear if you change a layout's type (**Layout Type** pop-up menu) and click OK.*

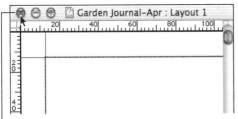

1 *Mac OS X: Click the red **close** button in the upper left corner of the project window to close a file.*

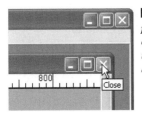

2 *Windows: If the project isn't maximized, click the close button in the upper right corner of the project window.*

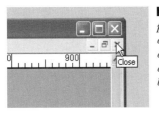

3 *Windows: If the project is maximized, click the close button directly below the application close button.*

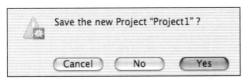

4 *If you attempt to close a file that has **never** been **saved**, this prompt will appear.*

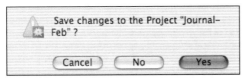

5 *If you try to quit/exit the application and **changes** were made to the file since it was last **saved**, this prompt will appear.*

Closing files

To close one file:

Mac OS X: Click the red close button in the upper left corner of the project window **1**.

Windows: If the project isn't maximized, click the project close button in the upper right corner of the project window **2**. If the project is maximized, click the project close button directly below the application close button **3**.

or

Choose File > Close (Cmd-W/Ctrl-F4).

TIP If you try to close a file that has never been saved, a prompt will appear. You can cancel the close operation (click Cancel), discard the file altogether (click No), or save the file before it's closed (click Yes) **4**.

To close all open QuarkXPress files:

Mac OS X: Option-click the red close button in the upper left corner of the project window or press Cmd-Option-W.

Windows: Choose Window > Close All.

To quit/exit the application:

In Mac OS X: Choose QuarkXPress > Quit QuarkXPress (Cmd-Q).

In Windows: Choose File > Exit (Ctrl-Q).

TIP When you try to quit/exit the application, a prompt will appear for each open file that has unsaved changes. You can cancel the quit/exit operation (click Cancel), close the file without saving the changes (click No), or save the changes before the file is closed (click Yes) **5**.

Appending specifications

Using the Append dialog box, you can append one or more style sheets, colors, H&Js, lists, and dashes & stripes from one project to another. In addition, as of QuarkXPress version 6, you can also append hyperlinks, menus, meta tags, font families, and cascading menus.

To append specifications from one project to another:

1. Open the file you want to append to.

2. Choose File > Append (Cmd-Option-A/ Ctrl-Alt-A).
or
Click Append in the Style Sheets, Colors, H&Js, Lists, or Dashes & Stripes, Hyperlinks dialog box (or Menus, Meta Tags, CSS Font Families, Cascading Menus in Web layouts).

3. Locate and click the name of the file that contains the components that you want to append, then click Open. You can append from a library file.

> **TIP** Only specifications that were saved with the file that you're appending from will show up on the list.

4. Click a category on the left side of the dialog box. 6.0!

5. In the Available column, click the name of the style sheet, color, H&J, list, dashes & stripes style, or other component you want to append **1**.
or
To append multiple components, click the first component in a series of consecutively listed components, then Shift-click the last in the series. Or Cmd-click/Ctrl-click to select/deselect individual components.

6. Click the right-pointing arrow **2**.

1 *In the **Available** column, select what you want to append.*

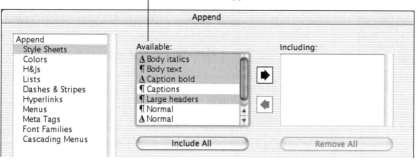

2 *Then click the **right-pointing** arrow to move those items to the **Including/Include** column.*

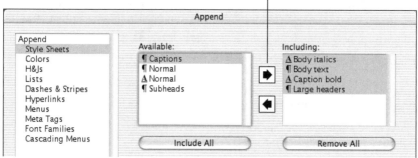

Quick-and-dirty append

If text to which a style sheet or sheets have been applied is pasted from another file using the Clipboard, drag-copied from another file, or retrieved from a library, the style sheet or sheets will be appended—barring any name conflicts. Colors and H&Js can also be appended this way.

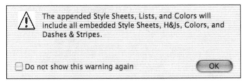

Click OK when this warning prompt appears.

2 *Click **Rename** or **Auto-Rename** to keep the existing item and append the new.*

3 *Or click **Use New** to replace the existing item with the appending item.*

4 *Or click **Use Existing** to prevent an item with the same name from appending.*

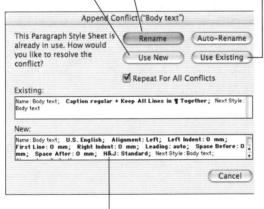

*In the **Append Conflict** dialog box, settings in a new (appending) style sheet that don't exactly match an equivalent setting in an existing style sheet of the same name in the file you're appending to will appear in boldface.*

7. Click OK. A warning prompt may appear **1**. Check "Do not show this warning again" to prevent the prompt from reappearing, if desired, then click OK again.

8. If an appending component has the same name as a component in the file you're appending to, the Append Conflict dialog box will open. Do one of the following for each conflict that arises:

Note: To have the same response be applied automatically to any remaining conflicts, check Repeat For All Conflicts before clicking Rename, Auto-Rename, Use New, or Use Existing.

To keep the existing component, append the new component, and rename an individual component yourself, click Rename **2**, type a new name, then click OK.

or

To have an asterisk be inserted automatically next to the name of any appending component that has a match in the open, destination project, click Auto-Rename.

or

To replace the existing item with the appending component, click Use New **3**.

or

To cancel the append of that item, click Use Existing **4**.

9. Click OK.

TIP To append all the components listed, instead of highlighting them, click Include All. Click Remove All to delete the whole list from the Including/Include column.

TIP If a style sheet that you're appending has the same keyboard equivalent as a style sheet in the project that you're appending to, the style sheet will append but not its keyboard equivalent.

(Illustrations on the following page)

Append

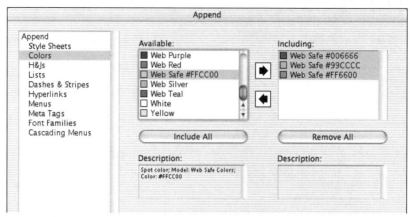

*Appending **colors***

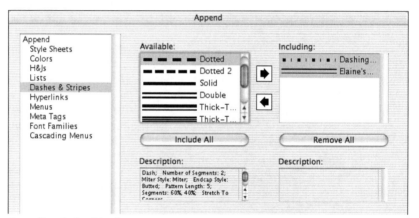

*Appending **dashes & stripes***

Append; Revert to Saved

Navigate/Undo 3

Zoom shortcuts

Fit in project window	Cmd-0/Ctrl-0 (zero)
Actual size	Cmd-1/Ctrl-1 (one)
Thumbnails	Shift-F6
Make all open windows Thumbnails view *(print layouts only)*	Option-Shift choose Window > Tile/Alt-Shift choose Window > Tile Horizontally or Tile Vertically
Fit pasteboard in project window	Cmd-Option-0/ Ctrl-Alt-0
Highlight view percent field	Control-V/ Ctrl-Alt-V
100%–200% toggle	Cmd-Option-click/ Ctrl-Alt-click

For the Zoom in and Zoom out shortcuts, see the following page.

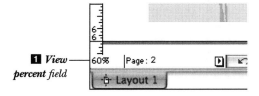

1 *View percent* field

Changing zoom levels

By learning how to switch zoom levels, you'll work more efficiently and minimize eye and neck strain. You can go back and forth between editing small details at a magnified zoom level to checking out the overall composition in Fit in Window view or a lower zoom level. Changing the zoom level doesn't alter a layout's output dimensions; it only changes its onscreen appearance.

To zoom in or out using the View menu or the view percent field:

Choose View > Fit in Window (Cmd-0/ Ctrl-0), 50%, 75%, Actual Size (Cmd-1/ Ctrl-1), 200%, or Thumbnails (Shift-F6).
or
Double-click the view percent field in the lower left corner of the project window **1** (Control-V/Ctrl-Alt-V), type a number between 10 and 800, then press Return/ Enter. You don't have to enter the % symbol. For Thumbnails view, enter "T", then press Return/Enter.

TIP Page elements can't be modified in Thumbnails view. Pages in a layout *can* be rearranged in Thumbnails view, however (see page 88), and whole pages can be drag-copied from one project to another, provided both projects are in Thumbnails view (see page 95).

TIP For an almost-thumbnails view in which page elements are editable, choose a very small view size, such as 25%.

Accessing the Zoom tool from the keyboard is much speedier than selecting and then deselecting the tool from the Tools palette. You can choose a different zoom level for each layout in a project.

Note: In Mac OS X, you need to be aware of a preferences setting when accessing the Zoom tool using the keyboard. If **Contextual Menu** is chosen as the Control Key Activates setting in QuarkXPress (Edit, in Windows) > Preferences > Application > Interactive, you can use the shortcuts as listed below. If Control Key Activates: **Zoom** is chosen, on the other hand, omit the Shift key from the shortcuts.

To zoom in or out using a shortcut:

Control-Shift-click/Ctrl-Spacebar-click on the page to zoom in **1**.
or
Control-Option-click/Ctrl-Alt-Spacebar-click on the page to zoom out.
or
Control-Shift-drag/Ctrl-Spacebar-drag a marquee across an area on the page that you want to magnify **2**.
or
In Mac OS X only, press Cmd-+ (plus) to zoom in or Cmd-- (minus) to zoom out. If the Content tool is chosen, deselect first.
or
Control-click/Right-click in a layout and choose Fit in Window or Actual Size.

TIP To set the Minimum, Maximum, and Increment percentages for the Zoom tool, double-click the tool, then click Modify.

TIP Click the project window zoom/maximize button to enlarge the window to full screen size (Mac OS X)/application window size (Windows). Click it again to restore the window's former size.

TIP The maximum zoom on a Windows monitor may vary depending on the current Display DPI value (screen resolution) in Edit > Preferences > Application > Display.

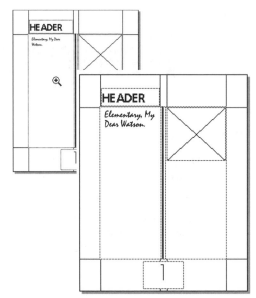

1 *Control-Shift-click/Ctrl-Spacebar-click on a page to zoom in.*

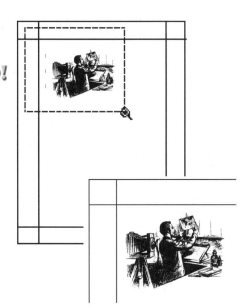

2 *Control-Shift-drag/Ctrl-Spacebar-drag over a section of a page to magnify that chosen area.*

Zoom In or Out

Screen redraw shortcuts

Forced redraw Cmd-Option-. (period)/
Ctrl-Alt-. Use this to correct
an incomplete screen redraw.

Stop redraw Cmd-./Ctrl-. (period) *or* Esc
or perform another action
(select an item, choose another
command, etc.)

1 *Click a **layout tab** at the bottom of the project window.*

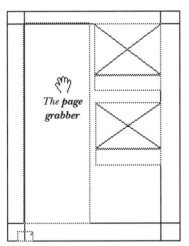

2 *Option-drag/Alt-drag to move a page in the project window.*

Moving around

To switch between layouts: 6.0!

Click a layout tab at the bottom of the
project window **1**.
or
From the Layout menu, choose Previous,
Next, First, or Last.
or
Choose from the Layout > Go To submenu.

Note: The page grabber isn't accessible
while the Zoom tool is chosen.

To move a layout in the project window using the page grabber hand:

Option-drag/Alt-drag to move a layout in
the project window. The cursor will temporarily turn into a hand icon **2**, and the
layout will redraw as you scroll. If Speed
Scroll is on in QuarkXPress (Edit, in
Windows) > Preferences > Application >
Interactive, pictures and blends may be
greeked (grayed out) as you scroll.

TIP Using the XPert Pilot palette in XPert
Tools Pro by a lowly apprentice production, inc. ("alap," for short), you can
choose user-defined view sizes, navigate
between pages, or quickly zip over to
any area of the currently displayed page
by clicking a thumbnail-sized replica.

Switch Between Layouts; Page Grabber

To move a layout in the project window using the scroll arrows, bars, or boxes:

Click a scroll arrow to scroll a short distance through a layout in the direction in which the arrow is pointing **1**.
or
Move a scroll box to move through a layout more quickly. The page number in the lower left corner of the project window will update if you move to a different page.
or
Click a gray scroll bar area to scoot quickly through a layout: Click above the right scroll box to jump upward, or click below it to jump downward. Click to the left of the bottom scroll box to jump to the left, or click to the right of it to jump to the right.

TIP The scroll speed and other scroll preferences are set in QuarkXPress (Edit, in Windows) > Preferences > Application > Interactive (see page 412).

To move through a layout using the extended keyboard:

Press Page Up or Page Down to move up or down one full screen **2**–**3**.
or
Press Shift-End/Ctrl-Page Down to go to the top of the last page in the layout.
or
Press Shift-Page Up to go to the top of the previous page.
or
Press Shift-Page Down to go to the top of the next page.
or
In Mac OS X, press Home to go to the top of the first page in the layout, or press End to go to the bottom of the last page (or the blank space to the right of the last page).

In Windows, press Ctrl-Home to go to the start of the current story, or press Ctrl-End to go to the end of the story.

For more shortcuts like these, see page 500.

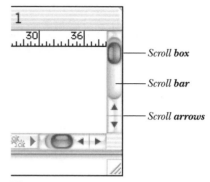

1 *The standard* **Macintosh** *window features:* **scroll boxes, bars,** *and* **arrows**

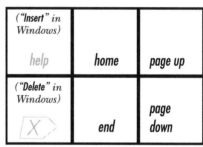

2 *Part of an extended keyboard in Mac OS X*

3 *The page that's currently showing in the* **upper left corner** *of the project window is the page that QuarkXPress considers to be displayed, even if only a small portion of that page is showing.*

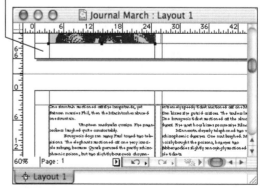

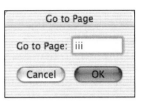

1 *Press Cmd-J/Ctrl-J to get to the* **Go to Page** *dialog box quickly.*

The **Page Layout** *palette*

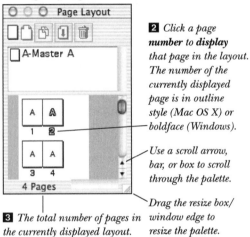

2 *Click a page* **number** *to* **display** *that page in the layout. The number of the currently displayed page is in outline style (Mac OS X) or boldface (Windows).*

Use a scroll arrow, bar, or box to scroll through the palette.

Drag the resize box/ window edge to resize the palette.

3 *The total number of pages in the currently displayed layout.*

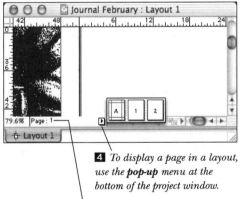

4 *To display a page in a layout, use the* **pop-up** *menu at the bottom of the project window.*

5 *Or double-click the current page number,* **enter** *the desired page number, then press Return/Enter.*

To go to a page using a command:

Choose Page > Previous, Next, First, or Last.
or
Choose Page > Go to (Cmd-J/Ctrl-J), enter the desired page number in the Go to Page field, then click OK **1**.

TIP If the desired page has a prefix that was applied using the Section command, be sure to enter that prefix along with the number in the Go to Page dialog box. Also make sure the number is entered in the correct format (e.g. lowercase Roman, numeric). To display a page based on its position in the layout rather than its applied Section number, enter "+" before the number. See page 96.

To go to a page using the Page Layout palette:

1. Choose Window > Show Page Layout (F10/F4).

2. Click the desired page number under the layout page icon **2**.
   or
   Double-click a layout page icon. (Single-clicking will highlight the icon but not display the page.)

TIP When a page icon is highlighted, its number displays in the lower left corner of the Page Layout palette. If a page begins a section, an asterisk will follow the number. If no page icon is highlighted, the total number of pages the layout contains will display instead (e.g., "8 Pages") **3**.

To go to a page using the Go-to-page menu or field:

Choose a page number from the Go-to-page pop-up menu at the bottom of the project window **4**.
or
Double-click the current page number at the bottom of the project window **5**, enter the desired page number, then press Return/Enter.

Arrange, Activate Projects

6.0! **To arrange multiple project windows:**

In Mac OS X, choose any of the following commands from the Window menu (or Shift-click the project window title bar and choose any of the commands from there):

Bring All to Front to bring all the currently open QuarkXPress project windows to the front of any other open application windows without changing their size, location, or stacking position.
or
Tile to stack all the currently open project windows in neat horizontal strips **1**.
or
Stack to stack project windows at full size in a stair-stepped arrangement.

In Windows, choose any of the following commands from the Window menu:

Cascade to stack project windows at full size in a stair-stepped arrangement.
or
Tile Horizontally to arrange project windows in horizontal strips.
or
Tile Vertically to arrange project windows in columns.

To activate an open project: 6.0!

Choose the name of any open project from the bottom of the Window menu.

In Mac OS X, you can also Shift-click a project title bar and choose from a list of open files.

In Mac OS X, a bullet will appear next to the name of any open but not active project that contains unsaved changes.

TIP If more than one monitor is hooked up, and Tile to Multiple Monitors is checked in Preferences > Application > Display, the open projects will be distributed among the monitors.

Freeze the frame

With **Save Document Position** checked in QuarkXPress (Edit, in Windows) > Preferences > Application > Save, projects will reopen in the same location, display size, and window size that they were in when they were last closed. With this option unchecked, projects will reopen at full window size in Fit in Window view.

Nifty tricks

In Mac OS X, hold down Option and choose Window > Tile or Stack to tile or stack all open projects into Thumbnails view. In Windows, hold down Alt-Shift and choose Cascade or a Tile command from the Window menu.

For Actual Size view in Mac OS X or Windows, while choosing the Tile or Stack command, hold down Control/Ctrl-Alt, or for Fit in Window view, hold down Cmd/Ctrl-Shift.

Or in Mac OS X, press Shift plus any of the above-mentioned keys, click the project window title bar, and choose Tile or Stack.

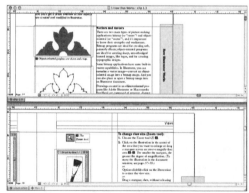

1 *This is after choosing Window >* **Tile** *in Mac OS X. In Windows,* **Tile Horizontally** *does the same thing.*

Undoing edits

If you're nervous about making mistakes, relax. You will never (okay, rarely) have to retrace your steps if you take advantage of all the safety mechanisms QuarkXPress has to offer. Your computer has a memory, and you can rely on it.

In most cases, the last maneuver you performed can be undone using the Edit > **Undo** command. If you change your mind again, choose Edit > **Redo.**

Get in the habit of **saving** after every couple of moves (see page 40). For some reason, beginning "Quarkers" are often reluctant to use this command (or are too absorbed with other tasks) and end up learning the hard way. Having learned a few hard lessons ourselves, we now save constantly, and we make a special point of saving before we perform any complicated maneuvers. Then, if we make the inevitable multiple-step blunder, we choose File > **Revert to Saved** to get back to the last-saved version of the file. (Also read about multiple undos/redos on the following three pages.)

The undo shortcut (Cmd-Z/Ctrl-Z) can also be used to **restore** the last-used settings in an open dialog box. To cancel out of a dialog box altogether without applying any values, click **Cancel** (Cmd-./Ctrl-.).

QuarkXPress has two features for backing up a whole project: **Auto Save** and **Auto Backup.** Read about these features on page 413.

And finally, if you're working on a complicated object, you can **duplicate** it (Item > Duplicate or Cmd-D/Ctrl-D) and set the copy aside for safekeeping (put it on the pasteboard). Then later you can compliment yourself on your great foresight.

Basic Undo

6.0! If you're accustomed to using a multiple undo feature in other applications, and have longed for the same thing in Quark-XPress, your prayers have been answered. Now you can undo up to 30 edits, in reverse order, or redo up to the same number of actions that you've undone. QuarkXPress stores those edits in memory (it's called the Undo History), replacing the oldest one on the list as each new edit is performed.

You may want to scan these pages and then reread them after you've learned how to perform some edits.

To undo via a shortcut or button:

As we said on the previous page, to reverse your last edit, one option is to choose Edit > Undo (Cmd-Z/Ctrl-Z). You can choose the same command again to undo the next most recent action, and so on, until no actions remain in the Undo History. *Note:* This is the default shortcut for Undo. If it doesn't work, see the preferences information on page 414.
or
Click the Undo button ⟲▸ at the bottom of the project window **1**–**2**. Keep clicking the button, if desired, to continue undoing. This button won't be available if the last edit can't be undone (see the sidebar on the following page) or if the Undo History is empty.

TIP If you perform an edit that affects the whole project, that edit is added to the Undo History for all the layout spaces in that project. See our chart on page 35, which lists the edits that affect whole projects and the edits that affect individual layouts.

Changing undo preferences

You can change the **shortcut** used to invoke the Redo function, as well as specify **how many** undos can be stored ("cached") at a time, in QuarkXPress (Edit, in Windows) > Preferences > Application > Undo. See page 414.

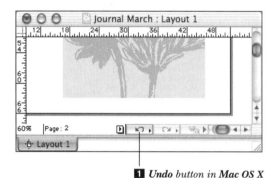

1 *Undo button in* **Mac OS X**

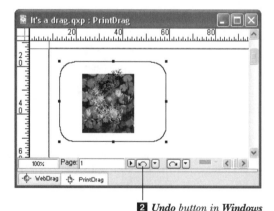

2 *Undo button in* **Windows**

Undo undoes more 6.0!

You can undo many edits in QuarkXPress 6 that you couldn't undo in previous versions, including:

- Get Text
- Get Picture
- Link/unlink text boxes
- Crop to Box for runaround and clipping paths
- Convert Text to Table, Convert Table to Text, and Convert Table to Group
- Edits made in the Edit > Style Sheets dialog box
- Layers palette commands, such as New Layer, Delete Layer, Duplicate Layer, Move Item to Layer, Merge Layers, Move Layer, Delete Layer, and Delete Unused Layers
- Colors palette shade percentage changes
- You can undo multiple color edits if those edits were made via a Colors palette context menu command, such as New Color, Edit Color, Duplicate Color, Delete Color, Make Spot, and Make Process.

These operations still can't be undone:

- Changes made in the Edit Colors dialog box
- Master pages changes (e.g., duplicating a master page or choosing commands from the context menu over the Page Layout palette while a master page is displayed)—once a layout page is redisplayed
- Edit Layer Attributes

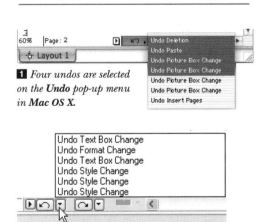

1 *Four undos are selected on the* **Undo** *pop-up menu in* **Mac OS X.**

2 *The* **Undo** *pop-up menu in* **Windows**

To undo via a menu command: 6.0!

Each reversible edit you perform is added to the Undo History pop-up menu, which opens when you press and hold the Undo button in Mac OS X **1**/the disclosure triangle next to the Undo button in Windows **2**. The most recently performed edit is listed at the top of the Undo History pop-up menu; the oldest edit is at the bottom.

When you make a selection on the Undo History pop-up menu, *all* subsequent edits (all the edits listed above the one you select on the menu) are selected and undone automatically. Unfortunately, you can't single out an edit from the middle of the list and undo just that one.

Beware! This doesn't make any sense to us, but the Undo History pop-up menu is *emptied* automatically whenever you perform any edit that's nonreversible or you choose File > Revert to Saved.

Regardless of what appears on the Undo History pop-up menu, the current maximum number of undos will still be available via the Undo command or button.

The Undo History *isn't* cleared when you perform nonreversible edits, such as those listed below, and thus they're exceptions to the above-mentioned rule:

- Choose File > Save
- Create a new master page
- Duplicate a master page
- Apply a master page to a layout page
- Create or move a ruler guide on a layout page
- Delete a ruler guide from a layout page
- Check the Use OPI option for a picture in Item > Modify > OPI

6.0! The Redo command redoes the last edit that you've undone. You can choose the command again and again to reverse multiple undos, going backward in history.

To redo edits that were undone:

Method 1

Choose Edit > Redo (Cmd-Shift-Z/Ctrl-Shift-Z). You can keep choosing the same command to reverse more undos, until the Redo History empties out. *Note:* If this command doesn't work, read about Undo preferences on page 414.

Method 2

Click the Redo button at the bottom of the project window. Click again to reverse more undos. This button won't be available if the Redo History is empty.

Method 3

Each edit you perform is added to the Redo History pop-up menu, which opens when you press and hold the Redo button in Mac OS X **1**/the disclosure triangle next to the Redo button in Windows **2**. The most recently performed undo will be listed at the top of the Redo History pop-up menu, and so on down in order. When you select an edit on the menu, that undo and all edits that are listed above it are selected and reversed.

Note: The Redo History is usually empty because QuarkXPress clears it automatically whenever you perform an edit other than Undo or Redo. When the Redo History is empty, the Redo button is unavailable.

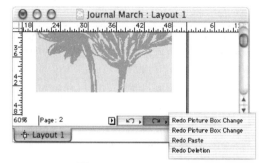

1 *The Redo pop-up menu in Mac OS X*

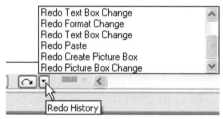

2 *The Redo pop-up menu in Windows*

Multiple Redo

Text Input 4

Continuing with your studies

Once you've read this chapter and learned the **rudiments** of manipulating text—getting it into a box, highlighting it, and rearranging it—you'll be ready to explore these other topics:

Paragraph formats   Chapter 6

Typography   Chapter 7

Style sheets   Chapter 13

Bézier text paths   Chapter 18

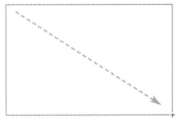

1 *Drag with a **Text Box** tool.*

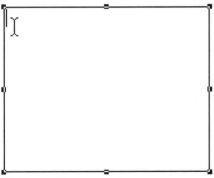

2 *A new text box is created.*

How does text get onto a page?

To input or import text in QuarkXPress, you first have to create a box to put it in or a text path to put it on. QuarkXPress has five tools that are expressly used for creating different-shaped text boxes, as well as two Bézier Text Box tools and four Text-Path tools. In addition, you can convert any item into a text box or text path.

Note: If you check Automatic Text Box in the New Project dialog box when you create a project, a text box will appear on all the pages in the default layout. This box is used to flow text from page to page, and you'll learn all about it in the next chapter. For now, you can just delete the auto text box if it gets in the way (click on it, then press Cmd-K/Ctrl-K—or, if you're in a lousy mood, Cmd-Option-Shift-K/Ctrl-Alt-Shift-K might cheer you up).

Text box basics

To create a text box:

1. Choose any Text Box tool except a Bézier text tool (they're covered in Chapter 18). A A A A A The cursor will turn into a crosshair.

2. Drag in any direction **1**. When you release the mouse, the finished box will be selected and ready for inputting **2**. When the Content tool is chosen and a text box is selected, a blinking text insertion marker appears in the box and the pointer turns into an I-beam.

TIP Remember the Edit > Undo command, which undoes most operations.

63

To resize a text box manually:

1. Choose the Item or Content tool (Shift-F8).

2. Click a box.

3. Drag any handle **1**–**2**.
   or
   To resize the box and preserve its original proportions, hold down Option-Shift/Alt-Shift while dragging. (Hold down Shift without Option/Alt to turn the box into a square.) Release Shift or Option-Shift/Alt-Shift after you release the mouse.

TIP Make sure the point of the cursor arrow is directly over one of the box handles before pressing the mouse. The cursor will change into a pointing-hand icon.

TIP If Delayed Item Dragging: Live Refresh is on in QuarkXPress (Edit, in Windows) > Preferences > Application > Interactive and you pause before dragging a handle of a text box, the text wrap will update continuously as you drag (the pointer will turn into a cluster of arrows) **3**. In the Delay field, you can specify the length of the pause required before dragging (0.1–5).

To resize a text box using the Measurements palette:

1. Choose the Item or Content tool.

2. Click a box.

3. Change the W value on the Measurements palette for the width of the box, then press Return/Enter **4**. You need to include an abbreviation for the measurement unit (e.g., "p" or "mm") only if the value you're entering is not in the current default unit. See page 30.
   and/or
   Change the H value on the Measurements palette for the height of the box, then press Return/Enter.

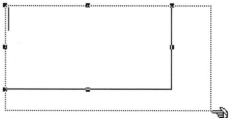

1 *Resize a box by dragging any of its four* **corner handles** *(note the hand pointer)…*

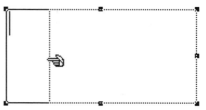

2 *…or drag any of its four* **midpoint handles.**

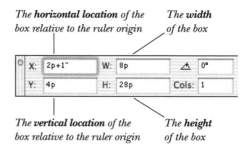

3 *Pause-dragging with* **Live Refresh** *on*

The **horizontal location** *of the box relative to the ruler origin*   *The* **width** *of the box*

X:	2p+1"	W:	8p	△	0°
Y:	4p	H:	28p	Cols:	1

The **vertical location** *of the box relative to the ruler origin*   *The* **height** *of the box*

4 *The current value can be replaced, or a plus or minus sign and then a value can be entered to the right of the current number to add to or subtract from it. In our example, the X field contains two different measurement units. When Return/Enter is pressed, the value is converted to inches (our default unit).*

Snap to it

If View > **Snap to Guides** is on (Shift-F7 toggles it on and off) and you drag the handle of a box or an anchor point near a guide, the handle or point will snap to the guide with a little tug. Turn Snap to Guides off to drag items manually without the little tug.

Mrs. Trenor was a tall, fair woman whose height just saved her from redundancy. Her rosy blondness had survived some forty years of futile activity without showing much trace of ill-usage except in a diminished play

EDITH WHARTON

1 *Pause before dragging to see the* **contents** *of the item as you move it…*

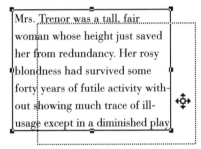

Mrs. Trenor was a tall, fair woman whose height just saved her from redundancy. Her rosy blondness had survived some forty years of futile activity without showing much trace of ill-usage except in a diminished play

2 *… or drag* **without pausing** *to see only the* **outline** *of the box as it's moved. Use this method on a slow machine.*

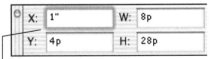

| X: | 1" | W: | 8p |
| Y: | 4p | H: | 28p |

3 *To* **position** *an object very precisely, enter new X and/or Y values on the Measurements palette.*

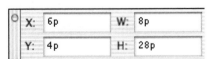

| X: | 6p | W: | 8p |
| Y: | 4p | H: | 28p |

4 *After pressing Return/Enter, the 1" value entered in the X field is converted to its equivalent in the* **default** *measurement unit (in this case, picas).*

To move a text box manually:

1. Choose the Item tool. Or if you're using the Content tool, hold down Cmd/Ctrl to turn it into a temporary Item tool.

2. Press inside a text box, pause briefly for the text to redraw, then drag the item to a new location on the same page or on a different page **1**–**2** (the pointer will be a cluster of arrowheads). The X and Y position values on the Measurements palette will update as you drag. To force scrolling, knock your pointer into the edge of the project window while dragging.

TIP Hold down Shift as you drag to constrain the movement to a horizontal or vertical axis. Release the mouse before releasing Shift. To use ruler guides to position an item, see page 201.

Use the Measurements palette to move the upper left corner of an item to a precise X/Y location, relative to the ruler origin.

To reposition a text box or any other item using the Measurements palette:

1. Choose the Item or Content tool.

2. Click the item you want to reposition.

3. Enter a new number in the X field on the Measurements palette to change the horizontal position of the item's bounding box relative to the ruler origin **3**, which, unless you change it, is located at the uppermost left corner of the project window.
   and/or
   Enter a new number in the Y field on the Measurements palette to change the vertical position of the box relative to the ruler origin.

4. Press Return/Enter **4**.

TIP To use arithmetic in the X or Y field, enter "+" after the current number, then the amount you want to add. To subtract, enter "-"; to multiply, enter "*"; or to divide, enter "/".

Working with text

To input text:

1. Choose the Content tool.

2. Click in a text box (or click on a text path) to create an insertion point.

3. Start typing **1**. Press Return/Enter whenever you want to begin a new paragraph **2**.

TIP Choose View > Show Invisibles (Cmd-I/ Ctrl-I) to reveal paragraph returns, spaces, and other non-printing characters.

TIP To move text inward from *all* sides of its box, select the box, choose Item > Modify, click the Text tab, then enter a Text Inset: All Edges value (click Apply to preview). Or to specify a different value for each side of a rectangular box, check Multiple Insets, then change the Top, Left, Bottom, or Right values (see page 71). And remember, you can always move the text box downward on the page!

What is the text overflow symbol?

If a text box is too small to display all the text that it contains, a text overflow symbol appears in the lower right corner of the box **3**. The text overflow symbol will disappear if the text box is enlarged enough to display all the type that it contains or if the box is linked to another box for the text to spill into.

The text overflow symbol doesn't print; it's merely an indicator that there's hidden text in the buffer. Only text that's visible in a box will print.

TIP If pages are mysteriously added to your layout when a text box becomes full, it means Auto Page Insertion is on in QuarkXPress (Edit, in Windows) > Preferences > Print Layout > General.

Keep the case open

UPPERCASE characters (input with Caps Lock or Shift pressed down) can't be converted back to lowercase. Lowercase characters, on the other hand *can* be converted into all caps or small caps with a flip of a switch. To typeset an all uppercase word, first type it all lowercase (or with just an initial cap), then select it and click the big "K" in the lower right corner of the Measurements palette (or click the little "K" for all small caps).

As soon as they were gone, Elizabeth walked out to recover her spirits; or in other words, to dwell without interruption on those subjects that must deaden them more. Mr. Darcy's behavior astonished

1 *Text is typed into a text box with the Content tool.*

As·soon·as·they·were·gone,·Elizabeth· walked·out·to·recover·her·spirits;·or·in· other·words,·to·dwell·without·interruption· on·those·subjects·that·must·deaden·them· more.·Mr.·Darcy's·behavior·astonished· and·vexed·her.¶
"Why,·if·he·came·only·to·be·silent,·
Jane Austen

2 *Press **Return** to begin a new **paragraph**.*

As soon as they were gone, Elizabeth walked out to recover her spirits; or in other words, to dwell without interruption on those subjects that must deaden them more. Mr. Darcy's behavior astonished ⊠

3 *The red **text overflow** symbol appears when a box is too small to display all the text that it contains.*

On an exceptionally hot evening early in July, a young man came

1 *Double-click anywhere in the middle of a **word** to highlight it **without** including any punctuation.*

On an exceptionally hot evening early in July, a young man came

2 *Double-click between a **word** and a **punctuation mark** or to the right of the punctuation mark to select both. Read more about **smart space** on page 192.*

On an exceptionally hot evening early in July, a young man came out of the garret in which he lodged in S. Place and walked slowly, as though in hesitation, towards K. Bridge.

He had successfully avoided meeting his landlady on the staircase. His garret was under the roof of a high, five-storied

3 *Triple-click to highlight a **line**.*

On an exceptionally hot evening early in July, a young man came out of the garret in which he lodged in S. Place and walked slowly, as though in hesitation, towards K. Bridge.

He had successfully avoided meeting his landlady on the staircase. His garret was under the roof of a high, five-storied

Fyodor Dostoevsky

4 *Click **four** times to highlight a **paragraph**.*

To highlight text:

1. Choose the Content tool.
2. Drag across the text you want to highlight.
or
Use one of these fast-clicking methods **1**–**4**:

Number of clicks	What gets highlighted
1 click	Creates an **insertion point**
2 clicks on word	A **word** (but *not* the space following it)
2 clicks between word and punctuation	A **word** *and* the punctuation following it (but *not* the space following it)
3 clicks	A **line**
4 clicks	A **paragraph**
5 clicks	A whole **story** (all the text in a box or in a series of linked boxes)

or
To highlight a whole **story,** click in a text box, then choose Edit > Select All (Cmd-A/Ctrl-A). Hidden overflow text, if any, will be included in the selection. *Note:* If the Item tool is selected when you choose Select All, all items on the currently displayed page or spread and surrounding pasteboard will become selected instead!
or
Click in a text box at the beginning of a **text string,** then Shift-click at the end of the text string.
or
To select from the current **cursor** position to the **end** of a story: Cmd-Option-Shift-down arrow/Ctrl-Alt-Shift-down arrow. (See page 501 for more shortcuts.)
or
To select a series of **words,** double-click the first word, keep the mouse button down on the second click, then drag. Or triple-click, then drag downward to highlight a series of **lines.**

Highlight Text

To delete text:

1. Choose the Content tool.

2. Click to the right of the character to be deleted **1**, then press Delete/ Backspace. (Press the left or right arrow on the keyboard to move the insertion point one character at a time.)
   or
   First highlight the text you want to delete **2** (see the previous page). Then in Mac OS X, press Delete or choose Edit > Clear. In Windows, press Backspace or Delete or choose Edit > Delete.

TIP To delete the character to the right of the cursor, press the del/Delete key on an extended keyboard or press Shift-Delete on a nonextended keyboard.

The Line Text-Path tool and Orthogonal Text-Path tool are discussed below. The Bézier Text-Path and Freehand Text-Path tools are discussed in Chapter 18.

To create a straight text path:

1. Choose the Orthogonal Text-Path tool ⁴⁺ to draw a straight horizontal or vertical text path **3**.
   or
   Choose the Line Text-Path tool ▽ to draw a straight-line path at any angle with no corners or bends **4**.

2. Drag to draw the path, and leave it selected.

3. Choose the Content tool.

4. Start typing. The text will march along the path.

Same ol' selection

If you deselect and then reselect a box with the Content tool, the **last** group of characters that were highlighted, if any, will re-highlight. To create a new insertion point, click once more in the text box.

1 *Pressing Delete with the cursor at this insertion point would remove the "S."*

2 *Pressing Delete with this selection highlighted would delete the "HES."*

3 *Drag vertically or horizontally with the **Orthogonal Text-Path** tool.*

4 *Drag at any angle with the **Line Text-Path** tool.*

Delete Text; Draw Straight Text Path

Hip. Well shone, moon—Truly, the
moon shines with a good grace.
Dem. Well roared, lion.
The. Well run, Thisbe.
The. Well moused, lion.

1 *To move text, highlight it, then choose Edit > **Cut**.*

Dem. Well roared, lion.
The. Well run, Thisbe.
The. Well moused, lion.

2 ***Click** to create a new insertion point.*

Dem. Well roared, lion.
The. Well run, Thisbe.
Hip. Well shone, moon—Truly, the
moon shines with a good grace.
The. Well moused, lion.
~ *William Shakespeare*

3 *Choose Edit > **Paste**.*

To delete any item:

Choose the Item or Content tool, click
the item you want to delete, then choose
Item > Delete (Cmd-K/Ctrl-K).
or
Choose the Item tool, and click the item
you want to delete. Then in Mac OS X,
press Delete or choose Edit > Clear. In
Windows, press Delete or Backspace or
choose Edit > Delete.

The Clipboard is a holding area that stores
one cut or copied selection at a time. The
current contents of the Clipboard can be
retrieved an unlimited number of times
via the Paste command. The current
Clipboard contents will be replaced if you
invoke the Copy or Cut command in any
application, and will be deleted if you turn
off your computer.

To rearrange text using the Clipboard:

1. Choose the Content tool.
2. Highlight the text you want to move **1**.
3. Choose Edit > Cut (Cmd-X/Ctrl-X)
   to place the highlighted text on the
   Clipboard and *remove* it from its current
   location.
   or
   Choose Edit > Copy (Cmd-C/Ctrl-C)
   to place a *copy* of the highlighted text
   on the Clipboard and leave the highlighted text in its current location.
4. Click in a text box to create a new
   insertion point **2**.
5. Choose Edit > Paste (Cmd-V/Ctrl-V) **3**.
   Smart Space takes care of adding
   spaces where needed (see page 192).

TIP The Clipboard can also be used to cut
   or copy any type of box, line, or group
   when the Item tool is selected, or a picture if the Content tool is chosen. Paste
   using the same tool that was used to
   Cut or Copy—unless you want the item
   to be anchored (see page 197)!

Delete Any Item; Rearrange Text

You can use the Drag and Drop Text feature to move or copy text quickly without having to use the Cut, Copy, or Paste command. You can drag and drop text within the same box or between linked boxes or table cells (a story), but not between unlinked boxes or cells. This is a very handy feature for making quick copy-edits.

Note: To enable the drag-and-drop feature, go to QuarkXPress (Edit, in Windows) > Preferences > Application > Interactive, then check Drag and Drop Text **1**.

In Mac OS X only, if the Drag and Drop Text option is off, you can still perform the command: Cmd-Control-drag the text to move it or Cmd-Control-Shift-drag to move a copy of it.

To drag and drop text:

1. Choose the Content tool.

2. Highlight the text you want to move or copy (see page 67).

3. Release the mouse.

4. To move the highlighted text, drag the blinking cursor to a new location in the same text box or table cell or in a box or cell that it's linked to. A hollow box will display under the pointer as you drag **2**–**3**.
   or
   To move a copy of the text, hold down Shift while dragging the blinking cursor to a new location (a hollow box and a plus sign will also display as you drag).

TIP Text that is dragged and dropped is also placed on the Clipboard, but you won't be aware of it unless you use the Paste command or choose Edit > Show Clipboard.

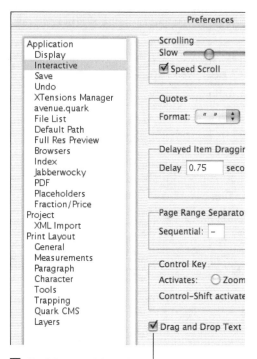

1 *Check* **Drag and Drop Text** *in QuarkXPress (Edit, in Windows) > Preferences > Application >* **Interactive**.

If you want to get somewhere else, you must run at least twice as fast as that. Now, *here*, you see, it takes all the running you can do, to keep in the same place.

2 *To* **drag and drop** *(move) text, highlight it, release the mouse, then drag the highlighted text (you'll see a blinking cursor) to a new position.*

"Now, *here*, you see, it takes all the running *you* can do, to keep in the same place. If you want to get somewhere else, you must run at least twice as fast as that..."

Lewis Carroll

3 *The sentences have been swapped.*

Drag-and-Drop Text

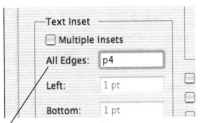

1 *To make the **Text Inset** uniform on all sides, leave Multiple Insets unchecked, and enter an **All Edges** value.*

> Promote then as an object of primary importance, institutions for the general diffusion of knowledge. In proportion as the structure of a government gives force to public opinion, it is essential that public opinion be enlightened.
>
> GEORGE WASHINGTON

2 *A text box with a **Text Inset** of 0 pt*

> Promote then as an object of primary importance, institutions for the general diffusion of knowledge. In proportion as the structure of a government gives force to public opinion, it is essential that public opinion be enlightened.

3 *The same text box with a **Text Inset** of 7 pt*

Working with text boxes

The Text Inset is the blank space between text and the four edges of the box that contains it. A Text Inset value greater than zero should be applied to any box that has a frame in order to create breathing space between the text and the frame.

To change the Text Inset:

1. Choose the Item or Content tool.

2. Click a text box.

3. Choose Item > Modify (Cmd-M/ Ctrl-M), then click the Text tab.

4. To apply a uniform Text Inset value to all four edges of the text box, leave Multiple Insets unchecked, then enter a value in the All Edges field (1 pt. is the default) **1**–**3**. If you're entering a value in points, you don't have to reenter the "pt."
   or
   To enter a different Text Inset value for each edge of a rectangular text box, check Multiple Insets **4**–**5**, then enter Top, Left, Bottom, and Right values.

5. *Optional:* Click Apply to preview, then readjust the Text Inset values, if desired.

6. Click OK.

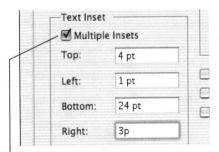

4 *To enter separate **Text Inset** values for the Top, Left, Bottom, and Right edges of a text box, first check **Multiple Insets**.*

> Promote then as an object of primary importance, institutions for the general diffusion of knowledge. In proportion as the structure of a government gives force to public opinion, it is essential that public opinion be enlightened.

5 *The text box with a **different Text Inset** value on each of its four sides*

Text Inset

These instructions apply to text boxes, pictures boxes, and contentless boxes.

To apply a frame to any type of box:

1. Choose the Item or Content tool.

2. Click a box (Bézier or standard).

3. Choose Item > Frame (Cmd-B/Ctrl-B).

4. Choose a preset Width from the pop-up menu or enter a custom Width **1**. You can enter fractions of a point.

5. Choose from the Style pop-up menu. (To create a custom dashed or multi-line frame, see pages 223–226.) *Note:* In Web layouts, only the Solid and Solid 3-D frames are available for HTML text boxes, which are boxes for which Convert to Graphic on Export is unchecked at the bottom of the dialog box. If this option is checked, an HTML text box will be converted to a raster box and any frame can be applied to it.

6. Choose from the Frame: Color pop-up menu.

7. Choose from the Frame: Shade pop-up menu or enter a Shade percentage.

Frame like a pro

■ Apply a Text Inset greater than zero in Item > Modify > Text to add breathing room between the text and the frame.

■ Use narrow, delicate frames rather than thick, ornate ones. Gaudy frames distract from, and overwhelm, the text. Less is more.

■ Unless you want the whole world to know you're new to graphic design, use frames sparingly here or there in a couple of spots—not frames, frames everywhere.

8. *Optional:* To recolor the white areas in a multiline or dashed style, choose from the Gap: Color and Shade pop-up menus.

9. Click Apply to preview, make any adjustments, then click OK (illustrations on the next page).

TIP To remove a frame, select the box, choose Item > Frame again, then enter 0 in the Width field.

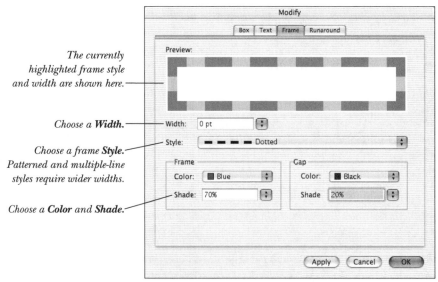

The currently highlighted frame style and width are shown here.

*Choose a **Width**.*

*Choose a frame **Style**. Patterned and multiple-line styles require wider widths.*

*Choose a **Color** and **Shade**.*

1 *The **Frame** pane of the Item > **Modify** dialog box*

Frames illustrated

Speak what you think now in hard words, and tomorrow speak what tomorrow thinks in hard words again, though it contradict every thing you said today.—"Ah, so you shall be sure to be misunderstood."—Is it so bad, then, to be misunderstood? Pythagoras was misunderstood, and Socrates, and Jesus, and Luther, and Copernicus, and Galileo, and Newton, and every pure and wise spirit that ever took flesh. To be great is to be misunderstood.

Ralph Waldo Emerson

Fish, like guests, smell after three days.

Ben Franklin

If you have built castles in the air, your work need not be lost; that is where they should be. Now put the foundations under them.

HENRY DAVID THOREAU

*Sometimes **simplest** is best.*

DO I CONTRADICT MYSELF?

VERY WELL THEN...

I CONTRADICT MYSELF;

I AM LARGE...

I CONTAIN MULTITUDES.

Walt Whitman

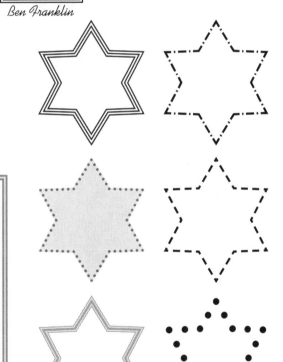

*These star-shaped Bézier boxes have **dashed** or **striped** frames. They were created using the Starburst tool.*

Frame Text or Picture Box

Text boxes can be made see-through so they can be layered on top of each other.

To make a text box see-through:

1. Choose the Item or Content tool.

2. If all the items you want to work with are on the same layer, click the text box that is to be on top. And if it's not on top, choose Item > Bring to Front (F5). If the items are on different layers, make sure the layers are in the correct stacking order (see page 280).

3. Choose Item > Runaround (Cmd-T/Ctrl-T).

4. Choose Type: None **1**, then click OK.

5. If the Colors palette isn't already open, choose View > Show Colors (F12).

6. Click the Background Color button on the Colors palette **2**.

7. Click None **3**–**4**. (Don't choose Black at a 0 shade percentage; that would make the box opaque white—not transparent.)

TIP To select an item that's behind another item, Cmd-Option-Shift-click/Ctrl-Alt-Shift-click. Each click will select the next item behind the currently selected items under the pointer (more about this on page 195).

TIP To group multiple items so they'll move in unison, see page 184.

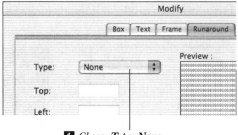

1 *Choose* **Type: None.**

2 *Click the* **Background Color** *button…*

3 *…then click* **None** *to make the box transparent.*

The **Colors** *palette*

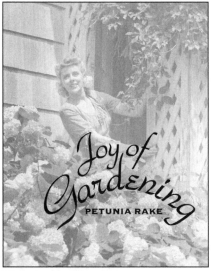

4 *Text in a* **transparent** *box on top of a picture*

Transparent Box

Get there fast

With the Item tool selected, you can double-click inside a text box (or picture box, line, or table) to open the Modify dialog box. Cmd/Ctrl double-click the item if the Content tool is selected.

Once upon a time there was a Pussy-cat called Ribby, who invited a little dog called Duchess to tea.
Beatrix Potter

Once upon a time there was a Pussy-cat called Ribby, who invited a little dog called Duchess to tea.

1 *First Baseline 0*   **2** *First Baseline 1p6*

3 *A **Text Angle** of 35°: The text is rotated; the box isn't.*

Sometimes I've believed as many as six impossible things before breakfast.
Lewis Carroll

4 *A rectangular text box **skewed** at a 40° angle: Both the text and the box are skewed.*

To move text downward in its box:

To move the first line of text downward from the top of its box, select the box, choose Item > Modify (Cmd-M/Ctrl-M), click the Text tab, then enter a First Baseline: Offset value greater than 0. This value will be in addition to the current Text Inset value. From the Minimum pop-up menu, choose whether, at minimum, the first line of text will be offset from the top of the box as measured from the line's largest Cap Height, Cap + Accent [mark], or Ascent (top of the tallest character, as in an "l" or a "T") **1**–**2**. This feature isn't available for HTML text (text in a Web layout for which Convert to Graphic on Export is unchecked in Item > Modify).
or
Choose Item > Modify (Cmd-M/Ctrl-M), check Text Inset: Multiple Insets, then enter a higher Top value.
or
This may feel like cheating, but sometimes simplest is best: Just yank the whole box downward on the page with the Item tool.

To rotate text in a box without rotating its box, follow these instructions. To rotate text and its box, see the following page.

To change the text angle:

1. Choose the Item or Content tool.

2. Click a text box of any shape (not HTML text). You can change the angle for text in only one item at a time.

3. Choose Item > Modify (Cmd-M/ Ctrl-M), then click the Text tab.

4. Enter a Text Angle value between –360° and 360°, then click Apply to preview.

5. Click OK **3**. The text can still be edited. You can restore the Text Angle to 0° at any time.

TIP To skew text **4**, follow the instructions above, except click the Box tab in Item > Modify, then enter a Skew value between –75 and 75.

To rotate a text box using the Measurements palette:

1. Choose the Item or Content tool.

2. Click a text box (not an HTML text box).

3. In the rotation field on the Measurements palette, enter a positive value between 0° and 360° to rotate the box counterclockwise **1** or a negative value to rotate it clockwise, then press Return/Enter. You can edit the text in its rotated position.

To rotate a text box using the Rotation tool:

1. Choose the Rotation tool. ↺

2. Click a text box (not an HTML text box).

3. Press to create an axis point for rotation, then drag the mouse away from the axis to create a "lever" **2**. The further you drag away from the axis before rotating, the easier the rotation will be to control.

4. Drag clockwise or counterclockwise **3**. Hold down Shift while dragging to rotate at an increment of 45° (release the mouse first).

The flip commands flip all the text in a box, but not the box itself. Text can be modified in its flipped position.

To flip text:

1. Choose the Content tool.

2. Click a text box (not an HTML text box).

3. Choose Style > Flip Horizontal or Flip Vertical.
or
Click the Flip Horizontal ➡ and/or Flip Vertical ⬆ button on the Measurements palette **4**–**5**.

Rotate Text Box; Flip Text

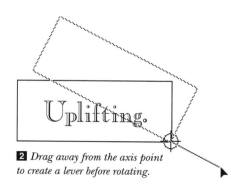

1 *The **rotation angle** of a text box*

X:	6p	W:	8p	∡	45°
Y:	4p	H:	28p	Cols:	2

Uplifting.

2 *Drag away from the axis point to create a lever before rotating.*

3 *The box rotated -90°*

It's a poor sort of memory that only works ƨbɿɒwʞɔɒd

Lewis Carroll

4 *The word "backwards" is in a separate text box, and it's **flipped horizontally**.*

Narcissus

5 *The text box containing the gray "Narcissus" was **flipped vertically**.*

Wrapping all around

Normally, text will wrap around only three sides of an item that's situated within a column. To wrap text around all sides of an item within a column, select the box that contains the text that's doing the *wrapping,* choose Item > Modify, click the Text tab, check **Run Text Around All Sides,** then click OK. See page 208.

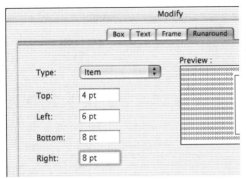

1 *In the **Runaround** pane of Item > Modify, choose Type: **Item**, then enter **Top, Left, Bottom,** and **Right** values.*

To wrap text around another item:

1. Stack the item that you want to wrap text around on top of a text box. To move a box to the front of its layer, select it with the Item or Content tool, then choose Item > Bring to Front (F5) (read about layers in Chapter 16).

2. With the new box still selected, choose Item > Runaround (Cmd-T/Ctrl-T).

3. Choose Type: Item **1**.

4. For a rectangular box, enter Top, Left, Bottom, and Right values for the space between the item in front and the type that's wrapping around it (press Tab to move quickly from field to field).
or
For a nonrectangular box, enter a single Outset value, which will apply to all of its sides.

Note: If you're entering a value in points, you don't have to reenter the "pt".

5. Click Apply to preview, make any adjustments, then click OK **2**–**3**.

We thus learn that man is descended from a hairy, tailed quadruped, probably arboreal in its habits, and an inhabitant of the Old World. This creature, if its whole structure had been examined by a naturalist, would have been classed amongst the Quadrumana, as surely as the still more ancient progenitor of the Old and New World monkeys.
The Quadrumana and all the higher mammals are probably derived from an ancient marsupial animal, and this through a long series of diversified forms, from some amphibian-like creature, and this again

> **We thus learn that man is descended from a hairy, tailed quadruped, probably arboreal in its habits, and an inhabitant of the Old World.**
> *Charles Darwin*

2 *Text will wrap around only **three** sides of an item that's situated within a column, unless Run Text Around All Sides is on for the text that's doing the wrapping (see the sidebar, above).*

We thus learn that man is descended from a hairy, tailed quadruped, probably arboreal in its habits, and an inhabitant of the Old World. This creature, if its whole structure had been examined by a naturalist, would have been classed amongst the Quadrumana, as surely as the still more ancient progenitor of the Old and New World mon- keys. The Quadrumana and all the higher mammals are probably derived from an ancient marsupial animal, and this through a long series of diversified forms, from some amphibian-like creature, and this again from some fish-like animal. In the dim obscurity of the past we can see that the early progenitor of all the Vertebrata must have

> **We thus learn that man is descended from a hairy, tailed quadruped, probably arboreal in its habits, and an inhabitant of the Old World.**
> *Charles Darwin*

3 *Text will always wrap around all four sides of an item if the item **straddles** more than one column.*

The Vertical Alignment options affect all the text contained in a box. Leading (line spacing) and interparagraph spacing, which affect one or more paragraphs, are discussed in Chapter 6.

To change vertical alignment:

1. Choose the Item or Content tool, then click a rectangular text box. Or choose the Item tool, then select multiple boxes (see page 183).

2. Choose Item > Modify (Cmd-M/Ctrl-M).

3. Click the Text tab.

4. From the Vertical Alignment: Type pop-up menu, choose Top, Centered, Bottom, or Justified **1**.

5. In vertically justified text with an Inter ¶ Max value of 0, space is added evenly between lines and paragraphs. An Inter ¶ Max value greater than 0 is the maximum space that can be added between paragraphs before leading is affected. Try raising this value and see what happens.

6. Click Apply to preview, then click OK **2**. *Note:* Make sure there isn't a return at the end of the last line in a box to which Bottom, Centered, or Justified Vertical Alignment has been applied, or the alignment will be thrown off. The Vertical Alignment options are also affected by the First Baseline and Text Inset: Top values.

TIP Vertical justification won't work if the justified text box is behind another box that has a Runaround setting other than None. To make justification work, change the Runaround Type to None for the top box in Item > Runaround.

TIP If you've chosen Centered alignment and your text happens not to have any descenders (characters that extend below the baseline), you may need to Baseline Shift the type downward slightly to make it look more centered (see page 129).

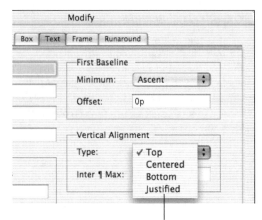

1 *The four **Vertical Alignment** options*

2

> Never put off till tomorrow what you can do the day after tomorrow.

Top *vertical alignment*

> Never put off till tomorrow what you can do the day after tomorrow.

Bottom *vertical alignment*

> Never put off till tomorrow what you can do the day after tomorrow.

Centered *vertical alignment*

> Never put off till tomorrow what you can do the day after tomorrow.
>
> *Mark Twain*

Justified *vertical alignment*

Vertical Alignment

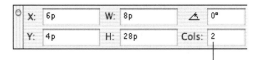

1 *The number of* **columns** *in a text box can be changed using the Measurements palette.*

There was a nice hot singey smell; and at the table, with an iron in her hand, stood a very stout short person staring anxiously at Lucie. Her print gown was tucked up, and she was wearing a large apron over her striped petti-	coat. Her little black nose went sniffle, sniffle, snuffle, and her eyes went twinkle, twinkle, twinkle; and underneath her cap—where Lucie had yellow curls—that little person had PRICKLES! *Beatrix Potter*

2 *A* **two-column** *text box...*

There was a nice hot singey smell; and at the table, with an iron in her hand, stood a very stout short person staring anxiously at Lucie.	Her print gown was tucked up, and she was wearing a large apron over her striped petti-coat. Her little black nose went sniffle, sniffle, snuffle,	and her eyes went twinkle, twinkle, twin-kle; and under-neath her cap—where Lucie had yel-low curls—that little person had PRICKLES!

3 *...is converted into a* **three-column** *text box.*

Follow either set of instructions on this page to change the number of columns and/or the gutter width in an individual box. To change the non-printing margin and column guides or to change the number of columns in a box originating from a master page, follow the instructions on page 243.

To change the number of columns using the Measurements palette:

1. Choose the Item or Content tool.
2. Select a text box.
3. Enter a number in the "Cols" field on the Measurements palette **1**.
4. Press Return/Enter **2**–**3**.

To change columns and/or gutter width using a dialog box:

1. Choose the Item or Content tool.
2. Select a text box.
3. Choose Item > Modify (Cmd-M/ Ctrl-M), then click the Text tab.
4. Change the number in the Columns field (1–30, depending on the width of the box) **4**.
   and/or
   Change the Gutter Width value for the blank space between the columns.
5. Click OK.

Change Columns, Gutter

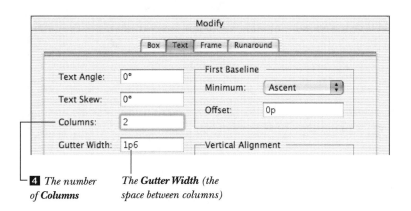

4 *The number of* **Columns**   *The* **Gutter Width** *(the space between columns)*

You can save text from a QuarkXPress file as a separate file into any of these formats: ASCII, HTML, XPress Tags, WordPerfect, Microsoft Word, or Rich Text. You can save all the text in a story, or just a highlighted portion.

To save text as a word processing file:

1. Choose the Content tool.

2. Highlight the text to be saved.
or
Click in a story.

3. Choose File > Save Text (Cmd-Option-E/Ctrl-Alt-E).
or
Control-click/Right-click and choose Save Text from the context menu.

4. Type a name for the text file in the Save As/File name field **1**–**2**.

5. If text is highlighted in the layout, you can click Entire Story or Selected Text. If you clicked in a story but didn't highlight any text, the Entire Story option will be chosen for you.

6. Choose a file format from the Format/Save as Type pop-up menu. A format's import/export filter must be enabled in order for it to appear on the list. Use the XTensions Manager to turn a filter on or off (see page 427).

7. *Optional in Windows:* If you've chosen ASCII as the format and you check Mac OS Line Endings, the standard Windows line break that's represented by a return and line feed character will be replaced by just a return character, which is standard in Mac OS X.

8. Choose a location in which to save the text file.

9. Click Save (Return/Enter).

TIP To learn more about XPress Tags, see the QuarkXPress documentation or David Blatner's *Real World QuarkXPress 6* (Peachpit Press).

Comparing the formats

ASCII strips all formatting.

HTML preserves font and type styling for importing and viewing in a browser.

WordPerfect and **Microsoft Word** may strip some formatting.

XPress Tags retains all formatting. Formatting codes will display with the text when viewed in a word processing application.

Rich Text Format preserves font, font size, type styling, and style sheet information from QuarkXPress.

1 *Type a name in the **Save As** field.*

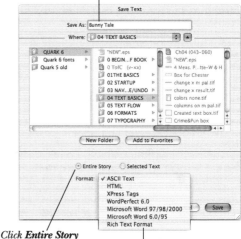

*Click **Entire Story** or click **Selected Text** (if available).* *Choose a file **format**. This is the Save Text dialog box in **Mac OS X**.*

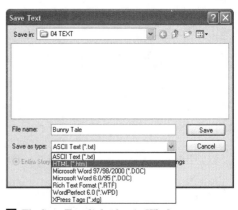

2 *The **Save Text** dialog box in **Windows***

Text Flow 5

What if

If you didn't turn on **Automatic Text Box** in the New Project dialog box but later on you decide you need an auto text box, you can add it "manually." See the instructions on page 254.

Adding pages

In the previous chapter, you learned how to get text into a box. The next step is to learn how to route overflow text from box to box and from page to page.

Auto page insertion is used for layouts in which a story flows consecutively from one page to the next, as in a book or booklet. You'll start by enabling the Automatic Text Box and Auto Page Insertion options. Then when you import or input text into an automatic text box, new pages will be added, if necessary, to contain any overflow text, and text boxes will be linked from page to page. Each layout can have up to 2,000 pages.

For layouts that contain multiple stories that may flow onto nonconsecutive pages, as in a newsletter, manual linking is a better choice (see page 89).

To turn on Auto Page Insertion for a new project:

1. Choose File > New > Project (Cmd-N/Ctrl-N) to create a new print project.

2. Check Automatic Text Box to have an automatic text box appear on every layout page in the default layout.

3. Choose or enter Page Size, Orientation, Margin Guides, and Column Guides options, then click OK.

4. Choose QuarkXPress (Edit, in Windows) > Preferences > Print Layout > General.

5. Choose Auto Page Insertion: End of Story, End of Section, or End of Document **1** (the location where you want new pages to be added).

6. Click OK.

Preferences

Display

Greek Text Below: `5 pt`   ☐ Greek Pictures

Guides

) In Front ○ Behind Snap Distance: `6`

Master Page Items

) Keep Changes ○ Delete Changes

Auto Picture Import

) Off ○ On ⦿ Verify

Hyperlinks

■ Anchor Color

■ Hyperlink Color

Framing

) Inside   ○ Outside

Page Insertion: ✓ Off
                   End of Story
                   End of Section
                   End of Document

Auto Constrain

(Cancel)   (OK)

1 *In QuarkXPress (Edit, in Windows) > Preferences > Print Layout > General, choose **Auto Page Insertion: End of Story, End of Section,** or **End of Document**.*

A text file created in a word processing or spreadsheet program can be imported into a text box or boxes in QuarkXPress, provided its import/export filter is installed and enabled (see page 427). Formats that can be imported include word processing files (such as WordPerfect and Microsoft Word), HTML files, XPress Tags, and ASCII text with or without XPress Tags.

To import text:

1. *Optional:* Turn on Auto Page Insertion (see steps 4–6 on the previous page).

2. Choose the Content tool.

3. Click in a text box. Click in an automatic text box for automatic page insertion. (If Auto Page Insertion is off, the imported text will flow into a box or a series of linked boxes, but new pages won't be added.)

4. Choose File > Get Text (Cmd-E/Ctrl-E).
   or
   Control-click/Right-click the text box and choose Get Text.

5. Locate and click a text file **1**, then click Open, or double-click the file. In Windows, you can use the "Files of type" drop-down menu to narrow or broaden the list.

6. Check Convert Quotes to convert foot and inch marks into quotation marks (see page 130) and double hyphens into em dashes.

7. *Optional:* Check Include Style Sheets to append style sheets from a Microsoft Word or WordPerfect file or when importing an ASCII file with XPress Tags codes.

8. Click Open (**1**–**4**, next page).

Word styles

■ To import style sheets applied to text in Microsoft Word, check **Include Style Sheets** in the Get Text dialog box. If any style sheet names in the Word file match style sheet names in the QuarkXPress file, an alert dialog box will appear. To learn about the options in that dialog box, see page 51 (the same dialog box appears if a conflict crops up while appending style sheets). Also check Include Style Sheets to import ASCII text with XPress tags as styled text (with typographic and formatting attributes included).

■ The **XPress Tags** filter must be enabled for the Include Style Sheets option to be available. Use the XTensions Manager to enable/disable this import/export filter.

1 *Click the* **text file** *to be imported.*

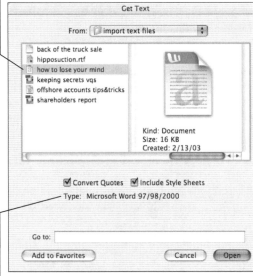

In Mac OS X, the currently highlighted file's format **Type** *is shown here. In Windows, the* **Name, Format, File Size,** *and modification* **Date** *of the currently highlighted file are shown.*

Auto Page Insertion on

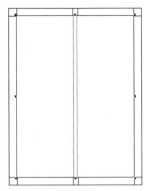

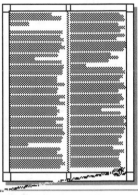

2 *New pages are created* **automatically** *to accommodate the imported text, and the text is linked in a continuous flow.*

1 *Auto Page Insertion is* **on,** *an automatic text box is selected, and then a text file is imported.*

Auto Page Insertion off

3 *Auto Page Insertion is* **off,** *a non-automatic text box is selected, and then a text file is imported.*

4 *The box can't accommodate all the text and it's not linked to any other boxes, so the* **text overflow** *symbol appears in the lower right corner.*

Import Text

New pages can be added to a layout using either the Insert Pages dialog box or the Page Layout palette. We tend to use the Page Layout palette to add single pages and the dialog box to add multiple pages.

To insert pages using a dialog box:

1. *Optional:* We take a methodical approach to adding pages, since it can have a domino effect on the existing pages in a layout. Our first step is to save our file, so we can use Revert to Saved if we need to. Our second step is to choose Page > Go to (Cmd-J/Ctrl-J), enter the number of the page we want pages inserted before or after, and then click OK.

2. If you want to link the new pages to an existing text chain, choose the Item or Content tool, then click a box in the chain.

3. Choose Page > Insert.

4. In the Insert field, enter the number of pages to be inserted (1–1999) 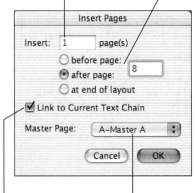.

5. Click "before page," "after page," or "at end of layout," and make sure the correct page number appears in the field. The number of the currently displayed page will appear there, but you can enter a different number. If the page has a prefix or Roman style that was assigned via the Section command, type it that way.

6. Choose Master Page: Blank Single, Blank Facing Page, or a master page.

   If you want to link the new pages using an automatic text box, choose a Master Page that contains an automatic text box on which to base the new page(s), and check Link to Current Text Chain. (Linking is covered on pages 89–91 in this chapter; Chapter 14 is devoted entirely to master pages.)

7. Click OK. The Insert Pages command can't be undone but the inserted pages can be deleted.

How many?

Need to know the total number of pages in a layout? Make sure no page icons are highlighted on the Page Layout palette, then look at the total **page count** readout in the lower left corner of the palette **1**.

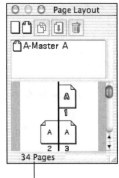

1 *The **total** number of pages in the layout*

*Choose a **location** for the inserted pages, and enter a number in the field.*

2 *Enter the **number** of pages to be added.*

*Check **Link to Current Text Chain** to link the new pages to the end of the currently selected text chain.*

*Choose whether the inserted pages will be based on an existing **master** page or a **blank** master page.*

Insert Pages Using a Dialog Box

Watch your masters

Master pages are used to add repetitively used items to layout pages, and you'll learn all about them in Chapter 14. For now, keep in mind that if you add an uneven number of pages to a facing-pages layout (unless you drag it manually to a spread by itself with the Force Down pointer), the left and right master pages will reapply automatically from the inserted pages forward. Master pages won't reapply if you add an even number of pages to this type of layout.

Single-sided blank   *Facing-pages blank*

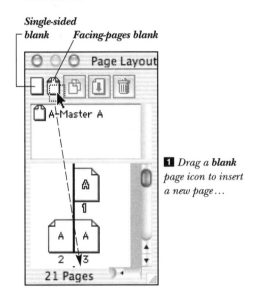

1 *Drag a blank page icon to insert a new page…*

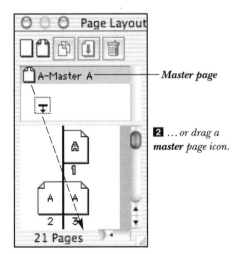

— *Master page*

2 *… or drag a master page icon.*

If you check Facing Pages in the New Project or New Layout dialog box for a print layout, all pages after the first page will be stacked in pairs along a central spine. This format is used for books and magazines. On the Page Layout palette, facing-page icons have a turned-down (dog-eared) corner.

If you uncheck Facing Pages in the New Project or New Layout dialog box, pages will be stacked singly. Single-sided page icons have square (not dog-eared) corners. To create a spread in a single-sided layout, you can arrange your layout page icons side by side (see the following page). To convert a layout from single-sided to facing-pages, or vice versa, see page 243.

Beware! There's a good chance the Undo command won't do a clean job of undoing changes made using the Page Layout palette, such as adding, deleting, or rearranging pages. So do yourself a favor and save your file before performing any of those operations. Then, if something goes awry, you can resort to File > Revert to Saved to rescue your file.

To insert pages using the Page Layout palette:

1. Choose Window > Show Page Layout (F10/F4).

2. Drag a blank or master page icon into the layout page area (**1**–**2**, this page and **1**–**4**, next page). A blank page won't be associated with a master page and won't have an automatic text box, but a master page can be applied to it at any time (see page 247).

TIP You can't insert a page to the left of the first page in a facing-pages layout, unless the layout begins with an even section number (see page 96).

TIP If you Option-drag/Alt-drag a blank or master page into the layout page area, the Insert Pages dialog box will open.

(More illustrations on the following page)

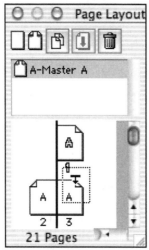

1 *To insert a page **between** spreads in a facing-pages layout, release the mouse when the **Force Down** pointer is displayed.*

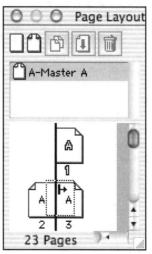

2 *In a facing-pages layout, if you release the mouse when the **Force Right** pointer is displayed, subsequent pages may reshuffle. Pages won't reshuffle in a single-sided layout.*

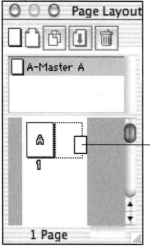

*If you see this **non-force** pointer (no arrow) when you release the mouse, no page reshuffling will occur.*

3 *To create a **spread** in a single-sided layout (print layouts only), drag a new page next to an existing page. Choose a very small view size for your layout so you can see how the new arrangement looks.*

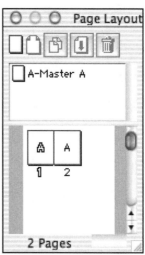

4 *With the page icons in this arrangement, pages 1 and 2 display side by side in the project window. The maximum overall width is 48″. Pages will print singly unless Spreads is checked in File > Print > Layout.*

Pages keep coming back

If, when you delete layout pages from a print layout, **Auto Page Insertion** is on in QuarkXPress (Edit, in Windows) > Preferences > Print Layout > General, and the master page has an intact (not broken) chain icon (which means an automatic text box is present), and the text in a linked chain doesn't fit completely on the pages that remain, new pages will be added automatically to accommodate the overflow text. If this makes you feel like the sorcerer's apprentice, turn Auto Page Insertion off; the overflow symbol will appear, and no new pages will be added. In both scenarios, the overflow text is preserved.

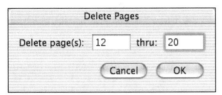

1 *Enter starting and ending page numbers if you want to delete a series of pages.*

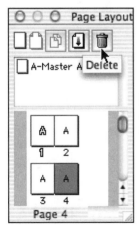

2 *To delete a page, click its icon, then click the **Delete** button.*

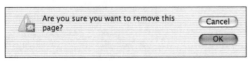

3 *Click OK when this prompt appears.*

Deleting pages

Both methods on this page work equally well for deleting pages. It all comes down to personal preference—whether you're a dialog box kind of person or a palette kind of person.

To delete pages using a dialog box:

1. Choose Page > Delete.

2. Enter a number in the first field to delete one page.
   or
   Enter numbers in both fields to delete a range of pages **1**. If a page has a prefix or Roman style that was assigned via the Section command, type it in exactly that manner. You can enter "end" in the second field to delete pages from the starting number through the end of the layout.

3. Click OK. You can't undo this.

To delete pages using the Page Layout palette:

1. On the Page Layout palette:
   Click a layout page icon **2**.
   or
   Click the icon of the first page in a series of pages to be deleted, then Shift-click the icon of the last page in the series.
   or
   Cmd-click/Ctrl-click nonconsecutive page icons. (Cmd-click/Ctrl-click a selected page icon if you need to deselect it.)

2. Click the Delete button on the palette, then click OK when the prompt appears **3**. You can't undo this, either.
   or
   Option-click/Alt-click the Delete button on the palette to bypass the prompt.

Rearranging pages

If you rearrange pages in Thumbnails view, you will be less likely to move the wrong ones, because you'll be able to see which ones you're moving.

Note: Before proceeding with the instructions on this page, which can't be undone, we recommend that you save your file.

To rearrange pages in Thumbnails view:

1. Choose View > Thumbnails (Shift-F6).
   or
   Press Control-V/Ctrl-Alt-V, press "t", then press Return/Enter.

2. In the project window, drag a page icon to a new location **1**. If automatic page numbering was applied to the layout, the numbers will update to reflect their new position.

3. Choose a different zoom level for the layout.

TIP To move more than one page at a time in Thumbnails view, click the first page in a series of consecutive pages, Shift-click the last page in the series, then drag. Or Cmd-click/Ctrl-click to select nonconsecutive pages, then drag.

TIP You can also rearrange layout pages using the Page > Move dialog box.

To rearrange pages using the Page Layout palette:

1. Choose Window > Show Page Layout (F10/F4).

2. Drag a layout page icon to a new location **2**–**3**.
   or
   Click the icon of the first page in a series of pages to be moved, Shift-click the icon of the last page in the series, release Shift, then drag the pages to a new location. Or Cmd-click/Ctrl-click to select nonconsecutive pages, then drag.

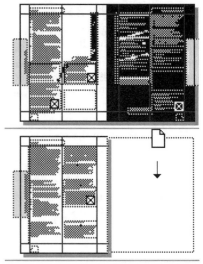

1 *A page being dragged to a new location*

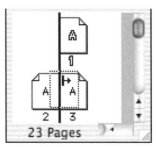

2 *If you force a page between two **pages** in a facing-pages layout, the remaining pages may reshuffle. Note the **Force Right** pointer.*

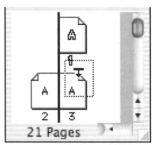

3 *If you force a page between two **spreads** in any kind of layout, the remaining pages won't reshuffle. Note the **Force Down** pointer.*

Rearrange Pages

Linking/unlinking text items

Text that flows from one box, path, or cell to another, whether linked manually or automatically, is called a story. Manual linking can be used in addition, or as an alternative, to automatic page insertion. In a print layout, you can manually link text boxes or paths on the same page or on different pages within the same layout. You can also link cells within the same table or from table to table. In a Web layout, the only thing you can link are boxes on the same page. (To link all the cells in a table, see pages 139–140.)

To link text items manually:

1. Choose the Linking tool.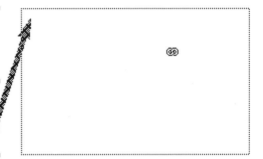

2. Click a text box, text path, or table cell. It can contain text or it can be empty. A "marching ants" marquee will appear **1**.

Keep on linkin'

Option-click/Alt-click the Linking tool to **keep it selected** so as to link multiple items. Click another tool when you're done linking. This also works with the Unlinking tool, as well as most other tools (e.g., text box, picture box, tables, line, text-path).

3. Click an **empty** text box, path, or table cell. An arrow will appear briefly, showing the new link **2**–**3**. A new item can be added at any juncture in an existing chain.

TIP If you click the wrong item initially with the Linking tool, choose a different tool or click outside the box to stop the ants from marching.

Again I see you're about to pounce,
alas, my poor computer mouse.

And losing this page I cannot afford,
but there you march across the keyboard.

You can't be hungry again so fast
Why the time's just barely passed.

Oh maybe I'll give you just a nibble,
just so you'll stay out of trib'l.

1 *Click a text box, text path, or table cell…*

2 *…then click an **empty** text item.*

Again I see you're about to pounce,
alas, my poor computer mouse.

And losing this page I cannot afford,
but there you march across the keyboard.

You can't be hungry again so fast
Why the time's just barely passed.

Oh maybe I'll give you just a nibble,
just so you'll stay out of trib'l.

I know it's warmer than my lap,
but the printer's not the place to nap.

And I don't need your claws to catch,
the printer's pages as they hatch.

To keep you from my papers chew'n
I guess I shouldn't leave them strew'n.

I just wish you wouldn't eat'm
before I've had a chance to read'm.

3 *The boxes are now **linked**.*

Link Text Boxes or Text Paths

To unlink text items:

1. Choose the Unlinking tool.

2. Click one of the text boxes, paths, or table cells in the chain to be unlinked.

3. Click the head or tail of the link arrow **1**. Links preceding the break will remain intact; the link to succeeding boxes, paths, or cells will be broken **2**. *6.0!* In QuarkXPress 6, you can undo this.

TIP If you're unable to unlink with the Unlinking tool, make sure there are no other items obstructing the one that you're trying to click on.

TIP If you click in a linked box with the Content tool, you can press the up or down arrow on the keyboard to jump from the first line in the box to the last line of the previous box in the chain or from the last line in the box to the first line in the next box in the chain.

TIP If you rearrange pages in a text chain, the links will stay intact.

Find the links

To see where the links are in a layout, choose a small display size (around 30%), then click one of the items in the link chain with the Unlinking tool. Choose a different tool when you're finished.

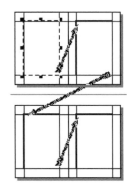

Ah, what can ever be more stately and admirable to me than mast-hemm'd Manhattan?

River and sunset and scallop-edg'd waves of flood-tide?

The sea-gulls oscillating their bodies, the hay-boat in the twilight, and the belated lighter?

What gods can exceed these that clasp me by the hand, and with voices I love call me promptly and loudly by my nighest name as I approach?

What is more subtle than this which ties me to the woman or man that looks in my face?

Which fuses me into you now, and pours my meaning into you?   *Walt Whitman*

1 *With the Unlinking tool, click a text item, then click the **head** or **tail** of the **arrow** that connects it to another item.*

Ah, what can ever be more stately and admirable to me than mast-hemm'd Manhattan?

River and sunset and scallop-edg'd waves of flood-tide?

The sea-gulls oscillating their bodies, the hay-boat in the twilight, and the belated lighter?

2 *The link is **broken**.*

Oronte. Do you find anything to object to in my sonnet?

Alceste. I do not say that. But, to keep him from writing, I set before his eyes how, in our days, that desire had spoiled a great many very worthy people.

Oronte. Do I write badly? Am I like them in any way?

Alceste. I do not say that. But, in short, I said to him: What pressing need is there for you to rhyme, and what the deuce drives you into print? If we can pardon the sending into the world of a

badly-written book, it will only be in those unfortunate men who write for their livelihood. Believe me, resist your temptations, keep these effusions from the public, and do not, how much soever you may be asked, forfeit the reputation which you enjoy...

Molière

1 *Choose the **Unlinking** tool, then **Shift-click** inside the item to be unlinked from the chain.*

Copy, paste, duplicate linked boxes

You can copy, paste, or duplicate a linked text box or boxes. You can also drag-copy a linked box between projects or into a library. Text preceding the box in the chain, if any, won't copy; overflow text will copy, but it will be hidden. To copy an entire story, be sure to copy the *first* box in the chain.

To delete a text item from a chain and preserve the chain:

1. Choose the Item or Content tool.

2. Select the text item to be deleted.

3. Choose Item > Delete (Cmd-K/Ctrl-K). Simple! The text will be rerouted to the next item in the chain. You can undo this.

To unlink a text item from a chain and preserve the item and chain:

1. Choose the Unlinking tool.

2. Shift-click inside the text box, path, or table cell to be unlinked **1**–**2**.

TIP Using Linkster from GLUON, Inc. or XPert TextLink in XPert Tools Pro from alap, inc., you can perform magic tricks, like unlinking a chain and having the text stay right where it is.

Oronte. Do you find anything to object to in my sonnet?

Alceste. I do not say that. But, to keep him from writing, I set before his eyes how, in our days, that desire had spoiled a great many very worthy people.

Oronte. Do I write badly? Am I like them in any way?

Alceste. I do not say that. But, in short, I said to him: What pressing need is there for you to rhyme, and what the deuce drives you into print? If we can pardon the sending into the

2 *The middle box has been **unlinked** from the chain.*

Unlink Text Boxes or Text Paths

Working with blocks of text

If you're doing a rough layout and you need some mock text to fill in some boxes on your page, you can have Jabberwocky do the work for you. You have a choice of five default "languages," in prose or verse. If you're ambitious or have a light schedule, you can create and edit your own jabber.

Jabberwocky, if you don't happen to know, is the name of a wonderful poem in the book *Through the Looking Glass* by Lewis Carroll ("Twas brillig, and the slithy toves did gyre and gimble in the wabe..."). Love that book.

To fill text boxes with dummy text:

1. *Optional:* To specify the kind of text to be inserted, choose QuarkXPress (Edit, in Windows) > Preferences > Application > Jabberwocky, choose English, Esperanto, Klingon, Latin, or a custom language from the "When Jabbering, use" pop-up menu 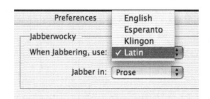, choose Prose or Verse from the "Jabber in" pop-up menu, then click OK.

2. To fill a text box/path or a series of linked boxes/paths with dummy text based on the parameters chosen in Jabberwocky Preferences, choose the Content tool, click in a text box or path, then choose Utilities > Jabber **2**–**3**. *Note:* The Jabberwocky.xnt XTension, which ships with QuarkXPress 6, must be enabled in order to access this feature (see page 427).

   Note: If Jabber is used to fill a chain of boxes or paths, the text will stop at the end of the last box or path in the chain; there will be no hidden, overflow text.

You can invent your own Jabberwocky language or edit an existing language.

To create or edit a Jabberwocky set:

1. Choose Edit > Jabberwocky Sets.

2. Click an existing set, then click Edit **4**. *or*

1 *Choose a "language" in Preferences > Application >* **Jabberwocky.**

Qo'noS Qagh reH
'ach wa' verengan jon vatlh Qav DenIbya' Qatlhs
Ach QI'tomer ah po' tlb tera'.
Wa' pov Quch HIv vatlh QaQ meHloDnI'S
Joq vagh QIp 'ejyo'S reH chop Qo'noS.
Vatlh DIvI'S tlha' wa' ych

2 *Klingon verse*

Two irascible lampstands laughed, and one sheep grew up, even though two pawnbrokers ran away almost drunkenly, and five wart hogs telephoned botulisms, although Batman bought Minnesota, and five aardvarks towed Quark. One bourgeois trailer quickly fights two fountains. One mat ran

3 *The point of using dummy text is to create a text "texture." If you find any of the jabber languages distracting or idiotic, by all means don't use them. This is QuarkXPress's* **English** *prose jabber.*

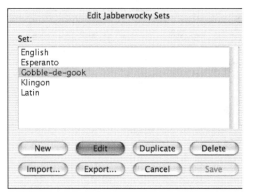

4 *You can create, edit, duplicate, or delete a Jabberwocky set using the* **Edit Jabberwocky Sets** *dialog box.*

Jabberwocky

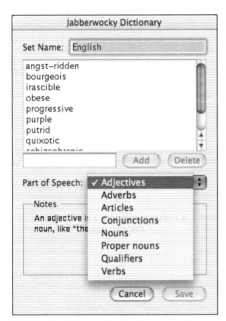

1 *Use the Jabberwocky Dictionary dialog box to add or delete words from a Jabberwocky set.*

Simoneyeh logega Cuplook kwan fala funo jala vata mopie heyso plineto nata palaty gwoglerog kumo Simoner izame hitu plineto luba wenenb bobega gosie fotin jekah rutil Katal cata Simoneyeh logega Cuplook kwan fala funo jala vata mopie heyso plineto nata palaty gwoglerog kumo Simoner izame hitu

2 *Custom jabber*

Waper Watershlash pladerwop sickwons pladerwap crapis wapils toyswos stickap irlis crabler swo florap blogubyap botens dogulis craler Momylis adylis evrop ofils woropwap glasulis flwowwo rumdeydume lickwick twoglis evroslis swols swigis eywoshlis cinbwlis irpulis swundedome crocklis ircks flopis

3 *More custom jabber*

Click New, then enter a name in the Set Name field.

3. Here's where the fun starts. Choose a Part of Speech from the pop-up menu, type a real or made-up word in the field, then click Add **1**. (To delete a word, click on it, then click Delete.)

4. Click Save **2**–**3**. The new set will appear on the first pop-up menu in the Jabberwocky Preferences dialog box.

The Line Check command can be used to find out how many overflow text boxes are present in a layout, along with other type-setting data, and if you want, it can get your cursor to each occurrence.

To use the Line Check command:

1. Choose Utilities > Line Check > Search Criteria.

2. Check or uncheck any boxes to include/exclude those criteria from the search **4**.

3. *Optional:* Click Count, note the quantities listed, then click OK.

4. To start the search, click in a text box, then choose Utilities > Line Check > First Line. The first instance found of any of the items you checked in step 2 will be highlighted in the layout.

5. To jump from one instance to the next, press Cmd-;/Ctrl-;.

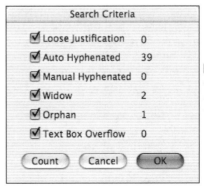

4 *In the Search Criteria dialog box, choose what you want QuarkXPress to search for.*

When text is linked between nonconsecutive pages, as in a newsletter or magazine, there is usually an indicator to guide the reader to the continuation of the story or article. These "Continued on" and "Continued from" indicators are called "jump lines." When the Next Box Page Number command is inserted, like magic, it instantly converts into the page number of the next linked box in the chain. If that text is relinked or moved to a different page, the page number will update automatically.

To insert a "Continued on" command:

1. Choose the Rectangle Text Box tool. Or if you want to get fancy, choose a Bézier Text Box or Text-Path tool.

2. Create a separate, small box or path that overlaps the text box that contains the story, and keep it selected.

3. Choose Item > Runaround (Cmd-T/ Ctrl-T).

4. Choose Type: Item.

5. Click OK.

6. Choose the Content tool.

7. Type any desired text into the small box, such as "Continued on page," or use a graphic symbol, such as an arrow. The keystrokes for entering Zapf Dingbat characters are in Appendix A.

8. Press Cmd-4/Ctrl-4 to insert the Next Box Page Number command **1**–**3**. Don't enter the actual page number— it will appear automatically.

TIP Press the down arrow on the keyboard to move the text insertion point from the last line of text in a box to the first line of text in the next box in the chain (or press the up arrow to do the reverse).

To insert a "Continued from" command:

Follow the instructions above, but for step 8, press Cmd-2/Ctrl-2 to insert the Previous Box Page Number command **4**.

Elizabeth here felt herself called on to say something in vindication of his behaviour to Wickham; and therefore gave them to understand, in as guarded a manner as she could, that by what she had heard from his relations in Kent, his actions were capable of a very different construction; and that his

Continued on page 3

1 *A text box containing the **Next Box Page Number** command is positioned so that it overlaps the main text box.*

Continued from page <None>

2 *If the characters <None> appear instead of a page number, either the text box or path that contains the Previous or Next Box Page Number command isn't overlapping a linked text box or the text box it overlaps isn't linked to a box on another page.*

Continued on page 3

3 *You can create a jump line on a text path.*

4 *The **Previous Box Page Number** command is inserted here.*

Continued from page 1

character was by no means so faulty, nor Wickham's so amiable, as they had been considered in Hertfordshire. In confirmation of this, she related the particulars of all the pecuniary transactions in which they had been connected, without actually naming her authority, but stating it to be such as might be relied on.

Jane Austen

Jump Lines

Rescuing an unsavable file

If you get an error message that says your file can't be saved, **DON'T CLOSE IT!** Take a deep breath, chant a mantra, create a whole new project or open a template that has the same dimensions as the problem file; next, use the method on this page to drag pages from the old project to the new (saving the new file periodically), then trash the corrupted file. If that doesn't work, try using the MarkzTools V XTension from Markzware Software to open and salvage your damaged files.

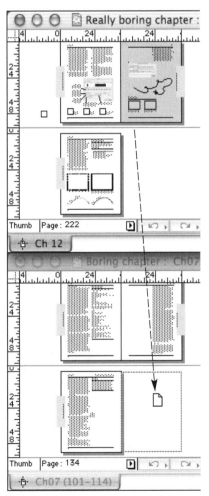

1 *Drag-copying pages* in *Thumbnails* view *from one project window to another*

Notes: You can't copy a page to a layout whose page size is smaller than the one you're copying. A page to which a facing-pages master has been applied can be copied to a single-sided layout, but items on the page may be repositioned as a result. Any style sheets, colors, dashes & stripes, lists, H&Js, or master pages on the appending pages will be added to the target layout. And finally, all the layers from the destination layout are copied to the target layout.

To drag-copy pages from one project to another:

1. Open the project (and display the layout) you want to copy from and the one you want to copy to.

2. In Mac OS X, choose Window > Tile. In Windows, choose Window > Tile Vertically. Then for each window, choose View > Thumbnails.

   TIP To make room for new pages at the end of a layout, drag the resize box on the target project window upward, click the down scroll arrow to scoot the layout pages all the way upward, then drag the resize box downward to lengthen the project window again (see the bottom window in the illustration at left).

3. Drag a page icon from one project window into the other. A copy of the page will appear in the target project window. Pages will reshuffle depending on where you release the mouse (watch for the Force Right, Force Left, Force Down, or non-force pointer).
   or
   To drag multiple pages, click the first page in a series of consecutive pages, Shift-click the last page in the series **1**, then drag. If the pages to be drag-copied contain linked text, copy all the linked pages at once instead of one by one. Otherwise, the text from the linked boxes will copy, but the links will be broken.

The Section command renumbers all or some of the pages in a layout with a user-specified starting number. This is useful for publications such as books that are composed of multiple files. You can choose a different page numbering format for each section. For example, in this book, the lowercase Roman format is used for the table of contents and the numeric format is used for the main body of the book. *Note:* To make the page numbers actually appear on your layout pages, follow the instructions on page 244.

To number a multifile layout automatically, you can use the Book feature (see Chapter 22).

To number a section of a file:

1. Display the layout page where the new section is to begin by double-clicking its icon on the Page Layout palette.
or
Choose Page > Go to (Cmd-J/Ctrl-J), enter the number of the page that is to begin the new section, then click OK.

2. Click the Section button at the top of the Page Layout palette.
or
Choose Page > Section.

3. Check Section Start ■.

4. Enter the desired starting Number for the section.

5. *Optional:* Enter a maximum of four characters in the Prefix field (e.g., "Page").

6. *Optional:* Choose a different numbering Format.

7. Click OK.

TIP If you section-number a facing-pages layout starting with an even number, the first page will become a left-hand page. The remaining pages won't necessarily follow suit and switch their right or left-hand positions, though.

Number a Section

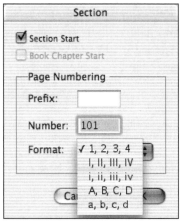

■ *Check **Section Start**, enter a **Prefix** (if desired), enter the starting **Number**, and choose a numbering **Format**. (Book Chapter Start is available only when a chapter is opened independently of its book.)*

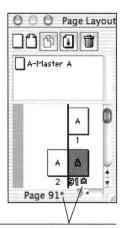

Why the asterisk?

An asterisk below a page icon on the Page Layout palette signifies that a **section** starts on that page. If the first page in a section is currently displayed in the project window, an asterisk will also appear next to the page number at the bottom of the Page Layout palette and at the bottom of the project window.

To have a page's **absolute** number (relative position in the layout) display at the bottom of the Page Layout palette instead of its number in a section, Option-click/Alt-click the layout page icon (see also the first tip on page 57).

Using the Next Box and Next Column characters

The Next Box character pushes text to the next box in a linked chain.
The Next Column character pushes text to the next column within
the same box (or in some cases, the next text box in the chain).

> I come from haunts of coot and hern,
> I make a sudden sally,
> And sparkle out among the fern,
> To bicker down a valley.
>
> By thirty hills I hurry down,
> Or slip between the ridges,
> By twenty thorps, a little town,
> And half a hundred bridges.
>
> Till last by Philip's farm I flow
> to join the brimming river,
> For men may come and men may go,
> But I go on for ever.
>
> I chatter over stony ways,
> In little sharps and trebles,
> I bubble into eddying bays,
> I babble on the pebbles.

> With many a curve my banks I fret
> By many a field and fallow,
> And many fair foreland set
> With willow-weed and mallow.
>
> I chatter, chatter, as I flow
> To join the brimming river,
> For men may come and men may go,
> But I go on for ever.
>
> *Alfred Tennyson*

The original text boxes

> I come from haunts of coot and hern,
> I make a sudden sally,
> And sparkle out among the fern,
> To bicker down a valley.
>
> By thirty hills I hurry down,
> Or slip between the ridges,
> By twenty thorps, a little town,
> And half a hundred bridges.
>
> Till last by Philip's farm I flow
> to join the brimming river,
> For men may come and men may go,
> But I go on for ever.

> I chatter over stony ways,
> In little sharps and trebles,
> I bubble into eddying bays,
> I babble on the pebbles.
>
> With many a curve my banks I fret
> By many a field and fallow,
> And many fair foreland set
> With willow-weed and mallow.
>
> I chatter, chatter, as I flow
> To join the brimming river,
> For men may come and men may go,
> But I go on for ever.
>
> *Alfred Tennyson*

*Instead of shortening the text box
to push the text to the next box, a
Next Box character (**Shift-Enter**)*
is inserted. Remove a Next Box
character as you would any text
character: Click to the right of it
with the Content tool, then press
Delete/Backspace.*

*The **Next Box** character (Shift-Enter)* (turn on View > **Show Invisibles** to see it)*

> I come from haunts of coot and hern,
> I make a sudden sally,
> And sparkle out among the fern,
> To bicker down a valley.
>
> By thirty hills I hurry down,
> Or slip between the ridges,
> By twenty thorps, a little town,
> And half a hundred bridges. ↓

> Till last by Philip's farm I flow
> to join the brimming river,
> For men may come and men may go,
> But I go on for ever.
>
> I chatter over stony ways,
> In little sharps and trebles,
> I bubble into eddying bays,
> I babble on the pebbles.

*The **Next Column** character (**Enter**)**

*Use the numeric keypad.

Next Box, Next Column Characters

Placing one header over two columns

Ruler guide

The Night in Isla Negra

The ancient night and the unruly salt
beat at the walls of my house;
lonely is the shadow, the sky
by now is a beat of the ocean,
and sky and shadow explode
in the fray of unequal combat;
all night long they struggle,
nobody knows the weight

of the harsh clarity that will go on opening
like a languid fruit;
thus is born on the coast,
out of the turbulent shadow, the hard dawn,
nibbled by the salt in movement,
swept up by the weight of night,
bloodstained in its marine crater.
Pablo Neruda

*One way to align text: Put the text in **separate boxes**, then manually drag each box so the first baseline of text lines up with the same horizontal **ruler guide** (turn off View > Snap to Guides). Make sure the leading is the same in both boxes.*

TIP *Choose the Item tool and press the up or down arrow key to nudge a selected box upward or downward 1 point at a time; press Option-arrow/Alt-arrow to nudge it in 0.1-point increments.*

The Night in Isla Negra

The ancient night and the unruly salt
beat at the walls of my house;
lonely is the shadow, the sky
by now is a beat of the ocean,
and sky and shadow explode
in the fray of unequal combat;
all night long they struggle,
nobody knows the weight

of the harsh clarity that will go on opening
like a languid fruit;
thus is born on the coast,
out of the turbulent shadow, the hard dawn,
nibbled by the salt in movement,
swept up by the weight of night,
bloodstained in its marine crater.
Pablo Neruda

*Here's another way to do it: Place the header in a separate box and put the main text in a **two-column box** below it.*

Formats 6

Formatting fundamentals

Well, you've managed to get some text onto your page, but it's just sitting there in a big clump, and it's hard to read. By adding space between lines and paragraphs, indents, and other paragraph formats, not only will your type look more elegant and professional, it will also be easier to read.

All the formatting commands described in this chapter affect entire paragraphs rather than individual characters. These commands, which are accessed via the Style menu when text is highlighted, include horizontal alignment, hyphenation and justification, indents, leading, space before and after, keeping lines together, rules, tabs, and paragraph style sheets 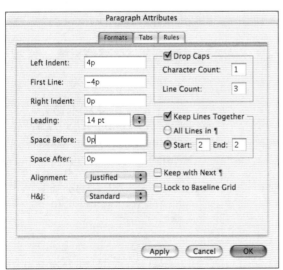. In the next chapter, you'll learn the ins and outs of typography (styling characters in different fonts, point sizes, and so on).

A paragraph consists of one or more characters or words, followed by an invisible Return character. A Return looks like this when View > Show Invisibles is on: ¶. Paragraph formats can be applied manually—or even more efficiently, using style sheets (see Chapter 13).

The following features are *not* available for HTML text boxes (boxes in Web layouts for which Convert to Graphic on Export is unchecked in Item > Modify): Force and Justified alignment; H&Js; Lock to Baseline Grid; Tabs; First Baseline; and Inter-Paragraph Max. These features *are* available for rasterized text boxes (boxes in Web layouts for which Convert to Graphic on Export is checked in Item > Modify), but this option increases a file's size and download time, so it use it only when necessary.

1 *Most of the commands that affect whole paragraphs are found in the* **Formats, Tabs,** *and* **Rules** *panes of the* **Paragraph Attributes** *dialog box.*

To indent a whole paragraph:

1. Choose the Content tool.

2. Click in a paragraph or drag downward through a series of paragraphs **1**.

3. Choose Style > Formats (Cmd-Shift-F/ Ctrl-Shift-F).

4. Enter a Left Indent and/or Right Indent value in any measurement system used in QuarkXPress **2**.

5. Click Apply to preview (Cmd-A in Mac OS X) **3**–**4**. Or Option-click/ Alt-click Apply to turn on continuous apply (Alt-A in Windows). Click in, or Tab to, another field to activate it.

6. Click OK.

Do it with style!

Once you learn the basics of paragraph formatting, learn how to apply these attributes via **style sheets** (see Chapter 13). Believe us, you'll save yourself a lot of monotonous work.

THE MAIN CONCLUSION ARRIVED AT IN THIS WORK, NAMELY, THAT MAN IS DESCENDED FROM SOME LOWLY ORGAN-ISED FORM, WILL, I REGRET TO THINK, BE HIGHLY DISTASTEFUL TO MANY. BUT THERE CAN HARDLY BE A DOUBT THAT WE ARE DESCENDED FROM BARBARIANS.

1 *A paragraph with 0 indents*

2 *Enter **Left Indent** and/or **Right Indent** values.*

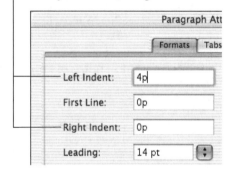

Paragraph Att

Formats | Tabs

Left Indent: 4p

First Line: 0p

Right Indent: 0p

Leading: 14 pt

THE MAIN CONCLUSION ARRIVED AT IN THIS WORK, NAMELY, THAT MAN IS DESCENDED FROM SOME LOWLY ORGANISED FORM, WILL, I REGRET TO THINK, BE HIGHLY DISTASTEFUL TO MANY. BUT THERE CAN HARDLY BE A DOUBT THAT WE ARE DESCENDED FROM BARBARIANS.

3 *A paragraph with a **left indent** of 2p (called a "block" indent)*

THE MAIN CONCLUSION ARRIVED AT IN THIS WORK, NAMELY, THAT MAN IS DESCENDED FROM SOME LOWLY ORGANISED FORM, WILL, I REGRET TO THINK, BE HIGHLY DISTASTEFUL TO MANY. BUT THERE CAN HARDLY BE A DOUBT THAT WE ARE DESCENDED FROM BARBARIANS.

CHARLES DARWIN

4 *A paragraph with a **right indent** of 2p*

Paragraph Indents

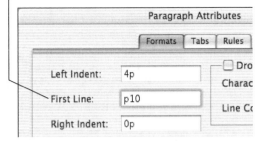

1 *The **First Line** indent field in Style > Formats (Paragraph Attributes dialog box)*

Oronte. [To Alceste] But for you, you know our agreement. Speak to me, I pray, in all sincerity.

Alceste. These matters, sir, are always more or less delicate, and every one is fond of being praised for his wit.

But I was saying one day to a certain person, who shall be nameless, when he showed me some of his verses, that a gentleman ought at all times to exercise a great control over that itch for writing which sometimes attacks us, and should keep a tight rein over the strong propensity which one has to display such amusements; and that, in the frequent anxiety to show their productions, people are frequently exposed to act a very foolish part.

Molière

2 *A **first line indent** enhances readability.*

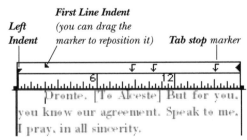

First Line Indent
Left (you can drag the
Indent marker to reposition it) **Tab stop** *marker*

3 *The width of the Paragraph **Formats** ruler matches the width of the currently selected text box.*

Don't try to indent type by pressing the Spacebar. The lines won't line up properly because typeset characters aren't equal in width, as they are on a typewriter. The proper way to indent type is by entering a value greater than zero in one or more of the three Indent fields in the Formats pane of the Paragraph Attributes dialog box.

To indent the first line of a paragraph:

1. Choose the Content tool.

2. Click in a paragraph or drag downward through a series of paragraphs.

3. Choose Style > Formats (Cmd-Shift-F/ Ctrl-Shift-F).

4. Enter a First Line value **1**. If you're not sure what value to use, start with the point size of the text you're indenting (e.g., for 9 pt. type, enter p9).

5. Click Apply to preview (Cmd-A in Mac OS X).

6. Click OK **2**.

TIP When the Paragraph Attributes dialog box is open, a tabs ruler displays over the currently selected text box (not HTML text boxes). Indents can be adjusted by dragging the indent markers in the ruler **3**. Ditto for tab stops. To insert a new tab stop, click in the ruler. (Read more about tabs in Chapter 8.)

TIP Don't indent the first paragraph in a story, especially if there's a headline or subhead right above it. Why not? It doesn't look good. Make the first paragraph flush left instead, and enhance it with a nice drop cap, large initial cap, or a few small caps characters. Try it both ways or take a peek at some magazines you have around the house, and you'll see what we mean.

TIP For each text box, the current paragraph indent value is added together with the current Text Inset value (see page 71).

Leading (line spacing) is the distance from baseline to baseline between lines of type, and it's measured in points. Three types of leading are used in QuarkXPress:

Absolute leading is an amount that remains fixed regardless of the point size of the type to which it's applied **1**.

We use absolute leading because we like the control it gives us, but there's an alternative, called auto leading, that you may as well know about. Auto leading is calculated separately for each line of text based on the point size of the largest character per line **2**. The percentage used for that calculation is specified in the Auto Leading field in QuarkXPress (Edit, in Windows) > Preferences > Print Layout or Web Layout > Paragraph, and it applies to the entire layout. For example, if 20% is the current percentage and the largest character in a line of text is 10 pt., the leading for that line would be 12 pt. You won't see a percentage in the Leading field; you'll just see the word "auto." Alternatively, you can enter an incremental value, such as +2 or –2, in the Auto Leading field. In this case the leading will be calculated based on the point size of the largest character in each line, plus or minus that increment; the increment will appear in the Leading field on the Measurements palette.

To change paragraph leading using the Measurements palette:

1. Choose the Content tool.

2. Click in a paragraph or drag downward through a series of paragraphs.

3. Change the Leading value on the Measurements palette **3**.
   or
   In the Leading area of the Measurements palette, click the up arrow to increase the leading in 1-point increments, or the down arrow to reduce the leading. Option-click/Alt-click an arrow to increase or reduce the leading in 0.1-point increments.

> **B**ut the moment that she moved again he recognized her. The effect upon her old lover was electric, far stronger than the effect of his presence upon her. His fire, the tumultuous ring of his eloquence, seemed to go out of him. His lip struggled and trembled under the words that lay upon it; but deliver them it could not as long as she faced him. His eyes, after their first glance…
>
> **THOMAS HARDY**

1 *A paragraph with 11 pt. **absolute** leading: The leading is consistent throughout, despite the fact that two different point sizes are applied to the type in the first line of the paragraph.*

> **B**ut the moment that she
>
> moved again he recognized her.
>
> The effect upon her old lover was
>
> electric, far stronger than the
>
> effect of his presence upon her.

2 *The same paragraph with **auto** leading: The large initial cap is throwing the whole thing off, and it ain't pretty.*

Auto leading

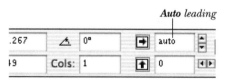

Absolute leading

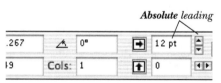

3 *The **Leading** area on the **Measurements** palette*

He put some sticking plaster on his fingers, and his friends both came to dinner. He could not offer them fish, but he had something else in his larder.

Sir Isaac Newton wore his black and gold waistcoat.

And Mr. Alderman Ptolemy Tortoise brought a salad with him in a string bag.

And instead of a nice dish of minnows they had a roasted grasshopper with lady-bird sauce, which frogs consider a beautiful treat; but I think it must have been nasty!   *Beatrix Potter*

*Use **roomy leading** to enhance readability if your text is set in a **wide column**, in a **sans serif** or **bold** font, or in a font that has a **large x-height, tall ascenders,** or **tall descenders**. This is 8 pt. Gill Sans Regular, with roomy 11 pt. leading.*

He put some sticking plaster on his fingers, and his friends both came to dinner. He could not offer them fish, but he had something else in his larder.

Sir Isaac Newton wore his black and gold waist-coat.

And Mr. Alderman Ptolemy Tortoise brought a salad with him in a string bag.

And instead of a nice dish of minnows they had a roasted grasshopper with lady-bird sauce, which frogs consider a beautiful treat; but I think it must have been nasty!

*You can use **tighter leading** for **serif** body text or multiple-line **headlines** or **subheads**. This is 8 pt. Bauer Bodoni with 10 pt. leading.*

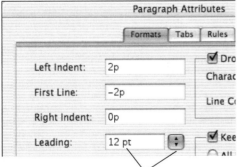

1 *The **Leading** area in the Paragraph Attributes dialog box (Formats pane)*

To change paragraph leading using the keyboard:

1. Choose the Content tool.

2. Click in a paragraph or drag downward through a series of paragraphs.

3. Press Cmd-Shift-"/Ctrl-Shift-" to increase leading or Cmd-Shift-:/Ctrl-Shift-: to decrease leading in 1-point increments. If the leading was on auto, it will switch to the nearest absolute value when you use this shortcut.

TIP Press Cmd-Option-Shift-" or :/ Ctrl-Alt-Shift-" or : to modify leading in 0.1-point increments.

TIP The traditional way to notate point size and leading is to divide the two values by a slash. For example, "8/11" represents 8-point type with 11-point leading.

To change paragraph leading using a dialog box:

1. Choose the Content tool.

2. Click in a paragraph or drag downward through a series of paragraphs.

3. Choose Style > Leading (Cmd-Shift-E/ Ctrl-Shift-E). The Paragraph Attributes > Formats dialog box opens.

4. Type a value in the highlighted Leading field in an increment as small as .001 **1**. You don't need to enter the "pt".

TIP Don't know what value to enter? Try adding 2 points to the current point size and see how it looks (e.g., 12 pt. leading for 10 pt. type). The point size of your type is shown in the point size field in the top right corner of the Measurements palette.

5. Click OK.

TIP Leading has no affect on the positioning of the first line of text in a box. To lower text from the top of its box, select the box, choose Item > Modify, click the Text tab, click Text Inset: Multiple Insets, then increase the Top value.

Leading

To change horizontal alignment:

1. Choose the Content tool.

2. Click in a paragraph or drag downward through a series of paragraphs.

3. Click one of the five horizontal alignment icons on the Measurements palette **1**. The Justified and Forced Justified options are not available for HTML text boxes.

Note: Forced Justified alignment justifies all the lines in a paragraph— including the last line. For this option, make sure the paragraph has a Return character (¶) at the end.

TIP Only one horizontal alignment option can be applied per paragraph.

TIP Horizontal alignment can also be changed by using the shortcuts listed at right; or the Style > Alignment submenu; or the Alignment pop-up menu in the Style > Formats dialog box.

TIP Turn on Hyphenation for justified text to help reduce the gaps between words (see pages 117–119).

Horizontal alignment shortcuts

Flush left, ragged right	Cmd-Shift-L/Ctrl-Shift-L
Centered	Cmd-Shift-C/Ctrl-Shift-C
Flush right, ragged left	Cmd-Shift-R/Ctrl-Shift-R
Justified	Cmd-Shift-J/Ctrl-Shift-J
Forced Justified	Cmd-Option-Shift-J/ Ctrl-Alt-Shift-J

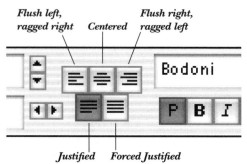

1 *The five **horizontal alignment** icons on the Measurements palette*

So we was all right now, as to the shirt and the sheet and the spoon and the candles, by the help of the calf and rats and the mixed-up counting; and as to the candlestick, it warn't no consequence, it would blow over by and by....
MARK TWAIN

Flush left, ragged right

So we was all right now, as to the shirt and the sheet and the spoon and the candles, by the help of the calf and rats and the mixed-up counting; and as to the candlestick, it warn't no consequence, it would blow over by and by....

Centered (for occasional use only; it's tiring to read).

So we was all right now, as to the shirt and the sheet and the spoon and the candles, by the help of the calf and rats and the mixed-up counting; and as to the candlestick,

Try to vary the line lengths in centered text (it usually looks better).

So we was all right now, as to the shirt and the sheet and the spoon and the candles, by the help of the calf and rats and the mixed up counting; and as to the candlestick, it warn't no consequence, it would blow over by and by....

Flush right, ragged left (also a bit tiring to read, but sometimes useful)

So we was all right now, as to the shirt and the sheet and the spoon and the candles, by the help of the calf and rats and the mixed-up counting; and as to the candlestick, it warn't no consequence, it would blow over by and by....

Justified

So we was all right now, as to the shirt and the sheet and the spoon and the candles, by the help of the calf and rats and the mixed-up counting; and as to the candlestick, it warn't no consequence, it would blow over by and by.

Forced Justified

1 *This is an awkward break.*

The night so luminous on the spar-deck, but otherwise on the cavernous ones below—levels so very like the tiered gal-leries in a coal-mine—the luminous night passed away. Like the prophet in the chariot disappearing in heaven and dropping his mantle to Elisha, the withdrawing night transferred its pale robe to the peeping day.

The night so luminous on the spar-deck, but otherwise on the cavernous ones below—levels so very like the tiered¶

galleries in a coal-mine—the luminous night passed away. Like the prophet in the chariot disappearing in heaven and dropping his mantle to Elisha, the withdrawing night transferred its pale robe to the peeping day.

2 *A paragraph Return creates a whole new paragraph—no good.*

The night so luminous on the spar-deck, but otherwise on the cavernous ones below—levels so very like the tiered galleries in a coal-mine—the luminous night passed away. Like the prophet in the chariot disappearing in heaven and dropping his mantle to Elisha, the withdrawing night transferred its pale robe to the peeping day. *Herman Melville*

3 *Pressing **Shift-Return/Shift-Enter** creates a **line break** within the same paragraph—much better.*

Use this method to adjust a headline or fix an awkward break in ragged left or ragged right copy. We have to admit, QuarkXPress doesn't do a fantastic job of wrapping and hyphenating text, and we often have to fiddle with our paragraphs manually to make them look better. Sigh. (Quark 7?)

To break a line without creating a new paragraph:

1. Choose the Content tool.

2. Click just to the left of a whole word that you want to bring down to the next line, then press Shift-Return/Shift-Enter **1**–**3**.
   or
   To insert a discretionary hyphen which will disappear if the text reflows (unlike a regular hyphen), click in a word where you want a hyphen to be inserted, then hold down Cmd/Ctrl and press "-" (hyphen).

TIP To remove a discretionary hyphen where it's being utilized, click at the beginning of the next line, then press Delete/Backspace.

TIP To find out where a word should be hyphenated, click in the word, then choose Utilities > Suggested Hyphenation (Cmd-Option-Shift-H/ Ctrl-Alt-Shift-H). If no hyphens display in the dialog box, it means that word isn't supposed to be hyphenated. This command isn't available for HTML text boxes.

6.0!

Line Break

Note: The values entered in the Space Before and Space After fields are added together, so try to be consistent and use one most of the time and the other for special circumstances. For example, we use Space After for body text and use Space Before for subheads to add extra space above them.

To change the spacing between paragraphs:

1. Choose the Content tool.

2. Click in a paragraph or drag downward through a series of paragraphs.

3. Choose Style > Formats (Cmd-Shift-F/ Ctrl-Shift-F).

4. Enter a Space Before or Space After value **1**.

5. Click Apply to preview (Cmd-A in Mac OS X).

6. Click OK **2**.

TIP The Space Before command has no effect on the first line of text in a box. To move text downward on a page, the simplest thing is to move the box itself—an obvious solution that's easy to forget! If you don't want to move the box, you can use First Baseline (see page 75) or Text Inset (see page 71).

Better Measurements palette

FullMeasure XT from Badia Software is a context-sensitive adjunct to the QuarkXPress Measurements palette. Options and values can be chosen for text (paragraph and character attributes), pictures, text paths, lines, guides, or groups, depending on what item or items are currently selected in your layout.

1 *The Space Before and Space After fields in Paragraph Attributes > Formats*

O to be a Virginian where I grew up! O to be a Carolinian!
O longings irrepressible! O I will go back to old Tennessee
and never wander more.

Mannahatta

I was asking for something specific and perfect for my city,
Whereupon lo! upsprang the aboriginal name.

Now I see what there is in a name, a word, liquid, sane, unruly,
    musical, self-sufficient,
I see that the word of my city is that word from of old,
Because I see that word nested in nests of water-bays, superb…

∾ WALT WHITMAN

2 *If you want to fine-tune the spacing between paragraphs, use the* **Space Before** *or* **Space After** *field. Don't insert extra Returns—it's so-o–o unprofessional.*

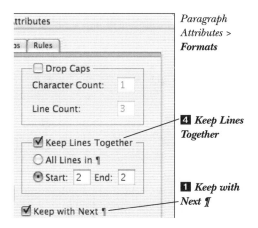

4 *Keep Lines Together*

1 *Keep with Next ¶*

2 *An unsightly widow*

> "I am dreadfully afraid it *will* be mouse!" said Duchess to herself— "I really couldn't, *couldn't* eat mouse pie. And I shall have to eat it, because it is a party. And *my* pie was going to be veal and ham. A pink and white pie-dish! and so is mine; just like Ribby's dishes; they were both bought at Tabitha Twitchit's."
>
> Duchess went into her larder and took the pie off a shelf and looked at it.
>
> "Oh what a good idea! Why shouldn't I rush along and put my pie into Ribby's oven when Ribby isn't there?"
>
> *Beatrix Potter*

> "I am dreadfully afraid it *will* be mouse!" said Duchess to herself— "I really couldn't, *couldn't* eat mouse pie. And I shall have to eat it, because it is a party. And *my* pie was going to be veal and ham. A pink and white pie-dish! and so is mine; just like Ribby's dishes; they were both bought at Tabitha Twitchit's."
>
> Duchess went into her larder and took the pie off a shelf and looked at it.
>
> "Oh what a good idea! Why shouldn't I rush along and put my pie into Ribby's oven when Ribby isn't there?"

3 *An unsightly orphan*

Apply the Keep with Next ¶ command to a subhead to ensure that if it falls at the end of a column or page, it won't become separated from the paragraph that follows it. Like all paragraph formats, Keep with Next ¶ can be applied manually or via a style sheet. Don't apply it to body text.

To keep two paragraphs together:

1. Choose the Content tool.
2. Click in a paragraph.
3. Choose Style > Formats (Cmd-Shift-F/ Ctrl-Shift-F).
4. Check Keep with Next ¶ **1**.
5. Click OK.

As QuarkXPress defines it, a widow is the last line of a paragraph that's stranded at the top of a column **2**. An orphan is the first line of paragraph that's stranded at the bottom of a column **3**. Both are typesetting no-no's. The Keep Lines Together command can be used to prevent orphan and widow lines. It can also be used to keep *all* the lines in a paragraph together.

To prevent orphan and widow lines:

1. Choose the Content tool.
2. Click in a paragraph.
3. Choose Style > Formats (Cmd-Shift-F/ Ctrl-Shift-F).
4. Check Keep Lines Together **4**.
5. Click All Lines in ¶ to keep all the lines of a paragraph together, even if the paragraph falls at the end of a column or page (we use this for subheads and the like).
   or
   Click Start to turn on orphan and widow control, then enter "2" (or even "3") in the Start and End fields to ensure that no fewer than two lines of a paragraph are stranded at the bottom or top of a column, respectively.
6. Click OK.

Formatting tips and tricks

A format in which the first line of a paragraph is aligned flush left and the remaining lines are indented is called a hanging indent. Hanging indents can be used to make subheads, bullets, or other special text more prominent or to hang punctuation (see page 132). A hanging indent that's created by following the steps below can be applied via a style sheet.

To create a hanging indent using a dialog box:

1. Choose the Content tool.

2. Click in a paragraph or drag downward through a series of paragraphs.

3. Choose Style > Formats (Cmd-Shift-F/ Ctrl-Shift-F).

4. Enter a Left Indent value. Need a suggestion? Try 1p or 2p **1**.

5. Enter a First Line value that's equal to or less than the number you entered in the previous step, preceded by a minus (-) sign.

6. Click Apply to preview (Cmd-A/Alt-A), make any adjustments, and then click OK **2**–**3**.

1 *Enter a positive* **Left Indent**... *...and a negative* **First Line.**

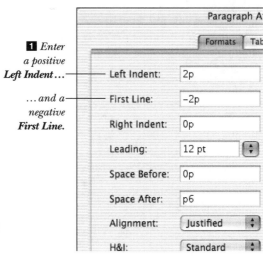

The Paragraph Attributes > **Formats** *pane*

A **tab** *stop is created automatically at the location of the indent. (To style this text, we used a character style sheet. A character style sheet could also be used to style bullets or dingbats/wingdings in a bulleted list.)*

I mean in singing; but in loving—Leander the good swimmer, Troilus the first employer of panders, and a whole book full of these quondam carpet-mongers, whose names yet run smoothly in the even road of a blank verse, why, they were never so truly turned over and over as my poor self in love.

Marry, I cannot show it in rhyme; I have tried; I can find out no rhyme to lady but baby—an innocent rhyme;

WILLIAM SHAKESPEARE

2 *In this example, a* **positive Left Indent** *and a* **negative First Line** *create a hanging indent formation in each paragraph.*

D. Pedro. He is in earnest.

Claud. In most profound earnest; and I'll warrant you for the love of Beatrice.

D. Pedro. And hath challenged thee?

Claud. Most sincerely.

D. Pedro. What a pretty thing man is when he goes in his doublet and hose, and leaves off his wit!

Claud. He is then a giant to an ape: but then is an ape a doctor to such a man?

WILLIAM SHAKESPEARE

3 *In this example, after the hanging indents were created via a positive Left Indent and a negative First Line, the* **Tab** *key was pressed after the bold text in each paragraph to align the text to the tab stop that QuarkXPress inserted automatically.*

THESEUS. |Now, fair Hippolyta, our nuptial hour draws on apace; four happy days bring in another moon: but, oh, methinks, how slow this old moon wanes! She lingers my desires, like to a step-dame or a dowager, long withering out a young man's revenue.

~ William Shakespeare

1 *To insert the* **Indent Here** *character, click in the text, then press* **Cmd-\/Ctrl-\.**

THESEUS. Now, fair Hippolyta, our nuptial hour draws on apace; four happy days bring in another moon: but, oh, methinks, how slow this old moon wanes! She lingers my desires, like to a step-dame or a dowager, long withering out a young man's revenue.

2 *A* **hanging indent** *is created.*

3 *The* **Indent Here** *character displays as a vertical dotted line when View > Show Invisibles is on. If you don't see it, zoom in.*

THESEUS. |Now, fair Hippol hour draws on days bring in oh, methinks,

On the positive side, the Indent Here character instantly creates a hanging indent wherever your cursor happens to be positioned. On the minus side, the Indent Here character has to be inserted manually into each paragraph, it can't be incorporated into a style sheet, and it can't be added or removed using Find/Change. It's very handy for quickly formatting a unique paragraph here or there. To create a hanging indent in multiple paragraphs, though, follow the instructions on the previous page instead.

To create a hanging indent using the Indent Here character:

1. Choose the Content tool.

2. Click in a paragraph where the indent is to be inserted (not in an HTML text box) **1**.

3. Press Cmd-\(backslash)/Ctrl-\ **2**.

To remove an Indent Here character:

1. Choose the Content tool.

2. Choose View > Show Invisibles (Cmd-I/ Ctrl-I), if invisibles aren't currently showing.

3. Click just to the right of the Indent Here character **3**. If you're having trouble locating the correct spot, you can press the left or right arrow key on your keyboard to move the text cursor one character at a time.

4. Press Delete/Backspace. Choose View > Show Invisibles again, if you prefer to work with this feature off.

Indent Here Character

An interesting drop cap (or caps) can add pizzazz to a page and spark your reader's interest. *Caution:* Because they're so easy to create, it's tempting to use drop caps here, there, and everywhere. Don't succumb— like hot chilis, they're best used sparingly.

To insert an automatic drop cap:

1. Choose the Content tool.

2. Click in a paragraph.

3. Choose Style > Formats (Cmd-Shift-F/ Ctrl-Shift-F).

4. Check Drop Caps **1**.

5. Click Apply to preview (Cmd-A/Alt-A), and move the dialog box out of the way, if necessary.

6. *Optional:* To "drop cap" more than one character, enter that number in the Character Count field (1–127).

7. *Optional:* To adjust the height of the drop cap, change the Line Count (2–16). The drop cap will adjust automatically to fit the line count.

8. Click Apply to preview again, then click OK **2**–**3**.

9. *Optional:* Highlight the drop cap and change its color, shade, or font (see the next chapter). Be bold and imaginative!

TIP To anchor any item (e.g., a picture box, text box, contentless box, or line) as a drop cap or a large initial cap, see page 197.

Line Count: The number of vertical lines of text the drop cap will adjust to fit into

1 *Check **Drop Caps** in Paragraph Attributes > Formats.*

Character Count: The number of characters to be "dropped"

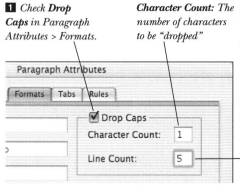

Not only was her first-floor flat invaded at all hours by throngs of singular and often undesirable characters but her remarkable lodger showed an eccentricity and irregularity in his life which must have sorely tried her patience. His incredible untidiness, his addiction to music at strange hours, his occasional revolver practice within doors, his weird and often malodorous scientific experiments, and the atmosphere of violence and danger which hung around him made him the very worst tenant in London. On the other hand, his payments were princely...

SIR ARTHUR CONAN DOYLE

2 *A **drop cap** with a **character count** of **1** and a line count of **5***

NOT only was her first-floor flat invaded at all hours by throngs of singular and often undesirable characters but her remarkable lodger showed an eccentricity and irregularity in his life which must have sorely tried her patience. His incredible untidiness, his addiction to music at strange hours, his occasional revolver practice within doors, his weird and often malodorous scientific experiments, and the atmosphere of violence and danger which hung around him made him the very worst tenant in London. On the other hand, his payments were princely...

3 *A **drop cap** with a **character count** of **3** and a line count of **2***

An anomaly which often struck me in the character of my friend Sherlock Holmes was that, although in his methods of thought he was the neatest and most methodical of mankind, and although also he affected a certain quiet primness of dress, he was none the less in his personal habits one of the most untidy
SIR ARTHUR CONAN DOYLE

1 *A drop cap is **highlighted**.*

An anomaly which often struck me in the character of my friend Sherlock Holmes was that, although in his methods of thought he was the neatest and most methodical of mankind, and although also he affected a certain quiet primness of dress, he was none the less in his per-

2 *The drop cap is **enlarged** to 125%.*

For those who like this sort of thing, this is the sort of thing they like.
ABRAHAM LINCOLN

3 *The cursor correctly positioned for **kerning** next to a drop cap.*

4 *The **tracking/kerning** section of the Measurements palette*

To resize an automatic drop cap manually:

1. Choose the Content tool.

2. Highlight the drop cap character or characters **1**.

3. Change the size percentage (16.7%–400%) in the upper right corner of the Measurements palette **2**.
or
Choose Style > Character (Cmd-Shift-D/Ctrl-Shift-D), then change the Size percentage.

To kern next to a drop cap:

1. Choose the Content tool.

2. Click in the first line of the paragraph between the drop cap and the character to the right of it (not in an HTML text box). You'll see a long blinking bar when the cursor has been inserted correctly **3**.

3. In the tracking/kerning section of the Measurements palette, click the left arrow to delete space or the right arrow to add space **4**. Option-click/Alt-click the left or right arrow to kern in finer increments.
or
To kern using the keyboard, press Cmd-Shift-[/Ctrl-Shift-[or Cmd-Shift-]/Ctrl-Shift-]. Add Option/Alt to the shortcut to kern in a finer increment.

To remove an automatic drop cap, just back out the same way you came in.

To remove an automatic drop cap:

1. Choose the Content tool.

2. Click in the paragraph that contains the drop cap.

3. Choose Style > Formats (Cmd-Shift-F/Ctrl-Shift-F).

4. Uncheck Drop Caps.

5. Click OK.

Automatic Drop Cap

There are many reasons to use the Paragraph Rules feature for creating rules. For one, a paragraph rule stays anchored to its paragraph even if the paragraph is moved or reflows (a line created with a line tool would stay put). Second, a paragraph rule can be applied using a style sheet. And finally, unlike the Underline type style, a paragraph rule can be modified in its appearance and position. Paragraph rules are horizontal only—no verticals.

To insert a paragraph rule:

1. Choose the Content tool.

2. Click in a paragraph or drag downward through a series of paragraphs.

3. Choose Style > Rules (Cmd-Shift-N/Ctrl-Shift-N).

4. Check Rule Above and/or Rule Below ◼.

5. Choose or enter a Width. Click Apply to preview (Cmd-A/Alt-A).

6. Choose Indents or Text from the Length pop-up menu. If you choose

Becoming unruly

To remove a paragraph rule, reopen the Rules dialog box (Cmd-Shift-N/Ctrl-Shift-N), then *uncheck* Rule Above and/or Rule Below. To remove a rule from a style sheet, click Rules in the Edit Style Sheet dialog box, then uncheck Rule Above and/or Rule Below.

*Choose a **Style**. To create a custom style, use the Dashes & Stripes feature.*

*Choose **Length**: **Indents** or **Text**.*

*The amount a rule is indented is equal to the **From Left** and/or **From Right** values— plus any existing paragraph Indents and Text Inset values.*

◼ *Check **Rule Below** (or **Rule Above**) to add a rule; **uncheck** the box to **remove** it.*

*Enter a number to **Offset** a **Rule Above** upward from the baseline of the **first** line of the paragraph or to Offset a **Rule Below** downward from the baseline of the **last** line of the paragraph.*

*Enter or choose a **Width**.*

*Choose a **Color**.*

*Choose a **Shade**.*

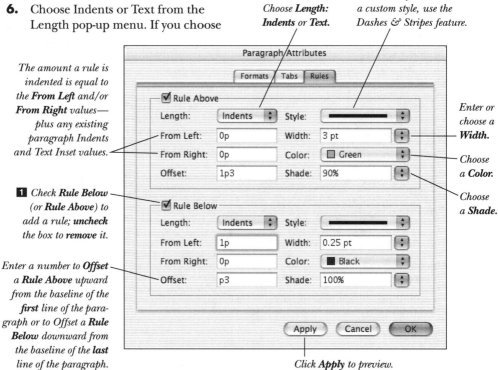

*Click **Apply** to preview.*

Paragraph Rules

Hey! diddle, diddle,
The cat and the fiddle,

1 *In this example, the first line of the paragraph is **indented**, which causes the rule to indent as well.*

Hey! diddle, diddle,
The cat and the fiddle,

2 *To align the rule with the left edge of the rest of the paragraph, as in this example, in the From Left field we entered the same value as the paragraph's left indent with a **minus** sign in front of it (–1p).*

Hey! diddle, diddle,
The cat and the fiddle,
The cow jumped over the moon;
The little dog laugh'd
To see such sport,
And the dish ran away with the spoon.

3 *A 2-pt Rule Above, Length: **Indents**, Offset p10*

Hey! diddle, diddle,
The cat and the fiddle,
The cow jumped over the moon;
The little dog laugh'd
To see such sport,
And the dish ran away with the spoon.

4 *A 2-pt Rule Above, Length: **Text**, Offset p10*

H*ey! diddle, diddle,*
The cat and the fiddle,
The cow jumped over the moon;
The little dog laugh'd
To see such sport,
And the dish ran away with the spoon.

5 *A 2-pt Rule Above, Length: Text, **From Left** 1p10, Offset p10*

Text, the rule will be the width of the first line of text in the paragraph for a Rule Above or the width of the last line of text in the paragraph for a Rule Below. If you choose Indents, the rule will be the width of the paragraph, unless you enter a number greater than 0 in the From Left and/or From Right field (see step 8). *Note:* The rule will also be shortened by any Indent values in Style > Formats and any Text Inset values in Item > Modify > Text **1**.

7. In the entire Offset field, enter the fixed distance, in any measurement unit, by which you want to offset the bottom of the Rule Above upward from the baseline of the first line of the paragraph or offset the top of the Rule Below downward from the baseline of the last line of the paragraph (not for HTML text boxes). For a Rule Above, enter an Offset that is equal to or greater than the point size of the type.
or
Enter a percentage Offset (0–100%). A Rule Below with a 20% Offset, for example, would position the rule closer to the bottom of the currently selected paragraph than would an 80% offset. If this method is used and the spacing between the paragraphs is altered, the rule position will adjust automatically. We're not wild about this option.

8. *Optional:* Raise the From Left and/or From Right values to indent, and thus shorten, the rule.

9. Choose a style from the Style pop-up menu. To create a custom style, see pages 223–224.

10. Choose a color from the Color pop-up menu.

11. Choose or enter a Shade percentage.

12. Click Apply to preview, make any adjustments, then click OK **2**–**5**.

(For more illustrations, see the next page.)

Paragraph Rules

ETHAN FROME

By Edith Wharton

I had the story, bit by bit, from various people, and, as generally happens in such cases, each time it was a different story.

If you know Starkfield, Massachusetts, you know the post-office. If you know the post-office you must have seen Ethan Frome drive up to it, drop the reins on his hollow-backed bay and

Rules can be used to jazz up subheads

Rules can be used to jazz up subheads

*Rules of varying **lengths** and **weights***

Norton Thorpe clapped the young Frenchman on the shoulder and, with a hearty smile, shook his hand. "My dear chap! How could I possibly object to my daughter becoming not only the new Countess d'Auvergne but also the wife of an up-and-coming electronics genius!" Lisa, her eyes moist with tears of joy, not

"How could I possibly object to my daughter becoming not only the new Countess d'Auvergne but also the wife of an up-and-coming electronics genius!"

only because of her future marriage but also because of her restored relationship with her father, threw her arms around Nancy in a warm embrace exclaiming: "Oh, Nancy, none of this could ever have happened if you hadn't worked so hard to solve

Carolyn Keene

Going in reverse

To create a **reverse rule,** color the text white, and use a negative Offset and a wide width (the point size of the type plus a few points) for the rule. A negative value of up to half the width of the rule can be used. This is a 16-point black Rule Above, Length: Indents, Left and Right Indents: 0, and Offset: -p4. The headline text is 9 pt.

Cumin
Cayenne
Coriander
Chervil
Cinnamon

*To add alternating **tints** behind text, use a wide Rule Above with a negative Offset. Apply it via a style sheet!*

*Need to fill up a page with horizontal **lines?** Apply a paragraph rule, then keep pressing Return/Enter.*

*Rules can be used as **decorative** elements or for **emphasis. In this** example, a Return was inserted after every line, making every line a separate paragraph.*

*Here paragraph rules are used to **separate** a pull quote from the main body text.*

ALL

THE

REALLY GOOD

IDEAS

I EVER HAD

CAME

TO ME

WHILE I WAS

MILKING

A COW.

Grant Wood

Do it without the grid

To align text without using the Lock to Baseline Grid feature, make sure the sum of the space before and after any subheads or between paragraphs is a *multiple* of the leading value. For example, if your body text has 14 pt. leading, add 8 points before each subhead and 6 points after (a total of 14). Use style sheets to ensure that all the leading in your body text is uniform.

There are several methods of making coffee, each highly recommended—I cannot decide which is best, but the following way is a good one:—

TO MAKE COFFEE.— Take fresh-roasted coffee (a quarter of a pound for three persons is the rule, but *less* will do;) allow two tablespoonfuls for each person, grind it just before making, put it in a basin and break into it an egg, yolk, white, shell and all. Mix it up with the spoon to the consistence of mortar, put in warm not *boiling* water in the coffee pot; let it boil up and *break* three times; then stand a few minutes, and it will be as clear as amber, and the egg will give it a rich taste.

ANOTHER WAY TO MAKE COFFEE.—Pour hot water into your coffee pot, and then

stir in your coffee, a spoonful at a time, allowing three to every pint of water; this makes *strong* coffee. Stir it to prevent the mixture from boiling over, as the coffee swells, and to force it to combine with the water. This will be done after it has boiled gently a few minutes. Then let it stand and boil slowly for half an hour; remove it from the fire, and pour in a tea-cup of cold water, and set it in the corner to settle. As soon as it becomes clear, it is to be poured, gently, into a clean coffee pot for the table.

Made in this manner it may be kept two or three days in summer, and a week in winter; you need only heat it over when wanted.

Sara Josepha Hale from *The Good Housekeeper,* 1841

1 *Text aligned across columns using **Lock to Baseline Grid***

The Lock to Baseline Grid command is used to precisely align text across columns (for an alternate method, see the sidebar). This command is not available for HTML text boxes, but it is available for table cells.

To align text to a grid:

1. Take note of what leading value is currently applied to your body text. Also, select your text box, go to Item > Modify > Text, then on a scrap of paper, jot down the current First Baseline: Offset value (paperless office? Ha!).

2. *Optional:* To display the nonprinting gridlines, choose View > Show Baseline Grid (Option-F7/Ctrl-F7).

3. Choose QuarkXPress (Edit, in Windows) > Preferences > Print Layout or Web Layout > Paragraph.

4. Enter as the Baseline Grid: Start value the First Baseline: Offset value that you got from Item > Modify.

5. Enter as the Baseline Grid: Increment the current leading value or a multiple of the leading value.

6. Click OK.

7. To snap the text to the grid lines, select the paragraphs you want to lock (or better yet, do this via a style sheet), choose Style > Formats, check Lock to Baseline Grid, then click OK **1**.

   Note: If Justified is chosen as the Vertical Alignment: Type in Item > Modify > Text, only the first and last lines in the column will lock to the grid.

   Note: Also see the information about Maintain Leading on page 423.

TIP You may not want to lock subheads to the grid.

You can use this trick to copy paragraph formats within the *same* text box or between *linked* text boxes, but not between unlinked boxes or table cells. Paragraph style sheet and local formatting specifications will copy; character attributes (font, size, color, etc.) won't.

To copy formats in the same story:

1. Click in a paragraph **1** or drag downward through a series of paragraphs that you want to reformat.

2. Option-Shift-click/Alt-Shift-click the paragraph whose formats you want copied to the paragraph(s) you selected in the previous step **2**.

> Then there was nothing but the air and the swiftness of the little cloud that bore me and those two men still leading up to where white clouds were piled like mountains on a wide blue plain, and in them thunder beings lived and leaped and flashed.
>
> *Now suddenly there was nothing but a world of cloud, and we three were there alone in the middle of a great white plain with snowy hills and mountains staring at us; and it was very still; but there were whispers...*
>
> JOHN G. NEIHARDT, FROM BLACK ELK SPEAKS

1 *Click in a paragraph (or highlight a series of paragraphs) to be **reformatted**...*

> Then there was nothing but the air and the swiftness of the little cloud that bore me and those two men still leading up to where white clouds were piled like mountains on a wide blue plain, and in them thunder beings lived and leaped and flashed.
> *Now suddenly there was nothing but a world of cloud, and we three were there alone in the middle of a great white plain with snowy hills and mountains staring at us; and it was very still; but there were whispers...*
>
> JOHN G. NEIHARDT, FROM BLACK ELK SPEAKS

2 *...then Option-Shift-click/Alt-Shift-click the paragraph whose formats you want to **copy**. In our example, the top paragraph reformats (its Left Indent, Space After, Alignment, and Space After values change) but the font remains the same because the font is a character attribute—not a paragraph attribute.*

Appending an H&J

To append an H&J from one project to another, choose File > **Append** or click Append in the H&J dialog box (either way you'll get to the same place). An H&J that is created when no files are open will appear on the H&J pop-up menu in all subsequently created files.

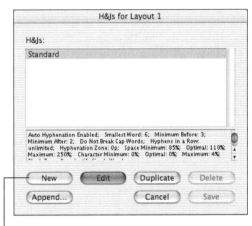

1 Click **New.** Or choose an existing H&J and click **Edit.** Click **Append** to append an H&J from another project.

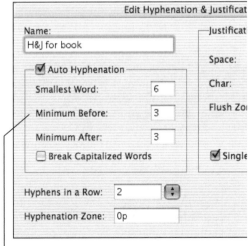

2 Choose hyphenation settings in the **Edit Hyphenation & Justification** dialog box.

Applying hyphenation

Auto Hyphenation lessens gaps between words in justified type and smooths ragged edges in nonjustified type. A set of hyphenation and justification settings is called an "H&J," and each project can contain up to 1,000 of them. To apply an H&J, follow the instructions on page 119. (Manual hyphenation, which is discussed in the sidebar on page 120, should be used only to correct an occasional awkward break here or there.)

To create or edit an H&J:

1. Choose Edit > H&Js (Cmd-Option-J/ Ctrl-Alt-J). (The shortcut is new.) **6.0!**

2. To create a new H&J, click New **1**, then enter a name.
   or
   Click an existing H&J, then click Edit. The Standard H&J can be modified.

3. Check Auto Hyphenation **2**.

4. Change any of the hyphenation settings:

   Smallest Word is the minimum number of characters a word must contain to be hyphenated. We use 5 or 6.

   Minimum Before is the minimum number (1–6) of a word's characters that must precede a hyphen.

   Minimum After is the minimum number (2–8) of characters that can follow a hyphen. For the sake of readability, we use 3 rather than the default 2.

   Check Break Capitalized Words if you want to permit words that begin with an uppercase character to be hyphenated.

   Hyphens in a Row is the number of consecutive lines that can end with a hyphen. More than two hyphens in a row can impair readability.

   Enter a Hyphenation Zone value greater than zero to create a more ragged edge (less hyphenation).

(Continued on the following page)

Create or Edit an H&J

5. To tighten word spacing in justified paragraphs, enter lower Space: Min./Minimum and Space: Max./Maximum values **1**. The subheads and thumb tabs in this book have slightly tightened word spacing. Headlines also tend to look better with tighter-than-normal word (and character) spacing. To loosen word spacing, enter higher values.

To tighten the character spacing in justified paragraphs, enter lower Char: Min./Minimum and Char: Max./Maximum values. To loosen character spacing, enter higher values. Experiment, and make your final judgment from a printout. The effect may vary depending on the font.

To change the word or character spacing in both justified and nonjustified paragraphs, change either or both of the Opt./Optimum values.

6. *Optional:* The Flush Zone, which is the span within which the last word in a justified paragraph must fall in order to be justified, can be widened.

Check Single Word Justify to force any single word that falls on a line by itself to be justified to the full width of the text box, minus any indents. Usually this occurs at the end of a paragraph.

Note: The Forced Justify horizontal alignment option justifies single words automatically. In fact, Forced Justify overrides both the Flush Zone and Single Word Justify setttings.

7. Click OK.

8. Click Save. To apply an H&J, follow the instructions on the next page.

TIP To delete an H&J, click its name, then click Delete. If the H&J is currently applied to text in your project, you'll be prompted to choose a replacement H&J for the deleted one **2**. The Standard H&J can't be deleted.

1 *The* **Space** *values affect inter-word spacing; the* **Char.** *values affect character (letter) spacing.*

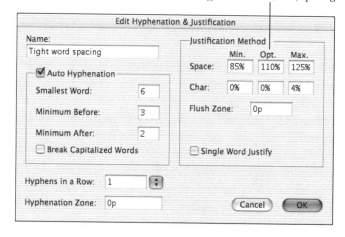

2 *This alert dialog box will open if you* **delete** *an H&J that is currently applied to text in your project.*

*In this illustration, **hyphenation** is **on** for
the **subheads** (a no-no!) and **off** for the
justified body text (another no-no because
it leaves ugly "rivers" of white space).*

*Here **hyphenation** is turned **off** for the **subheads** and turned **on** for the **justified** body
text. An improvement, don't you think?*

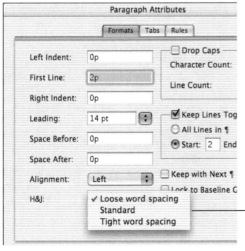

H&Js are applied to individual paragraphs
via the H&J pop-up menu in Style >
Formats. If you're using more than one
H&J setting in a project, the most efficient
way to apply them to your text is via a style
sheet (click Formats in the Edit Paragraph
Style Sheet dialog box; see Chapter 13).
The Normal style sheet will have the
Standard H&J associated with it unless a
different H&J is chosen for it. H&Js can't
be applied to HTML text.

To apply an H&J:

1. Choose the Content tool.
2. Click in a paragraph or drag downward
   through a series of paragraphs.
3. Choose Style > Formats (Cmd-Shift-F/
   Ctrl-Shift-F).
4. Choose from the H&J pop-up menu **1**.
5. Click Apply, if desired (Cmd-A/Alt-A),
   then click OK.

TIP The Expanded Hyphenation Method,
which uses a built-in hyphenation dictionary, creates better word breaks than
the other methods. Go to QuarkXPress
(Edit, in Windows) > Preferences > Print
Layout or Web Layout > Paragraph,
click a Language under Hyphenation,
then choose Expanded from the
Method pop-up menu. The Standard
and Enhanced methods are from
earlier versions of QuarkXPress. We
think even the Expanded Hyphenation
Method could stand some improvement.

TIP Use a nonbreaking (permanent)
hyphen if you want a word to *always*
hyphenate but never break at the end
of a line (a compound word, such as
"e-mail" or "two-thirds"). To insert one,
press Cmd-=/Ctrl-=.

1 *To apply an H&J to highlighted
text or to make it part of a style sheet,
choose from the **H&J** pop-up menu
in Paragraph Attributes > **Formats**.*

The Hyphenation Exceptions dialog box is used not only to enter words you don't want hyphenated, but also to specify how specific words are to be hyphenated.

To enter hyphenation exceptions:

1. Choose Utilities > Hyphenation Exceptions.

2. Type a word that you *don't* want hyphenated **1**. You can't type spaces or punctuation marks.
   or
   Specify how a word *will* be hyphenated by typing it with a hyphen.

3. Click Add (Return/Enter).

4. *Optional:* To edit an entry, click on it, edit it in the field, then click Replace.

5. Repeat steps 2–3 or 4 for any other words. Be sure to add any variations of a word, such as its plural form.

6. Click Save. Hyphenation exceptions are saved in the XPress Preferences file, and are layout-specific.

TIP To prevent a compound word from hyphenating, add each part of the word separately as a hyphenation exception.

TIP You can use the Line Check feature to search for manually and/or automatically hyphenated words (see page 93).

Hyphenating manually

Have you ever noticed, in your reading, a hyphen in the middle of a line that wasn't supposed to be there? Now that type is set in desktop publishing applications, it's an all too frequent occurrence.

If for some reason you want to hyphenate a word manually, don't use a regular hyphen, which will stay in your text if the text reflows. Instead, use a **discretionary** hyphen (Cmd-hyphen/Ctrl-hyphen), which will disappear if the text reflows (though the nonprinting marker for it will remain).

If you're not sure how to hyphenate a particular word, choose the Content tool, click in the word, then choose Utilities > **Suggested 6.0!** **Hyphenation** (Cmd-Option-Shift-H/Ctrl-Alt-Shift-H). If no hyphens display in the dialog box, it means that word isn't supposed to be hyphenated, period.

Neither feature is available for HTML text boxes.

*This word **won't** hyphenate under any circumstances.*   *This word **will only** hyphenate in the way the hyphen is entered here.*

1 *Using the **Hyphenation Exceptions** dialog box, you can specify how a word **is** to be hyphenated and also specify which words you **don't** want hyphenated.*

Typography 7

Reformat type the fast way

Once you've mastered the typographic basics, we urge you to read Chapter 13, **Style Sheets!**

*Enter a point size between 2 and 720 in the **Size** field.*

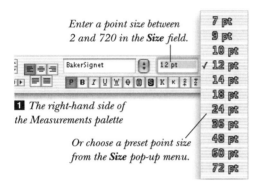

1 *The right-hand side of the Measurements palette*

*Or choose a preset point size from the **Size** pop-up menu.*

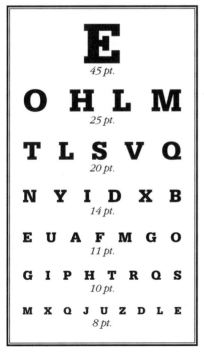

E
45 pt.

O H L M
25 pt.

T L S V Q
20 pt.

N Y I D X B
14 pt.

E U A F M G O
11 pt.

G I P H T R Q S
10 pt.

M X Q J U Z D L E
8 pt.

Typography basics

Tired of 12 pt. Helvetica? Now you'll have some fun. In this chapter, not only will you learn how to change basic type attributes (point size, font, etc.), you'll also learn how to add professional touches, such as smart quotation marks.

To resize type using the Measurements palette:

1. Choose the Content tool.

2. Highlight the text to be resized.

3. Double-click the Size field on the far right side of the Measurements palette **1**, enter a point size (2–720) in an increment as small as .001 point, then press Return/Enter. You don't have to enter the "pt."
   or
   Choose a preset size from the Size pop-up menu on the right side of the Measurements palette.

TIP Cmd-Shift-\/Ctrl-Shift-\ opens the Character Attributes dialog box and highlights the Size field in one keystroke.

Use this method to resize type if your highlighted text contains more than one point size—all the type will resize at once. (To scale type *and* its box, see page 128.)

To resize type using the keyboard:

1. Choose the Content tool.

2. Highlight the text to be resized.

3. Press Cmd-Shift-</Ctrl-Shift-< to reduce the text in preset sizes or > to enlarge it. Or press Cmd-Option-Shift-</Ctrl-Alt-Shift-< to reduce the text in 1-point increments or > to enlarge it.

Resize Type

If you're new to typography, read "Type for print" on page 135. For further reading on this topic, explore one of Robin Williams' terrifically helpful books, such as *The Non-Designer's Type Book* (Peachpit Press).

To change fonts:
1. Choose the Content tool.
2. Highlight the text to be modified.
3. Choose a font from the Font pop-up menu on the Measurements palette 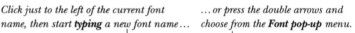.
   or
   On the Measurements palette, click in the Font field to the left of the current font name, type the first few characters of the desired font name, then press Return/Enter .
   or
   Choose a font from the Style > Font submenu.

TIP For information about managing fonts, see pages 437–438.

TIP To recolor type, see page 264.

Font shortcuts

Highlight font field on Measurements palette	Cmd-Option-Shift-M/ Ctrl-Alt-Shift-M
Apply next font on font menu	Option-F9/Ctrl-F9
Apply previous font on font menu	Option-Shift-F9/ Ctrl-Shift-F9

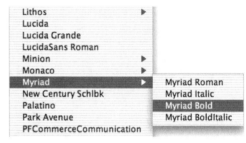

1 A **Font** submenu in Mac OS X

*Click just to the left of the current font name, then start **typing** a new font name… …or press the double arrows and choose from the **Font pop-up** menu.*

2 The **Font** area is on the right side of the Measurements palette.

One-stop styling

If you'd like to make all your Font, Size, Color, Shade, Scale, Track/Kern Amount, Baseline Shift, and Type Style choices from one dialog box, choose Style > **Character** (Cmd-Shift-D/Ctrl-Shift-D). Don't forget to click Apply to preview.

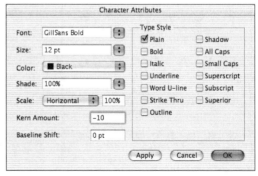

Type style shortcuts

First highlight the type, then hold down **Cmd-Shift/Ctrl-Shift** and press one of the following keys (use the same shortcut to remove a style):

Plain	**P**	Shadow	**S**
Bold	**B**	All Caps	**K**
Italic	**I**	Small Caps	**H**
Underline	**U**	Superscript	**+** *(Mac)* **0** *(Win)*
Word Underline	**W**	Subscript	**-** *(Mac)* **9** *(Win)*
Strike Thru	**/**	Superior	**V**
Outline	**O**		

Note: The word underline, outline, shadow, small caps, and superior styles aren't available for HTML text boxes.

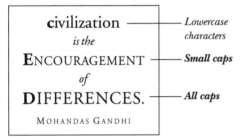

civilization — *Lowercase characters*
is the
ENCOURAGEMENT — ***Small caps***
of
DIFFERENCES. — ***All caps***
MOHANDAS GANDHI

Note: Looking for boldface or italics? Choose the actual bold or italic font from the Font menu—it's less likely to cause a printing error.

To style type:

1. Choose the Content tool.
2. Highlight the text to be styled.
3. Click one or more of the style buttons on the Measurements palette 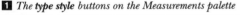.

TIP To remove *all* styling from highlighted type, click the "P" on the Measurements palette. To remove one style at a time, click any highlighted style button. If a style is half gray, it means not all the currently highlighted type has that style.

TIP Don't input text with the Caps Lock key down; lowercase characters can easily be converted into caps or small caps, but characters input with Caps Lock down can't be converted back to lowercase (unless you use a third-party case-conversion XTension). When the small caps style is applied, uppercase characters remain uppercase and lowercase characters turn into small caps.

TIP Superscript type sits above the baseline (as in ®). Subscript type sits below the baseline (as in ₂). Superior type aligns with the cap height of the type and is reduced in point size (as in 18ᵗʰ). Adjust the proportions of these styles in QuarkXPress (Edit, in Windows) > Preferences > Print Layout or Web Layout > Character (try reducing the "VScale" percentage).

Style Type

1 *The **type style** buttons on the Measurements palette*

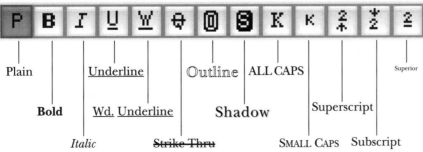

Kerning and tracking

Kerning is the manual adjustment of space between a pair of characters (the cursor is inserted between them). Tracking, the adjustment of the space to the right of one or more highlighted characters, can be used to create a variety of typographic effects. The same area of the Measurements palette is used for tracking as for kerning. *Note:* Before kerning manually, go to QuarkXPress (Edit, in Windows) > Preferences > Print Layout > Character and make sure Auto Kern Above is on, at or below the minimum type size of your text). The kerning and tracking commands aren't available for HTML text.

To kern or track type manually using the Measurements palette:

1. Choose the Content tool, and zoom in on the type you're going to kern or track.

2. For kerning, click between two characters ▮.
   or
   For tracking, highlight any number of consecutive characters.

3. Click the right Tracking & Kerning arrow to add space or the left arrow to remove space ▮–▮. To track or kern in a finer increment, Option-click/ Alt-click the right or left arrow.
   or
   Enter a value between -500% and 500% in the Tracking & Kerning field in an increment as small as .001.

TIP To restore normal tracking to highlighted text or to restore normal kerning at a text insertion point, enter 0 in the Tracking & Kerning field or click the left or right arrow until 0 appears in the field.

TIP To apply tracking or kerning values via a dialog box, choose Style > Track or Kern. To adjust the letterspacing for longer passages of text, use an H&J (see pages 117–119).

You can't kern/track HTML text

And that's not all you *can't* do! For a list of what is permissible and what isn't, see page 136.

Tomorrow

▮ *Click **between** two characters to **kern** them.*

14 pt				GillSans Bold
-16				P **B** *I* U

▮ *The **Tracking & Kerning** field and arrows on the Measurements palette*

Tomorrow

▮ *Now the "T" and the "o" are **closer** together.*

C I V I L I Z A T I O N
is the
E N C O U R A G E M E N T
of
D I F F E R E N C E S.
Mohandas Gandhi

▮ *A phrase with positive **tracking** values*

Nothing
great was
ever achieved
without
enthusiasm.

*Ralph Waldo
Emerson*

▮ *A phrase with a **negative** **tracking** value of -6*

Kern or Track

To Tr Ta Yo Ya Wo Wa We Va Vo

1 *These are a few of the character pairs that often need **extra kerning**, particularly if they're set in a large point size.*

THE TALE OF MRS. TIGGY-WINKLE
THE TALE OF MRS. TIGGY-WINKLE

---

2 *Wide tracking (letterspacing) is popular nowadays, especially since it's so easy to do. We use it only for **short** passages, though; it's tiring to read in long passages. Small caps, as in this illustration, look nice "tracked out," as does very chunky or very thin type (e.g., a condensed font).*

Style is self-plagiarism.

3 *This phrase has normal word spacing.*

Style is self-plagiarism.

∼ ALFRED HITCHCOCK

4 *Here the same phrase has a **Word Space Tracking** value of -10. Negative word space tracking adds a professional touch to headlines and other large-sized text.*

This is the quickest method for tracking—and it's our favorite.

To kern or track using the keyboard:

1. Choose the Content tool.
2. Click between two characters or highlight any number of characters.
3. Press Cmd-Shift-[/Ctrl-Shift-[(left bracket) to remove space, or] (right bracket) to add space **1**–**2**. To kern or track in a finer increment, include the Option/Alt key in the shortcut.

Use the Word Space Tracking* shortcut described in the following instructions to adjust inter-word spacing in an isolated phrase, such as a large headline.

Note: To adjust inter-word spacing in repetitive text (e.g., subheads) or in a larger body of text, create an H&J that has tightened word spacing and apply it via a style sheet. That's how we tightened the word spacing of subheads in this book (as in the words "To adjust inter-word spacing:" below).

To adjust inter-word spacing:

1. Choose the Content tool.
2. Highlight one or more words.
3. In Mac OS X, press Cmd-Control-Shift-[(left bracket) to remove space or] (right bracket) to add space **3**–**4**. For finer word space adjustments, include the Option key. In Windows, press Ctrl-Shift-1 or Ctrl-Shift-2.

To remove kerning and word space tracking:

1. Choose the Content tool.
2. Highlight the kerned text.
3. Choose Utilities > Remove Manual Kerning.* This command has no effect on tracking values.

*Word Space Tracking and Remove Manual Kerning are part of Type Tricks.xnt, an XTension that ships with QuarkXPress.

Some character pairs, because of their shape and how they happen to fit side by side, have noticeable gaps between them. To ameliorate this problem, fonts have hundreds of built-in kerning pairs—character duos that are nudged together slightly. To turn this pair kerning on, go to QuarkXPress (Edit, in Windows) > Preferences > Print Layout or Web Layout > Character, and check **Auto Kern Above.**

If you're unhappy with the default spacing in a particular kerning pair or pairs that appear repetitively in your layouts, you can use QuarkXPress's kerning editor to specify your own kerning values. You should try to correct any particularly large, toothy gaps (usually in large type) so they don't stand out in the crowd, but don't try to equalize the spacing between all characters. To adjust overall letterspacing, use an H&J (see page 115). Adjust headlines manually.

To use the Kerning Table Editor:

1. Choose Utilities > Kerning Table Edit. If it's unavailable, enable the Kern-Track Editor.xnt (see page 427).

2. Start typing or click the name of the font that you want to edit █, then click Edit.
   or
   Double-click the name of the font that you want to edit.

3. Click a kerning pair on the list.
   or
   In the Pair field, type a kerning pair.

4. Enter a new kerning Value or click the up or down arrow (a negative value will bring characters closer together). Option-click/Alt-click either arrow to kern in a finer increment.

5. When you're satisfied with the new kerning value, as shown in the Preview window █, click Replace to replace the existing pair or click Add to add it as a new pair.

6. Click OK, then click Save.

Keep project settings

Kerning table changes are made on a font-by-font basis, but they apply to the whole *application*. If the XPress prompt appears when you open a file and you want to preserve the project's existing kerning table values, click Keep Project Settings.

To restore a font's original, manufacturer-defined kerning values for all pairs, click *Reset* in the Kerning Values dialog box. QuarkXPress's kerning values don't affect font usage in other applications.

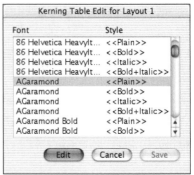

1 *Click the font whose kerning you want to edit, then click Edit.*

2 *Note the Preview as you change a kerning pair's Value. The most accurate preview, of course, is high-resolution output.*

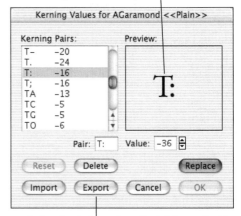

To save the kerning pairs you've adjusted for one font to apply to another font, click Export, then Save. To import those values, choose another font, then click Import.

Alligator

1 *This is Futura Regular,*
Horizontal Scale 0.

Alligator

2 *Here a condensed font*
is fudged by applying a
Horizontal Scale *value of*
30% to Futura Regular.

Alligator

3 *But we think the pro-*
portions are more balanced
in Futura Condensed
Regular, (Horizontal
Scale 0), a typeface that's
condensed to begin with.

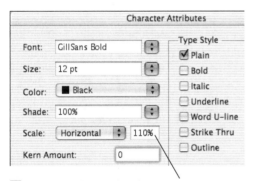

Character Attributes	
Font: GillSans Bold	**Type Style**
Size: 12 pt	☑ Plain
Color: ■ Black	☐ Bold
Shade: 100%	☐ Italic
Scale: Horizontal 110%	☐ Underline
Kern Amount: 0	☐ Word U-line
	☐ Strike Thru
	☐ Outline

4 *The **Scale: Horizontal** field in the Character*
Attributes dialog box

Whale *Expanded type*

Giraffe *Condensed type*

5 **Horizontal scaling** *is used for **stylizing** type.*

Typographic tips and tricks

Normal text has a horizontal scale of 100%. Raising this value makes type wider (extends it); lowering this value below 100% makes type narrower (condenses it). Changing the vertical scaling percentage changes only a character's height. This is different from changing point sizes!

Note: Because the Scale command affects only the vertical parts of letters—not the horizontals (or vice versa)—it causes letter shapes to become distorted. For more narrow (or expanded) characters that look more balanced, we recommend using a Condensed (or Expanded) typeface instead of applying the Horizontal Scale command to Regular characters **1**–**3**. Another option is to create custom weights for an Adobe Multiple Masters font. We rarely use the Scale feature (call us type purists).

To scale type using a dialog box:

1. Choose the Content tool.

2. Highlight the text to be scaled (not HTML text).

3. Choose Style > Horizontal/Vertical Scale. The Character Attributes dialog box will open, with the Scale field highlighted.

4. For horizontal scaling, choose Scale: Horizontal, then enter a percentage between 25 and 99 to condense the type (make it narrower than normal) or a percentage between 101 and 400 to expand the type (make it wider than normal) **4**. A Horizontal Scale of 60%, for example, will condense type by 40%; a Horizontal Scale of 125% will expand type by 25%.
or
Choose Scale: Vertical, then enter the desired percentage.

Note: You can scale type in one direction (horizontally or vertically) but not both.

5. Click Apply (Cmd-A/Alt-A), make any adjustments, then click OK **5**.

Scale Type Horizontally or Vertically

To scale type horizontally or vertically using the keyboard:

1. Choose the Content tool.

2. Highlight the text to be scaled (not HTML text).

3. Hold down Cmd/Ctrl and press [(left bracket) to condense or shorten the type in 5% increments, or] (right bracket) to expand or lengthen it **1**–**4**. Include the Option/Alt key to scale in 1% increments. Scaling will be horizontal or vertical depending on which option is currently selected in the Character Attributes dialog box.

This method for scaling type interactively rather than by specifying an exact point size is appropriate when you're working visually —trying to make a headline or a logo look just so. You can't use it on text in a linked box or on a text path created using the Line Text-Path or Orthogonal Text-Path tool.

To scale type interactively:

1. Choose the Item or Content tool.

2. To scale type while preserving the proportions of the type and the box or path, Cmd-Option-Shift-drag/Ctrl-Alt-Shift-drag a handle **5**–**6**. The leading will readjust proportionately. *Note:* To scale type on a path, make sure Item > Edit > Shape is off (Shift-F4/F10 toggles it on and off). You should see the handles of the bounding box when the path is selected, not the anchor points. *or*
   To scale type and its box (or path) without preserving their proportions, Cmd-drag/Ctrl-drag a side midpoint handle to scale horizontally or a top or bottom midpoint handle to scale vertically. The type will condense or expand to fit the shape of the box or path.

TIP To restore normal scaling to type, highlight it, choose Style > Horizontal/Vertical Scale, then enter 100 in the Scale field.

"It was much pleasanter at home," thought poor Alice, "when one wasn't always growing larger and smaller, and being ordered about by mice and rabbits."

1 *Normal (100%) horizontal and vertical scale*

"It was much pleasanter at home," thought poor Alice, "when one wasn't always growing larger and smaller, and being ordered about by mice and rabbits."

2 *75% vertical scale*

"It was much pleasanter at home," thought poor Alice, "when one wasn't always growing larger and smaller, and being ordered about by mice and rabbits."
~ *Lewis Carroll*

3 *80% horizontal scale*

"It was much pleasanter at home," thought poor Alice, "when one wasn't always growing larger and smaller, and being ordered about by mice and rabbits."

4 *110% horizontal scale*

"Oh, I'm not particular as to size," Alice hastily replied; "only one doesn't like changing so often, you know."

5 *The original text*

"Oh, I'm not particular as to size," Alice hastily replied; "only one doesn't like changing so often, you know."

6 *The text and box are scaled interactively, and the* **proportions** *of both are preserved.*

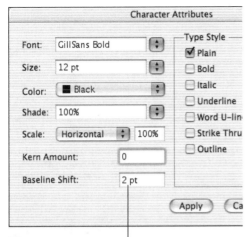

1 *A positive **Baseline Shift** value shifts characters above the baseline; a negative Baseline Shift shifts characters below the baseline.*

*The **baseline***

2 *The "C" was shifted downward. Baseline Shift is handy for creating signs, company logos, and the like.*

Using the Baseline Shift command, you can shift one or more characters above or below the baseline. Don't use this command to shift a whole paragraph—that's the job of leading. Use Baseline Shift only to fiddle with a little bit of type—to nudge a bullet, a dash, or an anchored item slightly upward or downward, or to shift the position of text on a Bézier path. A Baseline Shift value can be incorporated into a paragraph or character style sheet. Baseline Shift is not available for HTML text boxes.

To vertically shift type using a dialog box:

1. Choose the Content tool.

2. Highlight the characters to be shifted.

3. Choose Style > Baseline Shift. The Baseline Shift field will highlight automatically.

4. Enter a number up to three times the point size of the type to be shifted. Enter a minus sign (-) before the number to shift the type below the baseline **1**–**2**.

5. Click OK.

TIP If you change the point size of type that has a Baseline Shift value other than zero, the Baseline Shift value will adjust accordingly.

To vertically shift type using the keyboard:

1. Choose the Content tool.

2. Highlight the characters to be shifted.

3. In Mac OS X, press Cmd-Option-Shift-+ (plus) to raise the type above the baseline in 1-point increments or - (hyphen) to lower the type below the baseline.

In Windows, press Ctrl-Alt-Shift-) (close paren) or ((open paren).

It's easy to input the curly, smart quotation marks that professional typesetters use or foreign language quotation marks, such as guillemets (« »). With the Smart Quotes feature on, press ' to produce a single quotation mark in the style currently specified in the Interactive pane of the Preferences dialog box (' in English) or press Shift-' to produce a double quotation mark (").

To turn on Smart Quotes:

1. Choose QuarkXPress (Edit, in Windows) > Preferences (Cmd-Option-Shift-Y/Ctrl-Alt-Shift-Y).

2. Click Interactive under Application.

3. Check Smart Quotes.

4. Choose a style for the quotes from the Quotes: Format pop-up menu **1**.

5. Click OK **2**.

TIP Uncheck Smart Quotes to produce foot and inch marks when you type ' and ", respectively. To produce a single smart quote when Smart Quotes is unchecked or to produce a foot mark when Smart Quotes is checked, press Control-'/Ctrl-'. To produce a double smart quote when Smart Quotes is unchecked or to produce an inch mark when Smart Quotes is checked, press Control-Shift-'/Ctrl-Alt-'.

TIP If you import text with Convert Quotes checked in the Get Text dialog box, smart quotes will be substituted for straight quotes.

TIP Here's something we learned from Robin Williams' *Beyond the Mac Is Not a Typewriter*. In place of an absent letter, use an apostrophe, not a smart quote. For example, a date should be written like this: '94, not like this: '94. Here's another example: Sugar 'n' spice. To enter an apostrophe manually, press Option-Shift-]/Alt-].

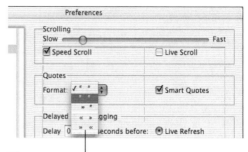

1 *In Preferences > Application > Interactive, check* **Smart Quotes** *and choose a quotes* **Format**.

"HATE THE SIN *and* LOVE THE SINNER"

—*Mohandas Gandhi*

2 *Use* **Smart Quotes** *for* **quotation marks** *and* **apostrophes**.

Prime time

Please—we beg of you—use straight quotes *only* for foot and inch marks **3** (not for quotation marks). Or better yet, use oblique foot and inch marks, called **prime** marks. To produce a prime mark in Mac OS X, press Cmd-Option-Q to insert a character in the Symbol font, then press Option-4; for a double prime mark, press Cmd-Option-Q, then Option-, **4**.

In Windows, for a prime mark, type Alt+2032; for a double prime mark, type Alt+2033.

The woman is 5'6" tall.

3 *You can use straight quotes to indicate feet, inches, minutes, or seconds…*

The woman is 5′6″ tall.

4 *…or better yet, use prime marks.*

A few special characters (all fonts)

©	Option-G/Alt-Shift-C
®	Option-R/Alt-Shift-R
™	Option-2/Alt-Shift-2
•	Option-8/Alt-Shift-8
¢	Option-4/Alt+0162*
¶	Option-7/Alt-Shift-7
°	Option-Shift-8/Alt+0176*

*Hold down Alt, press the numbers sequentially on the numeric keypad, then release Alt; the character will appear.

1 *A few **Zapf Dingbats** characters*

> Sir Isaac Newton wore his black and gold waistcoat. ❦ And Mr. Alderman Ptolemy Tortoise brought a salad with him in a string bag. ❦ And instead of a nice dish of minnows they had a roasted grasshopper with lady-bird sauce, which frogs consider a beautiful treat; but I think it must have been nasty! ❧
>
> *Beatrix Potter*

2 *You can use a symbol to separate sentences or paragraphs or to mark the end of a story or article. But don't limit yourself to the Zapf Dingbat and Symbol fonts—other symbol fonts are available. These symbols are from Adobe's **Minion Ornaments** font.*

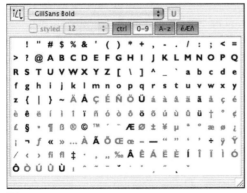

3 *The **PopChar X** palette inserts characters in your text.*

Note: To insert dingbats repetitively, as in a bulleted list, use a character style sheet.

To insert one Zapf Dingbat or Symbol character:

1. Choose the Content tool, then click in your text to create an insertion point.

2. For a Zapf Dingbat character, press Cmd-Option-Z/Ctrl-Shift-Z. For a Symbol character, press Cmd-Option-Q/ Ctrl-Shift-Q. *Note:* For this shortcut to work, in Preferences > Application > Undo, the Redo Key setting must be Cmd-Shift-Z/Ctrl-Shift-Z.

3. Press any key or keyboard combination to produce the desired Zapf Dingbat character **1**–**2**. If you continue to type, the original, non-Dingbat typeface will reappear automatically.

TIP Design idea: Make the Zapf dingbat, or any other dingbat, slightly smaller than the surrounding text, or make it huge, so it serves as a graphic.

Special characters in other fonts

To insert special characters, first you need to know which keystroke to use. Appendix A is a chart of Zapf Dingbat, Symbol, and other special characters. To find other characters, in Mac OS X, you can use Applications > Utilities > Key Caps. Choose from the Font menu, then study the keyboard map. Press Option, Shift, or Option-Shift to display other characters. Type the keystroke to confirm it, copy it (Cmd-C), choose the Content tool, click in your text, then paste (Cmd-V).

A faster approach is to buy the inexpensive PopChar X utility **3** (www.macility.com). To use PopChar X, click in a text box with the Content tool to create an insertion point, then click the desired character on the PopChar palette—the character will appear at your insertion point in the current font.

In Windows, you can use the Character Map to access special characters.

Special Characters

Hanging punctuation

If you're setting text that starts or ends with punctuation and that is larger or more noticeable than standard body text (a pull quote in an article, for example, or a quotation on a book jacket), the paragraph alignment will be more pleasing if the punctuation hangs outside the main body of the text.

How to do it. Unfortunately, it's not a flip-of-the-switch operation, like a drop cap. Here are a couple of methods: Create a **hanging indent** using either positive or negative indents (see page 108), or use the **Indent Here** character (see page 109) **1**–**3**. (You could also use either technique to hang a large initial cap.)

Here's one more way to hang punctuation: Type a space before the punctuation mark **4**, then apply **negative kerning 5**. If the box has a low Text Inset value, the first character may be partially or completely hidden, but it will still print.

Copyfitting

If you need to squeeze text into a tight space or bring up a stubborn orphan word or hyphenated word (horrors!) from the end of a paragraph, use whichever of these techniques you think your readers are *least* likely to notice:

- Use Auto Hyphenation.
- Turn on Auto Kern Above for the smallest type size you're using in QuarkXPress (Edit, in Windows) > Preferences > Print Layout or Web Layout > Character.
- Apply -.5, -1 or -2 tracking (not more!).
- Rewrite the copy—delete, add, rearrange, or substitute words (only if you have permission to do so or it's your writing!)
- Widen the column.
- Apply 99% scaling.
- Apply slightly tighter word spacing by using an H&J.
- Switch to a condensed font.

Breaking a rule

With the Orthogonal Line tool, draw a line. Use Item > Step & Repeat (Cmd-Option-D/Ctrl-Alt-D) to make horizontal duplicates (0 Vertical Offset), and then lengthen or shorten the lines, as needed.

Early American Cookery

"There is no such thing as a non-working mother."

1 *Non-hanging punctuation*

"There is no such thing as a non-working mother."

2 *Hanging punctuation, created using a **hanging indent**: The left alignment of the paragraph is cleaner.*

"There is no such thing as a non-working mother."

3 *Even better: Here the second line is aligned with the stem of the "T."*

"There is no such thing ↵ as a non-working mother."

4 *To create hanging punctuation using kerning, insert a space to the left of the first character in the paragraph…*

"There is no such thing as a non-working mother."

~ HESTER MUNDIS

5 *…and then apply **negative kerning**. It may look peculiar on screen but it will print just fine.*

How to get attention

- ■ Make the text you want to stand out larger.
- ■ Use **boldface** or *italics* in the same font family as the body text.
- ■ Choose a **contrasting** font or color.

Don't use the underline or ALL CAPS style to get attention. Those styles actually make type look more uniform, and thus harder to read.

A few embellishments

PUMPKIN PIE	Stew the pumpkin dry, and make it like squash pie, only season rather higher. In the country, where this *real yankee pie* is prepared in perfection, ginger is almost always used with other spices.

*To create **side-by-side paragraphs**, anchor a text box on the left side (Item > Modify > Align with Text: Ascent), Baseline Shift it upward, if need be, and create a hanging indent in the main paragraph (see page 108). Another option altogether: Put the text into adjacent **table** cells.*

Pumpkin pie
Stew the pumpkin dry, and make it like squash pie, only season rather higher. In the country, where this *real yankee pie* is prepared in perfection, ginger is almost always used with other spices.

*Here an anchored box with a 10% black background is used as a **drop cap**.*

S tew the pumpkin dry, and make it like squash pie, only season rather higher. In the country, where this *real yankee pie* is prepared in perfection, ginger is almost always used with other spices.
~ *Sara Josepha Hale*

*Ultra simple, but oh so elegant: We chose a different font for the first character (Bodoni Highlight), and enlarged it. This is called a **raised initial cap**.*

Type in reverse

There's no one-step method for creating reversed type. You have to change the type color to white (see page 264) and change the background of the text box to black (see page 265). You can also reverse type via a style sheet; choose a legible, sans serif typeface and a black or colored paragraph rule (see pages 112–114).

Get your dashes straight

When to use a regular **hyphen**: To write a compound word, as in "three-year-old."

When to use an **en dash** (Option-hyphen/ Ctrl-Alt-Shift-hyphen): Between a range of numbers, as in "Figures 4–6"; a time frame, as in "4–6 weeks"; a distance, as in "4–6 miles"; or a negative number, as in –8.

When to use an **em dash** (Option-Shift-hyphen/Ctrl-Shift-=): To break up a sentence, as in "Bunny rabbit—excuse me— stay here." Don't add a whole space around an em or en dash — it will be too noticeable (as in this sentence). Instead, you can add a little bit of space by kerning—as in this sentence—or use a narrow flex space, which is a variation of a standard en space (Option-Shift-Spacebar/Ctrl-Shift-5 inserts a breaking flex space). Specify a Flex Space Width percentage in QuarkXPress (Edit, in Windows) > Preferences > Print Layout or Web Layout > Character. Or use an em dash with built-in thin spaces around it from an expert font set.

To create a **nonbreaking standard hyphen** (as in "write-off"), press Cmd- =/Ctrl- =.

Dot, dot, dot

To produce an **ellipses** character (…), press Option-;/Alt+0133. If those dots are too close together for your comfort, you can type periods instead and then track them out a little bit (. . .).

Or you can type a period (.), then a nonbreaking flex space (Cmd-Option-Shift-Space bar/Ctrl-Alt-Shift-5), then a period, then a flex space, and so on (. . .).

Fractions

There are several ways to produce fractions in QuarkXPress:

- In Windows, for ¼, press Alt+0188; for ½, press Alt+0189; and for ¾, press Alt+0190.

- Use an expert character set, such as Adobe Garamond Expert. It looks like this: ¾. Or use a math font.

- Type the numerator, a slash, and the denominator, highlight all the characters, then choose Style > Type Style > Make Fraction. The fraction will look like this: ¾. You can kern between the characters in this type of fraction. You can specify Fraction/Price preferences in QuarkXPress (Edit, in Windows) > Preferences > Application > Fraction/Price (see page 419). Fraction/Price is part of Type Tricks.xnt, an XTension that ships with QuarkXPress.

- And lastly, you can build a fraction by hand, but it's a cumbersome process. First, type the numerator. Next, in Mac OS X, type a virgule (Option-Shift-1; in Windows, type a slash (preferably in an Expert font set). Type the denominator, apply the Superior style to the numerator, and finally, reduce the point size of the denominator by half. This is how it looks with a virgule: ¾. If you want to fuss even more, you can adjust the Superior style Offset, VScale, and HScale in QuarkXPress (Edit, in Windows) > Preferences > Print Layout or Web Layout > Character.

TIP Speaking of preferences, to choose default Character settings (e.g., Ligatures, Auto Kern Above, Subscript and Superior style) for future projects, close all QuarkXPress projects, then go to QuarkXPress (Edit, in Windows) > Preferences > Default Print Layout or Default Web Layout > Character.

Nonprinting characters

The character	The keystroke
Tab	→ Tab
Word space	. Spacebar
New paragraph	¶ Return/Enter
New line	↵ Shift-Return/ Shift-Enter
Next column	↓ Enter
Next box	⤓ Shift-Enter (on the keypad)
Indent here	┊ Cmd-\/Ctrl-\

Old-style numerals have graceful descenders, as in 3, 4, 5, 7, and 9. You can find them in the Adobe Expert and other special font sets. These numerals have variable widths, though, unlike modern numbers, so they shouldn't be used for tables. Use them only where their decorative value can be appreciated.

1 *The **Expert** fonts aren't just for fractions.*

Make your rags look pretty

When all the copy is in place and ready for imagesetting, stop for a moment to fine-tune the right edge of your left-aligned paragraphs. Try to make the second-to-last line longer than the third-to-the-last line:

Every child is an artist.
The problem is how to remain
an artist once he grows up.

PABLO PICASSO

Or make the last line longer than the second-to-last line:

Every child is an artist. The
problem is how to remain
an artist once he grows up.

But don't let the whole thing cave inward:

Every child is an artist. The problem
is how to remain an artist once
he grows up.

Typography terms

Sans serif *font*

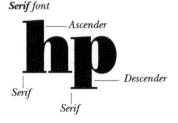

Baseline

Serif *font*

Ascender

Serif

Descender

Serif

Type for print

Our philosophy about choosing fonts for print output is similar to our philosophy about friendship: For body text, pick a few sturdy, dependable serif font families that you really like, and get to know them well. Serif fonts are the least tiring to read. A few of our current favorites in this category include New Baskerville (which you're reading now), Sabon, and Caslon. Garamond and Goudy are other good classics. Use fonts from the same family—not from different families: regular for the main text, bold and/or italics for emphasis.

For subheads, headers, and the like, pick a strong, contrasting sans serif face, such as Frutiger, Futura, Gills Sans, or Franklin Gothic.

Then, just as there are acquaintances that you enjoy seeing once in a while but would tire of if you saw them every day, there are special fonts that you should choose only for special occasions. Fonts that fall into this category include script faces and other decorative faces, such as Caflisch Script Bold, which you see in the sidebar headers in this book. They're great for party invitations, drop caps, headlines, and the like but would be tiring to read in long passages. We have a "Weird fonts" folder that we dig into once in a while when we're hunting around for something unusual. Just as it's good to stand by your old, reliable friends, it's also good to be open to meeting new "faces."

The best way to learn more about typography is to study typography in the real world around you and try to identify which fonts are being used. Whether it's a poster, year-end report, newspaper, newsletter, brochure, book, book cover, magazine, food label, cosmetics label, menu, matchbook cover, shopping bag, or even the credits you see at the movie theatre, wherever you see text (unless it's written by hand), it's typeset in a particular font.

Type for the Web

Unfortunately, the tried-and-true rules that designers are accustomed to following for print layouts don't always apply to Web layouts. When you choose a typeface for a print layout, for example, you can depend on your final output being crisp—and in the typeface you chose. A Web page, on the other hand, can (and probably will) look different on different monitors and in different operating systems. That's due to differing monitor resolutions and the fact that the fonts you chose may not be available on a user's station (in the case of the latter, font substitution may occur). Your job as a Web designer is to keep the strengths and pitfalls of your layout type in mind as you create your page. And at the present time, text on a Web page can be unreliable.

One solution to the font substitution dilemma is to convert text into graphics (raster text boxes), but this isn't universally useful, as it increases the download time for the page. Luckily, you can perform such a conversion on some text boxes and not others. It's a good solution for headlines, logos, and other text blocks that you want users to see in the original font. Then, for your body text, choose a font that's readily available on most users' systems, such as Times, Courier, or Helvetica.

Another solution is to create a CSS (cascading style sheet) Font Family—a list of substitute fonts to be used when a Web viewer lacks the fonts used in your Web layout. See the QuarkXPress User Guide for information about this feature.

Whereas as a print designer you won't see how your final work looks until it's printed, as a Web designer you can see your page in the actual environment in which it will be viewed—and the more variables you test, the better. View it on several browsers and operating systems so you'll know whether its download time is acceptable at various modem speeds and whether the layout works on different-sized screens. Based on that feedback, you can change a font here or there or convert text to graphics to improve the appearance and delivery of the page.

*Features that aren't available for HTML text boxes**

Typography

Fractional point sizes (e.g., 12.5 pt)

Outline, shadow, small caps, superior, and word underline type styles

Kerning and tracking

Baseline shift

Indent here, discretionary hyphen, nonbreaking hyphen, discretionary new line

Nonbreaking spaces; en, em, and flex spaces

Punctuation spaces and tabs are converted to standard spaces on export

Formats

Tabs

Lock to baseline grid

H&Js (can't be applied)

Justified and forced horizontal alignment

Box controls

Flip horizontal, flip vertical

First baseline

Inter-paragraph max

Box rotation

Disproportionate interactive resizing

Text box linking from page to page (you can link on the same page)

Skewing

Text paths and nonrectangular boxes are converted to raster boxes

Columns are converted to an HTML table on export

*Text boxes in Web layouts for which Convert to Graphic on Export is unchecked in Item > Modify

Tables and Tabs 8

What's a table?

A **table,** according to *The Oxford Modern English Dictionary* (Oxford University Press), is "a set of facts or figures systematically displayed, esp. in columns." In QuarkXPress, a table can contain text and/or numerals, pictures, or a combination thereof.

Shade plants

Genus	Hardiness zone	Height	Bloom time
Astilbe	4–8	24–36"	June–July
Dicentra	3–8	10–15"	May–Oct
Hosta	3–8	6–48"	Jul–Sep
Lamium	3–8	12"	Jun–Jul

1 *A* **table** *containing* **text**

Each block in a table is called a **cell.**

Perennials

GENUS		HARDINESS ZONE	HEIGHT	BLOOM TIME
Dianthus		3–8	6"	June–Oct
Hemerocallis		3–8	18–48"	June–Oct
Monarda		4–8	36–48"	July–Aug
Rudbeckia		4–8	30–40"	July–Oct

2 *A* **table** *containing* **pictures** *and* **text**

Tables and tabs

Using the table features in QuarkXPress, not only can you stack columns of text and/or numerals **1**, you can also create a table of pictures or even combine text and picture cells in the same table **2**. Best of all, the features are simple to use. Tables were introduced in QuarkXPress 5, and as with any new feature, they had some shortcomings. Many of those shortcomings have been addressed in version 6.

You can create a table first using the Tables tool and then put text and pictures into it, or you can convert existing text to a table. You can't convert existing pictures into a table, but you can cut and paste or import pictures into a table. All tables contain blocks, called cells, that you type or import text into or import a picture into. As you type into a text cell, the type wraps automatically.

Once a table is created, you can change the information or pictures that it contains; you can change the overall shape of the table itself; you can change the way the cells are configured by adding or removing rows or columns; and you can change the table's appearance by recoloring or restyling its outer frame and/or interior gridlines, or by changing the background color of any of its cells.

Note: If you need to line up numerals on the decimal point or align page numbers with a dot leader for a table of contents, you'll need to use tabs, which we start discussing on page 157. Tables will work for most of your chart-making needs, though. In fact, if you need to, you can insert tabs into text inside a table cell.

Creating tables

As we said on the previous page, you can create a table in either of two ways: Create the table and then enter type into it or convert existing text into a table. First, we'll show you how to create an empty table.

To create an empty text table:

1. Choose the Tables tool.⊞
2. Drag a box on any page in a layout (Shift-drag to make a square). The Table Properties dialog box appears.
3. Enter the desired number of Rows and Columns **1**.
   and
   Click Cell Type: Text Cells. The cell size will be calculated to fit within the overall table automatically.

   Note: The overall table dimensions, as well as the individual row and column sizes, can be changed later.

4. *Optional:* If you want the cells to be linked together so text can flow from box to box, click Link Cells (you can also link cells manually once the table is created). Then choose an option from the Link Order pop-up menu for the order in which cells will be linked. This can be changed later.
5. To specify the order in which the text insertion point will jump from cell to cell (see the sidebar), choose from the Tab Order pop-up menu. This, too, can be changed later.
6. Click OK.
7. Choose the Content tool.
8. Enter text into the cells **2**.
   or
   Click in a cell and import text into it using File > Get Text. The text will flow into that cell and any cells it's linked to.

   You can apply all the standard style and paragraph formatting attributes to table text, either manually (see

Jumping around

Note: These commands work only for cells that aren't linked.

Jump one cell to the **right** Control-Tab/Ctrl-Tab
or from the end of a **row** to
the beginning of the next row

Jump back to **previous** cell Control-Shift-Tab/
Ctrl-Shift-Tab

Jump one **character** at a Right arrow
time within a cell or from
the end of one cell to the
beginning of the next cell

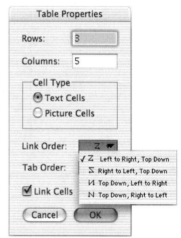

1 *Choose table parameters in the **Table Properties** dialog box.*

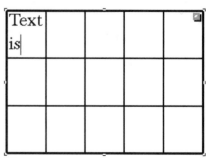

2 *Enter text in the **new table**.*

New, Empty Table

1 *None of the cells are linked in the original table.*

2 *After choosing the **Link Text Cells** command, all of the cells are linked.*

Chapters 6 and 7) or via paragraph and/or character style sheets (see Chapter 13). Style sheets can be applied to more than one cell at a time; to select multiple cells, see the sidebar on page 143.

TIP To reconfigure a table (e.g., add or delete rows or columns), see page 148.

TIP The table's overall size determines the maximum number of rows and columns it can contain.

If you want all your text cells to be linked together, then you'll be satisfied with the Link Text Cells option, described below. But what if you just want to link a few cells, and not all the cells in a table? You can do it manually with the Linking tool, just as you would non-table text (see page 89).

You can even link a text cell to a text box outside the table. Just remember the standard rule for all linking: You can't link to a box that already contains text, even if all that's left is a nonprinting character, such as a paragraph return. Also, you can't link a text cell to form controls in a Web layout.

To link all the text cells in a table: 6.0!

1. To begin with, the table must be empty or contain text in only one of its cells. It can contain picture cells; the links will just bypass those cells.

2. Choose the Item tool, then click the table **1**.

3. Choose Item (or Ctrl-click/Right-click the table) > Tables > Link Text Cells **2**. The cells will be linked in the Link Order currently chosen in the Table pane of Tables tool preferences.

TIP *Beware!* If Auto Page Insertion is on in Preferences > Print Layout > General, and you link all the cells in a table that contains overflow text, a new page (or pages) will be inserted automatically, and the new page(s) will be linked to the table.

Link Text Cells

6.0! The link order is the order in which text cells are linked together, either when you created the table initially or via the Link Text Cells command. It can be changed by choosing a command.

Note: If your table contains text cells that were linked manually, or if it contains text, you can't change the link order using the method below—you have to unlink all the linked cells and empty the table out first. If you don't want to empty out the table, you can manually relink cells in any order with the Linking tool.

The tab order is the order in which the text insertion point jumps between unlinked cells by using the shortcuts listed in the sidebar on page 138. The tab order has no effect on linked cells.

To change the link or tab order in a table:

1. Choose the Item or Content tool, then click the table **1**.

2. Choose Item > Modify, then click the Table tab.

3. Choose an option from the Link Order pop-up menu **2**.
and/or
Choose an option from the Tab Order pop-up menu.

The link order can be different from the tab order.

TIP To unlink cells, use the Unlinking tool (see pages 90–91).

TIP To choose the default link order for future tables, go to QuarkXPress (Edit, in Windows) > Preferences > Print Layout or Web Layout > Tools, click the Tables tool, click Modify, then choose an option from the Link Order pop-up menu. If you do this when no projects are open, the setting you choose will be the default for future projects.

1 *This is the table's original link order. (In order to make the links appear, for illustration purposes, we selected the table and chose the Linking tool.)*

2 *After choosing a new option from the **Link Order** pop-up menu, the text flows in a new direction.*

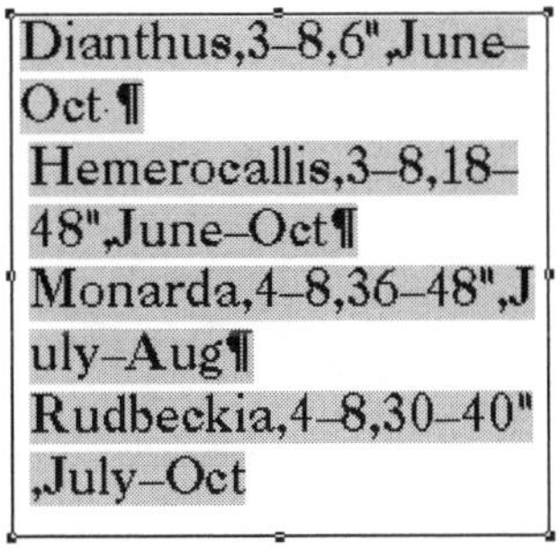

Dianthus,3–8,6",June–
Oct·¶
Hemerocallis,3–8,18–
48",June–Oct¶
Monarda,4–8,36–48",J
uly–Aug¶
Rudbeckia,4–8,30–40"
,July–Oct

1 *Select the text you want to appear in the table. Note that there are **no spaces** after the commas.*

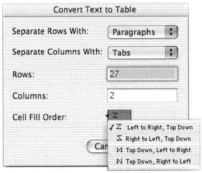

Convert Text to Table

Separate Rows With:	Paragraphs ⬍
Separate Columns With:	Tabs ⬍
Rows:	27
Columns:	2
Cell Fill Order:	Z

> ✓ Z Left to Right, Top Down
> Ƨ Right to Left, Top Down
> � Top Down, Left to Right
> N Top Down, Right to Left

Car

2 *The **Convert Text to Table** dialog box controls how text gets distributed into cells.*

Dia ⊠	·3–8	·6"	·⊠
He ⊠	·3–8	18⊠	⊠
Mo ⊠	·4–8	⊠	·⊠
Rud ⊠	·4–8	·	

3 *The resulting **table***

Dianthus	3–8	6"	June–Oct
Hemerocallis	3–8	18–48"	June–Oct
Monarda	4–8	36–48"	July–Aug
Rudbeckia	4–8	30–40"	July–Oct

4 *After **resizing** the table*

To create a table from existing text:

1. Decide which characters in the original text—returns, tabs, spaces, or commas—are to be used to determine how the text will be distributed into table cells (see steps 5 and 6), and add or delete those characters now, if necessary.

2. *Optional:* Choose View > Show Invisibles, if Invisibles is currently off.

3. Choose the Content tool, then select only the text that you want copied into the table cells **1**.

4. Choose Item > (or Control-click/Right-click the text) Convert Text to Table.

5. From the Separate Rows With pop-up menu, choose which character in the highlighted text (Paragraphs [Returns], Tabs, Space, or Commas) will be used to designate the start of each new row of cells **2**. If you choose Commas, for example, every comma in the text will start a new row.

6. Columns in the table will be set up according to the characters currently in the highlighted text, as reflected on the Separate Columns With pop-up menu. You can change this setting, too.

7. Change the Rows and Columns values only if you want to add blank rows or columns.

8. From the Cell Fill Order pop-up menu, choose the direction in which you want the existing text to flow into the new table. Each new paragraph will start at the next cell in the Cell Fill Order.

9. Click OK **3**. If there's more text than can fit into a cell (or into the last of a series of linked cells), the overflow symbol will appear in the lower right corner of that cell.

TIP To resize the table **4** (e.g., make it wider or narrower) or reconfigure the table (e.g., change the number of rows or columns), see pages 147–149.

We've devoted the entire next chapter to pictures, and Chapter 11 to combining pictures and text. You should learn those basics before you learn how to make picture tables!

Most of the Item > Modify controls that are available for a standard picture or text box are also available for individual cells in a table, such as Text Inset, Vertical Alignment, and Text Angle. In QuarkXPress 6, you **6.0!** can apply Clipping values to picture cells (see Chapter 11).

To create a picture table:

1. Choose the Tables tool.⊞

2. Draw a rectangle in a layout. The box shape and size can be changed later.

3. Enter the desired number of Rows and Columns **1**.
   and
   Click Picture Cells.

4. Click OK.

5. Choose the Content tool.

6. Click any cell, then use File > Get Picture to import a picture **2**.
   or
   Click a standard picture box that already contains an imported picture, copy the picture (Cmd-C/Ctrl-C), click a picture cell in the table, then paste (Cmd-V/Ctrl-V).

   Resize or move the pictures inside the cells as you would in a standard picture box.

TIP To reshape a column or row, see page 144. To reshape the overall table, see page 147. To convert any of the cells to text cells, see page 146.

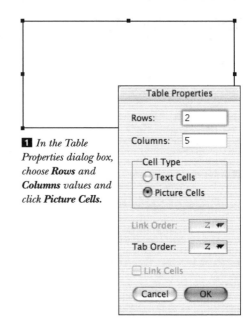

1 *In the Table Properties dialog box, choose **Rows** and **Columns** values and click **Picture Cells**.*

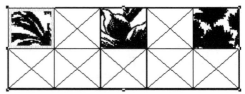

2 *After importing pictures into some of the cells*

Picture Table

Selecting table cells and their contents

Choose the **Content** tool, click the table, then:

Select the text in one **cell** or a story in **linked cells**	Cmd-A/Ctrl-A
Select all the cells in a **row**	Click just outside the left or right edge of the table (→ pointer)
Select all the cells in a **column**	Click just outside the top or bottom edge of the table (↓ pointer)
Select all the cells in a **series** of **rows** or **columns**	Drag along, and just outside of, any edge of the table
Select **adjacent** or **nonadjacent** cells	Shift-click cells

1 *Click at the top or bottom of a column to select it.*

2 *Click at the beginning or end of a row to select it.*

3 *Or Shift-click individual cells.*

To edit the contents of a table cell:

1. Choose the Content tool.

2. Click the cell whose attributes you want to change.
   or
   Select multiple cells by using one of the selection methods listed in the sidebar at left **1**–**3**.

3. Do any of the following:

   Each text cell is really a text box. Some of the options that you find in Item > Modify for standard text boxes are also available for text cells.

   To edit the typographic attributes of text in a table cell, use any of the standard methods (that is, Style > Character, the Measurements palette, or style sheets).

   To edit the paragraph attributes of text in a table cell, use Style > Formats or use style sheets.

   To move text from one cell to another, highlight it, then use the Cut (Cmd-X/Ctrl-X) and Paste commands (Cmd-V/Ctrl-V).

   To modify the attributes of a text cell, such as its width, background color, background shade, or Text Inset, use the Item > Modify > Cell and Text panes (Cmd-M/Ctrl-M). You can even rotate or skew text within its cell. The Cols and Gutter options aren't available for table cells.

   To modify picture cells, use the Picture, Clipping, or Cell pane in Item > Modify.

   To recolor the table border segments or gridlines, see pages 151–152 and pages 270–271.

   To recolor the overall table box or the table box frame, see page 269.

   To convert text cells to picture cells, or vice versa, see page 146.

Reconfiguring tables

To resize a column or row by dragging:

1. Choose the Item tool, then double-click the table.
   or
   Choose the Content tool, click the table, then press Cmd-M/Ctrl-M.

2. In the Table pane of the Modify dialog box:

   Check Maintain Geometry if you want the overall size of the table to remain fixed as you resize columns or rows. Other columns and rows will resize automatically to compensate.
   or
   Uncheck Maintain Geometry if you want to resize only one column or row at a time. The table will become larger or smaller to accommodate the new column or row size.

   Note: The current Maintain Geometry setting will remain in effect for each individual table; you don't have to choose it again every time you resize a column or row.

   Click OK.

3. Choose the Content tool.

4. Drag the vertical or horizontal gridline that separates any two columns or rows (the pointer will become a double-headed arrow ↔) **1**–**3**.

   If the column or row contains text, the text may rewrap inside each cell. If the row or column contains a picture or **6.0!** pictures, more of the pictures will become exposed or hidden as a result.

   If View > Snap to Guides is on, then a gridline will snap to the nearest guide if it's moved within the Snap Distance specified in QuarkXPress (Edit, in Windows) > Print Layout or Web Layout > General.

   TIP To resize the overall table, see page 147.

Maintain Geometry on the fly **6.0!**

To turn the Maintain Geometry option on or off without opening a dialog box, Control-click/Right-click the table, then choose **Table > Maintain Geometry** to add or remove the check mark.

1 *Move a gridline to* **resize** *a* **column** *or* **row.**

2 *The column is* **enlarged** *with* **Maintain Geometry checked,** *so the overall table size remains the same.*

3 *The column is* **enlarged** *with* **Maintain Geometry unchecked,** *so the overall table enlarges to accommodate the larger column.*

Resize Column or Row

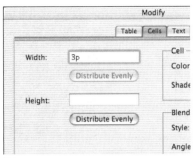

1 *In Item > Modify > Cell(s), enter new* **Width** *and/or* **Height** *values for a selected* **row** *or* **column**.

GENUS		HARDINESS ZONE	HEIGHT	BLOOM TIME
Dianthus		3–8	6"	June–Oct
Hemerocallis		3–8	18–48"	June–Oct
Monarda		4–8	36–48"	July–Aug
Rudbeckia		4–8	30–40"	July–Oct

2 *Five columns of uneven* **width** *are selected.*

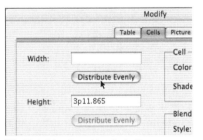

3 *Click* **Distribute Evenly** *in Item >* *Modify > Cell(s).*

GENUS		HARDINESS ZONE	HEIGHT	BLOOM TIME
Dianthus		3–8	6"	June–Oct
Hemerocal lis		3–8	18–48"	June–Oct
Monarda		4–8	36–48"	July–Aug
Rudbeckia		4–8	30–40"	July–Oct

4 *After clicking* **Width: Distribute Evenly,** *all the columns are now the* **same** *width. The text rewrapped in the first column.*

To resize a column or row by entering values:

1. Choose the Content tool.

2. Select the column(s) or row(s) you want to reshape or resize (see the sidebar on page 143).

3. Control-click/Right-click the table and choose Modify (Cmd-M/Ctrl-M).

4. In the Table pane, check Maintain Geometry to have the overall table size remain fixed as you resize columns or rows; unselected columns and rows will resize automatically. With this option checked, you can't resize the rightmost column or bottommost row.
or
Uncheck Maintain Geometry to have the table enlarge or shrink to accommodate the new column or row size. Unselected columns or rows will stay the same size.

Note: The Maintain Geometry setting remains in effect until it's changed.

5. Click the Cell(s) tab, then enter the desired Width or Height **1**. With Maintain Geometry on, one of these two fields won't be available. If the selected cells aren't uniform in size, a field will be blank, but a value can be entered.

6. Click Apply (Cmd-A/Alt-A), make any adjustments, then click OK.

To make columns and/or rows uniform in size:

1. Choose the Content tool.

2. Select the rows or columns you want to make uniform in size **2**.

3. Control-click/Right-click the table and choose Modify, then click the Cells tab.

4. Click Distribute Evenly under Width and/or Height **3**–**4**. A value will be entered automatically. This option won't be available if the selected columns or rows are already uniform in size.

5. Click Apply, if desired, then click OK.

Resize Column or Row; Distribute Evenly

A table can contain text cells, picture cells, contentless cells, or a combination thereof. Follow these instructions to change the content of existing cells.

Beware! If a cell contains a picture or text, that picture or text will be deleted if you change its content. You'll get a warning prompt, so you'll have a chance to change your mind at the last minute.

To change the content of a cell (picture, text, or none):

1. Choose the Content tool.

2. Select the cell or cells you want to convert (use one of the selection methods listed in the sidebar on page 143 if you want to select multiple cells) **1**.

3. Choose Item (or Control-click/Right-click the table) > Content > Picture, Text, or None. If you choose None, you'll be able to recolor the background of the cell or apply a blend to it but not put text or a picture inside it.

4. Respond in the alert dialog box, if one appears **2**–**3**.

1 *A column of cells is **selected**.*

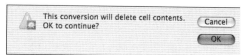

2 *Item > **Content** > **Picture** is chosen. The cells already contain text, so this alert dialog box appears.*

Dianthus		
Hemerocallis		
Monarda		
Rudbeckia		

3 *Clicking OK in the alert dialog box causes the text to be **deleted**. The cells in the third column are now empty picture cells.*

Modifier keys for resizing a table

Drag a **handle** of the table with the following keys held down:

Resize table, rows, and columns (not content) nonproportionally	No modifier keys
Resize table, rows, and columns (not content) proportionally	Option-Shift/ Alt-Shift
Resize table (not content) to a square	Shift/Shift
Resize table, rows, columns, and content nonproportionally	Cmd/Ctrl
Resize table, rows, columns, and content proportionally	Cmd-Option-Shift/ Ctrl-Alt-Shift

1 *A corner handle is dragged with **Option-Shift/ Alt-Shift** held down.*

2 *The table's dimensions—but not its content—are enlarged **proportionally.***

To resize a whole table:

1. Choose the Item tool, then click the table.

2. Using one of the shortcuts listed in the sidebar, drag any of the table's eight handles **1**–**2**. The cells will reshape to fit the new table dimensions.
   or
   Change the W (width) or H (height) value on the Measurements palette.
   or
   Control-click/Right-click the table and choose Modify, click the Table tab, enter new Width and/or Height values, click Apply if you want, then click OK.

TIP To move a selected table to a precise location on your page, change the Origin Across and Origin Down values in Item > Modify > Table or change the X and Y values on the left side of Measurements palette.

TIP The Live Refresh feature (where you pause before dragging, then see the item as you scale it) works for non-table items but not when resizing a table.

To add columns or rows to a table:

1. Choose the Content tool.

2. Before you add columns or rows, you need to decide whether to permit the overall width and height of the table to change as a result. Control-click/Right-click the table and choose Modify, then click the Table tab. With Maintain Geometry checked, the overall dimensions of the table will be preserved as columns or rows are added, but existing cells will become smaller in order to accommodate the new ones. With Maintain Geometry unchecked, the cell sizes won't change, but the overall table dimensions will increase.

3. Click OK, then click a cell or select the row or column that you want the new row or column to appear next to **1**.

4. Choose Item (or Control-click/Right-click the table) > Table > Insert Rows or Insert Columns.

5. *Optional:* Check Keep Attributes to have inserted cells and gridlines acquire the attributes of adjacent cells. If you choose Insert Above Selection, an inserted row will acquire the attributes of the row below it; if you choose Insert Below Selection, an inserted row will acquire the attributes of the row above it; if you choose Insert Left of Selection, an inserted column will acquire the attributes of the column to its right; if you choose Insert Right of Selection, an inserted column will acquire the attributes of the column to its left.

6.0!

Attributes that are duplicated include typographic specifications, style sheets, and settings in Item > Modify (Cell pane, Text, or Picture pane).

6. Enter the desired Number of Rows or Number of Columns **2**–**3**, and click where you want the new rows or columns to be inserted.

7. Click OK **4**.

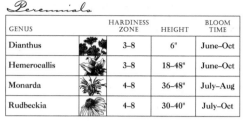

1 *The original table*

GENUS		HARDINESS ZONE	HEIGHT	BLOOM TIME
Dianthus		3–8	6"	June–Oct
Hemerocallis		3–8	18–48"	June–Oct
Monarda		4–8	36–48"	July–Aug
Rudbeckia		4–8	30–40"	July–Oct

Perennials

2 *In the **Insert Table Rows** dialog box, enter the number of **rows** you want to add, and click a location.*

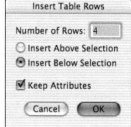

Insert Table Rows
Number of Rows: 4
○ Insert Above Selection
● Insert Below Selection
☑ Keep Attributes
Cancel OK

3 *Or in the **Insert Table Columns** dialog box, enter the number of **columns** you want to add, and click a location.*

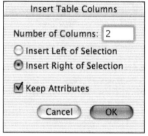

Insert Table Columns
Number of Columns: 2
○ Insert Left of Selection
● Insert Right of Selection
☑ Keep Attributes
Cancel OK

Perennials

GENUS		HARDINESS ZONE	HEIGHT	BLOOM TIME
Dianthus		3–8	6"	June–Oct
Hemerocallis		3–8	18–48"	June–Oct
Monarda		4–8	36–48"	July–Aug
Rudbeckia		4–8	30–40"	July–Oct

4 *In this case, we added two new **rows** to the **bottom** of the table.*

To delete a row or column from a table:

1. Choose the Content tool.

2. Before deleting a row or column, you need to decide whether to permit the overall width and height of the table to change. Click the table, choose Item > Modify (Cmd-M/Ctrl-M), then click the Table tab. With Maintain Geometry checked, the overall dimensions of the table will be preserved as columns or rows are deleted, but existing cells will be enlarged in order to fill the gap. With Maintain Geometry unchecked, the cell sizes won't change, but the overall table dimensions will decrease.

3. Click OK, then click just outside the edge of the table to select the entire row or column you want to delete **1**.

4. Choose Item > (or Control-click/Right-click any selected cell) Table > Delete Row(s) or Delete Column(s) **2**. You can undo this.

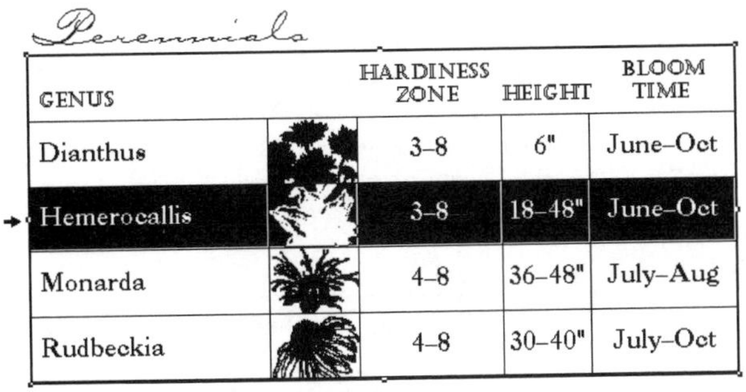

Perennials

GENUS		HARDINESS ZONE	HEIGHT	BLOOM TIME
Dianthus		3–8	6"	June–Oct
Hemerocallis		3–8	18–48"	June–Oct
Monarda		4–8	36–48"	July–Aug
Rudbeckia		4–8	30–40"	July–Oct

1 *A row is selected.*

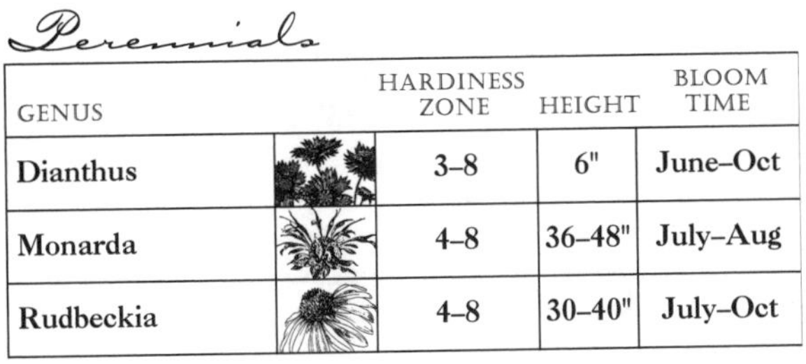

Perennials

GENUS		HARDINESS ZONE	HEIGHT	BLOOM TIME
Dianthus		3–8	6"	June–Oct
Monarda		4–8	36–48"	July–Aug
Rudbeckia		4–8	30–40"	July–Oct

2 *The Item > Table > **Delete Rows** command deleted the selected row.*

There are a number of reasons for combing cells. Maybe you want a header to span across the whole top of your table. Or perhaps you'd like to display a picture more prominently in a larger portion of the table.

To combine cells:

1. *Beware!* The text or picture in the topmost left selected cell will be preserved when you combine other cells with it, but any text or pictures in other selected cells will be **discarded** (you'll get a warning prompt). To preserve text or a picture for later use, take a moment now to copy and paste it either into a separate box outside the table or into a cell that you're not combining.

2. Choose the Content tool.

3. Shift-click a cell, then Shift-click the other cells you want to combine with it **1**.

4. Choose Item (or Control-click/Right-click) > Table > Combine Cells. If the cells currently contain text and/or pictures, an alert dialog box will appear **2**. If you want to live dangerously, click "Do not show this warning again," then click OK **3**.

   The selected cells will be combined into one. If the topmost left selected cell contained text, that text will now spread across or downward to fill the now larger cell size. If it was linked to another box, that linkage will be broken. If that cell contained a picture, the picture either will now fill, or can be scaled to fill, the whole combined cell.

To uncombine cells:

1. Choose the Content tool.

2. Click the cell you want to split up.

3. Choose Item (or Control-click/Right-click) > Table > Split Cell. The content of the cell will be placed inside the first of the newly divided cells.

Watch your links! **6.0!**

If you combine text cells that are linked, the combined cell will no longer be linked, but any other previously linked cells will remain linked. And if you split a combined text cell, the prior linkages won't be restored. You can restore them using the Linking tool.

Perennials for fall planting ☒	Genus		
Dianthus		3–8	6"
Hemerocallis		3–8	18–48"
Monarda		4–8	36–48"
Rudbeckia		4–8	30–40"

1 *Three cells in the top row are selected.*

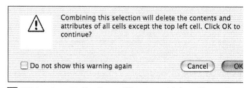

⚠ Combining this selection will delete the contents and attributes of all cells except the top left cell. Click OK to continue?

☐ Do not show this warning again ⟨ Cancel ⟩ ⟨ OK ⟩

2 *This alert dialog box will appear if the cells you're combining **contain** text or pictures.*

Perennials for fall planting		
Dianthus		3–8	6"
Hemerocallis		3–8	18–48"
Monarda		4–8	36–48"
Rudbeckia		4–8	30–40"

3 *Item > Table > **Combine Cells** is chosen: The top three cells are combined into one, preserving only the text from the first of the selected cells, and the text rewraps. We applied a blend to the combined cell (Item > Modify > Cell).*

Perennials for fall planting			
Dianthus		3–8	6"
Hemerocallis		3–8	18–48"
Monarda		4–8	36–48"
Rudbeckia		4–8	30–40"

1 *The original table*

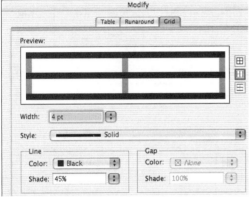

2 *Choose* **Width, Style, Color,** *and* **Shade** *options for gridlines in Item > Modify >* **Grid.**

Perennials for fall planting			
Dianthus		3–8	6"
Hemerocallis		3–8	18–48"
Monarda		4–8	36–48"
Rudbeckia		4–8	30–40"

3 *First we checked Maintain Geometry in the Table pane of Item > Modify. Then in the* **Grid** *pane, we clicked the* **Vertical gridlines only** *button, increased the Width, and changed the Shade to 45%.*

Restyling tables

You can dramatically change the appearance of a table by changing the line style, width, color, or shade of its gridlines and/or border, and this can be done using a dialog box (instructions on this page) or using submenus (see the next page). The default border and gridlines are black and 1 pt. in width.

For more about recoloring tables and their component parts, see pages 268–273.

To restyle the border or gridlines using a dialog box:

1. Choose the Item tool, then double-click the table **1**.

2. If you're going to change the width of the border/gridlines, you need to decide whether or not to permit the overall width and height of the table to change as a result. Click the Table tab. If you check Maintain Geometry, the overall dimensions of the table will be preserved, but existing cells will resize automatically in order to fill the gap. If you uncheck Maintain Geometry, the cell sizes won't change, but the overall table dimensions will.

3. Click the Grid tab.

4. On the right side of the dialog box, click one of the three icons for the gridlines and borders you want to restyle: Horizontal and Vertical ⊞, Horizontal only ☰, or Vertical only ⦀ **2**.

5. Choose a gridline Width, Style, Line: Color and Shade, and also choose a Gap: Color and Shade if the line style contains gaps. The horizontal gridlines will print on top of the vertical gridlines. To make the gridlines disappear, choose the Style: Solid, and choose a Width of 0 and/or a Color of None. 6.0!

6. Click Apply. At this point you can click another icon and apply different settings, if you like. Adjust any of the settings, then click OK **3**.

You can single out a handful of gridlines and/or border segments for restyling, or you can restyle all of them at once.

To restyle multiple border segments or gridlines via submenus:

1. Choose the Content tool.
2. Shift-click a gridline or border segment, then Shift-click additional horizontal or vertical gridlines or border (outer) segments. Gridlines and border segments can be selected at the same time. If a gridline is narrow, it may be hard to tell if it's selected.
or
Control-click/Right-click and choose Gridlines > Select Horizontal, Select Vertical, Select Borders (the outer frame of the table), or Select All (all gridlines and borders) **1**.
3. Choose attributes from the Style > Line Style, Width, Color, and Shade submenus **2–4**.
or
Control-click/Right-click one of the selected gridlines or border segments and make choices from the Width, Color, and Shade submenus on the context menu (Line Style isn't available).

TIP You can also change the gridline color and shade (but not the gap color) via the Color palette (see page 270).

TIP Shift-click a gridline or border segment, then use the Measurements palette to change the line width or style of just that gridline or segment.

Here's a zippity-quick way to restyle a single gridline or segment.

To restyle one border segment or gridline via submenus:

1. Choose the Content tool.
2. Control-click/Right-click a gridline or border segment and make choices from the Line Style, Width, Color, and Shade submenus.

1 *You can use the **Gridlines** submenu to select multiple gridlines, borders, or both.*

Perennials for fall planting			
Dianthus		3–8	6"
Hemerocallis		3–8	18–48"
Monarda		4–8	36–48"
Rudbeckia		4–8	30–40"

2 *The original table*

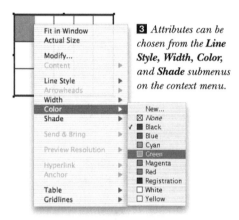

3 *Attributes can be chosen from the **Line Style, Width, Color,** and **Shade** submenus on the context menu.*

Perennials for fall planting			
Dianthus		3–8	6"
Hemerocallis		3–8	18–48"
Monarda		4–8	36–48"
Rudbeckia		4–8	30–40"

4 *The table after choosing different line styles and widths for the outer border segments and the first horizontal gridline and applying a color of None to the first vertical gridline (between the plant name cells and the picture cells)*

Restyle Border or Gridlines

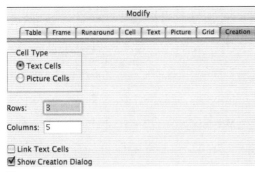

1 *Choose preference settings for future tables in the* **Creation** *pane of the* **Modify** *dialog box.*

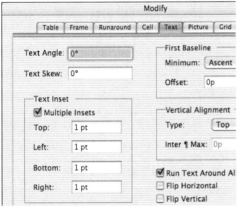

2 *Choose text preferences for future tables in the* **Text** *pane.*

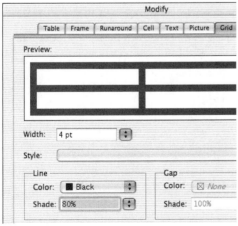

3 *Choose Width, Style, Color, and Shade preferences for gridlines in future tables in the* **Grid** *pane.*

Choosing Tables tool preferences

If you create tables frequently and you tend to choose the same parameters over and over for them, it's worth your while to take a moment to set a few preferences. These Creation preferences affect future tables that you create using the Tables tool but not tables created using the Convert Text to Table command.

To choose Tables tool preferences:

1. Double-click the Tables tool. ⊞
   or
   Choose QuarkXPress (Edit, in Windows) > Preferences > Print Layout or Web Layout > Tools, then click the Tables tool icon.

2. Click Modify, then click the Creation tab.

3. Choose whether you want future tables to contain text or picture cells, and make default Rows and Columns choices **1**.

4. To have text cells in future tables be linked automatically, click Link Text Cells.

5. *Optional:* To prevent the Table Properties dialog box from opening each time you use the Tables tool, uncheck Show Creation Dialog. If Link Text Cells is also checked, cells will be linked in the default order, which is Z. With Show Creation Dialog checked, the Table Properties dialog box will open each time you use the Tables tool, displaying your preferences.

6. Click the Table, Frame, Runaround, Cell, Text **2**, Picture, or Grid **3** tab, and change any of the available options in those panes, if desired.

7. Click OK twice.

153

Converting tables

When the Convert Table to Text command is applied to a table, a new text box is created, and it's filled with a copy of the text from the table. You can choose the order in which the text blocks from the table cells will flow into the new box, and whether they'll be separated by Returns, tabs, commas, or spaces. You can also choose whether you want the original table to be preserved (the default setting) or deleted.

Note: If the table contains pictures, those pictures will be inserted into anchored picture boxes within the new text box (see page 197).

To convert a table to conventional text:

1. Choose the Item or Content tool.

2. Click the table you want to convert **1**.

3. Choose Item (or Control-click/Right-click) > Table > Convert Table to Text.

4. From the Separate Rows With pop-up menu **2**, choose which character you want to have inserted at the end of each row (the default is Paragraphs).

5. From the Separate Columns With pop-up menu, choose which character you want to have inserted between each column (the default is Tabs).

6. Choose an option from the Text Extraction Order pop-up menu for the order in which text is to be extracted from the table (the default is Z, which is left to right, top to bottom).

7. Check Delete Table if you want the table to be deleted. Whether this box is checked or not, the converted text will appear in a new, separate box after you click OK.

8. Click OK **3**.

TIP If the table contains linked text and all you want to do is extract the text, just copy and paste it into a conventional text box instead of converting the table.

Dianthus	3–8	6"	June–Oct
Hemerocallis	3–8	18–48"	June–Oct
Iris	3–9	24–50"	June
Malva	4–7	36–48"	July–Oct
Monarda	4–8	36–48"	July–Aug
Rudbeckia	4–8	30–40"	July–Oct

1 *The original table*

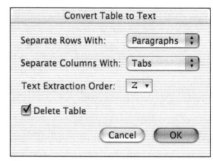

2 *Settings for the extracted text are chosen in the **Convert Table to Text** dialog box.*

Dianthus June-Oct	3–8	6"
Hemerocallis June–Oct	3–8	18–48"
Iris June	3–9	24–50"
Malva July–Oct	4–7	36–48"
Monarda July-Aug	4–8	36–48"
Rudbeckia July–Oct	4–8	30–40"

3 *After choosing Item > Table > **Convert Table to Text**, in this case, the columns are separated by tabs and the rows are separated by paragraph returns.*

Dianthus		*June-Oct*
Monarda		*July-Aug*
Rudbeckia		*July-Oct*

1 *Click a table.*

Dianthus		*June-Oct*
Monarda		*July-Aug*
Rudbeckia		*July-Oct*

2 *After choosing the **Convert Table to Group** command*

3 *After choosing the **Ungroup** command and then moving a few boxes*

Follow these steps if you'd like to convert your completed table to a group of separate but grouped conventional text boxes and/or picture boxes. Unlike the Convert Table to Text command, discussed on the previous page, this command doesn't copy the table—it converts it without copying.

To convert a table to a group: 6.0!

1. Choose the Item tool.
2. Click the table you want to convert **1**.
3. Choose Item > Table > Convert Table to Group. Leave the boxes grouped together **2**, or choose Item > Ungroup at any time **3**. Text from a series of linked cells will be preserved as a story.

On this page and the next, we'll discuss tables in Web layouts. You can export a table as an image to preserve any Quark-XPress formatting that isn't supported by HTML. Borders of tables created in Web layouts have a 3D appearance.

To specify that a whole table be exported as an image:

1. Display a Web layout, choose the Item tool, then click the table.
2. Choose Item > Modify (Cmd-M/ Ctrl-M), then click the Table tab.
3. Check Convert Table to Graphic on Export at the bottom of the dialog box. This option converts the whole table into a bitmap image; the cells will no longer be individually editable. If this option isn't checked, the table will be converted to HTML.
4. Click OK. The Rasterize icon 📷 will appear in the upper right corner of the table.

   Note: Each table has its own Convert Table to Graphic on Export setting, which means you have to remember to check it for each table you want rasterized. To read about the Export options, see pages 326–330.

If an entire table is exported as an image, all its cells will be included in the image; you won't be able to export individual cells as HTML content. If the Convert Table to Graphic on Export option is off for a whole table, you can specify that the contents of individual cells be rasterized upon export by following these instructions.

To have cell contents rasterize at export:

1. Display a Web layout in QuarkXPress, choose the Content tool, then select the cell(s) you want rasterized.

2. Choose Item > Modify (Cmd-M/Ctrl-M).
or
Control-click/Right-click the table and choose Modify.

3. Click the Cell(s) tab.

4. Make sure Convert Table to Graphic on Export is unchecked.

5. Check Convert Cell to Graphic on Export. The table layout will be converted to an HTML table, and the converted boxes will be rasterized as pictures.

6. Click OK.

Note: Picture cells and cells with a content of None are automatically exported as images; the Convert Cell to Graphic on Export option isn't available for them. To choose export options for picture cells or cells with a content of None, go to Item > Modify > Export.

TIP If you uncheck Convert Table to Graphic on Export in Item > Modify, only HTML-compatible formatting options will be available in the Text pane for that table. If you leave this option checked, all the formatting options will be available because the cell contents will be rasterized on export.

You can't have everything

For table **cells** that *won't* be converted to a graphic on export, these options are **not** available in Item > Modify > Grid:

- Dashes and stripes on table gridlines. Borders and gridlines must be solid.

- Varying widths for table gridlines. Gridlines must be uniform in width. That width will become the cell spacing in the HTML export.

And for **text** in a table cell that *won't* be converted to a graphic on export, these options are **not** available in Item > Modify > Text:

- First Baseline, Minimum, and Offset values

- Inter-Paragraph Max values

- The Flip Horizontal/Flip Vertical command for text

- Rotated or skewed text

- The Run Text Around All Sides option

On the right

Press **Option-Tab/Alt-Tab** to set a **right indent tab** that hugs the current right indent of the box, even if you resize the text box or table by dragging its right handle. You won't see a marker on the Tabs ruler for this kind of tab.

*A **decimal-aligned** tab with a dot leader*

*A **left-aligned** tab*   *An **outrageous** tab*

Setting tabs

Tabs are invisible commands that tell blocks of text where to line up **1**–**2**. If no custom tabs are set and you press Tab, text to the right of the Tab character will jump to the nearest default tab stop (they're ½ inch apart). Before you can set custom tab stops (next two pages), you must insert invisible tab characters → into your text. *Note:* Don't use spaces to create columns; it will look uneven due to variable character widths.

You can set up columns of text and/or numerals without tabs, by using the tables feature, but tabs are handy for inserting dot leaders or aligning numbers on the decimal. Tabs can be added to text in a table, but not to HTML text.

To insert tabs into text:

1. Choose the Content tool, then click in a text box.

2. Press Tab as you input copy before typing each new column. The cursor will jump to the next default tab stop. Don't press Tab again to move the type further along. If you're not happy with the location of the default stops (we rarely are), set custom stops (see next page).
   or
   To add tabs to existing text, click to the left of the text that is to start each new column and press Tab.

Insert Tabs into Text

Endangered vs. Non-Endangered Bears		
1930	**1992**	**2000** (Projected)
Pandas 1 million	4 thousand	0
Koalas 6 million	3 thousand	7
Poohs 1 million	2 billion	3 billion

2 *Use **tabs** to align columns of text.*

Endangered·vs.·Non-Endangered·Bears¶		
→ **1930** →	**1992** →	**2000**·(Projected)

*Choose View > **Show Invisibles** to reveal tab symbols and other non-printing characters.*

You can set a virtually unlimited number of custom tab stops per paragraph (one tab per point).

To set custom tab stops:

1. Choose the Content tool.

2. Zoom in on your layout to make it easier to see the tabs ruler increments, but make sure you can still see the full width of the text column.

3. Select *all* the paragraphs for which the tab stops are to be set.

4. Choose Style > Tabs (Cmd-Shift-T/ Ctrl-Shift-T), and move the dialog box if it's in the way. We also like to turn on Continuous Apply so we can preview our changes immediately (Option-click/Alt-click the Apply button).

5. Click the Left, Center, Right, Decimal, or Comma, or Align On button (**1**, next page). To align numerals, choose Decimal or Comma. To align to a character of your choosing, click Align On, then enter the character.

6. *Optional:* To create a leader, type one or two characters in the Fill Characters field (**1**–**4**, this page and **2**, next page). For a dot leader, type a period.

7. Click in the tabs ruler to insert a tab stop (**3**, next page). To move a marker, drag it to the left or the right.
or
Enter a position number (location on the ruler) in the Position field using any measurement system, then click Set (**4**, next page).

8. *Optional:* Repeat steps 5–7 to create additional tab stops.

9. Click OK.

TIP To set a series of tabs by specifying the distance between them, enter "+" and then the gap length in the Position field (e.g., "p10+p12"). If the list gets too long, click the last tab marker on the ruler, then continue on your way.

Work smart

Tabs, like all paragraph formats, can be applied via a **style sheet.** We usually create a style sheet based on a paragraph that already contains custom tab stops where we need them.

If you edit the tabs for the Normal style sheet or any other style sheet when no projects are open, you will in effect be creating your own default tab stops.

Steamed vegetable dumplings	3.50
Shrimp rolls	4.00

1 *To create a dot leader with extra space between the dots, enter a **period** and a **space** in the Fill Characters field.*

Steamed vegetable dumplings - - - - - - -	3.50
Shrimp rolls - - - - - - - - - - - - - -	4.00

2 *To create a dashed line with extra space between the dashes, enter a **hyphen** and a **space** in the Fill Characters field.*

Steamed vegetable dumplings _ _ _ _ _	3.50
Shrimp rolls _ _ _ _ _ _ _ _ _ _	4.00

3 *To change the point size, tracking, color, or other attributes of a tab leader, you have to do it manually for each instance or by using Find/Change. The tab leader in this example is tracked out, horizontally scaled, and baseline shifted downward.*

TIP *You can copy and paste a tab from one line of text to another. If you double-click the tab character, the whole leader will also become selected.*

Steamed vegetable dumplings ≈ ≈ ≈ ≈	3.50
Shrimp rolls ≈ ≈ ≈ ≈ ≈ ≈ ≈ ≈	4.00

4 *You can use **any character** as a fill character. Be creative! Mac OS X: This is Option-X and a space. Windows: This is Alt + 0187 in the Symbol font and a space. The font has to be changed manually.*

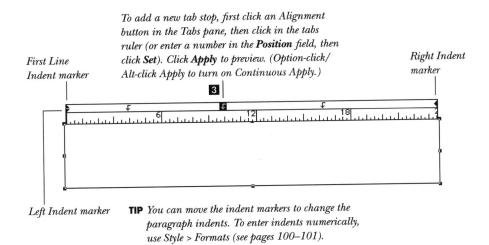

First Line
Indent marker

To add a new tab stop, first click an Alignment
button in the Tabs pane, then click in the tabs
ruler (or enter a number in the **Position** field, then
click **Set**). Click **Apply** to preview. (Option-click/
Alt-click Apply to turn on Continuous Apply.)

Right Indent
marker

3

Left Indent marker

TIP *You can move the indent markers to change the
paragraph indents. To enter indents numerically,
use Style > Formats (see pages 100–101).*

To align columns to a character of your
choosing, click the **Align On** alignment button,
then type the character in the **Align On** field.

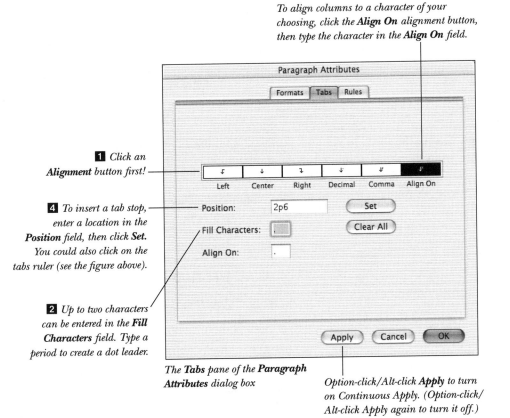

1 Click an
Alignment button first!

4 To insert a tab stop,
enter a location in the
Position field, then click **Set.**
You could also click on the
tabs ruler (see the figure above).

2 Up to two characters
can be entered in the **Fill
Characters** field. Type a
period to create a dot leader.

The **Tabs** pane of the **Paragraph
Attributes** dialog box

Option-click/Alt-click **Apply** to turn
on Continuous Apply. (Option-click/
Alt-click Apply again to turn it off.)

Set Custom Tab Stops

To edit or remove custom tab stops:

1. Choose the Content tool.

2. Select *all* the paragraphs that contain the stops you want to change or from which you want to remove tab stops.

3. Choose Style > Tabs (Cmd-Shift-T/ Ctrl-Shift-T).

4. Do any of the following:

To change the alignment of a stop, click its marker, then click a different Alignment button.
or
To change fill character(s), click a marker, then change the Fill Character(s).
or
To move a tab stop, drag it to the side manually. Or click on it, change its Position value, then click Set (Cmd-S/ Alt-S).
or
To remove one tab stop, drag its marker upward or downward off the ruler **1**.
or
To remove *all* the tab stops, click Clear All (Alt-C in Windows) **2** or Option-click/Alt-click the ruler.

5. Click Apply to preview (Cmd-A/Ctrl-A), readjust any of the settings, if desired, then click OK **3**.

Blank ruler?

If the paragraphs you highlight before choosing Style > Tabs contain more than one set of custom tab stops, only the tab stops for the first paragraph will display on the tabs ruler, but any new tab settings will affect *all* the currently highlighted text.

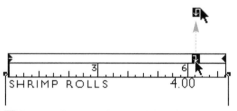

1 *Drag a tab stop marker **out** of the ruler to remove it.*

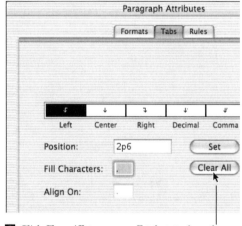

2 *Click **Clear All** to remove **all** tab stops from the currently highlighted text. The default tab stops will be restored to the text.*

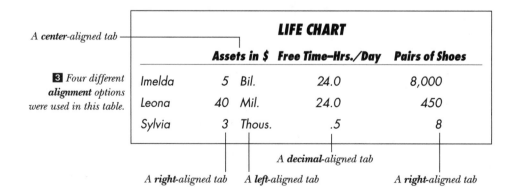

A **center**-aligned tab

3 Four different **alignment** options were used in this table.

LIFE CHART

	Assets in $		Free Time–Hrs./Day	Pairs of Shoes
Imelda	5	Bil.	24.0	8,000
Leona	40	Mil.	24.0	450
Sylvia	3	Thous.	.5	8

A **decimal**-aligned tab

A **right**-aligned tab   A **left**-aligned tab   A **right**-aligned tab

Pictures 9

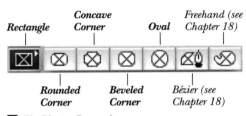

Rectangle | Concave Corner | Oval | Freehand (see Chapter 18)

Rounded Corner | Beveled Corner | Bézier (see Chapter 18)

1 *The **Picture Box** tools*

2 *Drag to create a **picture box**.*

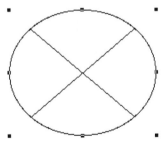

3 *An empty picture box has an "x" through its center.*

Picture basics

In QuarkXPress, a picture can be imported into a variety of different-shaped picture boxes. First you create a box using one of the Picture Box tools (Bézier or non-Bézier), then you import a picture into it.

File formats that can be imported include TIFF, PICT, EPS, GIF, JPEG, DCS, PCX, PDF, PNG, PhotoCD, Windows Metafile (WMF), and Bitmap (BMP).

Note: Most of the commands that are discussed in this chapter can also be applied to Bézier picture boxes. Béziers are covered in Chapter 18.

To create a picture box:

1. Choose any Picture Box tool **1** except the Bézier or Freehand Picture Box tool or the Starburst tool. The cursor will temporarily turn into a crosshair icon.

2. Drag in any direction **2**–**3**.

TIP Shift-drag a handle to turn a rectangular picture box into a square or an oval picture box into a circle. This also works with a text box.

TIP To apply a frame to a picture box, use Item > Frame (Cmd-B/Ctrl-B).

TIP Need more than one? Use the Item > Duplicate, Step and Repeat, or Super Step and Repeat command to create multiples of any item.

When a picture is imported into a picture box, a screen preview version of it is saved with the QuarkXPress file, for display purposes. Also saved with the QuarkXPress file is information about changes made to the picture within the layout, such as cropping or scaling. The original picture file isn't modified by such changes. Instead, a link is created to the original picture file, which the QuarkXPress file accesses when the layout is printed. If the link to the original picture file is broken (the original picture is missing) or the picture itself is modified, you must update the picture or it won't output properly (see pages 179–180).

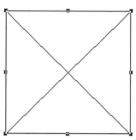

1 *Click a picture box. Note: If the box already contains a picture, the picture you import will replace the existing one.*

To import a picture:

1. Choose the Item or Content tool, then click a picture box.
or
Choose the Content tool, then click a picture box in a group or a picture cell in a table **1**.

2. Choose File > Get Picture (Cmd-E/ Ctrl-E). Or Control-click/Right-click the box or cell, then choose Get Picture from the context menu.

3. *Optional:* Check Preview to display a thumbnail of the picture (the picture has to have been saved with a preview).

4. Click a picture file name **2**–**3**, then click Open; or double-click the file name (twice, if necessary). If it looks as though the picture isn't there, see **1**–**2**, next page. There's a lot you can do to a picture, such as scaling, cropping, and rotating, and you can also scale, rotate, or distort the picture box. Instructions begin on page 167.

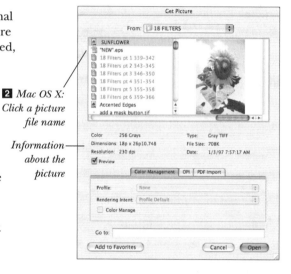

2 *Mac OS X: Click a picture file name*

Information about the picture

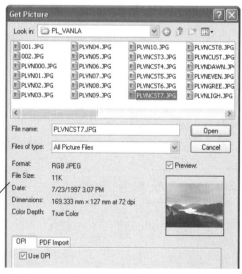

Information about the picture

3 *Windows: Click a picture file name or type the first character or two of the name in the File name field.*

Import Picture

Faster navigating

If you tend to import pictures over and over from the same folder, you can make that folder appear automatically in the Open dialog box by choosing it in QuarkXPress (Edit, in Windows) > Preferences > Application > **Default Path Preferences** (see page 415).

1 *The picture is imported using File > **Get Picture**—but where is it?! If it has a large white background, it may be off to one side.*

2 *Ctrl-click/Right-click and choose **Fit Box to Picture** to make the box fit the picture, or drag the picture using the **Content** tool.*

Formats you can import

You can import a TIFF, EPS, JPEG, DCS, GIF, PDF, PNG, PICT, PhotoCD, WMF (Windows Metafile), or Windows Bitmap (BMP) picture into a QuarkXPress picture box. (In Mac OS X, a Windows Metafile will convert into a PICT when it's imported.) QuarkXPress can color-separate an RGB or CMYK TIFF.

To import a picture in the JPEG, PDF, PCX, BMP, PhotoCD, or LZW TIFF format, make sure that format's import filter is enabled. If the required filter is disabled, you will get an error message that reads "This file requires XTensions software to be read properly." Use the Utilities > XTensions Manager to enable/disable filters.

If the QuarkXTensions software module for OPI is installed and enabled, a tab for that topic will be available at the bottom of the Get Picture dialog box; ditto for the PDF Filter and Quark CMS tabs. To read about OPI, see the QuarkXPress documentation. For a PDF, enter the number of the page you want to import in the Page field. For the Color Management tab to be available, the Color Management Active option also must be enabled (see page 432).

Pictures come in two basic flavors

A picture that is created in a bitmap program (e.g., Photoshop or Painter), or that is scanned, is actually composed of tiny pixels. You'll see the individual pixels only if you zoom way in on the image. The important thing to remember about a bitmap image is that enlarging it above 100% in QuarkXPress will diminish its resolution and output quality, whereas shrinking it will increase its resolution and output quality. If you're preparing an image in a bitmap program or scanning it for output from QuarkXPress, you should plan ahead and save it at the appropriate resolution, orientation, and size. You're

(Continued on the following page)

Import Formats; Picture Types

also better off making color adjustments to a picture in a bitmap program rather than in QuarkXPress.

A picture that's created in a drawing program, such as Adobe Illustrator or Macromedia FreeHand, is composed of mathematically defined objects. This type of picture is called "vector" or "object-oriented." A vector picture can be moved, scaled, recolored, and enlarged without affecting its output quality at all. It will be crisp at 20% and crisp at 120% (though enlarging it much beyond 100% may lengthen its print time). The higher the resolution of the output device, the sharper a vector picture prints. A vector picture can't be edited in QuarkXPress, however; it can be scaled, rotated, or skewed, but not recolored.

TIP If you rotate, crop, or scale your picture in its native application rather than in QuarkXPress, it will redraw and print from QuarkXPress more quickly.

Choosing the right resolution for a bitmap picture

For onscreen output, save the image in RGB color mode in its original application and at a resolution of 72 ppi.

For print output, choose one-and-a-half to two times the lpi (lines per inch) your commercial printer plans to use. For example, let's say your printer plans to use a 133 line screen. A color picture should be saved at twice the line screen. 133 times 2 equals 266, so you should save the picture in its original application at 266 ppi. For a grayscale picture, one-and-a-half times the line screen is sufficient (200 ppi, in our example).

Every rule has its exceptions. A bitmap image that contains sharp linear elements will require a higher resolution (600 ppi or higher). For a very painterly picture that contains amorphous shapes, on the other hand, a resolution value that's less than twice the output line screen may suffice.

Photoshop to QuarkXPress

You can import a single- or multi-layered Photoshop TIFF file into a QuarkXPress layout but not a native Photoshop (.psd) file.

For color separations, ask your output service provider or commercial printer whether to save your files in CMYK or RGB mode in Photoshop. If you choose the former, Photoshop will do the RGB-to-CMYK conversion; if you choose the latter, then either QuarkXPress or the output device will do it. Also be sure to ask which file format they prefer: TIFF, DCS (preseparated), or EPS.

Here, spot

If you import an EPS picture into a QuarkXPress layout, **spot** colors that were assigned to the picture will automatically append to the Colors palette for that project.

TIP To *prevent* applied colors from importing with an EPS picture, hold down Cmd/Ctrl as you click Open in the Get Picture dialog box.

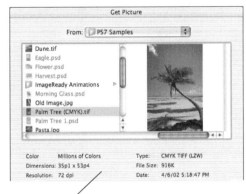

1 *Picture info*

A vector-based picture from a drawing application is resolution independent, which means it will print at the resolution of the output device. Just make sure it's saved in a file format that QuarkXPress can read.

If you're going to be outputting your QuarkXPress file to a color ink-jet printer, save your images at a high resolution in RGB color mode.

TIP A picture's file size, dimensions, color depth, and other information are listed in the Get Picture dialog box **1**. For information about an already imported picture, click on it, choose Utilities > Usage > Pictures, and check More Information.

Enlarge or shrink?

Scaling a bitmap picture in QuarkXPress affects its output resolution. If you shrink a bitmap picture in QuarkXPress, its output resolution will increase; if you enlarge a bitmap picture, its output resolution will decrease. Here's an example: Take a 150 ppi image and shrink it by half. Its ppi will increase to 300. Why should you bother paying attention to this? Because enlarging a bitmapped picture above 100% in QuarkXPress will diminish its print quality. A vector-based image (e.g., an Adobe Illustrator EPS) won't degrade in quality if it's enlarged in QuarkXPress, but it may take longer to print. You can also take a large picture and shrink it down in a QuarkXPress layout, but the picture will add significantly to the project's file size and also prolong its print time. So the moral of the story is…plan ahead.

EPS preview options

Every EPS picture has a PICT or TIFF preview built into it (unless it's specifically saved without one) so it can be viewed onscreen or printed on a non-PostScript printer. The higher a picture preview's bit

(Continued on the following page)

depth, the longer it may take to render onscreen and the larger the file storage size of the project into which it's imported.

When you save an EPS image for export to QuarkXPress, save it with a preview, if that option is available (both Adobe Illustrator and Macromedia FreeHand offer this option).

Any EPS picture that doesn't have a built-in preview will appear as a gray box in QuarkXPress, but it will print normally. To have QuarkXPress generate a full-resolution preview for the picture, select the gray box and choose Item > Preview **6.0!** Resolution > Full Resolution. Read more about the Full Resolution Preview option on pages 181–182 and about Full Res Preview preferences on page 416.

TIP To choose display options for TIFF pictures that you've already imported, go to QuarkXPress (Edit, in Windows) > Preferences > Application > Display (see page 411).

Looks like Greek to you

To speed up screen redraw, check **Greek Pictures** in QuarkXPress (Edit, in Windows) > Preferences > Print Layout or Web Layout > General. Greeked pictures look solid gray on screen at some view sizes, but they print normally. To ungreek a greeked picture, just click on it—the image will reappear.

Preview Options

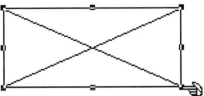

1 *Drag any of the four **corner handles** of a box...*

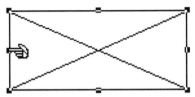

2 *...or drag any of the four **midpoint** handles of a box.*

*A new **Width** value is entered.*

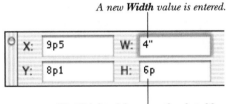

*The **Height** of the currently selected box*

3 *You can enter a value in the **Width** and **Height** field (or in any other field) in any measurement unit used in QuarkXPress.*

Scaling and positioning picture boxes

The dimensions of a picture box can be changed independently of the picture.

To scale a picture box manually:

1. Choose the Item or Content tool.

2. Click a picture box. For a Bézier picture box, turn off Item > Edit > Shape (Shift-F4/F10 toggles this command on and off).

3. Drag any handle **1**–**2**. Hold down Option-Shift/Alt-Shift while dragging to preserve the original proportions of the box.

To scale a picture box using the Measurements palette:

1. Choose the Item or Content tool.

2. Click on a picture box.

3. Double-click the W field on the Measurements palette, enter a number in an increment as small as .001 to modify the width of the box **3**, then press Return/Enter.
   and/or
   Double-click the H field on the Measurements palette, enter a number to modify the height of the box, then press Return/Enter.

TIP To enlarge or reduce the dimensions of a box by a specified amount, insert the cursor after the current value in the W or H field, enter a plus (+) or minus (-) sign, then enter the amount you want to add or subtract in any measurement unit used in QuarkXPress. You can also use / (slash) to divide the current value or * (asterisk) to multiply it.

Scale Picture Box

To delete a picture box:

1. Choose the Item or Content tool.

2. Click a picture box.

3. Choose Item > Delete (Cmd-K/Ctrl-K).

TIP A picture box that's selected with the Item tool can also be deleted by pressing Delete/Backspace on the keyboard or by choosing Edit > Clear.

To move a picture box manually:

1. Choose the Item tool or hold down Cmd/Ctrl if the Content tool is currently chosen.

2. With the pointer inside the picture box, drag in any direction. Pause before dragging to display the picture as it's moved (see the sidebar) **1** or drag without pausing to display only the outline of the box as it's moved **2**.

TIP You can drag a picture box or any other item from one page to another. To help you reach the desired page, you can force scrolling by knocking the pointer into the edge of the project window.

Take your pick

With **Delayed Item Dragging: Show Contents** chosen in QuarkXPress (Edit, in Windows) > Preferences > Application > Interactive, if you move or rotate an item that's behind other items, its full contents will be made visible temporarily as you move it. If **Live Refresh** is chosen instead, the item will stay as it actually looks in its layer as you move it, complete with any text wrap (it may be partially or completely obscured, if it's behind other items).

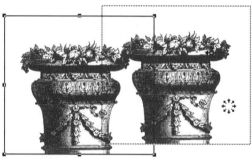

1 *To move a box, drag inside it with the **Item** tool. Pause before dragging to see the **picture** as you move it…*

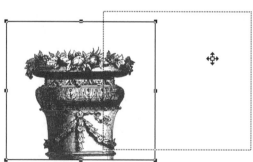

2 *…or drag without pausing to see only the **outline** of the box as it's moved.*

*The **horizontal** location of the upper left corner of a picture box relative to the ruler origin*

X:	4p4	W:	11p
Y:	9p2	H:	14p1

*The **vertical** location of the upper left corner of a picture box relative to the ruler origin*

1 *The Measurements palette*

2 *Add a positive or negative number to the right of the current value in the X or Y field, then press Return/Enter.*

X:	4p4+3p	W:	11p
Y:	9p2	H:	14p1

X:	7p4	W:	11p
Y:	9p2	H:	14p1

3 *The two numbers are added together and the box is repositioned.*

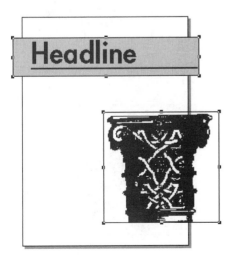

4 *These items are positioned for a bleed.*

To reposition a picture box using the Measurements palette:

1. Choose the Item or Content tool.
2. Click a picture box.
3. To change the horizontal position of the box relative to the ruler origin, which is normally located in the upper left corner of the layout, change the X value on the Measurements palette **1**.
   and/or
   To change the vertical position of the box, change the Y value on the Measurements palette.

TIP To move a box a specified horizontal or vertical distance, insert the cursor to the right of the current X or Y value, type a plus (+) or minus (-) sign, then enter a value in any measurement unit used in QuarkXPress **2**-**3**.

TIP To nudge a picture box or any other item 1 point at a time, select it with the Item tool, then press any of the four arrow keys on the keyboard. Or Option-press/Alt-press an arrow key to move an item in .1-point increments.

A bleed is the positioning of items so that they partially overhang the edge of the page. The overhanging portion is trimmed by the print shop after printing.

To create a bleed:

To create a bleed, position any item so that part of the item is on the page and part of it extends onto the pasteboard **4**. Items that are completely on the pasteboard won't print.

When you're ready to output your layout, you or your print shop will enter the width of the bleed area that you want to print and choose other print options in the Bleed pane in File > Print (see pages 440–441).

Fitting pictures into their boxes

To scale a picture:

1. Choose the Item or Content tool.

2. Click a picture.

3. Hold down Cmd-Option-Shift/Ctrl-Alt-Shift and press the > key to enlarge the picture 5% at a time or the < key to shrink it.
   or
   On the Measurements palette, enter new X% and/or Y% (picture size) values **1**–**5**.

TIP Press Tab to move from field to field on the Measurements palette (or press Shift-Tab to reverse your steps).

TIP You can copy values from one field on the Measurements palette and paste them into another field, such as from the X% field into the Y% field, or vice versa.

TIP To center a picture in its box, choose Style > Center Picture or press Cmd-Shift-M/Ctrl-Shift-M.

Horizontal scale of picture   *Horizontal location* of picture relative to upper left corner of picture box

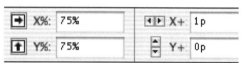

Vertical scale of picture   *Vertical location* of picture relative to upper left corner of picture box

1 *When the X and Y scale percentages differ from each other, it means the picture's proportions don't match those of the original.*

2 *When the X and Y scale percentages match, it means the picture's proportions do match those of the original.*

3 *A picture with an X scale of 55% and a Y scale of 55%*

4 *A picture with an X scale of 40% and a Y scale of 60%*

5 *A picture with an X scale of 60% and a Y scale of 40%*

To fit a picture to its box:

1. Choose the Item or Content tool.

2. Click a picture.

3. To scale the picture to fit completely within the box while maintaining its original proportions (aspect ratio), choose Style > Fit Picture To Box (Proportionally) or press Cmd-Option-Shift-F/Ctrl-Alt-Shift-F **1**–**2**.
or
To fit the picture into the box, but with its proportions altered relative to the original, choose Style > Fit Picture To Box (Cmd-Shift-F/Ctrl-Shift-F), or Control-click/Right-click the picture and choose Fit Picture to Box **3**.

1 *A picture before being resized*

2 *The **Cmd-Option-Shift-F/ Ctrl-Alt-Shift-F** keystroke fits the picture into the box while maintaining its proportions.*

3 *The **Cmd-Shift-F/Ctrl-Shift-F** keystroke stretches or squeezes the image to fit into the box.*

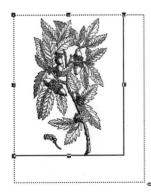

4 *Cmd-Option-Shift-drag/ Ctrl-Alt-Shift-drag a handle to resize a picture and its box simultaneously— and proportionally.*

Follow these instructions if the picture fits nicely in its box but you want to scale the whole shebang—picture and box.

To scale a picture and its box:

1. Choose the Item or Content tool.

2. If it's a Bézier picture box, turn off Item > Edit > Shape (Shift-F4/F10).

3. Hold down Cmd-Option-Shift/Ctrl-Alt-Shift, press a handle, pause briefly for the picture to redraw, then drag **4**.

Scale Picture

Along with resizing, cropping a picture can dramatically alter its impact on a page. Don't be afraid to crop drastically. Sometimes less is more. One caveat, though: If you're going to substantially crop a bitmapped picture, do it in the picture's original application. This will reduce the picture's file size and make it print faster.

To crop a picture by moving it within its box:

1. Choose the Content tool.

2. Drag inside the picture box (you'll see a hand icon) **1**.

TIP Click a picture and press an arrow key to nudge a picture 1 point at a time. Option-press/Alt-press an arrow key to nudge a picture 0.1 point at a time.

TIP You can also use a clipping path to prevent part of a picture from printing (see Chapter 11).

To crop a picture by resizing its box:

1. Choose the Item or Content tool, then click a picture box.

2. Drag any handle of the box **2**–**3**. For a Bézier box, turn off Item > Edit > Shape (Shift-F4/F10) first.

TIP To crop a picture by reshaping its box, read Chapter 18.

To fit a box to a picture:

1. Choose the Item or Content tool, then click a picture box.

2. Choose Style > Fit Box To Picture.
   or
   Control-click/Right-click the picture and choose Fit Box To Picture.

To delete a picture (and keep the box):

1. Choose the Content tool, then click a picture box.

2. Press Delete/Backspace.

1 *A picture being **moved** within its box*

2 *Drag any handle to **crop** a picture.*

3 *After cropping*

The *picture and box angle*

X:	7p4	W:	11p	⊿	0"
Y:	9p2	H:	14p1	⟋	0p

1 *The left side of the Measurements palette*

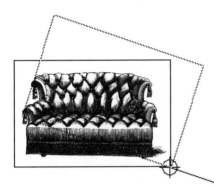

2 *Before rotating a box, you can create a lever by dragging away from the axis point. If you don't pause before dragging, only the outline of the box will be visible as you rotate it, not its contents.*

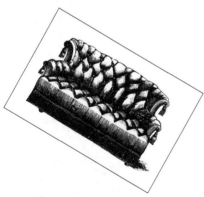

3 *A **picture** and its **box** being **rotated** together*

Picture tips and tricks

Note: Whenever possible, rotate, crop, or scale a picture in its original application before importing it into QuarkXPress—it will redraw, process, and print more quickly.

To rotate a picture and its box using the Measurements palette:

1. Choose the Item or Content tool.

2. Click a picture box.

3. In the picture and box angle field on the left side of the Measurements palette, enter a positive number between 0° and 360° to rotate the picture and box counterclockwise, or enter a negative number to rotate them clockwise **1**.

TIP To flip a picture, see page 178.

To rotate a picture and its box using the Rotation tool:

1. Choose the Rotation tool.

2. Click a picture box.

3. Press to create an axis point, drag the cursor away from the axis point to create a lever for better control **2**–**3**, then drag clockwise or counterclockwise.

TIP Shift-drag with the Rotation tool to rotate an item in increments of 45°.

TIP With Delayed Item Dragging: Show Contents chosen in QuarkXPress (Edit, in Windows) > Preferences > Application > Interactive, if you move or rotate an item that's behind other items, its full contents will be visible temporarily as you move it. If Live Refresh is chosen instead, you'll see the item as it actually looks (or is hidden, as the case may be) in its layer as you move it.

Rotate Picture

To rotate a picture (and not its box):

1. Choose the Item or Content tool.

2. Click a picture.

3. In the picture angle field on the right side of the Measurements palette, enter a positive value to rotate the picture counterclockwise or a negative value to rotate it clockwise **1**–**5**.

TIP To rotate the picture box and *not* the picture, first rotate the box and picture together using the angle field on the left side of the Measurements palette, then rotate just the picture using the angle field on the right side of the Measurements palette. For example, you could rotate the picture with its box 20°, then rotate the picture back –20°.

1 *The picture angle*

| X: | 35p10.4 | W: | 11p4 | △ | 0° | ➡ X%: | 75% | ◀▶ X+ | 0p | △ | 20° |
| Y: | 14p8.211 | H: | 15p7.989 | ⋌ | 0p | ⬆ Y%: | 75% | ↕ Y+ | 3p1 | ⟋ | 0° |

2 *0° rotation*

3 *40° rotation*

4 *90° rotation*

5 *180° rotation*

Rotate Picture

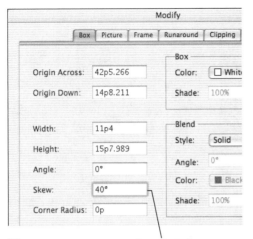

Modify

| Box | Picture | Frame | Runaround | Clipping |

Box

Origin Across: 42p5.266   Color: ☐ Whit

Origin Down: 14p8.211   Shade: 100%

Width: 11p4

Height: 15p7.989

Angle: 0°

Skew: 40°

Corner Radius: 0p

Blend

Style: Solid

Angle: 0°

Color: ■ Black

Shade: 100%

1 *To skew a picture (or text) box, choose Item > Modify, click the Box tab, then enter a **Skew** value.*

To skew a picture and its box:

1. Choose the Item or Content tool.

2. Click a picture box of any shape. Only one item can be skewed at a time.

3. Choose Item > Modify or Control-click/Right-click the box and choose Modify (Cmd-M/Ctrl-M).

4. Click the Box tab, then enter a Skew value between −75 and 75 **1**. Enter a positive value to skew it to the right or a negative value to skew to the left.

5. Click OK **2**–**4**. A picture (or text) can be edited in its skewed position.

TIP To skew a picture and *not* its box, click on it with the Content tool, then enter a value between −75 and 75 in the Skew field in the lower right corner of the Measurements palette. You could also enter a value in the Picture Skew field in Item > Modify > Picture.

2 *A picture box.*

3 *The box **skewed** 35%*

4 *The Box Skew feature was used to distort the top and side portions of this cube.*

Skew Picture and Box

The Contrast command can be used to perform coarse tonal or color adjustments to a picture—to, say, posterize it or make it high contrast. Hold onto your hat, though. Problem number one, you can't adjust a color TIFF unless the picture is imported with Color TIFFs: 8-bit as the setting in Preferences > Application > Display. At that setting, you'll be working off an 8-bit display, which is like drawing in the dark. And two, the Contrast controls are clunky (don't let Peter even get started on this topic). So play around with the Contrast command all you like, but do yourself a favor—don't mention it to Peter! We use Adobe Photoshop for this stuff, but that's probably not a big piece of news.

Note: Changes made using the Contrast dialog box don't affect the actual picture file—they affect only how a picture displays and prints from QuarkXPress.

To apply a custom contrast setting to a grayscale picture:

1. Choose the Item or Content tool.
2. Click a grayscale TIFF, JPEG, PICT, Windows bitmap (BMP), PCX, GIF, or PNG picture. You can't adjust an EPS or WMF picture.
3. Choose Style > Contrast (Cmd-Shift-C/ Ctrl-Shift-C). The availability of contrast options will vary depending on the picture file type.
4. Option-click/Alt-click the Apply button to turn on Continuous Apply.
5. Leave the Model setting on HSB.
6. Make any of the following adjustments:

    To posterize the picture **1**–**2**, click the Posterized Contrast (second-to-last) tool on the left side of the dialog box.
    or
    To make the picture high contrast, click the High Contrast tool **3**.
    or

1 *Normal contrast*

2 ***Posterization*** *reduces the number of grays in a picture to black, white, and four gray levels in between.*

3 *This is the original picture after clicking the **High Contrast** tool, then using the **Hand** tool to move the contrast curve downward and to the right.*

1 *This is the original picture after clicking the* **High Contrast** *tool, then using the* **Pencil** *tool to draw peaks and valleys in the contrast curve.*

To adjust the contrast manually, click the Hand tool, then drag the entire contrast curve.
or
Choose the Pencil tool, and draw a custom curve **1**.
or
Check Negative to create a negative of the picture.
or
Use more than one of the tools, in any order **2**.

To restore the picture's original contrast values at any time, click the Normal Contrast (sixth) tool.

7. Click OK.

TIP To apply color to a picture, see page 266. To adjust the shade of a 1-bit black-and-white picture, use Style > Shades.

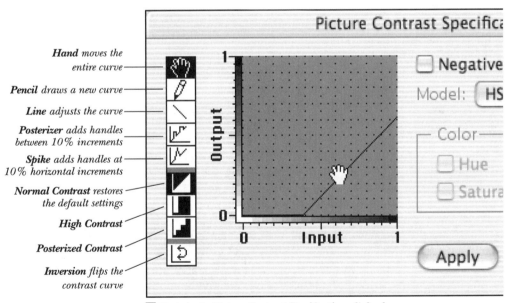

2 *Tools in the* **Picture Contrast Specifications** *dialog box*

The flip commands flip the contents of a box. A picture can be modified in its flipped position. (To flip a Bézier box and not its contents, see page 316.)

Note: As with cropping and rotating, it's better to flip a picture in its original application than in QuarkXPress—it will print and redraw more quickly.

To flip a picture:

1. Choose the Content tool.

2. Click on a picture box.

3. Choose Style > Flip Horizontal or Flip Vertical.
or
Click the Flip Horizontal and/or Flip Vertical button on the Measurements palette **1**–**2**.

TIP To undo a flip, stand on your head, or choose the command again, or click the button again on the Measurements palette.

Flip Horizontal button

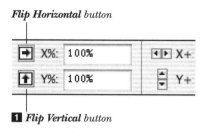

1 *Flip Vertical button*

2 *A copy of a picture flipped horizontally*

Cast a shadow

To add a soft drop shadow, bevel, emboss, or glow to any item, use the **ShadowCaster 3 XT** XTension from a lowly apprentice production, inc.

Status is everything

Modified The picture was modified in another application (but not moved).

Missing The picture was moved or renamed.

Wrong Type The picture's file format was changed (or the picture was compressed using a utility; you can't update this type).

No XTension The import filter for the picture's file format is disabled.

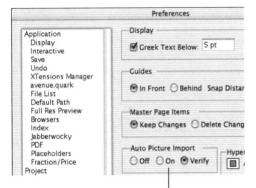

1 *In Preferences > Print Layout or Web Layout > General, click Auto Picture Import: Off, On, or Verify.*

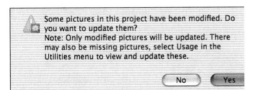

2 *With Auto Picture Import set to Verify, this alert dialog box will display if, upon opening the file, any pictures were modified outside QuarkXPress since the file was last closed.*

Updating pictures

When a picture is imported into a Quark-XPress file, the original picture file name and location is stored in the QuarkXPress file. If the original picture is then renamed or moved (is missing), its path to the QuarkXPress file must be reestablished in order for it to print correctly. QuarkXPress doesn't automatically update missing pictures. To do it yourself, follow the instructions on the next page.

If an original picture is modified in another application, on the other hand, its onscreen preview may or may not be updated automatically, depending on the current Auto Picture Import setting, which is discussed below. Unlike missing pictures, modified pictures will print correctly, whether you've chosen to have their onscreen previews update or not.

Thankfully, when a picture is updated, any scale, rotation, color, and offset values that were previously applied to it aren't changed.

To choose an import setting for modified pictures:

In QuarkXPress (Edit, in Windows) > Preferences > Print Layout or Web Layout (or Default Print Layout or Default Web Layout) > General, for Auto Picture Import, you can specify whether or not modified picture files in the project will be updated automatically when the project is reopened **1**.

If you reopen a project that was last saved with Auto Picture Import Off, the modified pictures won't be updated.

If the Auto Picture Import setting is On, the pictures will be updated automatically without a prompt appearing onscreen.

If Verify is the Auto Picture Import setting, a prompt will appear **2**. Click Yes to have the modified pictures update; no further steps are required.

6.0!

The path to missing (moved or renamed) picture files can be updated at any time using Utilities > Usage > Pictures. When pictures are updated, any scale, rotation, color, and other attributes that were previously applied to them are preserved.

The Usage dialog box can also be used to update modified pictures. You'll need to do this if Auto Picture Import was Off in Preferences > Print Layout or Web Layout > General when you opened the file (that is, if you opted not to have modified pictures update automatically), or if you modify any of the pictures outside of QuarkXPress after opening the file.

To update pictures using the Usage dialog box:

1. *Optional:* Choose the Content tool, then, in the layout, click the picture you want to update.

2. Choose Utilities > Usage (Option-F13 in Mac OS X).

3. Click the Pictures tab.

4. Click any file name whose Status is listed as Missing or Modified. If you clicked a picture in step 1, its name will highlight automatically.

Optional: Click Show to see the picture selected in the project window **■**.

5. Click Update **2**.

6. For any missing picture, locate and click the picture file name in the Find dialog box **3**, then click Open.

For any modified picture, click OK.

7. Click Done/Close.

TIP On Mac OS X, a dagger symbol † next to a page number in the Usage dialog box means the picture is located on the pasteboard for that page. In Windows, you'll see the letters "PB" instead.

What's its name?

If you want to know a picture's name, click the picture, choose Utilities > **Usage,** then click the Pictures tab. The name of the picture will be highlighted. Click Done to exit the dialog box.

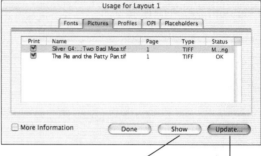

■ *Click Show to have the currently highlighted picture become selected in the layout.*   **2** *Click Update to search for a missing picture file.*

3 *Click the name of the missing picture, then click Open.*

1 *A couple of fine canines out on the town*

2 *A close-up of Amber, with Preview Resolution > Low Resolution chosen*

3 *The same picture and zoom level with Full Resolution chosen instead*

 One or more of the selected pictures has a resolution lower than 91 dpi and is limited to low resolution [10055]

4 *A low-resolution image can't be displayed at high resolution.*

Using full resolution preview 6.0!

In previous versions of QuarkXPress, when you placed a picture into a layout, the program displayed only a low-resolution preview **1**. This was a practical necessity years ago, when the video-processing horsepower of computers was lower than it is today, and scrolling around a document containing multiple full-color images was painfully slow. There was a drawback to this system, however: if you scaled the picture up, or zoomed in on the picture in order to crop it just so, the image you saw on your screen turned into a blocky, pixellated mess **2**.

QuarkXPress 6 allows you to take advantage of the high-octane video hardware in modern computers by providing a new option: full resolution preview. Pictures with this option applied will be displayed onscreen using the full resolution of the image file.

Note: Full resolution preview is not available for pictures in the GIF, PICT, or WMF format.

You can turn on full resolution preview for one or more selected pictures.

To turn on full resolution preview for specific pictures:

1. Choose the Item or Content tool, then click the picture you want displayed at full resolution. (Or to select multiple pictures, Shift-click them.)

2. Choose Item > Preview Resolution > Full Resolution **3**.
   or
   Control-click/Right-click the picture (or one of the selected pictures) and choose Preview Resolution > Full Resolution.

   Note: If the original picture file has a relatively low resolution to begin with, you'll get an error message when you try to choose the full resolution preview option **4**.

Full Resolution Preview

Of course, you can also reverse the setting.

To turn off full resolution preview for specific pictures:

1. Select the picture or pictures you want to display at low resolution.

2. Choose Item > Preview Resolution > Low Resolution.
or
Control-click/Right-click the picture (or one of the selected pictures)and choose Preview Resolution > Low Resolution.

Even on up-to-date machines, the process of scrolling through a layout can be slowed significantly if you have a lot of pictures set to display at full resolution. QuarkXPress allows you to turn off the display of full-resolution previews temporarily.

To disable full-resolution previews temporarily:

Choose View > Hide Full Res Previews. The pictures that have been set to display at full resolution will display at low resolution. (To make the full-resolution previews reappear, choose View > Show Full Res Previews.)

You can control several aspects of the handling of full-resolution previews via settings in the Full Res Preview pane in the Preferences dialog box. See page 416.

TIP The Full Res Preview XTension, which ships with QuarkXPress 6.0, is available only after you register your copy of the program! No, we didn't make this up.

Multiple Items

Moving multiple items

Constraining the movement of a multiple-item selection to the horizontal or vertical axis is a bit tricky. Once all the items are selected, start dragging the selection, then hold down Shift and continue dragging. Release the mouse, then release Shift.

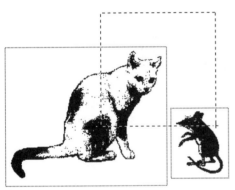

1 *Drag a marquee over multiple items with the* **Item** *tool.*

2 *Both picture boxes are* **selected,** *and the handles on both boxes are visible.*

It's one thing to create individual items, and quite another thing to arrange them into a pleasing composition. In this chapter you'll learn many layout skills, including how to group, lock, duplicate, rotate, scale, restack, anchor, and align multiple items.

Selecting and deselecting items

The position, size, angle of rotation, background color, and other specifications can be modified for a multiple-item selection. Available options will vary depending on whether the items are all text boxes, picture boxes, lines, text paths, or a combination thereof. Only items on unlocked layers can be selected (see page 282).

To select multiple items:

1. Choose the Item or Content tool.

2. Shift-click each item to be selected.
or
Position the cursor outside all the items to be selected, then drag a marquee that surrounds at least a portion of each item **1**–**2**. (To deselect any selected item, Shift-click it.)

To deselect all items:

Choose the Item tool, then press Tab.
or
Choose the Item or Content tool, then click a blank area in your layout.

To select all the items on a page or spread:

1. Choose the Item tool, and make sure the desired page is displayed (note the page number in the lower left corner of the project window).

2. Choose Edit > Select All (Cmd-A/Ctrl-A).

183

Grouping items

Grouped items remain associated and move as a unit unless they're ungrouped. In this book, each picture is grouped with its accompanying caption, and in some cases multiple picture/caption groups are themselves grouped together (nested) to form a larger group. Individual items in a group always remain editable.

To group items:

1. Choose the Item or Content tool.

2. Shift-click each item to be grouped (any item type except a table). (Shift-click any selected item to deselect it.)
   or
   Position the cursor outside all the items to be included in the group, then drag a marquee around them. You need to drag over only a portion of all the items—just make sure to grab at least one handle on each item.

3. Choose Item > Group (Cmd-G/Ctrl-G). Items stay on their original layers.

   Note: Use the Content tool to modify the size or contents of an item in a group. If the group is already selected 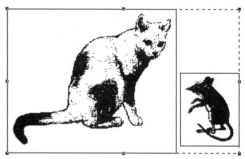, deselect it by clicking outside it, then with the Content tool, click the item you want to edit.

To move an item in a group:

1. Choose the Item or Content tool.

2. Hold down Cmd/Ctrl, press on the item to be moved, pause briefly for the item to redraw, then drag .

This method for removing an item from a group deletes the item from the layout altogether. To take an item out of a group without deleting it, see the following page.

To delete an item from a group:

1. Choose the Content tool.

2. Click the item to be deleted.

3. Choose Item > Delete (Cmd-K/Ctrl-K). This command *can* be undone.

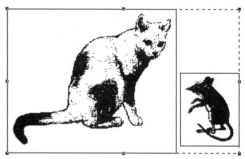
1 *A dotted **bounding box** surrounds a selected group.*

2 *To move an item in a group, **Cmd-drag/Ctrl-drag** the item with the Content tool.*

1 *If you resize a group while holding down **Cmd-Option-Shift/ Ctrl-Alt-Shift**…*

2 *…the items and their contents will **resize proportionally**.*

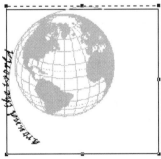

3 *If you resize a group with **no** keys held down, the **items** (box or path) will reshape, but not their contents (text or picture).*

To take an item out of a group and keep it:

Method 1

1. Choose the Content tool.

2. Click the item you want to take out of the group.

3. Press Cmd-D/Ctrl-D.

4. Click again on the item that's still in the group, then press Cmd-K/Ctrl-K.

Method 2

1. Choose the Item tool.

2. Choose Item > Ungroup.

3. Shift-click the item you want to take out of the group (the other grouped items will remain selected).

4. Choose Item > Group.

You can resize, move, cut, copy, duplicate, anchor, rotate, or recolor a whole group. To change a group's overall dimensions, angle, background color, or shade, or to apply a blend across a whole group, use Item > Modify > Group. Runaround options must be chosen individually for each item in a group (use the Content tool).

This method for resizing grouped items is a terrific timesaver. Frame widths and line weights won't change.

To resize a whole group:

1. Choose the Item tool, then click the group.

2. To resize the grouped items and their contents (text or picture) proportionally, drag a handle with Cmd-Option-Shift/Ctrl-Alt-Shift held down **1**–**2**.
or
To change the shape of the grouped items, but not their contents, drag a handle with no keys held down **3**.

To ungroup items:

1. Choose the Item tool, then click the group you want to ungroup.

2. Choose Item > Ungroup (Cmd-U/Ctrl-U).

Locking is a safety command that can be applied to any item to prevent it from being moved, resized, reshaped, or rotated *manually.* We lock items on our master pages (e.g., headers, footers) so they can't be moved manually.

Beware! Locking won't prevent the contents of a locked text box, picture box, or table, or the attributes of a line, such as its style, color, or width, from being edited. And a locked item can be moved or resized using the Measurements palette, or using a dialog box, such as Item > Modify or Space/Align. And one further warning: A locked item can be *deleted!*

To lock an item:

1. Choose the Item or Content tool.

2. Select the item to be locked (or select multiple items to be locked).

3. Choose Item > Lock (F6) 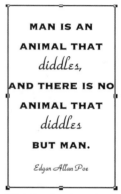. Choose the same command again to unlock any selected locked item or items.

TIP Looking for a stronger locking device? To lock items more completely so they can't be selected, moved, modified, or deleted by any means whatsoever, lock the layer they reside in (see page 282).

Creating multiples

To duplicate an item:

1. Choose the Item or Content tool.

2. Select the item or group you want to duplicate 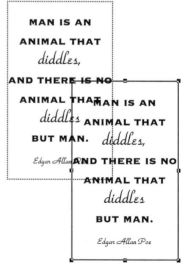.

3. Choose Item > Duplicate (Cmd-D/ Ctrl-D) 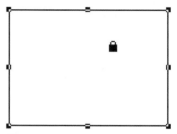. The default Duplicate offset values are 1p6 to the right and 1p6 downward. However, if the Step and Repeat dialog box was used in the current work session, the last-used offsets from that dialog box will be applied instead of the default offsets (see the following page).

TIP If you duplicate a locked item, the duplicate will be locked too.

1 *The pointer changes to a padlock when it's over a selected, locked item.*

> MAN IS AN
> ANIMAL THAT
> *diddles,*
> AND THERE IS NO
> ANIMAL THAT
> *diddles*
> BUT MAN.
> *Edgar Allan Poe*

2 *Select the item to be duplicated, then choose Item >* **Duplicate.**

> MAN IS AN
> ANIMAL THAT
> *diddles,*
> AND THERE IS NO
> ANIMAL THAT
> *diddles*
> BUT MAN.
> *Edgar Allan Poe*

3 *A duplicate is made.*

1 *Select an item.*

2 *Enter values in the Step and Repeat dialog box.*

3 *The bunny was duplicated using these values: Repeat Count 3, Horizontal Offset 0, and Vertical Offset 5p5.*

Using the Step and Repeat command, you can make multiple duplicates at one time and you can specify how far apart the duplicates will be from one another. The offset distance is calculated from the upper left corner of each item (or the bounding box, in the case of a Bézier box, line, or text path). You can use this command to reproduce any kind of item or group (e.g., you could generate multiple picture and caption groups in neat horizontal or vertical rows).

To step and repeat an item:

1. Choose the Item or Content tool.

2. Select an item or a group of items **1**.

3. Choose Item > Step and Repeat (Cmd-Option-D/Ctrl-Alt-D).

4. In the Repeat Count field, enter the number of duplicates to be made (1–99) **2**.

5. Enter a Horizontal Offset value. Enter a minus sign before the value to step and repeat items to the left of the original. Enter 0 in this field to have the duplicates align along their left edges without moving horizontally.
   and
   Enter a Vertical Offset value. Enter a minus sign before the value to step and repeat items above the original. Enter 0 in this field to have the duplicates align along their top edges without moving vertically.

   Enter positive values (or negative values) in both Offset fields to produce a stair-step arrangement.

6. Click OK **3**.

TIP If an alert prompt appears, reduce the Repeat Count and/or Offset values so that the duplicate items will be able to fit within the confines of the pasteboard. That should do it.

Super Step and Repeat.xnt, an XTension that ships with QuarkXPress, works like the Step and Repeat command, except that it also lets you choose rotate, scale, skew, and shade values for the duplicates and an axis point for the transformation.

To rotate, scale, or skew copies of an item using Super Step and Repeat:

1. Choose the Item or Content tool.

2. Select one text box, picture box, text path, or line 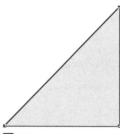. (Not a group—sorry!) To transform from a point on a Bézier, select that point now.

3. Choose Item > Super Step and Repeat.

4. In the Repeat Count field, enter the desired number of duplicates **2**.

5. In the Horizontal Offset field, enter the distance you want each copy to be offset on the horizontal *(x)* axis relative to the original. A positive value positions the copies to the right of the original; a negative value positions the copies to the left of the original. *and*
   In the Vertical Offset field, enter the distance you want the each copy to be placed on the vertical *(y)* axis relative to the original. A positive value positions the copies above the original; a negative value positions the copies below the original. The duplicates must be able to fit within the pasteboard.

   Enter 0 for both offset values to have the duplicate items land on top of the originals.

6. Intermediate duplicates, if any, will be assigned incremental angles, frame widths, line widths, shades, scale values, or skew values, depending on what end values are entered in the dialog box. Do any of the following:

   Change the Angle to have each duplicate be rotated counterclockwise by that amount, relative to the original or the previous duplicate **3**.

Power scaling

A number of XTensions offer powerful scaling tools, such as **ProScale** from GLUON, Inc., **Resize XT** from Vision's Edge, Inc., and **XPert Scale** in XPert Tools Pro from a lowly apprentice production, inc.

1 *Select an item.*

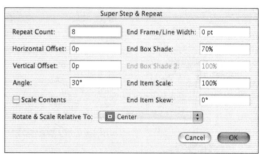

2 *Use the **Super Step & Repeat** dialog box for single or multiple **transformations**.*

3 *After using **Super Step and Repeat** to **rotate** copies of the item, using the settings shown in the previous figure*

Change the End Frame/Line Width or End Line Width for the final duplicate item. Each duplicate will be successively larger or smaller than the last, until the end width is reached. The current width of the selected line or frame is entered automatically; a different value can be entered. The end value must be able to fit on the resulting item(s).

Change the End Box Shade or End Line Shade (0%–100%) for the final duplicate box or line. Intermediate duplicates will be assigned incremental shades between the original and final shades. 100% is the default.

If your box contains a blend, change the End Box Shade 2 (0%–100%) for the background shade of the final box.

For a text path or line whose line style has multiple dashes or stripes, change the End Gap Shade (0%–100%) for the gap color in the final line. Intermediate gaps will be assigned incremental shades.

Change the End Item Scale or End Line Scale (1%–1000%) for the final duplicate.

If you want frames on the duplicate box(es) to be scaled, enter a final End Frame/Line Width size.

Change the End Item Skew (–75° to 75°) for the skew angle of the final duplicate. Both the box and its contents will be skewed. This option is available for boxes only, not for paths or lines.

7. To scale the contents of the item (text or picture) along with the box or path, check Scale Contents.

8. From the Rotate & Scale Relative To pop-up menu, choose the axis point around or from which the item will be rotated, scaled, or skewed. If a point is chosen on a Bézier item, the Selected Point option will be available.

9. Click OK **1**–**3**. Unfortunately, there is no Apply button. If you don't like the results, choose Undo or press Cmd-K/Ctrl-K—only the duplicates will disappear, not the original object.

Not so super

1 *Select an item.*

2 *From the **Rotate & Scale Relative To** pop-up menu, choose the point around or from which the item will be rotated or scaled.*

(More illustrations on the following page)

Not so super
Not so super
Not so super
Not so super
Not so super
Not so super

3 *These items resulted after using the **Super Step and Repeat** settings shown in the previous figure to create incrementally **larger** copies. Unfortunately, only absolute offset values can be entered—not a percentage—so the items are equidistant from each other and thus piled on top of each other.*

1 *The original item*

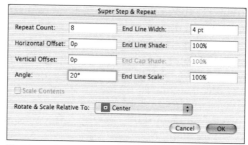

Super Step & Repeat

Repeat Count:	8	End Line Width:	4 pt
Horizontal Offset:	0p	End Line Shade:	100%
Vertical Offset:	0p	End Cap Shade:	100%
Angle:	20°	End Line Scale:	100%

Scale Contents

Rotate & Scale Relative To: Center

Cancel   OK

2 *The settings used to produce the next figure*

3 *The final items*

4 *The original item*

Super Step & Repeat

Repeat Count:	6	End Frame/Line Width:	0 pt
Horizontal Offset:	0p	End Box Shade:	80%
Vertical Offset:	0p	End Box Shade 2:	100%
Angle:	30°	End Item Scale:	20%
Scale Contents		End Item Skew:	0°

Rotate & Scale Relative To: Center

Cancel   OK

5 *The settings used to produce the next figure*

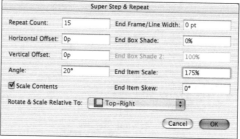

6 *The final items*

Vortex

7 *The original item*

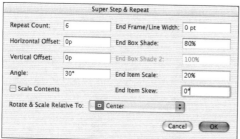

9 *The final items*

Super Step & Repeat

Repeat Count:	15	End Frame/Line Width:	0 pt
Horizontal Offset:	0p	End Box Shade:	0%
Vertical Offset:	0p	End Box Shade 2:	100%
Angle:	20°	End Item Scale:	175%
Scale Contents		End Item Skew:	0°

Rotate & Scale Relative To: Top-Right

Cancel   OK

8 *The settings used to produce the next figure*

Super Step and Repeat

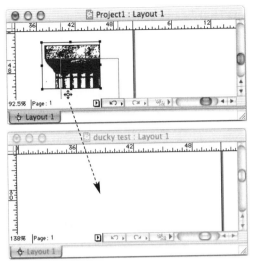

1 *Open two files, choose the **Item** tool, then drag an item from one project window into the other.*

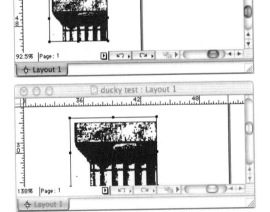

2 *A **duplicate** is made automatically as the item is dragged; the original item is unchanged.*

This method for copying items between projects doesn't use the Clipboard.

To drag-copy an item between projects:

1. Open two QuarkXPress files, and resize or move both project windows, if necessary, so you can see both of them on your screen. If you like, in Mac OS X, you can choose Window > Tile; in Windows, you can choose Window > Tile Horizontally or Tile Vertically.

2. Choose the Item tool (or hold down Cmd/Ctrl if the Content tool is chosen).

3. Display a layout in the "target" project. Drag any unlocked item or group from another project window (the "source" project) into the target project. Lo and behold, a duplicate of the item will appear in the target project **1–2**.

If your layout contains user-created layers, read the second set of instructions on page 279!

Any style sheets, H&Js, or custom colors that were applied to the item in the source project will also appear in the target project, unless there's a name conflict.

TIP If you drag-copy a box containing linked text, the text in that box will duplicate, along with any hidden overflow text from that point to the end of the story.

TIP Individual items can't be copied between projects in Thumbnails view, but entire pages can (see page 95).

Drag-Copy Item Between Projects

In these instructions, you'll use the Clipboard commands to copy items from one page to another within the same layout or between different layouts within the same project (you can't use drag and drop to do this). You could also use this method to copy items between projects (and you won't have to bother tiling your windows).

To copy and paste an item between pages, layouts, or projects:

1. Choose the Item tool.

2. Click the item or group to be copied.

3. Choose Edit > Copy (Cmd-C/Ctrl-C).

4. Click any page in any layout of the same output type, in either the same project or another project. (To activate an open project, you can choose it from the bottom of the Window menu.)

5. With the Item tool still chosen, choose Edit > Paste (Cmd-V/Ctrl-V). *Note:* If you copy an item with the Item tool and paste it into a selected text box with the Content tool, the item will be anchored—not copied! (Anchoring is discussed on pages 197–200.)

TIP To store an item for reuse, put it in a library, and then retrieve it from the library whenever you need it. You'll save time in the long run. See Chapter 20.

To cut or copy contents (picture or text) between pages, layouts, or projects:

1. Choose the Content tool.

2. Click the picture or highlight the text you want to copy or cut.

3. Choose Edit > Copy (Cmd-C/Ctrl-C) or Cut (Cmd-X/Ctrl-X).

4. Click another page in any layout in any project.

5. With the Content tool still chosen, click the picture box, text box, or text path that you want to paste into.

6. Choose Edit > Paste (Cmd-V/Ctrl-V).

Paste in place **6.0!**

Normally, an item will paste into the center of the project window. If you want to paste an item or group onto any page in the exact *x/y* location from which it was copied, choose Edit > **Paste in place** (Cmd-Option-Shift-V/Ctrl-Alt-Shift-V). This command can also be chosen from the context menu.

What smart space is

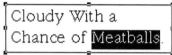

*If you double-click **inside** a word (or double-click then drag), only that word (or words) will become selected, not any adjacent spaces or punctuation.*

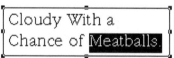

*If you double-click **between** a word and punctuation, both will become selected. If you copy and **paste** text, an **extra space** will be added, **if needed**.*

What smart space isn't
It isn't perfect.

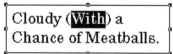

*If you cut text, the extra space left behind will be deleted, **except** if the gap occurs between a word and punctuation.*

Cloudy (**With**) a
Chance of Meatballs.

If you double-click a word that has opening and closing punctuation (e.g., parentheses or quotation marks), only the word will become selected. To select the word and punctuation, drag across them.

Who's afraid of Space/Align?

We were, until we got the hang of it. Now we use it all the time. This might help: When you choose between the Vertical and Horizontal options, think of the axis along which you want the items to *move*. If you want to align objects from left to right along their topmost edges, for example, check Vertical, click Space, leave the Space value at 0, and choose Between: Top Edges. Or to align objects along their left edges, check Horizontal instead and choose Between: Left Edges. Try it. Easier done than said.

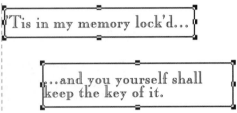

1 *Select* **two or more** *items.*

2 *Choose options in the* **Space/Align Items** *dialog box.*

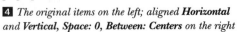

3 *Horizontal, Space: 0, Between: Left Edges is chosen. In this case the bottom box moves horizontally to the left to align with the leftmost box.*

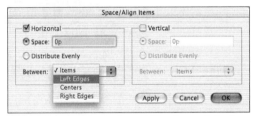

4 *The original items on the left; aligned* **Horizontal** *and* **Vertical, Space: 0, Between: Centers** *on the right*

Positioning items

The Space/Align feature aligns two or more selected items according to the position of the leftmost or topmost item, depending on which option you choose from the Between pop-up menu.

To align items:

1. Choose the Item or Content tool.

2. Shift-click each item that you want to align **1**. Items will stay in their layers.
   or
   Position the cursor outside the items to be aligned, then drag a marquee around them. *Note:* The Space/Align command *will* move locked items.

3. Choose Item > Space/Align (Cmd-,/ Ctrl-,).

4. Check Horizontal and/or Vertical **2**.

5. Click the Space button.

6. In the Space field, enter a positive or negative number between 0" and 10" in any measurement system in an increment as small as .001 to stair-step the items to the left or the right if Horizontal is checked, or upward or downward if Vertical is checked. Think of the Space field as an offset field.
   or
   Enter 0 to align the items along their edges or centers.

7. Choose from either or both Between pop-up menus. *Note:* If you choose Between: Bottom Edges for the Vertical option, the results may be contrary to what you'd expect; items will align to the bottom of the topmost item—not to the bottom of the bottommost item.

8. Click Apply to preview, make any adjustments, then click OK **3**–**4**.

TIP If you align a picture and an accompanying caption, remember to account for any Text Inset value above zero, which would position the text slightly inward from the left edge of its box.

If you choose the Horizontal and Distribute Evenly options in the Space/Align dialog box, the leftmost and rightmost of the currently selected items will remain stationary and the remaining selected items will be evenly spaced between them. If you choose the Vertical and Distribute Evenly options instead, the topmost and bottommost items will remain stationary. Items will stay in their respective layers.

To distribute items:

1. Select three or more items or groups 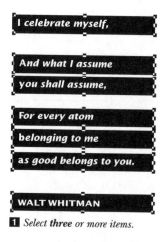 (if you don't know how to do this, follow steps 1–2 on the previous page).

2. Choose Item > Space/Align (Cmd-,/ Ctrl-,).

3. Check Horizontal and/or Vertical ▣.

4. Click Distribute Evenly under Horizontal and/or Vertical.

5. Choose an option from either or both of the Between pop-up menus. We tend to use the Items option the most.

6. Click Apply to preview. *Note:* If you change the settings and then click Apply again, the new settings will be added to the previously applied settings. Press Cmd-Z/Ctrl-Z to undo/ redo the last setting.

7. Click OK ▣.

1 *Select* **three** *or more items.*

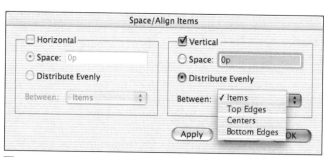

2 *Choose* **Distribute Evenly** *options in the* **Space/Align Items** *dialog box.*

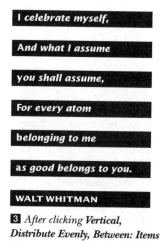

3 *After clicking* **Vertical,** **Distribute Evenly, Between: Items**

1 *The first click selects the text box, which is in front.*

2 *A second click selects the black cat. A third click would select the gray cat in the back.*

3 *The light gray cat is the backmost object.*

4 *The backmost object is* **moved** *in its layer.*

QuarkXPress automatically places the most recently created item in front of all the other items in your layout, or in front of all the other items on the currently active layer if your layout contains more than one layer. On this page, you'll learn how to dig through stacking levels.

On the next page, you'll learn a simple way to restack objects within a layer. To learn how to move an object to a different layer altogether, see Chapter 16.

If you just want to practice this technique, pile a few items on top of one another before you begin.

To select an item that's behind another item:

1. Choose the Item or the Content tool—whichever tool you're going to use to edit the item you want to select. If you're going to move the item, choose the Item tool; if you're going to edit its contents, choose the Content tool.

2. Cmd-Option-Shift-click/Ctrl-Alt-Shift-click an item **1**. Repeat to select each item behind it under the pointer in succession **2**. After the backmost item under the pointer is selected, the next click will reselect the topmost item in that spot.

To move an item that's behind other items:

1. Choose the Item tool.

2. Keep clicking with Cmd-Option-Shift/Ctrl-Alt-Shift held down. When you reach the item you want to move, drag immediately without releasing the mouse **3**–**4**. This little maneuver takes a bit of practice.

TIP To see an item as it looks in its layer as you drag it, including any text wrap, click Delayed Item Dragging: Live Refresh in QuarkXPress (Edit, in Windows) > Preferences > Application > Interactive, and pause before dragging.

Select, Move Obscured Items

You can use the Send to Back, Send Backward, Bring to Front, or Bring Forward command to change the stacking position of any item within its layer. Send to Back and Bring to Front move a selected item all the way to the front or back of its layer, whereas Send Backward and Bring Forward move an item backward or forward one level at a time within its layer.

To move an item forward or backward:

1. Choose the Item or Content tool.

2. Click an item ■.

3. Choose Item > Send to Back (Shift-F5) or Bring to Front (F5) **2**.

or

For the Send Backward command, press Option-Shift-F5/Ctrl-Shift-F5; or for the Bring Forward command, press Option-F5/Ctrl-F5. Or in Mac OS X, hold down Option and choose Item > Send Backward or Bring Forward. You may have to repeat the Send Backward or Bring Forward command several times to get the item to the desired stacking position.

or

In Mac OS X, if Control Key Activates: Contextual Menu is chosen in QuarkXPress (Edit, in Windows) > Preferences > Application > Interactive, Control-click the item and choose Send & Bring > Bring To Front, Bring Forward, Send To Back, or Send Backward. If Zoom is chosen as the Control Key preference, Control-Shift-click.

In Windows, Right-click and choose Send & Bring > Send Backward, Send To Back, Bring Forward, or Bring To Front.

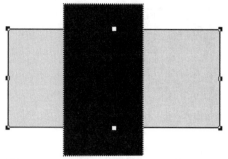

1 *A gray box (in **back** of a black box) is selected, as indicated by the eight handles, then Item > **Bring to Front** is chosen.*

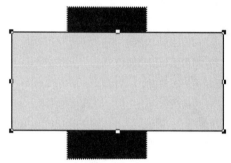

2 *The gray box is now **in front** of the black box.*

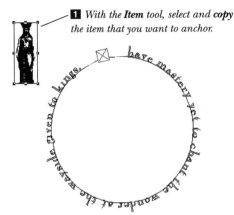

1 *With the **Item** tool, select and **copy** the item that you want to anchor.*

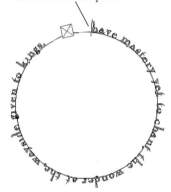

2 *Choose the **Content** tool, then click in the text to create an insertion point.*

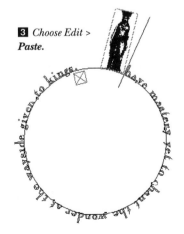

3 *Choose Edit > **Paste**.*

Anchoring items

You can paste (anchor) a line, picture box, text path, table, group, text box, or contentless box of any shape into any text box or onto any text path. Anchored items (inline graphics) function like characters in that they move with the text if the text reflows, and yet they remain fully editable.

Be sure to choose the right tools for these instructions!

To anchor an item into text:

1. Choose the Item tool.
2. Select the item to be anchored **1** (e.g., a table, a line, or perhaps an interesting graphic that you want to use as a drop cap).
3. Choose Edit > Copy (Cmd-C/Ctrl-C) or Cut (Cmd-X/Ctrl-X).
4. Choose the Content tool.
5. Click in a text box or on a text path to create an insertion point **2**.
6. Choose Edit > Paste (Cmd-V/Ctrl-V) **3**. You can do almost anything to an anchored item: reshape it, rotate it, recolor it, scale it, add a frame to it, change its contents (picture, text, or none), convert its shape, or apply a Runaround value to it (even a negative Runaround value!). Read more about anchored items on the next three pages.

Anchor Item into Text

197

To realign an anchored item:

1. Choose the Item tool.

2. Click an anchored picture box, text box, or table (not a group). Then, on the Measurements palette, click the Align with Text: Ascent button to align the top of the anchored item with the ascent (top) of the character to its right 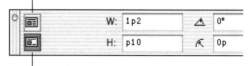. Or click the Align with Text: Baseline button to align the bottom of the anchored item with the baseline of the line of text in which it's anchored **3**.

To realign an anchored line (standard or Bézier) or a text path, click on it, choose Item > Modify > Line, then click Align with Text: Ascent or Baseline.

TIP To vertically offset a baseline-aligned anchored item, see the next page.

TIP Choose absolute—not auto—leading for text that contains an anchored box.

TIP You can change the Runaround for an item after it's anchored. Click on it, then choose Item > Runaround (Cmd-T/Ctrl-T).

TIP You can use a hanging indent (Style > Formats) or the Indent Here command (Cmd-\/Ctrl-\) to make an anchored item hang outside the paragraph **4**.

To move an anchored item to a new location:

1. Choose the Content tool.

2. To highlight the anchored item, click just to the left of it, then press Shift-right arrow (or click to its right, then press Shift-left arrow).

3. Choose Edit > Cut (Cmd-X/Ctrl-X).

4. Click in a text box where you want the item to reappear, then choose Edit > Paste (Cmd-V/Ctrl-V).

TIP To move an anchored item from one location to the next within the *same* text box, highlight it, then drag its left edge (Drag and Drop Text must be on in Preferences > Application > Interactive).

Align with Text: Ascent

1 *Align with Text: Baseline*

have mastery yet to chant the wonder at the wayside given to kings. Still by God's grace there surges within me singing magic grown to my life and power, how the wild bird portent hurled forth the Achaeans' twin-stemmed power single hearted, lords of the youth of Hellas, with spear and hand of strength to the land of Teucrus.   *Aeschylus*

2 *An anchored picture box, **Ascent** aligned*

ANTI-QUI-TIES

3 *An anchored picture box, **Baseline** aligned*

4 *An **Indent here** command is used to make the anchored item **hang** outside the paragraph.*

have mastery yet to chant the wonder at the wayside given to kings. Still by God's grace there surges within me singing magic grown to my life and power, how the wild bird portent hurled forth the Achaeans' twin-stemmed power single hearted, lords of the youth of Hellas, with

Realign, Move Anchored Item

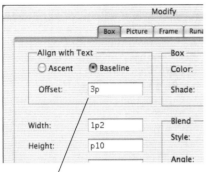

1 *Enter a number in this field to **offset** an anchored item that's baseline-aligned.*

2 *Resizing an anchored picture box*

3 *The anchored box enlarged*

The Offset option, which shifts an anchored item upward or downward, is available only for items that are baseline aligned, not for items that are ascent aligned.

To offset an anchored item:

1. Choose the Item or Content tool.
2. Click an anchored item (not a text path).
3. Choose Item > Modify (Cmd-M/ Ctrl-M), then click the Box, Line, or Table tab.
4. Enter a positive or negative Align with Text: Offset value **1**.
5. Click OK.

To resize an anchored item:

1. Choose the Item or Content tool. If the anchored item is a Bézier, turn off Item > Edit > Shape (Shift-F4/F10). (For Béziers, see Chapter 18.)
2. Click the anchored item.
3. For proportional scaling, Cmd-Option-Shift/Ctrl-Alt-Shift drag a handle (or drag an endpoint, if it's a line) **2**–**3**.

To delete an anchored item:

1. Choose the Item tool.
2. Click the item you want to delete.
3. Press Delete/Backspace.

TIP To do this another way, choose the Content tool, click just to the right of an anchored item (press the left or right arrow key to reposition the cursor), then press Delete/Backspace.

To create an unanchored copy of an anchored item:

Choose the Content tool, click the anchored item, then choose Item > Duplicate (Cmd-D/Ctrl-D).
or
Choose the Item tool, click the anchored item, choose Edit > Copy, click outside the text box, then choose Edit > Paste.

Offset, Resize, Delete, Copy Anchored Item

Drop anchor

To anchor highlighted text at its current location and convert it into a picture box at the same time, hold down Option/Alt and choose Style > Text to Box **1**–**3** (also see page 314).

 *did*

1 *Standard text characters are highlighted.*

 *did*

2 *Choosing Style > **Text to Box** with **Option/Alt** held down simultaneously converts the text into a picture box and anchors it at its current location.*

3 *We imported a picture into our anchored picture box.*

diddle diddle,

The *and the fiddle,*

The *jumped over*

the

The little *laugh'd*

To see such sport,

And the *ran away with the*

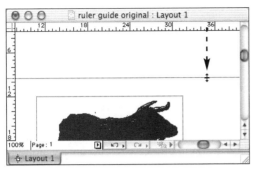

1 *Drag from a ruler to place a* **guide** *on a layout page or master page.*

Getting snappy

If you drag an item to a guide, the item will snap to the guide if View > **Snap to Guides** is on **2**. Specify a **Snap Distance** in QuarkXPress (Edit, in Windows) > Preferences > Print Layout or Web Layout > General (6 pixels is the default).

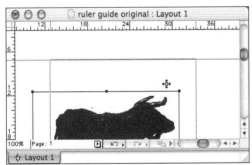

2 *An item will* **snap** *to a guide if it's dragged within the specified* **Snap Distance** *of the guide.*

Using guides

To position items precisely, use ruler guides (this page) or use the X and Y fields on the Measurements palette. To align items to each other, use Space/Align (see page 193).

To create a ruler guide manually:

1. If the rulers aren't showing, choose View > Show Rulers (Cmd-R/Ctrl-R). And if the margin guides aren't showing, choose View > Show Guides (F7).

2. Drag a guide from the horizontal or vertical ruler onto a layout page or master page **1**. As you drag, the guide's location will be indicated in the X or Y field on the Measurements palette and by a marker on the ruler. If you release the mouse over the pasteboard as you drag, the guide will extend across facing pages, if any, and onto the pasteboard.

TIP Ruler guides will display in front of or behind items depending on whether Guides: In Front or Behind is chosen in Preferences > Print Layout or Web Layout > General.

TIP To make a ruler guide visible only at or above a certain zoom percentage, choose that percentage, then hold down Shift as you create the guide.

To remove manual ruler guides:

To remove *one* ruler guide, choose the Item tool, then drag the guide back onto the ruler (the pointer will be a double arrowhead). If the guide is over an item, hold down Cmd/Ctrl and drag with the Content tool; this works only if Guides: In Front is chosen in Preferences > Print Layout or Web Layout > General. You can also move a guide using either tool.
or
To remove *all* horizontal guides or *all* vertical guides from a page (not the pasteboard), make sure no pasteboard is showing between the edge of the page and that ruler, then Option-click/Alt-click the ruler.

The Guide Manager command creates a custom grid of non-printing margin guides. You can control how many guides are created as well as their placement.

To create guides using Guide Manager:

1. If you want the guides to appear on only one page, go to that page now. Guides can't be placed on a master page. If guides aren't showing, choose View > Show Guides (F7).

2. Choose Utilities > Guide Manager, then click the Add Guides tab **1**. If the command isn't available, enable the Guide Manager.xnt XTension (see page 427).

3. From the Direction pop-up menu in the Guide Placement area, choose Horizontal, Vertical, or Both as the orientation for the guides.

4. *Optional:* Check Locked Guides to lock the new guides. They can be unlocked later.

5. From the Where pop-up menu, choose a location for the guides: Current Page, Current Spread, All Pages, or All Spreads. They can't be placed on a layer.

6. Do one or more of the following:

   To specify the interval between guides, check Spacing, then enter the desired interval in the Horizontal and Vertical fields. If no Spacing value is specified, the spacing will be calculated based on the Number of Guides values.

   If you don't want QuarkXPress to figure out how many guides to create, check Number of Guides, then enter Horizontal and/or Vertical values.

   From the Origin/Boundaries: Type pop-up menu, for the starting point of the grid: Choose Inset to inset the guides from the edges of the page/ spread, then enter inset values; or choose Absolute Position, then specify a starting location for the guides; or

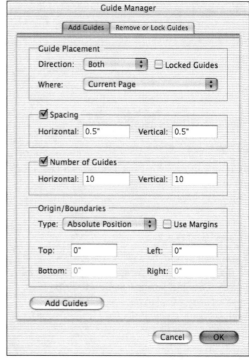

1 *Choose options in the* **Add Guides** *pane of the* **Guide Manager** *dialog box.*

Guide Manager

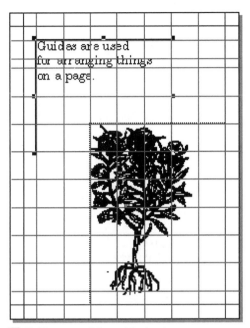

1 *Guides* are used for positioning items.

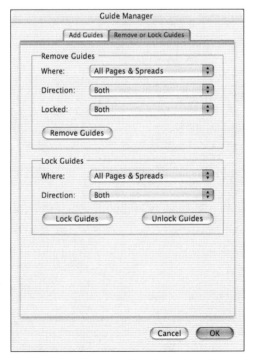

2 *The* **Remove or Lock Guides** *options are in a separate pane in the* **Guide Manager** *dialog box.*

choose Entire Page/Spread to have the grid originate from the upper left corner of the page or spread.

7. *Optional:* If Where: Current Page or All Pages is chosen, you can check Use Margins to have the grid be contained within the current margin guides.

8. Click Add Guides **1**.

9. Click OK. You can reapply this command to add more guides.

TIP The margin, ruler, and guide colors can be changed in Preferences > Application > Display.

To remove and/or lock/unlock Guide Manager guides:

1. Choose Utilities > Guide Manager.

2. Click the Remove or Lock Guides tab.

3. Under Remove Guides: Where **2**, choose which pages you want guides to be removed from: Current Page, Current Spread, All Pages, All Spreads, or All Pages & Spreads.
and
From the Direction pop-up menu, Choose Horizontal, Vertical, or Both.
and
From the Locked pop-up menu, choose whether you want Locked, Unlocked, or Both types of guides to be removed.

4. Click Remove Guides. All Guide Manager guides will be removed—as well as any guides that you dragged onto the page manually!

5. Under Lock Guides: Where, choose which pages you want guides to be locked or unlocked on: Current Page, Current Spread, All Pages, All Spreads, or All Pages & Spreads.
and
From the Direction pop-up menu, Choose Horizontal, Vertical, or Both.

6. Click Lock Guides or Unlock Guides.

7. Click OK.

Converting items

You can do more than convert a picture from one shape to another using the Shape submenu—you can also convert a standard picture box, text box, or content-less box into a Bézier box or convert any kind of picture box into a line. If you convert a text box into a line, it will become a text path. A table can't be converted into anything.

Note: If you convert a picture box that contains a picture into a line (any of the last three icons on the Shape submenu), the picture will be deleted.

To convert an item's shape:

1. Choose the Item or Content tool.

2. Click an item (don't select multiple items).

3. Choose a shape from the Item > Shape submenu –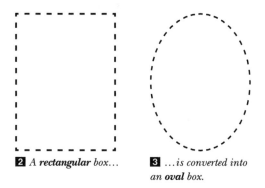.

TIP To make the corners of any of the first four shapes found under the Shape submenu more or less convex, choose Item > Modify (Cmd-M/Ctrl-M), click the Box tab, then change the Corner Radius value. 2″ is the maximum.

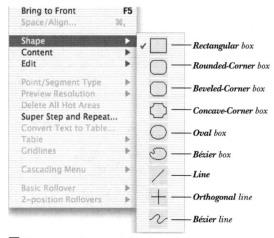

1 *An item can be converted into any shape on the Item > **Shape** submenu.*

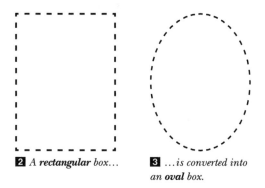

2 *A **rectangular** box...* **3** *...is converted into an **oval** box.*

Dinner one night consisted of lamb chops, becoming heavy at times, with occasional ketchup. Periods of peas and baked potatoes were followed by gradual clearing, with a wonderful Jell-O setting in the west.

~ *Judi Barrett*

4 *A **text box**...*

5 *...is converted into a **text path** by choosing the Line icon.*

1 *Choose **Picture, Text,** or **None** from the Item > **Content** submenu.*

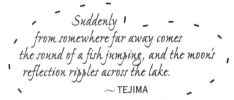

2 *A **picture** box…*

3 *…is converted into a **text** box (the text was added afterward).*

4 *A **contentless** box can contain a **frame** and a **solid color** or a **blend**—period.*

You can make a box or text path content-less, or vice versa; change a picture box into a text box, or vice versa; or change a line into a text path. Any text or picture the item originally contained will be removed; a frame will remain. *Note:* A Bézier line or Bézier text path can't be converted into a picture box.

To convert the contents of table cells, see page 146.

You can apply a solid color, blend, or frame to a contentless box, but you can't fill it with text or a picture. Contentless boxes function strictly as decorative elements.

To convert an item's contents:

1. Choose the Item or Content tool.

2. Click a text box, picture box, content-less box, line, or text path.

3. Choose Picture, Text, or None from the Item > Content submenu **1**–**4**.
or
Control-click/Right-click and choose Content > Picture, Text, or None.

4. Click OK if a warning prompt appears.

Design tips for Web and print

Just as a composer creates a musical score or an artist paints a picture, you have to arrange all the elements on your page so the message is understood clearly by your audience. If the writing is poor, your copywriter has more work to do, but your readers or viewers will become weary of even the most skillful writing if the layout and typography are poor. Your audience doesn't have to be spellbound, but you do want to capture their attention long enough to get the message across. Here are a few suggestions:

■ Let in some air. Leave a little **white space** around your text and pictures. How you do this depends on your subject matter. Use Text Inset values to add some air between a picture and its frame. Use ample gutters between columns (add delicate vertical rules for definition). Or gather elements up at the top of the page and leave the bottom of the page blank. Peaceful passages provide an important counterpoint to louder passages, and confident composers know how to play them off one another to their advantage.

■ Use a **grid** as an underlying structure to organize elements. Whether the grid is obvious to your readers or not, it makes for a more pleasing and orderly page, and it simplifies the layout process. In fact, many designers still use pencil and paper to sketch out broad design ideas before they create a layout on the computer.

■ **Break out** of the grid in select areas to add some punch. As an example, you could put thin rules around most of your pictures, then use a different type of picture with an irregular edge to add a more interesting, nonrectangular shape to the page.

■ Just as composers juxtapose opposing forces to create what we call **good tension**—slow versus fast, complex versus simple, loud versus soft, percussive versus melodic, and so on—you can create good tension in a layout in many ways. For example, instead of plopping two medium sized pictures smack in the middle of the page, put one large picture off to the side (let it bleed off) and a small picture in the opposing corner. Don't automatically stick everything in the center.

Elements that can be used to create pleasing tension include **scale** (large vs. small), **shape** (regular vs. irregular), **placement** (diagonal, vertical, and horizontal), **color** (raucous vs. subtle), and **shade** (light vs. dark).

■ When you arrange multiples of a similar object (e.g., pictures and their accompanying captions), the result doesn't have to be static. Use **repetition** to your advantage to create **texture** or **rhythm.** But do align the objects carefully— misalignments can be jarring (use Super Step and Repeat to make copies of an object or group, or use Space/Align to align existing objects). Keep in mind the **overall** shape multiple items will form when they're grouped together (e.g., the whole navigation bar, if you're designing a Web page). A good formation will have solidity and order. To see how the whole page looks, choose a small view size and turn guides off (it's the equivalent of squinting).

■ And last but not least, don't forget to set type like a professional (Chapter 7 is chock-full of tips for setting professional-looking type). The little **details** matter as much as the broad strokes.

Pictures and Text 11

1 *Click the text box that you want to be in front.*

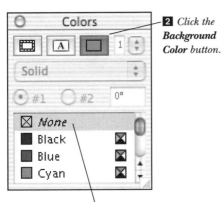

2 *Click the Background Color button.*

3 *Then click None to make the background of the top box transparent.*

4 *Now the text box is transparent.*

Pictures and text

There are many ways to combine text and pictures in QuarkXPress. For example, you can place a picture behind a text box that has a transparent background. Or you can have text wrap around the perimeter of a picture box, or wrap partially or completely around the irregular contours of the picture itself.

QuarkXPress not only gives you control over how text wraps around a picture, it also lets you create editable clipping paths that control how much of a picture prints. If you have a picture with a white background, for example, you can tell the program not to print the background. A clipping path can even be created from an embedded path or alpha channel that was saved with a picture in another application.

You can layer a text box over a picture box (or layer picture boxes or text boxes).

To make a text box see-through:

1. Choose the Item or Content tool.

2. Click the box that is to be in front. If it's not yet in front, choose Item > Bring to Front **1** or move the item to a higher layer (see page 278).

3. Choose View > Show Colors (F12).

4. Click the Background Color button on the Colors palette **2**, then click None at the top of the list of colors **3**–**4**. Don't select Black with a shade of 0%—you won't achieve transparency.

TIP If the item behind the text is so dark that the text is unreadable, switch gears and make the text white (see page 264).

To wrap text around an item:

1. The item the text is to wrap around must be on top of the text. It can be any kind of item (picture box, text box, contentless box, text path, Bézier shape, or table). To bring it forward, select it, then press F5 (or move it to a higher layer).

2. Choose the Item or Content tool.

3. Select the picture box.

4. Choose Item > Runaround (Cmd-T/Ctrl-T).

5. Choose Type: Item **1**.

6. To adjust the space between each side of a rectangular or square picture box and the text that's wrapping around it, enter Top, Left, Bottom, and Right values. For an item of any other shape, enter an Outset value.

7. Click Apply to preview the text wrap in the project window, then click OK **2**. *Note:* If the item straddles two columns, text will wrap around all its sides; if it's within a column, text will wrap around just three of its sides. (For a complete wrap in the latter case, click the text box, choose Item > Modify > Text, and check Run Text Around All Sides.)

TIP To choose default Runaround settings for any item creation tool, double-click the tool, click Modify, click Runaround, then choose settings.

TIP The Runaround value around a text path is calculated based on the path itself, not the text.

TIP If Maintain Leading is checked in Preferences > Print Layout or Web Layout > Paragraph and an item is positioned within a column of text, the first line of text that's forced below the item will snap to the nearest leading increment. With Maintain Leading off, the text will touch the bottom of the item, offset only by that item's current Runaround value.

The color code

The **Margin** color (the default is blue) is also used to represent an item's bounding box in the Runaround and Clipping dialog boxes. Similarly, the current **Ruler** guide color (the default is green) is used to represent the clipping path, and the current **Grid** color (the default is magenta) is used to represent the Runaround border. To change any of these colors, go to QuarkXPress (Edit, in Windows) > Preferences > Application > Display (Cmd-Option-Shift-Y/Ctrl-Alt-Shift-Y).

1 *Choose Type:* **Item** *in Item > Modify > **Runaround**.*

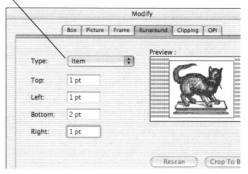

With my aversion to this cat, however, its partiality for myself seemed to increase. It followed my footsteps with a pertinacity which it would be difficult to make the reader comprehend. Whenever I sat, it would crouch beneath my chair, or spring upon my knees, covering me with its loathsome caresses. If I arose to walk it would get between my feet and thus nearly throw me down, or, fastening its long and sharp claws in my dress, clamber, in this manner, to my breast. At such times, although I longed to destroy it with a blow, I was yet withheld from so doing, partly by a memory of my former crime, but chiefly—let me confess it at once—by absolute *dread* of the beast...

This dread was not exactly a dread of physical evil—and yet... *Edgar Allan Poe*

2 *The text **wraps** around the picture box.*

Do you think it is said Pooh, "because ks. It is either Two night be, Wizzle, or zles and one, if so it ue to follow them." just a little anxious e animals in front of them were of Hostile Intent. And Piglet wished very much that his grandfather T.W.

1 *Before a clipping path is created, the white area around the photo* **prints.**

"Po⌐   ¹et. "Do you think it is
a⌐   " said Pooh, "because
ks. It is either Two
night be, Wizzle, or
zles and one, if so it
ue to follow them."
S   ⌐g just a little anxious
now,   three animals in front of
them were of Hostile Intent. And Piglet
wished very much that his grandfather T.W.

2 *A QuarkXPress* **clipping path** *is used to* **prevent** *the white area from printing. The text is still running behind the photo, though—it's not wrapping around it.*

"Pooh!" cried Piglet. "Do you think it is another Woozle?" "No," said Pooh, "because it makes different marks. It is either Two Woozles and one, as it might be, Wizzle, or Two, as it might be, Wizzles and one, if so it is, Woozle. Let us continue to fol-
                        A.A. Milne

3 *Finally,* **Runaround** *is turned on with the* *Type:* **Same As Clipping** *option for the photo to force the text to wrap around the* **image.**

What is a clipping path?

A clipping path is a mechanism that controls which parts of a picture **display** and **print** **1**–**3**. Areas of the picture within the clipping path are visible and will print; areas outside the clipping path are transparent and won't print. You may already know how to create a clipping path in another application, such as Adobe Photoshop. In that type of clipping path, the clipping information is saved in the picture itself. In QuarkXPress, when you use a clipping path that was saved with the original picture in another application, it's called an "embedded path."

Clipping paths in QuarkXPress work a little bit differently. They are also used to control which parts of an image will print, but they don't permanently clip areas of the image that extend outside it. Clipping path information in QuarkXPress is saved with the project, not in the image itself. This means that you can create a different clipping path for each instance in which you use an image. If you *want* to reuse a picture and its clipping path, on the other hand, you can simply drag and drop the picture box from one project to another; a copy will appear in the target project.

Another compelling reason to have Quark-XPress generate a clipping path is that as you reshape it or choose different settings for it, you'll be able to see immediately how it looks in your layout. What's more, you can adjust the shape of a clipping path to your heart's delight using any technique that you'd use to adjust a Bézier path.

You can have QuarkXPress create a clipping path based on the shape or silhouette of a picture, or you can create a custom path. QuarkXPress can also generate a new, editable clipping path based on any alpha channel (saved selection) or embedded path, provided the channel or path is saved with the picture file in its original application (e.g., Adobe Photoshop).

Runaround vs. clipping, in a nutshell

A clipping path controls which parts of a picture **display** and **print.** The Runaround feature controls how **text wraps** around a picture. The runaround text wrap or clipping path can be controlled by any of the following parameters 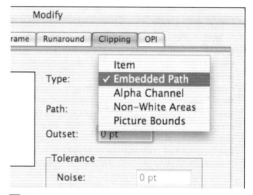–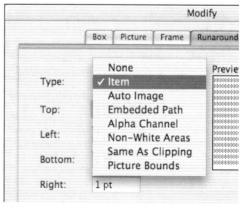:

Item: The edge of the picture box.

Embedded Path or **Alpha Channel:** An embedded alpha channel or path that was created and saved with the picture in a graphics application. You can use an embedded path in an imported picture if it was saved in any of these formats: TIFF, EPS, BMP, JPEG, PCX, or PICT. You can also use an alpha channel in a TIFF.

Non-White Areas: The non-white edge of a picture (the silhouette of an image, if it has a white background).

Picture Bounds: The picture's rectangular bounding box (not the QuarkXPress picture box).

To make matters even more confusing, for each Type there are additional options for controlling the placement of the clipping path or the runaround text wrap.

And for Runaround, there's an additional option: **Auto Image.** With Auto Image chosen, text will wrap around the edge of the image itself, not its bounding box. The runaround is created from the original, high-resolution image (not the preview), using Bézier curves, and works effectively on an image that has a clearly defined border and a flat, light background. It creates a combined, uneditable clipping and runaround path in one step (the edit clipping and runaround functions aren't available).

Choosing Type: **None** in the Runaround pane turns off Runaround altogether.

Though they may at first seem confusing, the Runaround and Clipping options offer a lot of control and flexibility, so they're worth spending some time to learn.

QuarkXPress and Photoshop

In Adobe Photoshop, if you convert a path into a **clipping path** and save the file in the EPS or TIFF format, you'll be able to select and edit the clipping path in QuarkXPress.

A Photoshop **vector mask** will display properly in QuarkXPress, but to have QuarkXPress make an editable clipping path from it, you have to save the file as a TIFF in Photoshop and then, in QuarkXPress, choose Non-White Areas as the clipping Type.

1 *The* **Type** *options in the* **Clipping** *pane of the* **Modify** *dialog box*

2 *The* **Type** *options in the* **Runaround** *pane of the* **Modify** *dialog box*

Clipping Paths

Choose a clipping path Type.

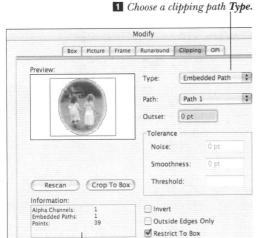

The Information area displays the number of alpha channels and embedded paths in the picture file, and the number of points that will be created for the QuarkXPress clipping path.

2 *Clipping Type:* **Item**—*the clipping path conforms to the box.*

3 *Clipping Type:* **Embedded Path**—*the clipping path conforms to a path that was saved with the image in its original application.*

To create a clipping path:

1. Import an EPS, TIFF, BMP, PCX, or PICT file into a rectangular picture box. For this first attempt, try using an image that has a white background.

2. To layer a picture, make sure its box has a background of None. (Select the box, click the Background Color button [ ] on the Colors palette, then click None.)

3. Choose Item > Clipping (Cmd-Option-T/Ctrl-Alt-T).

4. Note the green line in the preview window, which represents the clipping path, as you choose from the Type pop-up menu **1**:

   (Choose Item to turn off the clipping path function **2**. The picture will be cropped only by the picture box.)

   Choose Embedded Path to create a clipping path based on a clipping path that was saved with the picture in another application **3**. Choose Alpha Channel to create a clipping path based on the nonblack parts of an alpha channel that was saved with the picture in an image-editing program. *Note:* If the picture was saved with more than one alpha channel or path, choose the desired channel or path name from the Alpha or Path pop-up menu.

   Choose Non-White Areas to create a clipping path that follows the contours of the actual image and ignores nonwhite areas of the picture. The white areas have to be either close to white (e.g., very light gray) or absolute white for this to work.

   Choose Picture Bounds to have the path conform to the rectangular outer boundary of the picture (its bounding box) (**1**, next page). If Restrict To Box is unchecked, any areas of the picture that the picture box is cropping will become visible and may obscure items behind them.

(Continued on the following page)

Create Clipping Path

5. As you choose any of these *optional* settings, click Apply at any time to preview the current settings in the layout:

Click Crop To Box, if available, to have the clipping path stop at the edge of the box.

Click Rescan to restore the original path.

Check Invert to switch the cropped and visible areas **2**. This option isn't available when the Item or Picture Bounds Type is chosen.

Check Outside Edges Only for an Alpha Channel, Embedded Path, or Non-White Areas (not Item or Picture Bounds) clipping path if the picture contains a blank hole or holes where the background white shows through, and you don't want the clipping path to include them. With Outside Edges Only unchecked, an additional clipping path will be created for each hole **3**.

Check Restrict To Box to have only areas of the picture inside the picture box display and print (**1**–**2**, next page). Uncheck to let the entire picture display and print.

With any Type option except Item chosen, you can further expand or contract the clipping path to print more or less of the picture by entering a positive or negative value, respectively, in the Outset field. For Type: Picture Bounds, enter Top, Left, Bottom, and Right values. For Type: Embedded Path or Alpha Channel, the Outset value will expand or contract the entire clipping path relative to the original path or alpha channel. For the Non-White Areas type of clipping path, the Outset value will expand or contract the entire clipping path relative to the original nonwhite areas (**1**–**2**, page 214).

6. Choose Tolerance settings for an Alpha Channel or Non-White Areas type of clipping path:

1 *Clipping Type:* **Picture Bounds**—*the clipping path conforms to the outer perimeter of the image (its own bounding box).*

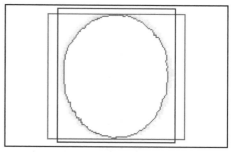

2 *Clipping Type:* **Non-White Areas** *with the* **Invert** *option on—only pixels in the outer fringe will print.*

3 *Clipping Type:* **Non-White Areas** *with* **Outside Edges Only** *off—the clipping path or paths surround any non-white areas in the image.*

Create Clipping Path

1 *Clipping Type:* **Picture Bounds** *with* **Restrict To Box** *on—only areas of the picture that are inside the picture box will print.*

2 *Clipping Type:* **Picture Bounds** *with* **Restrict To Box** *off—areas outside the picture box will print, even if they overlap the text.*

For an Alpha Channel clipping path, the Noise value (0–288 pt.) is the minimum size an area near the border of an alpha channel must be to be included in the clipping path (**3**–**4**, next page). Adjust the Noise value to exclude tiny, extraneous blobs in the background from the clipping path.

For an Alpha Channel or Non-White Areas clipping path, Smoothness (0–100) makes the path more or less smooth by adding or decreasing points (**5**–**6**, next page). The lower the Smoothness value, the more points the clipping path will contain; the higher the value, the fewer points the path will contain and the less precisely its shape will match that of the image. A low Smoothness could cause output problems, but the program can adjust this setting automatically during printing, if need be. You may need to play with this to achieve the optimal setting.

Threshold works with an Alpha Channel or Non-White Areas clipping path (**1**–**2**, page 215). It controls what percentages of gray on the alpha channel will be treated as white (and not mask the picture) and what percentages will be treated as black (and mask parts of the picture). At a Threshold setting of 10%, for example, gray values between 0% and 10% will be treated as white; gray values between 11% and 100% will be treated as black and will act as a mask. At a Threshold setting of 40%, more gray values will be treated as white, and less of the picture will be masked. For the Non-White Areas type of clipping path, the opposite is true: The Threshold is the percentage a color can be darker than white before it will be left outside the clipping path and thus won't print.

7. Click Apply, then click OK. If you'd like to reshape the clipping path, follow the instructions on page 217.

(Illustrations on the following two pages)

Create Clipping Path

1 *Clipping Type: **Non-White Areas, Outset -15**— the clipping path shrinks slightly inward.*

2 *Clipping Type: **Non-White Areas, Outset 15**— the clipping path expands slightly outward.*

3 *Clipping Type: **Non-White Areas** at the default **Noise** setting of **2 pt.**—the clipping path includes extraneous pixels outside the oval.*

4 *Clipping Type: **Non-White Areas, Noise 30 pt.** —the extraneous blobs aren't included in the clipping path.*

5 *Clipping Type: **Non-White Areas** at the default **Smoothness** setting of **2 pt.**—the clipping path has many points, and hugs the image precisely. (To display the points on the path, choose Item > Edit > Clipping Path.)*

6 *Clipping Type: **Non-White Areas, Smoothness 75 pt.**—here the clipping path is smoother, but it's less accurate.*

1 *Clipping Type: **Non-White Areas, Threshold 2*** *—the clipping path includes the gray background.*

2 *Clipping Type: **Non-White Areas, Threshold 10*** *—the clipping path ignores the gray background.*

setting the table 6.0!

With the Item tool and a table selected, you can choose Item > Runaround (Cmd-T/Ctrl-T) and enter Runaround values for the whole table. You still can't choose Clipping values for table cells— at least not yet (hint, hint).

Runaround and clipping: How they work together

If different Runaround and Clipping Types are chosen for the same picture, the text won't wrap at the edge of the picture. For example, if Picture Bounds is chosen as the Runaround Type, and Alpha Channel or Embedded Path is chosen as the Clipping Type (and assuming the picture's channel or path is smaller than the picture bounds), there will be a buffer area between the clipped picture and the text wrap.

If the Non-White Areas option is chosen for a picture as both the Runaround and the Clipping Type, text will wrap to the edge of a silhouetted image, plus or minus the current Outset width.

TIP To force text to flow into any holes in a picture where the white background shows through, uncheck the Outside Edges Only option in both the Clipping and Runaround panes.

TIP Don't wrap text *inside* a clipping path unless the text or picture's contrast has been carefully adjusted to ensure that the type is readable.

Runaround and Clipping

Here you'll be making text wrap around an image—not around an item's outer edge.

To wrap text around a picture:

1. Choose the Item or Content tool.

2. Select a picture box, and make sure it's in front of the text box. If it's not, Control-click/Right-click and choose Send & Bring > Bring To Front (or move it to a higher layer).

3. Choose Item > Runaround (Cmd-T/ Ctrl-T).

4. Choose Type: Non-White Areas.
   or
   Choose Type: Same As Clipping to have the text runaround conform to a QuarkXPress clipping path and utilize all the options that were chosen for that clipping path. To edit this type of wrap, edit the clipping path.

5. Enter an Outset value in points to adjust the space between the picture and the surrounding text. Try between 5 and 10 pt. Click Apply to preview.

6. Click Apply to preview again.

7. Click OK.

8. Press Cmd-Option-.(period)/Shift-Esc, if necessary, to force a screen redraw.

   Note: Normally, text will wrap around three sides of an obstruction (e.g., a picture or a box) if the obstruction is placed within a column. To wrap text completely around an item, select the text box in the back, go to Item > Modify > Text, check Run Text Around All Sides, then click OK **1**–**2**.

TIP *Beware!* If Picture Bounds is chosen as the Clipping Type and Non-White Areas is chosen as the Runaround Type, text will wrap to the edge of the image, but it may be obscured by the opaque background of the picture. That's because the edge of a picture box usually doesn't match up with the picture's bounding box.

Then, pray tell me what it is that you can infer from this hat?" He picked it up and gazed at it in the peculiar introspective fashion which was characteristic of him. "It is perhaps less suggestive than it might have been," he remarked, "and yet there are a few inferences which are very distinct, and a few others which represent at least a strong balability. That the man was highly intellectual is of course obvious upon the face of it, and also that he was fairly well-to-do within the last three years, although he has now fallen had foresight, but upon evil days. He has less now than ing to a moral ret- rogression, which, when taken with the decline of his fortunes, seems to indicate some evil influence, probably drink, at work upon him. This may account also for the obvious fact that his wife has ceased to love him…"   —*Sir Arthur Conan Doyle*

1 *You can make text run **completely** around a picture within the same column, but the text will be tiring to read, so don't use this option if you need to convey important information.*

Then, pray tell me what it is that you can infer from this hat?" He picked it up and gazed at it in the peculiar introspective fashion which was characteristic of him. "It is perhaps less suggestive than it might have been," he remarked, "and yet there are a few infer- ences which are very distinct, and a few others which represent at least a strong balance of probability. That the man was highly intellectual is of course obvious upon the face of it, and also that he was fairly well-to-do within the last three years, although he has now fallen upon evil days. He had fore- sight, but has less now than formerly, pointing to a moral retrogression, which, when taken with the decline of his for- tunes, seems to indicate some evil influ- ence, probably drink, at work upon him. This may account also for the obvious fact that his wife has ceased to love him…"

2 *To run text inside the holes of a picture, choose **Non-White Areas** for the runaround type and **uncheck Outside Edges Only**.*

1 *Option-click/Alt-click a line segment to add a point.*

*Reshape a clipping path to change which parts of a picture will **print**.*

2 *Option-click/Alt-click a point to delete it.*

*Hold down **Spacebar** to suspend redraw and rewrap as you reshape a runaround or clipping path.*

"Pooh!" cried Piglet. "Do you think it i
er Woozle?" "No," said Pooh, "because
different marks. It is either Two Woo
one, as it might be, W
Two, as it might be,
and one, if so it is,
Let us continue to
them." So they w
feeling just a little
now, in the case the th

*Reshape a runaround path to change how text **wraps** around a picture.*

3 *Dragging a segment*

"Pooh!" cried Piglet. "Do you think it i
er Woozle?" "No," said Pooh, "because i
different marks. It is either Two Woo
one, as it mi
Wizzle, or Tw
might be, Wizz
one, if so it is,
Let us continue to
them." So they went
ing just a little anxio

4 *The text rewraps.*

Note: QuarkXPress generates a clipping path based on the original, high-resolution picture file. When you manually edit a clipping path, however, if you work off a low-resolution screen preview, your edits won't be precise. To work off the high-resolution screen preview, choose Item > Preview Resolution > Full Resolution, and **6.0!** choose View > Show Full Res Previews (if this option is already chosen, the menu option will be Hide Full Res Previews).

To reshape a runaround or clipping path:

1. Choose the Item or Content tool.

2. Click a picture that has a clipping path or one of these Runaround types: Embedded Path, Alpha Channel, Non-White Areas, or Picture Bounds.

3. Choose Item > Edit > Runaround (Option-F4/Ctrl-F10).
   or
   Choose Item > Edit > Clipping Path (Option-Shift-F4/Ctrl-Shift-F10).

4. Use any of the techniques that you'd normally use to reshape a Bézier path (see pages 304–311) **1**–**4**. You can add or delete an anchor point; drag a point, segment, or control handle; or convert an anchor point from corner to curved (or vice versa).

   Beware! If you edit a clipping path and then reopen the Clipping pane, the clipping Type will be listed as User-Edited Path. If you choose a different Type at this point and click OK, you'll *lose* your custom path edits!

5. When you're done editing a runaround path, choose Item > Edit > Runaround again (Option-F4/Ctrl-F10). When you're done editing a clipping path, choose Item > Edit > Clipping Path again (Option-Shift-F4/Ctrl-Shift-F10).

   TIP To force the screen to redraw, press Cmd-Option-. (period)/Shift-Esc.

Reshape Runaround or Clipping Path

Wrapping text inside a hidden picture isn't something that you're going to do day in and day out, but it's a fun technique for special occasions.

To wrap text inside a hidden picture:

1. Choose the Item or Content tool, then click a silhouetted image on a solid white or off-white background **1**.

2. Make sure the picture box is in front of the text box. If necessary, Control-click/Right-click and choose Send & Bring > Bring To Front or move the picture box to a higher layer.

    Also make sure the picture box completely covers the text box; otherwise the text will be visible within the picture's clipping path and around the edge of the picture box.

3. Choose Item > Modify (Cmd-M/ Ctrl-M).

4. Click the Clipping tab, choose Type: Non-White Areas, and check Invert.

5. Click the Runaround tab, choose Type: Same As Clipping, then click OK.

    If necessary, press Cmd-Option-. (period)/Shift-Esc to force the screen to redraw **2**.

    Note: If the edge of the picture is showing (as in **2**), but you don't want it to print, click the picture, choose Item > Modify > Box, then check Suppress Output. It will still display onscreen, but it won't print.

TIP Choose a small point size and justified horizontal alignment for the type.

TIP To have the text wrap update as you move a picture, click Delayed Item Dragging: Live Refresh in QuarkXPress (Edit, in Windows) > Preferences > Application > Interactive.

1 *Click a picture that has a white background.*

brain *n.*

1 an organ of soft nervous tissue contained in the skull of vertebrates, functioning as the coordinating centre of sensation, and of intellectual and nervous activity. **2** (usu. in *pl.*; prec. by *the*) *colloq.* **a** the cleverest person in a group. **b** a person who originates a complex plan or idea. brain *n.* **1** an organ of soft nervous tissue contained in the skull of vertebrates, functioning as the coordinating centre of sensation, and of intellectual and nervous activity. **2** (usu. in *pl.*; prec. by *the*) col-

2 *The text is wrapping inside the clipping path instead of outside it.*

Lines 12

Need more than one of an item?

- Use the Duplicate shortcut (Cmd-D/Ctrl-D). Or if you want to control where the duplicates land, use Item > Step & Repeat.

- After you draw a line with a line tool, the tool automatically deselects. To keep a line tool selected so as to draw multiple lines, Option-click/Alt-click the tool on the Tools palette. When you're finished using it, choose a different tool.

1 *Choose the **Orthogonal Line** tool, then drag horizontally or vertically.*

2 *Choose the **Line** tool, then drag in any direction.*

Drawing lines

The line creation tools produce horizontal, vertical, and diagonal straight lines and arrows to which a variety of styles, endcaps, and colors can be applied. Using the Dashes & Stripes command, which is covered in this chapter, you can create custom line styles for use with the line tools, the Frame command, or the paragraph Rules command.

Note: To place rules under type, use the paragraph Rules feature (see pages 112–114). To anchor a line, see page 197. The Bézier Line, Freehand Line, Line Text-Path, and other Bézier tools are discussed in Chapter 18.

To draw a straight horizontal or vertical line:

1. Choose the Orthogonal Line tool.

2. Drag the crosshair icon horizontally or vertically **1**.

TIP To convert an orthogonal line into a Bézier line, select it, then choose the wiggly-line (last) icon from the Item > Shape submenu.

To draw a straight line at any angle:

1. Choose the Line tool.

2. Drag the crosshair icon in any direction **2**.

TIP Hold down Shift while drawing a line to constrain it to an increment of 45°.

TIP To choose preferences for a line tool, such as its default width, style, or color, double-click the tool to open the Tools Preferences dialog box, click Modify, then change any of the settings.

Modifying lines

To change the width of a line using the keyboard:

1. Choose the Item or Content tool.

2. Click a line (Bézier or other).

3. Press Cmd-Option-Shift->/Ctrl-Alt-Shift-> to widen the line, or press the < key to reduce the line width in 1-point increments. (Omit the Option/Alt key to change the line width to preset increments (Hairline, 1, 2, 4, 6, 8, or 12 pt).

   or

   Press Cmd-Shift-\/Ctrl-Shift-\. The Line Width field in Item > Modify > Line will highlight automatically. Enter the desired width (you don't have to type the "pt"), then click OK.

To restyle a line using the Measurements palette:

1. Choose the Item or Content tool.

2. Click a line (Bézier or other).

3. Do any of the following on the Measurements palette:

   Enter a Width value (.001–864 pt.) or choose a preset width from the pop-up menu **1**–**3**.

   Choose from the Style pop-up menu. (To create custom line styles, see pages 223–224.)

   Choose an arrowhead from the rightmost pop-up menu **4**.

TIP You can Control-click/Right-click a line and choose from the Line Style, Arrowheads, Color, or Shade submenu. These submenus are also found on the Style menu. Instructions for recoloring a line are on page 266.

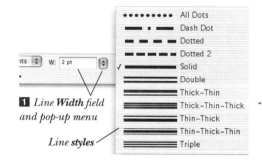

1 *Line **Width** field and pop-up menu*

*Line **styles***

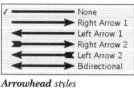

Arrowhead *styles*

2 *A line is selected.*

*Its **width** is increased.*

*A new **style** is applied.*

*An **arrowhead** is added.*

———————————————— Hairline

———————————————— .5 pt

———————————————— 1 pt

———————————————— 2 pt

———————————————— 4 pt

———————————————— 6 pt

3 *These are a few sample **line widths**. A Hairline prints as .125 pt. on a PostScript imagesetter.*

4 *A Bézier line with an arrow endcap and a gap color of 10% black*

Hidden force

You can use a non-printing line to create an off-beat text shape . Click a line, bring it to the front, choose Item > Modify, click the Line tab, check Suppress Output, click the Runaround tab, choose Type: Item, then specify an Outset value.

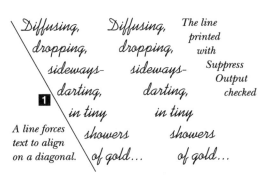

A line forces text to align on a diagonal.

The line printed with Suppress Output checked

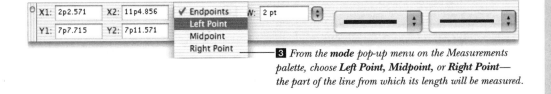

2 *Drag an endpoint to resize a line.*

To shorten or lengthen a line manually:

1. Choose the Item or Content tool.
2. Click a line.
3. Drag an endpoint to lengthen or shorten the line **2**. Option-Shift-drag/ Alt-Shift-drag to preserve the line's angle as you change its length.

To shorten or lengthen a line using the Measurements palette:

1. Choose the Item or Content tool.
2. Click a line.
3. From the mode pop-up menu on the Measurements palette **3**, choose which point you want the line to be measured from: Left Point (the beginning of the line), Midpoint, or Right Point.
4. In the Length (L) field on the Measurements palette, enter the desired length **4**.

3 *From the mode pop-up menu on the Measurements palette, choose Left Point, Midpoint, or Right Point— the part of the line from which its length will be measured.*

4 *The line Length field*

This icon represents the currently chosen mode: Left Point, Midpoint, or Right Point.

To move a line manually:

1. Choose the Item or Content tool.
2. Drag any part of a line other than an endpoint **5**.

5 *A line being moved*

To change the angle of a line:

1. Choose the Item or Content tool, then click a line.

2. To snap the line to an increment of 45° from the original angle, Shift-drag a handle 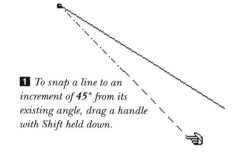 (this can't be done with an orthogonal line).
or
From the Measurements palette, choose Left Point, Midpoint, or Right Point (not Endpoints), then change the angle value **2**.
or
Choose the Rotate tool, ↻ press to establish an axis point, drag away from the line to create a lever, then drag clockwise or counterclockwise.

1 *To snap a line to an increment of **45°** from its existing angle, drag a handle with Shift held down.*

To reposition a line using the Measurements palette:

1. Choose the Item or Content tool, then click a line.

2. Choose, from the mode pop-up menu on the Measurements palette, the part of the line from which its position will be measured **3**–**4**.

3. Change the X and/or Y values. You can use math (add or subtract) in any field.

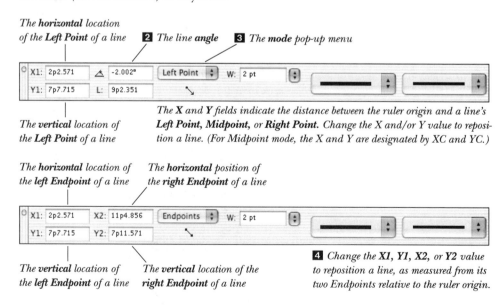

*The **horizontal** location of the **Left Point** of a line*   **2** *The line **angle***   **3** *The **mode** pop-up menu*

*The **vertical** location of the **Left Point** of a line*

*The **X** and **Y** fields indicate the distance between the ruler origin and a line's **Left Point, Midpoint,** or **Right Point.** Change the X and/or Y value to reposition a line. (For Midpoint mode, the X and Y are designated by XC and YC.)*

*The **horizontal** location of the **left Endpoint** of a line*   *The **horizontal** position of the **right Endpoint** of a line*

*The **vertical** location of the **left Endpoint** of a line*   *The **vertical** location of the **right Endpoint** of a line*

4 *Change the **X1, Y1, X2,** or **Y2** value to reposition a line, as measured from its two Endpoints relative to the ruler origin.*

How to apply dashes and stripes

Dash and stripe styles are available for all layouts in a project. This is how they're applied:

selected **box**   Frame dialog box

selected **line**   Style pop-up menu on Measurements palette; Style > Line Style; Item > Modify > Line

selected **text**   Style > Rules

*To narrow (or expand) the selection of dashes and stripes that display in the scroll window, choose a category from the **Show** pop-up menu.*

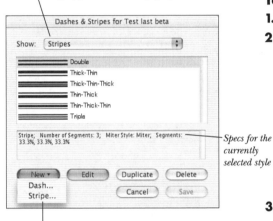

1 *To create a new style, choose **New: Dash** or **Stripe**.*

2 *Drag in the ruler to create a **new stripe** (or **dash**).*

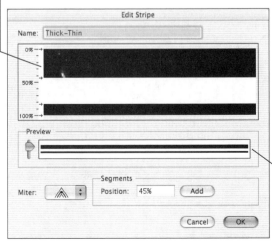

*The current stripe style **previews** here.*

Creating dashes and stripes

Using the Dashes & Stripes dialog box, you can create custom PostScript line styles for lines, frames, and paragraph rules. An edited dash or stripe style will update on all items to which it's already applied—in any and all layouts in the current project. **6.0!**

Note: To append a line style from one project to another, click Append in the Dashes & Stripes dialog box. Any dash or stripe style that's created when no projects are open will appear in future projects.

To create or edit dashes or stripes:

1. Choose Edit > Dashes & Stripes.

2. To create a new style, choose New: Dash or Stripe **1**, then type a name. (In Mac OS X, you can double-click the New pop-up menu to create a Dash style.)
   or
   To edit an existing style, double-click it. Or click its name, then click Edit.
   or
   To create a new style based on an existing one, click the style, click Duplicate, then change the name.

3. Note the Preview as you do any of the following:

   To add more dash or stripe segments, drag in the ruler, then drag again in another part of the ruler **2**. (Five is the maximum total number of dashes.)

   To move a dash or a stripe, drag inside it with the hand cursor.

   To shorten or lengthen a dash or widen or narrow a stripe, drag either of its arrows.

   To remove a dash, drag either of its arrows or the dash itself upward or downward off the ruler. To remove a stripe, drag either of its arrows or the stripe itself to the left or the right off the ruler.

   (Continued on the following page)

Create, Edit Dashes and Stripes

If you want to specify the distance between dashes, enter a number in the Repeats Every field **1**. The higher the Repeats Every value, the further apart the dashes will be. If you choose Times Width from the Repeats Every pop-up menu, dash segments will spread to fit the dimensions of the line or frame to which that style is applied. If you choose Points from the same pop-up menu, segments will maintain the same spacing no matter what.

Create a dash or stripe segment by entering the ruler % position where you want it to start in the Segment: Position field, then click Add.

4. Choose a Miter style for the corners of a Bézier frame or a multisegment line: Sharp, Rounded, or Beveled.

5. For dashes, you can choose a different Endcap style for the shape of the ends of the dash segments **2–4**. To enlarge the preview so you can see a closeup of how the endcap style looks, drag the Preview slider upward.

6. *Optional:* Check Stretch to Corners to have the dash or stripe design be stretched to fit symmetrically when chosen as a frame style for a box (**1–2**, next page).

7. Click OK.

8. Click Save.

TIP To remove a dash or stripe style, click on it, then click Delete. If the style you're deleting is currently applied to any items in your project, an alert dialog box will appear. Choose a replacement dash or stripe, then click OK.

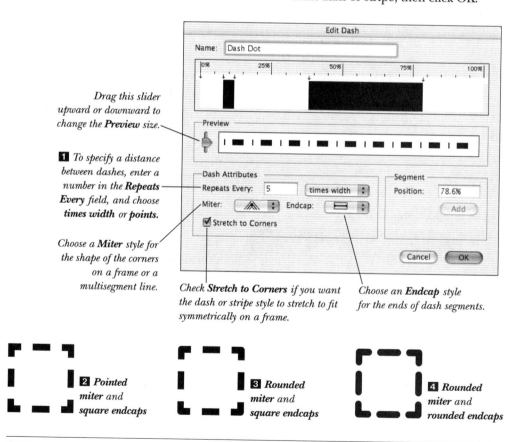

*Drag this slider upward or downward to change the **Preview** size.*

1 *To specify a distance between dashes, enter a number in the **Repeats Every** field, and choose **times width** or **points**.*

*Choose a **Miter** style for the shape of the corners on a frame or a multisegment line.*

*Check **Stretch to Corners** if you want the dash or stripe style to stretch to fit symmetrically on a frame.*

*Choose an **Endcap** style for the ends of dash segments.*

2 *Pointed miter and square endcaps*

3 *Rounded miter and square endcaps*

4 *Rounded miter and rounded endcaps*

Create, Edit Dashes and Stripes

1 *A custom dash style, with* **Stretch to Corners** *turned* **on**

2 *The same dash style with* **Stretch to Corners** *turned* **off**

To compare two dashes or stripes:

1. Choose Edit > Dashes & Stripes.

2. Cmd-click/Ctrl-click two dashes and/or stripe styles in the scroll window.

3. Option-click/Alt-click the Append button (it will turn into a Compare button). Differences between the two styles will be listed in boldface **3**.

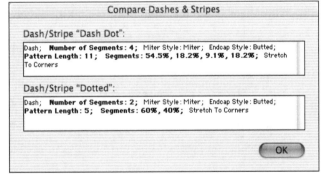

Compare Dashes & Stripes

Dash/Stripe "Dash Dot":

Dash; **Number of Segments: 4**; Miter Style: Miter; Endcap Style: Butted; **Pattern Length: 11**; Segments: 54.5%, 18.2%, 9.1%, 18.2%; Stretch To Corners

Dash/Stripe "Dotted":

Dash; **Number of Segments: 2**; Miter Style: Miter; Endcap Style: Butted; **Pattern Length: 5**; Segments: 60%, 40%; Stretch To Corners

OK

3 *Specifications for the Dash Dot style* **compared** *with specifications for the Dotted style.*

Compare Two Dashes or Stripes

Dashes and stripes are recolored on an object by object basis—not in the Edit Dash or Edit Stripe dialog box. In addition to recoloring dashes or stripes, if a style is applied as a frame or line, you can also recolor the gaps between them. Rules can also be recolored via a style sheet.

To recolor a dash or stripe:

1. Select the item that contains the dash or stripe you want to recolor.

2. For a frame, choose Item > Frame (Cmd-B/Ctrl-B); for a line, choose Item > Modify > Line; for a paragraph rule, go to Style > Rules (Cmd-Shift-N/ Ctrl-Shift-N).

3. In the Frame, Line, or Rules pane:

Choose a Color and Shade **2**–**5**. *and/or*

Choose a Gap: Color and Shade (this isn't available for a paragraph rule).

Dashes & stripes rule

Experiment and have fun with this feature! Once you have a dash or stripe you like, you can apply it quickly via a style sheet, as you would apply any other paragraph rule style **1**.

Subhead

1 *This is a custom* **stripe** *style applied as a paragraph* **Rule Above** *(Shade: 12% and Offset: -p.5)*

2 *This is a dashed frame with a 15% Black* **Gap** *color.*

3 *To polish it off, we added inner and outer frames in separate text boxes, both with a background color of None.*

Light Line color, dark Gap color

4

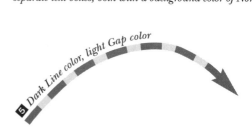

Dark Line color, light Gap color

5

Style Sheets **13**

*A **headline** style*

THE BILL OF RIGHTS

AMENDMENT I
Religious establishment prohibited. Freedom of speech, of the press, and right to petition

Congress shall make no law respecting an establishment of religion, or prohibiting the free exercise thereof; or abridging the freedom of speech, or of the press; or the right of the people peaceably to assemble, and to petition the Government for a redress of grievances.

AMENDMENT II
Right to keep and bear arms

A well-regulated militia being necessary to the security of a free State, the right of the people to keep and bear arms, shall not be infringed.

AMENDMENT III
Conditions for quarters for soldiers

No soldier shall, in time of peace be quartered in any house, without the consent of the owner, nor in time of war, but in a manner to be prescribed by law.

AMENDMENT IV
Right of search and seizure regulated

The right of the people to be secure in their persons, houses, papers, and effects, against unreasonable searches and seizures, shall not be violated, and no warrants shall issue, but upon probable cause, supported by oath or affirmation, and particularly describing the place to be searched, and the persons or things to be seized.

Creating and applying style sheets

A style sheet is a set of paragraph or character formatting specifications. Whatever text is highlighted when you click a style sheet on the Style Sheets palette (or execute its equivalent shortcut) is formatted instantly. But style sheets aren't used just for the initial formatting; they're also used for editing. If you modify a style sheet, all the text with which it is associated will update instantly. Each project can contain up to 1,000 style sheets, and they are 6.0! available to all layouts within the project.

Using style sheets will relieve you from zillions of hours of tedious styling and restyling, freeing you to concentrate on more exciting tasks. And here's another benefit: When you use style sheets, you can rest assured that your typography is consistent, whether you're working on a small brochure or a huge, multifile book. Every single character in this book was styled via a style sheet. Enough said?

— *A **body text** style*

— *A **subhead** style*
— *A **small subhead** style*

*Prevent carpal tunnel syndrome: Use style sheets to apply repetitive type specifications quickly. **Paragraph** style sheets are used in this illustration. A **character** style sheet is illustrated on the next page. In some other applications, style sheets are simply called "styles."*

Every new paragraph style sheet automatically has a default character style sheet associated with it that defines its character attributes. You can also create independent character style sheets 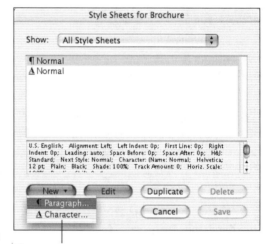. If you're unsure of the difference between paragraph and character style sheets, see "What's the difference?" on the next page and study the illustrations on page 234.

To create a style sheet the easy way:

1. For a paragraph style sheet, select either the first word of (or an entire) paragraph and apply any character or paragraph attributes, such as font, point size, type style, color, horizontal scaling, tracking, indents, leading, space after, H&J, horizontal alignment, tabs, rules, etc. that you want to be part of the style sheet. We will refer to this as the "sample" paragraph.
   or
   For a character style sheet, select and style a word or a string of words.

2. With the paragraph or text string still highlighted, choose Edit > Style Sheets (Shift-F11), then choose New: Paragraph or Character . In Mac OS X, you can double-click the New button to create a paragraph style.
   or
   Control-click/Right-click the paragraph (or character) style sheet area of the Style Sheets palette and choose New from the context menu **3**.

3. Type a descriptive Name for the new style sheet (**1**, next page).

4. *Optional:* Press Tab to move the cursor to the Keyboard Equivalent field. Then press a function key, or press a numeric keypad key with or without a modifier (Cmd, Option, Shift, or Control in Mac OS X; Ctrl or Ctrl+Alt in Windows).

5. *Optional:* To apply successive paragraph style sheets automatically as you input text, you can chain one style sheet to another. To do this, choose from the

"It is a very odd thing that Ribby's pie was **not** in the oven when I put mine in! And I can't find it anywhere; I have looked all over the house. I put **my** pie into a nice hot oven at the top. I could not turn any of the other handles; I think that they are all shams," said Duchess, "but I wish I could have removed the pie made of mouse! I cannot think what she has done with it? I heard Ribby coming and I had to run out by the back door!" *Beatrix Potter*

1 *A **character** style sheet was used to style the words "not" and "my."*

2 *Choose **New: Paragraph** or **Character**.*

3 *Control-click/Right-click the paragraph or character area of the Style Sheets palette, then choose **New** from the context menu.*

What's the difference?

A **character** style sheet contains only character attributes: font, type style, point size, color, shade horizontal/vertical scale, tracking, and baseline shift. A character style sheet can be applied to one or more characters. In this book, the step numbers (**2.**, **3.**), figure numbers (**4**, **5**), **boldface** words, and the word **TIP** were styled using character style sheets.

A **paragraph** style sheet, on the other hand, contains paragraph formats, tabs, and rules. It derives its character attributes from the character style sheet that's currently associated with it. A paragraph style sheet can be applied to, and affects, only entire paragraphs.

Next Style pop-up menu. When you press Return/Enter as you input text in your layout, the Next Style sheet will apply automatically to the next paragraph you type. The Next Style has no effect on existing paragraphs.

6. Click OK and then, if you're back in the Style Sheets dialog box, click Save to exit. Apply the new style sheet to the sample paragraph, if you like, and to any other paragraphs (see the next page). Two other methods for creating a style sheet are described on page 231.

1 *Enter a **name** for the style sheet. Use a descriptive name, such as "Body Text," or "Headline." Add a number to the name, if you like, as in "01Header" and "02Subhead."*

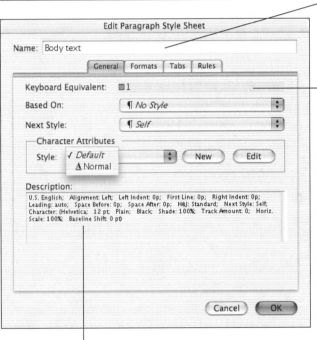

*Enter a **keyboard equivalent** for the style sheet. Note: Every function (F) key has a default, preassigned command (they're listed in Appendix B). If you choose an F key as a style sheet keyboard equivalent, the style sheet shortcut will override the preassigned command. To avoid this conflict altogether, use a number pad key, with or without a modifier key (e.g., Cmd/Ctrl, Option/Alt, or Shift).*

*The typographic and paragraph attributes for the currently highlighted style sheet are listed in the **Description** area.*

Create Style Sheet

*C*haracter style sheets can be used to style initial caps.

Extras —Or run-in subheads.

∿ Oregano
∿ Cumin
∿ Coriander
∿ Sage
∿ Thyme

*Typesetting bulleted lists or numbered paragraphs is a snap: Use a **paragraph** style sheet for the body text and then a **character** style sheet for the bullet or number.*

To apply a style sheet:

1. Display the Style Sheets palette (Window > Show Style Sheets or F11).

2. Choose the Content tool.

3. To apply a paragraph style sheet, click in a paragraph or drag through a series of paragraphs.

or

To apply a character style sheet, highlight the text you want to reformat.

4. Click a paragraph style sheet in the top portion of the Style Sheets palette **1**. The paragraph(s) will reformat instantly.

or

Click a character style sheet in the bottom portion of the Style Sheets palette. The highlighted text will reformat instantly.

or

Press the keyboard equivalent for the style sheet you want to apply, if one was assigned to it. The equivalents are listed on the Style Sheets palette.

or

Control-click/Right-click the text in your layout and choose a style sheet from the Paragraph Style Sheet or Character Style Sheet submenu **2**.

TIP A style sheet can be applied to one or more selected text cells in a table (see page 143).

Local formatting

Text formatted using a style sheet can be locally formatted at any time using the keyboard, the Measurements palette, or the Style menu. If you insert the cursor in or highlight locally styled text, a plus sign will appear on the Style Sheets palette next to the name of the style sheet that's associated with that paragraph.

You'll also see a plus sign next to a paragraph style sheet name if the text your cursor is in has both a paragraph style sheet and a character style sheet applied to it.

Local stripping

To strip a paragraph style sheet *and* all local formatting from a paragraph (including any character style sheets) and apply a new paragraph style sheet or reapply the same style sheet, click in the paragraph and then, on the Style Sheets palette, Option-click/Alt-click the style sheet you want to apply. (This is the equivalent of clicking No Style, then clicking a new style sheet.) This works for character style sheets, too (highlight only the characters you want to change).

*A plus sign preceding a style sheet name means that the currently highlighted characters contain **local formatting**.*

*Click **No Style** to disassociate a style sheet from your text.*

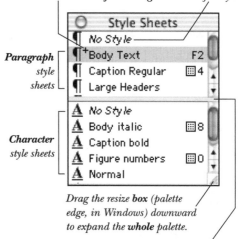

*Drag the resize **box** (palette edge, in Windows) downward to expand the **whole** palette.*

*Drag the **palette divider** downward to expand the **paragraph** style sheets area of the palette (expand the whole palette first).*

1 *To **apply** a style sheet, click its name on the Style Sheets palette or use the keyboard shortcut, if any, that was assigned to it. The shortcuts are listed on the palette.*

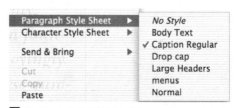

2 *Or Control-click/Right-click your text and choose a style sheet from the context menu.*

Disappearing text?

If you press a number key that was not assigned to a style sheet, any currently selected text will be *replaced* by that number character! (Use the Undo command to recover the text.) To avoid this, keep track of which numbers have assigned shortcuts and which don't.

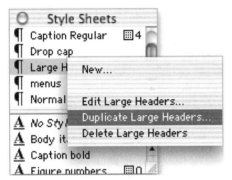

1 *Control-click/Right-click a style sheet name, choose **Duplicate** [style sheet name] from the context menu, then click OK.*

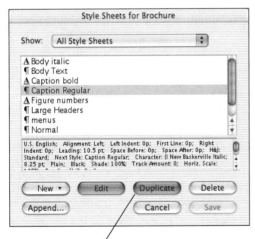

2 *Or in the Style Sheets dialog box, click a style sheet name, then click **Duplicate**. The word "copy" will automatically be added to the style sheet name. You can change the name, if you like.*

A fast way to create a variation on an existing style sheet is to duplicate it, and then edit the duplicate. Unlike a Based On style sheet (which is described on page 236), there is no linkage between a duplicate style sheet and the original from which it's generated.

To create a style sheet by duplication:

1. On the Style Sheets palette, Control-click/Right-click the style sheet you want to duplicate, then choose Duplicate [style sheet name] from the context menu **1**.
   or
   Choose Edit > Style Sheets (Shift-F11), click a style sheet, then click Duplicate **2**.

2. The Edit Paragraph (or Character) Style Sheet dialog box will open, and you'll see that the word "copy" was added to the style Name. Edit the name, if desired.

3. Edit the new style sheet (see the next page).

4. Click OK, then click Save, if necessary.

TIP Remember, style sheets are available to all the layouts in a project.

There's nothing to stop you from creating a new style sheet from scratch without clicking in a sample paragraph—it just takes longer.

To create a style sheet from scratch:

1. Choose Edit > Style Sheets.

2. Choose New: Character or Paragraph.

3. Enter a name for the new style sheet.

4. Follow steps 2–3 on the next page to assign character and paragraph attributes to the style sheet.

Edit Style Sheet

To edit a style sheet:

1. Open the Style Sheets palette, click in any text box to activate the palette, Cmd-click/Ctrl-click the style sheet you want to edit, then click Edit.

or

Choose Edit > Style Sheets (Shift-F11), click the style sheet you want to edit, then click Edit **1**. To narrow (or expand) the selection of style sheets on the list, choose a category from the Show pop-up menu.

or

Control-click/Right-click a paragraph style sheet on the Style Sheets palette and choose Edit [style sheet name] to go directly to the General pane of the Edit Style Sheet dialog box. Or do the same for a character style sheet to go directly to Edit Character Style Sheet dialog box **2**.

2. For a paragraph style sheet, use the General pane of the Edit Paragraph Style Sheet dialog box to rename the style sheet; to assign or change its keyboard equivalent or embedded character style sheet; or to assign a Next Style to it. To modify the style sheet's character attributes (e.g., the font or color), click Edit; to modify its formats, click the Formats tab (**1**, next page); to add, delete, or modify tabs, click Tabs; or to add, delete, or edit a rule, click Rules.

or

For a character style sheet, modify character attributes in the Edit Character Style Sheet dialog box (**2**, next page).

3. Click OK to exit the Formats, Rules, or Tabs pane (click OK twice if you're in the Character Attributes dialog box), then click Save, if necessary. Text that the style sheet was previously applied to in any layouts within the project will reformat instantly!

Hate digging through boxes?

To revise style sheets quickly using local formatting and a keystroke, try using the inexpensive **Redefine Style Sheets** XTension from XPedient Corporation.

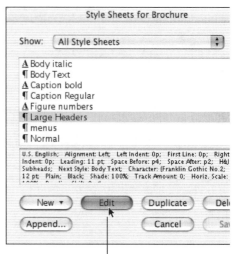

1 *To get to the Edit Paragraph or Character Style Sheet dialog box, click a style sheet name, then click **Edit**, or just double-click a style sheet name.*

2 *Control-click/Right-click a paragraph style sheet and choose **Edit** [style sheet name] to go straight to the General pane of the Edit Paragraph Style Sheet dialog box. Or do the same for a character style sheet to go straight to the Edit Character Style Sheet dialog box. You can edit only one style sheet at a time using this method, but it's speedy.*

Edit Paragraph Style Sheet

Name: Large Headers

General | **Formats** | Tabs | Rules

Left Indent: 1p3

First Line: −1p3

Right Indent: 0p

☐ Drop Caps

Character Count: 1

Line Count: 3

1 *For a **paragraph** style sheet, click the General, Formats, Tabs, or Rules tab to open that pane. Click Edit in the General pane to change character attributes.*

Edit Character Style Sheet

Name: Figure numbers

Keyboard Equivalent: ▦0

Based On: ⚠ *No Style*

Font: BundesbahnPi 1

Size: 9.5 pt

Color: ■ Black

Shade: 100%

Scale: Horizontal 100%

Track Amount: 8

Baseline Shift: 0 pt

Type Style

☑ Plain   ☐ Shadow

☐ Bold   ☐ All Caps

☐ Italic   ☐ Small Caps

☐ Underline   ☐ Superscript

☐ Word U-line   ☐ Subscript

☐ Strike Thru   ☐ Superior

☐ Outline

Cancel   OK

2 *For a **character** style sheet, change the Name, Keyboard Equivalent, Based On, Type Style, Font, Size, Color, Shade, Scale, Track Amount, or Baseline Shift attributes in the Edit Character Style Sheet dialog box.*

Edit Style Sheet

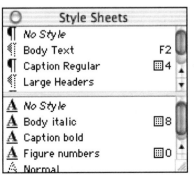

Style Sheets

¶ *No Style*

¶ Body Text   F2

¶ Caption Regular   ▦4

¶ Large Headers

A *No Style*

A Body italic   ▦8

A Caption bold

A Figure numbers   ▦0

A Normal

TIP *If the currently highlighted text has more than one style sheet applied to it, the ¶ or A symbol next to those style sheets will be dimmed (¶ A).*

Applying style sheets by example

Chapter xiv

Household economy

Clean paper walls = The very best method is to sweep off lightly all the dust, then rub the paper with stale bread—cut the crust off very thick, and wipe straight down from the top, then begin at the top again, and so on.

Wash carpets = The oftener these are taken up and shaken, the longer they will wear, as the dust and dirt underneath grind them out. Sweep carpets with a stiff hair brush, instead of an old corn broom, if you wish them to wear long or look well.

Black a brick hearth = Mix some black lead with soft soap and a little water, and boil it—then lay it on with a brush. Or mix the lead with water only.

SARA JOSEPHA HALE, FROM EARLY AMERICAN COOKERY

2 *A different paragraph style sheet is applied to the chapter number.*

3 *And yet another paragraph style sheet is assigned to the chapter name.*

1 *A **paragraph body text** style sheet is applied first to **all** the body text.*

Chapter xiv

Household economy

CLEAN PAPER WALLS ❦ The very best method is to sweep off lightly all the dust, then rub the paper with stale bread—cut the crust off very thick, and wipe straight down from the top, then begin at the top again, and so on.

WASH CARPETS ❦ the oftener these are taken up and shaken, the longer they will wear, as the dust and dirt underneath grind them out. Sweep carpets with a stiff hair brush, instead of an old corn broom, if you wish them to wear long or look well.

BLACK A BRICK HEARTH ❦ Mix some black lead with soft soap and a little water, and boil it—then lay it on with a brush. Or mix the lead with water only.

4 *A **character** style sheet is applied to each run-in **subhead**.*

5 *The Find/Change command is used to apply a character style sheet (ornament font) to every "=" character.*

Chapter xiv

Household economy

I CLEAN PAPER WALLS ❦ The very best method is to sweep off lightly all the dust, then rub the paper with stale bread—cut the crust off very thick, and wipe straight down from the top, then begin at the top again, and so on.

2 WASH CARPETS ❦ The oftener these are taken up and shaken, the longer they will wear, as the dust and dirt underneath grind them out. Sweep carpets with a stiff hair brush, instead of an old corn broom, if you wish them to wear long.

3 BLACK A BRICK HEARTH ❦ Mix some black lead with soft soap and a little water, and boil it—then lay it on with a brush. Or mix the lead with water only.

6 *A **drop cap** is added to the paragraph style sheet. Then, using a character style sheet, the drop caps are colored 30% gray and changed to the Adobe Garamond Expert font.*

Chapter xiv

Household economy

I CLEAN PAPER WALLS ❦ The very best method is to sweep off lightly all the dust, then rub the paper with stale bread— cut the crust off very thick, and wipe straight down from the top, then begin at the top again, and so on.

2 WASH CARPETS ❦ The oftener these are taken up and shaken, the longer they will wear, as the dust and dirt underneath grind them out. Sweep carpets with a stiff hair brush, instead of an old corn broom, if you wish them to wear long.

3 BLACK A BRICK HEARTH ❦ Mix some black lead with soft soap and a little water, and boil it—then lay it on with a brush. Or mix the lead with water only.

7 *Finally, the font in the run-in subhead character style sheet is changed to Bodoni Poster and the font in the body text paragraph style sheet is changed to Gill Sans. Now that style sheets have been assigned to all the text, making changes will be a snap!*

Removing character styling

Let's say you've applied a "Bold" character style sheet to a few phrases in a paragraph, and maybe you've also made some local formatting changes. You then decide you want to remove the character styling from one part of the paragraph. If you Option-click/Alt-click a paragraph style sheet (e.g., "Body Text"), all your other local formatting changes will be lost.

A better option is to create a Body Text character style sheet with the same type specs as the Body Text style and embed it into the Body Text paragraph style sheet. To remove the Bold character styling, select the Bold styled text, then apply the Body Text character style sheet. Local formatting will be removed from just the selected text.

A default character style sheet is automatically embedded into every paragraph style sheet. In fact, a paragraph style sheet's character attributes are derived from a character style sheet. You can change the individual character attributes of the default character style sheet for its associated paragraph style sheet (choose a different font or point size, for example).

If you want to change multiple character attributes for a paragraph style sheet all at once, you can embed a different or new character style sheet into it. The same character style sheet can be embedded into multiple paragraph style sheets.

This means, however, that if you change the specifications for a character style sheet, the character attributes for any paragraph style sheets into which it is embedded will update accordingly. And similarly, if you edit the character attributes in a paragraph style sheet, the character style sheet that's embedded into it will also update accordingly. If this seems like too much to keep track of, ignore this page and leave Default as the choice on the Character Attributes: Style pop-up menu!

To embed a character style sheet into a paragraph style sheet:

1. Choose Edit > Style Sheets (Shift-F11).

2. Click the paragraph style sheet that you want to embed the character style sheet into.

3. Click Edit.

4. From the Style pop-up menu in the Character Attributes area, choose an existing character style sheet **1**.
   or
   Click New **2**, type a name for a new character style sheet, choose character attributes, then click OK.

5. Click OK to exit the Edit Paragraph Style Sheet dialog box.

6. Click Save.

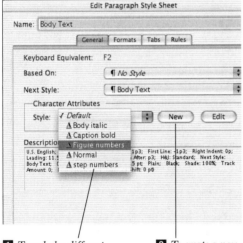

1 *To embed a different character style sheet into a paragraph style sheet, choose from the **Style** pop-up menu.*

2 *To create a new character style sheet, click **New**.*

One degree of separation: Based On

When one style sheet is based on another style sheet, the two remain associated. The Formats, Tabs, Rules, and Character Attributes: Style options from one style sheet (which we'll call the "child") are derived from a second style sheet (the "parent"). If the parent style sheet is modified, any child style sheets that are based on it will also change—with the exception of any specifications that are unique to the child style sheet. This is different from duplicating or embedding, which we discussed earlier.

If you'd like to try this option, choose a style sheet in Edit > Style Sheets, click Edit, then in the Edit [Paragraph or Character] Style Sheet dialog box, choose a parent style sheet from the Based On pop-up menu. For example, you could create a style sheet called Drop Cap that's based on a Body Text style sheet, and then, in the Drop Cap style sheet, turn on the automatic Drop Cap option in the Formats pane **1**. If you then change the Body Text style sheet (change the font, size, etc.), those changes will occur in the Drop Cap style sheet as well.

Using Find/Change to apply or change style sheets

To apply a style sheet to text using Edit > Find/Change (Cmd-F/Ctrl-F), uncheck Ignore Attributes on the Find/Change palette, enter a text string and/or choose character attributes on the Find What side of the palette, choose from the Style Sheet pop-up menu on the Change To side of the palette, then click the appropriate buttons at the bottom of the palette (see pages 290–294).

To use Find/Change to replace one style sheet with another on a case-by-case basis, choose both a Find What style sheet and a Change To style sheet. (If you were to delete and replace a style sheet in the Style Sheets dialog box instead, all occurrences of the style sheet would change.)

Parents and kids

- If you edit the Character Attributes Style: **Default** in the child style sheet, the parent (Based On) style sheet won't change. If you edit any nondefault, **embedded** character style that's present in both the parent and child style sheets (via Character Attributes: Edit), that change will affect both the parent and the child style sheets—and vice versa. In either place, what you're actually doing is editing the character style sheet.

- Let's say you've made some character attribute changes to a child style sheet and then you decide you want to reassociate it with the parent (Based On) style sheet. For the child, choose Based On: **No Style,** and then choose Based On: [the character style sheet used by the parent]. The parent and child style sheets will now have the same character attributes.

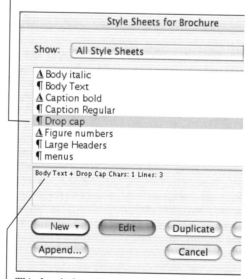

*1 Choose a "parent" style sheet from the **Based On** pop-up menu.*

*This **description** tells us that our Drop Cap style sheet consists of the Body Text style sheet plus the Drop Cap option.*

styling the master

A style sheet can be applied to any text box on a **master** page. You can even apply a style sheet to the automatic text box, though you can't enter text into it. The style sheet will then apply automatically to any text that's subsequently typed into that box on any associated layout page, but not to text that's imported using the Get Text command.

```
Style Name: Body Text          Style Name: Subhead
Font: New Baskerville          Font: FranklinGothic No.2
Size: 9.5 pt                   Size: 9.5 pt
Text Style: Plain              Text Style: Plain
Color: Black                   Color: Black
Shade: 100%                    Shade: 100%
Track Amount: 0p               Track Amount: 0p
Horiz Scale: 100%              Horiz Scale: 100%
Alignment: Left                Alignment: Left
Left Indent: 1p3               Left Indent: 0p
First Line Indent: -1p3        First Line Indent: 0p
Right Indent: 0p               Right Indent: 0p
Leading: p11.5                 Leading: p10.5
Space Before: 0p               Space Before: p4
Space After: p3                Space After: p2
Rule Above: None               Rule Above: None
Rule Below: None               Rule Below: None
Tabs: None                     Tabs: None

Style Name: Caption            Style Name: Sidebar
Regular                        body
Font: ITC Officina Serif       Font: GillSans
Bookitalic                     Size: 8.5 pt
Size: 8 pt                     Text Style: Plain
Text Style: Plain              Color: Black
Color: Black                   Shade: 100%
Shade: 100%                    Track Amount: 0p
Track Amount: 0p               Horiz Scale: 105%
Horiz Scale: 110%              Alignment: Left
Alignment: Left                Left Indent: 0p
Left Indent: 0p                First Line Indent: 0p
First Line Indent: 0p          Right Indent: 0p
Right Indent: 0p               Leading: p11
Leading: p10.5                 Space Before: 0p
Space Before: 0p               Space After: p3
Space After: 0p                Rule Above: None
Rule Above: None               Rule Below: None
Rule Below: None               Tabs: None
Tabs: None
```

1 *This list of style sheet specifications was generated by a third-party XTension.*

What's Normal?

The Normal paragraph and character style sheets are the default style sheets for all newly created text boxes. If the Normal style sheet is modified with a project open, text with which the Normal style sheet is associated will update just in that project.

If the Normal paragraph or character style sheet is modified when no projects are open, the modified style sheet will become the default for future projects. Similarly, any new style sheet that's created when no projects are open will appear automatically on the Style Sheets palette of future projects.

Managing style sheets

Appending style sheets

To append style sheets from one project to another, follow the instructions on pages 50–52. Or to append a style sheet the quick-and-dirty way, drag or copy and paste a text box that contains text to which the desired style sheet has been applied from a library or from another project into the current project—the applied style sheet will copy along with the item (as long as its name doesn't match a style sheet already present in the target project. We did say quick and dirty, didn't we?).

TIP There are a number of XTensions that will generate printed reports of the style sheet specifications used in a project **1**, as well as other data such as fonts, colors, H&Js, print styles, preferences, and picture files. Take a look at OfficialReport XT or Printools XT from Badia Software, or BureauManager from CompuSense Ltd.

If you delete a style sheet that's currently being used in your project, a dialog box opens automatically that you can use to choose a replacement style sheet for the deleted one. If you don't choose a replacement style sheet, the No Style (no style sheet) option will be applied by default.

To delete a style sheet:

1. On the Style Sheets palette, Control-click/Right-click the style sheet you want to delete and choose Delete [style sheet name] from the context menu **1**.

2. If the style sheet you're deleting is not currently being used in your project, click OK **2**.

   If the style sheet is currently being used in your project, a prompt will appear. From the "Replace with" pop-up menu, choose a replacement style sheet or choose No Style, then click OK **3**.

   Note: If you choose a replacement style sheet, any local formatting in the text will be preserved. If you choose No Style and then apply a new style sheet, on the other hand, all local formatting will be removed.

   6.0! You can undo the deletion of a style sheet.

TIP The Normal style sheet can be edited, but it can't be deleted.

TIP The method described above is the fastest one for deleting one, or even a few, style sheets. If you have to delete a whole slew of them, though, a faster method is to choose Edit > Style Sheets (Shift-F11), Cmd-click/Ctrl-click (or Shift-drag through) the style sheets you want to delete, then click Delete. Respond to any prompts that appear (as in step 2, above), then click Save.

1 *Control-click/Right-click a style sheet and choose* **Delete** *[style sheet name] from the context menu.*

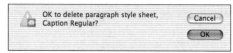

2 *If this prompt appears, click OK.*

3 *If this prompt appears, from the* **Replace with** *pop-up menu, choose a replacement style sheet or choose No Style.*

To delete all unused style sheets:

1. Choose Edit > Style Sheets (Shift-F11).

2. Choose Show: Style Sheets Not Used 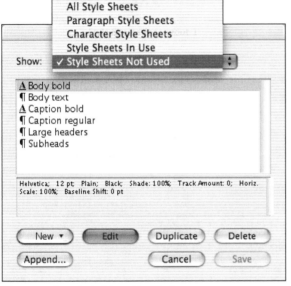.

3. Shift-drag upward or downward through the style sheet list to highlight all or some of the names.
or
Click a style sheet, then Shift-click the last style sheet in a series.

4. *Optional:* Cmd-click/Ctrl-click any style sheets that you don't want to delete.

5. Click Delete.

6. Click Save.

All Style Sheets
Paragraph Style Sheets
Character Style Sheets
Style Sheets In Use
Show: ✓ Style Sheets Not Used

A Body bold
¶ Body text
A Caption bold
¶ Caption regular
¶ Large headers
¶ Subheads

Helvetica; 12 pt; Plain; Black; Shade: 100%; Track Amount: 0; Horiz.
Scale: 100%; Baseline Shift: 0 pt

New ▾   Edit   Duplicate   Delete
Append...   Cancel   Save

1 *Choose* **Show: Style Sheets Not Used.**

To compare two style sheets:

1. Choose Edit > Style Sheets (Shift-F11).

2. Cmd-click/Ctrl-click the two paragraph style sheets or two character style sheets that you want to compare 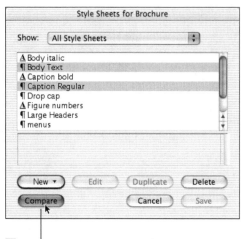. You can't compare a paragraph style sheet with a character style sheet—they're like apples and oranges...

3. Option-click/Alt-click the Append button—it will turn into a Compare button. The Compare [Paragraph or Character] Style Sheets dialog box will open 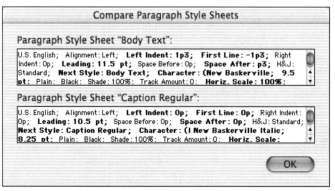. Any specifications that differ between the two style sheets will be listed in boldface.

4. Click OK when you're finished, then click Cancel.

TIP You can't compare style sheets from different projects using this method. You could append style sheets from one file to another, though, and then compare them once they're both in the same file.

1 *In the Style Sheets dialog box, Cmd-click/Ctrl-click two style sheets, then Option-click/Alt-click Append (it will turn into a* **Compare** *button).*

2 *Differences between the two style sheets are listed in* **boldface**.

Compare Two Style Sheets (side margin)

Master Pages

Master pages and layers

Items placed on a **master** page appear on the default layer for that layout and can't be moved to a different layer.

On **layout** pages, items that originate from the master page will initially reside on the default layer for that layout, but they can be moved to a different layer. If do you move any such item to a different layer, beware: The item will cease to be associated with the master page (you'll get an alert dialog box, so you can back out of the deal).

Using master pages

You can use the master pages in each layout as a blueprint for building your layout pages. For starters, they automatically contain a layout's margin and column guides. Then there are the items that you add to a master page yourself, such as headers, footers, picture boxes, logos, lines, and the all-important automatic page numbering command. Any item that you don't want to bother having to reconstruct over and over again on your layout pages can originate from a master page; it will appear automatically on every layout page that master page is applied to.

An item that's modified on a master page will also update on any layout pages that the master is currently applied to. Items that originate from a master page can be edited on any layout page, though, without affecting the master. Each new layout automatically contains its own Master A page, and you can add as many more as you need.

About Master Pages

Header and paragraph rule in a separate text box

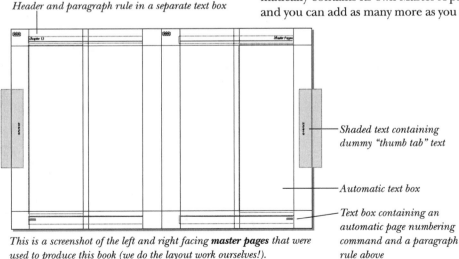

Shaded text containing dummy "thumb tab" text

Automatic text box

Text box containing an automatic page numbering command and a paragraph rule above

*This is a screenshot of the left and right facing **master pages** that were used to produce this book (we do the layout work ourselves!).*

Before you can learn how to use master pages, you need to learn how to navigate back and forth between master pages and layout pages. Master pages are created, modified, and applied using the Page Layout palette. Choose Window > Show Page Layout (F10/F4) to open it.

To switch between master page and layout page display:

On the Page Layout palette, double-click a master page icon or layout page icon, or click once on the page number below a layout page icon. The number of the currently displayed page will switch to outline/bold style **1**–**2**.

or

From the Go-to-page pop-up menu at the bottom of the project window, choose a layout or master page icon **3**.

or

From the Page > Display submenu, choose Layout or a master page name. If you choose Layout when a master page is displayed, the last displayed layout page will redisplay.

or

To view the master page that's applied to the currently displayed layout page, press Shift-F10/Shift-F4. To go back to the layout page, use the same shortcut.

Where are you?

The easiest way to tell whether you're on a layout page or a master page is to glance at the lower left corner of the project window. If you're on a layout page, the readout will say **Page: [such-and-such]**. If a master page is displayed, it will say **A-Master A**—or whatever the name of the master page is.

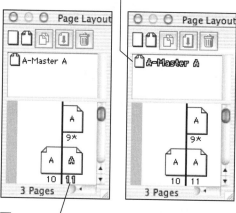

2 *Now a master page is displayed, so its name is in outline/bold style.*

1 *The number of the currently displayed layout page is in outline/bold style.*

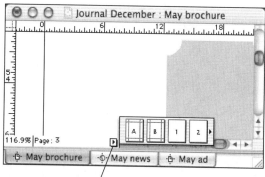

3 *You can use the Go-to-page pop-up menu to display any layout page or master page.*

Blank single-sided page icon

Blank facing-pages icon

Master page icon

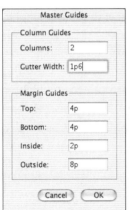

1 *The Page Layout palette for a **facing-pages** layout*

2 *The Page Layout palette for a **single-sided** layout*

3 *Change the non-printing margin guides and/or column guides in the **Master Guides** dialog box.*

4 *A **one-column** master...*

5 *...is changed to a **two-column** master.*

Single-sided vs. facing pages

If you check Facing Pages in the New Project or New Layout dialog box, you can specify Inside and Outside margins instead of Left and Right margins. In this type of layout, the first page is positioned by itself, and any subsequent pages are arranged in pairs along a central spine **1** (unless you've applied an even starting page number via the Section command). Facing master page and layout page icons on the Page Layout palette have a turned-down (dog-eared) corner. This format is used for books and magazines.

If Facing Pages is unchecked in the New Project or New Layout dialog box, pages will be stacked vertically (not in pairs) **2**. Single-sided master and layout page icons have square (not dog-eared) corners. You can create a spread in a single-sided layout by moving layout page icons so they're side by side (see page 85). To convert a layout from single-sided to facing pages, or vice versa, see the sidebar on page 253. The Facing Pages option isn't available in Web layouts.

If you modify the margin or column guides on a master page, all the layout pages with which that master is associated will display the updated guides. Any automatic text boxes that fit exactly within the margin guides before the guides were changed will exhibit the new column and gutter width values and will resize automatically to fit the new margins. Margin and column guides aren't available in Web layouts.

To modify the non-printing margin and column guides:

1. Double-click a master page icon on the Page Layout palette.

2. Choose Page > Master Guides.

3. Change the Column Guides and/or Margin Guides values **3**.

4. Click OK **4**–**5**, then redisplay a layout page.

If you enter the Current Page Number command on a master page, the current page number will appear on any layout pages to which that master is applied. If you then add or delete pages from the layout, the page numbers will update automatically.

Note: Many of the procedures discussed in this chapter can't be undone, like applying a master page or deleting pages. We suggest that you save your file before working with master pages and the Page Layout palette, so you'll have the Revert to Saved command to fall back on.

To number pages automatically:

1. Double-click the Master A icon on the Page Layout palette **1**. The words "A-Master A" or "L-A-Master A" will appear in the lower left corner of the project window.

2. Choose the Rectangle Text Box tool. A

3. Drag to create a small text box where you want the page number to appear (typically, it's placed at the bottom of the page, but any location is fine).

4. With the new box and the Content tool selected, press Cmd-3/Ctrl-3 (the Current Page Number command) **2**. It will look like this: <#>.

   In a facing-pages layout, you need to enter the command on both the left and right master pages (see **1**, next page)—it's easy to forget this!

5. Highlight the Current Page Number command, then style it as you would a regular character (choose a font, point size, etc.). (To add other master page items, such as headers, footers, and the like, see page 246.)

6. To see how the page numbers look, display any layout page: Click a layout page number on the Page Layout palette or press Shift-F10/Shift-F4 **3**.

TIP Unfortunately, automatic page numbers can't be manually kerned, and they are

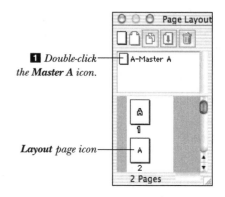

1 *Double-click the **Master A** icon.*

Layout page icon

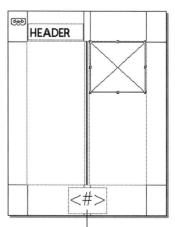

2 *The **Current Page Number** command displays as "<#>" on the master page.*

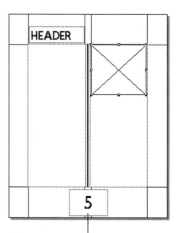

3 *The **Current Page Number** command displays as the **actual** page number on a layout page.*

Align the numbers

To make sure the two boxes that hold the Current Page Number command align vertically on the left and right master pages in a facing-pages layout, use Item > **Step and Repeat** (e.g., Horizontal Offset 10p, Vertical Offset 0) to duplicate the box, then Shift-drag the duplicate to the right page 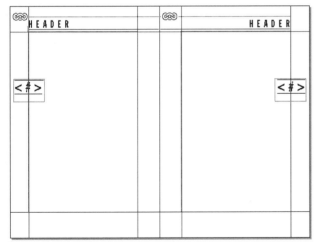. Remember to choose right paragraph alignment (click the Right Alignment icon on the Measurements palette) for the command on the right facing page.

If you use the **Duplicate** command to copy the box instead, the next step would be to select both boxes and use Item > **Space/Align** (Vertical, Space: 0, Between: Top Edges) to align their top edges. Another way to align the boxes vertically is to enter matching numbers in the **Y** field on the **Measurements** palette for both boxes (copy the value in the Y field for the first box, click the second box, then paste into the Y field for the second box).

unaffected by the Kerning Table Editor. You could track the Current Page Number command on the master page, but doing so would cause all the automatic page numbers in the layout to be tracked by the same value.

TIP You can enter the Current Page Number command on any layout page, but the page number will appear only on that individual page.

TIP To print a master page (or a set of facing-pages masters), display that page before choosing File > Print.

TIP If you're in a position to break with the norm, instead of automatically placing the Current Page Number command at the bottom of the page, try placing it in a new location . Then embellish it: Apply a color to it, make it very large, add a paragraph rule above and/or below it, etc. For more formal documents, you may type a prefix such as "Page" before the command.

1 *In a facing-pages layout, you must enter the Current Page Number command on both the **left** and **right** facing master pages.*

2 *This is how the page number looks on a **layout** page.*

Note: In a facing-pages layout, every master page has two parts: a left page and a right page. Items from the left master page appear only on left (even-numbered) layout pages; items on the right master page appear only on right (odd-numbered) layout pages.

To modify a master page:

1. Double-click a master page icon on the Page Layout palette ■ or choose a master page icon from the Go-to-page pop-up menu at the bottom of the project window.

2. Add or modify any master item— header, footer, line, ruler guide, picture box, or what have you. You can drag any item from a library onto a master page. You can't enter text into an automatic text box.

   Pages to which the master page has already been applied will be modified. See "Keep or Delete Changes?" starting on page 248.

3. To redisplay a layout page, click a layout page number on the Page Layout palette or choose a layout page icon from the Go-to-page pop-up menu.

   TIP If you checked Automatic Text Box in the New Project or New Layout dialog box, an automatic text box will appear on the default Master A page and on any layout pages to which Master A is applied. Text can't be entered into the automatic text box on a master page, but text can be entered into any other text box on a master page. You *can* reshape the automatic text box ■.

   TIP You can preformat any text box on a master page by applying a style sheet or individual type specifications. Text that you subsequently type into the box will take on those specifications.

Lock 'em up

Once your master items are positioned exactly where you want them, lock them, where appropriate, to prevent them from being moved on any layout pages (Item > Lock, or F6).

■ *Double-click a master page icon.*

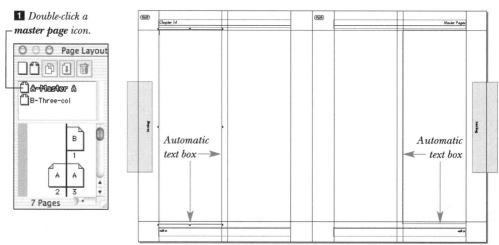

■ *These are the left and right **master pages** for this book. The automatic text box on each page was resized to fit into one column to make room for illustrations, and the number of columns in the box was reduced to one.*

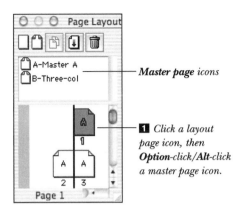

Master page icons

1 *Click a layout page icon, then* **Option**-*click/***Alt**-*click a master page icon.*

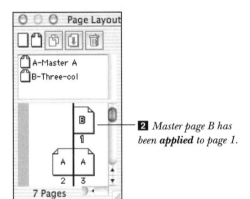

2 *Master page B has been* **applied** *to page 1.*

To apply a master page to a layout page:

Click a layout page icon on the Page Layout palette (or double-click the icon, if you also want the page to display on screen) **1**, then Option-click/Alt-click a master page icon **2**.

or

Drag a master page icon (labeled icon) over a layout page icon.

or

To apply a master page to multiple layout pages, click the page icon of the first page in the series, Shift-click the last page icon in the series **3** (or Cmd-click/Ctrl-click nonconsecutive icons **4**), then Option-click/Alt-click a master page icon.

TIP If you drag-copy a page or pages from one project to another in Thumbnails view, any master pages that were assigned to the source pages that differ from those in the target project will also be added to the target project. If the target project already contains a master page of the same name, the newly appended master page will be assigned the next letter of the alphabet.

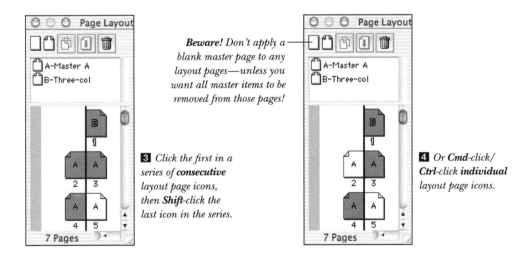

Beware! *Don't apply a blank master page to any layout pages—unless you want all master items to be removed from those pages!*

3 *Click the first in a series of* **consecutive** *layout page icons, then* **Shift**-*click the last icon in the series.*

4 *Or* **Cmd**-*click/* **Ctrl**-*click* **individual** *layout page icons.*

Apply Master Page

Keep/Delete Changes Preference

Keep or delete changes?

If Master Page Items: Delete Changes is chosen in QuarkXPress (Edit, in Windows) > Preferences > Print Layout or Web Layout > General (Cmd-Option-Shift-Y/Ctrl-Alt-Shift-Y), and a master page is applied or reapplied to a layout page, locally modified and unmodified master items will be deleted from the layout page **1**–**3**. If Keep Changes is chosen as the Master Page Items setting instead, only unmodified master items will be deleted **4**. Confused?

To learn the difference between these two settings, start by putting a couple of items on a master page (make them large and/or colorful so they'll be easy to spot). Next, locally modify one of those master page items on a layout page. Now reapply the master page to the same layout page. If the item you modified disappeared, Delete Changes is the current setting. Then do the same procedure with Keep Changes chosen instead. See the difference?

TIP Text contained in the automatic text box on any layout pages is preserved regardless of the current Master Page Items setting, even if the automatic text box is resized on the master page.

1 *This is an item on a master page.*

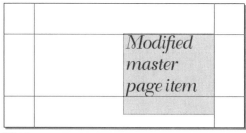

2 *The master page item is moved and modified on one of the layout pages.*

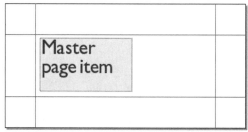

3 *With **Delete Changes** as the default setting, after the master is reapplied, the modified master item is deleted.*

4 *With **Keep Changes** as the default setting, after the master page is reapplied, the modified item remains.*

To further confuse matters

If master page items are edited on layout pages and the master page is reapplied, there's one more thing to keep in mind: Reapplying the master page can affect an item's attributes (color, size, shape, frame, etc.) and its contents (text or picture) differently.

The unmodified master page

The contents are modified on a layout page.

Delete Changes is in effect and the same master page is reapplied. The modified contents are replaced.

Scenario 1

On a layout page, you edit the **contents** of a text box that originated from a master page but you don't recolor, resize, or move the box itself. The same master page is reapplied with Master Page Items: **Delete Changes** as the current Preferences setting. The result: The locally modified text in the box on the layout page is replaced with the updated item from the master page.

The unmodified master page

The contents are modified on a layout page.

Keep Changes is in effect and the same master page is reapplied. The master item appears behind the modified item.

Scenario 2

On a layout page, you edit the **contents** of an item that originated from a master page but not its attributes. The same master page is reapplied, but this time with **Keep Changes** as the Preferences setting. The result: The reapplied master page item appears behind the modified layout page item, and it's hidden from view.

(Continued on the following page)

Keep/Delete Changes Preference

Scenario 3

You edit the **contents** of a box on a layout page and also edit **attributes** of the master item on the master page (but *not* its contents) with **Keep Changes** as the Preferences setting. The result: The attributes of the box, but not its contents, update on the layout page.

The unmodified master page

The contents on an associated layout page are modified.

An item attribute (background color, in this case) is modified on the master page.

Keep Changes is in effect. The background is changed; the modified contents remain.

Watch for reshuffling

If an **odd** number of pages is added to, deleted from, or moved within a facing-pages layout and layout pages are reshuffled as a result, the corresponding left and right master pages will be *reapplied* to the reshuffled pages automatically.

Scenario 4

You edit an item's **attributes** and **contents** on the master page with **Delete Changes** as the Preferences setting. The result: The item is completely replaced with the updated master page item—even if that item was modified on the layout page.

The unmodified master page

An item's attributes and contents are modified on the master page.

The contents of the item are modified on the layout page.

Delete Changes is in effect and the same master is reapplied. The item is completely replaced on the layout page.

Keep/Delete Changes Preference

You can use the Duplicate command on the Page Layout palette to create a variation on an existing master page. The new, duplicate master page will contain all the items from the master page from which it's copied, including an automatic text box or Current Page Number command, if any. You can make any additions or changes to the duplicate.

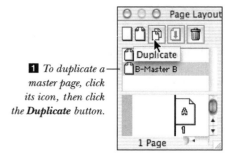

1 *To duplicate a master page, click its icon, then click the **Duplicate** button.*

To duplicate a master page:

1. On the Page Layout palette, click the icon of the master page you want to copy **1**.

2. Click the Duplicate button **2**.

TIP To copy a master page from one project to another, see the tip on page 247.

TIP If you duplicate a layout, all master pages and master page items from the original layout will be duplicated, too. 6.0!

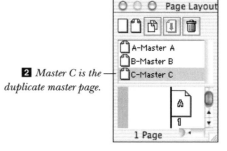

2 *Master C is the duplicate master page.*

To create a new, blank master page:

Drag a blank master page icon into the blank part of the master page icon area on the Page Layout palette **3**. Move the palette divider downward to enlarge the top portion of the palette, if necessary **4**–**5**. The next available letter of the alphabet will be assigned to the new master page.

Note: If you drag a new master page icon over an existing one (whether intentionally or not), an alert dialog box will open. Click OK to replace the existing master page with the new blank one, or click Cancel. You can't undo this, so be careful.

3 *To create a new, **blank** master, drag a blank page icon into the master page area.*

TIP To change the order of master page icons on the Page Layout palette, drag an icon upward or downward. The master page names won't change. Make sure you see the Force Down pointer as you do this; otherwise you'll end up replacing one master page with another (luckily for you, you'll get a prompt).

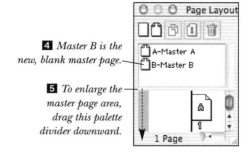

4 *Master B is the new, blank master page.*

5 *To enlarge the master page area, drag this palette divider downward.*

Duplicate Master; Create Blank Master

Facing to single, single to facing 6.0!

To convert a single-sided layout to a **facing-pages** layout, choose Layout > Layout Properties, check Facing Pages, click OK, then create any facing master pages that you need. No big deal.

Converting a facing-pages layout to a **single-sided** layout requires more steps. First create a single-sided master page, complete with an automatic text box (see the next page) and/or any other desired items. You can copy and paste items from the facing-pages master to this new single-sided master. Next, drag the single-sided master page over the existing facing-pages master, then click OK when the prompt appears. Click any layout page icon on the palette, choose Layout > Layout Properties, uncheck Facing Pages, then click OK. Any non-master items on layout pages will be preserved; any automatic text boxes that were resized on layout pages will be replaced but their content will be preserved. The single-sided layout page icons can be rearranged, if you like.

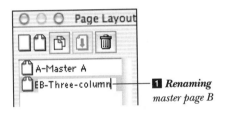
1 *Renaming master page B*

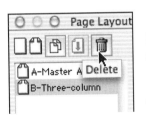
2 *To delete a master page, click its icon, then click the **Delete** button (this is the palette in **Mac OS X**).*

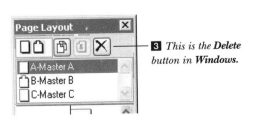
3 *This is the **Delete** button in **Windows**.*

To rename a master page:

1. In Mac OS X, click a master page name (not the icon) on the Page Layout palette. In Windows, double-click a master page name.

2. Highlight the prefix, then type up to three replacement characters. Don't delete the hyphen between the prefix and the master page name; if you do, QuarkXPress will insert its own prefix.
or
Highlight and change the characters following the hyphen **1**.
or
Highlight all the characters, including the prefix, type a master page name, then click elsewhere or press Return/Enter. The original prefix (letter in the alphabet) and a hyphen will be reinserted automatically as the first two characters.

Beware! If you delete a master page, any unmodified master items on any associated layout pages will also be deleted. If a layout page associated with the deleted master page contains an automatic text box from the deleted master and that text box isn't resized, it too will be deleted—*even if it contains text!* If, on the other hand, the automatic text box is resized on a layout page and the current Master Page Items setting in QuarkXPress (Edit, in Windows) > Preferences > Print Layout or Web Layout > General is Keep Changes, the box will be preserved.

To delete a master page:

1. Click a master page icon on the Page Layout palette.

2. Click the Delete button on the palette **2**–**3**.

3. If the master page is in use, an alert prompt will appear. You can't undo this, so click OK if you're confident (choose File > Revert to Saved if you make a boo-boo).

To create your own automatic text box:

1. Display the master page that you want to add an automatic text box to.

2. Choose Fit in Window view (Cmd-0/Ctrl-0) so you can see the whole page, and make sure the guides are showing (View > Show Guides).

3. Choose the Rectangle Text Box tool [A] or any other Text Box tool, then draw a text box **1**.

4. Choose the Linking tool. ⟨⟩

5. Click the link (broken chain) icon in the upper left corner of the page **2**.

6. Click the text box **3**, then click the Item or Content tool to deselect the Linking tool.

7. For a facing-pages layout, repeat all of the above steps on the opposing facing page for that master.

Note: If your automatic text box fits perfectly within the current margin guides and you later change the margin guides, the automatic text box will resize automatically to fit within the new guides.

To unlink

To unlink an automatic text box, choose the **Unlinking** tool, then click the **link** icon in the upper left corner of the master page (it will turn into a broken chain icon). If you're working on a facing-pages layout, be sure to do this on both the left and right master pages.

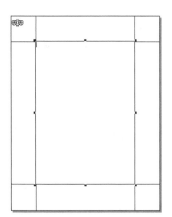

1 *To create an automatic text box, first draw a text box of any size on the master page with the **Rectangle Text Box** tool.*

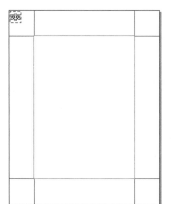

2 *Choose the **Linking** tool, then click the broken chain icon in the upper left corner of the master page.*

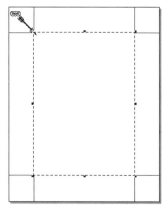

3 *Finally, click the text box.*

What can be recolored

- Text characters
- Text paths, with or without text
- Pictures in some file formats
- Lines
- Frames
- Paragraph rules
- Gaps between dashes or stripes
- Background of a text box, picture box, contentless box, or Web layout
- Table box, frame, cells, gridlines, or border segments
- Web hyperlinks (see page 344)

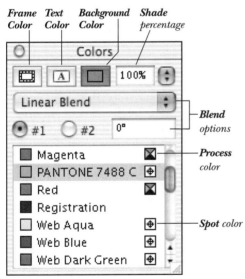

Frame *Text* *Background* *Shade*
Color *Color* *Color* *percentage*

Blend options

Process color

Spot color

The **Colors palette** *is used to apply colors to text, pictures, boxes, frames, lines, text paths, and tables, and to create blends.*

Note: Color management is covered in Chapter 23; trapping is covered in Chapter 24.

Creating colors

Each file can contain up to 1,000 colors, and they appear on the Colors palette and in any dialog box where colors are chosen, such as Frame, Character Attributes, and Modify. Colors that are created when no projects are open will be present in all subsequently created projects. Colors that are created with a project open will be saved only with that project. Regardless of which layout is displayed when you add a color, that color will be available for all the **6.0!** layouts in the current project.

Two basic methods are used for printing color—spot color and process color—and you can use both in the same file.

Color for print

Each spot color is printed using a separate plate. Spot color inks are mixed according to specifications defined in a color matching system, such as PANTONE. Various tints (percentages) of the same spot color will appear on the same printing plate.

In process color (CMYK) printing, four plates are used: cyan (C), magenta (M), yellow (Y), and black (K). A layer of tiny colored dots is printed from each plate, and the overlapping dots create an illusion of solid or graduated color. The only way to print the continuous tones in a photograph is by using process colors.

Computer monitors display additive color by projecting red, green, and blue (RGB) light, whereas printers produce subtractive color using ink. Because computer monitors don't accurately display ink equivalents,

(Continued on the following page)

solid colors for print output should be specified using formulas defined in a printed process or spot color matching system guide (swatchbook). If you mix colors for print output based on how they look onscreen, you may be in for a rude surprise when you see the final product.

Color for the Web

One important goal that Web designers have had to keep in mind from the outset has been to choose colors that will display consistently in a variety of settings, while avoiding colors that may not be available. Now that 16-bit monitors are becoming commonplace (and some monitors have even higher resolutions than that), choosing colors is less worrisome, as these monitors are capable of displaying a wide range of colors.

When designing Web graphics for viewers using 8-bit monitors, your color choices are more limited. The various platforms and browsers have only 216 colors in common, but if you stick with these "Web-safe" colors, you can pretty much depend on your colors looking as you intended. Steer clear of non-Web-safe colors, which can look different from one platform or browser to the next when viewed on an 8-bit monitor.

To simplify the process of choosing Web-safe colors, QuarkXPress offers two different models: Web Safe Colors and Web Named Colors. Every new project automatically contains 16 named Web-safe colors (in addition to the default process colors), which appear on the Colors palette. To create a Web-safe color, see page 262. *Beware!* When applying a Web-safe color, keep its shade at 100%. At any other percentage, it won't be Web-safe.

The color models

RGB

The computer's native color model. Use for onscreen output.

HSB

The traditional artist's method for mixing colors based on their individual hue (H), saturation (S), and brightness (B) components.

LAB

A device-independent color model used for color conversions across multiple devices, such as printers and monitors.

CMYK

A four-color process printing model that simulatse a multitude of colors by printing tiny dots of cyan (C), magenta (M), yellow (Y), and black (K) ink. You choose the percentages.

Multi-ink

A user-defined color comprising multiple spot and/or process colors.

PANTONE

Widely used spot and process color matching systems. In its Hexachrome matching system, two additional plates—orange and green—are added to the usual cyan, magenta, yellow, and black. Hexachrome ("high fidelity" or "HiFi") colors are more vibrant—and more expensive; speak with your commercial printer before using them!

TOYO, DIC

Spot color matching systems that are primarily used in the Far East.

FOCOLTONE, TRUMATCH

Four-color process matching systems for choosing predefined, prenamed process colors (not spot colors). FOCOLTONE colors were designed to lessen the need for trapping colors.

Web Safe Colors

Predefined Web-safe colors chosen by number or by swatch.

Web Named Colors

Predefined Web-safe colors chosen by name or by swatch.

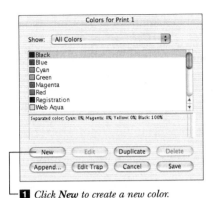

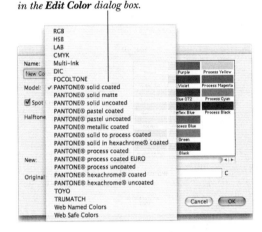

1 *Click New to create a new color.*

2 *Choose a PANTONE Model in the Edit Color dialog box.*

To create a spot color for print output:

1. Choose Edit > Colors (Shift-F12), then click New **1**.
   or
   If an item is selected in your layout, Control-click/Right-click the Colors palette and choose New.

2. From the Model pop-up menu in the Edit Color dialog box, choose one of the PANTONE options (nothing that says "process," though) **2**.

3. Click a color swatch (use the scroll arrows to scroll through the choices) **3**.
   or
   Click in the PANTONE field, then type a number from a PANTONE color guide.

4. Spot Color is checked automatically. (If this option is unchecked, the spot color will be converted into a process color.)

5. Click OK, then click Save, if necessary. The new color will appear on the Colors palette and in all dialog boxes that have a color option **4**.

TIP To access a PANTONE color or a color from any other matching system, that matching system file must be in the Color folder inside the QuarkXPress folder when the program is launched.

TIP To read about the Halftone pop-up menu, see page 440.

Check Spot Color.

3 *Click a color swatch (click a scroll arrow to scroll through the swatches)...*

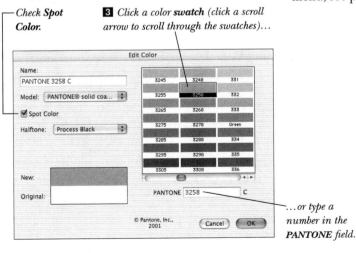

...*or type a number in the PANTONE field.*

4 *The new PANTONE color appears on the Colors palette.*

Create Spot Color

To create a process color for print output:

1. Choose Edit > Colors (Shift-F12), then click New.
or
If an item is selected, Control-click/Right-click in the Colors palette and choose New.

2. Choose Model: FOCOLTONE or TRUMATCH or choose one of the PANTONE process or hexachrome options **1**. Then enter the desired color number in the FOCOLTONE, TRUMATCH, or PANTONE field or scroll through the swatches and click a swatch **2**; a name will appear in the Name field. PANTONE solid colors are four-color process colors that simulate spot colors.
or
Choose Model: CMYK **3**, enter percentages (or move the sliders to the desired percentages) from a color matching book in the C, M, Y, and K fields **4**, then type a name for the color in the Name field. The vertical bar controls brightness (the amount of black in the color).

3. Click OK and then, if necessary, click Save. The color will appear on the Colors palette and in dialog boxes that have a color option, in all layouts in the current project.

TIP The Registration color is used for registration and crop marks, which commercial printers use to align color plates.

Fast track to Edit Color

If the Item > Modify dialog box is open, choosing Color: **Other** in the Box, Frame, Line, Picture, or Cell pane gets you to the Edit Color dialog box. You can also choose Other from the Color pop-up menu in Style > Formats > Rules and Style > Character.

1 *To choose a process color from a matching system, choose* ***Model: TRUMATCH*** *or* ***FOCOLTONE,*** *or choose one of the* ***PANTONE process*** *or* **hexachrome** *options. A Name will appear automatically when you choose a color.*

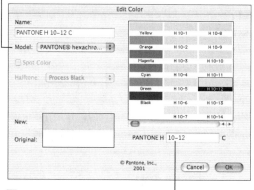

2 *Then enter a number in the* ***TRUMATCH, FOCOLTONE,*** *or* ***PANTONE*** *field or click a color swatch.*

3 *To mix your own process color, first choose* ***Model: CMYK.***

Type a Name for the new CMYK color.

For any process color, make sure ***Spot Color*** *is* ***unchecked.*** *(If this option is checked, the process color will be converted into a spot color.)*

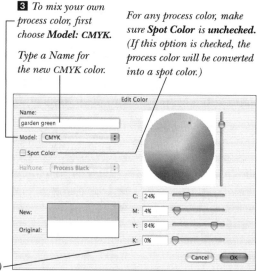

4 *For the CMYK Model, enter* ***C, M, Y,*** *and* ***K*** *percentages. (Don't use the color wheel; it's like picking a color blindfolded.)*

Appending colors

- To append colors from one project to another, click **Append** in the Colors dialog box or choose File > Append (Cmd-Option-A/ Ctrl-Alt-A) (see pages 50–52).

- For a quick-and-dirty append, **drag-copy** an item to which the desired color has been applied from a library into a project window or from one project window to another. Here's the dirty part: If there's a color with a matching name in the target project, the color won't append.

- If you **import** an EPS picture into Quark-XPress, any spot colors in the picture will be appended to the QuarkXPress Colors palette.

You can use a duplicate of an existing color as a starting point for a new color. This is for CMYK or RGB colors only—not for spot colors.

To create a color by duplicating an existing color:

1. Choose Edit > Colors (Shift-F12), click a color, then click Duplicate.
   or
   If an item is selected, Control-click/ Right-click in the Colors palette and choose Duplicate [color name].

2. Change the color Name, if desired.

3. Edit the color by adjusting any of the C, M, Y, or K (cyan, magenta, yellow, or black) or R, G, or B (red, green, or blue) percentages. You can also change the color Model.

4. Click OK and then, if necessary, click Save.

TIP To compare the components of two colors, in the Colors dialog box, Cmd-click/Ctrl-click two color names, then Option-click/Alt-click Append (it will turn into a Compare button). Any differences between the colors will be listed in boldface.

TIP Another quick way to get to the Edit > Colors dialog box is to Cmd-click/ Ctrl-click a color on the Colors palette.

Duplicate Color

To edit a CMYK or RGB color:

1. Choose Edit > Colors (Shift-F12, or Cmd-click/Ctrl-click a color on the Colors palette), then double-click the CMYK or RGB color that you want to edit (or click a color name, then click Edit) **1**.

or

If an item is selected, Control-click/Right-click a color on the Colors palette, then choose Edit [color name] **2**.

2. Change any of the C, M, Y, K or R, G, B percentages by entering new values or moving the sliders **3**. The vertical bar controls brightness (the amount of black in the color). You can also change the color Name or Model.

3. Click OK and then, if necessary, click Save. The color will update immediately on all items in the project where it's currently being used and will update on the Colors palette for all layouts in the project.

TIP To create a rich black, you can add some magenta (M) or cyan (C) to your black (K). Ask your commercial printer for advice.

TIP Click the Original color swatch in the Edit Color dialog box to restore the color's original formula.

*To limit how many colors appear on the list, choose a category from the **Show** pop-up menu.*

1 *Double-click the color you want to **edit**.*

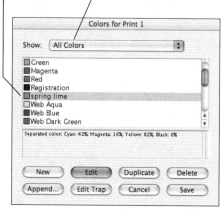

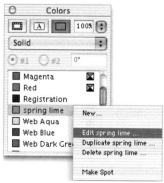

2 *Or choose **Edit** [color name] from the context menu (Colors palette).*

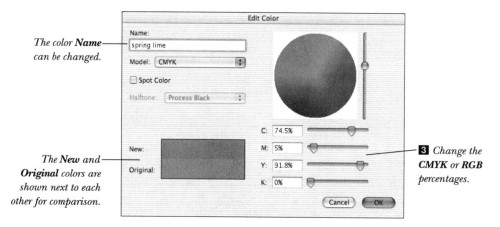

*The color **Name** can be changed.*

*The **New** and **Original** colors are shown next to each other for comparison.*

3 *Change the **CMYK** or **RGB** percentages.*

Edit CMYK or RGB Color

Switcheroo

Control-click/Right-click a color name on the Colors palette, and choose **Make Spot** or **Make Process** to convert the color.

Multi-ink is a color model for print output in which you can create new colors from a combination of process and/or spot colors. For example, you could create a new color by combining 50% of a PANTONE color and 20% of a CMYK color. Multi-ink colors print from more than one plate.

Note: Talk to your commercial printer before using multi-ink colors, as they can cause moiré patterns or other printing problems if the proper screen angles aren't used.

1 *Choose **Multi-Ink** from the **Model** pop-up menu.*   *Choose **Process Inks: CMYK** or **Hexachrome.***

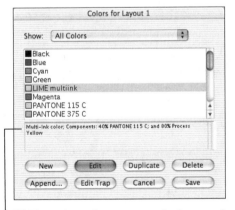

*Click a **color**, then choose a **Shade** for it.*

2 *The various color **percentages** for the currently selected multi-ink color are listed here.*

To create a multi-ink color:

1. Choose Edit > Colors (Shift-F12), then click New.
   or
   If an item is selected, Control-click/ Right-click in the Colors palette and choose New.

2. Choose Model: Multi-Ink **1**.

3. On the right side of the dialog box, choose Process Inks: CMYK or Hexachrome.

4. Click a color, then choose a Shade percentage for that color.

5. Repeat the previous step for the colors you want to combine with the first color.

   TIP To apply the same Shade percentage to more than one color at a time, Shift-click or Cmd-click/ Ctrl-click them before choosing a percentage.

6. Type a Name for the multi-ink color (tip: include "multi-ink" in the name).

7. Click OK **2**. Click Save, if necessary. The color will appear on the Colors palette and in dialog boxes that have a color option.

   TIP To see how color mixes look when printed, refer to the Color+Black (spot colors plus black) or Color+Color (spot color combinations) PANTONE swatch book.

QuarkXPress offers two color palettes for choosing Web-safe colors: Web Safe Colors (216 colors available) and Web Named Colors (123 colors available). The Web Named Colors are a subset of the 216 Web Safe Colors, and are listed by name instead of by number for easy reference.

To create a Web-safe color:

1. Choose Edit > Colors (Shift-F12), then click New.

or

If an item is selected, Control-click/ Right-click in the Colors palette and choose New.

2. From the Model pop-up menu, choose Web Named Colors or Web Safe Colors. Web Safe Colors are numbered according to their hexadecimal values.

3. Click a color swatch.

or

For a Web Named Color, start typing the name in the HTML field until the desired color becomes highlighted 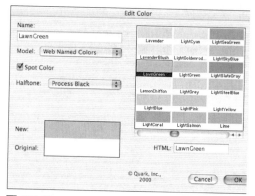. For a Web Safe Color, enter a number in the Hex Value field 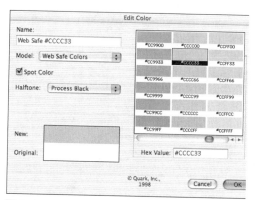. You can use a hexadecimal color guide or table for reference.

4. Click OK.

5. Click Save, if necessary. The new color will appear on the Colors palette and in any dialog boxes that have a color option.

1 *Web Named Colors: Love those yummy **names**.*

2 *Web Safe Colors are identified by their assigned **hexadecimal** numbers.*

Find/change colors

To find/change colors in text, use the Find/Change feature in QuarkXPress (see pages 290–292). To find and change colors in nontext items, you have to use a third-party XTension, such as **ColorManager,** courtesy of CompuSense Ltd.

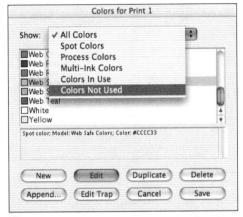

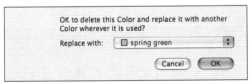

1 *In the* **Default Colors** *dialog box, click the color you want to delete, then click* **Delete.** *Or to delete all the colors that aren't currently being used in the project, choose Show:* **Colors Not Used,** *select the colors you want to delete, then click Delete.*

2 *Choose a replacement color from the* **Replace with** *pop-up menu.*

To delete or globally replace a color:

1. To delete or replace a color in all layouts in a project, leave the project open.
or
To delete or replace a color on the default Colors palette (the default palette for new projects), close any open projects.

2. Choose Edit > Colors (Shift-F12).

3. If you're going to replace the deleted color, create the replacement color now, if it doesn't already exist.

4. Click the color you want to delete. Cyan, Magenta, Yellow, Black, White, and Registration cannot be deleted.
or
To delete all the colors that aren't currently being used in the project (and reduce the file's storage size), choose Show: Colors Not Used **1**, then select the colors you want to delete. To do this, click the first in a series of consecutive colors, then Shift-click the last color in the series. Or Cmd-click/Ctrl-click to select nonconsecutive colors.

5. Click Delete. If the color you deleted was currently applied to any item in the active project, a prompt will appear. Choose a replacement color from the "Replace with" pop-up menu **2**, then click OK. You can undo this by clicking Cancel, but not after you've clicked Save.

6. Click Save.

TIP To quickly delete one color with the option to undo, Control-click/Right-click the color on the Colors palette, and choose Delete [color name]. Respond to the prompt, if it appears. In QuarkXPress 5 this couldn't be undone; now it can. **6.0!**

Applying colors

Use the following method to recolor a unique area of text, such as a headline. Since you can apply color to text using the Character Attributes dialog box, the fastest way to recolor repetitive instances or larger bodies of text is via a style sheet. You can also use Find/Change to apply a color, either directly or via a style sheet.

To recolor text:

1. Choose Window > Show Colors to display the Colors palette (F12).

2. Choose the Content tool.

3. Highlight the text that you want to recolor. The text can be in a table.

4. Click the Text Color button ⒶＡ on the Colors palette **1**.

5. Click a color.

6. Choose a percentage from the shade pop-up menu (**2** and **4**). The default shade value is 100%. To apply a custom shade, choose Style > Shade > Other, enter a percentage, then click OK.

   Note: A color or shade can also be applied to text via the Character Attributes dialog box (Cmd-Shift-D/ Ctrl-Shift-D) or via the Style > Color and/or Shade submenus.

TIP If you're coloring type white or restoring reversed type to black-on-white, change the type color first and then change the background color. That way, the text will be easier to highlight **3**.

CREATIVE MINDS
ALWAYS HAVE BEEN KNOWN TO SURVIVE ANY
KIND OF BAD TRAINING.
Anna Freud

3 *Choose a bold, chunky typeface for reversed type. Reversed serif letters (as in "Anna Freud") can look wispy.*

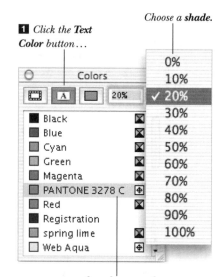

*Choose a **shade**.*

1 *Click the Text Color button…*

*… then choose a **color**.*

*The Colors palette when **text** is selected*

There is no such thing as a non-working mother.

~Hester Mundis

2 *A different **shade** percentage is applied to each character.*

TWENTYPERCENT

THIRTYPERCENT

FORTY PERCENT

FIFTY PERCENT

SIXTY PERCENT

SEVENTYPERCENT

EIGHTYPERCENT

NINETYPERCENT

HUNDREDPERCENT

4 *A range of **shades** applied to type*

Recolor Text

Go FullColor

FullColor XT by Badia Software offers enhanced palette-level features for creating, editing, finding, and applying solid colors and blends.

---

1 *To recolor the background of a text or picture box, click the* **Background Color** *button...*

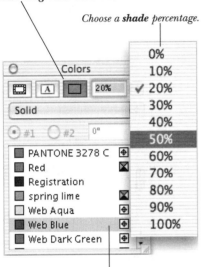

Choose a **shade** *percentage.*

...then click a **color.**

The Colors palette when a **text box,** **picture box,** *or* **contentless box** *is selected*

In the following instructions, you'll learn how to recolor the background of any kind of box. Want to have some fun? Create playful or dramatic graphic items using empty or contentless standard or Bézier boxes (or lines). Use your imagination! To create multiples of any item, use Item > Step and Repeat. To apply blends, see pages 273–274.

To recolor the background of an item:

1. Choose Window > Show Colors to display the Colors palette (F12).

2. Choose the Item or Content tool, then click a text box, picture box, contentless box, or group, or select multiple items. For a table, choose the Content tool, then select one or more table cells.

3. Click the Background Color (third) button 🔳 on the Colors palette **1**.

4. Click a color.

5. *Optional:* Choose a different percentage from the shade pop-up menu **2**–**3**. The default shade value is 100%.

TIP You can also recolor the background of an item by dragging a color swatch from the Colors palette over the item (see page 272) or by using Item > Modify (Box, Group, Table, or Cells pane).

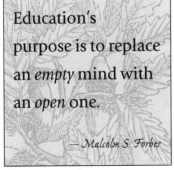

2 *Black type on top of a picture that has a 10% black background*

3 *Black type on top of a text box that contains 30% black type and has a 10% black background*

Education's purpose is to replace an *empty* mind with an *open* one.

— *Malcolm S. Forbes*

Recolor Background of Item

To recolor a picture:

1. Choose Window > Show Colors to display the Colors palette (F12).

2. Choose the Content tool.

3. Click a 1-bit or grayscale PICT or TIFF or a grayscale JPEG.

4. Click the Picture Color button ⊠ on the Colors palette **1**.

5. Click a color.

6. *Optional:* Choose a different percentage from the shade pop-up menu **2**. The default shade value is 100%.

TIP A color or shade can also be applied to a picture using the Style > Color and/or Shade submenus or using Item > Modify > Picture.

To recolor a line or a text path:

1. Choose Window > Show Colors to display the Colors palette (F12).

2. Choose the Item tool.

3. Select a standard line, Bézier line, or text path, or create a multiple-item selection.

4. Click the Line Color button ╱ on the Colors palette **3**.

5. Click a color.

6. *Optional:* Choose a different percentage from the shade pop-up menu. The default shade value is 100%.

TIP A line can also be recolored using the Style > Color and/or Shade submenus. In Item > Modify > Line, you can recolor a line and/or the gaps in a dashed or striped style.

1 *First click the* **Picture Color** *button... Choose a* **shade** *percentage.*

...*then click a* **color.**

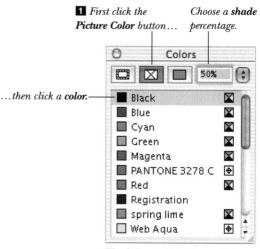

The Colors palette when a **picture** *is selected*

2 *TIFF line art with a 30% shade*

3 *First click the* **Line Color** *button... Choose a* **shade** *percentage.*

...*then click a* **color.**

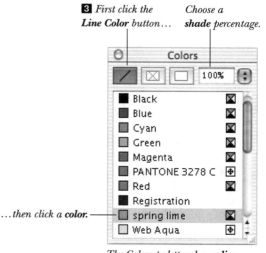

The Colors palette when a **line** *is selected*

1 *First click the*   *Choose a*
Frame Color button ...   *shade percentage.*

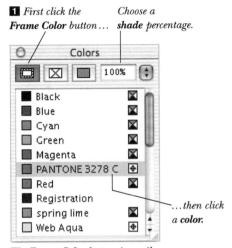

*The **Frame Color** button is available on the Colors palette when
a text or picture box is selected.*

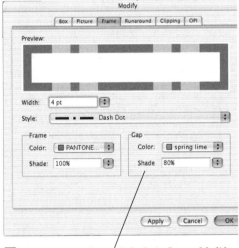

2 *Choose a **gap color** and **shade** in Item > Modify
(**Frame** or **Line** pane).*

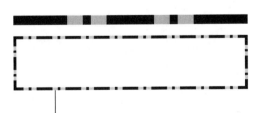

3 *This gap color is Black, 25%.*

Note: Specifying a color for a frame using the Colors palette doesn't actually place the frame on the box. To make the frame appear, you must specify a frame Width above zero in the Item > Frame dialog box (Cmd-B/Ctrl-B). You can choose a frame color before or after assigning a width.

To recolor a frame:

1. Choose Window > Show Colors to display the Colors palette (F12).
2. Choose the Item or Content tool.
3. Click a text box, picture box, or group of items, or create a multiple-item selection.
4. Click the Frame Color button 🔲 on the Colors palette **1**.
5. Click a color.
6. *Optional:* Choose a different percentage from the shade pop-up menu. The default shade value is 100%.

To recolor the gaps in a line, frame, or text path:

1. Choose the Item or Content tool.
2. Click the box or line that contains the gaps that you want to recolor.
3. For a box, choose Item > Modify, then click the Frame tab (Cmd-B/Ctrl-B gets you directly to the Frame pane).

   For a line or text path, choose Item > Modify, then click the Line tab (Cmd-M/Ctrl-M).

   The gap color can't be changed for a paragraph rule.
4. Choose from the Gap: Color pop-up menu **2**.
5. Choose or enter a Gap: Shade percentage.
6. Click Apply to preview, then click OK **3**.

6.0! You have more options for redecorating tables in QuarkXPress 6. Here's what you can apply:

- A color of None, a solid color, or a blend to the background of one or more cells

- A solid color or a blend to the background of a table box (the overall box that contains all the table cells)

- A solid color or a blend to the gridlines between cells

- A color of None or a Width of 0 to a gridline or border segment (to make it disappear)

- A solid color to a table's outer frame

Note: By default, table cells are white. To change this default color for future tables, double-click the Tables tool, click Modify, click the Cell tab, then choose a Cell: Color and Shade.

To recolor the background of table cells:

1. Choose the Content tool.

2. Click in one cell or Shift-click to select multiple cells.

3. Click the Background Color button 🔲 on the Colors palette, click a color, and choose a shade. You can also apply a blend (see pages 273–274) **1**.
   or
   Choose Item > Modify (Cmd-M/Ctrl-M), then click Cell(s). Choose a color from the Cell: Color pop-up menu and a percentage from the Shade pop-up menu. Or to apply a blend, choose from the Blend: Style, Angle, Color, and Shade pop-up menus.

Quick coloring

Select the table with the Content tool, then drag a color swatch from the Colors palette over a table **cell, gridline,** or **border segment.** The color will be applied at the shade percentage of the last color that was applied to that part of the table. For example, if a cell has a shade of 40% Tangerine, and you drag Lemon Chiffon over that cell, Lemon Chiffon will replace Tangerine and will be applied at 40%. Option-drag/Alt-drag a color to apply it at full strength (100% shade), regardless of the percentage that was last applied to that component.

AROMATIC HERBS		
NAME	**FLAVOR AROMA**	**LATIN NAME**
BASIL, SWEET	CLOVE	*Ocimum basilicum*
BAY, SWEET	EARTHY	*Laurus nobilis*
FENNEL	ANISE	*Foeniculum vulgare*
LAVENDER	SWEET	*Lavandula*
LEMON BALM	LEMON	*Melissa officinalis*
LOVAGE	CELERY	*Levisticum officinale*
MARJORAM	HONEY	*Origanum majorana*
PEPPERMINT	MENTHOL	*Mentha × piperata*
ROSEMARY	RESIN	*Rosmarinus officinalis*
SAGE, PINEAPPLE	PINEAPPLE	*Salvia elegans*

1 *We applied a **solid tint** to the background of some table cells and a subtle **blend** to the topmost cell.*

Aromatic Herbs

NAME	AROMA	LATIN NAME
BASIL, SWEET	CLOVE	*Ocimum basilicum*
BAY, SWEET	EARTHY	*Laurus nobilis*
FENNEL	ANISE	*Foeniculum vulgare*
LAVENDER	SWEET	*Lavandula*
LEMON BALM	LEMON	*Melissa officinalis*
LOVAGE	CELERY	*Levisticum officinale*
MARJORAM	HONEY	*Origanum majorana*
PEPPERMINT	MENTHOL	*Mentha × piperata*
ROSEMARY	RESIN	*Rosmarinus officinalis*
SAGE, PINEAPPLE	PINEAPPLE	*Salvia elegans*

1 *We applied a blend and a frame to our table box. The border segments have a Width of 0; at a Width above 0, they'd be visible just inside the table box frame.*

By default, the background of the table box, which holds all the table cells, is white. To change it, follow these instructions.

Note: If you apply a color to the background of a table box, you won't be able to see the color unless the cells have a color of None.

To recolor the background of a table box: 6.0!

Method 1

1. Choose the Item tool, then click a table.

2. On the Colors palette, click the Background Color button,■ then choose a color and shade **1** or apply a blend (see pages 273–274).

Method 2

1. Choose the Item tool, then double-click a table to open the Modify dialog box.

2. Click the Table tab, choose a Box: Color and Shade, or choose Blend options, then click OK.

The default color of the table box frame is 100% black, but it too can be recolored. It can't have a color of None.

To recolor the table box frame: 6.0!

Method 1

1. Choose the Item tool, then double-click a table to open the Modify dialog box.

2. Click the Frame tab, enter or choose a Width greater than 0, choose a Style, and choose a Frame: Color and Shade.

3. For a dashed or multistripe style, choose a Gap: Color and Shade.

4. Click OK.

Method 2

1. Choose the Item tool.

2. Click a table.

3. Click the Frame Color button ▣ on the Colors palette.

4. Click a color swatch on the palette.

Recolor Table Box, Frame

The border segments and gridlines in a table can be recolored individually or all at once. Their default color is 100% black.

6.0! In QuarkXPress 5, you couldn't apply a color of None or a width of 0 to a gridline to make it disappear. In version 6 you can.

Note: To recolor individual table gridlines or segments in a Web layout, you must first convert the table to a graphic (see page 155).

To recolor table border segments and/or gridlines:

Method 1

1. Choose the Content tool.

2. Click a gridline or border segment, then Shift-click additional gridlines or segments, if desired. You can select both horizontals and verticals. The outer border has four segments. (If you have trouble selecting individual gridlines or segments, use one of the commands described next, then deselect the ones you don't want to recolor.)
or
Control-click/Right-click the table and choose Gridlines > Select Horizontal, Select Vertical, Select Borders (the outer frame segments of the table), or Select All (all the gridlines and borders) **1**.
or
Click the table and choose Item > Gridlines > Select Horizontal, Select Vertical, Select Borders, or Select All.

3. Choose from the Style menu (or Control-click/Right-click the table) > Color and Shade submenus. While you're at it, you can also change the line width via this menu, but be aware of the current Maintain Geometry setting if you do so (see pages 144–145).
or
Click the Line Color button ✏ on the Colors palette, click a swatch, then choose a shade from the pop-up menu **2**.

Seeing colors?

Selected border segments and gridlines are temporarily colored with their **complementary** color; the correct color displays when you **deselect.** If the item doesn't redraw properly, click on it again, then deselect again.

1 *You can select gridlines or border segments manually or via the **Gridlines** submenu.*

Aromatic Herbs		
NAME	**AROMA**	**LATIN NAME**
BASIL, SWEET	CLOVE	*Ocimum basilicum*
FENNEL	ANISE	*Foeniculum vulgare*
LAVENDER	SWEET	*Lavandula*
LEMON BALM	LEMON	*Melissa officinalis*
LOVAGE	CELERY	*Levisticum officinale*
PEPPERMINT	MENTHOL	*Mentha x piperata*
ROSEMARY	RESIN	*Rosmarinus officinalis*
SAGE, PINEAPPLE	PINEAPPLE	*Salvia elegans*

2 *We applied various shades of black to the **gridlines** and **borders** and also changed their width.*

Method 2

1. Choose the Item tool, then double-click a table to open the Modify dialog box.

2. Click the Grid tab ■.

3. Click one of the three icons at the right side of the dialog box for the components you want to recolor: All gridlines and border segments ⊞, only vertical gridlines and segments ⊞, or only horizontal gridlines and segments. ⊟

4. Choose a Line: Color and Shade, and also choose a Gap: Color and Shade if there are gaps in the line style.

5. Click Apply, adjust any of the settings, then click OK.

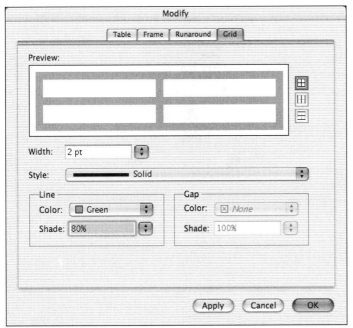

1 *In the Line and Gap areas in the Grid pane of the Item > Modify dialog box, choose Color and Shade percentages.*

Use the drag color feature to apply color to (or to preview colors on) a frame; a line; a text path; the background, gridlines, or border segments of a table; or the background of any type of box. You can't recolor text or a picture this way.

To recolor by dragging:

1. For any type of item except a table, choose the Item or Content tool. To recolor border segments or gridlines in a table, choose the Content tool.

2. Select any item in your layout to activate the Colors palette (it doesn't have to be the item you're going to recolor).

3. Drag a swatch from the Colors palette over a text box, picture box, contentless box, frame, line, or text path, or a table cell, gridline, or border segment **1**.

4. To apply the color, release the mouse over the item **2**. If you're applying a color to something narrow, such as a frame, line, text path, or table gridline, release the mouse when the *tip* of the arrow is directly over the component that you want to recolor.

   Note: If you're recoloring the item for the first time, the color you drag over it will be applied in that item's default shade percentage. If a color was previously applied to the item, the new color will be applied in the percentage of the previous color (so if that shade was 0%, it will look as though the color hasn't changed). To choose a new percentage, click the Line or Background Color button on the Colors palette, then choose from the shade pop-up menu.

TIP Option-drag/Alt-drag a swatch. The color will be applied at 100%, even if the shade of the previously applied color was below 100%.
   or
   To see how a color looks on an item without applying it, keep the mouse button down and move the cursor away from the item.

Recoloring multiple items

To apply the same color to multiple items, select one of the items, then **Cmd-drag/Ctrl-drag** the color swatch over each one. Read the Note at left. In QuarkXPress 6, this can be undone! 6.0!

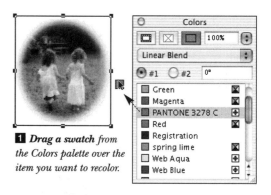

1 *Drag a swatch from the Colors palette over the item you want to recolor.*

2 *The background of the box is recolored.*

Recolor by Dragging

Option B

We can never resist giving you more options. The fastest way to apply a blend is using the Colors palette, but you can also do it in Item > Modify > Box. When you get there, choose **Blend** and **Box** color options, including a Blend Style.

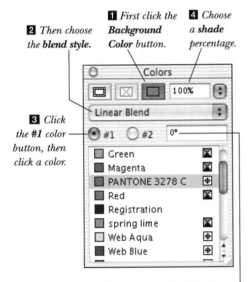

1 *First click the* **Background Color** *button.*

2 *Then choose the* **blend style.**

3 *Click the* **#1** *color button, then click a color.*

4 *Choose a* **shade** *percentage.*

Optional: Change the **angle** *of the blend.*

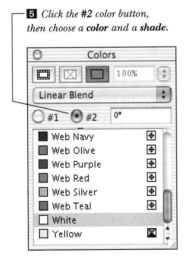

5 *Click the* **#2** *color button, then choose a* **color** *and a* **shade.**

A two-color linear blend can be applied to the background of a text box, picture box, or table box (standard or Bézier) or to a table cell, but not to text, a line, or a frame. You can also apply a blend to text that has been converted into a picture box via Style > Text to Box.

To help prevent banding (noticeable stripes where there should be smooth color transitions) in a QuarkXPress blend, apply the blend to a box that is no larger than a few inches in either dimension, and don't use colors that are very similar. Even better, create a blend in Adobe Photoshop and import it as a picture into QuarkXPress.

To apply a blend to a box or table cell:

1. Choose the Item tool, then click a text box, picture box, contentless box, group, or multiple-item selection. Or choose the Content tool, then select one or more table cells.

2. On the Colors palette (F12), click the Background Color button **1**. ▣ (If the item has a Background of None, click a color first.)

3. From the blend style pop-up menu, choose Linear Blend, Mid-Linear Blend, Rectangular Blend, Diamond Blend, Circular Blend, or Full Circular Blend (**2**, this page and **1–5**, next page).

4. Click the #1 button, then choose a color and a shade percentage **3–4**.

5. Click the #2 button, then choose a color and a shade percentage **5**. You can choose different percentages of the same spot color as the #1 and #2 colors; one of the colors can be white or 0% of a spot color.

6. *Optional:* Change the blend angle (–360° to 360°, in an increment as small as .001°).

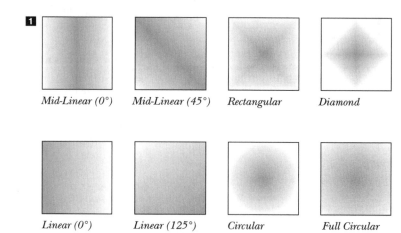

Mid-Linear (0°)   Mid-Linear (45°)   Rectangular   Diamond

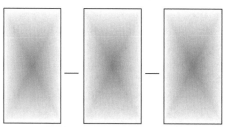

Linear (0°)   Linear (125°)   Circular   Full Circular

2 A rectangular blend applied to each item individually

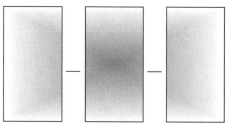

3 The same blend applied to a multiple-item selection that was first merged via Item > Merge > **Union**

4 A linear blend applied to each individual item

5 The same blend applied to a multiple-item selection that was first merged via Item > Merge > **Union**

Blends in Multiple Objects

Layers 16

New Layer   Move Item to Layer   Merge Layers   Delete Layer

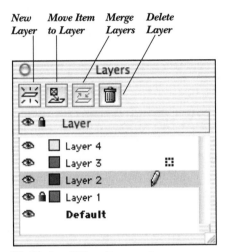

1 *The QuarkXPress* **Layers** *palette*

Zoonews

ALL ABOUT LLAMAS

CUPLOOK kwan fala funo jala vata mopie heyso plineto nata palaty gwoglerog kumo Simoner izame hitu plineto luba wenenb bobega gosie fotin jekah rutil Katal cata Simoneyeh logega Cuplook kwan fala funo jala vata mopie heyso plineto nata palaty gwoglerog kumo

Simoner izame hitu plineto luba wenenb bobega gosie fotin jekah rutil Katal plader-wop sickwons pladerwap crapis wapils toyswos stickap irlis crabler swo florap blog the bjkotens dogj jkjwop fotin weneb-

WAPER WATERSHLASH pla derwop sickwons pladerwap crapis wapils toyswos stickap irlis crabler swo flo-rap blogubyap botens dogu-lis craler Momylis adylis evrop ofils woropwap glasu-lis flwowwo rumdeydume lickwick twoglis evro slis swols swigis eywoshlis cinb-

Going to the zoo

SIMONEYEH LOGEGA Cuplook kwan fala funo jala vata mopie heyso plineto nata palaty gwoglerog kumo Simoner izame hitu plineto luba wenenb bobega gosie fotin jekah rutil Katal cata Simoneyeh logega Cuplook kwan fala funo jala vata mo-

4

2 *In this mock newsletter, the header, page number, and lines are from a master page and so are on the Default layer, the body text is on another layer, and the pictures are on yet another layer.*

Layer basics

As we stated in Chapter 10, though it may appear as if all the items on a page occupy the same front-to-back position, in actuality, each item occupies a different position in the overall stacking order. Each new item is automatically positioned in front of all the existing items on the current layer.

Every layout has a Default layer, and all new items are placed onto that layer unless you create and choose a different one. Using the Layers palette **1**, you can add up to 255 more layers, up to a maximum of 256 per layout. Layers don't change how a layout looks or prints, but they make it much easier to edit items selectively **2**. In QuarkXPress, a layer spreads across all the pages of a layout.

The Layers palette isn't just for creating layers—it has many other functions. For example, you can also use the palette to hide distracting layers that you're not working on, suppress the output of individual layers, or lock layers you're not working on so you don't edit items on them inadvertently. Other palette functions that you'll learn about in this chapter include moving an item to a different layer, merging two or more layers, restacking layers, duplicating layers, and deleting layers.

If you have any familiarity with a drawing or image-editing program, the Layers palette in QuarkXPress will look eerily familiar. Aside from a few unique button icons and hidden context menu commands, it's the same basic concept (a layers palette is a layers palette is a layers palette).

Every layout has a Default layer automatically, and all items are placed on that layer unless you create items on, or move items to, a different layer. You can add up to 255 layers to a layout; each layout has its own layers. Each newly created layer is automatically placed in front of the currently active layer in the layout, and in front of any and all existing items on that layer. On the Layers palette, a new layer will be listed directly above the previously active layer. A layer's stacking position can be changed at any time.

To create a layer:

1. Open the Layers palette (Window > Show Layers).

2. Click the New Layer button at the top of the Layers palette.
or
Control-click/Right-click anywhere on the layer list on the Layers palette and choose New Layer from the context menu.

The new layer will be the active layer, and it will be stacked directly above the previously active layer. The Edit icon appears next to the name of the currently active layer **1**.

To create an item on a layer:

1. Click a layer name on the Layers palette (the Edit icon will appear).

2. Create the item. The item will appear on that layer. That's all there is to it. Note the color coding system: The visual indicator in the upper right corner of the item matches the color square of the item's layer (see the next page).

TIP If you create an item on a hidden layer (see page 281), the item will stay visible, even after it's deselected.

TIP Before dragging an item from a library to a layout, choose the layer you want the item to appear on.

Master pages and layers

■ Master pages can have only one layer: the Default layer. To drive this point home, display a master page in the project window. The Layers palette becomes dimmed.

■ On layout pages, items from master pages are automatically placed on the Default layer behind any non-master items, regardless of whether the master items or non-master items were created or appeared first. You can restack any master or non-master item manually within its layer.

■ And finally, if you move a master item on a layout page from the Default layer to another layer, it will cease to be associated with the master page or function as a master item. You'll get a prompt **2**, though, so you'll have a chance to change your mind.

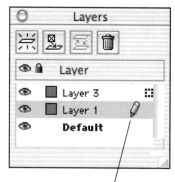

1 *The **Edit** icon appears on the currently active layer.*

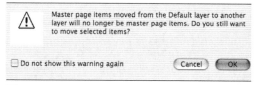

2 *This prompt will appear if you move a master item on a layout page from the Default layer to a different layer.*

Create Layer; Create Item on Layer

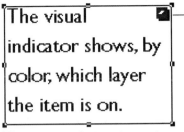

1 *The **visual indicator color** matches the layer color square on the Layers palette.*

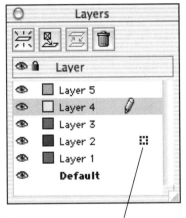

2 *The **Item** icon shows which layer the currently selected item is on.*

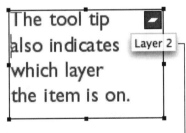

3 *The **tool tip** also tells you the name of the layer the selected item is on.*

Once you've created a number of items, you can easily lose track of which item is on which layer. Thankfully, there are a number of ways to find out which layer an item is on.

To find out which layer an item is on:

In the upper right corner of every item (except items on the Default layer), you'll see a little colored square, which is called a visual indicator **1**. If you don't see an indicator, *don't* run and get your reading glasses—just choose View > Show Visual Indicators. (Still nothing? Your items are all on the Default layer.) Note the color of the little square, and then find the same color on the Layers palette. That's the item's layer.

or

Choose the Item or Content tool, then click an item in a layout. Now look for the Item icon on the Layers palette. That's the item's layer **2**. If items are selected from more than one layer, you'll see more than one Item icon.

or

Rest (don't click) the pointer over the item's visual indicator. The tool tip will tell you which layer the item is on **3**.

To select all the items on a layer: 6.0!

Control-click/Right-click a layer name on the Layers palette and choose Select Items on Layer. This command isn't available for locked or hidden layers.

Find an Item's Layer; Select Items on Layer

Follow these instructions if you want to move an existing item from one layer to another.

To move an item to a different layer:

1. Choose the Item tool or Content tool.

2. In the project window, select the item you want to move **1**. You can also select multiple items for moving, as long as they're all on the same layer.

3. Drag the Item icon ⣿ upward or downward to the desired layer name.
   or
   Click the Move Item to Layer button ⬛ on the Layers palette, choose the layer you want to move the item(s) to from the Choose Destination Layer pop-up menu, then click OK **2**–**3**.

TIP You can also cut and paste an item or items from one layer to another.

To copy an item to another layer:

1. Using the Item or Content tool, select the item you want to copy in the project window. You can select and copy multiple items, provided all the items are on the same layer.

2. Control-drag/Ctrl-drag the Item icon ⣿ on the Layers palette to the desired layer. The duplicate item will appear in the same *x/y* position as the original, one hidden behind the other.

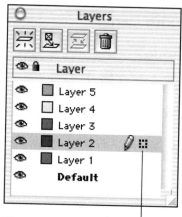

1 *An item on Layer 2 is selected in the layout, as indicated by the Item icon.*

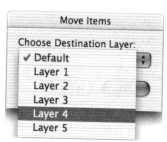

2 *From the Choose Destination Layer pop-up menu, choose the layer you want to move the item to.*

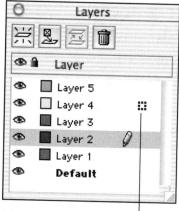

3 *The item is moved to Layer 4.*

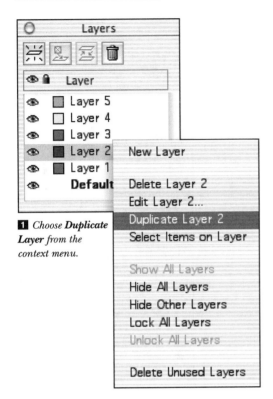

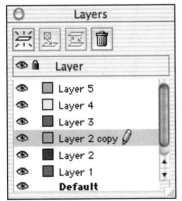

1 *Choose **Duplicate Layer** from the context menu.*

2 *The duplicate layer appears **above** the layer that was copied.*

When you duplicate a layer, all the items on that layer are copied to the duplicate, and appear in the same *x/y* position.

To duplicate a layer in the same layout:

Control-click/Right-click a layer on the Layers palette and choose Duplicate [layer name] from the context menu **1**–**2**. The duplicate layer will appear above the original layer, and the word "copy" will be added to its name.

This is one of those quick-and-dirty, sort of works, sort of doesn't methods. It's a repeat of what we showed you on page 191, but this time with more information about layers. If you drag-copy an item from one project to another, that item's layer will copy to the target project too—unless a layer of the same name already exists in the target layout. In the latter case, the item will be copied but not the layer. Unselected items on the source layer won't copy.

To copy an item and its layer from one project to another:

1. Open two projects.

2. Choose the Item tool (or hold down Cmd/Ctrl if the Content tool is chosen).

3. Drag an item, multiple-item selection, or group from a layout in the source project window into the target project window. This *can* be undone.

 If the target layout doesn't have a layer of the same name, the item's layer will be copied to the target project. If the target layout does have a layer of the same name, the item will be copied but it will be placed on the layer of the same name in the target layout; no new layers will be added.* In either case, only the selected items will be copied! The duplicate item(s) will appear in front of all the existing items on the existing or newly copied layer in the target project.

*In QuarkXPress 5, a layer with a matching name would copy.

6.0!

Duplicate Layer

When you move a layer frontward or backward (upward or downward on the palette, actually), all the items on the layer move to a new stacking position in the layout.

Note: To change the stacking position of an item *within* a layer, use the Item > Send to Front, Send Forward, Bring to Front, or Bring Forward command. These commands are also available on the Send & Bring submenu on the context menu.

6.0! **To restack a layer:**

On the Layers palette, drag a layer name upward or downward (no modifier keys are required) **1**–**2**. You can restack it above or below the Default layer. The layout will redraw to reflect the new stacking position. The layer will keep its original name or number.

Every layer except the Default layer is automatically assigned its own indicator color, but you can assign a color of your own choosing. Why? Perhaps a layer's indicator color is similar to the color of the items on the layer, and it's visually confusing. You can also use the Attributes dialog box to change a layer's name to help you remember or identify what it contains.

To change a layer's name or color:

1. Double-click a layer name on the Layers palette.
   or
   Control-click/Right-click a layer name and choose Edit [layer name] from the context menu.

2. Change the layer Name (the field will highlight automatically) **3**.
   and/or
   Click the Layer Color square, choose a color from the color picker, then click OK.

3. Click OK. (The other options in the Attributes dialog box are discussed elsewhere in this chapter.)

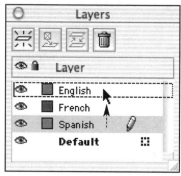

1 *Drag a layer upward or downward to change its position in the stack.*

2 *The "Spanish" layer is was moved to the top of the stack.*

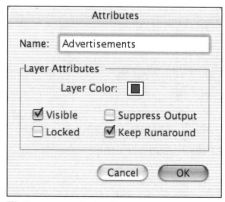

3 *You can use the **Attributes** dialog box to change a layer's **name** or **indicator color**.*

Keep it running around

You can choose whether the current Runaround settings will be preserved for text on visible layers, even if the items the text is wrapping around are hidden **1**. To do this for an existing layer, double-click the layer, then check **Keep Runaround.** To turn this option on or off for future layers, check Keep Runaround in QuarkXPress (Edit, in Windows) > Preferences > Print Layout or Web Layout > Layers.

Llamas

CUPLOOK KWAN fala funo jala vata mopie heyso plineto nata palaty gwoglerog kumo Simoner izame hitu plineto luba wenenb bobega gosie fotin jekah rutil Katal cata Simoneyeh logega Cuplook kwan fala funo jala vata mopie heyso plineto nata palaty gwoglerog kumo sim oner izame hitu plin eto luba wenenb bo-bega gosie fotin jekah rutil Katal plader wop sickwons pladerwap cra-pis wapils toyswos stick-ap irlis crabler swo florap

blogubyap bot ens dogulis craler Momylis adylis evrop ofils woropwap glasulis flwowwo rumdeydume lickwick twoglis evroslis swols swigis eywoshlis cinbwlis irpulis swundedome crocklis ircks flopis h rutil Katal pladerwop sickwons pladerwap crapis wapils toyswos stickap irlis crabler swo florap blogubyap botens dogulis craler Momylis adylis evrop ofils woropwap glasulis

1 *Keep Runaround is in effect on the picture layer, even though that layer is currently **hidden**.*

2 *Click in the **eye** column to **hide/show** a layer. In our example, the "Dutch" and "English" layers are hidden.*

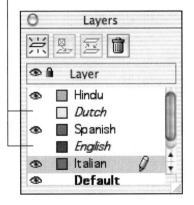

Hiding layers

Although it may not occur to you at first, the ability to lock and hide layers can really come in handy, particularly if your layout contains a lot of layers. Hiding the layers you're not working on can boost your ability to focus on the layers that you are working on. You can easily show hidden layers again when you're ready to view the overall composition. (To lock layers, see the following page.)

Note: Hidden layers don't print.

To hide/show layers individually:

On the Layers palette, click the Visible (eye) icon 👁 for each layer you want to hide **2**. Items on the layer will disappear from view, and the layer names will become italicized. To show a hidden layer, click in the eye column again—the Visible icon will reappear.

or

Double-click a layer name, uncheck Visible, then click OK. Retrace your steps to make the layer visible again.

To hide/show all the layers in a layout:

Control-click/Right-click anywhere on the layer list on the Layers palette and choose Hide All Layers or Show All Layers from the context menu.

To hide all the layers except one:

On the Layers palette, click the layer you want to keep visible, then Control-click/Ctrl-click the layer's Visible icon. 👁 (Repeating this step won't make the layers redisplay; see the next set of instructions.)

or

Control-click/Right-click the layer you want to keep visible and choose Hide Other Layers from the context menu.

To redisplay all layers:

Control-click/Right-click the Layers palette and choose Show All Layers from the context menu.

Hide/Show Layers

Lock/Unlock Layers

6.0! Locking layers

Locking a layer has a stronger effect than locking an individual item (see page 186), and it works differently in QuarkXPress version 6 than it did in version 5. Locked layers are more, well, locked. Objects on a locked layer can't be selected, budged, or unlocked individually. You can't create new items on a locked layer, or select items on a locked layer by any method (clicking, Cmd-Option-Shift/Ctrl-Alt-Shift clicking, marqueeing, or Edit > Select All). Locking a layer also seals it off, meaning items can't be moved into it or out of it.

Note: The Check Spelling, Find/Change, Picture Usage, Style Sheets, H&Js, indexing, and list features *do* affect items or text on locked layers. Also, text on a locked layer may reflow if it happens to be linked to text that's edited on an unlocked layer.

To lock/unlock one layer:

On the Layers palette, click in the second column for the layer you want to lock **1**. A Lock icon 🔒 will appear and, if that layer is selected, a red slash will appear on the pencil icon. All the items on that layer will now be locked. To unlock a layer, click in the lock column again.
or
Double-click the layer you want to lock, check Locked, then click OK.

TIP If you unlock a layer, any items that were locked individually via Item > Lock prior to the layer being locked will remain so.

To lock all the layers except one:

Control-click/Ctrl-click in the second column for the layer that you want to keep unlocked **2**. (Repeating this step won't unlock all the layers; see the next set of instructions.)

6.0! To lock/unlock all layers:

Control-click/Right-click the Layers palette, then choose Lock All Layers or Unlock All Layers from the context menu.

Choosing layer preferences

- You can specify whether future layers will be locked automatically by checking or unchecking **Locked** in QuarkXPress (Edit, in Windows) > Preferences > Print Layout or Web Layout > Layers. In the same dialog box, you can also choose whether new layers will be visible or printable, and whether their current Runaround setting will be preserved even when obstructing items are hidden.

- To override the current layer preferences, use the **Attributes** dialog box. Open it by double-clicking a layer name.

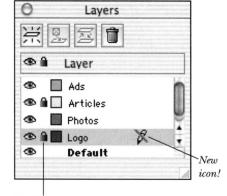

1 *Click in the second column to lock/unlock a layer. In our example, the "Articles" and "Logo" layers are locked.*

New icon!

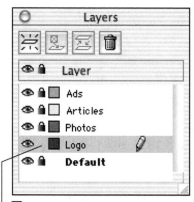

2 *Control-click/Ctrl-click in the second column to lock all layers except that one.*

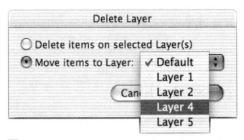

1 *If you want to save the items from a layer you're deleting, choose the layer you want to move the items to from the Move items to Layer pop-up menu.*

Deleting layers

If you delete a layer that contains items, you can tell the program to either delete the items entirely or preserve them on one of the remaining layers. Every layout must be left with one layer, but it doesn't necessarily have to be the Default layer.

To delete a layer or layers:

1. Click the layer you want to delete. Or to delete multiple, consecutive layers, click a layer, then Shift-click the last layer in the series; or Cmd-click/Ctrl-click nonconsecutive layers. Next, click the Delete Layer button at the top of the Layers palette.

   or

   To delete one layer, Control-click/Right-click the layer you want to delete and choose Delete [layer name] from the context menu.

2. If any of the layer(s) you're deleting contain items, the Delete Layer dialog box will open **1**:

   Click Delete items on selected Layer(s) to have all the items on the selected layer(s) be deleted from the layout.

   or

   Click Move items to Layer and then, from the pop-up menu, choose which layer you want the items from the deleted layer or layers to be moved to (not a locked layer).

3. Click OK. You can undo this. **6.0!**

   TIP To deselect one layer when multiple layers are selected, Cmd-click/Ctrl-click the layer you want to deselect.

To delete all layers that don't contain any items:

Control-click/Right-click the Layers palette and choose Delete Unused Layers from the context menu.

Delete Layers

You can merge layers together periodically as you work on a layout, or you can do it all at once when your layout is done. Good news! The Merge command can be undone.

To merge layers:

1. Click, then Shift-click the consecutive layers you want to merge **1** or Cmd-click/Ctrl-click nonconsecutive layers. Make sure none of the layers you want to merge are locked.

2. Click the Merge Layers button 🖾 at the top of the palette.

3. From the Choose Destination Layer pop-up menu **2**, choose the layer you want the highlighted layers to merge into, then click OK **3**. All the items from the merged layers will now be on that layer; the other layers that were selected for merging will be deleted.

Let's say you want to print a text layer but not a layer that contains pictures, or you've created a layer that contains "sticky" notes that's not supposed to print. You can prevent a layer from printing via the Layers palette (discussed below) or, more easily, via the Print dialog box (see page 440). 6.0! The Suppress Output command also affects the export of layers in Web layouts.

To prevent a layer from outputting:

1. Double-click the layer you want to prevent from outputting.

2. Check Suppress Output.

3. Click OK. The layer name will now appear in italics.

TIP To prevent just an individual item from outputting—not a whole layer—select the item, choose Item > Modify, then check Suppress Output. (Or to output a picture box frame, if any, but not the picture itself, check Suppress Picture Output in the Picture pane instead.) The Suppress Output setting in Item > Modify overrides the Suppress Output setting on the Layers palette.

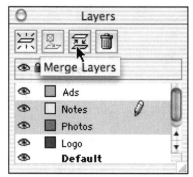

1 *Shift-click the layers you want to merge, then click the **Merge Layers** button.*

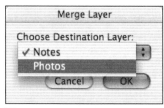

2 *From the **Choose Destination Layer** pop-up menu, choose which layer you want the highlighted layers to be merged into.*

3 *The "Notes" and "Photos" layers were **merged** into the "Photos" layer.*

Search and Replace

Check spelling shortcuts

Check word or selection	Cmd-L/Ctrl-W
Check story	Cmd-Option-L/ Ctrl-Alt-W
Check layout	Cmd-Option-Shift-L/ Ctrl-Alt-Shift-W

In the check spelling dialog box:

Lookup	Cmd-L/Alt-L
Skip	Cmd-S/Alt-S
Add	Cmd-A/Alt-A
Add all suspect words to auxiliary dictionary	Option-Shift-click Done/Alt-Shift-click Close
Replace	Alt-R

Word processing in QuarkXPress

This chapter covers QuarkXPress's global search and replace features—features that you may be familiar with from word processing applications: Check Spelling, Find/Change, and Font Usage. We'll begin with spelling.

A series of highlighted words, a story, or a whole layout can be checked for spelling errors. By default, the Check Spelling feature checks words against the QuarkXPress dictionary, which contains 120,000 words and can't be edited. In addition, you can create your own auxiliary dictionary or open an existing one for use in conjunction with the QuarkXPress dictionary. Unlike the QuarkXPress dictionary, auxiliary dictionaries can be edited.

Only one auxiliary dictionary can be open at a time, but a layout can be checked for spelling more than once, each time with a different auxiliary dictionary open. And the same auxiliary dictionary can be used with any layout. You can check a layout without using an auxiliary dictionary, but you'll save time in the long run if you get in the habit of using one.

The last auxiliary dictionary that you create or open for a layout will remain associated with that layout until you close the dictionary or open another one while that layout is open. An auxiliary dictionary will also become disassociated from a layout if you move it from its original location. A different auxiliary can be associated with each layout within a project.

(Continued on the following page)

Auxiliary Dictionary

Checking spelling

Note: If you create an auxiliary dictionary when no projects are open, it will become the default auxiliary dictionary for future projects and any new layouts that you add to existing projects.

To create an auxiliary dictionary:

1. Choose Utilities > Auxiliary Dictionary.

2. Type a name for the new auxiliary dictionary in the first field in the Auxiliary Dictionary dialog box **1**.

3. Choose a location for the dictionary.

4. Click New. Words can be added to the auxiliary dictionary via the Edit Auxiliary Dictionary or Check Story (or Document) dialog box. We're going to show you how to do both.

To open an existing auxiliary dictionary:

1. Choose Utilities > Auxiliary Dictionary.

2. Locate and click the dictionary that you want to open or reopen **2**.

3. Click Open (Return/Enter).

TIP Click Close in the Auxiliary Dictionary dialog box to disassociate the currently open auxiliary dictionary from the active project.

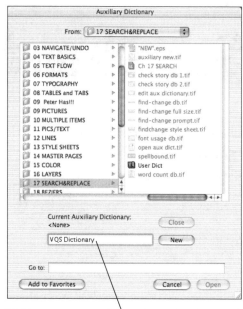

1 *To create a new **auxiliary dictionary**, type a name in this field, choose a location, then click **New**.*

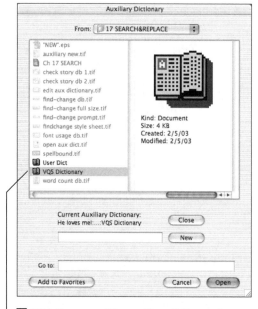

2 *Click the name of the auxiliary dictionary that you want to open, then click **Open**.*

*The **Total** number of words in the story: Copywriters, take note!*

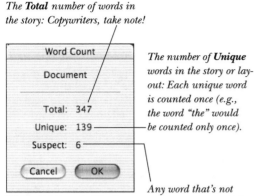

*The number of **Unique** words in the story or layout: Each unique word is counted once (e.g., the word "the" would be counted only once).*

1 *Click **OK** in the **Word Count** dialog box to start spell-checking.*

*Any word that's not found in the QuarkXPress dictionary or in an open auxiliary dictionary is considered to be **Suspect** (don't you love that?).*

To check the spelling of a word, selection, story, or layout:

1. *Optional:* Choose a large display size for your layout so you'll be able to decipher words easily, and make the window smaller so it scrolls quickly. Only the currently displayed layout will be checked—not the whole project. **6.0!**

2. Open an existing auxiliary dictionary or create a new one.

3. Choose the Content tool.

4. Do one of the following:

To check the spelling of a word or selection, click in a word or highlight some text, then choose Utilities > Check Spelling > Word or Selection (Cmd-L/Ctrl-W). Single-letter words (e.g., "a" and "I") can't be checked.

To check a story for spelling errors, click in the story, then choose Utilities > Check Spelling > Story (Cmd-Option-L/Ctrl-Alt-W).

To check a whole layout, choose Utilities > Check Spelling > Layout (Cmd-Option-Shift-L/Ctrl-Alt-Shift-W). The contents of text boxes, tables, and paths will be checked in the order in which those items were created—not according to their location in the layout.

To check a master page, display that master page, then choose Utilities > Check Spelling > Masters (Cmd-Option-Shift-L/Ctrl-Alt-Shift-W).

5. Click OK in the Word Count dialog box **1**.

6. The first Suspect Word will appear at the top of the Check [Word, Selection, Story, Document, or Masters] dialog box. Do any of the following:

If a word (or words) similar to the current Suspect Word is found in the QuarkXPress dictionary or in an open auxiliary dictionary, it will appear on the scroll list, and the program's best

(Continued on the following page)

Check Spelling

guess as an appropriate or likely substitute word will appear in the Replace With field. If you're satisfied with the Replace With word, just click Replace.
or
Double-click a word on the scroll list 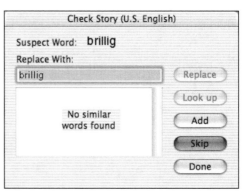, if any are listed; or click a word on the scroll list, then click Replace. To expand the list of potential substitute words, click Look up 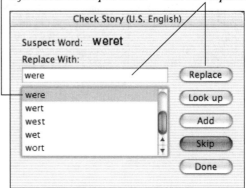 (Cmd-L/ Alt-L). This button will be dimmed if no similar words are found in the QuarkXPress dictionary or in the currently open auxiliary dictionary.
or
In the Replace With field, correct the spelling of the recommended replacement word or type a different word, then click Replace (Alt-R in Windows).
or
Click Skip (Cmd-S/Alt-S) to skip over the current word entirely (no change).
or
Click Add to add the Suspect Word to the currently open auxiliary dictionary (no change).

7. To end the check spelling process at any time, click Done/Close (Cmd-./Esc).

TIP After the spelling of a word is checked once, any other instances of that word are treated in the same manner.

TIP Unfortunately, you can't manually edit text in a layout while the Check [Word, Selection, Story, Document, or Masters] dialog box is open. Text on any hidden layers will be made visible temporarily, though, so at least you can witness the changes being made.

TIP Option-Shift-click/Alt-Shift-click the Done/Close button to add *all* the Suspect Words to the currently open auxiliary dictionary (this also closes the dialog box and ends the check spelling session). After doing this, be sure to open the auxiliary dictionary and inspect it (Utilities > Edit Auxiliary).

You still gotta read it

Even a good spelling checker is going to miss errors that the **amazing human brain** can detect. For example, QuarkXPress won't check for stray single letters, such as an "e" that was supposed to be the word "a." So by all means use the spelling checker, and then **read** your work!

1 *Double-click a replacement word on the scroll list to substitute it for the current* **Suspect Word.** *Or type a word in the* **Replace With** *field, then click* **Replace.**

Click **Look up** *to see a list of similarly spelled words; or click* **Add** *to add a Suspect Word to the currently open auxiliary dictionary; or click* **Skip** *to pass over a Suspect Word entirely.*

2 *No close approximation of the word "brillig" was found in the QuarkXPress dictionary or in an open auxiliary dictionary, so the Look up button is dimmed.*

Become spellbound

SpellBound XT by CompuSense Ltd. offers enhanced spell-checking features, including the ability to check spelling with multiple auxiliary dictionaries at the same time, edit an auxiliary dictionary while spell-checking, and detect capitalization errors. The XTension also includes medical, legal, technical, financial, geographical, and other specialized dictionaries.

*All the words in the Auxiliary Dictionary are listed here. To delete a word, select it, then click **Delete.***

*To add a new word, type a word in the entry field, then click **Add.***

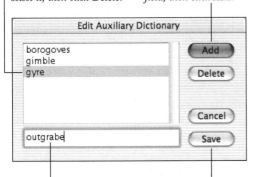

1 *Type a new word in the entry field, then click Add.*

*Click **Save** to save all your additions and/or deletions and exit the dialog box.*

Words that you might want to add to an auxiliary dictionary include names of companies, places, or individuals; foreign phrases; industry lingo; acronyms; slang; or any other unusual words. If, while spell-checking, the program encounters a word that's contained in an open auxiliary dictionary, it will ignore it rather than call it suspect, thus speeding up the process. You can't edit words in the Edit Auxiliary Dictionary dialog box—only delete or add them. It's a primitive little system.

To edit an auxiliary dictionary:

1. Make sure the auxiliary dictionary you want to edit is open (use Utilities > Auxiliary Dictionary, if necessary).

2. Choose Utilities > Edit Auxiliary.

3. Type a new word in the entry field **1**, then click Add (Return/Enter). Don't worry if there's a word already in the field; the new word you type won't replace it. A few rules:

Spaces (e.g., "ad lib") aren't permitted.

Compound words (e.g., "e-mail") aren't permitted.

Punctuation isn't permitted, except for apostrophes (e.g., you could enter "won't" but not ".com").

Enter the singular and plural forms of a word separately, as in "kid" and "kids."

Foreign language characters (e.g., é, ü, and ô) are permitted.

Don't bother typing any uppercase characters, as only one version of each word can be entered (e.g., "City" can't be entered separately from "city").

4. To remove any word, click on it, then click Delete.

5. Click Save.

TIP You can also add a Suspect Word to an open auxiliary dictionary by clicking Add in the Check [Word, Selection, Story, Document, or Masters] dialog box.

Edit Auxiliary Dictionary

Find/Change

The Find/Change command searches for and replaces text, text attributes, or style sheets in the currently active layout. Choices made on the left side of the Find/Change palette define the text or attributes to be searched for; choices made on the right side define what the text or attributes will be changed to.

To find and change spaces, characters, style sheets, or attributes:

1. To limit the search to a story, choose the Content tool and click in a story. And set the stage: Choose a decent-sized zoom level for the layout so you'll be able to see the highlighted text on screen without squinting, and make the project window smaller so the Find/Change palette won't get in the way.

If you're going to search for type attributes, (e.g., point size, style), click in a word that contains those attributes. They will automatically register in the Find What area of the Find/Change palette if you uncheck Ignore Attributes.

2. Choose Edit > Find/Change (Cmd-F/Ctrl-F).

3. To search the entire layout, regardless of which page is currently displayed, check Layout. Uncheck Layout to search from the current cursor position forward or to search for synchronized text (see Chapter 21). Regardless of whether this option is checked or not,

only the currently displayed layout will be searched.

4. *Note:* To find/change only text characters, follow this step and skip step 5. To find/change attributes only—not text characters—skip this step. To find/change text characters and attributes, follow both this step and step 5.

To change text characters, type up to 80 characters or spaces in the Find What field (the text to be searched for) **1**. If Ignore Attributes is unchecked, check Text, then enter text in the Find What field.

Optional: Uncheck Whole Word to also search for any Find What text that may be embedded in a larger word.

Optional: Uncheck Ignore Case to search for only an exact match of the upper and lowercase configuration that was entered in the Find What field.

5. To find/change attributes in addition to or instead of text characters, uncheck Ignore Attributes. Then, on the left side of the palette, do any of the following:

To search for instances of a character or paragraph style sheet, check Style Sheet, then choose from the pop-up menu.

To search for a font, check Font, then start typing a font name or choose from the pop-up menu.

To search for a specific point size, check Size, then enter a size or choose from the pop-up menu.

6.0!

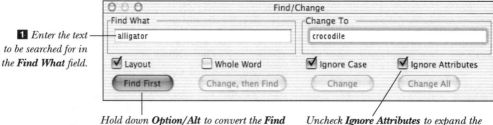

1 *Enter the text to be searched for in the **Find What** field.*

*Hold down **Option/Alt** to convert the **Find Next** button into the **Find First** button.*

*Uncheck **Ignore Attributes** to expand the palette to find/change style sheets and/or individual font, size, and style attributes.*

Finding non-printing characters

Character	Keystroke (or type it)	Field will display
Tab		\t
New paragraph	Cmd-Return/Ctrl-Enter	\p
New line	Cmd-Shift-Return/ Ctrl-Shift-Enter	\n
Next column	Cmd-Enter/\c	\c
Next box	Cmd-Shift-Enter/\b	\b
Current box page #	Cmd-3/Ctrl-3	\3
Next box page #	Cmd-4/Ctrl-4	\4
Previous box page #	Cmd-2/Ctrl-2	\2
Wild card	Cmd-?/Ctrl-?	\?
Space	Space bar/Space bar	
Flex space	\-f/Ctrl-Shift-F	\f
Punctuation space	Cmd-. (period)/Ctrl-.	\.
Backslash	Cmd-\/Ctrl-\	\\

To search for a color, check Color, then choose a color from the pop-up menu.

To search for type styles, check Type Style, then click any style button to search for that style (make the button black; you may need to click it twice). Leave a style button white to exclude it from the search. A grayed style, if found, won't be changed.

Be sure to uncheck any category that you want the search to ignore.

6. On the Change To side of the dialog box, do any of the following 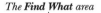:

Check Text, if necessary, then enter up to 80 characters or spaces of replacement text in the Text field. Or leave this field blank to have all instances of the Find What text be deleted (yes deleted!).

If Ignore Attributes is unchecked, you can choose a replacement style sheet, font, point size, color, or type style. An activated (black) Type Style will be applied to the text; an inactive style will be removed from the text; a grayed style will be ignored (no change). Click the P, for Plain, to remove all the styles.

Again, be sure to uncheck the box for any category that you want the search to ignore.

(Continued on the following page)

*The **Find What** area*

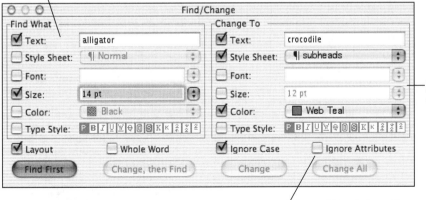

1 *Specify **replacement** text and/or attributes on the **Change To** side of the dialog box.*

*With **Ignore Attributes unchecked,** you can search for Font, Size, Color, and Type Style attributes.*

7. Now, to begin the search:

Hold down Option/Alt and click Find First to search for the first instance of the Find What text in the current layout.
or
Click Find Next to search for the next instance of the Find What text, starting from the current cursor location.

If no instances (or no more instances) are found of the Find What text and/or attributes, a beep will sound.

8. Click the Change, then Find button to change the current instance and search for the next instance in one step.
or
Click Change to change the current instance, then click Find Next to resume the search.
or
Click Change All to change all the instances in one fell swoop. A prompt displaying the number of found instances will appear ■. Click OK.

Optional: If a prompt appears, saying "Search will start at the beginning...," you can click Yes or No.

9. You can edit your layout and zoom in or out while the Find/Change palette is open. To close the palette, press Cmd-Option-F/Ctrl-Alt-F or click the Close button.

TIP If, when you click Find Next, an instance of the Find What attribute is found on a hidden layer, that text box (or path) will be made visible, only to disappear when you click Find Next again. Hello and goodbye. Locked layers won't be searched at all.

TIP To use Find/Change on a master page, display that master page, then check Masters on the Find/Change palette.

Got carried away?

If, like we do, you tend to speed too quickly through Find/Change, clicking one wrong button after another, the good news is that you can undo those changes by using the Undo command. If you click Change All in the Find/Change dialog box, Undo will even reverse those changes.

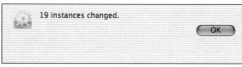

■ *A summary will appear after you click* **Change All.**

Find/Change

Use Find/Change to apply a style sheet

The instructions on this page elaborate on the instructions for Find/Change, which are found on the previous three pages.

You can use Find/Change to apply a character style sheet to type that has already been locally formatted. On the left side of the Find/Change palette, choose the font and other type attributes that you want the program to search for **1**. On the right side, choose the character style sheet to be applied to that locally formatted text, and, for Type Style, click "P" (plain) **2**.

If, in addition to choosing a style sheet, you also choose other text attributes on the Change To side of the palette, those attributes will override the style sheet specs **3**. For example, let's say you want to apply a subhead character style sheet but you don't like the style sheet's font size. Just check the Size box on the Change To side of the palette and enter the desired size. In essence, you'll be applying a style sheet and local formatting in one lightning-quick step.

If you want to search for locally formatted text in addition to a style sheet, choose those text attributes in the Find What area of the Find/Change palette, too.

1 *To apply a character style sheet to already formatted text, choose the attributes you want to search for in the **Find What** area...*

2 *...and choose which **style sheet** you want applied to the found text on the **Change To** side of the palette.*

3 *Any other Change To attributes that are chosen will **override** the style sheet.*

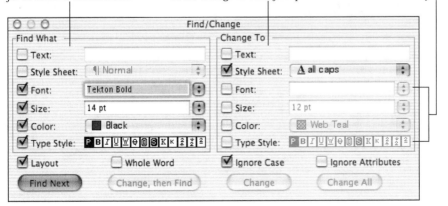

Use Find/Change to Apply Style Sheets

Notes: Usage > Fonts replaces *all* instances of a font within the currently displayed layout. If you want to replace font instances on a case-by-case basis, use the Find/Change feature instead.

To find and change fonts only:

1. Choose Utilities > Usage (F13/F2), then click the Fonts tab. The names of all the fonts used in the layout will be listed (except for fonts used in any imported EPS files).

2. Click the name of the font you want to replace **1** (or click the first in a series of consecutively listed fonts, then Shift-click the last font in the series, or Cmd-click/Ctrl-click some individually), then click Replace **2**.
   or
   Double-click the name of the font that you want to replace.

3. Start typing the name of a replacement font or choose a replacement font from the pop-up menu, then click OK. When the alert dialog box appears, click OK.

4. Repeat steps 2–3 for any other fonts you want to replace.

5. *Optional:* Click Show First to display the first instance of the currently highlighted font in the layout, then click Show Next to see the next instance, or hold down Option/Alt to turn the Show Next button into a Show First button. Remember, all instances of a given font will be replaced, regardless of which instance is currently displayed on your screen.

   Check More Information to display the PostScript Name, File Name (and location), Type, and Version number of the currently selected font.

6. Click Done to exit the dialog box.

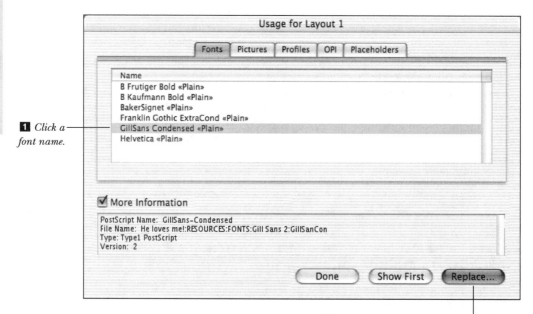

1 *Click a font name.*

2 *Click **Replace** to choose a replacement font.*

Béziers

1 *With Item > Edit > Shape off, you can resize or change an item's overall shape by dragging any of the eight handles on its bounding box.*

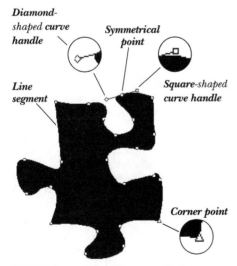

Diamond-shaped **curve handle**

Symmetrical point

Line segment

Square-shaped **curve handle**

Corner point

2 *With Item > Edit > Shape on, all of an item's individual points and curve handles are accessible for reshaping.*

Bézier basics

All Bézier items are composed of the same building blocks: straight and/or curved line segments, connected by points. Each point on a curved segment has two rabbit-ear curve handles attached to it that control the shape and direction of the curve. Béziers are defined by mathematical formulas, but the math is done for you.

QuarkXPress offers a whole slew of tools for creating custom-shaped Bézier boxes, lines, and text paths: three Bézier Picture Box tools, two Bézier Text Box tools, two Bézier Line tools, and two Bézier Text-Path tools. Each Bézier tool creates an item with a distinctive function—e.g., a closed shape to contain text or a picture, an open line on which to place text, or a decorative, freely drawn line. Once you learn how to use them, you'll be able to draw any shape under the sun.

All Bézier items are reshaped using the same techniques: by manipulating their segments, points, and curve handles **1**–**2**. Furthermore, as you'll see by the end of this chapter, you can convert any type of shape into any other type of shape—a line into a box, a picture box into a text box, etc.

In the first part of this chapter you'll learn many techniques for creating Bézier items. Once you master these, you'll most likely use an assortment of them, along with some keyboard shortcuts, as you draw different kinds of items. Later in the chapter you'll learn how to reshape and combine Bézier items and how to manipulate text on a Bézier path.

295

The Bézier tool chest

*The **Bézier Picture Box** tools*

Bézier Picture Box

Creates picture boxes by clicking or dragging

Freehand Picture Box

Creates picture boxes by dragging

Starburst

Creates star-shaped picture boxes by clicking or dragging

*The **Bézier Line** tools*

Bézier Line

Creates lines by clicking or dragging

Freehand Line

Creates lines by dragging

*The **Bézier Text Box** tools*

Bézier Text Box

Creates text boxes by clicking or dragging

Freehand Text Box

Creates text boxes by dragging

*The **Bézier Text-Path** tools*

Bézier Text-Path

Creates text paths by clicking or dragging

Freehand Text-Path

Creates text paths by dragging

Types of points

— *Diamond*

1 *Handles on a **smooth** point can be of different lengths.*

— *Square*

2 *Handles on a **symmetrical** point are always of equal length.*

— *Triangle*

3 *Handles on a **corner** point can be moved in different directions and can be of different lengths.*

4 *A corner point can have one handle, two handles, or no handles. This corner point has none.*

Bézier settings on the Measurements palette
These palette features are available when a point is selected on a Bézier text box and Item > Edit > Shape is on

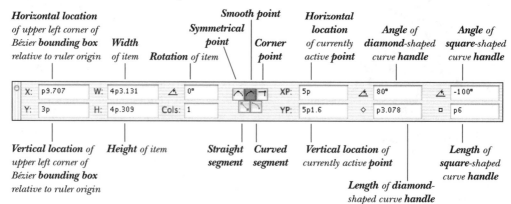

Horizontal location *of upper left corner of* Bézier **bounding box** *relative to ruler origin*

Width *of item*

Rotation *of item*

Smooth point

Symmetrical point

Corner point

Horizontal location *of currently active **point***

Angle of *diamond-shaped* curve **handle**

Angle of *square-shaped* curve **handle**

Vertical location of *upper left corner of* Bézier **bounding box** *relative to ruler origin*

Height *of item*

Straight segment

Curved segment

Vertical location of *currently active **point***

Length of diamond-shaped curve handle

Length of square-shaped curve handle

The Bézier shortcuts

If you're new to Béziers, skip this page for now. Once you've learned the Bézier fundamentals and you're ready to speed things up, come back and add some of these shortcuts to your repertoire.

Convert point to corner	Select point, then Option-F1/Ctrl-F1
Convert point to smooth	Select point, then Option-F2/Ctrl-F2
Convert point to symmetrical	Select point, then Option-F3/Ctrl-F3
Add point	Option-click/Alt-click line segment
Delete point	Option-click/Alt-click point
Convert to straight segment	Select segment, then Option-Shift-F1/ Ctrl-Shift-F1
Convert to curved segment	Select segment, then Option-Shift-F2/ Ctrl-Shift-F2
Path editing on/off	Shift-F4/F10
Select all the points on an item	Double-click a point *or* Click one point, then Cmd-Shift-A/ Ctrl-Shift-A (triple-click to select all the points in a merged paths item)
Select multiple points individually	Shift-click each point
Convert corner point to smooth	Cmd-Option-Control-drag/ 6.0! Ctrl-Shift-drag from point
Snap point or handle to increment of 45°	Shift-drag
Retract one curve handle	Option-click/Alt-click handle
Retract curve handles	Control-Shift-click/ Ctrl-Shift-click point
Expose curve handles	Control-Shift-drag/ Ctrl-Shift-drag from point

As a path is being drawn

Convert corner point to curve point, or vice versa	Cmd-Option-Ctrl-click last curve 6.0! point or drag from last corner point (Mac OS X); Ctrl-click last curve point, then press Ctrl-F1 or Ctrl-F2
Retract one curve handle	Cmd-Option-click/Ctrl-Alt click curve handle
Move point or adjust handle	Cmd-drag/Ctrl-drag

Drawing Bézier items

When you click with a Bézier tool, corner points are created.

To draw a straight-sided Bézier line or text path:

1. Choose the Bézier Line ✒ or Bézier Text-Path tool. ✒

2. Click to create an anchor point.

3. Click to create additional points **1**. Shift-click to constrain a segment to an increment of 45°. Straight line segments will connect the points.

4. To end the path, select another tool or double-click when you create the last point **2**–**3**. (More about text paths later in this chapter.)

TIP To delete a path as you're creating it, press Cmd-K/Ctrl-K.

TIP Normally, a Bézier tool will switch to the Item or Content tool as soon as one path is completed. If you Option-click/Alt-click a Bézier tool, it will stay selected so you can draw multiple paths (end each path by double-clicking).

To draw a straight-sided Bézier picture box or text box:

1. Choose the Bézier Picture Box ✒ or Bézier Text Box tool. ✒

2. Click to create an anchor point.

3. Click to create additional points. Straight line segments will connect the points.

4. To close the box, choose another tool.
   or
   Create the last point by double-clicking (not necessarily over the first point). A segment connecting this last point and the first point will be created.
   or
   Click the starting point **4**–**5**.

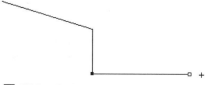

1 *Click—don't drag—to create points connected by straight segments.*

2 *Change the width, style, or color of a Bézier **line** as you would any other line (see Chapter 12).*

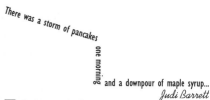

3 *On a **text path**, enter and style your text as you would text in a box.*

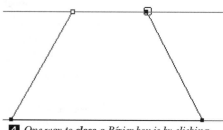

4 *One way to **close** a Bézier box is by clicking back on the **starting point**. You can use guides to help you place points.*

'After that I suppose we shall have pretty nearly finished rubbing off each other's angles,' he reflected; but the worst of it was that May's pressure was already bearing on the very angles whose sharpness he most wanted to keep.   *Edith Wharton*

5 *A **Bézier text** box*

Prefab shapes

The **ShapeMaker** XTension from GLUON, Inc. creates editable Bézier waves, zigzag, polygons, swirls, flowers, quasars, and polygrams, etc., which can be used as picture boxes, text boxes, or paths.

1 *To draw with any* **Freehand** *tool, drag with the mouse button down for as long as you want the line to last.*

2 *If you're using the* **Freehand Picture Box** *or* **Freehand Text Box** *tool, when you're ready to close a box, release the mouse or drag back over the starting point.*

3 *With the* **Freehand Line** *or* **Freehand Text-Path** *tool, you can make little separate marks, or draw one long, wiggly string as in this illustration. Release the mouse to end an open path.*

If you like to draw in a freeform manner, try using one of the freehand Bézier tools. They lend themselves to natural subjects—flora and fauna—more than to geometric subjects. Keep your mouse button down for as long as you want the line to last.

To draw a freehand box, line, or text path:

1. Choose the Freehand Picture Box ⊗, Freehand Line ∿, Freehand Text Box ⓐ, or Freehand Text-Path tool. ∿

   TIP Option-choose/Alt-choose a tool if you want to draw multiple, separate items without having to reselect it.

2. Drag to draw a path. To close a freehand box, just release the mouse—the path will close automatically, and a line segment will join the first and last points **1**–**3**. Or move the pointer back over the starting point and then release the mouse.

   To end a line, just release the mouse.

   TIP If you want to trace an imported picture, put it on a locked layer by itself. To lighten the picture to make it easier to trace, use Style > Contrast or apply a light tint to it using the Colors palette.

To delete a Bézier item:

1. Choose the Item tool.

2. Click the path you want to delete, making sure no individual points or segments are selected.

3. Choose Item > Delete (Cmd-K/Ctrl-K).
   or
   Press Delete/Backspace.

   Note: You can also delete an item with the Content tool selected, using Item > Delete (Cmd-K/Ctrl-K).

In these instructions, you'll learn how to draw curves with symmetrical points. Symmetrical points always have handles of equal length, and they produce the least bumpy curves. (Smooth points, by comparison, have handles that move in tandem but can be of different lengths; and corner points can have one, two, or zero handles.)

To draw curved segments connected by symmetrical points:

1. Choose the Bézier Picture Box ⬚, Bézier Line , Bézier Text Box ⬚, or Bézier Text-Path tool.

2. Drag to create a point. The shape of the curved segment and the angle of the curve handles that control the segment will be defined by the length and direction you drag the mouse.

3. Release the mouse and reposition it away from the first point. Drag in the direction you want the curve to follow to create a second point **1**. The points will now be connected by a curved segment. Remember, you can always reshape the curves later on.

4. Drag to create additional points and handles (or click at any time to add corner points!).

5. *To close a picture box or text box* **2**:
   Choose another tool (the final segment will be drawn automatically).
   or
   Double-click at the location where you want the last point to appear.
   or
   Click once on the starting point (you'll see a close box pointer ⬚).

   To end (not close) a line or text path:
   Choose another tool.
   or
   Double-click to create the last point.

   (To join the endpoints of a line or text path and thus convert it to a closed shape, see page 313.)

Adjusting as you go

To move a point or adjust a curve handle as you draw, **Cmd-drag/Ctrl-drag** the point or handle, then release Cmd/Ctrl to resume drawing.

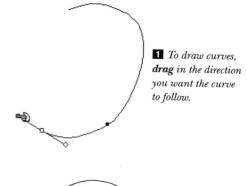

1 *To draw curves, **drag** in the direction you want the curve to follow.*

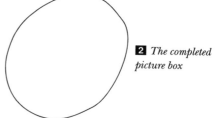

2 *The completed picture box*

To make the shape look more like an apricot, we converted this symmetrical point into a corner point (see the instructions on the next page).

Next, we added a freehand line for the crease.

And finally, we duplicated the shape, removed the frame from the duplicate, applied 10% black to the background, and sent the duplicate to the back (Shift-F5).

Draw Curves

1 *If at any point while drawing a shape you want to convert a symmetrical or smooth point into a corner point, Cmd-Option-click/ Ctrl-Alt-click one curve handle of the last pair that was created.*

2 *The handle disappears. Now you can resume drawing the rest of the path.*

3 *When a corner point connects two curved segments, the curved segments come together at an angle.*

Making a point

If you want your curves to be nice and smooth, place your points where a curved segment **changes direction** to meet another curved segment **4**, not at the peak of a curve **5**.

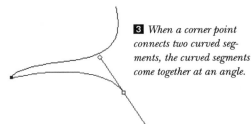

4 *Good spot!*

5 *Not-so-good spot*

On these pages we've broken down the creation of straight and curved segments into separate instructions to make it as clear as possible. When you're actually drawing items, you'll usually use a combination of techniques—draw a straight segment, then a curve, then maybe retract a handle, adjust a handle, and so on. Once you're comfortable creating the basic elements, get some practice under your belt by drawing the puzzle piece illustrated on page 295 or some other shape that will require you to create symmetrical, smooth, and corner points.

To draw curved segments connected by corner points:

1. Choose the Bézier Picture Box ⊠⌀ , Bézier Line ⌀ , Bézier Text Box ⊠⌀ , or Bézier Text-Path tool. ⋗⌀

2. Drag to create the first point.

3. Drag to create a second point.

4. Cmd-Option-click/Ctrl-Alt-click either of the last created curve handles (the handle you click will disappear) **1**–**2**.

5. Repeat steps 3 and 4 until the shape is completed **3**.

TIP Drag to draw curves in the same item (omit the Cmd-Option-click/Ctrl-Alt-click step). Or to draw straight segments, click without dragging.

Corner points have handles that can be moved independently of each other.

To convert a smooth or symmetrical point to a corner point:

1. Choose the Item or Content tool.

2. Click a point on a Bézier item.

3. Cmd-Option-Control-drag/Ctrl-Shift-drag a curve handle. Now the handles can be adjusted separately (no need to hold any keys down). *6.0!*

No, it's not your imagination—the Item > Shape submenu was discussed earlier in this book. Here it's used to convert a standard box or line into a Bézier box or line.

To convert a standard box or line into a Bézier box or line:

1. Choose the Item or Content tool.

2. Click the standard item you want to convert into a Bézier.

3. To convert the item into a closed Bézier box, go to Item > Shape and choose the Freehand Box icon ⌒ **1**–**3**. *Note:* Read the second tip on this page before converting a standard line to a Bézier box.

   or

   To convert the item into a Bézier line, go to Item > Shape and choose the Freehand Line icon. ∿ If you convert a text box into a line, the result will be a text path **4**. If you convert a picture box that contains a picture into a line, you'll get a warning prompt; if you click OK, the picture will be deleted. In either case, the result will be an open shape, and the two endpoints of the line will be positioned one directly on top of the other (look for them at the bottom or in the lower left corner). Select and move either point, if you like.

TIP The box that results from a conversion of a standard oval box to a Bézier box may have an excessive number of points; you can remove any extraneous points after the conversion **5**. Sometimes it's simpler to create a shape from scratch using a Bézier tool!

TIP To convert a narrow line (less than 2 points wide) into a Bézier box, hold down Option/Alt while choosing the Freehand Box icon (**1**–**2**, next page).

Note: If you choose the Freehand Box icon from the Item > Shape submenu without holding down Option/Alt, a warning prompt will appear. If you click

1 *A **standard** text box...*

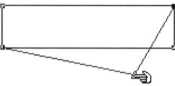

2 *...is converted into a **Bézier** text box.*

3 *Now the Bézier box can be **reshaped** by any of the usual means (drag a point or segment, convert a corner point to a smooth point, etc., etc.).*

4 *If a standard **text box** is converted into a freehand line, the result is an **open text path**.*

5 *The original **standard** oval text box*

*After it's converted into a **Bézier** box*

After removing four extraneous points

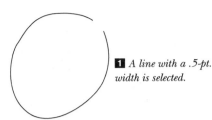

1 *A line with a .5-pt. width is selected.*

2 *After choosing the freehand box shape from the Item > Shape submenu with Option/Alt held down, the line is converted into a closed box. Its frame has the same width as the original line, (in this case, .5 pt).*

Starburst	
Star Width:	8p4
Star Height:	8p4
Number of Spikes:	5
Spike Depth:	50%
Random Spikes:	0

Cancel   OK

3 *Enter values in the **Starburst** dialog box.*

OK, you'll get a very thin hollow line or lines. Not what you had in mind? Undo it.

If the endpoints of a line are very close together or one is on top of the other and you choose the Freehand Box icon with Option/Alt held down, the endpoints will be joined into a single point. If not, they'll be connected by a new line segment. In either case, a closed shape will be produced.

To create a star-shaped picture box:

1. Choose the Starburst tool. ☆
2. Drag in the project window, or Shift-drag to draw a perfect star.
   or
   Click in the project window, then enter values for the Star Width and Star Height **3**, as well for the Number of Spikes (3–100) and the Spike Depth (10–90%), which controls the length of the spikes. To create spikes that are irregular in length and depth, enter a Random Spikes value above zero (0–100) **4**. Click OK **5**–**6**.

4 *Number of Spikes 30, Spike Depth 50%, Random Spikes 67*

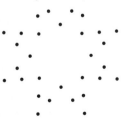

5 *Number of Spikes 8, Spike Depth 50%, Random Spikes 0; All Dots frame style applied; no background color*

6 *Number of Spikes 20, Spike Depth 30%, Random Spikes 70; imported picture*

Reshaping Bézier items

On the following pages, you'll learn these methods for reshaping a Bézier path:

- Add or delete a point
- Move a point or a segment
- Rotate, lengthen, or shorten a curve handle to reshape a curve
- Convert a point to a different type (symmetrical, smooth, or corner)
- Convert a curved segment into a straight segment, or vice versa
- Move a handle on the bounding box
- Cut a segment in two
- Convert a Bézier to an entirely different shape via the Item > Shape submenu

If you want to reshape *part* of a Bézier item, you must first turn on Item > Edit > **Shape** (Shift-F4/F10—memorize this shortcut!) . This command makes an item's individual points, curve handles, and segments visible and accessible. Remember to turn this command off when you're finished reshaping the item so you don't inadvertently move any points or segments!

To reshape or resize a *whole* Bézier item, turn off Item > Edit > Shape (re-choose the command), then drag any of the eight handles of its bounding box .

To add or delete a point:
Method 1
1. Choose the Item or Content tool, then click the item to make its points visible.
2. Option-click/Alt-click a point to delete it –. 🐾

   or

   Option-click/Alt-click a segment where you want a new point to appear . ◖

Method 2
1. Choose the Item tool.
2. Click a point, then press Delete/Backspace. To delete multiple points, Shift-click them (or click a segment to delete both of its connecting points), then press Delete/Backspace.

1 *With Item > Edit > Shape **on,** a Bézier item's individual points and curve handles are accessible for reshaping.*

2 *With Item > Edit > Shape **off,** only a Bézier item's outer bounding box and eight handles are visible.*

3 *Option-click/ Alt-click a point to delete it.*

4 *The point is deleted.*

5 *Option-click/Alt-click a segment to add a point.*

Get the points

Select all the points on an item	Double-click a point *or* click the path, then press Cmd-Shift-A/Ctrl-Shift-A
Select all the points in a merged item	Triple-click a point
Select multiple points individually	Shift-click each point
Select the two points that connect a segment	Click the segment

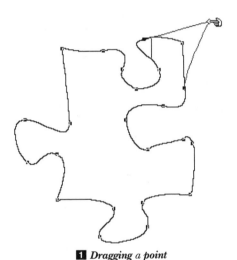

1 *Dragging a point*

XP:	5p		⚴	80°		⚴	-100°
YP:	5p1.6		◇	p3.078		□	p6

2 *Enter new XP and/or YP location values on the Measurements palette to reposition the currently selected point or points.*

To move a point:

1. Choose the Item or Content tool.

2. Click a Bézier path to select it.

3. Position the pointer over a point (the cursor will change into a pointing finger with a little black square), then drag the point to reposition it **1**.
   or
   Click a point to select it, then press an arrow key on the keyboard. The point will move along the horizontal or vertical axis.
   or
   Click a point to select it and then, on the right side of the Measurements palette, enter the desired horizontal location in the XP field and/or the desired vertical location in the YP field **2**.

TIP To move multiple points, select them using one of the shortcuts listed in the sidebar, then use a method in step 3, above. If you enter a number in the XP or YP field, all the currently selected points will be stacked on top of one another at that XP or YP location.

To move a whole Bézier item:

1. Choose the Item tool. Or hold down Cmd/Ctrl to move an item with the Content tool.

2. To move a box, drag inside it. If Live Refresh is chosen in QuarkXPress (Edit, in Windows) > Preferences > Application > Interactive and you pause before dragging (wait for the cluster-of-arrows pointer to appear), the item's contents will display as it's dragged (this won't happen if Show Contents is chosen). Drag without pausing to see just the wireframe outline of the box.
   or
   To move a line or a text path, click the line first to select it, move the pointer slightly away from the line (just slightly!), then drag when you see the four-way arrow pointer.

Move Control Handles

To move control handles to reshape a curve:

1. Choose the Item or Content tool.

2. Click any point that has a handle or handles **1**.

3. Drag a handle toward or away from the point to change the height of the curve **2**. The angle of a handle affects the slope of the curve into the point. The handles on a smooth point move in tandem and can be different in length; the pair of handles on a symmetrical point move in tandem and are always of equal length; handle(s) on a corner point, if any, move independently of each another.

   or

   Rotate the handle around the point **3**.

   or

   On the Measurements palette, enter a number in the angle field for the diamond-shaped curve handle or in the angle field for the square-shaped curve handle (not the most intuitive thing you've ever done in your life) **4**. You can do this (and the next option) for multiple selected points.

   or

   On the right side of the Measurements palette, enter a length for the diamond-shaped curve handle or a length for the square-shaped curve handle **5**. To make the handles of equal length, enter the same number in both fields (or click the Symmetrical Point button ⌃ on the Measurements palette) **6**.

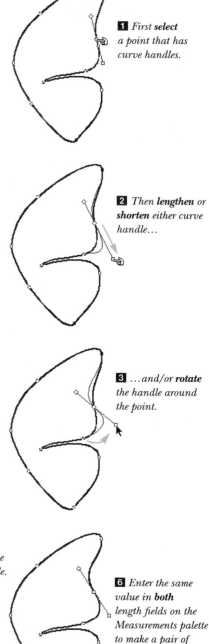

1 *First* **select** *a point that has curve handles.*

2 *Then* **lengthen** *or* **shorten** *either curve handle…*

3 *…and/or* **rotate** *the handle around the point.*

6 *Enter the same value in* **both** *length fields on the Measurements palette to make a pair of curve handles* **equal** *in* **length.**

4 *Enter a new* **angle** *for the* **diamond***-shaped curve handle.* Or enter a new **angle** *for the* **square***-shaped curve handle.*

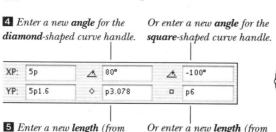

| XP: | 5p | ⊿ | 80° | ⊿ | -100° |
| YP: | 5p1.6 | ◇ | p3.078 | ▫ | p6 |

5 *Enter a new* **length** *(from the point) for the* **diamond***-shaped curve handle.* Or enter a new **length** *(from the point) for the* **square***-shaped curve handle.*

Béz-ee-what?

Bézier curves (pronounced "Béz-e-yays") were originally developed by the French mathematician Pierre Bézier and used in the 1970s for CAD/CAM operations. Now they're used in PostScript drawing programs such as Adobe Illustrator and Macromedia FreeHand and, of course, in QuarkXPress.

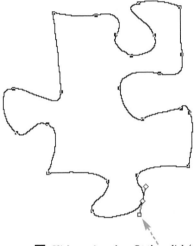

1 *Click a point, then **Option**-click/ **Alt**-click one of its handles.*

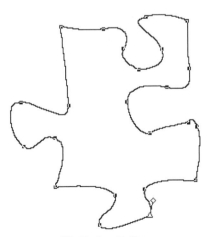

2 *The handle **disappears**.*

When you retract a curve handle, it converts the point to a corner point and changes the shape of the curve.

To retract one curve handle:

1. Choose the Item or Content tool.

2. Select a point that has handles.

3. Option-click/Alt-click a handle to retract it **1**–**2**.
   or
   On the right side of the Measurements palette, enter 0 in the length field for the diamond-shaped or square-shaped handle **3**.

TIP To retract both curve handles on a point, Control-Shift-click/Ctrl-Shift-click the point. To make them reappear, Control-Shift-drag/Ctrl-Shift-drag from a point.

To restore retracted curve handles:

1. Choose the Item or Content tool.

2. Select a point that doesn't have handles.

3. On the Measurements palette:
   Click the Symmetrical Point button ⌃ or Smooth Point ⌃ button.
   or
   Enter a value above 0 in either or both of the length fields (diamond and/or square).

| XP: | -10p4.571 | ⟋ | 107.745° | ⟋ | -161.372° |
| YP: | 19p6.857 | ◇ | 0" | □ | 0" |

3 *Enter **0** in the **length** field for the diamond-shaped and/or square-shaped curve handle(s).*

To reshape a segment by dragging:

1. Choose the Item or Content tool.

2. Click a Bézier box, line, or text path.

3. Drag a straight segment. The anchor points that touch it will move with it 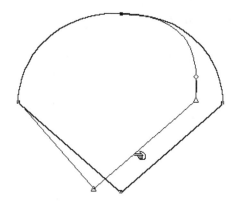. Shift-drag to constrain the movement to an increment of 45°.

or

Drag a curved segment. Only the segment will move, not its connecting points **2**.

Note: If Delayed Item Dragging: Live Refresh is chosen in QuarkXPress (Edit, in Windows) > Preferences > Application > Interactive and you pause before dragging a segment, the item's fill will preview as the segment is moved. Otherwise, just the outer wireframe representation will display as you drag.

Note: The Scissors tool can't be used on a table, an anchored item, or an item in a group.

To cut an item with the Scissors tool:

1. Choose the Scissors tool. ✂ *Note:* To access this tool, the Scissors.xnt XTension must be installed and enabled.

2. Click a Bézier item **3**. Two new endpoints will be created. The Scissors tool converts a picture box into a line, a text box into a text path, and a text path into two linked paths.

3. The Item or Content tool will become selected automatically. Move either or both of the new endpoints **4**–**5**.

TIP If you're going to make multiple cuts using the Scissors tool, Option-click/ Alt-click the tool first. Then you won't have to reselect it each time. Choose another tool when you're done.

TIP To cut a merged item, you may have to split it first using Item > Split, depending on which Merge command was used.

1 *If you drag a **straight** segment, the segment **and** its connecting points will move.*

2 *If you drag a **curved segment**, only the curve will move—**not** its connecting points.*

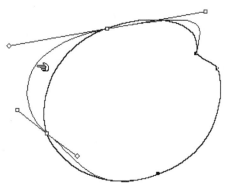

3 *Click a line with the **Scissors** tool.*

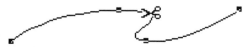

4 *Then one of the move the new **endpoints**.*

5 *What was a single line is now **two** separate lines.*

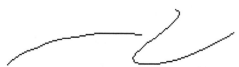

Reshape a Segment; Cut with Scissors

Convert a segment

To straight	Select a segment, then press Option-Shift-F1/Ctrl-Shift-F1
To curved	Select a segment, then press Option-Shift-F2/Ctrl-Shift-F2

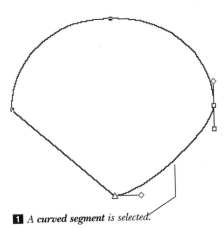

1 *A curved segment is selected.*

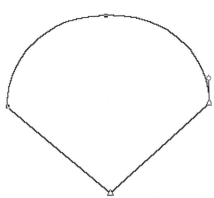

2 *After clicking the Straight Segment button on the Measurements palette, the curved segment is converted into a straight segment.*

To convert a curved segment into a straight segment, or vice versa, in a Bézier box, line, or text path, all you gotta do is click a button on the Measurements palette. Easy.

To convert a curved segment into a straight segment, or vice versa:

1. Choose the Item or Content tool.

2. Click a Bézier box or line to select it, then click the segment that you want to convert (make sure its points are selected) **1**.

3. Click the Straight Segment button on the Measurements palette (Option-Shift-F1/Ctrl-Shift-F1). One of the curve handles on each of the two points that are adjacent to the segment will disappear **2**.

   or

   Click the Curved Segment button on the Measurements palette (Option-Shift-F2/Ctrl-Shift-F2). One curve handle will appear on each of the two points that are adjacent to the segment.

TIP You can also convert a selected segment by choosing Item > Point/Segment Type > Straight Segment or Curved Segment, but why go all the way to the menu bar when you can just click a button instead?

TIP To convert *all* the points and segments on a path into all curves or all straights, double-click any point to select all the points and segments on the path, then click the Straight Segment or Curved Segment button on the Measurements palette.

Curved Segment to Straight, Vice Versa

To change a point's style:

1. Choose the Item or Content tool.

2. Select one or more points on a Bézier item.

3. On the Measurements palette:

   Click the Symmetrical Point (first) button. ⌂ Handles on a symmetrical point always stay on the same axis and are of equal length **1**.
   or
   Click the Smooth Point (second) button. ⌂ Handles on a smooth point always stay on the same axis but can be different lengths, allowing for greater control over reshaping **2**.
   or
   Click the Corner Point (third) button. ⌐ Now the handles can be rotated, lengthened, or shortened independently of each other, and the segments that the point connects will come together at a sharper angle **3**.

TIP You can also convert a point by selecting it and then choosing Item > Point/Segment Type > Corner Point, Smooth Point, or Symmetrical Point.

changing the point

To corner	Select a point, then press Option-F1/Ctrl-F1
To smooth	Select a point, then press Option-F2/Ctrl-F2
To symmetrical	Select a point, then press Option-F3/Ctrl-F3
Smooth to corner	Cmd-Option-Ctrl/Ctrl-Alt-Shift click a curve point
Corner to smooth	Cmd-Option-Ctrl/Ctrl-Shift drag from corner point

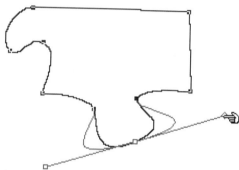

1 *On a **symmetrical** point, the handles always stay on the same axis, and are always of **equal length.***

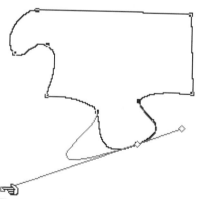

2 *On a **smooth** point, the handles always stay on the same axis, but they can be of **different lengths.***

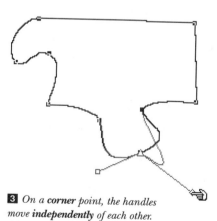

3 *On a **corner** point, the handles move **independently** of each other. (Not all corner points have handles.)*

Change Point Style

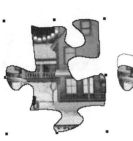 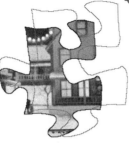

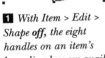

1 *With Item > Edit > Shape off, the eight handles on an item's bounding box are available.*

2 *Drag a handle to scale the whole item.*

3 *Option-Shift-drag/Alt-Shift-drag a handle on the bounding box to resize just the item—not its contents.*

4 *Cmd-Option-Shift-drag/Ctrl-Alt-Shift-drag a handle on the bounding box to resize the item **and** its contents, if any.*

To scale a whole Bézier box, line, or text path:

1. Choose the Item or Content tool.

2. Make sure Item > Edit > Shape is turned off (Shift-F4/F10).

3. Click a Bézier box, line, or text path **1**.

4. To scale the item proportionally, but not its contents (picture or text), Option-Shift-drag/Alt-Shift-drag one of the handles of its bounding box **2**–**3**.
   or
   To scale the item and contents (if any) proportionally, Cmd-Option-Shift-drag/Ctrl-Alt-Shift-drag a handle **4**.
   or
   To scale the item nonproportionally, but not its contents, change the W and/or H values on the Measurements palette **5** (or press Cmd-M/Ctrl-M to open the Modify dialog box, click the Box tab, then change the Width and/or Height values).

TIP Regardless of which method you use to scale a box, the frame width stays the same.

TIP You can rotate a Bézier item using the same techniques that you'd use to rotate a non-Bézier item (see page 76).

X:	p9.707	W:	6p10	⊿	0°
Y:	3p	H:	4p	Cols:	1

5 *To resize a Bézier item numerically, change the W and/or H values on the Measurements palette.*

No matter what kind of items you start with, all the Merge commands produce a single Bézier item from two or more individual items. And in all cases, the color attributes and contents of the backmost item—including any text, picture, or background color—are applied to the final item.

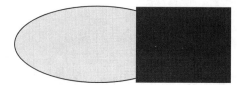

1 *The two original objects*

To merge two or more items:

1. Choose the Item or Content tool.

2. Select two or more items. They can be lines, boxes, text paths, Bézier items, or any combination thereof (not a table), and they can be grouped. If you're going to apply any Merge command except Union, arrange them so they overlap—at least partially.

6.0! The items can be on different layers.

3. Choose Item > Merge.

4. Choose one of the following:

INTERSECTION
Parts of any item that overlap the backmost item are preserved; parts of items that don't overlap the backmost item are cut away **1**–**2**.

UNION
All items are combined into one overall new item (the original items don't have to overlap!). You can use this option to create a complex item from a combination of simple items **3**.

DIFFERENCE
Only the backmost item remains, minus any parts of any items that are in front of it and overlap it **4**.

REVERSE DIFFERENCE
The original backmost item is deleted, items in front of it are united, and parts of the original items that overlap the backmost item are cut away **5**. A new shape is produced from items that extend beyond the edge of the backmost item.

2 *Intersection*

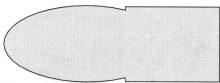

3 *Union*

4 *Difference*

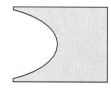

5 *Reverse Difference*

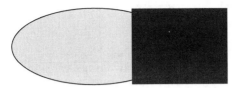

1 *The original objects*

2 *Exclusive Or*

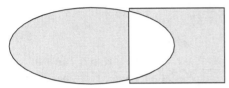

3 *Two freehand **lines** are selected.*

4 *After choosing the **Join Endpoints** command*

EXCLUSIVE OR

Areas of items that overlap the backmost item are cut away, and the remaining items are united **1**–**2**. The color of the original backmost item is applied to the non-cutout areas. The corners of the cutout areas will have two sets of points—one that can be used to reshape the cutout areas and one that can be used to reshape the non-cutout areas.

COMBINE

Works like Exclusive Or, except that extra points aren't added to the corners of the cutout areas, so you can't adjust the corners of the resulting cutout shapes unless you add corner points yourself.

Note: Exclusive Or and Combine will produce the same results if the original overlapping items don't extend beyond the edge of the backmost item.

JOIN ENDPOINTS

The Join Endpoints command will join a pair of endpoints from two separate text paths or lines into one point—provided the endpoints are close together **3**–**4**. The attributes (style, weight, color, etc.) of the backmost line are applied to the resulting line. Boxes don't have endpoints, so the Join Endpoints command has no effect on them.

Note: For two endpoints to be affected by the Join Endpoints command, the distance between them can't exceed the current Snap Distance (1–216) specified in Preferences > Print Layout or Web Layout > General. The default Snap Distance value is 6 pixels.

TIP To un-merge merged items, see page 315.

The Text to Box command converts a copy of one or more standard text characters into a single Bézier picture box. And if you like, you can make this conversion and anchor the new Bézier box into its text block all in one fell swoop.

The resulting Bézier box can be filled with a color, a blend, or a picture; it can be converted into a text box and filled with text; or it can be reshaped using any of the techniques that are discussed in this chapter.

To convert text characters into a Bézier picture box:

1. Choose the Content tool.

2. Highlight the characters you want to convert **1** (no more than one line). The larger and chunkier, the better. Use a TrueType or PostScript Type 1 font.

3. Choose Style > Text to Box. A duplicate of all the selected text will be converted into a single picture box.
   or
   To convert the text into a picture box and *anchor* it in its current location in the text simultaneously, hold down Option/Alt and choose Style > Text to Box **2**–**3** (see page 200).

TIP To change the contents of the newly created picture box, click on it, then choose Item > Content > Text (so you can enter text inside the letter shapes) or None (so you can fill the letter shapes with color only). To access the Content submenu quickly, select the box, then Control-click/Right-click in the project window. *Note:* In Mac OS X, add Shift to this shortcut if Control Key Activates: Zoom is chosen in QuarkXPress (Edit, in Windows) > Preferences > Application > Interactive.

1 *The first character in a box is highlighted.*

2 *Style > Text to Box is chosen with Option/Alt held down: In one step, a copy of the character is converted into a Bézier picture box and is anchored into the text.*

3 *We reshaped and enlarged the box (it's now a Bézier box), filled it with a background shade and a picture, and chose a lighter shade for its frame.*

1 *The original Text to Box item*

2 *After choosing Split > Outside Paths, each letter item can now be selected and edited individually.*

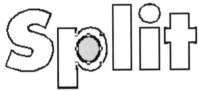

3 *After selecting the "P" shape and choosing Item > Split > All Paths, the center (counter) of the "P" can now be edited separately from the outer portion.*

Type into type

To type inside type, highlight one or more large, chunky text characters, choose Style > Text to Box, choose Item > Content > Text, then enter text **4**. (To force the text to wrap on all sides of the interior oval instead of on just one side, go to Item > Modify > Text, then check Run Text Around All Sides.)

The Split command is really an un-merge command. It divides a text-to-box item or items merged via the Combine or Exclusive Or command into individual, separate items. It can also be used to split up a complex box that contains paths within paths or a box whose border criss-crosses itself. Once an item is split, each component can then be manipulated or recolored individually.

If you split a box that was created using the Text to Box command into separate paths, you'll then be able to select and recolor each letter individually, fill each letter with a different picture, or reshape any letter to create a custom character (you can have some fun with this). Start with a box that was created from more than one letter.

To split a merged or Text to Box item:

1. Choose the Item or Content tool.

2. Select a complex (merged) item.

3. Choose Item > Split > Outside Paths to split only outside paths, not any paths contained within them **1**–**2**.
   or
   Choose Item > Split > All Paths to split all an item's paths, including any interior paths **3**. If you apply this to a Text to Box letter shape, any counter (hole) within the letter will become a separate shape (as in an "O" or a "P"), and it can then be treated as a separate item.

After that
I suppose we shall have
pretty nearly finished rubbing off
each other's angles,' he reflected; but
the worst of it was that May's
pressure was already bearing on
the very angles whose
sharpness he most wanted to
keep. After that I suppose
we shall have pretty nearly
finished rubbing

EDITH WHARTON

4

You can flip any type of Bézier item. Try flipping a Bézier text path vertically.

To flip an item:

1. *Optional:* To create a mirror image, duplicate the item (Cmd-D/Ctrl-D) before you flip it.

2. Choose the Item or Content tool.

3. Click the item, and turn off Item > Edit > Shape.

4. So you'll be able to restore the original dimensions to the item after it's flipped, on the Measurements palette, highlight the W or H field, depending on which way you want to flip the box— horizontally (W field) or vertically (H field)—and copy the current value (Cmd-C/Ctrl-C).

5. If you copied the W value, drag a side midpoint handle all the way across the item to the other side **1**–**2**. Or if you copied the H value, drag the top or bottom midpoint handle.

6. Re-highlight the field that you chose for step 3 above, paste (Cmd-V/Ctrl-V), then press Return/Enter **3**.

TIP To flip the *contents* of a selected box, choose the Content tool, then choose Style > Flip Horizontal or Flip Vertical or click the Flip Horizontal button ➡ or Flip Vertical button ⬆ on the Measurements palette.

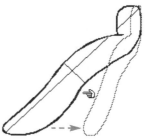

1 *After copying an item's width or height from the Measurements palette, drag a midpoint handle all the way across the shape.*

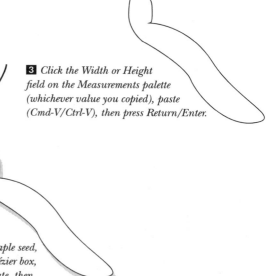

2 *Continue dragging to the opposite side.*

3 *Click the Width or Height field on the Measurements palette (whichever value you copied), paste (Cmd-V/Ctrl-V), then press Return/Enter.*

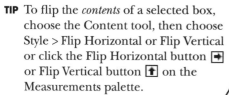

To produce this maple seed, we duplicated a Bézier box, flipped the duplicate, then positioned them side by side.

Flip an Item

1 *Select a line, then choose Item > Content >* **Text.**

2 *The line becomes a* **text path.**

Creating Bézier text paths

In addition to creating a text path using any of the Text-Path tools, you can also produce a text path by converting an existing line.

To convert a line into a text path:

1. Choose the Item or Content tool.
2. Click a line that was created using the Orthogonal Line, Line, Bézier Line, or Freehand Line tool **1**.
3. Choose Item > Content > Text (or choose it from the context menu).
4. With the Content tool chosen, type, paste, or import text onto the path **2**.

Text on a fat path

We converted a round text box into a freehand line via Item > Shape, made the path 20% black and wider in Item > Modify > Line, added type, and in Item > Modify > Text Path, chose Align Text: Descent and Align with Line: Bottom. To fine-tune the position of the text on the path, we used Style > Baseline Shift. (The picture is in a picture box.)

After clicking the Flip Text button on the Measurements palette

Tip for drawing text paths

Try not to create acute concave angles when you draw a text path—the letters will bunch together and be unreadable.

Try to draw smooth, shallow curves instead.

Other ways to play with text paths

To change the width and other attributes of a text path, select it using the Item tool, then choose attributes from the Style menu or in Item > Modify > Line. Any dash or stripe style can be applied to a text path **1**.

To recolor a text path, select it with the Item tool and choose from the Style > Color and Shade submenus. Or select it with the Item or Content tool, click the Line Color button ⬜ on the Colors palette, then click a color and choose a shade. (To make the path invisible, click the Line Color button, then click None.)

Change the attributes of text on a path as you would text in a box: Select it using the Content tool, then choose attributes from the Style menu or the right side of the Measurements palette; or apply a style sheet or sheets to it.

To flip text to the opposite side of a path, click the path with the Content tool, then click the Flip Text button ⬛ on the Measurements palette **2**–**3** or choose Style > Flip Text. Or click the path with the Item or Content tool, then check or uncheck Flip Text in Item > Modify > Text Path.

To turn a text box into a text path, select the box, then from the Item > Shape submenu, choose the Line icon ╱ **4** or Orthogonal Line icon. ➕ An open text path will be created. Or if you choose the Bézier Line icon ∿ instead, a path will be created in the shape of the original box **5**.

1 *To create this text path, we converted a standard round text box into a Bézier line.*

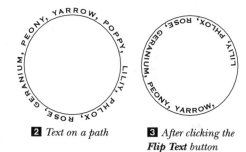

2 *Text on a path*   **3** *After clicking the* **Flip Text** *button*

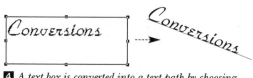

4 *A text box is converted into a text path by choosing the* **Line** *icon* ╱ *from the Item >* **Shape** *submenu.*

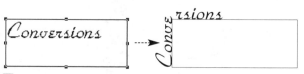

5 *A text box is converted into a text path by choosing the* **Bézier Line** *icon* ∿ *from the Item >* **Shape** *submenu.*

To change the orientation of text on a curvy path:

1. Choose the Item or Content tool.

2. Click on a text path.

3. Choose Item > Modify (Cmd-M/ Ctrl-M), then click the Text Path tab.

4. Click any of the four Text Orientation buttons **1**.

5. Click Apply to preview.

6. Click OK.

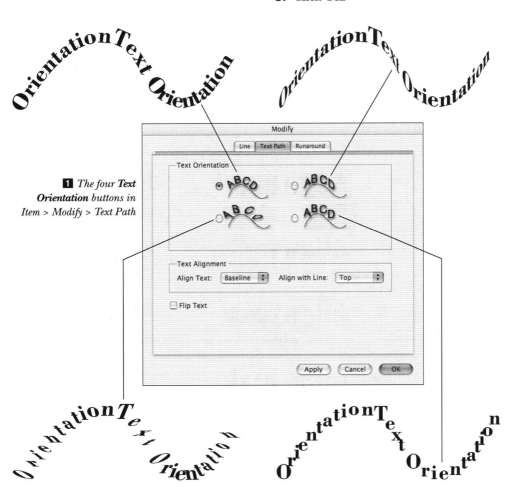

1 *The four **Text Orientation** buttons in Item > Modify > Text Path*

To raise or lower text on its path:

1. Choose the Item or Content tool.

2. Click on a text path.

3. Choose Item > Modify (Cmd-M/ Ctrl-M), then click the Text Path tab.

4. Choose Align Text: Ascent, Center, Baseline, or Descent **1**–**2** (to specify the part of the text that touches the path).

5. Choose Align with Line: Top, Center, or Bottom (to specify the part of the path the text connects to) **3**. The wider the path, the more dramatic the shift.

6. Click Apply to preview.

7. Click OK.

TIP In a print layout, you can use Style > Baseline Shift to further raise or lower text on a path.

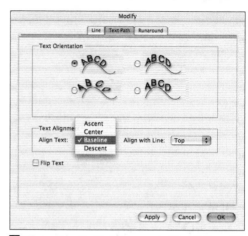

1 *Choose from the* **Text Alignment: Align Text** *and/or* **Align with Line** *pop-up menus in Item > Modify > Text Path.*

2
Align text
Align Text: Ascent

Align text
Align Text: Center

Align text
Align Text: Baseline

Align text
Align Text: Descent

3
Align text
Align with Line: Top

Align text
Align with Line: Center

Align text
Align with Line: Bottom

Raise, Lower Text on Path

Web Layouts 19

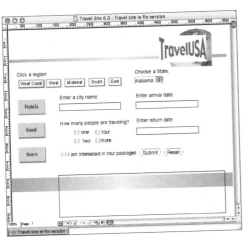

1 *A Web layout in QuarkXPress*

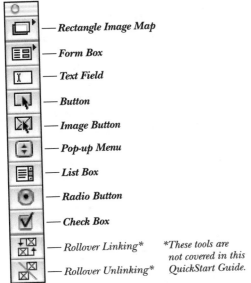

*These tools are
not covered in this
QuickStart Guide.*

— *Rectangle Image Map*

— *Form Box*

— *Text Field*

— *Button*

— *Image Button*

— *Pop-up Menu*

— *List Box*

— *Radio Button*

— *Check Box*

— *Rollover Linking**

— *Rollover Unlinking**

2 *The tools on the **Web Tools**
palette are used for creating various
types of controls for Web pages.*

Creating Web layouts

In this chapter we'll show you how to create Web layouts **1**, as well as how to preview them in whichever browser is currently installed in your operating system. The good news is that you can apply all your existing print layout skills to building Web layouts—you don't have to leave those skills by the wayside. Another piece of news is that in addition to the standard tool palette you're already familiar with, you'll also need to learn to use an assortment of Web tools **2** and some new techniques and commands that are unique to Web layouts. This is a big, fat chapter for a reason.

6.0! Print and Web layouts can reside in the same project, and you can add as many of each as you like. To build a Web page, you can create new items right in a Web layout or copy and paste items from any existing Web or print layout in any project. If you don't want to start from scratch, you can duplicate a print layout and then convert the duplicate into a Web layout.

Any or all of the following elements can be added to a Web layout:

- Text, which will be exported either as HTML text or as a rasterized graphic

- Picture files in most graphic formats, which will be converted to an appropriate Web graphics file format, such as JPEG, GIF, or PNG, upon export

- Tables, lines, or any other standard items

- Interactive elements, such as image maps and rollovers, that link the viewer to additional information

(Continued on the following page)

Web Layouts

- Buttons and forms with text entry fields and check boxes that collect information entered by the viewer and send it to a script program that, in turn, submits the data to a Web server for processing and possible feedback information

TIP You can use layers in a Web layout, but they'll be flattened in the export file.

TIP To make an item appear on every page of a Web layout, create or paste the item onto the master page for that layout.

Both the file storage size of a Web page and the modem speed of the user's system affect the time it takes a page to download for display in a browser. The smaller the file storage size, the less data there is to be downloaded. The faster the modem speed, the quicker the data travels between the Web server and the user's browser. The essence of good Web design is to produce a Web page that looks good *and* downloads in a reasonable time frame.

Every Web page is actually an HTML file that contains HTML code and conforms to the HTML language structure. The page is composed of text as well as path references to picture files. The HTML code instructs the browser how to display the text and pictures as a Web page.

Since QuarkXPress Web layouts are stored in the standard QuarkXPress format, you can create and revise them using the same QuarkXPress features that you'd use to construct a print layout. You don't have to enter or work with HTML code—at least not directly.

When your Web layout is finished, you can export it as HTML files directly from QuarkXPress. Then, following the instructions from your Internet service provider (ISP), you can use other software to upload the HTML files and any picture files used in the pages to the ISP's server for display on the Web.

Web layout to Website

Here's the basic scenario:

In QuarkXPress, you'll create a Web layout, adding text, pictures, lines, paths—whatever.

Next you'll export your finalized layout pages from QuarkXPress as HTML files and export any pictures that are used on those pages as separate files (in the GIF, JPEG, or PNG format).

The HTML file or files will be placed, along with the picture files that you've used, into a site folder of your choosing. The browser will then open the multiple files from that folder and display them as a cohesive whole—a Website. Your original QuarkXPress Web layout will be preserved in its original form, separate and apart from any HTML file that you decide to generate from it.

To navigate through pages in a Web layout in QuarkXPress, you'll use the Page Layout palette. To navigate between HTML files in the Website, you first need to link one file to the next in QuarkXPress using hyperlinks. Then, when a user views your HTML files in a browser and clicks a link, the browser reads the link and displays the designated linked file.

Keeping things organized

- In Item > Modify > Export in QuarkXPress, create and label a separate folder for each picture file format, such as GIF, JPEG, and PNG. Then, when you export the pictures that you've used in a Web layout, put them in the folder/directory that you've allocated for that format. This will help keep things organized.

- In QuarkXPress, you can designate a site folder/directory for your exported HTML files and any image folders/directories that contain pictures used in your Web layout (see page 420).

- Before uploading your Website to a server for viewing on the Web, ask your Internet service provider how it wants files and folders named and organized in the site folder/directory that you've designated.

A Web layout isn't a Web page—at least not yet. It's a layout that can, if exported as HTML, be turned into a Web page. Let's begin.

To create a Web layout:

6.0!

1. To create a new project, choose File > New > Project (Cmd-N/Ctrl-N).
   or
   With an existing project open, choose Layout > New.

2. Choose Layout Type: Web.

3. Enter a Layout Name.

4. In the Colors area 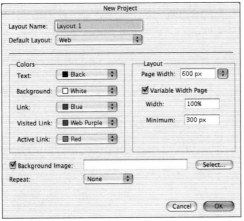, choose colors for the Background of the page, for a Link (hyperlink) that gets a user to additional data, for a Visited Link (a link that's already been clicked), and for an Active Link (a link that's currently being clicked on). (The Visited Link and Active Link colors display only when a page is viewed in a browser.)

5. In the Layout area, enter a Page Width value or choose a preset width from the pop-up menu.

6. *Optional:* Check Variable Width Page, then enter a Width percentage and Minimum width value. When this option is checked, variable HTML text boxes will have the capacity to

Web page size

When calculating the appropriate size for a Web page, consider common monitor sizes and modem speeds. Nowadays, you can safely design for a 800 x 600-pixel viewing area and a 56 Kbps modem. The page won't occupy the whole browser window, though; the browser's navigation buttons and toolbar will also occupy some space (see **1**, next page). Realistically, you'll be working with an area about 10 inches wide (740 pixels) by 7.5 inches high (550 pixels). You can increase the page height, but your viewers will have to scroll downward to view the whole page.

stretch or shrink in width down to the Minimum width value as the user resizes their browser window; HTML text within the box will reflow. To make a text box variable, select the box, choose Item > Modify, click the Text tab, then check Make Variable Width.

7. *Optional:* Check Background Image, click Select (Mac OS X)/Browse (Windows), then locate and open a picture file to be displayed behind all the other items on the Web page. From the Repeat pop-up menu, choose:

   Tile for continuous horizontal and vertical repetition of the image.

   Horizontally for continuous horizontal (but not vertical) repetition of the image.

   (Continued on the following page)

1 *The New* **Project** *dialog box*

Vertically for continuous vertical (but not horizontal) repetition of the image.

None to display the image in only one location—the upper left corner of the browser window.

8. Click OK. (The blue vertical line represents the rightmost edge of the page, as specified in the Page Width field.) You will learn how to add forms, form controls, interactive Web elements, and hyperlinks to a page later in this chapter.

TIP QuarkXPress won't create a new layout if more than 25 layouts are currently open (like, dude—who's going to have 25 layouts open?).

TIP The options or values entered in the New Layout or New Project dialog box apply to the default master page for the layout. Every site page created from that master will have these settings.

To add pages to a Web layout:

With a Web layout open, choose Page > Insert, enter in the Insert [   ] pages field the number of pages you wanted inserted, then click OK.
or
On the Page Layout palette, drag a master page icon into the layout page area, below any existing layout page icon **2**.

The methods for moving through a Web layout are the same as for a print layout. Here's a quick summary.

To go to another page in a Web layout:

Choose Page > Previous, Next, First, or Last.
or
On the Page Layout palette, double-click a layout page icon.
or
Choose a layout page number from the Go-to-page pop-up menu at the bottom of the project window.

Creating text and picture items

You'll use the same tools to create **text** for a Web layout that you would use to create text in a print layout (draw a box with a text box tool, then enter or import text), but the attributes you can assign differ between these two types of layouts due to their unique quirks, limitations, and requirements. For example, you can't link text boxes in a Web layout. To learn more, read "Type for the Web" on page 136.

To get a **picture** into a Web layout, use the same method you'd use in a print layout: Draw a box with any picture box tool, then use File > Get Picture to import a picture.

1 *A Web page has to fit within the standard size* ***browser window,*** *and allowance must be made for the browser's navigation and toolbar areas.*

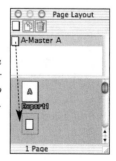

2 *To add a page to a Web layout, drag a master page icon downward into the layout page area.*

If you've created a Web layout but are unhappy with any of the color, layout width, or background image properties choices you made in the New Layout dialog box, you can change them at any time for the current page via the Page Properties dialog box. And while you're at it, you can also enter a title for the Web page.

To change the properties of an existing Web page:

1. Choose Page > Page Properties (Cmd-Option-Shift-A/Ctrl-Alt-Shift-A).

2. Enter a name in the Page Title field 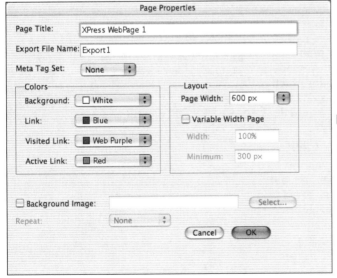. This title will display in the title bar of the browser window.

3. Change the Export File Name. This name is used for the page on the Page Layout palette and when the page is exported as an HTML file. Don't enter spaces or slashes (/)—they aren't accepted as characters on the Windows and Unix platforms.

   If you leave the default Export File Name as is and you export the page as an HTML file, there's a good chance the program may discover an export

What's changed?

Changes made in the Page Properties dialog box affect only the currently displayed layout page. Changes made in the Layout Properties dialog box affect any layout pages that are subsequently produced by dragging the Blank Single Page icon on the Page Layout palette; these new pages won't initially be associated with any master page.

file with the same name in the same folder. (An alert dialog box will ask if you want to replace the existing export file, to which you can respond by clicking Yes to replace or No to cancel.) To avoid this confusion altogether, we prefer to enter a custom name in the Export File Name field.

4. Choose a Meta Tag Set from the pop-up menu. (To learn about meta tag sets, see pages 374–376.)

5. Change any of the other settings in the dialog box (see page 323).

6. Click OK. Each Web layout page has its own set of Page Properties. These properties don't apply to a whole layout.

1 *Use the **Page Properties** dialog box to change the name, colors, width, or background image of an existing Web page.*

Page Properties

Web viewers who download your page may not have all the fonts you used to design the page. In this case, the viewer's Web browser will substitute a commonly used, standard font for yours, and this can affect the look and layout of your page. By specifying that your display type (e.g., a header or logo) be converted to a graphic on export, you can be confident that it will look the same in the browser. Keep in mind, however, that because this conversion adds a graphic to your Web page, it increases the file's size and download time.

To convert a text box into a bitmap graphic:

1. With the Item or Content tool, select a text box in your layout.

2. Choose Item > Modify, then click the Export tab.

3. Check Convert to Graphic on Export **1**. For other options in the Export pane, see the instructions that follow.

4. Click OK.

To choose a Web graphics format for a picture file:

1. With the Item or Content tool, select a picture box in your layout.

2. Choose Item > Modify, then click the Export tab.

3. *Optional:* Enter a description in the Alternate Text field to be displayed in lieu of the image in browsers for which the show images option is turned off or on Websites for which it's required by law. Alt text helps make a site accessible to viewers with disabilities.

4. The Export As formats will compress the image to reduce its storage size and will modify colors in the image to get it in sync with the display capabilities of the browser. (To learn more about these formats, see pages 328–330.)

How big?

To find out the file size of an exported picture file, in Mac OS X, highlight the file name in the Finder, then choose File > **Get Info** (Cmd-I). In Windows, Right-click the file in Windows Explorer and choose **Properties** from the pop-up menu.

Once you know the exact file size of the compressed image, you can calculate how long it will take to transmit over the Web. For example, a 50K file traveling on a 56 Kbps modem will take approximately 9 seconds to download.

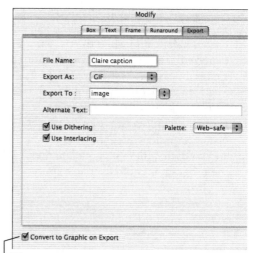

1 *Check* **Convert to Graphic on Export** *in Item > Modify > Export for a text box.*

Watch that excess baggage!

When a picture is exported, QuarkXPress exports the whole thing, regardless of whether it was cropped or scaled in QuarkXPress. Exporting a larger picture than you need will increase a site's download time unnecessarily. For this reason, it's best to crop or scale your pictures in an image-editing application (e.g., Adobe Photoshop) to the desired size before importing them into QuarkXPress.

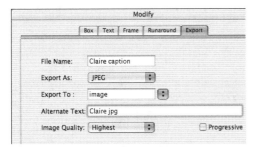

1 *Export options for the JPEG format*

2 *Export options for the GIF format*

3 *Export options for the PNG format*

From the Export As pop-up menu, choose:

JPEG (Joint Photographic Experts Group) **1** for a photographic, continuous-tone image that doesn't contain solid colors or whose edges aren't distinct. Choose from the Image Quality pop-up menu (the higher the quality setting, the better the image display and the less data loss, but the larger the file size and thus the slower the download time). Check Progressive to have the image download in progressively greater detail.

GIF (Graphics Interchange Format) **2** for an image that has solid-color areas and sharp edges, as in a logo or display type. This format reduces an image's colors to a 256-color palette. Choose a palette from the Palette pop-up menu to be used when the image is converted into the GIF 256-color format. Web-safe, the best choice, guarantees that solid colors are converted to browser-safe colors. Check Use Dithering to allow solid-color areas that aren't contained in the browser palette to display as a mixture of two browser colors (see the sidebar on the next page). Check Use Interlacing to have the image download in progressively greater detail; this option increases the file size.

PNG (Portable Network Graphics) **3** for a photographic, continuous-tone image. Its compression scheme causes no data loss. Click True Color to convert the image using the maximum number of colors (this option produces the largest file size). Or click Indexed color, then check Use Dithering to allow solid-color areas that aren't contained on the browser palette to display as a mixture of two browser colors. For the Indexed color option, choose a palette from the Palette pop-up menu to be used for reducing the image

(Continued on the following page)

Export Formats for Images

colors to 256 colors. Web-safe guarantees that solid colors will be converted to browser-safe solid colors (the best choice). Check Use Interlacing to have the image download in progressively greater detail; this option increases the file size.

5. In the Export To field, enter a name for a new folder/directory to hold the exported image or leave this location as the default "image" folder/directory. The folder will be created when the Web layout is exported. Any folders/directories that have already been created will be listed on the Export To field pop-up menu.

6.0!

6. Click OK.

More about the export formats

The GIF, JPEG, and PNG formats, with their built-in compression schemes, significantly reduce the storage size of image files while causing only a minor reduction in image quality. Compressed images download faster on the Web.

- Images with a solid background color and a few solid-color shapes will compress the most (expect a file size in the range of 20–50K), whereas images that have many color areas, textures, or patterns won't compress nearly as much, especially large images (100K and up).

- The GIF format may compress continuous-tone, photographic images less than it will images that contain only solid-color areas, so JPEG is a better format choice for a these types of images.

- For onscreen output, save your images at a resolution of 72 ppi, with a sufficient width and height in pixels to produce an acceptable image size in the browser.

In summary, images that must be large (500 x 400 pixels or larger) ideally should contain only a handful of large, solid-color shapes. Try to restrict the size of images

Dithering

Dithering is the intermixing of two palette colors to create the impression of a third color. It makes images that contain a limited number of colors (256 or fewer) look as if they contain a greater range of colors and shades, and thus they are more pleasing to the eye. Dithering is usually applied to continuous-tone images to increase their tonal range, but unfortunately, it can also make them look a bit dotty.

Dithering usually doesn't produce aesthetically pleasing results in images that contain solid colors. This is because the browser palette will dither pixels to re-create any colors that the palette doesn't contain. For images that contain solid colors, it's better to create colors in an image-editing program that lets you work with a Web-safe color palette.

Continuous-tone imagery is, in a way, already dithered. Some continuous-tone imagery looks fine on a Web page without dithering and in the allotted 256 colors. Dithering adds noise and additional colors to a file, though, so compression is less effective when dithering is on than when it's off. With dithering enabled, you may not be able to achieve your desired degree of file compression. As is usually the case with Web output, you'll need to strike an acceptable balance between aesthetics and file size.

What's in a name?

To rename the default "image" folder/directory, go to QuarkXPress (Edit, in Windows) > Preferences > Web Layout > General, then enter the desired folder/directory name in the Image Export Directory field (see page 420).

Separation of Web and print

To set preferences for a Web layout, go to QuarkXPress (Edit, in Windows) > Preferences (Cmd-Option-Shift-Y/Ctrl-Alt-Shift-Y). To set preferences for all future Web layouts, close all projects, then open the Preferences dialog box. The Default Web Layout preferences are listed below the Default Print Layout preferences. Preferences for the two types of layouts are set separately, whereas Application preferences apply to both print and Web layouts. Web and print layouts have many of the same Preferences options in their separate panes, but some preference options are unique to one type of layout or the other. Read more about preferences in Chapter 23.

1 *GIF is a suitable export format for this image, which contains only solid-color shapes.*

2 *For this continuous-tone image,* **JPEG** *is a more suitable export format.*

that contain intricate shapes and colors to just a portion of the Web browser window.

GIF

GIF is the standard file format used for Web graphics. It's an 8-bit format, which means a GIF image can contain a maximum of 256 colors. Most browser palettes are also 8-bit, which means they too can display a maximum of 256 colors—not the thousands or millions of colors that are needed to make images look pleasing to the eye. Colors that a browser palette lacks are simulated by dithering, a display technique that intermixes color pixels to simulate other colors. Since color substitutions are more noticeable in solid-color areas than in continuous-tone areas, GIF is a good format choice for images that contain solid-color areas or shapes with well-defined edges, such as type **1**. GIF can save fully transparent pixels (one level of transparency).

JPEG

The JPEG format may be a better choice for preserving color fidelity if your image is continuous-tone (contains gradations of color or is photographic) and your viewers have 24-bit monitors, which have the capacity to display millions of colors **2**.

On the plus side, the JPEG format can compress a 24-bit image to the same file size as the GIF format can compress an 8-bit image.

On the down side, JPEG is a poor choice for images that contain solid colors or type, because its compression methods tend to add unwanted pixels (artifacts) along the well-defined edges of these kinds of images. Also, not all Web users have 24-bit monitors. A JPEG image will be dithered on an 8-bit monitor, although dithering in a continuous-tone image will be less noticeable than in an image that contains solid colors.

(Continued on the following page)

Export Formats for Images

If you choose JPEG as your export format, decide which degree of compression is acceptable by weighing the exported file size versus diminished image quality 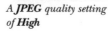. The lower the image quality option you choose, the greater the degree of compression and the greater the image data loss.

PNG Indexed and PNG True Color

The two PNG formats, Indexed and True Color, have the capacity to save partially transparent pixels and are especially useful for saving images that have soft, feathered edges. The PNG Indexed format allows for only 256 colors in the optimized image and is similar to the GIF format. The PNG True Color format allows for millions of colors in the optimized image and is similar to the JPEG format. Both PNG formats use a lossless compression method (they don't cause data loss).

Unfortunately, PNG isn't very popular yet, even though it's supported directly by Internet Explorer 4.0, Netscape Navigator 6, and later versions of both these browsers.

*A **JPEG** quality setting of **High***

*A **JPEG** quality setting of **Lowest**: Note the artifacts along the edges of the shapes.*

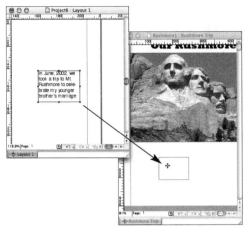

1 *Drag an existing item into a Web project.*

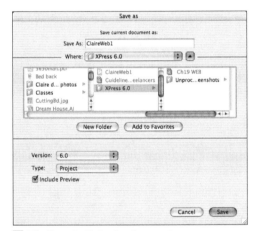

2 *The Save As dialog box for a project*

Items can be created directly on a Web page or they can be drag-copied or copied and pasted from other layouts.

To add items to a Web page by drag-copying:

1. Create a Web layout (see page 323).

2. Open an existing QuarkXPress print or Web project that you want to copy items from. Drag any items (text boxes, picture boxes, contentless boxes, lines, text paths, or tables) into the new Web layout window **1**. The items will be copied automatically.

3. Choose export options for any of the items (see page 326). If desired, you can also add interactive elements (see page 345) or form controls (see page 357) to the layout.

TIP If you drag-copy a text box or table from a print layout to a Web layout, the Convert to Graphic on Export option will be enabled for the item automatically, but you can go to Item > Modify and uncheck this option for any selected item.

The "saving" we're talking about here is just plain ol' saving as a QuarkXPress project—not exporting. The steps for previewing and exporting Web layouts are discussed next.

To save a Web project:

For an already saved project, choose File > Save (Cmd-S/Ctrl-S).

or

For a new, as yet unsaved project, choose File > Save, enter a name, choose a location, then click Save **2**.

Previewing and exporting Web layouts

In order to preview your Web page in a browser, you need to tell QuarkXPress which Web browsers are present in your system.

Note: QuarkXPress is a robust page layout program—not a full-featured Web-page creation program. Although QuarkXPress can export PostScript page layout descriptions and convert them to HTML code, it can't convert HTML code into the page layout environment; you can open an "export.htm" file in a browser at any time, but not in QuarkXPress.

To choose browser preferences:

1. Go to QuarkXPress (Edit, in Windows) > Preferences > Browsers.

2. Click Add ▮, locate a browser in your system, then click Open. Click Add again if you want to locate any other browsers in your system.

3. *Optional:* If you want to change which browser is the default, click in the Default column in the Available Browsers scroll window next to a different browser name (a check mark will appear).

4. Click OK to exit the Preferences dialog box.

TIP To modify the name used to list a browser in the Preferences > Browser pane (let's say you want the name to reflect the browser version), click the browser name, click Edit, change the Display Name, then click OK. This change affects only the browser name that QuarkXPress displays on its own menus, not the name of the actual browser application.

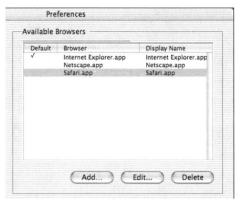

▮ *You can use the **Browsers** pane of the Preferences dialog box to tell QuarkXPress which Web browsers are available in your system or to specify a different browser as the default.*

No surprises!

The same Web page may display differently in different browsers (e.g., Microsoft Internet Explorer and Netscape Navigator) and on different platforms (Mac OS, Windows). Be sure to view your Web page, at a minimum, in the two main browsers and on the two main platforms so you'll know how it will look on different viewers' systems.

1 *HTML Preview button*

2 *HTML Preview pop-up menu*

You can preview any individual pages prior to exporting your whole Web layout. For the preview, QuarkXPress creates a temporary page in memory. (To preview hyperlinks, on the other hand, you have to export the whole layout; see page 335.)

Note: In order to follow the instructions below, a browser must be installed in your system.

To preview a Web page in a browser:

1. Click the HTML Preview button at the bottom of the project window **1**. The page will open in the default browser currently chosen in QuarkXPress (Edit, in Windows) > Preferences > Application > Browsers (whichever browser has a check mark in the Default column).
or
Choose a browser from the HTML Preview pop-up menu at the bottom of the project window **2**.
or
Control-click/Right-click a blank area of your Web layout and choose from the Preview HTML submenu.

2. When you're done previewing, close the browser window, then click back in the QuarkXPress project window.

TIP You can also choose a browser from the Page > Preview HTML submenu, but why go to all that trouble?

TIP If you do a lot of previewing, you might want to refresh your browser window to get a fresh, clean look at your work. In Explorer, click the Refresh button; in Netscape, click the Reload button.

Preview Page in Browser

When your Web layout is finished, it's ready to be exported as HTML. Here's how to do it.

To export a Web layout as HTML:

1. Choose File > Export > HTML.

2. Enter a page number or a range of page numbers to be saved, or choose All (the default choice) from the pop-up menu 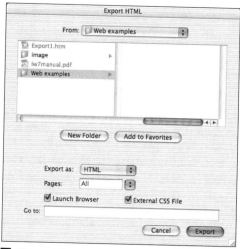.

3. Choose or create a folder in which to save the HTML file.

4. *Optional:* Check Launch Browser to have the default browser launch automatically and display the exported page(s).

5. *Optional:* Check External CSS File to have QuarkXPress generate and place a CSS (cascading style sheet) file into the folder you chose in step 3.

6. Click Export. A separate Export.htm file will be created for each page specified in step 2 above. The file name will match the name entered in the Export File Name field in the Page > Page Properties dialog box. The ".htm" extension is added automatically.

   Note: If you reexport a Web page to the same folder location, an alert dialog box will appear after you click Export. Decide whether you want to replace individual export files, replace all files, or not replace individual files.

TIP Any images in the Web layout will be exported in the formats you've chosen and will be stored in a default folder/directory called "image" unless you specified a different folder/directory in Item > Modify > Export (see page 328). This folder will be inside the folder/directory that contains the exported HTML page(s).

6.0!

Cascading style sheets

The color, font, and styling information in a **CSS** (cascading style sheet) file affects how the browser displays text in an exported HTML file. Cascading style sheets control HTML text formatting just as style sheets in a QuarkXPress layout control text formatting. Style sheets that are applied to text in a QuarkXPress Web layout are converted into a CSS file *automatically* by QuarkXPress upon export.

Note: Text boxes that are converted to a graphic prior to export won't be affected by a CSS.

■ If you change the styling of text in a Web layout and then reexport it, remember to check the **External CSS File** option so QuarkXPress will update the existing CSS file.

■ In order for the browser to use the CSS file when it displays the HTML file, you must keep the **.htm** file and its corresponding **.css** file in the same folder.

■ To view the simple CSS format coding, open the external CSS file in a plain text editor (e.g., TextEdit or NotePad).

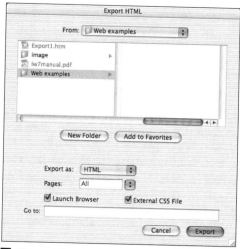

1 *Choose options in the **Export HTML** dialog box.*

PDFs and hyperlinks

Hyperlinks can be used in **PDF** files in order to create links between different areas of text (usually within the same file or to other URLs). Hyperlinks are interactive in an exported PDF file only when the file is viewed in Acrobat Reader.

New Hyperlink button

1 *On the* **Hyperlinks** *palette, destinations can be shown by Name (as shown in this figure) or by Link (as shown in the next figure).*

2 *If the list on your Hyperlinks palette gets to be overly long, via the* **Show** *buttons, you can choose not to show (or hide) URLs* ⊕*, anchors* ⚓*, or pages* ▯ *to make it more compact.*

Creating hyperlinks

Websites have to present information in an organized, controlled manner so users can access the information they need without getting confused. To help orient users, a Website's introductory usually lists, by topic, the other pages in the site.

Let's say you've created a multipage Web layout and you've filled the new page(s) with the relevant text and graphics. The next step is to place navigation hyperlinks ("links," for short) on the page to enable users to get to other locations on the same page, to other pages in the Website, or even to another Website. For example, to get users to a page bearing product information, you would set up a "Products" link.

Various visual devices are used to designate hyperlinks, including underlined text, image maps, rollovers, and cascading menus. We'll delve into all of these techniques later in this chapter. The Hyperlinks palette in QuarkXPress **1**–**2** is used to assign a link destination to a selected linking device. That device can be highlighted text, an image map area, or a picture box. Hyperlinks are interactive only when viewed in a browser.

First we'll show you how to create a URL link.

To create a URL hyperlink:

1. Choose Window > Show Hyperlinks.

2. *Optional:* Choose the Item or Content tool, then click a picture box to use as a linking device, or choose the Content tool and select some text to use as a linking device.

   Note: If you create a Hyperlink destination without first selecting text or a picture box, that link won't be assigned, though you can assign it later (see "To create a hyperlink for an existing destination," on page 337).

(Continued on the following page)

Create URL Hyperlink

3. Click the New Hyperlink button 🔗 on the Hyperlinks palette.
or
Choose Style > Hyperlink > New.
or
With the pointer over an item, Control-click/Right-click, then choose Hyperlink > New from the context menu **1**–**2**.

The latter two options are available only if you have selected text or an item.

4. Enter a Name to be listed on the palette as the link destination, and leave URL as the choice on the Type pop-up menu **3**. The other Type choices are discussed on pages 338 and 342.

6.0!

5. Enter a location in the URL field. Acceptable locations include an anchor in the active layout (see page 338), the URL for a file on the Internet, or the name of an exported HTML file that's located in the same folder as the exported .htm file for the active layout.
or
Choose a destination from the URL pop-up menu **4**. Exported HTML files and URLs that are present in the active layout will appear on this pop-up menu. The name of the exported QuarkXPress Web page that displays on this pop-up menu is taken from the Export File Name field in the Page Properties dialog box. From the URL pop-up menu, you can choose one of the four standard protocols ("– http://," "https://," "ftp://," or "mailto: –").
or
Click Select/Browse to the right of the URL field, locate the desired file name, then click Link. You can link to an exported HTML file from another folder, but keep in mind that for the link to work properly on the Internet, the file will need to be uploaded to the Internet service provider's server along with your exported HTML files. Click

What's on the menu?

The Hyperlink > **New** submenu on both the context menu and the Style menu lists only those exported HTML files that are located in the same folder as the active project. You can choose one of those file names as the destination for a hyperlink.

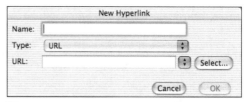

1 *The* **New Hyperlink** *dialog box looks like this if you create an* **unassigned** *hyperlink (didn't select text or an item for step 2 in the instructions on the previous page).*

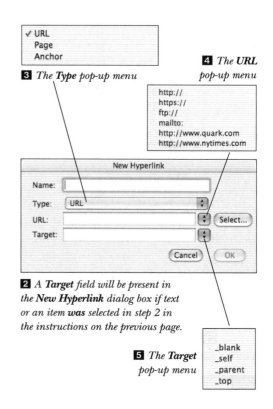

3 *The* **Type** *pop-up menu*

4 *The* **URL** *pop-up menu*

2 *A* **Target** *field will be present in the* **New Hyperlink** *dialog box if text or an item* **was** *selected in step 2 in the instructions on the previous page.*

5 *The* **Target** *pop-up menu*

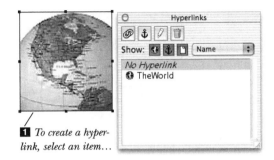

1 *To create a hyper-link, select an item...*

2 *...then click a destination name on the palette. If you reselect the item, the destination name on the palette will become selected.*

*With **Name** chosen from this pop-up menu, destinations are listed by their assigned names.*

3 *With **Link** chosen from this pop-up menu, destinations are listed by their URL, page name, or anchor name.*

the Link/Open button to enter a destination as a complete path name.

6. If text or an item was selected in step 2, choose an option from the Target pop-up menu to designate where any destination HTML pages should display (**5**, previous page). These frame targets are needed only if the item is embedded within a frameset on your Web page. Choose:

None (the empty space at the top) or "_self" to load the target page in the same frame or window that holds the current page.

"_blank" to load the target page in a new, unnamed window.

"_parent" to load the target page into the parent frame, if there is one, of the current page.

"_top" to load the target page into the full browser window, replacing any framesets.

7. Click OK. The new destination will appear on the palette.

TIP The Hyperlinks palette can list destinations that aren't assigned to any item or text, and you don't have to use them in the Web layout.

This is a method for creating a hyperlink without using a dialog box.

To create a hyperlink for an existing destination:

1. Show the Hyperlinks palette.

2. Highlight some text or select a text or a picture box to be used as a linking device **1**.

3. Click an existing destination or anchor name on the Hyperlinks palette **2**–**3**.
or
Control-click/Right-click an item and choose a destination from the Hyperlink submenu. Either the link icon or a text underline will appear in the box you're using as a linking device.

To edit a hyperlink:

1. On the Hyperlinks palette, click a name or a link, then click the Edit button.

2. Edit text in the URL field and/or the Target field.

3. Click OK. The hyperlink listing will update on the palette.

Anchors are special names that are attached to existing items on a page and that function as place markers either for a specific page in a Website or for a specific location on a Web page. If an anchor is chosen as a destination for a hyperlink, a user can click that hyperlink on a Web page to get to the destination page or location where the actual anchor item resides.

To create an anchor:

1. *Optional:* Highlight some text or select a text or picture box to assign to the anchor you'll be creating in the following steps. You can also assign an item to the anchor later (see the following page).

2. Click the New Anchor button ⚓ on the Hyperlinks palette.
or
Choose Style > Anchor > New.
or
Control-click/Right-click an item, then choose Anchor > New.

The latter two options are available only if text or an item is selected.

3. Change the picture or text Anchor Name that was entered automatically, or leave it as is. If you type a space or other character that isn't acceptable, an alert dialog box will appear when you click OK.

4. Click OK **1**. Anchor names are preceded by a "#" on pop-up menus, submenus, and the Hyperlinks palette.

New Anchor button

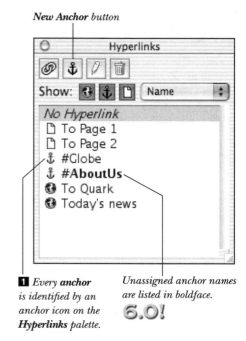

1 *Every* **anchor** *is identified by an anchor icon on the* **Hyperlinks** *palette.*

Unassigned anchor names are listed in boldface.

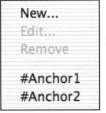

1 *Select an item to be attached to an anchor...*

2 *...then choose an anchor name from the Anchor submenu.*

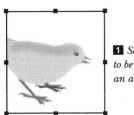

3 *The Anchor icon signifies that this item is attached to an anchor.*

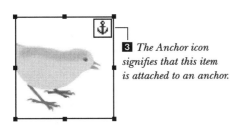

4 *These items are attached to an anchor destination. The item on the left has a link icon, whereas the text on the right has a link underline. In a browser, clicking a link item like either of these will take you to the location of an anchor item (as in **3**, above).*

When you attach an anchor to an item in your layout, that item's location becomes the anchor's destination.

To assign an existing anchor to an item: 6.0!

1. Highlight some text or select a text or picture box **1**.
2. Choose Style > Anchor.
   or
   Control-click/Right-click the selected item, then choose Anchor.
3. Choose an anchor name from the submenu **2**–**3**. (These names also display on the Hyperlinks palette when Link is chosen from the palette pop-up menu.)

Here is how to create a link to an anchor.

To create a link to an anchor destination: 6.0!

1. Highlight some text or select a text or picture box to become the linking device.
2. In the Hyperlinks palette, click the anchor destination for the text or picture box to link to **4**. In the browser, clicking this text or item will take the user to the page where the anchor is located. Use this method to create a "back to top" link on a page.

You can rename an anchor at any time.

To rename an anchor:

1. Click an anchor name on the Hyperlinks palette.
2. Click the Edit button.
3. Change the name.
4. Click OK.

TIP An anchor can also be edited via Style > Anchor > Edit or via the Anchor > Edit command on the context menu.

Link, Rename Anchor

If you want to break the link between the hyperlink text or object and the destination, you must remove the hyperlink to that destination. No text or items will be removed from the layout—only the link information will be removed. (To delete a destination, see the following page.)

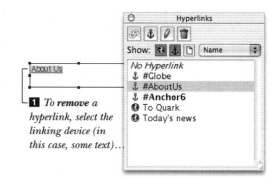

1 *To **remove** a hyperlink, select the linking device (in this case, some text)...*

6.0! To break a hyperlink:

1. In your Web layout, select a text or picture box that is functioning as a linking device. On the Hyperlinks palette, the destination name for that linking device will be highlighted **1**.

2. Click "No Hyperlink" on the Hyperlink palette **2**.
   or
   Choose Style > Hyperlink > Remove.
   or
   Control-click/Right-click the selected item, then choose Hyperlink > Remove.

   The destination name will remain, but the link between it and the text or picture box will be broken.

2 *...then click **No Hyperlink** on the Hyperlink palette.*

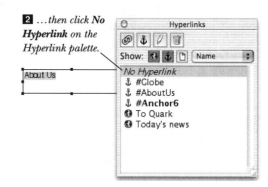

TIP If a text box or picture box is deleted from a layout, any hyperlinks that the item contained will also be deleted. The listing on the Hyperlinks palette will update to reflect the change; the destination name will remain.

TIP If an item or text that hasn't been linked to a destination is selected, "No Hyperlink" automatically becomes highlighted on the Hyperlinks palette.

Remove Hyperlink

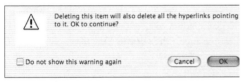

1 *On the Hyperlinks palette, click a destination name, then click the **Delete** button. The destination and any hyperlink references to that destination will be deleted from the palette.*

2 *This prompt appears when you delete a destination link or anchor.*

When a destination name or anchor listing is deleted from the Hyperlinks palette, only the hyperlink references to it are deleted from the palette—not the actual destination item or linking device.

To delete a destination or anchor:

1. On the Hyperlinks palette, click a destination name or anchor name **1**.

2. Click the Delete button on the palette, then click OK when the alert box appears **2**. The destination or anchor listing and all hyperlink references that point to that destination will be deleted from the palette; the items will remain.

You can also use the Hyperlinks palette to quickly navigate through a Web layout and locate a destination page or item.

To go to a hyperlink destination:

Double-click a hyperlink or anchor name on the Hyperlinks palette **3**. The page or anchor item will be displayed in the project window.
or
Control-click/Right-click a hyperlink or anchor name on the Hyperlinks palette, then choose Go To.
or
On the Hyperlinks palette, double-click a link to an HTML file that resides either in the current site folder or in another folder/directory on your hard drive. The default browser will open and that file will be displayed. *Note:* If you're not connected to the Internet when you double-click a URL destination, a dialog box will alert you that the server can't be found.

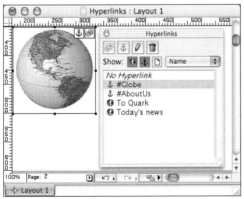

3 *On the Hyperlinks palette, double-click a link name. QuarkXPress will locate and select that hyperlink item and display it in the project window.*

This technique creates internal (relative) hyperlinks that take a viewer to different pages within the same Website.

To create a hyperlink from one page to another in a Web layout:

1. Create or display a Web layout that contains at least two pages.

2. On the first page, select an item or some text to use as a linking device 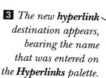.

3. Click the New Hyperlink button ☍ on the Hyperlinks palette.
   or
   Choose Style > Hyperlink > New.

4. Enter a destination name for the palette to display.

5. **6.0!** Choose Page from the Type pop-up menu.

6. **6.0!** Choose a page from the Page pop-up menu **2**. (The page names you entered into the Export File Name field in the Page Properties dialog box will be listed here.)

7. Click OK. The new hyperlink with the destination name you entered will now be listed on the Hyperlinks palette **3**.

TIP You could also have created a page destination with no text or item selected (omit step 2) and then later assigned that page destination to some text or an item in the layout.

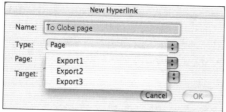

2 *A destination name is entered and a destination page is chosen from the **Page** pop-up menu in the **New Hyperlink** dialog box.*

Absolute vs. relative hyperlinks

An **absolute** hyperlink assigns either a complete path location for the destination file, including the name of the hard disk, or the complete http://www... listing. When a browser attempts to link to this destination, it has to go to the Internet to search for the appropriate Web path, which takes time. To preview getting to another Website via an absolute hyperlink using the HTML Preview button, your browser must be connected to the Web.

A **relative** hyperlink includes only the path to a folder/directory within the current Website's folder hierarchy. It's faster, because the browser need only go to that folder/directory on the current Web server or hard disk to retrieve the destination file. What's more, you can preview getting to a page in your Website linked via a relative hyperlink even when your browser is offline.

As a general rule, you should use an absolute hyperlink to link to a destination on another Website and a relative hyperlink to link to a destination in the current Website.

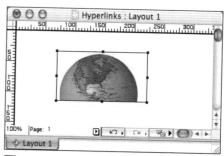

1 *A **picture** box is **selected** in a Web layout.*

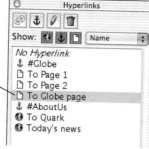

3 *The new **hyperlink** destination appears, bearing the name that was entered on the **Hyperlinks** palette.*

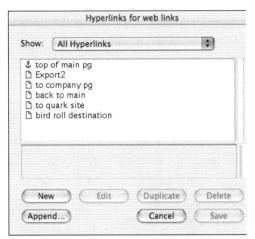

1 *In the* **Hyperlinks** *dialog box, click* **New** *to create a new destination.*

2 *The same destination names appear in the* **Hyperlinks** *dialog box (shown in the previous figure) as on the Hyperlinks palette.*

URL, page, and anchor destinations can **6.0!** also be created via the Hyperlinks dialog box. This can be done with or without any text or item being selected in your layout.

To create hyperlink destinations using the Hyperlinks dialog box:

1. *Optional:* Highlight some text or select a text or picture box to become the linking device.

2. Choose Edit > Hyperlinks **1**.

3. In the Hyperlinks dialog box, click New to create a new destination.

4. Follow the steps on pages 335–337 to enter options in the New Hyperlink dialog box, then click OK.

5. Repeat steps 3–4 to create additional destinations.

6. Click Save.

TIP The destinations listed in the Hyperlinks dialog box will match the names listed on the Hyperlinks palette **2**.

TIP As with the Show buttons on the Hyperlinks palette, you can use the Show pop-up menu in the Hyperlinks dialog box to control how many destinations are listed in the dialog box at a time.

The other buttons in the Hyperlinks dialog box

To append hyperlink destinations from another project, click Append, locate a project that contains hyperlink destinations, then click Open (see pages 50–52).

Click Duplicate to duplicate the currently selected hyperlink destination. Save the copy under a new name.

Click Delete to delete the currently selected hyperlink destination.

Hyperlinks Dialog Box

The restyling that you will be doing here will affect all the hyperlink text on the current page—but just the current page. *Note:* Since most browsers let users choose their own page and link colors, their choice may override yours.

To style hyperlink text:

1. Choose Page > Page Properties (Cmd-Option-Shift-A/Ctrl-Alt-Shift-A).

2. In the Colors area **1**, choose new color options from the Link and Visited Link pop-up menus.

3. Click OK. *Note:* Colors chosen for hyperlink text via the Style menu or Colors palette override colors chosen via the Link pop-up menu in the Page Properties dialog box.

You can choose which colors will be used to represent hyperlinks and anchors in a text box in Web layouts (and PDF exports). These colors will display in the Quark-XPress layout but not in the exported file.

To change the anchor icon color for a Web layout:

1. Display a Web layout.

2. Go to QuarkXPress (Edit, in Windows) > Preferences > Web Layout > General.

3. In the Hyperlinks area, click the Anchor Color square, choose a new color, click OK, then click OK to exit the Preferences dialog box.

To change the anchor and/or hyperlink icon color for a PDF export:

1. Display a print layout that will be exported to PDF.

2. Go to QuarkXPress (Edit, in Windows) > Preferences > Print Layout > General.

3. In the Hyperlinks area, click the Anchor Color and/or Hyperlink Color square **2**, choose a new color, click OK, then click OK to exit the Preferences dialog box.

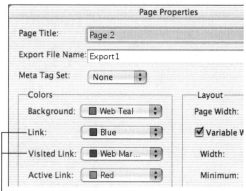

1 *Make Colors:* **Link** *and* **Visited Link** *choices in the* **Page Properties** *dialog box.*

2 *The* **Hyperlinks** *area of QuarkXPress (Edit, in Windows) > Preferences > Print Layout >* **General** *for a* **print** *layout*

Style Hyperlink; Change Icon Color

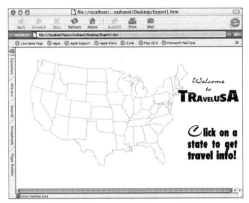

1 *In this **image map**, each **hot area** represents one of the 48 Continental States. When users click a state, they jump to another Web page.*

2 *The **URL** link for a selected hot area in the image is listed at the bottom of the browser window.*

Creating image maps

Images can do more than just make a Website look nice—they also can be used to create interactive image maps to link users to other pages or sites. To do this, first an image is divided into regions, which are called "hot areas," and then each region is assigned a unique link **1**. If a user clicks a hot area, he or she is taken to another Web page or site **2**. Image maps are fun to use, and they look better than text links!

Image maps are an HTML feature, but to code an image map directly in HTML would be very laborious. Instead, in QuarkXPress 6, you can create image maps by defining hot areas over one or more picture boxes (this doesn't affect or change the picture). Each hot area is assigned a hyperlink to another page in the same Web layout or to another site on the Web. Then, when the Web layout is exported as an HTML file, QuarkXPress automatically creates the code for the image map. To create an image map, follow the instructions that begin below.

A picture can contain one or more image map hot areas.

To create an image map with a URL link:

1. The Image Map XTension must be enabled before you begin. To enable XTensions, see page 427.

2. Display a Web layout and choose View > Show Guides (F7) so the newly created image map areas will be visible.

3. *Optional:* Select a picture box.

(Continued on the following page)

4. Choose the Rectangle or Oval Image Map tool , then drag across a picture. *Optional:* Shift-drag to constrain a rectangle to a square or an oval to a circle.
or
Choose the Bézier Image Map tool, then draw a polygon over a picture (the same way you would draw a Bézier text or picture box). To close the box, click the starting point, or create the final point by double-clicking **2**.

Note: Any hot areas that extend outside the picture box will be cropped to the edges of the box when the page is exported.

5. To add a hyperlink to the hot area, keep the hot area selected, then:

Display the Hyperlinks palette, then click the New Hyperlink button **3**.
or
Choose Style > Hyperlink > New.
or
Control-click/Right-click the hot area and choose Hyperlink > New.

6. In the New Hyperlink dialog box (**1**, next page):

Enter a name.

Choose URL from the Type pop-up menu. 6.0!

Enter a URL in the URL field.
or
From the URL pop-up menu, choose a URL or an exported HTML file that has already been created and is listed as a destination on the Hyperlinks palette.
or
Click Select/Browse, locate an exported HTML file, then click Link/Open.

7. To designate where the linked Web page will display, enter a Target destination or choose a destination from the Target pop-up menu. If the Target field is left blank, the target destination will be ignored. A Target destination is

1 *The **Rectangle, Oval,** and **Bézier** tools on the Image Map tool pop-out menu on the Web Tools palette*

2 *A **hot area** created with the **Bézier Image Map** tool*

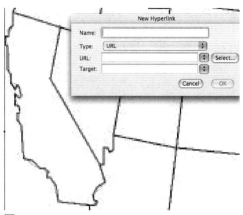

3 *Click the **New Hyperlink** button on the **Hyperlinks** palette.*

Commonly used URL protocols *(http://, https://, ftp://, etc.)*, other existing URL destinations, and other exported HTML files are listed on the **URL** pop-up menu.

http://
https://
ftp://
mailto:
http://www.xyzconn.com
http://www.xyzwash.com
http://www.xyzcalif.com
http://www.xyzoregon.com

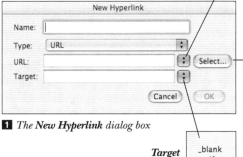

1 *The* **New Hyperlink** *dialog box*

Target destinations

_blank
_self
_parent
_top

Use the **Link to File** *dialog box to locate and link to a local HTML file.*

2 *In the* **Image Map Properties** *dialog box, specify the maximum number of points on polygonal hot areas.*

needed only if your Web page contains a frameset.

"_blank" displays the linked Web page in a new unnamed window.

"_self" displays the linked Web page in the same frame as the image map.

"_parent" displays the linked Web page in the parent frame (window) of the image map. If no parent exists, the link will be displayed in the same frame as the image map.

"_top" displays the linked Web page in the full browser window and eliminates any frames.

To learn more about the Hyperlinks palette, see page 335–338.

8. *Optional:* Repeat steps 3–7 to create other hot areas on the same picture.

9. To preview the image map effect, see page 351. The hot area borders won't display in the browser.

TIP QuarkXPress converts oval and Bézier hot areas into polygons. To control the precision with which it does so (the number of points that the polygon will be composed of), go to QuarkXPress (Edit, in Windows) > Preferences > Web Layout > Tools, click the Oval Image Map or Bézier Image Map tool icon, then click Modify. In the Image Map Properties dialog box, enter a Flatten Shape: Maximum Points value **2**.

TIP To create a hyperlink to an existing destination, click a hot area on an image map, then click the destination link (or name, if your hyperlinks are being shown by name) on the Hyperlinks palette. **6.0!**

TIP To link a hot area on an image map to an anchor or to another page in the current site, for step 6 on the previous page, choose Anchor or Page from the Type pop-up menu and choose an existing destination from the Anchor or Page pop-up menu. **6.0!**

An image's hot areas will move if the image is moved and will be scaled if the image is scaled. You can also edit an image map directly, as in these instructions.

Beware! If a different (new) image is imported into a picture box that contains hot areas, any existing hot areas and hyperlinks in that picture box will be deleted!

To edit an image map:

1. Make sure guides are showing (View > Show Guides or F7).

2. Select the picture box and the hot area.

3. To resize a hot area, drag its handles.
or
To reshape a hot area, edit its points as you would a standard Bézier box.
or
To move a hot area, select it, move the pointer over the area **1**, then drag **2**.
or
To delete a hot area, select it (make sure its handles are visible), then press Delete/Backspace.

4. To edit a hyperlink, click the name or link in the Hyperlinks palette, then click the Edit button *✐* at the top of the palette **3**.

5. In the Edit Hyperlink dialog box **4**, do any of the following: Edit the existing name; or for a URL, choose another URL from the pop-up menu or click the Select button to locate a file to link to; or for a Page or Anchor link, choose another page or anchor from the appropriate pop-up menu.

6. Click OK.

1 *To reposition an existing hot area within an image, move the pointer over the hot area...*

2 *...then drag it to a new location.*

3 *Click the Edit button on the Hyperlinks palette.*

6.0!

4 *Make changes in the Edit Hyperlink dialog box.*

Edit Imge Map

1 *Two modes in a* **rollover**

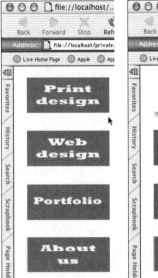

A list of option buttons

When the mouse is moved **over** *one of the buttons, its appearance changes. If a user clicks the item, they're linked to another page.*

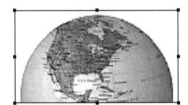

2 *Select a* **picture.**

3 *In the* **Rollover** *dialog box, choose a* **Rollover Image** *and a* **Hyperlink.** *Use the Select/Browse buttons to locate the image files quickly.*

Creating rollovers

A rollover is an image on a Web page whose appearance changes when the mouse is moved over it **1**. If a user clicks the item, they're linked to another Web page. Rollovers are used as visual cues to help users find links on a page or to show them additional information about a link, and are a fun way to add interactivity to Web pages.

Rollovers can't be produced in HTML; some programming help is required (usually JavaScript). Fortunately, you can create rollovers right in QuarkXPress 6, and it's not hard to do. First you select a default image and a rollover image, then you choose a hyperlink to another page in the same Website or in another Website. QuarkXPress does the rest for you.

To create a rollover:

1. Select a picture **2** or select a text box for which the Convert to Graphic on Export option is on in Item > Modify, then choose Item > Basic Rollover > Create Rollover.
or
Control-click/Right-click a picture and choose Basic Rollover > Create Rollover.

2. In the Rollover dialog box **3**, the path and file name for the Default Image will be filled in already—that's the picture that's currently selected. If you change this information, a different picture will be imported into the box.

To choose a Rollover Image, click Select/Browse, locate an image to appear when the image is rolled over, then click Open.

3. For the Hyperlink destination:

From the Hyperlink pop-up menu, choose a URL or HTML file that's currently being used as a link in the active layout.

(Continued on the following page)

or
Click Select/Browse, then choose either an HTML file on your hard drive or a URL.

4. Click OK **1**. To preview the rollover, see the instructions on the next page.

TIP If the rollover image is larger than the default image, the rollover image will need to be scaled and cropped to fit the picture box that contains the default image. See the next set of instructions.

To view a rollover image: 6.0!

Select an item that contains a rollover, then choose Item > Basic Rollover > Rollover Image.
or
Control-click/Right-click an item that contains a rollover and choose Basic Rollover > Rollover Image.

Now that the rollover image is visible **2**, you can move, scale, or crop it to make it fit better in the picture box.

TIP When a default image or rollover image is displayed and selected, you can choose an export format for it in Item > Modify.

To edit a rollover:

1. Select the item that contains a rollover.

2. Choose Item > Basic Rollover > Edit Rollover.
or
Control-click/Right-click the item and choose Basic Rollover > Edit Rollover.

3. In the Rollover dialog box, change the Default Image, Rollover Image, or Hyperlink destination.

4. Click OK.

TIP You can also edit a rollover hyperlink by clicking the destination listing on the Hyperlinks palette, clicking the Edit button, and then changing the URL.

Linking pages

To create a rollover that links two pages of a Web layout, start by exporting those two pages. Next, display the first page, and follow our steps on page 349 to create a rollover. And finally, for step 3, from the Hyperlink pop-up in the Rollover dialog box, choose the export file name of the second page as the link for the rollover.

Hyperlink icon

6.0! *Default Image icon*

Rollover icon

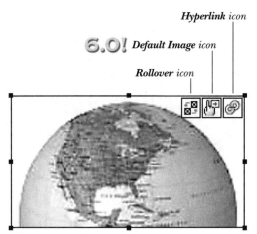

1 *A default rollover image*

Rollover icon

2 *When the rollover image is displayed, the Hyperlink and Default Image icons are hidden; only the Rollover icon remains visible.*

(sidebar) View Rollover Image; Edit Rollover

1 *In the browser, the normal state of a rollover displays when the pointer is **not** over the item.*

2 *In the browser, if you position the pointer **over** a rollover, the hand pointer and the substitute rollover image display.*

Follow these instructions if you want to remove a rollover from an item without deleting the item or its contents.

To remove the rollover function from 6.0! an item:

1. Select the picture box that contains a rollover.

2. Choose Item > Basic Rollover > Remove Rollover.
   or
   Control-click/Right-click and choose Basic Rollover > Remove Rollover.

TIP You could also, of course, delete a picture box containing a rollover altogether; the rollover will be deleted along with the item.

To preview an image map or rollover:

1. Display a page that contains an image map or rollover item.

2. Click the HTML Preview button ![button] at the bottom of the Web project window.

3. In the browser, position the pointer over the image map hot area or rollover (the hand pointer will display). For a rollover, the rollover image should appear **1**–**2**. Click the image map area or rollover. If the browser can locate the link page, that page will display. If the browser can't locate the link page or if the link is a URL and the browser isn't currently connected to the Internet, an alert box will display. Click OK, then click back in a Quark-XPress project window.

Remove, Preview Rollover

6.0! Creating cascading menus

When the user rolls over an area of a Web page that contains a cascading menu, only the top-level menu items on the cascading menu are visible. If the user rolls over a menu item, the submenu items under that menu item are revealed (they cascade). If the user chooses a submenu item to which a link has been attached, that link becomes activated **1**–**2**. Aside from being fun to use, cascading menus allow a Web page designer to orchestrate how much information appears onscreen and keep a page from looking cluttered.

To create a cascading menu, you'll define menu and submenu items and the menu group's properties. Then later, you'll attach the menu group to an item.

To define a cascading menu group:

1. Choose Edit > Cascading Menus.

2. Click New. The Edit Cascading Menu dialog box will open.

3. Enter a Menu Name for the cascading menu group. This is just a definition, not the actual menu items that will appear on the Web page.

Use options in the **Menu Properties** pane of the Edit Cascading Menu dialog box to style the cascading menu (**1**, next page):

1. From the Background Color pop-up menu, choose a background color to appear behind the main menu items.

2. From the Style Sheet pop-up menu, choose a style sheet to be applied to all the menu items.

3. In the Text Inset field, enter a value to be used to offset the first main menu name from the left edge of the box that holds the menu, and to further indent any submenu items.

4. In the Menu Orientation area, click Horizontal or Vertical for the axis on which the menu and submenu items will be arranged.

1 *This text item stays visible onscreen. A cascading menu (not currently visible) is attached to it.*

2 *When the pointer is over an item that contains a cascading menu, the* **menu** *items display.* *When the pointer is over a menu item,* **submenu** *items display.*

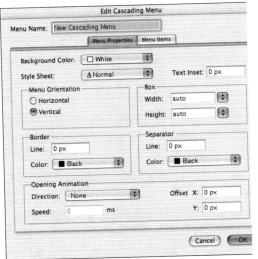

1 *Options in the **Menu Properties** pane of the **Edit Cascading Menu** dialog box control the appearance of the cascading menu.*

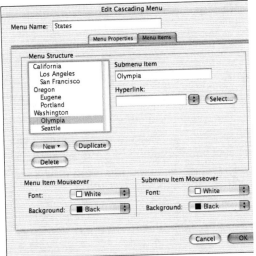

2 *Options in the **Menu Items** pane of the **Edit Cascading Menu** dialog box control the content of the menu, including submenu items and hyperlinks.*

5. In the Box area, enter Width and Height values for the overall cascading menu, or leave the choice as "auto" to have the program calculate the menu size based on character count and font size of the text it contains.

6. *Optional:* In the Border area, enter a Line width and choose a Color for a border to enclose every listing on the cascading menu.

Optional: In the Separator area, enter a Line width and choose a Color for a separator line to be inserted between each submenu item.

7. In the Opening Animation area, from the Direction pop-up menu, choose the direction in which you want menu items to cascade. If None is chosen, they will appear all at once (they won't cascade).

8. When a direction other than None is chosen from the Direction pop-up menu, the Speed field becomes available. Enter a value (0–10,000 milliseconds) for the speed at which submenu items will display upon rollover. At a Speed setting of 0, there will be no delay.

9. In the Offset fields, enter X and Y values to offset the cascading menu downward and to the right so it doesn't obscure the object it's attached to. These values are in addition to the Text Inset value.

Use options in the **Menu Items** pane of the Edit Cascading Menu dialog box **2** to control the wording, links, and rollover effect for the cascading menu.

1. Click New, and choose Menu Item from the pop-up menu.

2. In the Menu Item Name field, select the default text and replace it with the name of your menu item. Main menu names usually don't have hyperlinks attached to them.

3. Click the new main menu name in the Menu Structure window and then,

(Continued on the following page)

from the New pop-up menu, choose
Submenu Item .

4. Select the default text in the Submenu
Item Name field and replace it with the
name of your submenu. *Note:* You can't
use the same name for menu and submenu items.

5. Press Tab, or click in the Hyperlink
field. This field controls which link the
Web user will get to when he or she
clicks the submenu item in the browser.

Enter a URL or HTML file name.
or

Choose an existing link from the
Hyperlink pop-up menu (only names
of exported HTML files, URLs, and
anchors currently being used as links
in the active layout will appear on this
pop-up menu).
or

Click Select/Browse, locate and click
an existing exported HTML file or URL
to use as the hyperlink, then click Open.

6. To add more submenu names to
appear under the current menu item,
repeat steps 3–4. Any additional submenu items will be indented under
the currently highlighted menu item.

7. To add another menu item, click a
menu item in the Menu Structures
window that you want the new one to
appear below (the menu items will
appear in this order in the cascading
menu). Click New and choose Menu
Item. Follow steps 2–5, above, to create
the menu item and any submenu items.

8. In the Menu Item Mouseover area,
choose a font color and a background
color that will display in the browser
behind the text when the user's pointer
is over a menu item.

9. In the Submenu Item Mouseover area,
choose a font color and a background-
color that will display behind the text
in the browser when a user's pointer is

1 *You can add, duplicate, or delete
selected menu items from a cascading
menu. Here, we're adding a **New:
Submenu Item** to the menu group.*

Mind your sizes

A cascading menu will display in the browser only when a user's pointer is over the bounding box of the item that it's attached to. By scaling the box in QuarkXPress before converting it to a graphic on export, you can control how close a user's pointer must be to it before the cascading menu will be revealed. The smaller the box, the closer the viewer's pointer must be for the cascading menu to display.

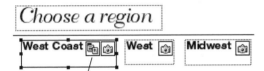

1 *A cascading menu is attached to this item in the Web layout, as indicated by the* **Cascading Menu** *icon. Make the box relatively small and be sure it doesn't overlap any other items (which may also have cascading menus attached to them) to avoid confusing the viewer as to which text belongs to which menu.*

Choose a region

West Coast	West	Midwest
California	Los Angeles	
Oregon	San Francisco	
Washington	Berkeley	
	San Diego	

2 *This is the cascading menu in a browser when the viewer's pointer is close to the box that contains the words "West Coast."*

over a submenu item. Theoretically, a different highlight color could be chosen for each item in a cascading menu.

TIP To delete a menu or submenu item from the Menu Structure window, select it, then click Delete. Or click Duplicate to duplicate it.

10. Finally, click OK. At this point you can either create another cascading menu group by clicking New and then choosing options in the Menu Properties and Menu Items panes of the Edit Cascading Menu dialog box, or you can click Save to close the Cascading Menus dialog box and be done with it. Now follow the next set of instructions to attach the menu group to an item in your Web layout.

In the long-winded instructions that you just followed, you created a cascading menu group. The last step is to attach your cascading menu group to an object in your layout (usually text or an image) that will stay visible and stationary onscreen and that identifies the cascading menu. This way, a user will be tempted to roll over that area, and the cascading menu that you've slaved over will appear!

To attach a cascading menu to an item:

1. Create or select an item. If it doesn't have a Rasterize (camera) icon, choose Item > Modify and check Convert to Graphic on Export, then click OK.

2. From the Item > Cascading Menu submenu, choose a cascading menu name.
or
Control-click/Right-click the item and choose from the Cascading Menu submenu.

The Cascading Menu icon 🖿 will appear in the upper right corner of the item **1**–**2**.

To preview a cascading menu:

1. Display the page in your Web layout that contains a cascading menu, then click the HTML Preview button ▢▧▶ at the bottom of the project window.

2. In the browser, roll the pointer over a menu name to watch the submenu items cascade—Ta-Dah! (**2**, previous page)—then roll over any submenu item and watch it change colors. (You chose that color in the Edit Cascading Menu dialog box.)

3. Click back in the QuarkXPress project window.

To edit an existing cascading menu:

1. Choose Edit > Cascading Menus.

2. Click an existing cascading menu name on the list, then click Edit, or just double-click a name.

3. Choose options in the Menu Properties and/or Menu Items panes of the Edit Cascading Menu dialog box, following the steps on pages 352–355. When you're done, click OK, then click Save to close the Cascading Menus dialog box.

When you remove a cascading menu from an item, the item's contents are left intact. The cascading menu group also remains in the project, and can be edited and attached to any item at any time.

To remove a cascading menu from an item:

1. Choose the Item or Content tool, then select an item that has a cascading menu attached to it.

2. Choose Item > Cascading Menu > Remove Cascading Menu.
   or
   Control-click/Right-click the selected item and choose Cascading Menu > Remove Cascading Menu.

   The cascading menu icon will disappear from the item.

Cascading Menus dialog box options

To append a cascading menu group or groups from another project, click Append, locate a project that contains cascading menu groups, then click Open (see pages 50–52).

Click Duplicate to duplicate the currently selected cascading menu group. Save the copy under a new name.

Click Delete to delete the currently selected cascading menu group.

Preview, Edit, Remove Cascading Menu

Opening the Web Tools palette

Unless you close it, the Web Tools palette displays automatically when a Web layout is displayed. To open the palette if it was closed, choose Window > Tools > **Show Web Tools.**

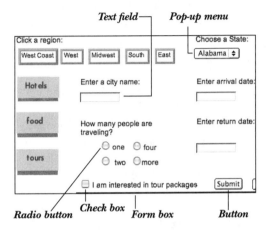

❶ *Various types of* **form controls** *within a* **form box** *on a Web page*

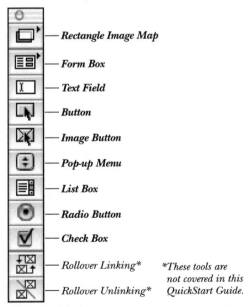

❷ *The tools on the* **Web Tools** *palette are used to create various types of* **controls** *for Web pages.*

Creating forms

Viewers use forms ❶ on a Web page to enter information, check options, or make choices from a list. Then they click a Submit button to send the data to the Web server for processing. Forms for data collection can be used to order products, request documents, perform searches on a Website, or send user information to a Website. The HTML language supports form tags that can be used on a Web page. The Web browser reads the form tags and creates the field, box, or button. A form box is the container that holds text fields, buttons, etc.

Data can be entered or chosen on a form in a variety of ways, such as via text entry fields, lists, pop-up menus, check boxes, or radio buttons, along with the requisite Submit and Reset buttons. QuarkXPress calls these various parts of a form "controls," and provides several tools on the Web Tools palette for creating them ❷. The tool name matches the kind of form control that it creates. For example, the Pop-up Menu tool creates a pop-up menu control.

A server-based script or application is required to process form data. Most often, CGI (Common Gateway Interface) scripts are used for this purpose. QuarkXPress doesn't provide the means to create these scripts; a third-party application is required. Talk with your Webmaster to learn more about the creation of CGI or other server-based scripts.

To create a form box:

1. Choose the Form Box tool 📧 from the Web Tools palette.

2. Position the pointer over a blank area of a Web layout, then drag to create a form box. Form boxes can't overlap each other.

TIP Use Item > Content > Form to convert an existing item into a form box. Any existing box content will be deleted!

Create Form Box

To choose options for a form box:

1. Choose the Item or Content tool, then click a form box.

2. Choose Item > Modify (or Control-click/Right-click and choose Modify), then click the Form tab **1**.

3. *Optional:* Change the Name. You can leave the default name as is, but remember that each form box must have a unique name.

4. Choose an option from the Method pop-up menu to be used for submission of form data:

   Post to send the user-entered data as a separate packet to the Web server. This is usually the preferred option.

   Get to append the user-entered data to the end of the URL or to the end of the file specified by the URL in the Action field. The Get method may append excess data, thus exceeding the URL length limit and resulting in data loss.

5. From the Target pop-up menu, choose where you want any server-returned data (usually an HTML page) to display. *Note:* These frame targets are needed only if your form is embedded within a frameset on your Web page. Choose:

   None (the empty line on the pop-up menu) or _self to load the return page into the same frame or window that holds the form.

   "_blank" to load the return page into a new, unnamed window.

   "_parent" to load the return page into the parent frame, if there is one, of the form.

   "_top" to load the return page into the full browser window, replacing any framesets.

6. If Post was chosen for the Method in step 4, you need to choose a MIME encoding option (that's short for Multi-purpose Internet Mail Extension).

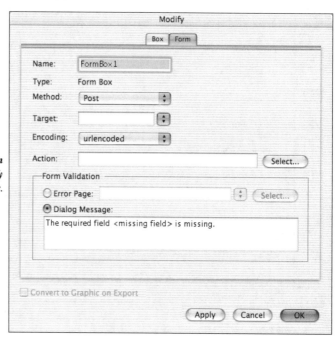

1 *This is the **Form** pane in the **Modify** dialog box for a form box.*

MIMEs are helper applications that aid in the translation of data. Choose one of the following:

"urlencoded" to make the user-data submitted to the Web server follow the urlencoded specifications so the data can be used on most operating system platforms and software applications.

"form-data" to alert the Web server that the user-data is being submitted as a separate attached file and should be encoded as multipart form-data. This way, the server will read the multiple parts of the form submission and not just the name of the attached file.

"plain" to specify that user-data submitted to the Web server not be encoded.

7. In the Action field, enter a URL for the CGI script that will process the user-data submitted to the Web server.
or
Click Select (Mac OS X)/Browse (Windows), then locate and open an existing script file.

8. In the Form Validation area, choose the response method for a submitted form that lacks an entry in a required field:

Click Error Page to have an existing HTML page display in response to an error. Enter a URL for that page; or choose an HTML file from the pop-up menu; or click Select (Mac OS X)/ Browse (Windows), then locate an HTML file (its path will be entered automatically in the URL field).
or
Click Dialog Message, then enter an alert message in the text field or leave the default message as is. The "<missing field>" tag allows the name of the first empty required field to be entered automatically into an alert message.

9. Click OK.

You can specify dimensions for the form box that is created automatically when any form *control* tool is used (not the Form tool). The settings you specify will remain in effect until they're changed.

To choose default dimensions for form boxes:

1. Choose QuarkXPress (Edit, in Windows) > Preferences > Web Layout > Tools, then click the Form Box tool icon 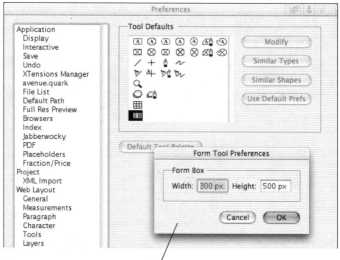 at the bottom of the Tool Defaults window.
   or
   Double-click the Form Box tool on the Web Tools palette.

2. Click Modify.

3. Enter default Width and Height dimensions for the form box in pixels **1**, click OK, then click OK to close the Preferences dialog box.

Form can-do's

■ When you move a form box, any form controls within the box will move along with it.

■ A control can be duplicated within the same form box, provided there's sufficient room for the duplicate in the box.

■ You can scale a form box as you would any other box (click the box with the Item or Content tool, then drag any handle).

■ Form boxes can be positioned on any layer on a page; layer features are fully functional.

■ Form boxes are deleted in the same way other standard items are: Click the box with the Item or Content tool, then press Delete/Backspace or Cmd-K/Ctrl-K.

■ To copy a control, Copy or Cut it using the Item tool, then Paste it into its current form box or into another form box (the box must be large enough to accommodate it). A control can also be dragged from one form box to another.

1 *Choose* **Form Tool Preferences** *in QuarkXPress (Edit, in Windows) >* *Preferences > Web Layout >* **Tools.**

Editing controls

To edit an existing control, select the *control box*—not the surrounding form box—choose Item > Modify, click Form, then change any of the settings.

Visual indicators for forms 6.0!

*The visual indicator for an **image button control***   **1** *The visual indicator for a **form box***

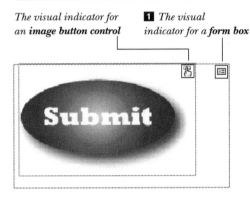

- The Group command is available for controls inside a form box.

- Form boxes can be created in table cells. If a project containing such an item is saved in QuarkXPress 5.0 format, the 6.0! form box will convert to a table cell with a content of None.

- To apply a background color and shade to a form box, use the Colors palette or Item > Modify > Box. Some form con- 6.0! trols (e.g., radio buttons, check boxes) have opaque white backgrounds. Image Button, Radio Button, and Check Box controls can have a background of None.

Form can'ts

- Controls are always contained inside a form box—they can't be hanging around loose somewhere.

- A control can't overlap or reside inside another control. You'll get an alert prompt if you try to draw a new control inside an existing control. Form boxes can't overlap each other, even if they're on different layers. You can duplicate form controls, but the duplication must not result in any overlapping.

- Text can't be entered into, or pictures placed within, a form box or form control.

The other form tools

The Text Field, Button, Image Button, Pop-up Menu, List Box, Radio Button, Check Box, and File Selection tools on the Web Tools palette can be used either to create a control within a whole new form box or to add controls to an existing form box. If you drag with any of these tools in a blank area of your layout, a new form box will be created in the default size, with the control inside it **1**. If you drag inside an existing form box, the control will be added to, and contained within, that box. More than one control can be created within an existing form box, provided you don't try to draw a new control on top of an existing one.

This page and the next 11 pages of this chapter are devoted to form controls.

Text field controls are added to a Web page to allow the user to enter characters, or to type a password that shows up in the field as a series of asterisks.

To create a text or password field control:

1. Choose the Text Field tool ⌷ from the Web Tools palette.

2. Drag in a blank area of the Web page.
or
Drag inside a blank area of an existing form box.

3. Choose Item > Modify (or Control-click/Right-click the control and choose Modify), then click the Form tab ◼.

4. Change the Name or leave the default name as is. Each control must have a unique name.

5. Choose one of these options from the Type pop-up menu:

Text-Single Line to create an entry field that can contain only one line of text.

Text-Multi Line to create an entry field that can contain multiple lines of text and a scroll bar.

Password to create an entry field that will display a user-entered password as a series of asterisks in Mac OS X, bullets in Windows. *Note:* A password field control doesn't perform the actual processing of password protection; that processing is a function of the CGI script.

Hidden Field to create a text field that will be invisible to the user but that can contain pre-entered text to be submitted along with the form data. No other options are available when Hidden Field is chosen.

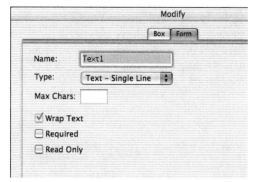

◼ *The **Form** pane in the **Modify** dialog box for a **Text Field** control*

shifting the scale

In HTML, text field controls are sized based on the character count in the field as well as the font size specified in the browser preferences, whereas in a QuarkXPress Web layout, controls and other items are sized based on pixels. As a result, a control that you create in QuarkXPress will probably look different in scale or even positioning when viewed in a browser. Hopefully, these discrepancies will be resolved in a future version of QuarkXPress.

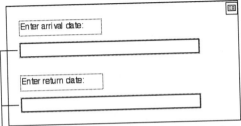

1 *These two **text field** controls are inside a form box in a Web layout. The explanatory text is in separate, standard boxes.*

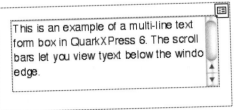

2 *A **text field** control with **Text-Multi Line** chosen (note the presence of a scroll bar)*

6. Enter a value in the Max Chars field to specify the maximum number of characters the field can hold. Leave this field blank to have the Web browser determine the maximum number of characters.

7. *Optional:* If you chose Text-Multi Line for step 5, you can check Wrap Text to have multiple lines of text automatically wrap within the multi-line text field control.

8. *Optional:* Check Read Only to prevent the user from editing any text in the text field control when it's displayed in a browser.

   Optional: Check Required to specify that the text field control must contain an entry before the submitted form can be considered valid. With this option checked, if the user tries to submit the form with a required field empty, the chosen Form Validation method will be activated (see step 8 on page 359).

9. Click OK **1**–**2**.

In a browser, if a user enters more text in a field than the field can display, the entered text scrolls to the left. When this happens, the user doesn't see the complete entry and is more likely to make an input error. Whenever possible, make sure your controls—particularly Text-Single Line controls—are wide enough to display a user's complete entry.

To scale a control:

Choose the Item or Content tool, click a control, then drag a handle **1**–**2**. A single-line text field control can only be resized horizontally; a multi-line text field control can be resized in any direction, using any handle.

To move a control:

Choose the Item tool or hold down Cmd/ Ctrl if the Content tool is chosen, then drag the control to a new position within the form box. You can select and then move more than one control at a time.

TIP You can't drag a control or any of its handles outside its form box.

To delete a control:

Click a control using the Item tool, then press Delete/Backspace.
or
Click a control using the Content tool, then press Cmd-K/Ctrl-K.

It's not the same!

You align your controls nicely in QuarkXPress, and then view your Web page in a browser—and lo and behold, the alignment looks out of whack. To help avoid this problem, make sure the controls don't overlap each other or overlap any noncontrol items (e.g., standard text or picture boxes). Also, align your items carefully using Item > Space/Align or using ruler guides in conjunction with View > Snap to Guides.

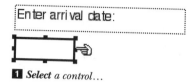

1 *Select a control…*

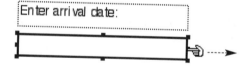

2 *…then drag a handle to scale it.*

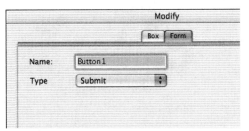

1 *This is the* **Form** *pane in the* **Modify** *dialog box for a* **button** *control. In this case, a submit button will be created.*

Enter arrival date:

Enter return date:

| Submit | | Reset |

2 *Here, the* **Submit** *and* **Reset** *buttons and two text field controls are inside the same form box. The Submit button sends text that the user enters into the text field controls to the Web server. The Reset button clears any user data from the text field controls. The other text was entered into two standard text boxes.*

A requisite submit button control is used to send user data from a Web page form to the Web server. A reset button control is used to clear user-data from fields and boxes in a form so a user can reenter data, if need be. Submit and reset buttons must be created within the same form box as the check box, text field, and radio button controls; otherwise they won't know which data to submit or reset. The submit and reset button functions can be previewed only in a browser.

To create a submit or reset button control:

1. Choose the Button tool 🔲 from the Web Tools palette.

2. Click a blank area of a Web page.
or
Click a blank area in an existing form box.

3. Choose Item > Modify (or Control-click/Right-click the control and choose Modify from the context menu), then click the Form tab **1**.

4. Change the Name or leave the default name as is. Each control must have a unique name.

5. From the Type pop-up menu, choose the kind of button you want to create:

Reset restores all controls within a form box to their default values (usually a blank state).
or
Submit sends the data contained within a form box to the target CGI script.

6. Click OK **2**.

7. Choose the Content tool, click the control, then enter the desired button name. The button will automatically scale to fit the length of the name.

You can't style the button text. It will be displayed in the browser's default sans serif font, as specified by the browser preferences.

An image (picture) can be used as a submit button control **1** instead of text.

Note: At the present time, for this type of control, there is no Type pop-up menu in the Form pane in Item > Modify that would allow you to switch between the submit or reset functions, so the button can be used only for the submit function.

To create a submit button control using an image:

1. Choose the Image Button tool.

2. Drag in a blank area of the Web page, or inside an existing form box.

3. Choose File > Get Picture, locate a picture file, then click Open. Scale the picture as desired.

4. Choose Item > Modify (Cmd-M/ Ctrl-M) (or Control-click/Right-click the control and choose Modify from the context menu), then click the Export tab **2**.

5. From the Export As pop-up menu, choose a graphics file format: JPEG, GIF, or PNG. To learn more about these formats, see pages 327–330.

6. In the Export To field, enter a name to create an additional folder/directory to hold the image, or leave the default "image" folder selected. Any folders that have already been created will be listed on the Export To pop-up menu.

7. In the Alternate Text field, enter a text description that can be substituted for the image, or leave the default entry as is. Alternate Text is used when image display is turned off for the browser, and is also used by visually impaired users to help them navigate through a site.

8. The remaining options in the Export pane will vary depending on which Export As format you chose in step 5.

For **JPEG,** choose an option from the Image Quality pop-up menu: Highest,

1 *To create this button, we created a button shape and text in Adobe Illustrator, saved the file as a GIF, created an image button control in QuarkXPress, and then imported the .gif file into the image button control box.*

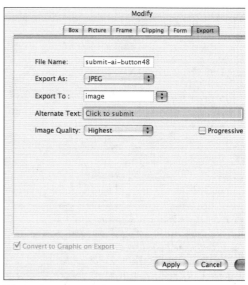

2 *This is the **Export** pane of the Modify dialog box for an **image button** control, with **JPEG** chosen from the Export As pop-up menu.*

Renaming a control

Each and every control to be used on a Web page must have a *unique* name. To rename an image button or any other type of control, select the control, go to Item > Modify > Form, change the Name, then click OK.

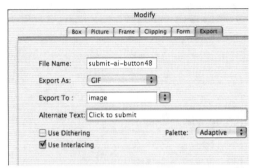

1 *This is the* **Export** *pane of the Modify dialog box for an* **image button** *control, with* **GIF** *chosen from the Export As pop-up menu.*

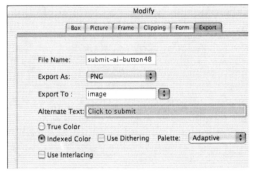

2 *This is the* **Export** *pane of the Modify dialog box for an* **image button** *control, with* **PNG** *chosen from the Export As pop-up menu.*

High, Medium, Low, or Lowest. The higher the quality setting, the less the image will be compressed but the larger its file storage size and the longer its download time. Check Progressive to have the image display in progressively more detail as it downloads.

or

For **GIF 1**, check Use Dithering to have any image colors that aren't found on the browser palette display as a combination of two colors. Check Use Interlacing to have the image display in progressively more detail as it downloads. And choose an option from the Palette pop-up menu (Web-safe, Adaptive, Windows, or Mac OS) to be used for reducing the number of colors in the image to the 256 colors that a browser can display. We recommend choosing Web-safe, since this palette contains only those colors used by both the Navigator and Explorer browsers.

or

For **PNG 2**, click True Color to preserve the maximum possible number of existing image colors for display in the browser, or click Indexed Color to limit the number of image colors to 256. If you clicked Indexed Color, you can check Use Dithering to have any image colors that aren't found on the browser palette display as a combination of two colors; and choose an option from the Palette pop-up menu (Web-safe, Adaptive, Windows, or Mac OS) to be used for reducing the number of colors in the image to the 256 that a browser can display. Web-safe is a good choice, since this palette contains only those colors used by both the Navigator and Explorer browsers. Check Use Interlacing to have the image display in progressively more detail as it downloads.

9. Click OK.

Pop-up menus and scroll lists on a Web page allow users to make choices or navigate to supplementary information. A list control offers several options at a time, whereas a pop-up menu has to be clicked on in order for its contents to be revealed.

To create a pop-up menu or list control:

1. Choose the Pop-up Menu tool ⬚ or the List Box tool ⬚ from the Web Tools palette.

2. Click a blank area of the Web page.
   or
   Click a blank area in an existing form box.

3. With the pop-up menu control still selected, choose Item > Modify (or Control-click/Right-click the control and choose Modify from the context menu), then click the Form tab **1**–**2**.

4. Change the Name or leave the default name as is. Remember, as we've said before, each control must have a unique name.

5. From the Type pop-up menu, choose Pop-up Menu to create a pop-up menu control, or choose List to create a scroll list control. Either way, the resulting effect can be previewed only in a browser.

6. Choose an existing menu set from the Menu pop-up menu, or choose New to create a new menu set. For more information about menu sets, see page 370.

7. *Optional:* If you chose List in step 5, above, check Allow Multiple Selections to enable users to choose more than one item at a time on the scroll list.

8. *Optional:* Check Required to require that the user make a selection from the pop-up menu or list before the submitted form will be considered valid. If the user attempts to submit the form

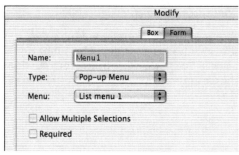

1 *This is the **Form** pane of the **Modify** dialog box for a **pop-up menu** control.*

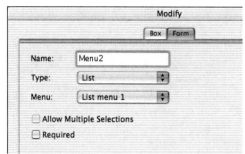

2 *This is the **Form** pane of the **Modify** dialog box for a **list box** control.*

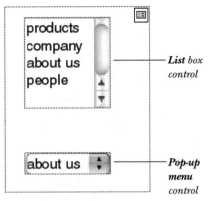

List *box*
control

Pop-up
menu
control

1 *These list box and pop-up menu controls use the same menu set, so the same entry names are available in both. The default entry in this menu set is "about us." It displays on the collapsed pop-up menu box and will also be highlighted in the list box when the Web page is viewed in a browser. (Instructions for creating a menu set begin on the following page.)*

without making a selection, the chosen Form Validation error method will be activated (see step 8 on page 359).

9. Click OK **1**.

Note: We recommend that you also create a separate text box containing instructions on how and why the user should use the pop-up menu or list control, and place this text box next to the control.

Follow the instructions on the next page to create the text content for the list or pop-up menu control.

TIP To scale a list control vertically, select the control, then move the top or bottom midpoint handle. A pop-up menu control can't be resized manually. This type of control is scaled automatically to fit the largest text entry in the applied menu set.

TIP A list control will have a scroll bar only if the chosen menu set items overflow the current list box in the QuarkXPress Web layout.

Pop-Up Menu or List Control

List controls and pop-up menu controls are the containers for lists of items a user will choose from. A menu set provides that list of items to a control, along with values or URL addresses for each item.

To create a menu set:

1. Choose Edit > Menus, then click New.
   or
   Select a pop-up menu or list control, choose Item > Modify > Form, then choose Menu: New.

2. Type a Name for the set and check Navigation Menu if the items to be created will be used to link a user to another Web page .

3. Click Add, then enter a name for the individual item.

4. If you checked Navigation Menu in step 2, above, and you want the menu item to link the user to another page, enter a valid URL or path for that Web page in the URL field 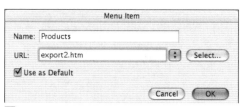. To have the path name be entered automatically, choose a file name from the URL pop-up menu or use the Select/Browse button to locate an existing external file. Only names of exported HTML files, URLs, and anchors that are currently being used as links in the active layout will appear on the URL pop-up menu.

   If you didn't check Navigation Menu in step 2, enter a Value for the item. The information entered into the Value field will be sent to the Web server when the item is selected and the form is submitted .

5. Check Use as Default to have the current menu item be highlighted on the list when viewed in a browser. In a pop-up menu control, this default menu item will be the only visible item when the pop-up menu is collapsed. You can also specify a default item in the main Edit Menu dialog box (see step 7).

6. Click OK .

The other buttons

In the **Edit Menu** dialog box, click Duplicate to copy a selected item; or click Edit (or just double-click the item name) to edit a selected item; or click Delete to delete a selected item.

In the **Menus** dialog box, click Edit to edit a selected menu set; or click Duplicate to copy a selected menu set; or click Delete to delete a selected menu set.

1 *Use the **Edit Menu** dialog box to create a menu set. With **Navigation Menu** checked, each menu item must contain a URL as its Value.*

2 *With Navigation Menu **checked** in the Edit Menu dialog box, you can enter a URL in the **Menu Item** dialog box for the current menu item to link to.*

3 *With the Navigation Menu option **unchecked** in the Edit Menu dialog box, you can enter **Value** data in the **Menu Item** dialog box to be sent to the Web server when the current menu item is selected by a user in the browser.*

Create Menu Set

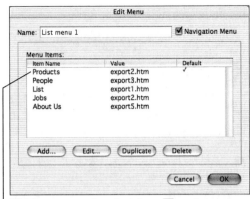

 *The new menu item from figure* 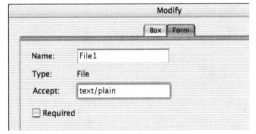 *on the previous page appears in the* ***Item Name*** *column in the* ***Edit Menu*** *dialog box.*

2 *Drag with the* ***File Selection*** *tool to create a* ***browse*** *button control.*

3 *This is the* ***Form*** *pane of the* ***Modify*** *dialog box for a file selection control.*

7. *Optional:* Click in the Default column for an item to make it the current default for a control that uses this menu set.

8. Click OK, then click Save to save the menu set. If you're in the Modify dialog box, click OK to exit.

Next, we'll show you how to create a Browse button. A user will click this button when they're required to locate and select a file to be submitted with their form to a Web server.

To create a separate file selection control:

1. Choose the File Selection tool ⬆ (it's on the Form Box tool pop-out menu on the Web Tools palette).

2. Drag in a blank area of the Web page.
or
Drag in a blank area inside an existing form box **2**.

3. Choose Item > Modify (Cmd-M/ Ctrl-M) (or Control-click/Right-click the control and choose Modify from the context menu), then click the Form tab **3**.

4. Change the Name or leave the default name as is. Each control must have a unique name.

5. *Optional:* In the Accept field, enter the names of MIME types, separating the names with a comma. This list will be used by the Web server to help it interpret the separate file that will be submitted with the form.

6. *Optional:* Check Required to make it mandatory for the user to click Browse and choose a file to be submitted with the form.

7. Click OK.

Users can select only one option from among a group of radio buttons, whereas they can check as many check boxes as they like (that's how they work in dialog boxes, too).

To create a radio button or check box control:

1. Choose the Radio Button tool ⦿ or the Check Box tool ☑ from the Web Tools palette.

2. Drag in a blank area of the Web page.
   or
   Drag in a blank area inside an existing form box. For radio button controls to be in the same group, they must be created within the same form box.

3. With the control selected, choose Item > Modify (or Control-click/Right-click the control and choose Modify from the context menu), then click the Form tab **1**–**2**.

4. Change the name or leave the default name as is. Each check box control must have a unique name, whereas radio buttons require a group name. If you want radio button controls within the same form box to be in the same group (e.g., to ensure that only one button in the form can be highlighted at a time), they must all use the same Group name.

   TIP If you've created several radio buttons, you can select them, choose Item > Modify > Form, and then enter a name for the whole group.

5. From the Type pop-up menu, choose "Check box" to create a check box control, or choose "Radio button" to create a radio button control.

6. Enter a Value to be sent to the Web server when the control is selected and the form is submitted. The Value informs the data-controlling script what the chosen option signifies

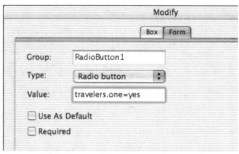

1 *This is the **Form** pane of the **Modify** dialog box for a **radio button** control.*

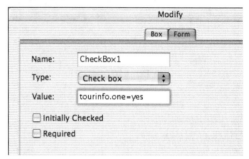

2 *This is the **Form** pane of the **Modify** dialog box for a **check box** control.*

1 *These are **radio button** and **check box** controls within a form box on a Web page. **Submit** sends the value that was entered in the Value field in Item > Modify > Form for the radio button controls that are clicked and the check box controls that are checked. **Reset** unhighlights and set all the controls in the form box back to their default state.*

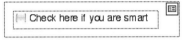

2 *Enter text **inside** the control box…*

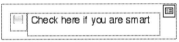

3 *…or enter text into a **separate** box.*

(e.g., a "yes" to a question or an amount from a category).

7. *Do any of the following optional steps:*

For a check box control, check Initially Checked to have the current control be checked when the Web page initially displays or the form is reset.

For a radio button, check Use As Default to have the current button control be selected when the Web page initially displays or the form is reset. In a group of radio buttons, only one button can be preselected at a time.

Check Required to require that the control be clicked or checked before the submitted form will be considered valid. If the user tries to submit the form without the required selection, the chosen Form Validation method will be activated (see step 8 on page 359).

8. Click OK **1**.

9. Enlarge the box that holds the control by dragging any of its handles (the control can't extend outside the form box). Choose the Content tool, then enter text to identify the button or box **2**. The text can be styled or indented using commands on the Style menu or the Measurements palette.
or
Enter text into a separate text box, and then align that box with the control box **3**.

Radio Button or Check Box Control

Creating meta tags

When generating a search list and index-ing Web pages, Web search engines use the first lines of text on a Web page as the description for that page. Attaching a meta tag to a Web page—an HTML tag that describes the content of the page—gives you control over what text a search engine will examine, and helps prevent your page from being described and categorized incorrectly. If your Web page is properly described and indexed on a search list, Web users will be able to find your site more readily via the search engine, and hopefully more traffic will be attracted to your site.

The various categories and options used in meta tags are derived from the data-transfer system and data organization used by Web servers. In QuarkXPress, meta tag categories are organized into meta tag sets, which in turn are incorporated into code for a Web page. It's all behind the scenes, though; meta tags don't produce any visible items on a Web page.

To create a meta tag set:

1. With a Web layout open, choose Edit > Meta Tags, then click New .

2. Enter a Name for the set.

3. Click Add.

4. In the Edit Meta Tag dialog box, choose an attribute from the Meta Tag pop-up menu or enter an attribute in the field:

Name to designate the category of tag names that describe information about the Web page, such as the author, any copyrights, a brief page description, the application used to create the page, or keywords to be used for indexing the page.

or

http-equiv to designate a category of tag names that instruct the browser to perform specific actions when display-ing the page, such as which character

Where they're stored

If a set is created using the Meta Tags command when a Web layout is open, that set will be stored only with that layout. If a set is created when no projects are open, it will be stored as a default in the XPress Preferences file.

Meta Tags, like all the commands listed on the lower half of the Edit menu, follow this directive: Settings that are chosen when a project is open will be stored only with that project; settings that are chosen when no projects are open become the defaults for future projects.

1 *The **Edit Meta Tag Set** dialog box for a new **tag set***

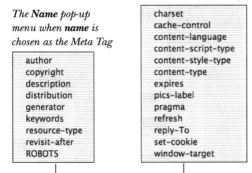

1 *The* **Name** *pop-up menu when* **http-equiv** *is chosen as the Meta Tag*

The **Name** *pop-up menu when* **name** *is chosen as the Meta Tag*

set to use for the page, how to cache the page in the browser, when the page should expire from the browser cache, and when to automatically refresh (reload) the page into the browser.

5. Choose a value from the Name pop-up menu or enter a value in the field **1**. The values displayed on the pop-up menu will vary depending on which attribute was chosen in the previous step. (For a description of the Name field options, see the QuarkXPress 6 documentation.)

6. In the Content field, enter descriptive content text, separating the phrases with a comma.

7. Click OK.

8. To create additional meta tags, click Add, then repeat steps 4–7. You may repeat steps 4–7 several times in order to create meta tags for the author's name, for the generator program and version used to create the page, for a description of the page (entered in the Content field), and for keywords (entered in the Content field, with the phrases separated by commas) **2** (see also **2**, next page).

9. When you're done, click OK **3**, then click Save to save the whole set.

TIP In the Meta Tags dialog box, click Duplicate to duplicate the current set.

TIP In the Meta Tags dialog box, click Delete to delete the current set. If a meta tag set is attached to the active Web layout, an alert dialog box will appear. From the pop-up menu, choose a replacement meta tag set or choose None; click OK, then click Save.

TIP If no Web project is open when you choose Edit > Meta Tags, you will create a default meta tag set that isn't associated or stored with any particular project.

2 *In the* **New Meta Tag** *dialog box, the "keywords" Name was chosen and a list of keywords to be used in a search were entered into the* **Content** *field.*

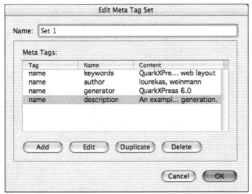

3 *The* **Edit Meta Tag Set** *dialog box lists the* **Tag,** **Name,** *and* **Content** *of each meta tag.*

Create Meta Tag Set

To edit a meta tag set:

1. Choose Edit > Meta Tags.

2. Choose a set name, then click Edit.

3. Click a tag in the scroll window, then click Edit.

4. Choose new options from the pop-up menus and/or modify the Content text.

5. Click OK twice, then click Save.

You can attach a different meta tag set to each page in a Web layout.

To attach a meta tag set to a Web page:

1. Display the desired Web layout and go to the desired page.

2. Choose Page > Page Properties (Cmd-Option-Shift-A/Ctrl-Alt-Shift-A).

3. Choose a meta tag set from the Meta Tag Set pop-up menu **1**.

4. Click OK **2**. The attached meta tag set can be changed to a different set at any time.

You can append a meta tag set from one Web project to another.

To append a meta tag set:

1. Open the Web project to which you want to append a meta tag set.

2. Choose Edit > Meta Tags.

3. Click Append. Locate the Web project that contains the desired meta tag set, then click Open.

4. In the Available window, click a meta tag set name (or Shift-click multiple set names).

5. Click the right arrow to include the selected set(s), then click OK.

6. Click Save.

1 *In the Page Properties dialog box, choose from the Meta Tag Set pop-up menu.*

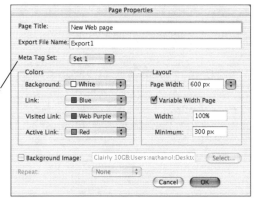

2 *This is source code in the Internet Explorer browser, showing meta tags that were created in QuarkXPress and then attached to a Web layout page.*

Libraries 20

Our "6.0!" logo

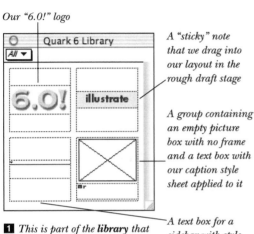

1 *This is part of the **library** that was used to produce this book (in Mac OS X).*

A *"sticky" note that we drag into our layout in the rough draft stage*

A *group containing an empty picture box with no frame and a text box with our caption style sheet applied to it*

A *text box for a sidebar with style sheets applied to it*

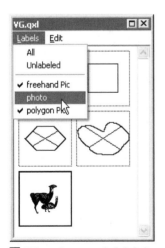

2 *Library items can be **labeled** and shown by category (this is a library palette in Windows).*

Using libraries

A library is a special kind of file that's used to organize and store items of any type: text boxes or picture boxes, empty or filled; contentless boxes; lines; text paths; tables; and even groups of items. Each library is displayed as a floating palette **1**–**2** and can contain up to 2,000 items. When you drag an item from a library palette into any QuarkXPress project window, a copy of the item appears in the active layout. An unlimited number of libraries can be created.

Note: The version of a picture that is stored in a library is just its low-resolution preview; this keeps library file sizes relatively small. However, if you send a file containing library elements for imagesetting—as with any picture used in a QuarkXPress layout—you'll need to supply the original picture files. A library can also serve a supporting role as an onscreen picture catalog.

To create a library:

1. Choose File > New > Library (Cmd-Option-N/Ctrl-Alt-N).

2. Type a name for the library in the Save As/Save as Type field.

3. Select a drive or folder in which to save the library.

4. Click Create. A new library palette will appear on your screen. To put items into the library, see the instructions on the following page.

To put an item in a library:

1. Create a new library or open an existing library.

2. Choose the Item tool, or hold down Cmd/Ctrl if the Content tool is chosen.

3. Drag any item, group, or multiple-item selection into the library 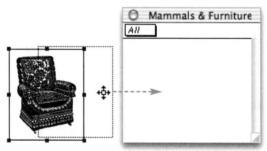. When the pointer is over the library, you'll see an eyeglasses icon 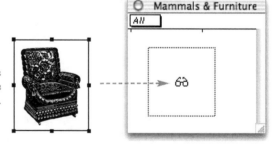. When you release the mouse, a thumbnail of the item will appear in the library 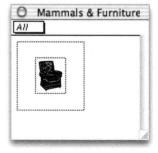; the original item will stay on your page. A multiple-item selection will be stored as one entry.

   You can't undo an addition to a library, but you can remove any item from a library (see page 380).

TIP Items can be dragged from one library to another.

Auto library save

If **Auto Library Save** is checked in QuarkXPress (Edit, in Windows) > Preferences > Application > Save, a library will be resaved each time an item is added to it or deleted from it. You may notice a slight processing delay each time this occurs. With this option unchecked, libraries are saved only when they're closed or when you quit/exit QuarkXPress.

*■ Drag an item into a library with the **Item** tool.*

*■ The pointer turns into an **eyeglasses** icon as the item is dragged into the library.*

■ The item is automatically duplicated, and the original is left intact in the layout. To move an item to a different spot in a library, just drag it.

Colors and libraries

■ If you retrieve an item from a library that has a color applied to it, the color will be appended to the Colors palette of the active file—unless there's a color with a matching name in the target file, in which case the item will append but not the color. The same holds true for a style sheet, dash/stripe, list, or H&J.

■ If you recolor or otherwise modify an item in a layout that originated from a library, the item in the library won't update. To update the library item, you'll have to remove the old item and add the updated one.

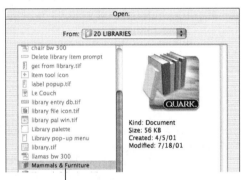

1 *Double-click a **library** file.*

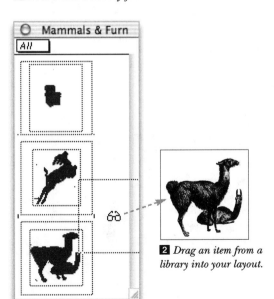

2 *Drag an item from a library into your layout.*

Any libraries that are open when you quit/exit QuarkXPress will reopen automatically when you relaunch the application.

To open an existing library:

1. Choose File > Open (Cmd-O/Ctrl-O).

2. Locate and click the library that you want to open **1**, then click Open (or double-click the icon). Library files are represented by a book icon.

TIP To open a library from the Desktop, double-click the library file icon. The extension for libraries is ".qxl". A library created in Mac OS X can't be opened in Windows, and vice versa.

TIP To close a library palette, click its close button. Don't use File > Close.

Picture paths

When a picture is added to a library, information about the path to the original picture file is stored with the library item. Similarly, when a picture is retrieved from a library, the picture's path information is stored with the project. For an image to print properly, the original picture file must be kept in the same location, with the same file name. If you move or rename the original picture file, you should update it in the library.

One way to update a library item is to relink the picture in the layout, select it with the Item tool, copy it (Edit > Copy in Mac OS X; Copy on the Edit menu on the library palette in Windows), click the library item to be replaced, paste, then click OK in the alert dialog box.

To retrieve an item from a library:

1. Choose the Item or Content tool.

2. If the layout has multiple layers, choose a layer for the library item.

3. Drag an item from a library into a layout page (you can enlarge the palette or use the scroll arrows to display items that are out of view) **2**. Simple as that.

If a library contains a lot of items, it can become difficult to find the items you need. By labeling related library items, you can limit the number of items that are displayed at a given time. You can assign a different label to each item or assign the same label to multiple items.

To label a library item:

1. Double-click a library item.

2. Enter a name in the Label field ■.
   or
   Choose an existing label, if there are any, from the Label pop-up menu ■. You can retype the same label for various items, but it's easier to choose an existing label, and you'll be less likely to make a typing error.

3. Click OK. If you created a new label, it will appear on the pop-up/drop-down menu at the top of the palette.

To display items by label:

Choose from the pop-up menu (Mac OS X) ■/Labels drop-down menu (Windows)■. More than one label category can be displayed at a time.

Choose All to display all the items in the library, both labeled and unlabeled.

Choose Unlabeled to display only those items that don't have a label.

To hide items bearing the same label:

A check mark on the pop-up/drop-down menu on a library palette means that that label category is displayed. Reselect a selected label to uncheck it.

To delete an item from a library:

1. Choose the Item or Content tool.

2. Click a library item.

3. In Mac OS X, choose Edit > Clear or press Delete. In Windows, choose Delete from the Edit menu on the library palette or press Ctrl-X (Cut).

4. Click OK. You can't undo the deletion!

Making arrangements

Arranging library items in a logical order on the palette makes it easier to locate them. Just drag a library item to a different spot on the palette (note the arrowheads as you do this).

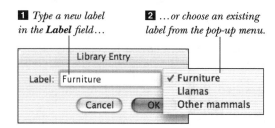

■ *Type a new label in the **Label** field...*

■ *...or choose an existing label from the pop-up menu.*

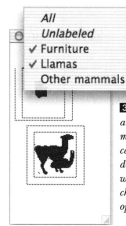

■ *On the pop-up menu on a library palette, a check mark appears next to each category that's currently displayed. In **Mac OS X**, when more than one label is chosen and the menu isn't open, it says Mixed Labels.*

■ *In **Windows**, you'll see a check mark on the **Labels** drop-down menu for each category that's displayed.*

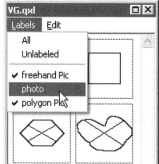

Synchronize

New chapter! 6.0!

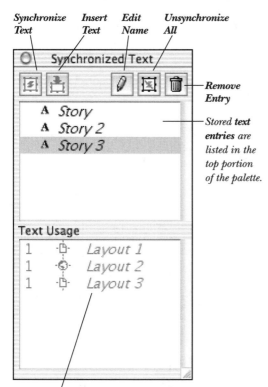

Synchronize Text · Insert Text · Edit Name · Unsynchronize All

Remove Entry

Stored **text** *entries are listed in the top portion of the palette.*

1 *Layouts that contain the currently selected text entry are listed in the* **Text Usage** *area of the* **Synchronized Text** *palette.*

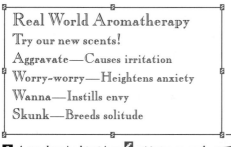

2 *A synchronized text icon* 🅂 *appears on each handle of items that contains synchronized text.*

Synchronizing text

What is synchronized text?

Synchronized text is text that's stored on the Synchronized Text palette and that's added, via the palette, to one or more layouts within the same project **1**. When it's on the palette it's called an "entry"; when it's inserted into a layout it's called an "instance."

Here's what's special about synchronized text: When one instance is edited, all other instances in the project that contain the same text update instantaneously **2**. This feature allows you to standardize your text content across multiple layouts, from print to Web. Whereas style sheets control text attributes and formats, synchronization controls just the text content.

Once a text entry is added to the Synchronized Text palette (Window > Show Synchronized Text), it can be stored there indefinitely and can be added to any layout within the same project if and when the need arises. An entry can consist of anything from a word or phrase to a series of paragraphs.

When an entry is selected on the Synchronized Text palette, all the layouts that contain a synchronized instance of that text are listed in the Text Usage area in the lower portion of the palette. If no layouts are listed in the Text Usage area, it means that at the moment the currently selected entry isn't synchronized in any layouts.

Synchronized Text

6.0! In these instructions, we'll show you how to add a text entry to the Synchronized Text palette. The text that is added to the palette simultaneously becomes a synchronized instance.

To add an entry to the Synchronized Text palette:

1. If the text you want to synchronize isn't already in your layout, choose any text tool, draw a text box or path, and enter text. (It can't be on a master page and it can't contain an anchored item.) Apply whatever typographic attributes you want to the text, either "by hand" or via a style sheet.

2. Choose the Content tool.

3. Click in the text box or on the text path **1**. *All* the text in the item is going to be synchronized (it can't be a portion).

4. Display the Synchronized Text palette (Window > Show Synchronized Text), then click the Synchronize Text button **⑤** on the palette.
 or
Control-click/Right-click the text item in your layout and choose Synchronize Text.
 or
Choose Style > Synchronize Text.

5. The Synch Content dialog box will open. Leave the current Item Name as is or enter a new, more descriptive name for the text entry **2**.

6. Click OK. The new entry will appear on the Synchronized Text palette **3**.

When a synchronized text box is selected, little **⑤** icons appear on its handles; in table cells, they'll appear in the corners; on a text path, they'll appear on the anchor points **4**.

TIP If you duplicate a layout that contains synchronized text, that text will also appear, and be synchronized, in the duplicate layout.

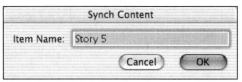

Real World Aromatherapy
Customer favorites!

By-Gones—Renews past grudges
Gluttony—Heightens greed
Spite—Promotes bad will

1 *Click in an item that contains text.*

2 *In the **Synch Content** dialog box, leave the **Item Name** as is or enter a new name.*

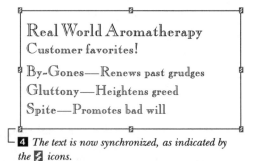

3 *The new **text entry** (Story 5, in this case) appears on the Synchronized Text palette.*

Real World Aromatherapy
Customer favorites!

By-Gones—Renews past grudges
Gluttony—Heightens greed
Spite—Promotes bad will

4 *The text is now synchronized, as indicated by the **⑤** icons.*

Text attributes

When text is added to the Synchronized Text palette, its current attributes (e.g., font, point size) will also apply to any instances of that text that are inserted into a layout. If you edit a style sheet that's associated with an entry on the Synchronized Text palette, all synchronized instances in your layouts will update accordingly, but the entry on the palette will not.

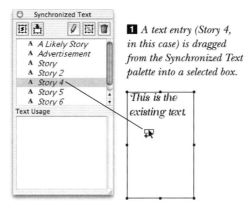

1 *A text entry (Story 4, in this case) is dragged from the Synchronized Text palette into a selected box.*

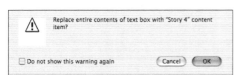

2 *This prompt will appear if the item you insert synchronized text into already contains text.*

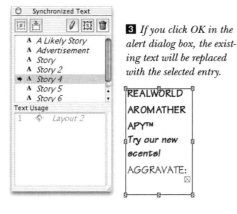

3 *If you click OK in the alert dialog box, the existing text will be replaced with the selected entry.*

Once an entry has been added to the Synchronized Text palette, it can then be inserted into text items in any layouts—Web and/or print—within the same project.

To insert synchronized text in a layout: 6.0!

1. To insert text into a new item, choose any text tool and create a new, empty text box, text cell, or text path in any layout. It can be on any layer, but it can't be on a master page. Leave the item selected.
    or
    Click in a box that already contains text (synchronized or not). In this case, the new, synchronized text will replace the existing text (a warning prompt will appear)!

2. Choose the Content tool.

3. Click an entry on the Synchronized Text palette.

4. Click the Insert Text button.🔼
    or
    Control-click/Right-click an entry on the palette and choose Insert Content into Box.
    or
    Drag the text entry from the Synchronized Text palette to the selected text box, cell, or path **1**.

5. If the text item you clicked on already contains text, an alert dialog box will appear **2**. Click OK to replace the existing text with the entry **3** (or click Cancel if you change your mind).

    When an instance is selected, it exhibits the little **2** icons, and an arrow appears next to the corresponding entry on the Synchronized Text palette.

6. To see how this feature works, add one or two more instances (maybe add one more in the same layout and a second one in another layout), following steps 1–5 above. Next, edit the text in any one of those instances; the other instances will update instantaneously!

Insert Synchronized Text

The more apt a name you assign to an entry, the more easily you'll be able to identify it. The more entries there are, the more imperative this becomes.

6.0! To rename an entry on the Synchronized Text palette:

1. Click an entry on the Synchronized Text palette, then click the Edit Name button.

   or

   Control-click/Right-click an entry on the Synchronized Text palette and choose Edit Name.

2. Edit the Item Name in the Edit Name dialog box ◘.

3. Click OK.

Along with learning how to synchronize text, you also need to know how to unsynchronize it so you can back out of the deal. You can unsynchronize one instance at a time (instructions on this page) or you can unsynchronize all the instances of a particular entry (instructions on the following page).

When a text instance (or instances) is unsynchronized, it remains in the text box, but its link to the Synchronized Text palette and any other instances is broken. In other words, when you edit text that's been unsynchronized, no other text items are affected.

To unsynchronize one instance: 6.0!

1. Choose the Content tool.

2. Click a synchronized text instance in any layout, then choose Style > Unsynchronize Text.

   or

   Or Control-click/Right-click a synchronized text instance and choose Unsynchronize Text.

3. When the alert dialog box appears ◙, click Yes.

Quick unsynchronize

If you copy or cut and paste synchronized text, the pasted text won't be synchronized.

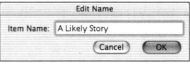

◘ *A story can be renamed via the **Edit Name** dialog box.*

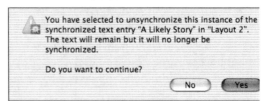

◙ *This prompt will appear if you **unsynchronize one** instance of a text entry.*

All means all—*all* instances in all layouts in the project.

To unsynchronize all instances of an entry:

1. On the Synchronized Text palette, click the entry you want to unsynchronize.

2. Click the Unsynchronize All button ⊠ on the palette.
   or
   Control-click/Right-click in the layout and choose Unsynchronize All.

3. When the alert dialog box appears **1**, click Yes. This can be undone.

   The text entry will remain on the Synchronized Text palette and can be reused.

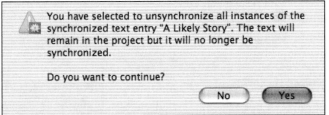

You have selected to unsynchronize all instances of the synchronized text entry "A Likely Story". The text will remain in the project but it will no longer be synchronized.

Do you want to continue?

    No   Yes

1 *This prompt will appear if you **unsynchronize all** the instances of a text entry.*

6.0! If the Synchronized Text palette starts to fill up with entries that you no longer have any use for, then it's time to weed some of them out. If you remove an entry from the Synchronized Text palette, any instances of that text will remain in the layout(s), but they will no longer be synchronized with one another and can be edited independently of one another.

To delete an entry from the Synchronized Text palette:

1. On the Synchronized Text palette, click the entry that you want to remove, then click the Remove Item button on the palette.
or
Control-click/Right-click an entry on the palette and choose Remove Content Item.

2. When the alert dialog box appears **1**, click Yes. This can be undone.

TIP If you delete a layout that contains synchronized text, any synchronized text in the remaining layout(s) will stay synchronized.

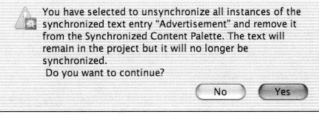

You have selected to unsynchronize all instances of the synchronized text entry "Advertisement" and remove it from the Synchronized Content Palette. The text will remain in the project but it will no longer be synchronized.
Do you want to continue?

No   Yes

1 *This prompt will appear if you **delete** an **entry** from the Synchronized Text palette.*

Delete Entry

Elaine's Book

Like libraries, book palettes
have their own unique
file icons and can be
opened using File > Open.

Move Chapter Up

Add
Chapter   *Move Chapter Down*

Print Chapter   *Remove Chapter*

Synchronize Book

M	Chapter	Pages	Status
M	.:master vqs 6	1★	Modified
	.:toc book vqs 6	i★–ii★	Modified
	1 How Illus Works	1★–8★	Available
	.:..:2 Startup	9–16	Modified
	.:...:3 Views	17–24	Modified
	4 Objects Basics	25–35	Modified

Book ver6

1 *A master file and several chapter files are displayed on this Book palette.*

Books, lists, and indexes

In this chapter we cover three features: books, lists, and indexing.

In QuarkXPress, a book is an umbrella file that's used for organizing and synchronizing multiple chapter files. A book can be any kind of publication that comprises more than one QuarkXPress file (e.g., magazine, newsletter, manual). Once individual book chapter files are united into a book, all of its style sheets, colors, H&Js, lists, and dashes & stripes are then derived from the file that you designate as the master, and page numbering flows continuously from one file to the next. In a workgroup situation, individual chapters of a book can be open and edited simultaneously on a network. If a book is edited at one station, any open copies of the same book on other stations will update automatically. Each book has its own Book palette **1** and can contain up to 1,000 chapters.

A list is a compilation, from one or more projects, of text passages that have the same paragraph style sheet applied to them. A common use for this feature would be to construct a table of contents. Via the Lists palette, you can choose options, such as whether the list will be alphabetized and whether it will include page numbers.

And lastly, you can create an index by manually tagging individual entries in a layout and then assigning an indent level and other formats to each entry via the Index palette (yup, it's as time-consuming as it sounds!). You can generate a different index for each layout in a project.

First, let's learn about the books feature.

Books

Creating books

To create a book:

1. Decide which file is to be the master. Specifications from this master will be applied to all the book chapters. To create a master file:

   Create a new file that contains only the master page(s), style sheets, colors, H&Js, lists, and dashes & stripes that you want all the chapter files to share. Apply the Current Page Number command (Cmd-3/Ctrl-3) to a text box on the master page. Save the file (you can include the word "master" in the title to help prevent confusion later).
   or
   Open an existing file, and use File > Save As to save a copy of it (use the word "master" in the name). Delete all the text and all the pages except the first page, then resave the file. As with a new file, make sure it contains only the master pages, style sheets, colors, H&Js, lists, and dashes & stripes that you want all the chapter files to share, and make sure it contains the Current Page Number command in a text box on the master page.

   You can use File > Append to append style sheets, colors, lists, etc. from any other file to the master.

2. Choose File > New > Book.

3. Enter a name for the book, and choose a location in which to save it 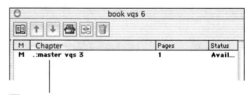.

4. Click Create (Return/Enter).

5. In the top left corner of the Book palette that opens, click the Add Chapter button.

6. Locate and click the name of the file that you want to serve as the master **2**, then click Add (Return/Enter) **3**. Now you can start adding chapters to the book (follow the instructions on the next page).

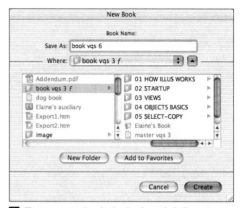

1 *Type a name for the book, then click* **Create**.

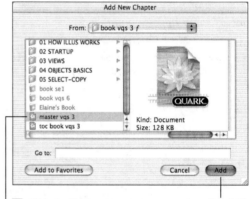

2 *Click the file that you want to have function as the* **master***...* *...then click* **Add**.

(book vqs 6)

3 *The* **Master** *file name appears on the* **Book palette**.

Create a Book

To add chapters to a book:

1. Prepare the chapter files. You can use File > Save As to generate copies of the master file, or you can use existing files. Chapters in an individual book don't have to have the same page size.

2. Click the Add Chapter (leftmost) button ▦ on the Book palette, locate and click the name of a file that you want to add as a chapter in the book, then click Add (Return/Enter) **1**. Repeat this step for any other files that you want to add as chapters. The actual files don't have to be open.

   Note: If no chapter name is highlighted when you click the Add Chapter button, the new chapter will be added at the end of the list. If a chapter name is highlighted when you click the Add Chapter button, the new chapter will be added directly after the highlighted one.

Note: A project can be added to a book only if it contains one, and only one, print layout. If it contains more than one layout, make copies of the project using Save As, delete all the layouts but one in each copy, then add any of those separate files to the book.

3. Click the Synchronize Book button **2**. ▣

4. In the Style Sheets, Colors, H&Js, Lists, and Dashes & Stripes panes of the Synchronize Selected Chapters dialog box, click the items from the master chapter that you want to add to all the chapter files (click, then Shift-click to select consecutive items; or Cmd-click/Ctrl-click to select nonconsecutive items), then click the right arrow in the middle of the dialog box to add the selected items **3**. (Click the left arrow at any time to remove the currently selected items.)

   or

   Click Include All to include all the items in the currently displayed category.

(Continued on the following page)

1 *After* **adding** *chapters to the book...*

2 *...click the* **Synchronize Book** *button.*

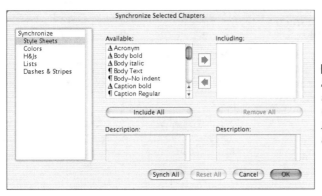

3 *Use the* **Synchronize Selected Chapters** *dialog box to specify which Style Sheets, Colors, H&Js, Lists, and Dashes & Stripes are to be added to all the chapter files.*

Add Chapters to a Book

TIP Remove All removes all the items in the current category from the Including window; Reset All eliminates your selections from all categories.

5. Click Synch All to synchronize everything from the master file to the chapter files.

6. Click OK, and answer any warning prompts. Page numbering will advance incrementally through the chapter files (unless any files contain section numbering, in which case an asterisk will appear next to those page numbers).

7. Close the Book palette by clicking the close button. All open book chapters will also close; you'll be prompted to save changes, if any were made.

TIP Once chapters have been added to a book, all you have to do is double-click a chapter name on the palette to open that chapter.

TIP A chapter file can be part of only one book at a time. To get around this, you can copy a chapter file using File > Save As or choose File > Duplicate in the Finder. Then you can use the copy in a different book.

To change the chapter order:

On the Book palette, click a chapter name, then click the Move Chapter Up button ⬆ or Move Chapter Down button ⬇ **1**–**2**.
or

6.0! Drag a chapter name upward or downward to a new spot on the chapter list **3**.

To delete a chapter from a book:

1. On the Book palette, click the name of the chapter that you want to delete.

2. Click the Remove Chapter button.

3. Click OK.

TIP You can't change a layout's output medium from print to Web while it's part of a book.

Change Chapter Order; Delete Chapter

No backing out

Book changes, such as adding or rearranging chapters, **can't be undone,** nor can the Revert to Saved command be used to restore a book to an earlier version.

Edits to a book are **saved** when you close the Book palette or quit/exit QuarkXPress. Save edits to an individual chapter as you would any project.

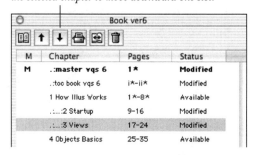

1 *Click the chapter you want to* **move.**

2 *Clicking the* **Move Chapter Down** *button causes the selected chapter to move downward one slot.*

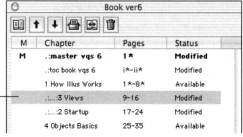

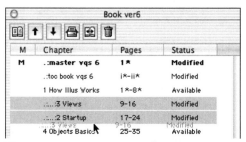

3 *You can also* **restack** *a chapter by dragging it upward or downward.*

Out of sync?

You may add style sheets, colors, and so on to any individual chapter file. But bear in mind that those added elements won't appear in any other chapter files unless they're added to the master file and then the chapters are resynchronized.

If you resynchronize, any style sheet, color, etc. in an individual chapter file that doesn't have a double in the master file will be left alone. A style sheet, color, etc. that *does* have a matching name in the master file, but whose specifications don't match, will be updated in the chapter file to match the master file. A component that is present in the master file but not in a chapter file will be added to the chapter file.

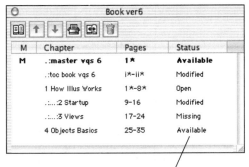

1 *The **Status** column on the Book palette tells you whether individual chapters are **Available**, already **Open**, have been **Modified** (edited), or are **Missing** (were moved).*

If you work with a book on a network, you'll need to look in the Status column on the Book palette to find out if someone else on the network has a chapter of that book open. On a network, chapters should always be opened and closed from the server.

Deciphering the Status column

Available 1 means that the chapter can be opened.

Open means that the chapter is open at your station.

[Other station name] means that the chapter is open at another station on the network.

Modified means that the chapter was opened and edited outside the book when the Book palette was closed. To update it, double-click the chapter name on the Book palette, then close the newly opened project window.

Missing means that the chapter was moved. To relink the chapter to the book, double-click its name on the palette, then locate and open the file.

To edit the master file:

1. Double-click the master file on the Book palette.

2. Create new style sheets, colors, H&Js, lists, and dashes & stripes in the master file, or use the File > Append command to add any of those elements from another file to the master file.

3. Make sure all the chapters in the book have a status of Available. If a chapter has a Modified status, double-click it, then close it.

4. Click the Synchronize Book button to add the new elements from the master file to all the book chapters.

5. Click OK.

Numbering pages in a book

There are two ways to number pages in a book, both of which we discuss below. With either method, for any numbering to show up on any layout pages, the Current Page Number command (Cmd-3/Ctrl-3) must be inserted into a text box on the master page of the master file.

One option is to let the page numbering occur automatically without doing anything. Chapters will be numbered sequentially, and Book Chapter Start will be checked in the Section dialog box for each one 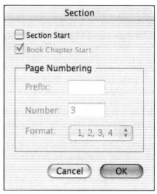.

A second option is to control the numbering yourself. On the Book palette, double-click the name of the chapter that is to begin a section, choose Page > Section, check Section Start 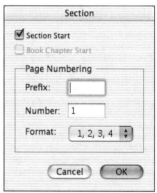, then enter a Number. Choose other options just as you would for a normal file. Section numbering will proceed through subsequent chapters up to the next section start, if there is one. You can make the first chapter (not the master) the beginning of the section, thus keeping the master outside the main flow of pages.

All book chapters adopt either the number format used in the first chapter file that's listed on the Book palette or any manual Section Start that occurs in any chapter that's listed above other chapters. Also, any master file counts as a page. To have chapter 1 start as page 1, set up a custom page number of 1 in the Section dialog box for that chapter.

1 *This is the default setting in the* **Section** *dialog box for a book.*

2 *To apply custom page numbering, click* **Section Start**, *then enter a starting page* **Number**. *If you want, you can also enter a* **Prefix** *and/or choose an alternative numbering* **Format**.

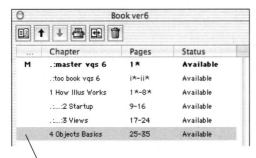

1 *To designate a different chapter file as the master, click on it, then click in this blank area to the left of it.*

2 *Chapter 4 is now the master file.*

To print book chapters:

1. To print an individual chapter in a book, click its name on the Book palette. Only a chapter file with a status of Available or Open will print. The chapter doesn't have to be open.
or
To selectively print more than one chapter, Cmd-click/Ctrl-click individual chapter names, or click and then Shift-click to select consecutively listed chapters.
or
To print a whole book, make sure no chapter names are highlighted (click in the blank area below the chapter names), and make sure no chapters have a Missing or Modified status or are open at another station on the network.

2. Click the Print Chapter button.

3. Choose the desired Print settings (including a Print Style, if desired), then click Print.

To designate a different chapter as the master:

1. On the Book palette, click the name of the chapter that you want to become the new master **1**.

2. Click in the blank area to the left of the chapter name **2**.

Creating lists

The purpose of the Lists feature is to generate a table of contents or other list for a layout (or a book), with or without page reference numbers, and with or without alphabetization **1**. It works by grabbing chapters names and numbers, section subheads, captions, sidebars, reference tables, etc. from a layout by searching for the style sheets that are assigned to those paragraphs.

For example, let's say you want all your text that has been assigned a subhead style to be gathered into a table of contents. First you use the Edit List dialog box to specify which style sheets are to be searched for. Then you decide how the list will be formatted. And finally, you use the Lists palette to preview and build the actual list.

To summarize, these are the basic steps you'll follow to create a list:

- Create a list definition by choosing which style sheets you want the program to search for throughout the layout or book, and by choosing format options.

- Preview the list in the scroll window on the Lists palette.

- Build the actual list in a text box in a layout.

To create and build a list definition for a project, follow the instructions starting on this page. To create and build a list for a book, follow the instructions on pages 398–399. The list definition you create draws only from the currently active layout when you preview and build it, but it can be reused for any other layouts in the same project or appended to other projects.

To create a list definition for a project:

1. Create separate style sheets for styling the list. And make sure your project's style sheets are consistent and are applied correctly to the categories of text that you want to appear in the table of contents.

allspice	cloves	paprika
basil	coriander	parsley
bay leaf	cumin	red pepper
caraway	dill	rosemary
cardamom	ginger	saffron
cayenne	lavender	sage
chervil	mace	savory
chives	mint	tarragon
cilantro	nutmeg	thyme
cinnamon	oregano	turmeric

1 *A* **list** *can consist of anything from a simple alphabetized shopping list to a whole table of contents for a book.*

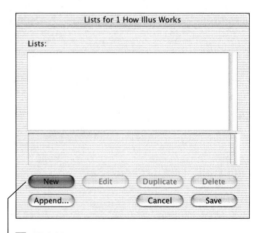

2 *Click* **New***.*

1 *Enter a name.*

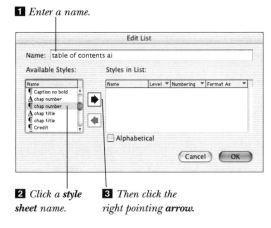

2 *Click a style sheet name.* **3** *Then click the right pointing arrow.*

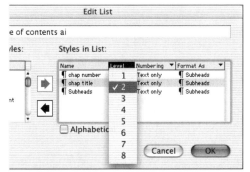

4 *For each style sheet category, choose an indent Level,...*

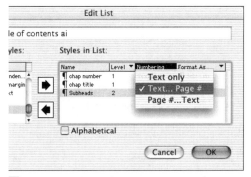

5 *...choose a Numbering option,...*

2. If you're generating a table of contents from one project, open that project now.

3. Choose Edit > Lists, click New (**2**, previous page) then enter a Name for the list definition **1**.

4. On the Available Styles scroll list, click the style sheet name (text category) to be searched for in the project **2**, then click the right-pointing arrow to add that style sheet to the Styles in List window **3**. Or just double-click the style sheet name.

To add multiple style sheets at a time, click and then Shift-click to select a consecutive series, or Cmd-click/Ctrl-click to select multiple style sheet names individually, then click the right-pointing arrow. (Click the left-pointing arrow if you need to remove a style sheet from the Styles in List window.) Character style sheets are allowable.

5. Click a style sheet in the Styles in List window and then, from the drop-down menus, choose the following:

The **Level** of indent text you want that style sheet content to have in the list (1, 2, 3, and so on) **4**. For example, you might assign level 1 to chapter names, the level 2 to headers, the level 3 to subheads, and so on.

A page **Numbering** style **5**. Choose Text...Page # if you want the page number to follow the text; choose Page #...Text if you want the page number to precede the text. Choose "Text only" if you don't want page numbers to appear at all.

Which style sheet (from the **Format As** drop-down menu) will be applied to

(Continued on the following page)

that text category **1**. If you created a style sheet(s) specifically for the list, this is the time to choose it.

Do the same for the other style sheets.

6. *Optional:* Check Alphabetical to have items on the list appear in alphabetical order rather than the order in which they appear in the layout.

7. Click OK.

8. Click Save. Follow the instructions on the next page to build (generate) the list.

TIP In the Lists dialog box, click Duplicate to duplicate the currently highlighted list if you want to create a variation of it; click Delete to remove the currently highlighted list. To append a list from another project, follow the general intructions for appending specifications on pages 50–52.

TIP The maximum number of style sheets that can be chosen for a list definition is 32. The maximum number of characters per paragraph that a list can contain is 256.

TIP For a list level that contains page number references, choose a style sheet with a right tab and a dot leader. The tab character will be inserted automatically.

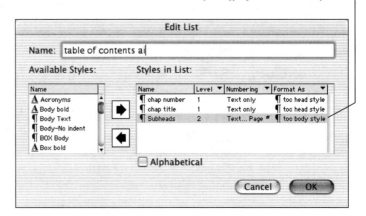

1 *Choose a **style sheet** from the **Format As** drop-down menu. In our example, the Format As styles differ from the Name styles.*

Create List Definition

Get there fast

If any project is open (even a chapter in a book) and you **double-click** a line of text on the Lists palette, the chapter that contains the text will open automatically and that text will be highlighted in the layout.

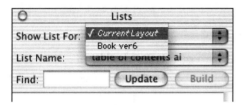

1 *From the* **Show List For** *pop-up menu in the Lists dialog box, choose* **Current Layout**.

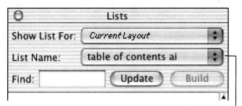

2 *Choose an existing list from the* **List Name** *pop-up menu.*

3 *This* **Lists** *palette is displaying a layout's* **table of contents**.

Once a list definition has been created and saved with your Levels, Numbering, and Format As (style sheet) choices, it's time to use the Lists palette to preview and build the actual list.

To preview and build a list for a layout:

1. Display the layout for which you want to build a list.

2. Choose Window > Show Lists (Option-F11/Ctrl-F11).

3. Choose Show List For: Current Layout **1**.

4. From the List Name pop-up menu, choose the name of the list that you want to build **2**. The list will preview in the scroll window on the palette. If necessary, click Update.

5. Choose the Content tool, and in the same layout, click in an empty text box to create an insertion point. It can be either a new box or the first in a chain of linked text boxes.

   A list also can be appended to the end of a block of text. For example, you can write an introductory paragraph, and then have the list start after that paragraph.

6. Click Build on the Lists palette **3**. The list will be built in the selected text box (or series of linked boxes), using your list definition, that is, the formatting options that were chosen in Edit > Lists.

TIP *Beware!* Don't delete any Styles (style sheets) from a project that were used in a list. If you do, text that those style sheets were assigned to won't appear on the list when you build it.

TIP The stacking order of text boxes determines how entries will be listed, with the frontmost box on a page appearing first. If your chapter title box is stacked in front of the chapter number box, the chapter title will be listed first.

Build List for Layout

Note: Before executing these instructions, make sure the book's master file contains all the style sheets that are used in the book and a list definition has been created for that master. Also make sure that all the book chapters have a status of Available.

To create a list definition for a book:

1. Close all open files, open the book file (its Book palette will also open), and open the master file.

2. Choose Edit > Lists.

3. Create a new list definition (see pages 394–396).
   or
   Click Append, locate and open the file that contains the list definition you want to use, click the name, click the right-pointing arrow, click OK **1**, and finally, respond to any name conflicts.

4. Click Save, then save and close the master file.

5. On the Lists palette (Window > Show Lists or Option-F11/Ctrl-F11), make sure the book file is chosen in the Show List For pop-up menu.

6. Deselect all chapter names, then click the Synchronize Book button on the Book palette.

7. In the Synchronize Selected Chapters dialog box, click Lists, select the desired list definition name, click the right-pointing arrow to include that list definition, then click OK. (Click OK in any alert dialog boxes.)

8. Make sure the list definition chosen in the previous step appears on the List Name pop-up menu on the Lists palette, then click Update. The list that's generated from all the chapters will display on the palette **2**–**3**. Note: If the list doesn't preview correctly, try opening the master file first, then click Update.

TIP If you renumber or rearrange pages in a book, you'll have to update and rebuild the list to make it current.

1 *Click the right-pointing arrow to **append** the list.*

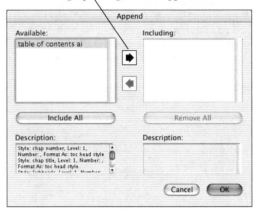

2 *Click **Update** to display the list.*

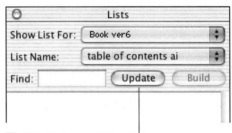

3 *The list previews on the **Lists** palette.*

Create List Definition for Book

*This is part of a **list** (table of contents) that was built from a book. This list is styled using style sheets that were created specifically for the list and assigned via the Format As drop-down menu in the Edit List dialog box.*

Perform the following steps after creating and updating a list definition for your book file (instructions on the previous page).

To build a list for a book file:

1. Create a new chapter for the book. One way to do this is by opening the master file, generating a copy of it using File > Save As, and stripping out the text from the new chapter. If it's going to be a table of contents and you want it to have its own numbering format, choose Page > Section, check Section Start, enter a Number, and choose a Format. And finally, make *6.0!* sure the file contains only one layout!

2. Add the new chapter to the book: Click the Add Chapter button 📖 on the Book palette, then locate and open the new chapter.

3. Click the Synchronize Book button 🔃 on the Book palette to copy the style sheets, colors, etc. from the master file to the new file, then click OK.

4. Click in a blank text box in the newly created chapter file.

5. On the Lists palette, choose Show List For [book name].

6. *Optional:* Turn on Auto Page Insertion in QuarkXPress (Edit, in Windows) > Preferences > Print Layout or Web Layout > General for the new chapter if you want overflow text from the list, if any, to flow into linked boxes on additional pages.

7. If the Build button is dimmed, click Update.

8. Click Build. The list will appear in the text box (or boxes).

Build List for Book

To revise a list:

1. Open the project and open the Lists palette (Option-F11/Ctrl-F11).

2. Choose a List Name.

3. For a nonbook file, double-click an entry; that text will become highlighted in the project window **1**. With any book chapter file open, if you double-click an entry from any chapter file, the chapter file will open and the text will become highlighted.

4. Make any modifications to the text in the layout. For example, to prevent a text passage from appearing on the list, apply any style sheet to it that isn't being searched for in the list.

5. Click Update on the Lists palette to update the list preview.

6. If you're going to rebuild the list in the same project, click in the text box that contains the list. Or if you're going to insert the rebuilt list and leave the old list unchanged, click exactly where you want the new one to appear. If the list is in a separate chapter of a book, open that chapter now.

7. Click Build.

8. Click Insert to build a new list and leave the old list unchanged **2**.
   or
   Click Replace to replace the current list with the new list **3**.

   You can't undo either operation.

TIP You can reformat a built list or apply different style sheets to it, but such changes will be lost if you rebuild the list using the Replace option.

TIP If the list on the palette is long and you want to quickly find a particular line, type the first word of the line in the Find field; a line will become highlighted after you start typing **4**. You have to type enough of the entry to differentiate it from similar entries.

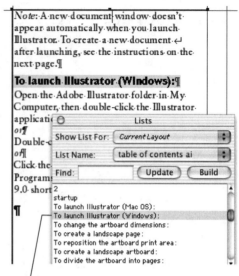

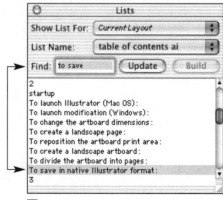

1 *For a nonbook file, **double-click** an entry on the Lists palette to view that entry in the project window.*

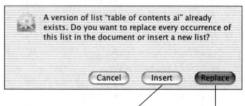

2 *Click **Insert** to build a new list at the current insertion point and leave the old list unchanged.*

3 *Or click **Replace** to replace the old list with the new list.*

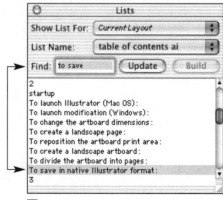

4 *An entry that was typed into the **Find** field on the Lists palette is searched for and found in the list.*

A
anchor points, 2-3

I
Illustrator, 1-6; Adobe, 1; closed paths, 2; FreeHand, 1; Macintosh, 1; object-oriented, 1; Objects, 1; precision tools, 5; Stroke, 3; tools, 2; vector image, 1; Windows, 1

O
object-oriented, 1 vector, 3; versus raster, 4; paths, 5; Pen tool, 5-7; printing, 8; resolution, 7

P
Pencil. See tool

1 *Portions of a built index in the **Run-in** format*

Indexing

Indexes are layout-specific, so you'll need **6.0!** to build a different index for each layout in a project. Building an index requires four main steps, in roughly this order:

- Create the style sheets for the index itself, for letter headings, for the entries themselves, etc.
- Mark all the text that is to be referenced in the index.
- Build the index **1**–**2**.
- Look over the index, and edit it, where necessary.

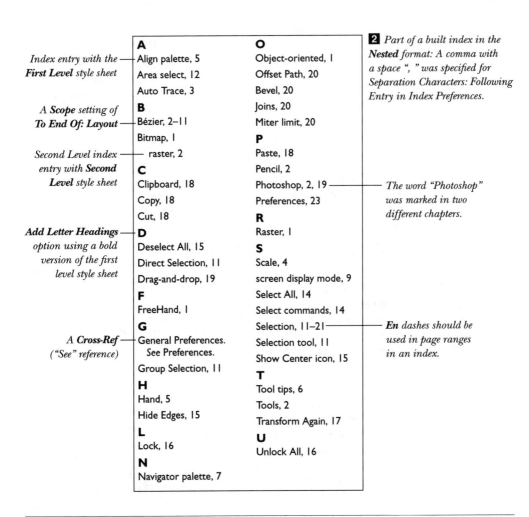

Index entry with the **First Level** *style sheet*

*A **Scope** setting of* **To End Of: Layout**

*Second Level index entry with **Second Level** style sheet*

Add Letter Headings *option using a bold version of the first level style sheet*

*A **Cross-Ref** ("See" reference)*

A
Align palette, 5
Area select, 12
Auto Trace, 3
B
Bézier, 2–11
Bitmap, 1
 raster, 2
C
Clipboard, 18
Copy, 18
Cut, 18
D
Deselect All, 15
Direct Selection, 11
Drag-and-drop, 19
F
FreeHand, 1
G
General Preferences. See Preferences.
Group Selection, 11
H
Hand, 5
Hide Edges, 15
L
Lock, 16
N
Navigator palette, 7

O
Object-oriented, 1
Offset Path, 20
Bevel, 20
Joins, 20
Miter limit, 20
P
Paste, 18
Pencil, 2
Photoshop, 2, 19
Preferences, 23
R
Raster, 1
S
Scale, 4
screen display mode, 9
Select All, 14
Select commands, 14
Selection, 11–21
Selection tool, 11
Show Center icon, 15
T
Tool tips, 6
Tools, 2
Transform Again, 17
U
Unlock All, 16

2 *Part of a built index in the **Nested** format: A comma with a space ", " was specified for Separation Characters: Following Entry in Index Preferences.*

The word "Photoshop" was marked in two different chapters.

En dashes should be used in page ranges in an index.

Indexing

Mark Layout for Indexing

Use the Index palette to mark and format index references for individual text strings in a layout. This is a time-consuming process. After that you'll build the index itself in the same file or in a separate file.

To mark a layout for indexing:

1. Enable Quark's Index.xnt XTension, if it's not already enabled.

2. Display a layout to mark for indexing or create a new layout to be marked as you enter text.

3. If you're going to do any "see also " cross-referencing or if you want page number references to appear in a different style from the index entries, create the character style sheet(s) that you want to apply to those references.

   This is also a good time to create all the other style sheets that you want to use in the built index. An index can have either a nested or run-in format (see the illustrations on the previous page). You can edit the style sheets later.

   For a nested index, you'll need a style sheet for the First Level text passages as well as a style sheet for each subsequent indent level. In the Style Sheet dialog box, you can use the Based On option for this, and apply progressively larger Left Indent values for the Second, Third, and Fourth Level styles.

   Also create a style sheet for letter headings if you're going to use them (A, B, C, and so on). Apply a Space Before value via Style > Formats, and choose a bolder font than the body text for that style sheet so it stands out.

4. Choose Window > Show Index.

5. In the layout, highlight a word or phrase that you want to include in the index **1**. You'll be choosing settings for each individual entry separately.
   or
   Select any text in the layout that you want to create an entry for; it will

Building a nest

To create **nested** (indented) entries, follow the instructions on this page and the next two pages, with this additional step: Click in the palette scroll window to the left of an existing First Level entry to move the indent arrow to that entry, then choose Level: Second Level, Third Level, or Fourth Level. When you add the entry, it will appear below, and indented from, the chosen First Level entry.

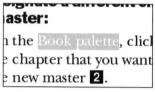

1 *Start by highlighting a word or a phrase in a layout that you want included in the index.*

2 *Text that's currently highlighted in the layout will display in the* **Text** *field on the Index palette.*

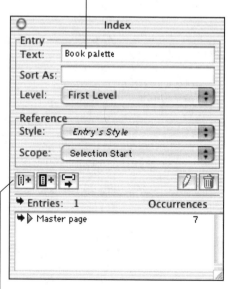

These buttons are, from left to right, **Add, Add All,** *and* **Find Next Entry.**

1 *Optional: Realphabetize an entry by retyping it differently in the **Sort As** field.*

2 *Choose a **Level** of indentation for each entry.*

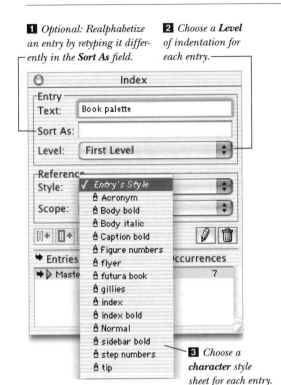

3 *Choose a **character** style sheet for each entry.*

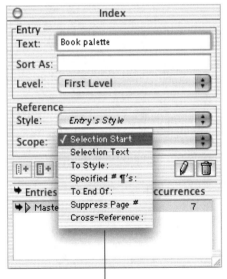

4 *Choose a **Scope** (range of pages) for each entry. For example, to index "Mark a layout for indexing," in this book, if we choose To Style and choose our subhead style, that topic will be listed on pages 402–404 in our index.*

display in the Text field on the Index palette (**2**, previous page). Change the text in this field if you want to create a broad category for the entry as opposed to having the item be indexed as written.

6. On the Index palette, review the text in the Text field, and change any capitalization or word endings, if desired.

7. *Optional:* In the Sort As field, enter a different method for alphabetizing **1**. For example, if you spell out a number in this field (e.g., "Seven-Up" instead of "7-Up"), that number will be sorted alphabetically in the index rather than be placed at the top of the index. The Sort As spelling won't affect the spelling of the entry in the layout.

8. Choose indent Level: First Level **2**.

9. *Optional:* From the Style pop-up menu **3**, choose a custom style to be assigned to any cross-reference words (see step 10) and page number(s) for this entry.

10. From the Scope pop-up menu, specify the range of pages to be referenced in the index for the current entry **4**:

Selection Start to specify the page on which the entry is located. If the entry spans more than one page, the page where the selection starts will be used.

Selection Text to specify the page(s) of a block of text.

To Style to specify the range from the selection start (or cursor position) to a style sheet you choose from the adjoining pop-up menu.

Specified # ¶'s to specify a range spanning the exact number of paragraphs that you enter in the adjoining field.

To End Of to specify either the end of the story or the end of the layout, whichever you choose from the pop-up menu. Choose this option for the title of any section that you want listed as a range of pages (e.g., "42–58").

(Continued on the following page)

Mark Layout for Indexing

Mark Layout for Indexing

Suppress Page # to suppress the page number. This is a good idea when you want to include a broad category, say "Preferences," that will have second-level items, such as "Application preferences" and "Layout preferences."

Cross-Reference to create a cross-reference for the current text. Choose "See," "See also," or "See herein" and enter the reference in the text field on the right.

11. Click the Add button **1**. The newly added entry will preview at the bottom of the palette and will be listed alphabetically in its chosen indent level. While the Index palette is open, an index marker (red brackets) will surround that passage in the layout **2**. When text is typed directly into the Text field on the palette, a square box appears in the layout at the location of the cursor.

12. Repeat steps 5–11 for all the remaining text in the layout that you want the index to include.

TIP If you double-click an index entry's page number on the palette, the text will display and highlight in the layout.

TIP To delete an entry, click it in the scroll window on the Index palette, click the Delete button on the palette, then click OK (you can't undo this!). No need to highlight the text in the layout; the brackets will be removed automatically.

delete a chapter from a b
⌐On the ⌐book palette⌐, click t⌐
of the chapter that you wan⌐
⌐Click the Remove Chapter ⌐

2 *If you highlight a word or phrase in a layout with the Index palette open, left and right* **index marker brackets** *will surround that passage. The hollow square marks where text was entered directly into the* **Text** *field on the Index palette.*

Index palette shortcuts

Display palette/ highlight **Text** field	Cmd-Option-I/Ctrl-Alt-I
Click **Add** button	Cmd-Option-Shift-I/ Ctrl-Alt-Shift-I

Index palette buttons

■ To find, mark, and add all instances of the current text as an entry, using the current settings, click the Add All button. ▣✛

■ To zip through a story to review the entries you've marked, keep clicking the Find Next Entry button. ↴

■ Hold down Option/Alt to turn the Add button into Add Reversed, which creates an entry based on the last word in the currently highlighted text; do the same to turn Add All into Add All Reversed, which does what Add Reversed does for all occurrences of that phrase. Option/Alt also turns Find Next Entry into Find First Entry.

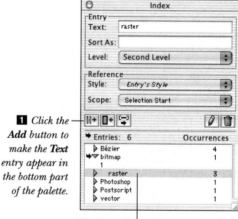

1 *Click the* **Add** *button to make the* **Text** *entry appear in the bottom part of the palette.*

The "raster" entry has been specified as a **Second Level** *indent under the "bitmap" entry. Note the position of the indent arrow (which appeared when we clicked in the arrow column for "bitmap") and the indentation of the "raster" entry in the scroll window.*

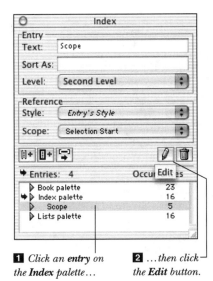

1 *Click an* **entry** *on the* **Index** *palette...*

2 *...then click the* **Edit** *button.*

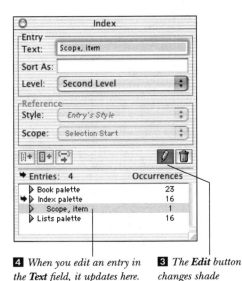

4 *When you edit an entry in the* **Text** *field, it updates here.*

3 *The* **Edit** *button changes shade when clicked.*

uilding an index f
separate file for it
red [Master] Page, he

5 *The* **second** *index entry marker box appears when a word is indexed more than once.*

To edit an index entry:

1. Click an index entry in the scroll window on the Index palette **1**.

2. Click the Edit button **2**. 🖋 The button will change shade **3**.

3. Edit the text in the Text field and/or the Sort As field **4**, change the Level value, then press Tab. The entry will update immediately.
   and/or
   Click the entry's reference (page number or cross-reference) in the scroll window (click the arrowhead/+ to reveal it, if necessary), then change the Reference: Style or Scope. The reference will update immediately.

4. Click on and edit any other entries.

5. Click the Edit button again when you're finished editing.

If you want to add an entry a second time, as a Second Level entry under a different First Level entry, you can't add it the same way. You'll need to follow these instructions instead.

To add an already marked word again to an index:

1. Click in the original marked word in the layout (don't highlight it).

2. Click in the Text field on the Index palette, then retype the entry.

3. Choose other Entry and Reference options.

4. To create a nested entry, click in the indent arrow (leftmost) column next to the entry below which you want the new entry to nest.

5. Click Add. A small hollow square will display inside the index marker brackets in the layout **5**.

To cross-reference an index entry:

1. Click in the text box in the layout that contains the indexed word.

2. Click the entry in the scroll window on the Index palette.

3. Choose Scope: Cross-Reference, choose a "See" option from the next pop-up menu, then type the cross-referenced word.

4. Click Add **1**. Click the arrowhead/+ next to the entry to preview. Click the arrowhead again to hide the entry.

Before building or rebuilding an index, you can use the Index Preferences dialog box to specify which punctuation marks will be used in the index.

To choose Index preferences:

1. Choose QuarkXPress (Edit, in Windows) > Preferences > Index.

2. *Optional:* To change the Index Marker Color (the brackets in marked text), click the color square, choose a new color, then click OK.

3. Change any or all of the settings in the Separation Characters fields **2**:

Between Entries is the punctuation between entries in a run-in style index (as in "frog, 17; toad, 18") and the ending punctuation in paragraphs in a nested style index.

Following Entry is the punctuation to follow each index entry (e.g., the comma in "Biscuit,").

Between Page Numbers is the punctuation between nonconsecutive page numbers (as in "34, 77").

Between Page Range is the punctuation used to define a range of pages (as in "24–102"). Use an en dash (Option-hyphen/Ctrl-Alt-Shift-hyphen).

Before Cross-Reference is the punctuation that's used before a "See" cross-reference (as in "Biscuit, 20. *See also*

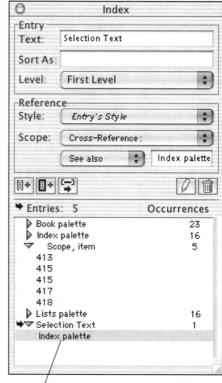

1 A *"see also"* reference added to an index

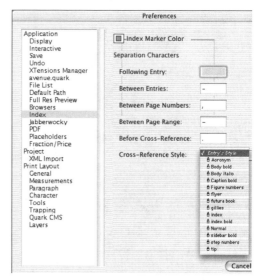

2 Choose **Index Preferences** before building or rebuilding an index.

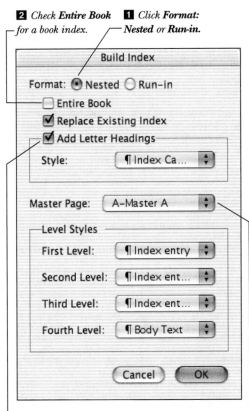

3 *Check **Add Letter Headings** to have each alphabetical group of index entries be separated by the appropriate alphabet letter.*

4 *Choose a **Master Page** format for the index.*

Rolls"). (This character will replace the chosen "Following Entry" character, when necessary.)

The **Cross-Reference Style** pop-up menu lists all the character style sheets in your project. Choose a style for the cross-referenced words, such as "See" or "See also."

4. Click OK.

Follow these instructions to build the actual index after the layout or book project has been marked for indexing and the pagination is finalized.

Note: Before building an index, you can choose Index Preferences (previous page).

To build an index:

1. For a book, create a new chapter file to hold the index, and make it the last chapter. Or open a nonbook project to create an index for just that marked project.

2. Turn Auto Page Insertion on in General Preferences if you're building a large index.

3. *Optional:* If you haven't already done so, create style sheets for each level of indentation and for alphabet letter headings. For a book, do this in the master file and then Synchronize.

4. Choose Utilities > Build Index.

5. Choose Format: Nested to indent each progressive level in the index **1**.
or
Choose Format: Run-in to string the index entry levels together in paragraph form following the First Level entry. They will be separated by the Between Entries punctuation mark that you chose in Index Preferences.

6. *Do any of these optional steps:*
Check Entire Book to index an entire set of book files **2**.

(Continued on the following page)

Build an Index

Check Replace Existing Index to replace an existing, previously built index with the newly built index.

Check Add Letter Headings to separate each alphabetical group of index entries by the appropriate letter of the alphabet (**3**, previous page). Choose a Style sheet for the headings from the pop-up menu.

7. Choose a Master Page for the index (**4**, previous page).

8. In the Level Styles area of the dialog box:

   For the Nested format, choose a paragraph style sheet for each level of indent (First Level, Second Level, Third Level, and Fourth Level).
   or
   For the Run-in format, choose a First Level style sheet.

9. Click OK (see the illustrations on page 401). The index will be built and a new page will be added to the end of your layout. (You don't have to select a text box first.)

TIP After building an index, if you want to edit any of the style sheets that were assigned via the Level Styles area of the Build Index dialog box, use Edit > Style Sheets. This index, and any other index that uses those style sheets, will update to reflect your changes. These changes will also be applied if you rebuild the index.

Stash it away

If you manually restyle an index using style sheets that are different from those that were chosen in the Build Index dialog box, you will lose those changes if you then rebuild the index with the Replace Existing Index option checked. We recommend that you keep the final, restyled index in a **separate** layout so you don't accidentally build over it.

Build an Index

Preferences 23

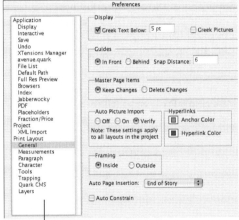

Preferences shortcuts

Preferences dialog box   Cmd-Option-Shift-Y/
                                     Ctrl-Alt-Shift-Y

Paragraph preferences   Cmd-Option-Y/Ctrl-Alt-Y

Tools preferences   Double-click item creation
                                  or Zoom tool

1 *Click a name on the left side of the* **Preferences** *dialog box to display that pane.*

Preferences that are covered in other chapters

For avenue.quark, Placeholders, and XML Import preferences, see the QuarkXPress documentation.

Getting to the preferences

The Preferences dialog boxes

Preferences are the default values that automatically apply when a feature or a tool is used. For example, when the Line tool is used, a line is automatically drawn in a particular width; that width is one of its default settings. Other default settings for the Line tool include its color and style.

Print Layout or Web Layout preferences that are chosen when a layout of that output medium is displayed will apply only to that layout. The current unit of measure for the rulers, dialog boxes, and palettes falls into that category. To set defaults for future layouts, make sure no projects are open when you open the Preferences dialog box.

Other preferences, such as whether the XTensions Manager displays at startup, apply to the whole application, regardless of whether any projects are open when you choose them.

To open a preferences dialog box **1**, you can use any of these three methods:

- Choose QuarkXPress (Edit, in Windows) > Preferences (Cmd-Option-Shift-Y/Ctrl-Alt-Shift-Y).
- Press one of the keyboard shortcuts listed in the sidebar at left.
- Control-click/Right-click a blank area in a layout and choose Preferences.

Other kinds of preferences

In addition to the preferences that you can choose via the Preferences dialog box, you can also set other kinds of very useful defaults for the application. For example, any paragraph or character style sheet that's created or appended when no projects are open will appear on the Style Sheets palette of subsequently created projects. The same holds true for colors, H&Js, lists, dashes & stripes, the default auxiliary dictionary, and in Web layouts, meta tags, menus, and cascading menus. Normal, the default style sheet that automatically appears in every new project and in any text box to which type specifications have not yet been applied can be edited for all future layouts when no projects are open. Don't overlook these kinds of defaults—they're enormous time-savers!

Tracking and kerning table settings, custom frame data, and hyphenation exceptions are stored in individual projects and in User Name/Library/Preferences/Quark/ QuarkXPress 6.0, in a file called XPress Preferences.prf. If, upon opening a file, the project settings don't match the XPress Preferences settings, an alert dialog box will appear. Click Use XPress Preferences (Cmd-./Esc) to apply the preferences resident on that machine, or click Keep Document Settings (Return/Enter) to leave the project as is (see the sidebar).

If you trash your XPress Preferences.prf file, the application will create a new one automatically, but in the process all your custom settings will be lost. For this reason, you should trash the Preferences file only if you absolutely have to (e.g., the application becomes corrupted and unusable) or if you intentionally want to restore the program defaults for some reason. You can copy your Preferences file and stash the copy for safekeeping. The Preferences file can also be copied to the same folder location on another computer.

Inside XPress Preferences

Saves in XPress Preferences and affects all projects immediately
Application Preferences (Display, Interactive, Save, Undo, XTensions Manager, avenue.quark, File List, Default Path, Full Res Preview, Browsers, Index, Jabberwocky, PDF, Placeholders, Fraction/Price), PPD Manager, Profile Manager, and Default Print Layout or Default Web Layout settings

Saves in XPress Preferences and affects all projects after relaunch
XTensions Manager, Print Styles

Saves in the current layout and in XPress Preferences
Kerning Table Edit, Tracking Edit, Hyphenation Exceptions

Saves only in the current print layout
Print Layout Preferences (General, Measurements, Paragraph, Character, Tools, Trapping, Quark CMS, and Layers), open or create auxiliary dictionary

Saves only in the current Web layout
Web Layout Preferences (General, Measurements, Paragraph, Character, Tools, Layers)

Choosing application preferences

Display

To choose the color for **Margin** or **Ruler** guides, or the **Grid,** click the appropriate square, then choose a color from the Color Picker. The Margin color is also used to represent the item boundary in the Runaround and Clipping dialog boxes and the Page Width Reference Guide in Web layouts; the Ruler color also represents the clipping path; and the Grid color also represents the runaround path.

In Mac OS X, with **Tile to Multiple Monitors** on, if you choose Window > Tile, multiple projects will be distributed across multiple monitors.

In Mac OS X, with **Full-screen Documents** on (the default setting is off), a project window will fill the entire screen when it's opened.

With **Opaque Text Box Editing** on, if you click a text box with the Content tool, it will look opaque, making it easier to edit the text, whether or not the box actually has a background color. With this option off (the default), a text box will keep its current background color, whether it's a solid color, a blend, or None (transparent).

Choose a color depth for the screen preview that QuarkXPress creates for imported **Color TIFFs.** A picture's screen preview affects its redraw speed and the storage size of the QuarkXPress file. The 8-bit (256 possible colors) option produces a faster redraw speed and smaller file size, but with an inferior screen preview. Style > Contrast isn't available for a picture that has a 16-bit preview (thousands of possible colors) or 32-bit (Mac OS)/24-bit (Windows) preview (millions of possible colors).

Choose a color depth for the screen preview for imported **Gray** [grayscale] **TIFFs.**

The **Pasteboard Width** is the percentage of the total width of the layout that's allocated to the pasteboard. 100% is the default. (48″ is the maximum total width.)

If you clicked "Do not show this warning again" in any alert dialog box, you can click **Show All Alerts** here to allow alert dialog boxes to redisplay.

Windows only: The **Display DPI Value** is the monitor resolution. Read about this setting in the QuarkXPress documentation.

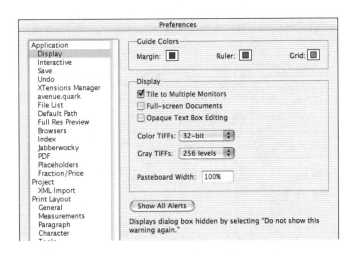

Display Preferences

Interactive

Move the **Scrolling** slider to choose a rate of speed for the scroll arrows and boxes on the project window.

With **Speed Scroll** on, on a slow machine, large pictures and blends will be greeked (display as solid gray) as you scroll and then redraw when you stop scrolling.

With **Live Scroll** on, the layout will redraw as you drag a scroll box on the project window. Turn this option off if you have a slow machine. Option-drag/Alt-drag a scroll box to temporarily turn Live Scroll on or off. The Page Grabber always produces a live scroll.

With **Smart Quotes** on, smart quotation marks are inserted automatically when the ' or " key is pressed (see page 130). Choose a Format (style) for the quotes. Professional typesetters always use Smart Quotes. Un-smart quotes look, well, un-smart.

Click Delayed Item Dragging: **Live Refresh** to see an item as it really looks in its layer as you pause-drag it, complete with any text wrap. Click **Show Contents** to temporarily display the full contents of an item as you drag it, even if the item is behind other items (pause for the Delay period before

Screen redraw shortcuts

Forced redraw	Cmd-Option-. (period)/Shift-Esc
Stop redraw	*Mac OS X:* Cmd-. (period)
	Mac OS X and Windows: Esc *or* perform another operation (e.g., select an item, choose another command)

dragging). Enter the number of seconds (or fraction of a second) in the Delay field that you want to pause before dragging.

Choose **Page Range Separators** for the symbols to be used in the Print dialog box to separate the page numbers you want to print.

Mac OS X only: Choose which function you want the **Control Key** to have: to Zoom in/out or to access Contextual Menus (the default).

With **Drag and Drop Text** on, you can highlight text and drag it to a new location within the same story (one or more linked text boxes or table cells). See page 70.

If **Show Tool Tips** is checked and you rest the pointer on a tool or a palette button, the name of that tool or button will display.

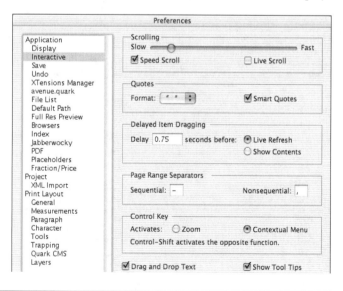

Save

Auto Save and Auto Backup are like system or power failure insurance. With **Auto Save** enabled, modifications are saved in a temporary file at the interval specified in the "Every [ ] minutes" field. Five minutes is the default. There may be a short (but potentially annoying) interruption in processing while an Auto Save occurs. If a system or power failure occurs while you're modifying a layout and you restart and then reopen the project, a prompt will appear. Click OK to reopen the last auto-saved version. *Beware!* Auto Save can't retrieve a project that's never been saved!

To restore the last manually saved version of an open project, choose File > Revert to Saved. To restore the last auto-saved version of a project, hold down Option/Alt while choosing File > Revert to Saved.

Unlike Auto Save, which saves only modifications made to a project in a temporary file, **Auto Backup** creates a backup version of the entire project when the Save command is executed. Progressively higher numbers are appended to the backup names. To specify how many backup versions will be created before the oldest

backup version is deleted, enter a number between 1 and 100 in the "Keep [ ] revisions" field.

Auto backups are saved in the current document (project) folder, unless you specify a different destination. Designating a different location for the backups can help prevent confusion. If you want to designate a different destination, click Other Folder, then click Select/Browse. In the Backup Folder/Browse for Folder directory dialog box, locate and open an existing folder (or to create a new folder in Mac OS X, choose a destination, click New Folder, enter a name, and click Create), then click Choose/OK. To reset the destination as the current project folder at any time, click Document Folder.

With **Auto Library Save** on, a library will be saved whenever an item is added to it. With Auto Library Save off, a library will be saved only when it's closed or when you quit/exit the application.

With **Save Document Position** on, when a project is reopened, it will have the same zoom level, window size, and position on-screen that it had when it was last closed.

*The **Auto Save** prompt*

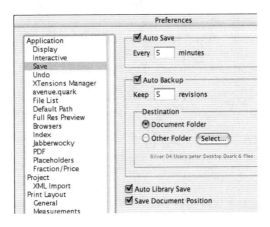

6.0! Undo

In Mac OS X, Cmd-Shift-Z is the default keyboard shortcut for Redo. To change this shortcut, choose Cmd-Z or Cmd-Y from the **Redo Key** pop-up menu. *Note:* If you choose Cmd-Z for Redo, you'll need to press Cmd-Option-Z when you want to reverse your steps back through the Undo History.

In Windows, Ctrl-Y is the default keyboard shortcut for Redo. To change this shortcut, choose Ctrl-Shift-Z or Ctrl-Z from the Redo Key pop-up menu. *Note:* If you choose Ctrl-Z for Redo, you'll need to press Ctrl-Alt-Z to reverse your steps back through the Undo History.

If you choose Cmd-Z/Ctrl-Z as your shortcut for Redo, you can then toggle back and forth between undoing and redoing the last edit, as in previous versions of QuarkXPress.

In the **Maximum History Actions** field, you can specify the maximum number (1-30) of edits (actions) that can be stored in your Undo History. The default setting is 20. If the number of actions in a work session exceeds this maximum, the oldest action will be removed from the Undo History pop-up menu.

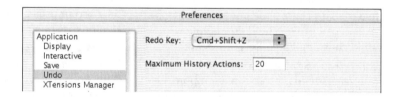

XTensions Manager

With **Show XTensions Manager at Startup: Always** on, the XTensions Manager will open automatically whenever the application is launched.

With **When: "XTension" folder changes** on instead, the XTensions Manager will open during launch only if you've added or

removed an XTension or XTensions from your XTension folder since the application was last open.

With **When: Error loading XTensions occurs** on, the XTensions Manager will open during a launch only if QuarkXPress encounters a problem while loading XTensions.

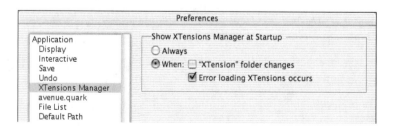

File List

Enter the maximum **Number of Files** (3–9) (recently opened and saved files) that can be listed on the File menu.

Click **Append Files to File Menu** to have file names be listed on the first level of the File menu, or click **Append Files to Open Menu Item** to have file names be listed on the File > Open submenu.

Check **Alphabetize Names** to have file names be listed in alphabetical order. With this option unchecked, names will appear in the order in which they were opened or saved.

Check **Show Full Path** to have a file's location (drive and folder) be listed next to its name on the File menu.

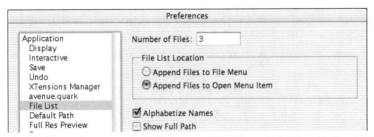

*The **File List** preferences are in the **Dejavu.xnt** XTension, which ships with QuarkXPress.*

Default Path

If you tend to navigate to the same folder each time you use the Open, Save/Save As, Get Text, or Get Picture command, it's worth your while to use Default Path preferences to designate a default path for those dialog boxes.

Click any or all of the four check boxes, and for each one you check, click Select/

Browse, choose a designated folder, then click Choose.

TIP To disable a default path, simply uncheck that box in the Default Path preferences dialog box. The default path will still be listed, but it won't be active.

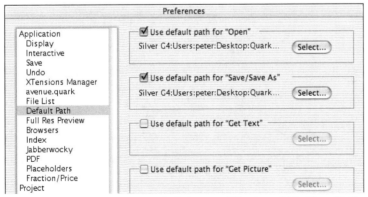

*The **Default Path** preferences are in the **Dejavu.xnt** XTension, which ships with QuarkXPress.*

6.0! Full Res Preview

High-resolution previews aren't stored in the project the pictures are imported into. Rather, they're stored in a folder called Preview Cache, which, by default, is located in the **QuarkXPress Folder**. To change this Preview Cache Location, click **Other Folder**, click Select/Browse, navigate to the folder that you want the preview cache to be stored in, then click Choose.

Enter the **Maximum Cache Folder Size** (200–4000 MB) for storage in the designated preview cache location.

With Display Full Resolution Preview for: **All Full Resolution Previews** chosen, if you apply View > Full Resolution Preview to pictures in a QuarkXPress project and

then open the project on another computer, the application will have to generate new previews, which can take a while. If you click **Selected Full Resolution Previews** instead, QuarkXPress won't display (or generate) any high-resolution previews until or unless a picture is selected.

To turn off the display of high-resolution previews, check **Disable Full Resolution Previews on Open.** Then, if and when you're ready to see the high-resolution previews, you can turn them back on again by choosing View > Show Full Res Previews.

By the way, the Full Res Preview XTension, which ships with QuarkXPress 6.0, is available only after you register your copy of the program!

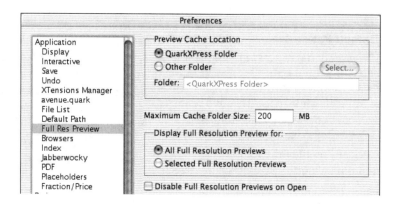

Browsers

The currently available browsers are listed in the **Browser** column. To access these browsers, use the HTML Preview pop-up menu at the bottom of the project window when a Web layout is displayed.

Click in the **Default** column to specify which browser is to launch when you click the HTML Preview button (rather than chose a browser from the HTML Preview pop-up menu), or when Launch Browser is checked in the Export HTML dialog box.

To add other browsers to the list of available browsers, click Add, locate and select a browser, then click Open. To change the Display Name (to be used only by Quark-XPress) of the currently selected browser, click Edit. To remove a selected browser from the list, click Delete.

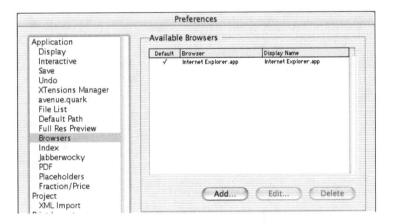

PDF

If you choose File > Export > Layout as 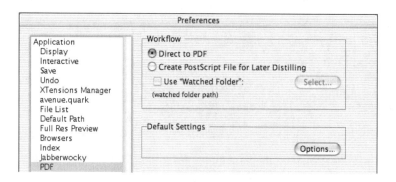 PDF to export a layout to PDF format and Workflow: **Direct to PDF** is chosen as the Preferences setting, QuarkXPress will export the layout directly into the PDF format. If the setting is **Create PostScript File for Later Distilling** instead, when you choose the Layout as PDF command, QuarkXPress will create a PostScript export file that you can later convert to PDF using Adobe Acrobat Distiller.

If you check **Use "Watched Folder"** and then click Select/Browse to designate a folder for exported PostScript files to be saved into, Acrobat Distiller will periodically check this folder and automatically distill any PostScript files that are saved to it.

Click Options in the Default Settings area to open the PDF Export Options dialog box, then click any of the four tabs in that dialog box to choose PDF options. See the QuarkXPress documentation for more information about the settings in this dialog box.

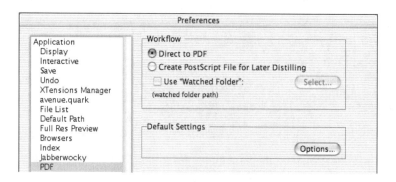

Fraction/Price

Fraction/Price preferences control the proportions of fractions (e.g., ½, ¼) and prices (e.g., $24^{99}, $99.^{99}). To produce a fraction in QuarkXPress, type the normal characters (e.g., 1/4), then select them and choose Style > Type Style > Make Fraction. Or for a price, type and select the characters, then choose Style > Type Style > Make Price. When the preferences are changed, only subsequently created fractions and prices are affected.

For fractions, you can change the **VScale** (vertical scale) and **HScale** (horizontal scale) for the Numerator, Slash, or Denominator to make them chunkier or thinner, and you can enter a **Kern** value for the space between the numerals and the slash or virgule. With **Virgule** (Mac OS X only) unchecked, the program will insert a normal backslash; with this option checked (we recommend checking it), a special slash that fits better around the numerals will be used instead.

For the Make Price command, check **Underline Cents** if you want the cents digits be underlined, as in $24^{99}. Whether or not you opt to have underlining, the cents will appear in the Superior style. Check **Delete Radix** to have a radix (decimal point or comma) appear in prices (as in $10.^{99}); or uncheck this option to produce prices without a radix (as in $10^{99}).

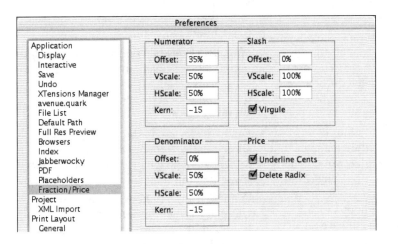

Choosing Print Layout and Web Layout preferences

(Default Print Layout or Default Web Layout, if the
Preferences dialog box is opened when no projects are open)

General *(See the figures on the following page)*

Greek Text Below is the point size below
which text will display as solid gray bars
to help speed up screen redraw. Greeking
is also affected by the current zoom level.

With **Greek Pictures** on, unselected pictures display as solid gray and selected
pictures display normally. This speeds up
screen redraw but is unnecessary if your
computer is reasonably fast.

Set ruler **Guides** to display In Front of or
Behind items on a page (see page 201).
The Snap Distance is the range in pixels
within which an item (or table gridline)
will snap to a guide if View > Snap to
Guides is on.

The **Master Page Items** options, Keep
Changes and Delete Changes, affect
whether modified master page items on
layout pages are kept or deleted when
master pages are applied or reapplied (see
page 248).

The **Auto Picture Import** options control
whether upon reopening a project, pictures being used in the project are updated
if they were modified after the project was
last closed. Choose On to have pictures
reimport automatically without a dialog
box opening; choose Verify to have an alert
dialog box appear if pictures were modified (see page 179); or choose Off to turn
this feature off.

Click the **Anchor Color** square to choose
a color for the hyperlink anchor icon in
print and Web layouts (see page 344).

Click **Hyperlink Color** to choose a color
for hyperlinks created in print layouts that
will be exported in the PDF format.

Framing is added either to the Inside (the
default) or Outside edges of a box. With
Outside chosen, framing increases the
dimensions of a box and changes its x/y
location; with Inside chosen, those settings
are unaffected. The Framing setting affects
only subsequently created boxes.

In print layouts, with **Auto Page Insertion**
on, pages will be added to a chain of automatic text boxes, when necessary, at the
location of your choosing: End of Story, End
of Section, or End of Document (see page
81). Choose Off to turn this feature off.

With **Auto Constrain** on, each newly created
item (child) is constrained by the dimensions of an existing (parent) item—a hold-
over from the early days of QuarkXPress.
We don't use this feature.

For a Web layout, in the **Image Export
Directory** field, enter the name of the
folder where image files are to be placed
when the project is exported (see page 328).

For a Web layout, choose a **Site Root
Directory** as the root folder to be used to
hold both the exported version of the layout and the image folders/directories that
you've designated to hold the exported
images. Click Select/Browse, then locate
and select a folder to be used as the site
root folder.

*General preferences for a **Print** layout*

*In **General** preferences for a **Web** layout, you'll see the options shown in the previous figure, except for the Auto Page Insertion option. The Image Export Directory and Site Root Directory options, shown in this figure, are available only for Web layouts.*

Measurements

For Measurements, choose the default **Horizontal** and **Vertical** unit separately: Inches, Inches Decimal, Picas, Points, Millimeters, Centimeters, Ciceros, or Agates (see page 30). For a Web layout only, you can also choose Pixels as the unit. These units are used for the Measurements palette, rulers, and dialog boxes—except for font size, leading, frame width, and line width, which always display in points, regardless of the current default unit.

TIP You can also Control-click/Right-click the horizontal or vertical ruler in the project window, then choose a unit from the Measure submenu.

72 points/inch is the current standard **Points/Inch** ratio in desktop publishing, so there's no need to change it. Ditto for **Ciceros/cm,** the ciceros-to-centimeter conversion ratio (2.197 is the default).

Print layouts only: With **Item Coordinates: Page** chosen (the default setting), horizontal ruler increments start anew at zero on each page. With **Spread** chosen, horizontal ruler increments advance uninterrupted across any multipage spreads.

Abbreviations

Inches	**in** *or* **"**
Inches Decimal	**in** *or* **"** with a decimal
Picas	**p**
Points	**pt** *or* **p** followed by a number (as in "p6")
Millimeters	**mm**
Centimeters	**cm**
Ciceros	**c**
Agates	**ag**
quarter of a millimiter	**q** *(used in Japan)*
Pixels	**px***

*In a print layout, pixels can't be chosen as the unit, but "px" can be used when entering values.

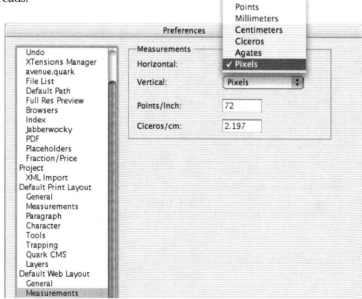

Default Web Layout > Measurements preferences

Paragraph

Auto Leading is enabled when "auto" or "0" is entered in the Leading field on the Measurements palette or in the Formats dialog box. When Auto Leading is used, you may see variable spacing between lines within the same paragraph, because it calculates the leading separately for each line based on the point size of the largest character per line. An increment can be entered instead of "auto" or "0." If you enter "+2," for example, 2 points will be added to the point size of the text to arrive at the leading amount (thus, 10-point text would have 12-point leading). The Auto Leading setting affects both newly created and *existing* text.

If **Maintain Leading** is on and an item is positioned within a column of text, the first line of text that's forced below the obstructing item will snap to the nearest leading increment (allowing for the current Item Runaround value), thereby enabling text baselines to align across columns. With Maintain Leading off, text will be offset from the bottom of an obstructing item only by any existing Item Runaround value, making it difficult, but not impossible, to align text across columns.

With **Mode: Typesetting** chosen, leading is measured from baseline to baseline, as in traditional typesetting. In **Word Processing** mode, leading is measured from ascent to ascent.

By aligning text or items in a layout across columns using the non-printing **Baseline Grid,** you can make your pages look more symmetrical and uniform. To use this feature for text, specify an Increment that's equal to or a multiple of the current text leading. The Start value should match the vertical (*y*) position of the first baseline of the text. To snap text to the gridlines, choose Style > Formats, then check Lock to Baseline Grid. To display the grid, choose View > Show Baseline Grid. *Note:* If Justified is currently chosen as the Vertical Alignment: Type in Item > Modify > Text, only the first and last lines in a column will lock to the grid.

The choices for **Hyphenation: Method** are, in order of appearance and quality from earlier versions of QuarkXPress to this version: Standard, Enhanced, and Expanded. Click a Language to access this drop-down menu.

Paragraph Preferences

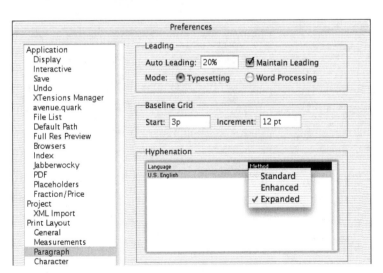

Character

The **Superscript** Offset is the distance a superscript character is raised above the baseline, and it's measured as a percentage of the current point size. The **Subscript** Offset is the distance a character is lowered below the baseline. The Superscript, Subscript, and Small Caps VScale (height) and HScale (width) are calculated as a percentage of a normal uppercase letter.

TIP Increase the HScale for Small Caps (it looks better), or better yet, use an expert font with built-in small caps.

Mac OS X only: A **ligature** is a pair of serif characters (such as an "f" followed by an "l") that are joined into one character to prevent them from ungracefully knocking into each other (**1**, next page). The hyphenation and check spelling features treat ligatures that are produced this way as normal characters. **Break Above** is the amount of tracking or kerning in a line of type above which characters won't be joined as ligatures (for justified type, try 3 or 4). Each font may require a different Break Above amount (experiment). Some, but not all, fonts include ligatures for "ffi" and "ffl." Ligatures apply to the whole layout.

The **Auto Kern Above** value is the point size above which characters will be kerned automatically, based on each particular font's built-in kerning values as well as any user-defined QuarkXPress Tracking Edit or Kerning Table Edit values. Kerning is essential for professional-looking type.

The increment used for tracking in QuarkXPress is ¹⁄₂₀₀ of an em space. With **Standard Em Space** off (the default setting), an em space equals the width of two zeros in the current font. With this option on, an em space equals the point size of the text.

The **Flex Space Width** (0–400%) is a percentage of an en space in the current font. To enter a breaking flex space in your text, press Option-Shift-Spacebar/Ctrl-Shift-5. To enter a nonbreaking flex space, press Cmd-Option-Shift-Spacebar/Ctrl-Alt-Shift-5. To make the flex space the same width as an em space, enter 200%.

Check **Accents for All Caps** to permit foreign-language accent marks on small caps or all caps text (**2**, next page). Note that they're acceptable in some languages and not others. To learn the keystrokes for producing foreign-language accent marks (e.g., é, ö, ã, à), see Appendix A.

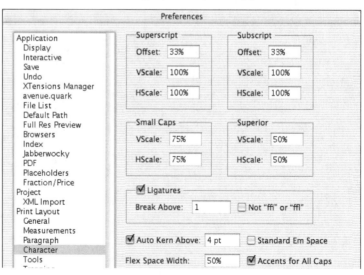

> "By the time she had caught the flamingo and brought it back, the fight was over..." *Lewis Carroll*

> **Accent** *n.:* a mark (as **É, À, Õ, Ü**) used in writing or printing to indicate a specific sound value, stress, or pitch.

1 *The "fl" and "fi"* **ligatures** *(boldface added for emphasis)*

2 *With* **Accents for All Caps** *on, accent marks can be inserted above uppercase characters.*

Tools

To choose default settings for a tool, click its icon in the Tools pane or double-click the tool on the Tools palette. Click **Modify** to change the default settings for the currently highlighted tool icon(s). Among the many tool settings that you can change are the background color, Frame Width, and Runaround Type for any Picture Box tool or Text Box tool, the Text Inset for the Text Box tools, and the Width for the Line tool. For the Zoom tool, you can specify Minimum and Maximum values 10–800%) and an Increment value (1–400%).

To set preferences for more than one tool at a time, first Cmd-click/Ctrl-click their icons individually. Or click one tool icon, then click **Similar Types** or **Similar Shapes** to change the default settings for related tools. Fewer Modify dialog box settings may be available when more than one tool icon is highlighted.

To restore the default *settings* for the currently highlighted tool icon or icons, click **Use Default Prefs.**

To restore the default *arrangement* of tools on the Tools palette and pop-out menus, click **Default Tool Palette.**

For a Web layout, you can choose default height and width values for the Forms Box tool (see page 360) and default settings for the Oval Image Map and Bézier Image Map tools. For either Image Map tool, click Modify and then, in the Image Map Properties dialog box, either enter a Maximum Points value (3–1000) for the maximum number of points used to produce curves on an image map shape, or move the Granularity slider. The closer this slider is to Fine, the more closely the points will follow the shape you drew and the more points will be created.

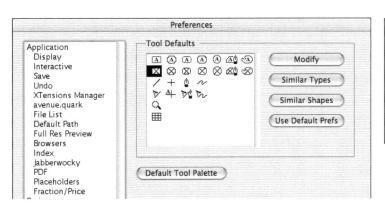

Layers

Choose whether newly created layers will be **Visible.** We suggest you leave this option checked unless you enjoy playing tricks on yourself. Invisible layers don't print.

Choose whether to **Suppress Output** of all items on subsequently created layers (this affects both print output and HTML export).

TIP To control the printing of individual items on a layer instead of all the items on a layer, use the Suppress Output or Suppress Picture Output option in Item > Modify.

Choose whether you want new layers to be **Locked.**

We leave the Suppress Output and Locked options unchecked.

Check **Keep Runaround** to preserve the current Runaround settings for text on visible layers, even if the items the text is wrapping around are hidden. The default setting for this option is checked, and we leave it that way.

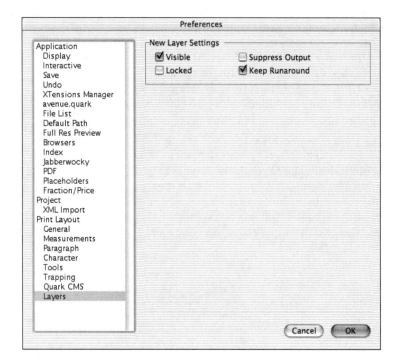

Layers Preferences

What does "!Error" mean?

The word **!Error** in the Status column for an XTension is a warning that QuarkXPress had a problem loading that XTension while launching.

*Choose an XTensions set from the **Set** pop-up menu.*

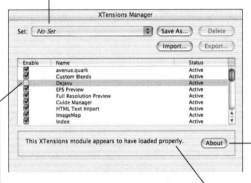

1 *Click in the **Enable** column in the **XTensions Manager** to enable or disable a Quark XTension, import/export filter, or third-party XTension.*

Read more information about the status of the currently highlighted XTension here.

*Click **About** (or double-click an XTension name) to learn more about an XTension, such as its own version number and whether it's optimized for the current version of QuarkXPress.*

Managing XTensions

XTensions are add-ons to QuarkXPress that extend the program's capabilities. Some XTensions are included with the application, such as the filters for importing word processing files, whereas others are produced by third-party developers and must be purchased separately (see page 29).

Using the XTensions Manager, you can enable or disable program and/or third-party XTensions from within the application, as long as they're located either in the XTension folder or the XTension Disabled folder. To conserve memory, you should disable any XTensions that you're not using. You can also use this utility to save, export, import, or delete XTension sets, which are user-defined groups of XTensions.

To enable/disable XTensions or import/export filters:

1. Choose Utilities > XTensions Manager.

2. Click a check mark to disable an XTension, or click an empty checkbox to enable it **1**. Repeat for any other XTensions you want to turn on or off.
   or
   Choose an XTensions set from the Set pop-up menu (see the next page).

3. *Optional:* Click About or double-click an XTension name to display information about the currently highlighted XTension. Click in the info dialog box to return to the Manager.

4. Click OK. The XTensions Manager changes won't take effect until you quit/exit and relaunch QuarkXPress.

To help you organize XTensions and make it easier to turn them on and off (this XTension on, that XTension off, etc.), you can save your custom XTensions Manager settings as a set. You can also choose which set will be in effect when the application is launched. XTensions sets are saved in the XPress Preferences file.

Whichever set is chosen from the Set pop-up menu when you quit/exit QuarkXPress will be in effect when the program is relaunched.

To create an XTensions set:

1. Choose Utilities > XTensions Manager.

2. Disable any XTensions that you don't want included in your set, and enable any XTensions that you do want included by clicking the box in the far left column.

3. Click Save As ◼.

4. Enter a name for the current set ◼.

5. Click Save. Your custom set will appear on the Set pop-up menu in the XTensions Manager ◼, and it will be enabled when the application is relaunched.

6. Click OK.

TIP To enable all the XTensions, choose Set: All XTensions Enabled. To disable them all, choose All XTensions Disabled from the same pop-up menu.

TIP To delete a user-defined set, choose it from the Set pop-up menu, then click Delete. This can't be undone!

◼ *Click **Save As** in the **XTensions Manager** to create a custom set.*

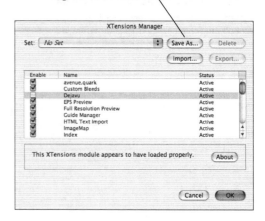

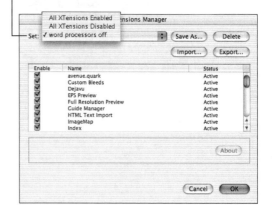

◼ *Enter a **name** for the XTensions set.*

◼ *The new set name appears on the **Set** pop-up menu.*

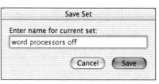

Create XTensions Set

XTensions Manager at startup

If you want the XTensions Manager to open automatically whenever the application is launched, go to QuarkXPress (Edit, in Windows) > Preferences > Application > XTensions Manager, then click **Show XTensions Manager at Startup: Always.** If either of the other two preference options are chosen, you can force the XTensions Manager to open as you launch Quark-XPress by holding down the Spacebar. Keep the Spacebar pressed until the Manager opens.

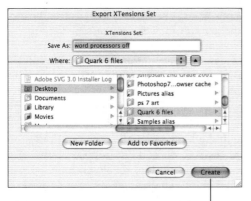

1 *Choose a location in which to save the XTensions file, then click* **Create.**

2 *This is what an* **XTensions** *set file icon looks like.*

User-defined XTensions sets are stored in the XPress Preferences file. This means that if you delete the XPress Preferences file, your custom sets will be deleted. If, however, you save your XTensions set to a separate file for safekeeping using the Export command, you'll be able to reimport them at any time using the XTensions Manager.

To save an XTensions set as a separate file:

1. Choose Utilities > XTensions Manager.

2. Create an XTensions set (instructions on the previous page).
   or
   Choose an existing user-defined set from the Set pop-up menu.

3. Click Export.

4. Choose a location in which to save the file, then click Create/Save **1**.

5. Click OK.

TIP To import a previously saved custom set that's not already listed on the Set pop-up menu, click Import, locate and click the set file that you want to import, then click Open **2**.

Managing color

What is color management?

Every device, whether it's a monitor or a printer, defines color within its own unique color range (called its "gamut") when it represents or reproduces color. The purpose of color management is to ensure consistent color by coordinating and matching color among various device gamuts—from monitor color (RGB) to final print output color (CMYK). If a color on a source device (monitor or scanner) is within the gamut of the destination device (printer), then color matching is straightforward. If a color on a source device is outside the gamut of the destination device, then the color management system adjusts the color (alters its hue, lightness, or saturation) to match the color between the source and destination devices. A monitor can't display, nor can a printing device output, all the colors in the visible spectrum.

Today's computers use color matching systems (CMS) to maintain color consistency between input and output devices. A CMS is built into the latest versions of both the Macintosh and Windows operating systems. In Mac OS X it's called ColorSync; in Windows it's called Image Color Management, or ICM.

All color matching systems work in basically the same way. First, they provide a method for identifying the color characteristics of various hardware devices, and save the information as profiles. Each profile records how the device's color response differs from a reference color space (usually CIE LAB). Each CMS also has a color engine that does the work of converting a document's color from its original profile to the reference color space and then

again to the output device's color profile. These systems work in conjunction with QuarkXPress's Color Management System XTension (Quark CMS.xnt) to ensure color accuracy between monitor representation and final output by taking into account variations between different color models (RGB color and CMYK color) and device gamuts.

The device profiles are sometimes called ICC profiles because their format was defined by the International Color Consortium (in Windows, they often bear the .icc suffix). They can also be used to match color between applications. Let's say you create a picture in Photoshop and then import it into a QuarkXPress layout. If you choose the same profiles (particularly the monitor and output profiles) in both applications, the picture will, hopefully, look the same onscreen in Quark-XPress as it does in Photoshop, and in both applications it will closely match the final output color. Once this color consistency is established, if you then change the monitor or the final output printer type, you must choose a new profile for each device in both applications.

Two critical steps in color matching are monitor calibration (generating and maintaining accurate screen characteristics, such as the white point and gamut) and choosing the correct color profile for each device. Although there are applications that you can use specifically for creating device and printer profiles, for most QuarkXPress users, the CMS built into your operating system and the profiles that ship with each device do an adequate job.

No CMS for Web layouts?

The Quark CMS preferences aren't accessible for Web layouts. According to Quark, Inc., this is because at the present time the monitors used by Web viewers don't have uniform standards for color definition, representation, or calibration. So for Web layouts, there wouldn't be any guidelines for choosing preferred or optimum settings in Quark CMS Preferences anyway.

Color in QuarkXPress

Two kinds of color are used in Quark-XPress projects: colors that are applied to items created within the application and colors that are saved in imported pictures. In the case of colors that are applied in QuarkXPress, the CMS generates color data based on either the monitor profile or the profile for the target output device. These item color profiles are assigned in QuarkXPress (Edit, in Window) > Preferences > Print Layout > Quark CMS.

When a picture is imported, the CMS looks to see if the picture contains a profile. The profile can be for the scanning device, for the monitor used in the image-editing program, or for the final output device that was chosen for the picture. If an imported picture lacks a profile, you can use the CMS to assign a source profile to it. For an RGB picture, this will be a scanning device, camera, or monitor profile—whichever is appropriate; for a CMYK picture, this will be the profile for the final output device.

An imported picture to which no profile was assigned will be assigned a default profile as per the current settings in Preferences > Print Layout > Quark CMS. The default profile can be overridden via either the Profile Information palette or the Get Picture dialog box.

Destination profiles, source profiles, and other parameters for onscreen color correction are chosen in the Quark CMS preferences dialog box, and these settings affect the whole layout.

To turn on color management:

1. Choose QuarkXPress (Edit, in Windows) > Preferences > Print Layout > Quark CMS.

2. To turn on color management, check Color Management Active **1**.

3. Make choices from the Destination Profiles pop-up menus for the target color output device.

   From the Monitor pop-up menu, choose a monitor profile. If the correct monitor profile name isn't listed, choose an Apple monitor that closely approximates your target monitor.

   For composite printer output (where all colors print on one sheet), choose a Composite Output printer profile. This type of printer is usually used for a limited run or to produce color proofs for review before producing separations.

   For color separations, choose a Separation Output printer profile.

Where the profiles are

In Mac OS X, the profile names listed on the pop-up menus in Quark CMS preferences and in the Profile Manager dialog box derive from the System/Library/ColorSync/Profiles folder and the Library/Color Sync/Profiles folder.

In Windows, the profiles are in *systemroot*System32\Color. You can use the Profile Manager dialog box to select *systemroot*System32\Spool\Drivers\Color as an auxiliary profile folder.

4. Choose a Default Source Profile for the source device that created the pictures that you imported into QuarkXPress.

   Choose profiles to manage specific color spaces (models) for colors and pictures in three categories: RGB, CMYK, and Hexachrome (six-plate printing).

   For the RGB color source, click the RGB tab, and from the Solid Colors: Profile pop-up menu, choose the exact monitor or the closest match that you can find. This kind of color derives from the monitor profile used by the program that created the color.

1 *Check **Color Management Active**.*

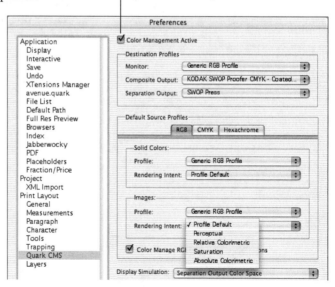

Know your intents

Choose a **Rendering Intent** to determine how colors will be changed as they're moved from one color space to another:

Perceptual changes colors in a way that seems natural to the human eye, and is appropriate for continuous-tone images. It does this by attempting to preserve the overall relationships among colors while squeezing them into a narrower range. This option works well for pictures that contain a lot of out-of-gamut colors.

Relative Colorimetric compares the white point, or extreme highlight, of the source color space to that of the destination color space. It keeps colors that are inside the destination color space unchanged, but changes (sometimes drastically) colors that are outside the color space of the destination device. The accuracy of this intent depends on the accuracy of the white point information in an image's profile. If your image doesn't contain many out-of-gamut colors, this rendering intent is probably a better choice than Perceptual, because fewer colors will be changed.

Saturation changes colors with the intent of preserving vivid colors, although it compromises their accuracy. It's appropriate for charts and business graphics.

Absolute Colorimetric is similar to Relative Colorimetric in that source colors within the destination gamut remain unchanged, but it doesn't remap source white to destination white. In other words, if the "white" in your source space has a color cast, the conversion to the destination space will try to reproduce that cast.

Note: Differences between rendering intents are visible only on a printout or upon conversion to a different color space.

For a scanned picture or camera picture, choose the scanner or camera profile from the Images: Profile pop-up menu. For a picture created in a graphics application, from the Image pop-up menu, choose the profile that was used by that graphics application to define the color space.

For Rendering Intent, choose or leave it as Profile Default unless you have a reason to change it (see the sidebar).

For the CMYK color source, click the CMYK tab, then choose the desired Solid Colors and Images printer profiles for color proofing or final output.

For the Hexachrome color source, click the Hexachrome tab, then choose the target output printer profile, if available. To color-separate Hexachrome colors, you also need to select a Hexachrome profile from the Separation Output menu.

5. For Display Simulation, choose the destination space (the device gamut or color range) you want the CMS to use for onscreen color correction. The bottom three categories on the pop-up menu match the three Destination Profile categories. For each Display Simulation choice, the profile you chose in the matching Destination Profile category will be used. Choose Off if or when you need to turn off onscreen color correction.

6. Click OK to close the dialog box and save your changes.

TIP Profiles assigned using the CMS are saved in the QuarkXPress file.

The Profile Information palette displays a selected picture's characteristics and offers you a limited means for modifying onscreen color correction for just that picture. To access this palette, color management must be enabled (see page 432).

To use the Profile Information palette:

1. Choose Window > Show Profile Information.

2. Click a picture box that contains an imported picture.

3. Examine the three information fields to learn about the current picture's Picture Type (Color, Grayscale, or Line Art [black-and-white]); File Type (TIFF, EPS, etc.); and Color Space (RGB; CMYK; or Unknown for an EPS file whose exact color space information isn't accessible to QuarkXPress, etc.).

4. Normally, the Profile 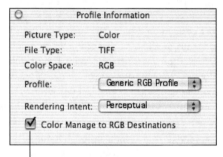 will be an embedded profile or the default profile currently chosen in the Default Source Profiles portion of Quark CMS preferences. If the picture has a profile of None, or the wrong profile, you can choose a source profile from the Profile pop-up menu. For an RGB picture, the Profile pop-up menu will list monitor, scanner, or camera names; for a CMYK picture, the Profile pop-up menu will list output device names.

   Note: A profile chosen from this palette will override any embedded or default profile assigned to the picture via the Quark CMS preferences dialog box.

5. Check Color Manage to RGB (or CMYK) Destinations to enable onscreen color correction for the selected picture (and thus override the Quark CMS preferences) **2**. Choosing a different profile name when this option is checked will immediately change the onscreen appearance of the currently selected picture.

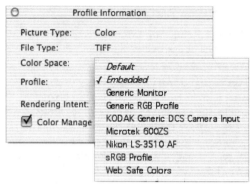

1 *If necessary, choose from the **Profile** pop-up menu on the **Profile Information** palette.*

2 *Check **Color Manage to RGB (or CMYK) Destinations** to turn on QuarkXPress' onscreen color correction for the currently selected picture.*

Profile Information Palette

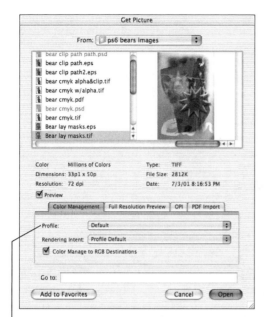

1 *You can choose a different **Profile** for an imported picture in the **Color Management** pane of the **Get Picture** dialog box.*

TIP Both the Profile pop-up menu and Color Manage to RGB (or CMYK) Destinations options are dimmed for grayscale pictures (there is no color to correct) and EPS pictures (EPS pictures are encapsulated; their color information can't be changed using any QuarkXPress command).

You can get information about a picture and assign a profile to it as you import it using the Get Picture dialog box. A profile chosen in this dialog box will override any embedded or default profile chosen in the Quark CMS preferences dialog box.

To turn on color management for a picture as it's imported:

1. Choose the Item or Content tool, then click a picture box.

2. Choose File > Get Picture.

3. Locate and click the name of the picture you want to import.

4. The picture's Color (depth), Dimensions, Resolution, Type, File Size, and the Date it was last modified will be listed in the dialog box.

5. The current Profile pop-up menu choice will be either Default, for the default source profile currently chosen in Quark CMS preferences for pictures that lack an embedded profile, or Embedded, if an embedded profile was assigned to the picture in an image-editing application. To override either of these profiles, make a choice from the pop-up menu **1**.

6. Check Color Manage to RGB (or CMYK) Destinations to enable Quark-XPress's color correction for the picture.

7. Click Open to import the picture.

Color Management for Imported Picture

Use the Profile Manager to view which profiles are currently installed in your system and/or to include or exclude individual profiles for use with the CMS.

To include/exclude profiles in QuarkXPress:

1. Choose Utilities > Profile Manager.

2. Click to remove a check mark from the Include column to exclude that profile from the CMS, or click to place a check mark in that column to include that profile **1**. By default, all profiles in the system are automatically included (checked).

3. *Optional in Windows:* By default, QuarkXPress looks to the *Systemroot* System32\Color folder for profiles. If you want to show QuarkXPress where other profiles are located, click Auxiliary Profile Folder: Select/Browse, then locate and choose a folder.

4. Click OK.

TIP Click Update in the Profile Manager dialog box if you've just installed/ uninstalled profiles in your system and you want the Profile Manager to update its list of current system profiles.

1 *The* **Profile Manager**

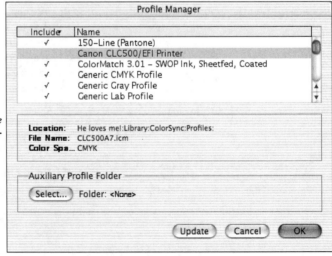

Profile Manager

Managing fonts

Using fonts in Windows 2000/XP

Dealing with fonts in recent versions of Windows is fairly straightforward. OpenType, TrueType, Type 1, and raster (bitmap) formats are supported. Font files are kept in the Fonts folder, at the top level of the folder that contains your installation of Windows. The default name for this folder is Windows.

A font management utility can be used to streamline your workflow, allowing you to store fonts in a folder of your choosing on your hard drive, activate sets of fonts for particular projects, and avoid having to copy large numbers of fonts into your Windows folder. For more information, see the next page.

Using fonts in Mac OS X

Just when you thought you had a handle on the Bitmap, TrueType, and PostScript formats, not to mention Adobe Type Manager (ATM), Suitcase, and other font-management utilities, the font world on the Mac was turned upside down. Hopefully, this information will help you navigate through the morass of changes in font storage and management.

By default, Mac OS X installs more than 50 professional-quality fonts. These fonts are in the .dfont format, which is a new variation on the Mac TrueType format. Mac OS X also supports the Mac PostScript Type 1, Multiple Master, Mac and Windows TrueType, and OpenType font formats.

The Quartz rendering engine, which is built into Mac OS X, eliminates the need for separate PostScript print and screen fonts and makes Adobe Type Manager (ATM) obsolete. In System Preferences > General, users can customize onscreen font smoothing for small point sizes to their liking. What's more, Mac OS X checks font integrity at startup and deactivates corrupt fonts without altering them. All the fonts that are currently installed in active font folders will be available to QuarkXPress or any other software you're using, and a virtually unlimited number of fonts can be used at a time.

Mac OS X is a multiuser environment, meaning that different people using the same computer can set up independent, individual accounts, complete with unique preferences, desktop display, fonts, applications, etc. Fonts can be stored in up to six locations, with each location offering a different kind of control over user access.

(Continued on the following page)

Managing Fonts

Mac OS X searches for and uses the first font name match it finds and ignores further matches, in the sequence listed below.

- Application fonts: A font folder can be stored inside an application folder. It will be used only by that application; it won't be available to other applications.

- Private fonts: Users can install their own fonts in Startup Drive/Users/ [User's Name]/Library/Fonts; they'll be available only to the user account that's currently logged in.

- Main font collection: This is the library of fonts that's installed by Mac OS X, and it's located in Startup Drive/ Library/Fonts. These fonts are usable by any account but can be altered only by an Administrator account.

- Network fonts: These fonts can be made available to large numbers of users logging in over a network and are accessible to all user accounts. See your network administrator for information on how to access these fonts.

- System fonts: These essential system fonts are stored in Startup Drive/ System/Library/Fonts. Don't fool around with them unless you're an experienced administrator.

- Classic fonts: These fonts, stored in the Fonts folder inside the OS 9 System Folder, can be used by all applications.

TIP With the exception of the Classic fonts, the fonts stored in the font folders listed above contain all the requisite point sizes and variations. You won't be able to open or inspect them in QuarkXPress, but there are some previewing utilities available that provide that capability.

Managing fonts in Windows and Mac

In Mac OS X, fonts can be installed or removed manually by moving them in or out of any of the five recognized font folders (except for System) listed at left. The System recognizes folder hierarchies within its active font folders, but unlike earlier operating systems, it doesn't recognize aliases. Copies of stored fonts must be moved into active font folders in order to be recognized.

In Windows, fonts can be moved or in or out of the Fonts folder in the Windows folder.

In Mac OS X and Windows, in order to remove a font, you must delete it from every location where it's being stored. QuarkXPress, unlike some other applications, automatically updates its font menu when fonts are activated or deactivated; you don't have to relaunch the application.

In a professional environment where frequent font changes are made, a third-party font management utility that makes easy work of opening and closing fonts is a must. As of this printing, we can confidently recommend Font Reserve (www.diamondsoft.com), Suitcase (www.extensis.com), and Font Agent Pro (www.insidersoftware.com)—utilities that have been around for years in previous incarnations.

Note: Suitcase and Font Reserve use plug-ins in order to auto-activate the fonts needed by QuarkXPress projects; we haven't tested the reliability of these plug-ins.

Managing Fonts

Printing files

To output a print layout on a PostScript printer:

1. Display the print layout you want to print. Only one layout can be printed at a time. For Web layouts, see page 445.

2. Open the Print dialog box by choosing File > Print (Cmd-P/Ctrl-P).

3. In Windows, choose a printer from the Printer drop-down menu.

4. *Optional:* Choose an existing print style from the Print Style pop-up menu (see page 447). If you want to override the current print style settings, enter new settings via the panes in the Print dialog box, then print. These changes will be only temporary; they won't affect the

Quick-and-dirty print

Once you've established your Print dialog box settings and you want to print an entire layout, press Cmd-P/Ctrl-P or Control-click/Right-click and choose **Print**, then press Return/Enter. Or to specify a range of pages, press Tab, type the starting page number, a hyphen, and the ending page number, then press Return/Enter.

original print style. A bullet will appear before the original print style name to signal that a temporary change was made.

5. Enter the number of Copies of each page you want to print ▮. 1 is the default.

6. To specify which pages will print, leave the default Pages setting on All; or enter nonconsecutive page numbers

(Continued on the following page)

▮ *Enter the number of **Copies** to be printed. 1 is the default.*

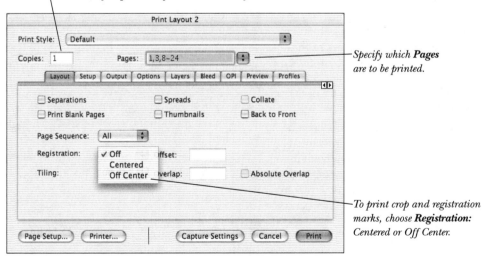

*Specify which **Pages** are to be printed.*

*To print crop and registration marks, choose **Registration:** Centered or Off Center.*

*This is the **Print** dialog box, **Layout** pane, in Mac OS X. For the Print dialog box in Windows, see page 443.*

439

divided by commas; or enter a range of numbers divided by a hyphen (you can type "end" after a hyphen to print to the end of a layout). (See "Which page?" on page 444.)

7. These instructions are lengthy, yes, but you don't necessarily have to follow all of them each and every time you send a print layout to the printer.

Use the **Layout** pane to turn on Separations, Spreads, Include Blank Pages, Registration (crop marks), and other settings.

Use the **Setup** pane to choose the correct Printer Description **1**, which will automatically establish the default Paper Size, Paper Width, and Paper Height settings. You can also change the printout size (Reduce or Enlarge), Page Positioning, and Orientation here.

Use the **Output** pane to choose a Print Colors setting (Black & White, Grayscale, or Composite CMYK, Composite RGB, As Is, or DeviceN), Halftoning, and printer Resolution options. The Print Colors options are controlled by the current Printer Description in the Setup pane.

Use the **Options** pane to turn on the Quark PostScript Error Handler (QuarkXPress's alert boxes) or to change the Output type (Normal, Low Resolution, or Rough), Data encoding, Full Resolution TIFF Output, or other image settings.

Use the **Layers** pane to turn printing temporarily on or off for individual layers **2**. Check Apply to Layout to have the current on/off settings for printing be applied to those layers in the layout (as reflected on the Layers palette).

The halftoning options

If you choose a process color from the **Halftone** pop-up menu in the Edit Color dialog box (Spot Color box checked), the halftone Frequency, Angle, and Function options that are currently set for that process color (C, M, Y, or K) will be assigned to it. To view or change the current settings, choose File > Print, click the Output tab, then choose Halftoning: Conventional. When you're all set to print the file, check Separations in the Layout pane. For more information, see page 449. Settings chosen in the Print dialog box override settings in the Edit Color dialog box.

1 *The* **Setup** *pane in the QuarkXPress* **Print** *dialog box*

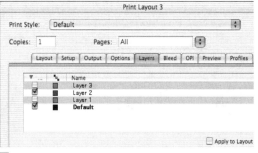

2 *The* **Layers** *pane in the QuarkXPress* **Print** *dialog box*

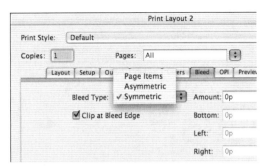

1 *When the **Custom Bleeds.xnt** XTension is enabled (the application installs and enables it by default), a **Bleed** pane is available in the Print dialog box. When this XTension is disabled, a simplified Bleed field appears in the Layout pane instead.*

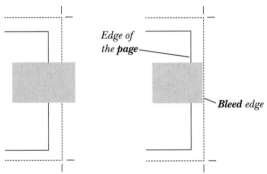

2 *With **Page Items** chosen, the whole item prints—as long as at least part of it is on the page.*

3 *With **Asymmetric** (or **Symmetric**) chosen and **Clip at Bleed Edge** checked, items print only up to the specified Amount (the bleed edge).*

Use the **Bleed** pane to choose bleed options. From the Bleed Type pop-up menu, choose Page Items to allow any items that are at least partially on the page to print in their entirety **1**–**2**. Asymmetric and Symmetric let you define the width of the bleed area. For Symmetric, enter one Amount value; for Asymmetric, enter Top, Bottom, Inside, and Outside values. With Clip at Bleed Edge checked, items won't print beyond the bleed area **3**; when it's unchecked, items that at least partially overlap the bleed area will print in their entirety, within the limits of the output device. For more about the bleed options, see the QuarkXPress documentation.

Use the Preview pane to preview any Bleed values in the preview window. (If Asymmetric is chosen in a facing-pages layout, you can click the Left of Spine or Right of Spine button below the preview window in the Preview pane.)

Options in the **OPI** pane apply only if you're outputting to an OPI prepress system that's going to replace your pictures with high-resolution picture files stored on that OPI system. Click the OPI tab and check OPI Active to have QuarkXPress write OPI comments for all the pictures in the file. Only pictures you target to be exchanged will be replaced by the full-resolution version. If a proxy of a picture is used in the file and the proxy contains OPI instructions, check Include Images for TIFF or EPS. Both picture data and comments will be sent to output. (See the QuarkXPress documentation.)

Note: If the OPI XTension is active, the OPI tab is available and the OPI pop-up menu in the Options pane becomes unavailable.

(Continued on the following page)

Print

Use the **Preview** pane to view a thumbnail of the current page with the chosen printing parameters **1**. The icon below the preview window indicates whether a cut-sheet print device (individual pieces of paper) ⬜ or a roll-fed print device (a roll of continuous paper) ◇ was chosen from the Printer Description pop-up menu in the Setup pane. To see a key for the different colors used in the preview window, press and hold the ? button.

If Color Management Active is checked in Preferences > Print Layout > Quark CMS, profiles chosen from the pop-up menus in the **Profiles** pane will override the current Destination profile for the Separation Output and/or Composite Output device chosen in Quark CMS preferences. Check Composite Simulates Separation to have the composite output simulate the appearance of the profile chosen for the target separation device.

8. When you're done switching between panes and choosing settings, click Print (Return/Enter).

If a missing pictures prompt appears, click List Pictures, click Update, locate and highlight the missing picture(s), click Open, then click Print.

Page Setup

In Mac OS X, clicking Page Setup in the Print dialog box opens the Page Setup dialog box **2** for the System's device driver; in Windows, clicking Properties opens the Properties dialog box (see the following page).

Changes made in the Setup pane of the Print dialog box, such as the Reduce or Enlarge or Orientation settings, update automatically in the Page Setup dialog box, and vice versa. Exception: A change to the Paper Size in either dialog box won't update in the other dialog box.

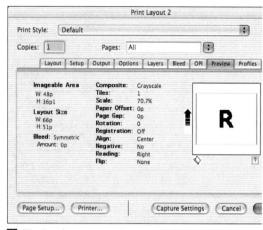

1 *The **Preview** pane in the Print dialog box*

*Choose a **Paper Size** option.*

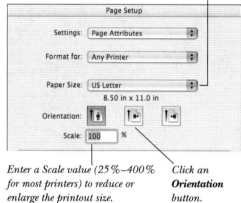

Enter a Scale value (25%–400% for most printers) to reduce or enlarge the printout size.

*Click an **Orientation** button.*

2 *This is the **Page Setup** dialog box in Mac OS X. You can choose the same Reduce/Enlarge and Orientation settings in the Setup pane of the Print dialog box.*

(sidebar) Page Setup

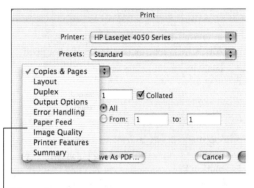

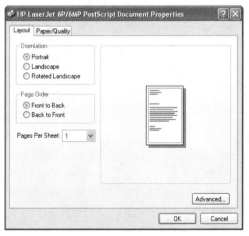

1 *In Mac OS X, clicking* **Printer** *in the Print dialog box opens the dialog box for the System's printer driver. Related panes can be accessed via this pop-up menu.*

2 *In the* **Print** *dialog box in Windows, clicking the* **Properties** *button opens the Properties dialog box.*

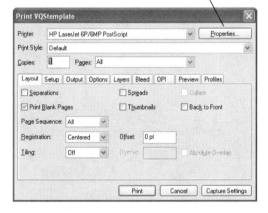

System printer

Mac OS X only

Clicking the Printer button at the bottom of the Print dialog box opens the Print dialog box for Mac OS X. There, via the pop-up menu on the left **1**, you can access additional panes pertaining to any installed printers currently chosen on the Printer pop-up menu. However, to ensure that QuarkXPress will handle the output, we recommend that you choose printing options from QuarkXPress's Print dialog box instead. One exception is using the Image Quality pane (accessed via the pop-up menu) to adjust how a laser printer or non-PostScript ink jet printer handles halftoning of images. To exit and accept the system's Print dialog box settings, click Print (this *won't* actually initiate printing).

Windows only

Clicking the Properties button **2** opens the printer's Properties dialog box **3**. Settings chosen in this dialog box will override the current settings in the Print dialog box in QuarkXPress.

Except for a Paper Size choice, changes made to settings in the Setup pane of the QuarkXPress Print dialog box, such as Copies and Orientation, update automatically in the Properties dialog box, and vice versa.

Options in the printer's Properties dialog box will vary depending on which printer is currently selected.

When you're done choosing Properties settings, click OK to return to the Quark-XPress Print dialog box.

3 *In the* **Layout** *pane of the Properties dialog box, choose Orientation and Page Order options for the currently chosen printer.*

Which page?

If your layout contains section numbering, be sure to enter the page number accurately, including any prefix (as in "Page xii") in the Pages field in the Print dialog box. To print a page based on its position within the layout instead (its absolute page number), type a plus sign, then the number. To print the third and fourth pages in a layout, for example, you'd enter "+3-+4."

TIP If your page numbers contain a hyphen (e.g., "Page A-8"), as specified in the Prefix field in the Section dialog box, you can't use a hyphen as a page range separator in the Pages field in the Print dialog box. To specify a different character for the Print dialog box, go to Preferences > Application > Interactive and enter the desired character in the Page Range Separators: Sequential and Nonsequential fields. A better idea: Use an en dash for page numbers on your layout pages instead!

DeviceN 6.0!

DeviceN composite color is a printing feature that allows a project containing colors of various types (e.g., a combination of CMYK colors, spot colors, blends, multi-inks, colorized TIFFs) to be output as a single composite print while preserving the file's color separation information. A print layout can be output as a composite or as separations, with no adjustments needed to the file. As an example, this dual output option would be useful for a project that is to be output to both PDF and to color separations for offset printing.

DeviceN can be chosen as a print option and when exporting to PDF and EPS. To specifiy DeviceN for print output, choose File > Print > Setup, choose a PostScript device from the Printer Description pop-up menu (only a PostScript level 3–compatible device can utilize DeviceN). Then, in the Output pane, choose DeviceN from the Print Colors pop-up menu.

Non-PostScript printers 6.0!

For improved output when outputting high-resolution EPS pictures to non-PostScript printers (such as ink-jet printers), turn on Item > Preview Resolution > Full Resolution.

Low-res output

If you choose Low Resolution from the Output pop-up menu in File > Print > Options, all pictures in a layout, including those set to Full Resolution Preview, will print at a low resolution, regardless of what type of printer is being used.

Section Numbers; DeviceN

Layout-specific print options 6.0!

Just as QuarkXPress displays or outputs only one layout at a time, the print options apply only to the currently active print layout. When you duplicate a print layout, its print options (along with other properties) also appear in the duplicate.

As Is 6.0!

With the As Is composite color option chosen, an item in a print layout will output on a PostScript device using that item's original source color space. This option is helpful when you have, say, an RGB image from an RGB scanner or image-editing program that you want to print as an RGB color composite on a PostScript device. The final output device—not QuarkXPress—will color manage the output. As with DeviceN, As Is color can be chosen for print output (PostScript level 3 printers only), and for PDF and EPS export.

Note: The As Is composite color option isn't available when Quark CMS is active. Turn Quark CMS off in the Preferences dialog box first if you want to access the As Is color option in the Print dialog box.

To specify As Is composite color for print output, go to File > Print > Setup, and then, from the Printer Description pop-up menu, choose a PostScript level 3–compatible device. Next, click the Output tab and then, from the Print Colors pop-up menu, choose As Is.

Printing Web layouts

You can't print a Web layout from Quark-XPress, but you can have the program export it as an HTML file to your currently available browser and print it from there. To do this, choose File > Print. Your chosen browser will launch, and then the System's Print dialog box will open. Click Print.

You can change which Web browsers are available for previewing or printing Web layouts in QuarkXPress (Edit, in Windows) > Preferences > Application > Browsers.

Capture the settings

Click Capture Settings in the Print dialog box to save the current print settings in the current print layout. The next time you open the Print dialog box, those captured settings will be the Default settings. Each time you choose other print options or choose another print style and then click Capture Settings, the new settings become the Default settings.

TIP To create a print style that contains print settings for use with other layouts, use Edit > Print Styles (see the following page).

With automatic tiling, any layout whose page size is larger than the standard paper size, such as a tabloid, can be printed in sections on multiple sheets of standard-size paper. QuarkXPress automatically prints crop marks to be used as guides for trimming the page sections, as well as margin label codes notating the order for reassembling them into the larger whole.

To print using automatic tiling:

1. Display the layout you want to print, then choose File > Print (Cmd-P/ Ctrl-P).

2. In the Setup pane, choose the appropriate Orientation icon. Portrait is a good choice for a tabloid page.

3. In the Layout pane, choose Tiling: Automatic **1**.

4. Enter a number in the Overlap field. 3" (18p) is the default. *Note:* If you want your pages to be centered within the overall arrangement of tiles, don't check Absolute Overlap.

5. Adjust any other print settings, then click the Preview pane to preview.

6. Click Print.

TIP To print an oversized layout on one standard size sheet of paper, check Fit in Print Area in the Setup pane.

Get some help

Just to whet your appetite, here's an abbreviated list of output-related XTensions and their features. Some of these XTensions are available for Mac OS X only, and some are available for both Mac OS X and Windows.

BureauManager (CompuSense Ltd.) prepares files for an output service provider, generates a report and list of instructions, collects files, and searches for missing picture files.

Printools XT (Badia Software) previews printed pages, tiles oversized layouts, allows you to change print settings from a palette, prints individual items, produces document reports, and tracks revisions.

BigPicture XT (Badia Software) manages links between pictures files and QuarkXPress projects, lists picture data, displays picture thumbnails, renames picture files, and searches for missing pictures.

XPert ItemMarks XT (in XPert Tools Pro, by a lowly apprentice production, inc.) creates customized crop marks, registration marks, color bars, etc. for whole pages or individual items.

SpecTackler (GLUON, Inc.) marks each item on a page with a tag containing either text and paragraph specifications or picture data (e.g., scale, resolution, dimensions, name).

1 *The* **Tiling** *options are located in the Layout pane of the Print dialog box.*

Stashing your styles

By default, print styles are saved in the XPress Preferences.prf file, but you can also save the print style currently selected in Edit > Print Styles to a separate file via the **Export** button. Then, if that style is deleted via the Delete button in the same dialog box (or the XPress Preferences.prf file is deleted), you can restore it via the Import button. In Mac OS X, the XPress Preferences.prf file is located in Users/UserName/Library/Preferences/Quark/QuarkXPress 6.0. In Windows, it's in Documents and Settings\ [user]\Application Data\Quark\QuarkXPress 6.0.

1 *Click* **New** *in the* **Print Styles** *dialog box.*

2 *We created a* **print style** *named "Rough" that has a Pictures: Output setting of Rough for faster printing (the pictures won't print).*

Print styles work like style sheets, except in this case they contain custom print settings. Once you've created a print style, you can then choose it from the Print Styles pop-up menu in the Print dialog box for *any* QuarkXPress print layout in any project, existing or future.

You can temporarily override settings from the currently chosen print style simply by choosing new settings from any pane in the Print dialog box. Print styles aren't available for Web layouts.

To create or edit a print style:

1. A project can be open or not (it doesn't matter). If a project *is* open, make sure a print layout is displayed— not a Web layout. Choose Edit > Print Styles.

2. Click an existing print style, then click Edit to modify it or click Duplicate to edit a copy of it.
   or
   Click New to create a new print style **1**.

3. For a new or duplicate print style, type a name in the Name field. Use a client or project name or the name of a print option, such as the printer name, to help you identify the print style.

4. Choose settings in the Layout, Setup, Output, and Options panes. (The Print dialog box has the same four panes).

5. Click OK, then click Save **2**.

TIP To remove a print style from the list, click on it, click Delete, then click Save. The Default print style can't be deleted.

Print Styles

To suppress printing of a picture:

1. Choose Utilities > Usage.

2. Click the Pictures tab and then, in the Print column, click to delete the check mark for any picture(s) . The picture won't print, but a frame, if any was applied to the box, will print. (Click the blank box at any time to restore the check mark and turn printing back on.)

3. Click Done.

TIP This can also be done for a selected picture by checking Suppress Picture Output in Item > Modify > Picture.

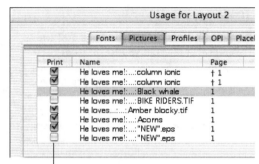

1 *To suppress the printing of a picture, remove its check mark in the Print column in Utilities > Usage > Pictures.*

You can print a layout minus *all* pictures to speed up printing or to help you see the naked, "bare bones" composition.

To suppress printing of all pictures:

Choose File > Print and then, in the Options pane, choose Output: Rough **2** (print layouts only). On the printout, an X will appear in each picture box. Ornate frame styles won't print.

Another way to hasten printing is to choose Output: Low Resolution. The low-resolution version of the picture that was saved automatically with the QuarkXPress file will print instead of the full-resolution version.

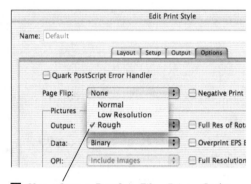

2 *Choose Output: Rough in File > Print > Options.*

To suppress printing of an item:

To suppress printing of an entire item (box, text path, line, or table) from a print layout, including its contents, and including any frame applied to the item, select the item, go to Item > Modify > Box (or Line or Table)(Cmd-M/Ctrl-M), then check Suppress Output **3**. We use this option to create non-printing "sticky" notes.

6.0! ## To suppress printing of a layer:

Choose File > Print and then, in the Layers pane, click the check mark in the left column for any layer (or select multiple layers, then choose No from the drop-down menu). To suppress printing of a layer via the Layers palette, see page 284.

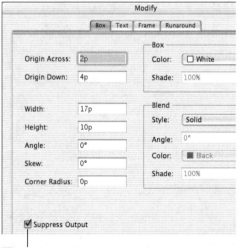

3 *To prevent a picture (and frame, if any) from printing, check Suppress Output in Item > Modify > Box.*

Suppress Printing

To modify the halftoning used by QuarkXPress

1. Choose File > Print and then, in the Layout pane, check Separations.

2. Click the Output tab **1**.

3. From the Plates pop-up menu (not the Plate column):

   Choose Used Process & Spot to choose halftoning options for only the process and spot colors that are being used in the layout.
   or
   Choose Convert to Process to convert all spot colors in the file to process colors.
   or
   Choose All Process & Spot to choose halftoning options for all colors—process, spot, and RGB.

4. Turn the printing of any individual plate on or off by checking or unchecking its box in the Print column.

5. Click the name of the plate (or plates) that you want to choose halftoning settings for, and then, as per your output service provider's instructions, choose settings from the Frequency, Angle, and Function drop-down menus. Each

Read all about it

To learn more about the complicated world of color separation, see one of the many useful reference books available, such as *Real World Color Management* by Bruce Fraser, Fred Bunting, and Chris Murphy (Peachpit Press).

spot color is assigned the screen values of one of the four process colors. Via the Halftone drop-down menu, you can apply screen values from another process color to the currently selected spot color.

6. Choose other print settings, then click Print.

TIP With Separations unchecked in the Layout pane, Printer becomes available as a choice on the Halftoning pop-up menu in the Output pane. With this option chosen, the printing device handles halftoning (with no modifications allowed); no halftone information is sent to the printer by QuarkXPress.

TIP To save yourself from repetitive setup work, create a print style that contains the desired halftoning options. Then you can choose that style from the Print Style pop-up menu in File > Print.

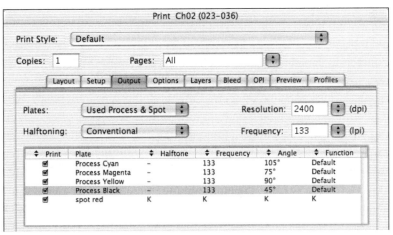

1 *Select a plate or plates, then choose settings for that plate from the **Halftone, Frequency, Angle,** and **Function** drop-down menus, as per your output service provider's instructions.*

Halftoning

What's a PPD?

A PPD, short for PostScript Printer Description, is a text file that contains information about a particular PostScript printer's parameters (how's that for alliteration?), such as its default resolution, usable paper and page sizes, and PostScript version number.

The PPD Manager, which facilitates the loading of PPDs into QuarkXPress, is helpful in any setting where more than one kind of printer is used. It controls which of the System's PPDs (and thus printer names) are available on the Printer Description pop-up menu in these three locations: File > Print > Setup, Edit > Print Styles > New > Setup, and Print Styles > Edit > Setup.

Although an unlimited number of PPDs can be loaded at a time, you can restrict the ones that are loaded to just the printers you output to from QuarkXPress.

To use the PPD manager:

1. Choose Utilities > PPD Manager.

2. Click a printer name ▉.

3. In the Include column, click the check mark to exclude that printer or restore the check mark to include it.

4. Click OK. All the Printer Description pop-up menus in QuarkXPress will update to reflect the new settings.

Where your PPDs are

It's a good idea to leave the PPDs in the default location for your platform so they can be found and accessed by all your applications, including QuarkXPress. In Mac OS X, dozens of PPDs are installed in folders in Library/Printers/PPDs. QuarkXPress creates a PPD folder in the user's library: [User Name]/Library/Preferences/Quark/QuarkXPress 6.0/PPD. QuarkXPress also looks for PPDs in the Classic System folder and the root level Library folder.

In Windows, PPDs are stored in *systemroot*System32\Spool\Drivers\W32x8613.

Changes made using the PPD Manager affect only QuarkXPress—not other applications.

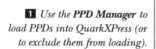

▉ *Use the **PPD Manager** to load PPDs into QuarkXPress (or to exclude them from loading).*

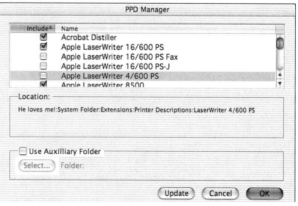

To add PPDs to the PPD Manager list:

1. Install PPDs in the folder listed in the sidebar on the previous page.

2. If QuarkXPress isn't running, launch it now.

3. Choose Utilities > PPD Manager.

4. Make sure the path listed for the PPD folder at the bottom of the dialog box is the same as the location used for step 1. If it is, skip ahead to step 5.

   If it's not the same path, check Use Auxiliary Folder, click Select, and locate the folder that contains the System's PPD files. When the correct folder name appears on the From pop-up menu, click Choose.

5. In the PPD Manager, click Update. Any PPDs that you just added to the System or Library folder will also be added to the current PPD list (unless you checked Use Auxilliary Folder and selected a substitute folder).

6. Make sure a check mark is present in the Include column for any PPD that you want listed as a choice on the Printer Description pop-up menu in File > Print > Setup and Edit > Print Styles > Setup.

7. Click OK.

TIP By default, QuarkXPress looks to several folders for PPDs. If you want QuarkXPress to look to only one folder, follow the second paragraph in step 4, above.

Add PPDs

Exporting files

Some print shops need a PostScript file of your layout for output. To do this, first prepare your layout as per your output service provider's instructions.

Note: Before creating a PostScript file, make sure the proper Printer Description file for the final print output device is enabled via the PPD Manager so it's available in the Setup pane of the Print dialog box.

To create a PostScript file in Mac OS X:

1. Display the layout you want to create a PostScript file of, then choose File > Print (Cmd-P).

2. Ask your output service provider which settings to choose in the Setup and Output panes.

3. Click Printer at the bottom of the dialog box, then click OK in the alert box.

4. Choose Output Options from the pop-up menu on the left side of the dialog box, check Save as File, choose Format: PostScript **1**, then click Save.

5. Choose a location in which to save the PostScript file, enter a name, such as "Ch1" or "1–10," then click Save again. The .ps extension will be appended to the PostScript file name automatically.

6. The QuarkXPress Print dialog box will become active again. Adjust any other settings, then click Print (not Cancel). Be sure to send along the live (non-PostScript) file and pictures to the output service provider, just in case.

To create a PostScript file in Windows:

1. Display the layout you want to create a PostScript file of, then click Start button > Printers and Faxes.

2. Right-click the name of your printer and choose Properties.

3. Click the Ports tab.

4. On the "Print to the following port(s)" list **2**, check the box for FILE: Print to File, then click OK.

5. Click in the QuarkXPress layout window, and choose File > Print (Ctrl-P).

6. From the Printer pop-up menu, choose the printer you chose in step 2, then click Print. *Note:* A warning will appear if you didn't check the box for FILE: Print to File in step 4, above.

7. Ask your output service provider what settings to choose in the Setup and Output panes.

8. In the Print To File dialog box, type a name for the output file in the File name field and choose a folder in which to save it.

9. For normal printing, remember to go back to the Properties > Ports tab and check the box for LPT1: Printer Port.

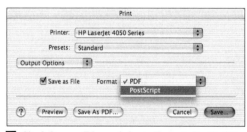

1 *Check Save as File, and choose Format: PostScript.*

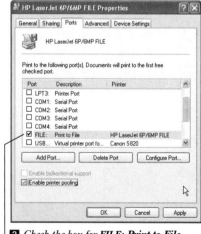

2 *Check the box for FILE: Print to File.*

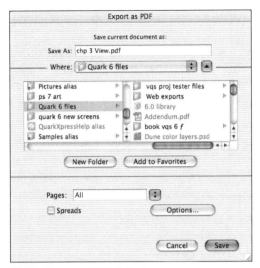

1 The **Export as PDF** dialog box

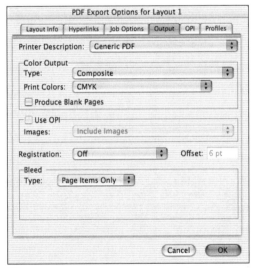

2 For information about choosing **PDF Export Options**, see the QuarkXPress 6 documentation.

If a layout is saved in the PDF file format, users will be able to view it in all its glory in either Adobe Acrobat or Acrobat Reader, on any platform, complete with pictures, colors, hyperlinks, and type as you intend it to be seen—without having to launch or even own a copy of QuarkXPress. The Layout as PDF command in QuarkXPress 6 boasts a number of enhancements. In the instructions below, you'll choose which layout and layout pages you want saved.

To save a layout as a PDF file: 6.0!

1. Display the layout you want to save as a PDF, then choose File > Export > Layout as PDF.
or
Control-click/Right-click in the layout and choose Export > Layout as PDF.

2. Enter a name, and choose a location for the file **1**. (Mac OS X users, keep the .pdf extension.)

3. *Optional:* To change the current PDF preferences, click Options, then choose settings under the various tabs **2**. See the QuarkXPress documentation for information about these options.

4. At the bottom of the dialog box, enter a range of Pages to be exported, or leave the setting as All to export all the pages in the currently displayed layout.

5. *Optional:* Check Spreads to produce full spreads (not separate pages) in the PDF file.

6. Click Save. The PDF file will appear in the location you chose in step 2, above.

TIP A PDF file can also be opened in Adobe Photoshop and Adobe Illustrator.

Save Layouts as PDF File

The Save Page as EPS command converts a QuarkXPress page into a single picture. Potential reasons for using this feature:

■ Your output service provider or commercial printer requests an EPS file for color-separations.

■ You want to import a QuarkXPress page into another application, such as Adobe Photoshop or Adobe Illustrator.

■ You want to create a resizable page within a page (e.g., an advertisement or logo ).

To save a page as an EPS file:

1. Display the layout that contains the page you want to save as an EPS file, then choose File > Save Page as EPS (Cmd-Option-Shift-S/Ctrl-Alt-Shift-S). *Note:* EPS files can't be edited in Quark-XPress, so be sure to save the original file from which it's generated so you'll be able to edit it or generate another EPS file from it later on!

2. Change the file name in the Save As/File name field, if desired (, next page) and choose a location for the EPS file.

3. The page number that appears in the Page field will be saved as an EPS. The number of the currently displayed page appears here automatically, but you can enter a different number.

Using a file saved as EPS

Save Page as EPS comes in handy if you have an ad or a logo that you created in QuarkXPress that you need to use in various sizes . To place an EPS into a layout, create a picture box and use File > Get Picture. As with any EPS file, in order to output it, the printer fonts must be available for any text it contains and the original files must be available for any pictures it contains.

1 *This is an **EPS** of the next page in this book—a page within a page.*

2 *This logo was created in QuarkXPress, **saved as an EPS** file, and then imported into various-sized picture boxes.*

4. Enter a Scale percentage (10%–100%).

5. *Optional:* Check Spread to save a multi-page spread instead of just the current single page. Check Transparent Page to save the file with a transparent background instead of a white background.

6. Choose Format: Color, B&W, DCS, or DCS 2.0. To color-separate a page before printing, you can save it in either of the two DCS (Desktop Color Separation) file formats. DCS produces five separate files (cyan, magenta, yellow, black, and a preview); DCS 2.0 produces color-separations in one file, plus a preview file, and can include spot color plates.

Ask your output service provider which file format you should choose for your target output device.

7. Choose Space: CMYK, RGB, As Is, or DeviceN. Read about As Is composite color on page 445; read about DeviceN on page 444. **6.0!**

8. Choose a Preview of None, TIFF, or PICT for the file. PICT is available only in Mac OS X.

9. If you're saving the page for color separation, ask your commercial printer which Data and OPI settings to choose. Binary files print more quickly and are smaller in size than ASCII files, so use ASCII only if Binary can't be used. Clean 8-bit produces a more portable output format using a combination of ASCII and binary data.

10. Click Save.

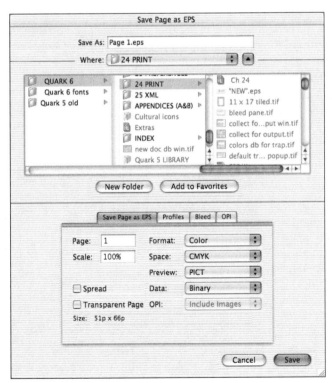

1 The **Save Page as EPS** *dialog box*

When you hand off a file to an output service provider, you must supply the project and layout names, names of fonts and colors used in the project, and other data. You also must supply the original files for any pictures being used in the file, or they won't output properly. The Collect for Output command gathers copies of all the required elements together for you automatically, and also produces a text report with information about the active layout. You can selectively choose whether the layout, linked pictures, embedded pictures, color profiles, screen fonts, and printer fonts will be included in the output folder.

To collect for output:

1. Save the project, display the print layout you want to collect output for, then choose File > Collect for Output. If any pictures can't be located or were modified after they were imported into the QuarkXPress file, an alert dialog box will appear. Click List Pictures, update the pictures, click OK, then respond to the next prompt by clicking Save.

2. Choose a location for the folder **1**–**2**.

3. In Mac OS X, click New Folder, change the folder name, if desired, then click Create. In Windows, click the New Folder button, change the folder name, if desired, then double-click the folder icon to open it.

4. *Optional:* Change the report name in the Save As/File name field.

5. Under Collect, check the file components you want QuarkXPress to place in the folder: Layout, Linked Pictures, Embedded Pictures (e.g., PICT, BMP, and WMF files), and Color Profiles (ICC profiles). In Mac OS X, you also have Screen Fonts and Printer Fonts checkboxes; Windows has a Fonts checkbox.

6. Click Save. If a dire warning prompt regarding collecting fonts appears, read it and decide which button to click. A folder containing the current

Just the facts, ma'am

To have QuarkXPress produce a report only without gathering any files, check **Report Only** before clicking Save in the Collect for Output dialog box. If you hold down Option/Alt when you choose File > Collect for Output, Report Only will be checked automatically.

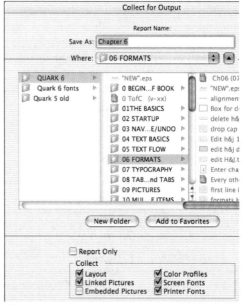

1 *The Collect for Output dialog box in Mac OS X*

2 *The Collect for Output dialog box in Windows*

Sidebar: Collect for Output

1 *Fill out this form.*

ELECTRONIC OUTPUT REQUEST

CLIENT INFORMATION
Contact Person: _____
Company: _____
Address: _____
City, St., ZIP: _____
Office Phone: _____
Home Phone: _____

DELIVERY INFORMATION
__ Deliver   __ Hold For Pickup   __ Call When Complete
Delivery Address: _____
City, St., ZIP: _____

TURNAROUND INFORMATION
__ Normal   __ Rush   __ Emergency

FONT INFORMATION
__ Adobe/Linotype   __ Agfa   __ Bitstream
__ Monotype   __   __

COLOR MANAGEMENT INFORMATION
__ Match colors according to assigned source profiles. (Include necessary profiles with job.)

COPYRIGHT INFORMATION
All that appears on the enclosed medium (including, but not limited to, floppy disk, modem transmission, removable media) is unencumbered by copyrights. We, the customer, have full rights to reproduce the supplied content.
Signature: _____
Date: _____

OUTPUT MEDIA (CHECK ALL THAT APPLY)
__ Film   __ RC Paper   __ Color Proof
__ Laser Print   __ Color Slides
__ Negative   -or-   __ Positive
__ Emulsion Down   -or-   __ Emulsion Up

LAYOUT:
Source Path Name: Silver G4:Users:peter:Desktop:Quark 6 files:junk 1
Destination Path Name: Silver G4:Users:peter:Desktop:Quark 6 files:junk 1 report
Last modified: 3:28 PM; 6/10/03
Layout Size: 2740K
Most recently saved version: 6.00r0
Project has been saved by the following versions of QuarkXPress:
          6.00r0
Total Pages: 4

OUTPUT SPECIFICATION
__ Output All Pages
__ Output The Following Specified Pages...
From: _____   To: _____

CROP MARKS
__ Yes   __ No

RESOLUTION/DPI
__ 1200/1270   __ 2400/2540   __ 3000+

SCREEN RULING/LPI
__ 65   __ 85   __ 133
__ 150   __ 175   __

COLOR SEPARATION PLATES
__ Cyan   __ Magenta   __ Yellow   __ Black
__   __   __   __

COLOR PROOF SPECIFICATION
__ Proof All Pages
__ Proof The Following Specified Pages...
From: _____   To: _____

LASER PROOF PROVIDED WITH JOB?
__ Yes   __ No

OTHER INFORMATION
Type information about the job here.

2 *And import the **report file** into the bottom box.*

ELECTRONIC OUTPUT REQUEST FOR: YOUR COMPANY NAME HERE   PAGE 2

Page Width: 51p
Page Height: 66p

REQUIRED XTENSIONS:
                              None

ACTIVE XTENSIONS:

	Cool Blends;	GIF Filter;	HTML Export;
Hyperlinks;	JPEG Filter;	Layers;	Placeholders;
SpellChecker;	Table;	Web Tools;	avenue.quark;
CompressedImage Import;	Custom Blends;	Dejavu;	EPS Preview;
Full Resolution Preview;	Guide Manager;	HTML Text Import;	ImageMap;
Index;	Item Sequence;	Jabberwocky;	Kern-Track Editor;
MS-Word 6-2000 Filter;	OPI;	PDF Filter;	PNG Filter;
Quark CMS;	RTF Filter;	Scissors;	Script;
Shape of Things;	Super Step and Repeat;	Type Tricks;	WordPerfect Filter;
XML Import;	XPress Tags Filter		

LAYOUT FONTS

Font Name	PostScript Name	File Name
»Plain»Helvetica	Helve	
»Plain»Sabon	Sabonita	
»Italic»Sabon	Sabonita	
»Bold»Italic»Sabon	Sabonita	
»Plain»GillSans BoldCondensed		GillSanBolCon
»Plain»I New Baskerville Italic		NewBaslta
»Plain»B Sabon Bold	SabonBol	
»Plain»Bundesbahn Pi 1	BundePiOne	
»Plain»Zapf Dingbats	ZapfDin	
»Plain»Bellevue	Belle	
»Plain»I Sabon Italic	Sabonita	
»Plain»BI Sabon BoldItalic	SabonBolIta	

MASTER FONTS

Font Name	PostScript Name	File Name
»Plain»Helvetica	Helve	
»Plain»R Frutiger Roman	FrutiRom	
»Plain»GillSans Bold	GillSanBol	
»Plain»GillSans BoldCondensed		GillSanBolCon
»Plain»Garamond	GaramLig	

PICTURE FONTS

PICTURE	FONT NAME
eps & type.eps	CaslonOpenFace

---

project, the components that you checked in the previous step, and a detailed report file, will be created.

After using the Collect for Output command, you can email or send the report file as is, or you can flow it into the Output Request template that QuarkXPress provides and then print that file or supply it as a PDF. One way or the other, your output service provider will want this information —not to mention the layout and the original files for any pictures used in the layout!

Note: In order to import the report file, the XPress Tags Filter.xnt XTension must be enabled. Use the XTensions Manager to do this, and then relaunch QuarkXPress.

To create an output request form:

1. Choose File > Open, and locate and open a file called Output Request Template.qxt. By default, it's installed in QuarkXPress/Templates/English.

2. Choose File > Save As (Cmd-Option-S/ Ctrl-Alt-S), type a name for the report, then click Save. For simplicity's sake, save the request form to your new Collect for Output folder.

3. Choose the Content tool.

4. Fill out the top portion of the Electronic Output Request **1**.

5. Choose the Content tool, then click in the text box at the bottom of page 1, below the horizontal line **2**.

6. Choose File > Get Text (Cmd-E/ Ctrl-E).

7. Locate and highlight the report file.

8. Check Include Style Sheets, then click Open (Return/Enter). New pages will be added automatically to accommodate all the text.

9. Save the project **3**.

3 *This is page 2 of a report. Note: Fonts used in any EPS graphics will be listed in the Picture Fonts category.*

Output Request Form

Imagesetting tips

An imagesetter is a device that produces high-resolution (1,250–3,540 dpi) paper or film output from electronic files. The paper or film output, in turn, is used by commercial printers to produce printing plates. *Note:* Some printers skip the intermediary film output step entirely and go directly to plate—so ask your printer! The following is a checklist of things to do to help your imagesetting run successfully:

■ Find out if your commercial printer can output your electronic files. Since they're intimately familiar with the printing press—its quirks and its requirements—they're often the best candidate for imagesetting.

■ If you're outputting the file with an output service provider, ask your commercial printer for specific advice regarding such settings as the lpi (lines per inch), emulsion up or down, and negative/positive. Tell your output service what output settings your commercial printer specified, and they'll enter the correct values in the Print dialog box (Output pane) when they output your file. Don't guess on this one. Also ask whether you should set trapping values yourself or have the output service do the trapping on their high-end system. You can also ask your commercial printer to talk directly with your output service provider.

■ Make sure any pictures in the layout are saved at final printout size and at the appropriate resolution for the final output device, which means approximately 1½ times the final lpi for a black-and-white or grayscale picture and 2 times the final lpi for a color picture. If a picture (especially an EPS) requires cropping, rotating, or scaling down, do so in the picture's original application, if possible—it will output more quickly.

■ Use the File > Collect for Output command to collect your project and associated images and to produce a report file. If you don't supply your output service provider with the original picture files, the low-resolution versions will be used for printing (yech!). The report file lists important specifications that they need in order to output your file properly, such as the fonts used in the layout.

■ If your output service provider needs a PDF or PostScript file of your layout, ask them for specific instructions.

■ Some output service providers will supply the necessary fonts—at least the Adobe fonts—but some printers prefer to have you supply them all. Include both the screen and the printer fonts, and don't forget to supply the fonts used in any imported EPS pictures.

■ Include printouts of your file (unless you're transferring the file electronically), with Registration marks turned on, or send a PDF version of the file.

■ If your layout doesn't print or takes an inordinately long time to print on your laser printer, don't assume it will print quickly on an imagesetter. Large pictures, irregularly shaped picture boxes, and clipping paths are some of the many items that can cause a printing error. If you are using the same high-resolution picture more than once, but in very different sizes, import copies of the picture saved at those specific sizes.

■ To reduce the amount of information the imagesetter has to calculate, delete any extraneous items from the layout's pasteboard. To find out if there are any pictures on the pasteboard, choose Utilities > Usage, and click the Pictures tab. If you see a dagger icon in Mac OS X or the letters "PB" in Windows, it means that picture is on the pasteboard.

What's on your plate?

In standard four-color process printing, a layout is color-separated onto four plates, one each for cyan, yellow, magenta, and black. Other potential combinations include printing a spot color and black on two separate plates or printing a spot color and the four process colors (a total of five plates).

Hexachrome (high-fidelity) colors color-separate onto six process color plates, with the result being greater color fidelity due to the wider range of printable colors. An RGB picture can be color-separated using this method.

Printing a spot

Be sure to check **Spot Color** in the Edit Color dialog box for any spot color that you want to color-separate onto a separate plate. To output a particular color, choose File > Print, check Separations in the Layout pane, and then, in the Output pane, choose **Used Process & Spot** from the Plates pop-up menu.

Spot colors, if they're saved in an Adobe Illustrator or Macromedia FreeHand file in the EPS format, will append to the Colors dialog box in the QuarkXPress layout and will also display in the plate scroll window in File > Print > Output. Make sure the name that's assigned to any spot color being used in both QuarkXPress and Adobe Illustrator is exactly the same in each program; otherwise two plates will print instead of the desired single plate.

Color separation tips

- Always refer to a printed swatch book when choosing colors (e.g., a PANTONE swatch book). Computer screens only simulate printed colors, so you won't get reliable results by choosing colors based on how they appear onscreen.

- Don't change the shade percentage for a process color via the Colors palette or Item > Modify. Instead, mix a color that has the desired shade percentage built into it. It's perfectly okay to change the shade percentage for a spot color (e.g., PANTONE), though.

- If your layout contains continuous-tone pictures, such as scanned photographs or artwork produced in an image-editing program, ask your output service provider or commercial printer in which file format (e.g., TIFF, EPS) and in which image mode (e.g., CMYK, RGB) those pictures should be saved. You can use an image-editing program, such as Adobe Photoshop, to change a picture's file format, resolution, or image mode.

- Ask your output service provider whether to use QuarkXPress or an image-editing program to convert any color pictures from RGB to CMYK for separations. Pictures scanned into CMYK color mode don't require conversion.

- RGB spot colors from imported Illustrator EPS files will remain as RGB spot colors, and will be listed as such in the Colors dialog box.

- If your layout contains hand-drawn registration or crop marks, apply the Registration color to them to ensure that they appear on all the separation plates.

- For color work, order a color proof of the layout (e.g., Iris, Xerox DocuColor, Matchprint, or a high-end inkjet proof) so it can be inspected for color accuracy.

Trapping colors

Trapping is the deliberate overlapping of colors to help safeguard against gaps that may result on press due to the misalignment of plates, paper shifting, or paper stretching.

In QuarkXPress, trapping is applied according to the way colors in each object interact with color(s) below it. Use the mini-glossary at right to familiarize yourself with trapping terminology.

Before exploring the circumstances in which trapping is necessary, we'll discuss a couple of circumstances in which trapping is unnecessary.

When not to apply trapping

Trapping is unnecessary when black type or a black item or frame is placed on top of a light background color. In this case, the black type will overprint (print on top of) the background color. You can specify a minimum percentage of black to control when and if overprinting will occur (see page 463).

Trapping is also unnecessary if process colors and adjacent or overlapping colors contain a common color component (C, M, Y, or K). Let's say you have a red, which contains a percentage of magenta, that touches a blue area that also contains a small percentage of magenta. The two colors both contain magenta, so trapping is unnecessary.

When to apply trapping

Trapping is necessary when you print spot colors, print process colors that don't have a common color component, or print a light color on a dark background.

In QuarkXPress, trapping values are assigned to the foreground color. A light foreground color spreads into the background color by a specified amount, and a light background color chokes the foreground color. To produce a choke trap in QuarkXPress, the foreground color is assigned a negative trapping value.

Trapping mini-glossary

Overprint

The foreground object color prints on top of the background color, so the inks actually mix together. Overprint is used if black is the foreground object color or if inks are intentionally mixed to produce a third (overlap) color.

Knockout

To prevent inks from overprinting, the foreground item's color shape is cut out (knocked out) of the underlying background color on the background color plate. Although this eliminates the problem of ink mixing, it creates a potential problem of a gap between the edges of the foreground and background colors. Trapping closes this gap.

Spread

The spread method of trapping is used when colors knock out and the foreground color is lighter than the background color. The edge of the foreground color object is enlarged slightly to make the foreground color spread into the background color on press **1**.

Choke

The choke method of trapping is employed when the foreground color is darker than the background color. The edge of the foreground color object shrinks slightly as a result of overprinting. This is because the background color spreads into (chokes) the foreground color on press.

1 *In a **spread** trap, the foreground object color spreads into the background object color.*

Intro to Trapping

Shut your trap!

If you feel queasy about setting traps in QuarkXPress, let your output service provider do it for you.

To turn off trapping, go to QuarkXPress (Edit, in Windows) > Preferences > Print Layout > Trapping, and click Trapping Method: Knockout All. Choose this option if you're producing a PostScript file for a high-end separation system. It's also appropriate for some color composite printers.

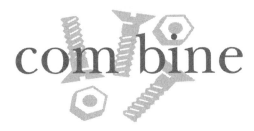

All of these objects (type and artwork) contain the process color magenta. Because they have this color **in common,** *trapping is unnecessary.*

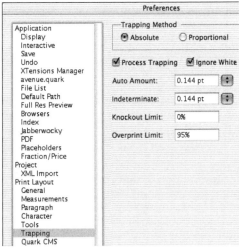

1 *Trapping preferences*

In QuarkXPress, trapping can be controlled using several features:

- On a **layout** basis using QuarkXPress (Edit, in Windows) > Preferences > Print Layout > **Trapping.**

- On an individual **color** basis using Edit > **Colors** (click Edit Trap).

- On an individual **item** basis using the **Show Trap Information** palette (Option-F12/Ctrl-F12).

The settings in Colors > Edit Trap override the settings in Trapping preferences. Trap Information palette settings override both the Edit > Colors > Edit Trap and the Trapping preferences settings.

To define automatic trap values and specify the defaults used by QuarkXPress for trapping object colors, you'll choose settings in the Trapping preferences dialog box.

To choose Trapping preferences for a whole layout:

1. Choose QuarkXPress (Edit, in Windows) > Preferences > Print Layout > Trapping **1**.

2. In the Trapping Method area (**1**, next page), choose Absolute to use the trapping value entered in the Auto Amount or Indeterminate field. The Auto Amount value is used if the foreground color is on top of a flat color. The Indeterminate value is used if the foreground color is on top of multiple shades or colors or over an imported picture. When the object color is darker, the background color chokes into the object color by the Auto Amount. When the foreground object color is lighter, the object color spreads into the background color by the Auto Amount.
or
Choose Proportional to use the trapping value entered in the Auto Amount field, multiplied by the difference in

(Continued on the following page)

Trapping Preferences

luminosity (lights and darks) between the foreground object color and the background color. The width of the trap will vary and be calculated by multiplying the Auto Amount value by the difference in luminosity between the object and background colors.

or

Choose Knockout All to turn trapping off for all objects. Objects will print with 0 trapping.

3. Check or uncheck Process Trapping. With Process Trapping on, each process component (cyan, magenta, yellow, and black) is spread or choked, depending on which one is darker—the foreground object or the background color. For example, if the cyan in the foreground object color is lighter than the cyan in the background color, the foreground object cyan is spread into the background cyan—but only on the cyan plate.

The trap width is equal to half the Auto Amount value when Absolute trapping is specified. When Proportional trapping is specified, the trap width will equal the Auto Amount value multiplied by the difference in luminosity values between the foreground object and background colors.

If Process Trapping is off, the same trapping value will be applied to all the process-color components, using the trapping settings for those colors as specified in the Colors > Edit Trap area.

4. Enter a trapping value in the Auto Amount field **2** or choose Overprint from the pop-up menu. Either the value entered or the Overprint setting will be used in the Trap Specifications dialog box (Edit > Colors > Edit Trap) and on the Trap Information palette whenever a field in either of these two locations is set to Auto Amount (+/-).

1 *Click a **Trapping Method**.*

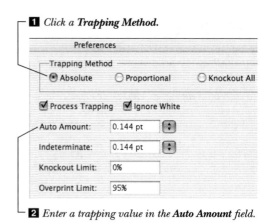

2 *Enter a trapping value in the **Auto Amount** field.*

Knockout Limit

If a color's gray value falls within the current Knockout Limit, that color knocks out the background color. The gray value is determined by subtracting a color's luminance value (as measured from its RGB components) from the number 1. This produces a percentage. The lighter the color, the lower the percentage. When the Knockout Limit is set to 10%, very light foreground colors knock out background colors, and medium light and darker foreground colors trap to the background color.

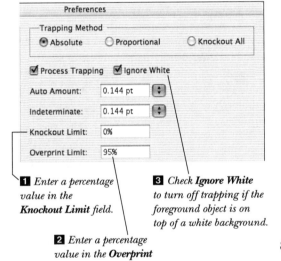

1 *Enter a percentage value in the **Knockout Limit** field.*

3 *Check **Ignore White** to turn off trapping if the foreground object is on top of a white background.*

2 *Enter a percentage value in the **Overprint Limit** field.*

5. Enter a trapping value in the Indeterminate field or choose Overprint from the pop-up menu. If a foreground object is over a background that consists of multiple shades or colors, or is over an imported picture, either the value you entered or the Overprint setting will be used.

6. Enter a Knockout Limit percentage **1** to set the gray (light and dark) value limit at which a foreground object color will knock out the background color (see the sidebar).

7. Enter an Overprint Limit value **2** for the shade percentage limit below which the foreground object color won't overprint the background color. For example, if the Overprint Limit is 92%, a foreground object that's 85% black won't overprint, even if that color or object is set to overprint via Edit > Colors > Edit Trap > Trap Specifications. The object will trap according to the Auto Amount value.

An Overprint setting chosen on the Trap Information palette will cause the selected object to overprint regardless of the current trap settings or any Overprint Limit value entered in any other dialog box.

8. Leave Ignore White checked **3** to turn off trapping for any instance in which the foreground object is on top of background areas that contain white and other colors. This is the preferred situation, since the white area won't be considered when the trap is calculated for the other colors.

With Ignore White unchecked, objects on a white background will overprint. If an object is set to spread over a background color, the Indeterminate value will be used for the spread.

9. Click OK to close the Preferences dialog box.

The Trap Specifications dialog box controls trapping on a color-by-color basis. The default settings for each color display in, and can be modified using, this dialog box.

Note: For these instructions, Absolute should be chosen as the Trapping Method in QuarkXPress (Edit, in Windows) > Preferences > Print Layout > Trapping.

To choose trapping values for a color (Trap Specifications):

1. Choose Edit > Colors (Shift-F12).
2. Click a color, then click Edit Trap **1**.
3. The name of the foreground color you chose will appear in the title bar of the Trap Specifications dialog box. Click one of the remaining colors listed, any of which could potentially be a background color **2**.
4. From the Trap drop-down menu **3**, choose:

   Default to have QuarkXPress determine how colors will be trapped. With Default chosen, black always overprints.

   Overprint to have the foreground color overprint the selected background color when the foreground color shade is equal to or greater than the Overprint Limit value specified in QuarkXPress (Edit, in Windows) > Preferences > Print Layout > Trapping.

   Knockout to have the foreground color knock out the selected background color.

   Auto Amount (+) to use the auto spread value for the foreground color.

   Auto Amount (–) to use the auto choke value for the foreground color.

   Custom to enter a custom spread or choke (negative) value for the foreground color.

   The Auto Amount and Overprint Limit settings were established in

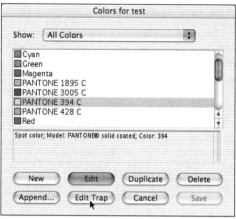

1 *Click a color, then click* ***Edit Trap***.

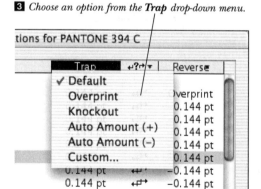

2 *The* ***Trap Specifications*** *dialog box opens.*

3 *Choose an option from the* ***Trap*** *drop-down menu.*

1 *Choose **Dependent Traps** or **Independent Traps** from the ↵?↷ drop-down menu.*

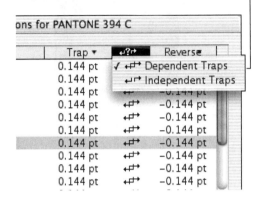

2 *Choose an option from the **Reverse** drop-down menu.*

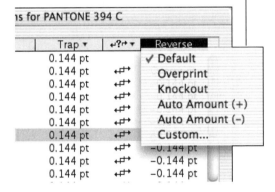

QuarkXPress (Edit, in Windows) > Preferences > Print Layout > Trapping.

5. From the second drop-down menu ↵?↷ ▼, choose Dependent traps (the default) to create the reverse trap situation for the colors you chose in steps 2 and 3, based on the current setting in the Trap column. Or choose Independent traps to create a unique trap setting in the Reverse column for these two colors **1**.

6. If Independent Traps is chosen in the second column, a different Trap setting for the currently highlighted color can be chosen **2**. This Reverse Trap setting will be used when the current highlighted color traps to the color named in the title bar of the dialog box. (If an option other than Default is chosen from the Reverse drop-down menu, an asterisk displays in the Reverse column.) The options are the same as in step 4.

Remember that when traps have a Dependent relationship, the Reverse column setting automatically derives from the current Trap column setting, and vice versa. Change either of these columns, and the other will change automatically. When traps have an independent relationship, unique settings can be set in these two columns.

7. Click OK, then click Save to close the Colors dialog box.

TIP Settings in the Trap Specifications dialog box override the settings in QuarkXPress (Edit, in Windows) > Preferences > Print Layout > Trapping.

TIP If a print layout is open when Edit > Colors is chosen, Edit Trap changes will apply only to the current layout. If no project is open, changes will apply to all subsequently created projects.

Trap Specifications

Note: Trap Information palette settings override the settings chosen in the Trapping preferences and Trap Specifications dialog boxes.

Note: For these instructions, Absolute should be chosen as the Trapping Method in QuarkXPress (Edit, in Windows) > Preferences > Print Layout > Trapping.

To choose trapping values for an object (Trap Information palette):

1. Choose Window > Show Trap Information to open the palette **1**.

2. Select the item to which you want to apply trapping.

3. Choose a new trap setting from any of the pop-up menus on the left side of the palette (the options will vary depending on the type of item chosen) **2**:

   Default to have the settings in Trapping preferences or Edit Trap be used to determine how colors will trap.

   Overprint to have the foreground item color overprint any background color.

   Knockout to have the foreground item color knock out any background color.

   Auto Amount (+) to have the auto spread value be used for the foreground color or Auto Amount (–) to have the auto choke value be used for the foreground color. The auto amount settings are established in QuarkXPress (Edit, in Windows) > Preferences > Print Layout > Trapping.

   Custom to enter a custom spread or choke (negative) value for the foreground color.

TIP Choosing Overprint from the palette will cause that item to overprint, regardless of the foreground or background color shade or the Overprint Limit value.

TIP To set trapping for text, highlight the text—the Text option on the palette will become available.

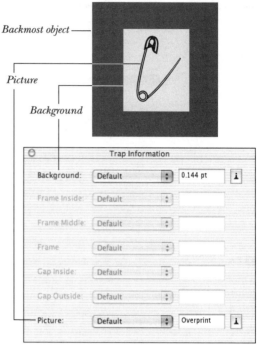

1 *This is the **Trap Information** palette with a picture box selected. Here, the Background color of the picture box (20% Black) defaults to a spread trap of the Auto Amount over the darker color underneath.*

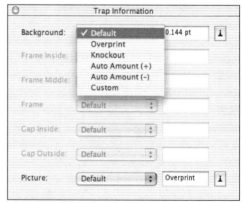

2 *The pop-up menu for trapping the **Background** color of a picture box*

Trap Information Palette

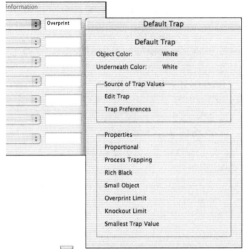

1 *Press the* [i] *icon on the Trap Information palette to display an explanation of the **Default Trap** setting. Here, the names of the two colors are listed; either the Edit Trap or the Trap Preferences dialog box is listed as the source of the trap decision (the **Source of Trap Values**); and the significant trap option (Property) Overprint Limit should be in boldface. We say "should be" because as of this writing, it's not working.*

2 *In this example, the text only partially overlaps a background color.*

What follows are guidelines for common trapping situations that may occur.

Trapping type

When it comes to trapping, a text box is treated like a single foreground object. The text box color will trap to the background color based on the current trap settings. When a text box with a background of None is on top of a background color, QuarkXPress will trap the type, even if the type itself isn't overlapping the background color **1**. This can occur with type that appears inside a large text box.

To control how text traps, select the text and set it to Overprint or Knockout via the Trap Information palette. You can also highlight individual characters or words and apply a unique trap setting to them that's different from the remaining characters in the box. Any box that's layered on top of a text box will trap to the background color of the text box—not to the type **2**.

QuarkXPress regards type that's partially on top of a paragraph rule as trapping to an indeterminate background color. If the type is completely within the paragraph rule, the type is trapped based on the type color-to-rule color relationship as per the Edit > Colors trap settings. This relationship can be changed only via Edit > Colors > Edit Trap.

Trapping a frame

A frame is layered on top of the contents of the box the frame is attached to. Using the Trap Information palette, you can apply different trapping settings to the inside, middle, and outside parts of a single-line or multiline frame, and to the gaps in a dashed frame.

Trapping imported pictures

In QuarkXPress, a picture can't be spread or choked to a background color.

Trapping adjustments that are made to a vector (object-oriented) picture in a

(Continued on the following page)

Trap Type, Frame, Pictures

drawing program, such as Adobe Illustrator, will output successfully from QuarkXPress. The Trap Information palette provides no trapping controls for the picture itself. *Note:* Don't scale an imported vector picture that was created with built-in trapping, because such scaling will also resize the trapping areas in the picture.

You can use the Trap Information palette to specify that a raster (bitmap) picture knock out or overprint a background color. This is helpful if you're colorizing a grayscale TIFF picture in QuarkXPress. Click on a picture, then choose Overprint or Knockout from the Picture pop-up menu on the Trap Information palette—whichever setting your commercial printer instructs you to choose.

A line art (black and white) picture to which you've applied a shade of black that's equal to or greater than the Overprint Limit in QuarkXPress will overprint any background color(s) it's positioned on top of. Use the Trap Information palette to set the picture to knock out, if desired.

Lines and boxes in QuarkXPress can knock out, overprint, or trap to pictures that are underneath them. Use the Trap Information palette to set the type of trap. Type can knock out, overprint, or spread to a picture underneath it.

Trapping bitmaps

You can apply trapping to some types of bitmap pictures via the Trap Information palette, including:

Grayscale TIFF (8-bit)

Black-and-white TIFF (1-bit)

RGB TIFF

CMYK TIFF

Colorized grayscale TIFF

Trapping can't be applied to an EPS in QuarkXPress.

Trap Pictures

XML "basics"

XML (Extensible Markup Language) is a simple structured language that helps manage information by identifying data, be it data you enter directly into the XML file or data in a text or database file. Once identified, that data can be selectively extracted and placed in other files or organized in ways that differ from the original source. XML data can be output as HTML files for the Web or can be used for print output. The avenue.quark XTension, which converts QuarkXPress content into XML format, is included with QuarkXPress 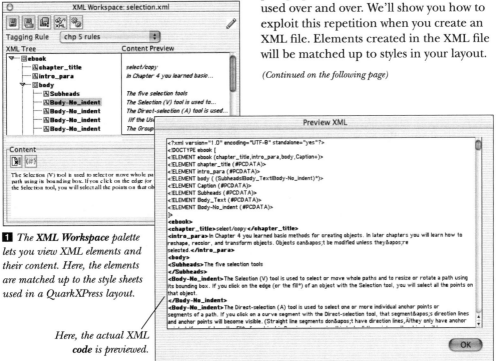.

In this chapter you'll be working with elements, which are fields of text or data. Each element can hold a specific piece of content (e.g., name, address, zip code). XML is used to define elements and the relationships among those elements. When generating the final XML output, elements can be selectively chosen and arranged.

Publications such as books, magazines, and newsletters have styles that appear repetitively. For example, a book's chapter header is repeated in every chapter. Similarly, magazine layouts have title, byline, intro paragraph, and body copy styles that are used over and over. We'll show you how to exploit this repetition when you create an XML file. Elements created in the XML file will be matched up to styles in your layout.

(Continued on the following page)

XML in QuarkXPress

❶ The **XML Workspace** palette lets you view XML elements and their content. Here, the elements are matched up to the style sheets used in a QuarkXPress layout.

Here, the actual XML **code** is previewed.

In QuarkXPress, style sheets are applied to different categories of text (header, intro paragraph, body, caption, etc.). The avenue.quark XTension matches up each element name with a style sheet name. Text from any paragraph that has a style sheet applied to it can be placed into a specific XML element. In this chapter, you'll learn how to create some basic XML elements and then associate them with existing style sheets in a QuarkXPress layout.

A person experienced in writing XML can go on to control the arrangement of the elements that hold the QuarkXPress content. Elements can be assigned a specific order to determine how the content is to be displayed in its output format, whether that format is print, the Web, or CD-ROM. By separating the content of a QuarkXPress file (text and pictures) from the structure of the original QuarkXPress layout (the arrangement of style sheets on a page), XML makes it possible to display that content in a variety of ways and in a variety of different output media.

For QuarkXPress users, the power of XML is that it can automatically extract content from any QuarkXPress layout based on style sheets that were assigned to that content. The XML elements will contain only the text content, though—not the style information from the style sheet or the appearance of the layout (see the sidebar at upper right).

Furthermore, a dynamic link can be set up between an XML file and the original QuarkXPress file. With this link in place, if text in the QuarkXPress file is edited, the elements that hold the content in the XML file will update automatically.

XML blues

Currently, only the Internet Explorer 5 (and later) and Netscape 6 (and later) Web browsers can translate XML code into properly styled, readable content. These browsers, though, don't always comprehend all the XML code (read: lots of alert error boxes).

If you drag your completed XML file into a browser window, you'll probably see both the text content and the XML tag codes. This is because the browser needs some sort of style sheet file, usually a cascading style sheet (CSS) file, to help it interpret the display style of the text (and hide the code). (Cascading style sheets aren't covered in this book.)

Neither browser supports the XML code that references external picture files. So even if the XML text does display, no pictures will display on an XML page. Sorry.

Just a start

From this introductory chapter to XML, you'll get a glimpse of the many roles XML plays. XML is very complex, though, and worthy of many books on its own. If and when you're ready to learn more, check out these sources:

XML for the World Wide Web: Visual QuickStart Guide, by Elizabeth Castro, Peachpit Press.

www.w3.org, the Web site for the World Wide Web Consortium, which is the main standards body for all things Web.

Using elements

Elements in a DTD are similar to fields in a database. The more specific the fields are, the more specific will be the content they contain, and the more varied the ways the content can be extracted and organized, depending on the desired output medium (print or Web).

For comparison, think of a mail merge function, where each line of an address is defined as an individual element. Rearranging the elements would alter how the individual lines of the address could be displayed. Specified lines of the address could be used in an output document (say, using just names and business titles) without using the remaining lines of the address. In the case of XML, all the rearranging and reorganizing is controlled by selectively choosing which elements will be in the XML file.

DTDs?!? Relax...

Writing a DTD is neither the most necessary nor most critical part of using XML with QuarkXPress. In fact, it may be better to use an industry-standard DTD that's already been written for your type of business. Using an industry-standard DTD assures compatibility when XML data is exchanged with other users in similar businesses.

The critical parts of learning the avenue.quark XTension for XML are one, understanding how to use the XML Tree on the XML Workspace palette, and two, setting up the tagging rules for the XML file. These areas will be explained in this chapter. So relax!

XML and DTDs

A DTD (short for "document type definition") is a plain text file that's created using a simple text editor. A DTD specifies which elements will be in an XML file, the kind of information that can be put into an element, the order of the elements in the XML file, and which elements can contain subelements (nested elements). Although a DTD isn't required for creating XML files, it helps control the relationships among elements and helps keep elements consistent between different XML files. QuarkXPress's implementation of XML requires a DTD file.

Complex DTDs are usually created by specialized administrative or technical support personnel. For the individual designer using QuarkXPress, a variation of an existing DTD can serve as a framework for creating individual DTDs for each type of QuarkXPress layout that will be translated into HTML or other output media.

The XML format is best suited for extracting and transferring text content from multiple QuarkXPress files whose style sheets have an orderly progression (e.g., title, subhead, body copy, and so on). For small, individual HTML projects, you can create a new Web layout right in Quark-XPress. In fact, this whole XML step in between may be overkill for a small project, but the decision is yours.

Starting out with XML

Before you can create an XML file and tag existing content in a QuarkXPress file, you have to define a DTD. To make things easier, you can base the new DTD on an existing one. A simple DTD need only contain elements that represent the style sheet names used in an existing Quark-XPress layout. You will also create a container element to define the order and interrelationships among elements in the XML file.

(Continued on the following page)

In QuarkXPress, DTD elements display on the XML Tree, which is located on the XML Workspace palette. On the XML Tree, elements are displayed hierarchically, from top level to sublevel, as defined in the DTD file.

Key parts of a DTD

The DTD references a root element, which is the overall keyword that categorizes all the data to be contained in the XML elements. Technically, the XML file will specify the root element, but for clarity, the DTD should reference a root element in an opening comment.

Each element must be declared (defined) in order to establish what kind of content it can contain. If an element is going to contain child elements (subelements of the parent element), those child elements must be listed in the declaration of the parent element. A parent element is just a container for child element names. Child elements are nested under parent elements on the XML Tree on the XML Workspace palette.

If content from the QuarkXPress file is to be arranged in a particular sequence, the container element declares the layout order of its child elements for the resulting XML file. This order can be the exact layout order of content in the QuarkXPress layout, or it can be given a new structure so that its order differs from that of the content in the QuarkXPress layout.

The DTD you'll create by following the instructions on the next page contains a parent element, which in turn contains child elements that will be matched up with the various style sheets that were applied to a story in a QuarkXPress layout. This arrangement will allow you to quickly place the content of the entire story into the child elements.

Mind your p's and q's

XML and DTD element names are case-sensitive. Switching between capital and lowercase letters for different occurrences of an element name could cause an XML parser (the software that interprets XML data) to interpret each occurrence as a different element. XML and DTD element names must begin with a letter or an underscore (_); the remaining characters in the name can be letters, underscores, numbers, colons, hyphens, or periods—but NOT spaces or tabs!

Parent and child elements

- Declaring an element as a container element makes it a parent and determines which elements are nested within it (its children).

- The XML Tree on the XML Workspace palette represents element relationships as defined in the DTD. On the XML Tree, a parent element occupies a higher position (is less indented), and each child element is nested below its parent **1**.

- Sibling elements reside on the same indent level on the tree.

- The topmost element on the tree is usually the root element. All elements that are declared within this element in the DTD will occupy the next level on the tree.

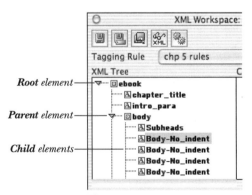

1 *The XML Tree, showing three types of elements*

Note: Before creating a DTD, make sure your QuarkXPress layout contains paragraph style sheets for different categories of text, such as a title style sheet and an intro paragraph style sheet, and make sure they're applied to the appropriate text. Use your style sheet names for the element names to be created in the following steps (they don't have to match ours) **1**.

To create a simple DTD:

1. Open a plain-text editor, such as TextEdit in Mac OS X or WordPad in Windows. If you use Microsoft Word, you must save the file in Text Only file format.

2. Type the first line, and type a comment line stating what the root element will be. Comment lines are written as follows: <!-- comment text here --> **2**. For each separate line of code, press Return/Enter only after the ">".

3. Declare (define) the root element as an element, and, in parentheses after the root element name, type the elements that are to be listed on the next

top level on the XML Tree on the XML Workspace palette **3**. All elements are contained in the root element. Create elements with names taken from your style sheets that are applied to the text that you want to include in the XML file. For example, all of our layouts contain a chapter title that's styled with a "chapter title" style sheet. We want title text in the XML file, so we'll create an XML element (named "chapter_title," for simplicity's sake) to hold that text.

All elements must be enclosed, meaning that the line of code must start with "<!" and end with ">".

Note: Our layouts have only one chapter title item, intro paragraph item, and body item, but many caption items. We therefore placed a "+" after the Caption element name to force avenue.quark to create multiple caption elements during the tagging phase. See the sidebar on the next page for more information on symbols. Tagging is discussed on pages 480–483.

(Continued on the following page)

```
<?xml version="1.0" encoding="UTF-8"?>
<!--    NAME:     vqs-ebook-txt    -->
<!--    Root element is ebook       -->
<!ELEMENT ebook (chapter_title, intro_para, body, Caption+)>
<!ELEMENT body (Subheads | Body_Text | Body-No_indent)*>
<!ELEMENT Subheads (#PCDATA)>
<!ELEMENT Body_Text (#PCDATA)>
<!ELEMENT Body-No_indent (#PCDATA)>
<!ELEMENT chapter_title (#PCDATA)>
<!ELEMENT intro_para (#PCDATA)>
<!ELEMENT Caption (#PCDATA)>
```

1 *This **DTD** code was created in a text editor. The element name (the word after "<!ELEMENT") was declared using style sheet names from our layout (Subheads, Body_Text, Body-No_indent, chapter_title, intro_para, Caption). You should use style sheet names from your layout as the element names.*

```
<!--    Root element is ebook       -->
```
2 *Comment line*

```
<!ELEMENT ebook (chapter_title, intro_para, body, Caption+)>
```
3 *Declaring the root element*

Create a DTD

4. Declare the elements that were listed in the parentheses in the previous step. End each noncontainer (nonparent) element line with "(#PCDATA)" (parsed character data). This code tells the XML parser (the software that interprets XML data) that those elements may contain text or processing instructions **1**. The elements can be declared in any order within the DTD.

5. For an instance such as a story that contains more than one paragraph style sheet, we've defined a body element. Now we need to declare it. List the element "body," and then, in parentheses, create all the child elements to be included in this parent element, using names based on the paragraph style sheet names whose content you want placed into the XML file **2**. Don't create elements for style sheet names that define content you don't want. Remember, you're trying to control which content will be included in the XML file.

The vertical bar "I" represents an either/or option. Any one of these style sheet names can be present in the story. The exact order and presence of style sheets in the story isn't important, because the body element will gather content from any one of or all of those styles for placement into its elements.

DTD quantity symbols

When placed at the end of an element name, the DTD symbols listed below indicate how many times that nested element will occur within the main element above it. These symbols provide greater flexibility for handling the order and frequency of content to be tagged into elements. They also display on the DTD Tree in the Edit Tagging Rules dialog box (see page 482).

Symbol	Indicates
No symbol	only once
?	zero (none) or once
+	one or more times
*	zero (none), one, or more times

```
<!ELEMENT chapter_title (#PCDATA)>
<!ELEMENT intro_para (#PCDATA)>
<!ELEMENT Caption (#PCDATA)>
```
1 *Declaring elements*

```
<!ELEMENT body (Subheads | Body_Text | Body-No_indent)*>
```
2 *The **body element** is declared as a **container** element and is the parent to the child elements that are listed within the parentheses. These child elements will match up with style sheet names used in the QuarkXPress story. On the XML Tree on the XML Workspace palette, the child elements will be nested under the parent body element. Type each line of code as one line.*

```
<!ELEMENT Subheads (#PCDATA)>
<!ELEMENT Body_Text (#PCDATA)>
<!ELEMENT Body-No_indent (#PCDATA)>
```

1 *Declare the **child elements** (listed in the body element) that will hold content from style sheets with the same name in the QuarkXPress story.*

An asterisk "*" symbol after the closing parenthesis indicates that zero (none), one, or more than one occurrence of an element may occur in body text. (This code symbol helps prevent the XML parser from returning an error.) By placing the symbol outside the parentheses, the body element can have none, one, or all of the listed style sheet names present, in any order and in any frequency, when the content of a QuarkXPress story is tagged to the body element. If an asterisk is inserted immediately after an element name, it will apply only to that element.

Note: Currently, when a line of code that defines a parent container element includes a quantity symbol outside the parentheses, none of the child elements will initially display on the XML Tree. The child elements will display once you tag an item in your layout to the parent element (see our instructions for tagging on page 482).

6. Declare the child elements listed in the parent element in the previous step **1**. At this point, you've matched up XML elements with paragraph style sheets in the layout whose content you want in the XML file. Elements are defined either in the first element line ("ebook," in our example) or in the body element line. All the defined elements are then declared in subsequent lines. You can only declare an element that's been referenced in the first element line or in a parent container line.

7. Using your style sheet names, make sure your file matches the structure of our DTD example. Then save the file as plain text or text only, with the .dtd extension. In Mac OS X, TextEdit files require the .txt extension.

Now you'll incorporate the DTD file into a new XML file.

To create an XML file:

1. Display a QuarkXPress print layout that is to be tagged.

2. Choose File > New > XML (Cmd-X/ Ctrl-X).

3. In the New XML dialog box, click Custom.xmt on the Template list to create an XML file **1**.
   or
   Click an existing XML template file (.xmt) on the Template list on which to base the new XML file. Any .xmt files that are located in the QuarkXPress/ Templates folder or directory will be listed. Read more about templates on page 478.

4. Click Import, locate your DTD file, then click Open.

5. Make sure the root element you referenced in the DTD is chosen from the Root Element pop-up menu.

6. Click OK. The XML Workspace palette will open **2**–**3**. Leave this palette open as you proceed with the next set of instructions.

TIP Once you click OK, you can't change which DTD or root element is assigned to this XML file. If you want to edit a DTD or choose a different DTD or root element, you'll have to make a new XML file.

TIP On the XML Tree on the XML Workspace palette, click the arrowhead/+ sign to the left of an element to expand/collapse the outline and view its nested child elements, if any. In our example, the body element won't display any child elements until after it's tagged (see page 482).

To open an existing XML file:

1. Choose File > Open.

2. Locate the .xml file, then click Open.

(left margin) **Create, Open XML File**

XML Tree symbols

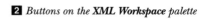

■ An element defined as (#PCDATA)

▣ A parent element

☐ An empty element

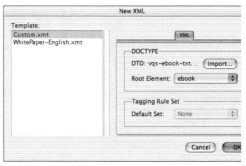

1 *The New XML dialog box*

2 *Buttons on the XML Workspace palette*

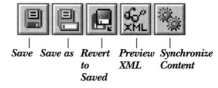

Save   Save as   Revert   Preview   Synchronize
to   XML   Content
Saved

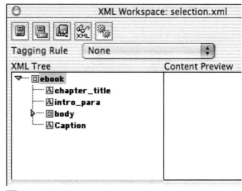

3 *The XML Tree on the XML Workspace palette derives its structure from the DTD, with the root element at the top and the elements contained in the root element declaration below.*

The first step in the process of converting QuarkXPress files to XML is to link paragraph style sheet names in a QuarkXPress layout to elements that have been defined in a DTD and that are listed on the XML Tree on the XML Workspace palette. After that, you'll follow the steps on page 480 to associate an XML file with a tagging rule set, and finally, you'll tag the content of a layout for inclusion in the XML elements.

To create tagging rules:

1. Display your QuarkXPress layout, then choose Edit > Tagging Rules.

2. Click New Set.

3. Type a Name for the rule set **1**.

4. Click an element name on the DTD Tree, click Add Rule, check Style Sheet in the Rule Settings area, then choose the desired paragraph style sheet name from the pop-up menu.

5. Check "New tag for each paragraph" to have avenue.quark tag each paragraph style sheet occurrence as a separate element in the XML file.

Where the DTD Tree comes from

The DTD Tree shown in the Edit Tagging Rules dialog box derives from the parent and child elements as defined in the DTD. To change what's listed on the DTD tree, you'd have to redefine (rewrite) the elements in the DTD file.

6. Repeat steps 4 and 5 for each of the other elements that you want matched up with style sheet names. At any time, you can click Duplicate to duplicate the currently selected rule or click Delete to delete the currently selected rule.

7. Click OK.

8. Click Save to save the rule set. The new tagging rule set will be listed on the Tagging Rule Set pop-up menu on the XML Workspace palette.

TIP The DTD and <root element> used by the current XML file will appear in the DOCTYPE: field in the Tagging Rules dialog box and on the title bar of the Edit Tagging Rules dialog box.

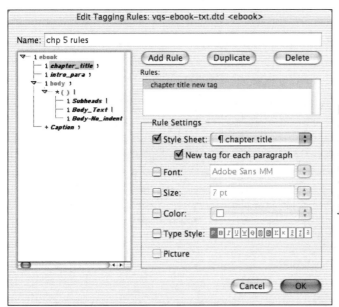

1 *In the Edit Tagging Rules dialog box for our file, the "chapter_title" element has a rule setting that links it to the chapter title style sheet. The words "new tag" appear next to the chosen style sheet name because New tag for each paragraph is checked.*

Once a relationship is established between QuarkXPress style sheets and XML elements, as defined in the tagging rule set, the contents of any QuarkXPress layout that uses style sheets of the same name can be selectively copied into the elements of that particular XML file. By controlling which elements are used when outputting an XML file, you can control which QuarkXPress content will be output. The original content of the QuarkXPress layout is preserved and is used as the content source.

To save an XML file:

1. Click the Save (first) button 🖺 on the XML Workspace palette.

2. Enter a name in the Save As/File name field and choose a location **1**.

3. From the Type pop-up menu, choose XML Document or avenue.quark Template.

4. From the Encoding pop-up menu, choose UTF-8 (this is a Unicode specification that includes European and Asian font characters).

5. Check Save XML as Standalone to embed the DTD code into the XML file. If this option is left unchecked, for the XML file to be reopened and worked with, an external DTD file associated with this XML file must be available to avenue.quark.

   Technical note: This option sets the value of the standalone=yes/no declaration in the first line of XML code, and it also determines whether the DTD code will be stored internally in the XML file or referenced as an external file.

6. *Optional:* Check Exclude avenue.quark Processing Instruction to save the XML file without the extra avenue.quark code. With this option checked, you won't be able to reopen the XML file in avenue.quark.

7. Click Save.

DTD Tree symbols

The symbols that appear to the left of element names on the DTD Tree in the Edit Tagging Rules dialog box reflect how many times that nested element will occur within the main parent element above it. (For a definition of each symbol, see the sidebar on page 474.)

■ If an element name is bold and black, it means tagging rules can be created for it.

■ If an element name is bold, black, *and* italic, it means at least one tagging rule has already been assigned to that element.

The character next to an element name (the "," or "|") is the same character that was used to separate elements that were declared in a container element in the DTD. The container element defines what the child elements are and how frequently they occur.

XML templates

New XML files can be based on an existing **XML template** (such files have an .xmt extension). The new file won't write over the template. By default, XML templates are saved in the QuarkXPress/Templates folder.

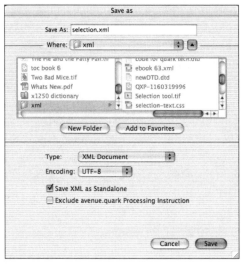

1 *The **Save as** dialog box for an **XML** file*

Preview XML tips

■ You can select and/or copy lines of text in the Preview XML dialog box, but you can't edit the code or the content.

■ A preview of the XML code in our example of a DTD would show a "<body>" tag, followed by a child tag named for the style sheet that's applied to the first paragraph in the story. The child's text content would be surrounded by "< >" brackets. The "</body>" tag marks the end of the body element.

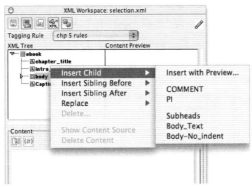

1 The **XML Tree** submenus, showing options for modifying the XML Tree

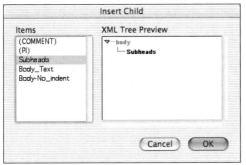

2 This dialog box opened after we chose Insert Sibling Before > **Insert with Preview** on the XML Workspace palette. From the list on the left, we chose an element to be inserted. The XML Tree previews on the right.

TIP To save a variation of an XML file, click the Save As (second) button on the XML Workspace palette. Change the name and/or location, change any of the options as discussed in steps 3–6 on the previous page, then click Save.

To preview an XML file:

Click the Preview XML button on the XML Workspace palette. XML code, the code from the DTD, and any tagged content will be listed in the dialog box. Click OK when you're done.

To edit the XML Tree:

1. On the XML Workspace palette, click an element on the XML Tree.

2. Control-click/Right-click the element, and then, from the XML Tree sub-menu, choose one of these options **1**:

Insert Child: A nested element will be inserted.

Insert Sibling Before or Insert Sibling After: An element on the same level of the tree will be inserted.

Replace: The selected element will be replaced by another element.

Delete: The selected element will be deleted.

Show Content Source: The selected element's content will be highlighted in the current QuarkXPress layout.

3. From one of the Insert Child or Sibling submenus or the Replace submenu:

Choose Insert (or Replace) with Preview to preview changes to the XML Tree. Elements that are available for insertion or replacement will be listed on the left side of the dialog box **2**. Click OK to accept the change (or click Cancel to reject it).

or

Choose an element from the list at the bottom of the submenu to have that

(Continued on the following page)

element be inserted or replaced at the currently selected point on the tree.

The XML Tree will update accordingly.

TIP To revert an XML file to its last saved state, click the Revert to Saved button ![icon] on the XML Workspace palette.

To close an XML file:

Click the close button in the upper left corner (Mac OS X)/upper right corner (Windows) of the XML Workspace palette.

Your next step is to tag the QuarkXPress content to the elements in the XML file. avenue.quark will read through an existing QuarkXPress layout and match the style sheet names found in the text with the tagging rules (the name connections) that you just assigned to elements defined in the DTD and that are contained in the XML file. The process is automatic: All you have to do is Cmd-drag/Ctrl-drag the selected text box onto an element on the XML Tree on the XML Workspace palette, and avenue.quark will do the rest.

To tag the content of a QuarkXPress layout:

1. Open an XML file, then display the QuarkXPress layout that you're going to use as the content source for that XML file.

2. Choose a tagging rule set from the Tagging Rule pop-up menu.

3. Choose the Item tool, click in a text box, then Cmd-drag/Ctrl-drag the box over an element name on the XML Tree **1**. A + (plus) icon will display as you drag. Release the mouse when a rectangular selection frame appears around the element name.

4. Click OK. The content of the selected element will display in the Content Preview panel on the XML Workspace palette.

Multiple palettes

More than one XML file can be open at a time, and each file will have its own XML Workspace palette. The palette title bar will indicate the file to which the palette belongs. The currently active XML Workspace palette has an edit icon ![pencil icon] in its upper right corner.

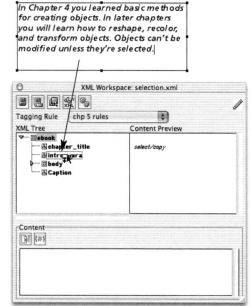

1 *Cmd-drag/Ctrl-drag a text box onto the appropriate element name on the **XML Tree**. The first few words of content will display in the **Content Preview** panel. Here we're dragging a text box containing a paragraph styled with the "intro para" style onto the "intro_para" element name. The connection between the style sheet and the element was created in the Edit Tagging Rules dialog box.*

Note: If the element already contains text, then that existing text will be replaced by the newly tagged text.

TIP Tagged QuarkXPress text is enclosed within yellow highlighted < and > brackets in the layout.

TIP Any QuarkXPress file whose content has been tagged to elements in an XML file will also open when you open that XML file.

To remove the content of an element:

1. Click an element on the XML Tree on the XML Workspace palette.

2. Control-click/Right-click an element name, and then, from the Replace submenu, choose the same element name to remove its current content (e.g., to remove "intro_para" element content, you would choose "intro_para" from the submenu). Retag to add new content to the element.

TIP The Delete Content option on the context menu isn't available for content that's placed via tagging.

The method described on this page is the fastest way to convert QuarkXPress text content into XML. If you've structured your "body" XML element according to the parent/child relationship used in our DTD, this method should work. *Note:* In order for a paragraph with an applied style sheet to become the source of content for a declared element, you first have to create a rule that links the style sheet name to an element name by using the Edit Tagging Rules dialog box.

To tag a story that uses multiple style sheets:

1. Make sure the desired tagging rule set is chosen from the Tagging Rule pop-up menu on the XML Workspace palette **1**. The Tagging Rules command created connections (links) between the layout's style sheet names and the XML elements.

2. Click in a story (text box) in a QuarkXPress print layout.

3. Cmd-drag/Ctrl-drag the text box over the desired element on the XML Tree (using our example, the "body" element gained nested child elements on the XML Tree) **2**. Each child element represents a style sheet that was declared in the DTD, specified as a rule in the tagging rule set, and found in the story in the QuarkXPress layout. (This is the main reason we specified that these elements were to be organized within the body container element in the DTD. Without this parent/child relationship, you couldn't automatically tag an entire story!)

TIP More than one story can be tagged to the same parent element. The child elements of the second story will display on the palette following the elements of the first story that was tagged, regardless of where the stories are located in the QuarkXPress layout.

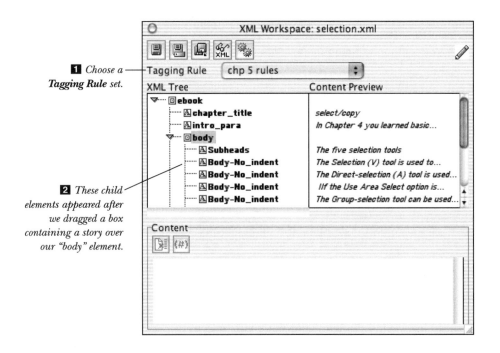

1 *Choose a Tagging Rule set.*

2 *These child elements appeared after we dragged a box containing a story over our "body" element.*

XML Workspace: selection.xml

Tagging Rule — chp 5 rules

XML Tree — Content Preview

- ebook
  - chapter_title — select/copy
  - intro_para — In Chapter 4 you learned basic...
  - **body**
    - Subheads — The five selection tools
    - Body-No_indent — The Selection (V) tool is used to...
    - Body-No_indent — The Direct-selection (A) tool is used...
    - Body-No_indent — IIf the Use Area Select option is...
    - Body-No_indent — The Group-selection tool can be used...

Content

Tag a Story

Do you know where your pictures are?

We don't have room in this QuickStart Guide to show you the code that would be required in the DTD for avenue.quark to tag picture boxes and store picture file names. Besides, as of this writing, neither Internet Explorer nor Netscape can interpret the XML code that's used to reference external picture files, so no pictures would display on the XML page in those browsers anyway.

Guidelines for tagging multiple caption boxes

The following comments apply to the Caption element that we declared in the DTD code (see page 473).

- To tag a single caption text box to the XML Tree, you can drag the box over the Caption element **1** or over its parent element, ebook.

- To tag multiple caption text boxes to the XML Tree, you need to drag each caption text box over its parent element, ebook. Doing this will create multiple caption elements, each one containing the content of a single caption box.

  Remember, in the DTD, we inserted a + after the word "Caption" when we declared it as part of the ebook element.

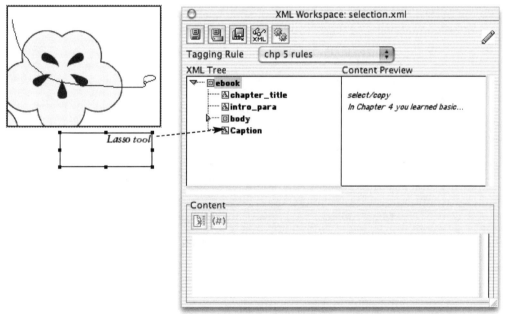

1 *In this example, a caption box is being tagged using our DTD structure. The caption content will be contained in the Caption element.*

Text in a QuarkXPress layout that's been tagged to elements in an XML file is, by default, dynamically linked, meaning that if you edit the text in the QuarkXPress file, the element content will update automatically. To manually update the content in an XML file to match the current content of the QuarkXPress layout, click the Synchronize Content button on the XML Workspace palette **1**, then click Yes. You'll need to do this manual update any time you choose Revert to Saved in the Quark-XPress file or if Enable Dynamic Content Update is unchecked in QuarkXPress (Edit, in Windows) > Preferences > Application > avenue.quark.

Beware! You can't undo the Break Dynamic Link command, which you'll learn to use in these instructions. What you can do, however, is use the Replace command on the context menu to remove any text content and then retag the QuarkXPress text to the element to reestablish a dynamic link.

To break the link between an element and its content:

1. On the XML Tree on the XML Workspace palette, click the element you want to break the link from **2**.

2. Click the Break Dynamic Link button 🔳 in the lower part of the palette **3**.

1 *Synchronize Content button*

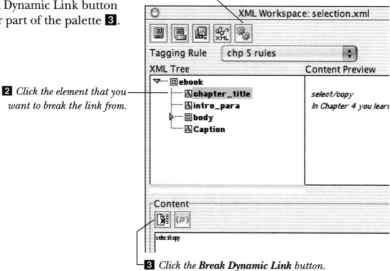

2 *Click the element that you want to break the link from.*

3 *Click the Break Dynamic Link button.*

Creating sequences

The Sequences palette enables you to create a sequence (list) of items contained in a QuarkXPress layout and then tag the entire sequence to the elements in the XML Tree in a single step.

To create a new sequence:

1. Display a QuarkXPress print layout.

2. Open the Sequences palette, then click the New Sequence button **1**.

3. Leave the sequence name selected on the palette.

4. Select an item in the QuarkXPress layout.

5. Click the Add Item button on the Sequences palette to add the item to the newly-named sequence. This button is available only when a sequence or item name is selected on the palette and an item is selected in a Quark-XPress layout.

6. Repeat steps 4–5 to add other items to the sequence.

TIP To delete an individual item or an entire sequence from the list, click the applicable name, then click the Delete button. This can't be undone.

Create Sequence

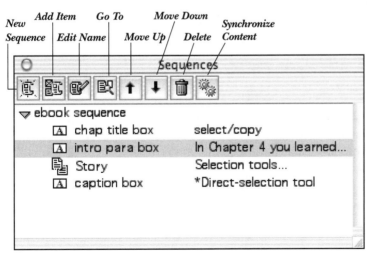

New Sequence Add Item Edit Name Go To Move Up Move Down Delete Synchronize Content

⬇ ebook sequence
  [A] chap title box   select/copy
  [A] intro para box   In Chapter 4 you learned...
  🗐 Story   Selection tools...
  [A] caption box   *Direct-selection tool

1 *The Sequences palette, showing a sequence of items: The first few words of text are listed next to each item.*

To rename a sequence or any item on the list:

1. Click a sequence or item name on the Sequences palette, then click the Edit Name button. 🗹

or

Cmd-click/Ctrl-click an item name on the list.

2. Type the desired Box Name **1**, then click OK.

The order in which items are selected and added to the sequence determines their order on the list and in the XML file. The position of any item on the list can be changed.

To move an item to a different position on the list:

1. Click an item name on the Sequences palette list **2**.

2. Click the Move Up ⬆ or Move Down button ⬇ on the palette **3** to move the item one step upward or downward at a time. Keep clicking the arrow, if desired, to move the item further upward or downward.

To add an item to a sequence:

1. Expand a sequence list on the Sequences palette by clicking its arrowhead/+ sign.

2. Click the name of the item on the sequence list below which you want the new item to be added.

3. Select an item in the QuarkXPress layout.

4. Click the Add Item button 🔲 on the Sequences palette. The new item will be listed on the palette, below the item you selected in step 2.

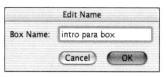

1 *Use the Edit Name dialog box to rename an item or sequence.*

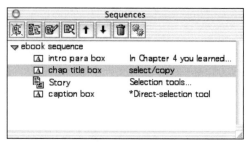

2 *Click an item name on the Sequences palette.*

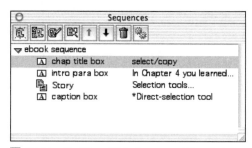

3 *Clicking the Move Up button caused the selected item to move upward on the list.*

Rename Sequence; Move, Add Item

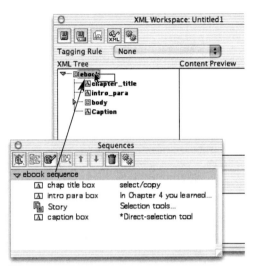

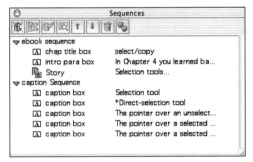

1 *Cmd-drag/Ctrl-drag a sequence name over the root element (topmost element) on the **XML Tree** on the XML Workspace palette.*

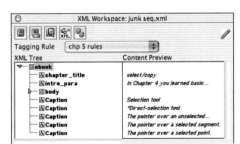

2 *The **Sequences** palette displays a new sequence that was created for caption boxes.*

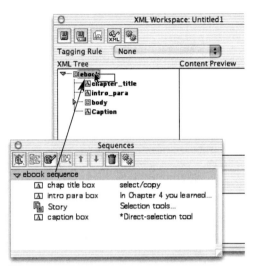

3 *After the new sequence is tagged onto the XML Tree, a new caption element is generated for each caption box from that sequence.*

Before a sequence can be tagged, a tagging rule set must be chosen for the current XML file. The rules define the associations between the style sheets in the currrent QuarkXPress layout and the elements in the XML file.

To tag a sequence:

1. Display the Sequences palette, the relevant XML file, and the QuarkXPress layout.

2. Make sure the appropriate tagging rule set is chosen from the pop-up menu on the XML Workspace palette.

3. Cmd-drag/Ctrl-drag the sequence name from the Sequences palette over the root element (the topmost element) on the XML Tree on the XML Workspace palette **1**. avenue.quark will automatically tag all the items listed.

TIP Defined nested child elements are matched up automatically with style sheet names that occur in a story if two conditions are met: First, a DTD container element that defines which child elements can be contained within that parent element was declared, and second, the style sheets were assigned to DTD elements via a tagging rule set.

To create a sequence of several caption boxes on the Sequences palette for quick tagging, follow these steps:

To tag multiple caption boxes to an element:

1. On the Sequences palette, create a new sequence, then select and add each caption box to that new sequence **2**.

2. Cmd-drag/Ctrl-drag the new sequence name from the Sequences palette over the root element on the XML Tree. A caption element will be created for each box in the new sequence **3**.

Tag Sequence

You can use the Sequences palette to navigate through an open QuarkXPress layout.

To go to an item in a layout:

Click an item name on the Sequences palette list **1**, then click the Go To button **2**. ▣
or
Double-click an item name on the palette.

The chosen item will become selected, and it will be displayed in the current QuarkXPress project window.

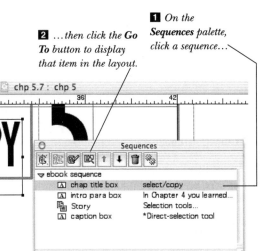

2 *...then click the* **Go To** *button to display that item in the layout.*

1 *On the* **Sequences** *palette, click a sequence...*

After a sequence of items has been created in a QuarkXPress layout, you can automatically update the item content listed on the Sequences palette with the current contents of the QuarkXPress layout.

Note: Even if you don't synchronize the content that's displayed for an item in a sequence, the most current QuarkXPress content will be used when the sequence is tagged to the XML elements.

To synchronize the content of a QuarkXPress layout with items in a sequence:

With the QuarkXPress file open, on the Sequences palette, click the Synchronize Content button. ▣ The content that's displayed for all the items in the sequence will be updated with the current content of the QuarkXPress layout.

Go To Item; Synchronize Content

Special Characters A

Zapf Dingbats: Mac OS X and Windows

Dingbat	Key Combo Mac/Win	ASCII	Dingbat	Key Combo Mac/Win	ASCII
	space	32	✙	: (Shift-;)	58
✂	! (Shift-1)	33	✚	;	59
✂	" (Shift-')	34	✛	< (Shift-,)	60
✄	# (Shift-3)	35	✝	=	61
✄	$ (Shift-4)	36	✞	> (Shift-.)	62
☎	% (Shift-5)	37	✟	? (Shift-/)	63
✆	& (Shift-7)	38	✠	@ (Shift-2)	64
✈	'	39	✡	A	65
✈	((Shift-0)	40	✢	B	66
✉	) (Shift-9)	41	✣	C	67
☛	* (Shift-8)	42	✤	D	68
☞	+ (Shift-=)	43	✥	E	69
✌	,	44	✦	F	70
✍	-	45	✧	G	71
✎	.	46	★	H	72
✏	/	47	☆	I	73
✐	0	48	✪	J	74
✑	1	49	✫	K	75
✒	2	50	✬	L	76
✓	3	51	✭	M	77
✔	4	52	✮	N	78
✕	5	53	✯	O	79
✖	6	54	✰	P	80
✗	7	55	✱	Q	81
✘	8	56	✲	R	82
✙	9	57	✳	S	83

Dingbat	Key Combo Mac/Win	ASCII		Dingbat	Key Combo Mac	Key Combo Win
✳	T	84		▼	t	116
✳	U	85		◆	u	117
✳	V	86		❖	v	118
✳	W	87		❭	w	119
✳	X	88		❙	x	120
✳	Y	89		❙	y	121
❋	Z	90		❚	z	122
✲	[	91		❛	{	123
✳	\	92		❜	|	124
✴	]	93		❝	}	125
✿	^ (Shift-6)	94		❞	~	126
❀	_ (Shift--)	95		❨	Opt-U Shift-A	Alt+0128
❁	`	96		❩	Opt-Shift-A	Alt+0129
❂	a	97		❪	Opt-Shift-C	Alt+0130
❁	b	98		❫	Opt-E Shift-E	Alt+0131
✳	c	99		❴	Opt-N Shift-N	Alt+0132
❄	d	100		❵	Opt-U Shift-O	Alt+0133
❅	e	101		❬	Opt-U Shift-U	Alt+0134
❆	f	102		❭	Opt-E, A	Alt+0135
✳	g	103		❮	Opt-`, A	Alt+0136
✳	h	104		❯	Opt-I, A	Alt+0137
✲	i	105		❲	Opt-U, A	Alt+0138
✳	j	106		❳	Opt-N, A	Alt+0139
✳	k	107		❴	Opt-A	Alt+0140
●	l	108		❵	Opt-C	Alt+0141
○	m	109		♣	Opt-Shift-8	Alt+0161
■	n	110		❦	Opt-4	Alt+0162
❑	o	111		❧	Opt-3	Alt+0163
❒	p	112		♥	Opt-6	Alt+0164
❑	q	113		❡	Opt-8	Alt+0165
❐	r	114		❢	Opt-7	Alt+0166
▲	s	115		❦	Opt-S	Alt+0167

Dingbat	Key Combo Mac	Key Combo Win	Dingbat	Key Combo Mac	Key Combo Win
♣	Opt-R	Alt+0168	⑨	Opt-Shift-\	Alt+0200
♦	Opt-G	Alt+0169	⑩	Opt-;	Alt+0201
♥	Opt-2	Alt+0170	❶	Opt-space	Alt+0202
♠	Opt-E	Alt+0171	❷	Opt-`, Shift-A	Alt+0203
①	Opt-U	Alt+0172	❸	Opt-N, Shift-A	Alt+0204
②	Opt-=	Alt+0173	❹	Opt-N, Shift-O	Alt+0205
③	Opt-Shift-'	Alt+0174	❺	Opt-Shift-Q	Alt+0206
④	Opt-Shift-O	Alt+0175	❻	Opt-Q	Alt+0207
⑤	Opt-5	Alt+0176	❼	Opt-hyphen	Alt+0208
⑥	Opt-Shift-=	Alt+0177	❽	Opt-Shift-hyphen	Alt+0209
⑦	Opt-,	Alt+0178	❾	Opt-[	Alt+0210
⑧	Opt-.	Alt+0179	❿	Opt-Shift-[	Alt+0211
⑨	Opt-Y	Alt+0180	→	Opt-]	Alt+0212
⑩	Opt-M	Alt+0181	→	Opt-Shift-]	Alt+0213
❶	Opt-D	Alt+0182	↔	Opt-/	Alt+0214
❷	Opt-W	Alt+0183	↕	Opt-Shift-V	Alt+0215
❸	Opt-Shift-P	Alt+0184	↘	Opt-u, Y	Alt+0216
❹	Opt-P	Alt+0185	→	Opt-U, Shift-Y	Alt+0217
❺	Opt-B	Alt+0186	↗	Opt-Shift-1	Alt+0218
❻	Opt-9	Alt+0187	→	Opt-Shift-2	Alt+0219
❼	Opt-0	Alt+0188	→	Opt-Shift-3	Alt+0220
❽	Opt-Z	Alt+0189	→	Opt-Shift-4	Alt+0221
❾	Opt-'	Alt+0190	→	Opt-Shift-5	Alt+0222
❿	Opt-O	Alt+0191	→	Opt-Shift-6	Alt+0223
①	Opt-Shift-/	Alt+0192	→	Opt-Shift-7	Alt+0224
②	Opt-1	Alt+0193	→	Opt-Shift-9	Alt+0225
③	Opt-L	Alt+0194	➤	Opt-Shift-0	Alt+0226
④	Opt-V	Alt+0195	➤	Opt-Shift-W	Alt+0227
⑤	Opt-F	Alt+0196	➤	Opt-Shift-R	Alt+0228
⑥	Opt-X	Alt+0197	➡	Opt-I, Shift-A	Alt+0229
⑦	Opt-J	Alt+0198	➡	Opt-I, Shift-E	Alt+0230
⑧	Opt-\	Alt+0199	➧	Opt-E, Shift-A	Alt+0231

Zapf Dingbats

Dingbat	Key Combo Mac	Key Combo Win
➡	Opt-U, Shift-E	Alt+0232
⇨	Opt-`, Shift-E	Alt+0233
⇩	Opt-E, Shift-I	Alt+0234
⇦	Opt-I, Shift-I	Alt+0235
⇨	Opt-U, Shift-I	Alt+0236
⇩	Opt-`, Shift-I	Alt+0237
⇨	Opt-E, Shift-O	Alt+0238
⇨	Opt-I, Shift-O	Alt+0239
[not used]	Opt-Shift-K	Alt+0240
⇨	Opt-`, Shift-O	Alt+0241
⟳	Opt-E, Shift-U	Alt+0242
⟫⟶	Opt-I, Shift-U	Alt+0243

Dingbat	Key Combo Mac	Key Combo Win
↘	Opt-`, Shift-U	Alt+0244
➤	Opt-Shift-B	Alt+0245
➚	Opt-I, space	Alt+0246
↖	Opt-N, space	Alt+0247
➤	Opt-Shift-,	Alt+0248
➴	Opt-Shift-.	Alt+0249
→	Opt-H	Alt+0250
↔	Opt-K	Alt+0251
➤	Opt-Shift-Z	Alt+0252
➤	Opt-Shift-G	Alt+0253
⇒	Opt-Shift-X	Alt+0254

Special Characters: Mac OS X *(not font specific)*

Character	Key Combo	ASCII Code
Ä	Opt-U, Shift-A	0128
Å	Opt-Shift-A	0129
Ç	Opt-Shift-C	0130
É	Opt-E, Shift-E	0131
Ñ	Opt-N, Shift-N	0132
Ö	Opt-U, Shift-O	0133
Ü	Opt-U, Shift-U	0134
á	Opt-E, A	0135
à	Opt-`, A	0136
â	Opt-i, A	0137
ä	Opt-U, A	0138
ã	Opt-N, A	0139
å	Opt-A	0140
ç	Opt-C	0141
é	Opt-E, E	0142
è	Opt-`, E	0143

Character	Key Combo	ASCII Code
ê	Opt-I, E	0144
ë	Opt-U, E	0145
í	Opt-E, I	0146
ì	Opt-`, I	0147
î	Opt-I, I	0148
ï	Opt-U, I	0149
ñ	Opt-N, N	0150
ó	Opt-E, O	0151
ò	Opt`, O	0152
ô	Opt-I, O	0153
ö	Opt-U, O	0154
õ	Opt-N, O	0155
ú	Opt-E, U	0156
ù	Opt`, U	0157
û	Opt-I, U	0158

Special Characters: Mac OS X

Character	Key Combo	ASCII Code		Character	Key Combo	ASCII Code
ü	Opt-U, U	0159		Ω	Opt-Z	0189
†	Opt-T	0160		æ	Opt-'	0190
°	Opt-Shift-8	0161		ø	Opt-O	0191
¢	Opt-4	0162		¿	Opt-Shift-/	0192
£	Opt-3	0163		¡	Opt-1	0193
§	Opt-6	0164		¬	Opt-L	0194
•	Opt-8	0165		√	Opt-V	0195
¶	Opt-7	0166		ƒ	Opt-F	0196
ß	Opt-S	0167		≈	Opt-X	0197
®	Opt-R	0168		Δ	Opt-J	0198
©	Opt-G	0169		«	Opt-\	0199
™	Opt-2	0170		»	Opt-Shift-\	0200
´	Opt-E, space	0171		…	Opt-;	0201
¨	Opt-U, space	0172		non-brk space	Opt-space	0202
≠	Opt-=	0173		À	Opt-`, Shift-A	0203
Æ	Opt-Shift-'	0174		_	Opt-N, Shift-A	0204
Ø	Opt-Shift-O	0175		Õ	Opt-N, Shift-O	0205
∞	Opt-5	0176		Œ	Opt-Shift-Q	0206
±	Opt-Shift-=	0177		œ	Opt-Q	0207
≤	Opt-,	0178		–	Opt-hyphen	0208
≥	Opt-.	0179		—	Opt-Shift-hyphen	0209
¥	Opt-Y	0180		"	Opt-[	0210
µ	Opt-M	0181		"	Opt-Shift-[	0211
∂	Opt-D	0182		'	Opt-]	0212
Σ	Opt-W	0183		'	Opt-Shift-]	0213
Π	Opt-Shift-P	0184		÷	Opt-/	0214
π	Opt-P	0185		◊	Opt-Shift-V	0215
∫	Opt-B	0186		ÿ	Opt-u, Y	0216
ª	Opt-9	0187		Ÿ	Opt-U, Shift-Y	0217
º	Opt-0	0188		⁄	Opt-Shift-1	0218

Special Characters: Mac OS X

Character	Key Combo	ASCII Code	Character	Key Combo	ASCII Code
€	Opt-Shift-2	0219	Ó	Opt-E, Shift-O	0238
‹	Opt-Shift-3	0220	Ô	Opt-I, Shift-O	0239
›	Opt-Shift-4	0221		Opt-Shift-K	0240
fi	Opt-Shift-5	0222	Ò	Opt-`, Shift-O	0241
fl	Opt-Shift-6	0223	Ú	Opt-E, Shift-U	0242
‡	Opt-Shift-7	0224	Û	Opt-I, Shift-U	0243
·	Opt-Shift-9	0225	Ù	Opt-`, Shift-U	0244
‚	Opt-Shift-0*	0226	ı	Opt-Shift-B	0245
„	Opt-Shift-W	0227	^	Opt-I, space	0246
‰	Opt-Shift-R	0228	~	Opt-N, space	0247
Â	Opt-I, Shift-A	0229	¯	Opt-Shift-,	0248
Ê	Opt-I, Shift-E	0230	˘	Opt-Shift-.	0249
Á	Opt-E, Shift-A	0231	·	Opt-H	0250
Ë	Opt-U, Shift-E	0232	°	Opt-K	0251
È	Opt-`, Shift-E	0233	¸	Opt-Shift-Z	0252
Í	Opt-E, Shift-I	0234	˝	Opt-Shift-G	0253
Î	Opt-I, Shift-I	0235	˛	Opt-Shift-X	0254
Ï	Opt-U, Shift-I	0236	ˇ	Opt-Shift-T	0255
Ì	Opt-`, Shift-I	0237			

Special Characters: Windows *(not font specific)*

Character	Key Combo (Alt+ANSI code)	Character	Key Combo (Alt+ANSI code)
€	Alt+0128	[*not used*]	Alt+0160
[*not used*]	Alt+0129	¡	Alt+0161
‚	Alt+0130	¢	Alt+0162
ƒ	Alt+0131	£	Alt+0163
„	Alt+0132	¤	Alt+0164
…	Alt+0133	¥	Alt+0165
†	Alt+0134	¦	Alt+0166
‡	Alt+0135	§	Alt+0167
ˆ	Alt+0136	¨	Alt+0168
‰	Alt+0137	©	Alt+0169
Š	Alt+0138	ª	Alt+0170
‹	Alt+0139	«	Alt+0171
Œ	Alt+0140	¬	Alt+0172
[*not used*]	Alt+0141	-	Alt+0173
Ž	Alt+0142	®	Alt+0174
[*not used*]	Alt+0143	¯	Alt+0175
[*not used*]	Alt+0144	°	Alt+0176
'	Alt+0145	±	Alt+0177
'	Alt+0146	²	Alt+0178
"	Alt+0147	³	Alt+0179
"	Alt+0148	´	Alt+0180
•	Alt+0149	µ	Alt+0181
–	Alt+0150	¶	Alt+0182
—	Alt+0151	·	Alt+0183
˜	Alt+0152	¸	Alt+0184
™	Alt+0153	¹	Alt+0185
š	Alt+0154	º	Alt+0186
›	Alt+0155	»	Alt+0187
œ	Alt+0156	¼	Alt+0188
[*not used*]	Alt+0157	½	Alt+0189
ž	Alt+0158	¾	Alt+0190
Ÿ	Alt+0159	¿	Alt+0191

Special Characters: Windows

Character	Key Combo (Alt+ANSI code)	Character	Key Combo (Alt+ANSI code)
À	Alt+0192	à	Alt+0224
Á	Alt+0193	á	Alt+0225
Â	Alt+0194	â	Alt+0226
Ã	Alt+0195	ã	Alt+0227
Ä	Alt+0196	ä	Alt+0228
Å	Alt+0197	å	Alt+0229
Æ	Alt+0198	æ	Alt+0230
Ç	Alt+0199	ç	Alt+0231
È	Alt+0200	è	Alt+0232
É	Alt+0201	é	Alt+0233
Ê	Alt+0202	ê	Alt+0234
Ë	Alt+0203	ë	Alt+0235
Ì	Alt+0204	ì	Alt+0236
Í	Alt+0205	í	Alt+0237
Î	Alt+0206	î	Alt+0238
Ï	Alt+0207	ï	Alt+0239
Ð	Alt+0208	ð	Alt+0240
Ñ	Alt+0209	ñ	Alt+0241
Ò	Alt+0210	ò	Alt+0242
Ó	Alt+0211	ó	Alt+0243
Ô	Alt+0212	ô	Alt+0244
Õ	Alt+0213	õ	Alt+0245
Ö	Alt+0214	ö	Alt+0246
×	Alt+0215	÷	Alt+0247
Ø	Alt+0216	ø	Alt+0248
Ù	Alt+0217	ù	Alt+0249
Ú	Alt+0218	ú	Alt+0250
Û	Alt+0219	û	Alt+0251
Ü	Alt+0220	ü	Alt+0252
Ý	Alt+0221	ý	Alt+0253
Þ	Alt+0222	þ	Alt+0254
ß	Alt+0223	ÿ	Alt+0255

Keyboard Shortcuts B

	Mac OS X	**Windows**
Show/hide palettes		
Tools	F8	F8
Measurements	F9	F9
Display Measurements palette and highlight first field (item selected)	Cmd-Option-M	Ctrl+Alt+M
Page Layout	F10	F4
Style Sheets	F11	F11
Colors	F12	F12
Find/Change	Cmd-F	Ctrl+F
Trap Information	Option-F12	Ctrl+F12
Lists	Option-F11	Ctrl+F11
Index	Cmd-Option-I	Ctrl+Alt+I
Dialog boxes		
OK (or heavy bordered button)	Return *or* Enter	Enter
Display next pane	Cmd-Option-Tab	Ctrl+Tab
Display previous pane	Cmd-Option-Shift-Tab	Ctrl+Shift+Tab
Cancel	Cmd-. (period) *or* Esc	Esc
Apply *(Mac OS X only)*	Cmd-A	
Yes	Cmd-Y	Y
No	Cmd-N	N
Highlight field	Double-click	Double-click
Select consecutive items on list	Shift-click	Shift+click
Select nonconsecutive items on list	Cmd-click	Ctrl+click
Dialog boxes and palettes		
Highlight next field	Tab	Tab
Highlight previous field	Shift-Tab	Shift+Tab
Add	+	+
Subtract	-	-
Multiply	*	*
Divide	/	/
Revert to original values	Cmd-Z or F1	Ctrl+Shift+Z

	Mac OS X	**Windows**
Tools palette		
Select next tool	Cmd-Option-Tab	Ctrl+Alt+Tab
Select previous tool	Cmd-Option-Shift-Tab	Ctrl+Alt+Shift+Tab
Item tool/Content tool toggle	Shift-F8	Shift+F8
Turn Content tool into temporary Item tool	Cmd	Ctrl
Keep a tool selected	Option-click tool	Alt+click tool
Clipboard		
Cut	Cmd-X *or* F2	Ctrl+X
Copy	Cmd-C *or* F3	Ctrl+C
Paste	Cmd-V *or* F4	Ctrl+V
Paste in place	Cmd-Option-Shift-V	Ctrl+Alt+Shift+V
Whole project		
New Project dialog box	Cmd-N	Ctrl+N
New Library dialog box	Cmd-Option-N	Ctrl+Alt+N
Open dialog box	Cmd-O	Ctrl+O
Save	Cmd-S	Ctrl+S
Save As dialog box	Cmd-Option-S	Ctrl+Alt+S
Quit/Exit	Cmd-Q	Ctrl+Q or Alt+F4
Append	Cmd-Option-A	Ctrl+Alt+A
Revert to last Auto Save	Option-Revert to Saved	Alt+Revert to Saved
Close active project	Cmd-W	Ctrl+F4
Mac OS X only:		
Close all open QuarkXPress files	Cmd-Option-W *or* Option-click Close button	
Hide QuarkXPress	Cmd-H	
Hide Others	Cmd-Option-H	
Undo/Redo		
Undo	Cmd-Z *or* F1	Ctrl+Z
Redo *(see page 414)*	Cmd-Shift-Z	Alt+Shift+Z
Display		
Fit in Window	Cmd-0 (zero) *or* Ctrl-click > Fit in Window	Ctrl+0 (zero) *or* Right-click > Fit in Window
Fit pasteboard in project window	Option-choose Fit in Window *or* Cmd-Option-0	Alt+Fit choose in Window *or* Ctrl+Alt+0 (zero)
Actual Size	Cmd-1 *or* Ctrl-click > Actual Size	Ctrl+1 *or* Right-click > Actual Size

	Mac OS X	**Windows**
Zoom in	Control-Shift-click* *or* drag *or* Cmd- + (plus)**	Ctrl+Space bar click *or* drag
Zoom out	Control-Option-click *or* Cmd- – (minus)**	Ctrl+Alt+Space bar click
Highlight view percent field	Control V	Ctrl+Alt+V
Thumbnails	Shift-F6 *or* enter "T" in View Percent field (press Return)	Shift F6 *or* enter "T" in View Percent field (press Enter)
Change to 200%, then toggle between 100% and 200%	Cmd-Option-click	Ctrl+Alt+click
Stop redraw	Cmd-. (period)	Esc
Force redraw	Cmd-Option-. (period)	Shift+Esc
Show/hide Baseline Grid	Option-F7	Ctrl+F7

*If Control Key Activates: Zoom is chosen in Preferences > Interactive, omit Shift

*For Cmd- + or Cmd- –, if Content tool is chosen, deselect all items first

Rulers and guides

Show/hide Guides	F7	F7
Snap to Guides (toggle)	Shift-F7	Shift+F7
Show/hide Rulers	Cmd-R	Ctrl+R
Delete all horizontal ruler guides from page *(no pasteboard showing)*	Option-click horizontal ruler	Alt+click horizontal ruler
Delete all vertical ruler guides from page *(no pasteboard showing)*	Option-click vertical ruler	Alt+click vertical ruler

Project windows

Stack or tile/cascade or tile project windows	Shift-click project title bar and choose Stack or Tile	Window > Cascade, *or* Tile Horizontally, *or* Tile Vertically (no shortcut)
Maximize project window	Click zoom button	F3
Activate open project window *(Mac OS X only)*	Shift-click project window title bar and choose file name from pop-up menu	
Stack or tile/cascade or tile to Actual Size	(Hold Control) Window > Stack/Tile†	(Hold Ctrl+Alt) Window > Cascade/Tile
Stack or tile/cascade or tile to Fit in Window	(Hold Cmd) Window > Stack/Tile†	(Hold Ctrl) Window > Cascade/Tile
Stack or tile/cascade or tile to Thumbnails	(Hold Option) Window > Stack/Tile†	(Hold Alt) Window > Cascade/Tile

†Or add Shift to shortcut, click project window title bar, and choose command from pop-up menu

	Mac OS X	**Windows**
Navigate in a layout		
Go To Page dialog box	Cmd-J	Ctrl+J
Start of layout/story	Control A *or* Home	Ctrl+Home
End of layout/story	Control D *or* End	Ctrl+End
Up one screen	Control K *or* Page Up	Page Up
Down one screen	Control L *or* Page Down	Page Down
To first page	Control Shift-A *or* Shift-Home	Ctrl+Page Up
To last page	Shift-End	Ctrl+Page Down
To previous page	Shift-Page Up	Shift+Page Up
To next page	Shift-Page Down	Shift+Page Down
To previous even or odd page	Option-Page Up	Alt+Page Up
To next even or odd page	Option-Page Down	Alt+Page Down
Page Grabber Hand (any tool except Zoom)	Option-drag	Alt+drag
Toggle master/layout page display	Shift-F10	Shift+F4
Display next master page	Option-F10	Ctrl+Shift+F4
Display previous master page	Option-Shift-F10	Ctrl+Shift+F3
Enable Live Scroll if off in Preferences > Interactive, or disable if on	Option-drag scroll box	Alt+drag scroll box
Items		
Modify dialog box	Cmd-M *or* double-click item with Item tool	Ctrl+M *or* double-click item with Item tool
Modify dialog box, Frame pane	Cmd-B	Ctrl+B
Lock/Unlock	F6	F6
Delete item	Cmd-K	Ctrl+K
Constrain rotation to increment of 45° with Rotation tool	Shift while rotating	Shift while rotating
Move item (Content tool)	Cmd-drag	Ctrl+drag
Nudge item 1 point	Arrow keys	Arrow keys
Nudge item ⅒ point	Option-arrow keys	Alt+Arrow keys
Constrain movement to horizontal/ vertical (Item tool)	Shift-drag	Shift+drag
Constrain movement to horizontal/ vertical (Content tool)	Cmd-Shift-drag	Ctrl+Shift+drag

	Mac OS X	**Windows**
Multiple items		
Select All (Item tool)	Cmd-A	Ctrl+A
Select multiple items (Item tool)	Shift-click *or* marquee	Shift+click *or* marquee
Group	Cmd-G	Ctrl+G
Move item in a group (Content tool)	Cmd-drag	Ctrl+drag
Resize group proportionally	Cmd-Option-Shift drag handle	Ctrl+Alt-Shift+drag handle
Ungroup	Cmd-U	Ctrl+U
Duplicate	Cmd-D	Ctrl+D
Step and Repeat dialog box	Cmd-Option-D	Ctrl+Alt+D
Select behind other items	Cmd-Option-Shift-click	Ctrl+Alt+Shift+click
Bring to Front	F5	F5
Send to Back	Shift-F5	Shift+F5
Bring Forward one level	Option-Item menu > Bring Forward *or* Option-F5	Ctrl+F5
Send Backward one level	Option-Item menu > Send Backward *or* Option-Shift-F5	Ctrl+Shift+F5
Space/Align dialog box (multiple items selected)	Cmd-, (comma)	Ctrl+, (comma)
Select text		
Show/Hide Invisibles	Cmd-I	Ctrl+I
One word (no punctuation mark)	Double-click	Double-click
One word (with punctuation mark)	Double-click between word and punctuation	Double-click between word and punctuation
One line	Triple-click	Triple-click
One paragraph	Click four times quickly	Click four times quickly
Entire story (Content tool)	Click five times quickly *or* Cmd-A	Click five times quickly *or* Ctrl+A

With cursor in text (keep pressing arrow to extend the selection):

	Mac OS X	**Windows**
Previous character	Shift-left arrow	Shift+left arrow
Next character	Shift-right arrow	Shift+right arrow
Previous line	Shift-up arrow	Shift+up arrow
Next line	Shift-down arrow	Shift+down arrow
Previous word	Cmd-Shift-left arrow	Ctrl+Shift+left arrow
Next word	Cmd-Shift-right arrow	Ctrl+Shift+right arrow

From the text insertion point to:

	Mac OS X	**Windows**
Start of paragraph	Cmd-Shift-up arrow	Ctrl+Shift+up arrow
End of paragraph	Cmd-Shift-down arrow	Ctrl+Shift+down arrow

	Mac OS X	**Windows**
Start of line	Cmd-Option-Shift-left arrow	Ctrl+Alt+Shift+left arrow *or* Shift+Home
End of line	Cmd-Option-Shift-right arrow	Ctrl+Alt+Shift+right arrow *or* Shift+End
Start of story	Cmd-Option-Shift-up arrow	Ctrl+Alt+Shift+up arrow *or* Ctrl+Shift+Home
End of story	Cmd-Option-Shift-down arrow	Ctrl+Alt+Shift+down arrow *or* Ctrl+Shift+End

Move the text insertion point

Character-by-character	Left and right arrows	Left and right arrows
Line-by-line	Up and down arrows	Up and down arrows
Word-by-word	Cmd-left and right arrows	Ctrl+left and right arrows
Paragraph-by-paragraph	Cmd-up and down arrows	Ctrl+up and down arrows
Start of line	Cmd-Option-left arrow	Ctrl+Alt+left arrow *or* Home
End of line	Cmd-Option-right arrow	Ctrl+Alt+right arrow *or* End
Start of story	Cmd-Option-up arrow	Ctrl+Alt+up arrow *or* Ctrl+Home
End of story	Cmd-Option-down arrow	Ctrl+Alt+down arrow Ctrl+End

Drag and drop text

Drag-move*	Drag	Drag
Drag-copy* (Drag and Drop Text on in Preferences > Interactive)	Shift-drag	Shift+drag

If Drag and Drop Text is off in Preferences > Interactive, press Cmd-Control to move, or press Cmd-Ctrl-Shift-drag to move a copy

Delete text

Previous character	Delete	Backspace
Next character	Shift-Delete *or* Del key	Delete or Shift+Backspace
Previous word	Cmd Delete	Ctrl+Backspace
Next word	Cmd-Shift-Delete	Ctrl+Delete *or* Ctrl+Shift+Backspace
Selected characters	Delete	Backspace

Resize text

Open Character Attributes dialog box, Size field highlighted	Cmd-Shift-\	Ctrl+Shift+\
Increase size to preset size	Cmd-Shift->	Ctrl+Shift+>
Increase size by 1 point	Cmd-Option-Shift->	Ctrl+Alt+Shift+>
Decrease size to preset size	Cmd-Shift-<	Ctrl+Shift+<

	Mac OS X	**Windows**
Decrease size by 1 point	Cmd-Option-Shift-<	Ctrl+Alt+Shift+<
Resize text and box*	Cmd-drag handle	Ctrl+drag handle
Resize text and box proportionally*	Cmd-Option-Shift-drag handle	Ctrl+Alt+Shift+drag handle

Works on nonlinked text items only. For type on a path, turn off Item > Edit > Shape.

Text flow

Get text dialog box (Content tool)	Cmd-E	Ctrl+E
Current page number (use on master page or layout page)	Cmd-3	Ctrl+3
Previous text box page number	Cmd-2	Ctrl+2
Next text box page number	Cmd-4	Ctrl+4
Next column	Enter	Keypad Enter
Next box	Shift-Enter	Shift+Keypad Enter
Save Text	Cmd-Option-E	Ctrl+Alt+E
Open Insert Pages dialog box	Option-drag master page into layout page area	Alt+drag master page into layout page area
Delete selected page icons on Page Layout palette, bypass prompt	Option-click Delete button	Alt+click Delete button
Apply master page	Select layout page icon(s), then Option-click master page icon	Select layout page icon(s), then Alt+click master page icon

Paragraph formats

Paragraph Attributes dialog box, Formats pane	Cmd-Shift-F	Ctrl+Shift+F
Paragraph Attributes dialog box, Leading field	Cmd-Shift-E	Ctrl+Shift+E
Paragraph Attributes dialog box, Tabs pane	Cmd-Shift-T	Ctrl+Shift+T
Paragraph Attributes dialog box, Rules pane	Cmd-Shift-N	Ctrl+Shift+N
Increase leading 1 point	Cmd-Shift-"	Ctrl+Shift+"
Decrease leading 1 point	Cmd-Shift-:	Ctrl+Shift+:
Increase leading $\frac{1}{10}$ point	Cmd-Option-Shift-"	Ctrl+Alt+Shift+"
Decrease leading $\frac{1}{10}$ point	Cmd-Option-Shift-:	Ctrl+Alt+Shift+:
Delete all tab stops	Option-click tabs ruler	Alt+click tabs ruler
Right indent tab	Option-Tab (in text box)	Shift+Tab
Display Suggested Hyphenation	Cmd-Option-Shift-H	Ctrl+Alt+Shift+H
Set button in Tabs pane in Paragraph Attributes dialog box	Cmd-S	Alt+S

	Mac OS X	**Windows**
Open H&Js dialog box	Cmd-Option-J *or* Option-Shift-F11	Ctrl+Alt+J *or* Ctrl+Shift+F11
Copy formats from one paragraph to another in the same story	Select paragraph to be formatted, then Option-Shift-click in source paragraph	Select paragraph to be formatted, then Alt+Shift+click in source paragraph

Fonts

Display measurements palette and highlight font field	Cmd-Option-Shift-M	Ctrl+Alt+Shift+M
Display measurements palette and insert cursor in font field	Shift-F9	Shift+F9
Select next font	Highlight text, then Option-F9	Highlight text, then Ctrl+F9
Select previous font	Highlight text, then Option-Shift-F9	Highlight text, then Ctrl+Shift+F9
Insert one Zapf Dingbats character*	Cmd-Option-Z, then type character	Ctrl+Shift+Z, then type character
Insert one Symbol character	Cmd-Option-Q, then type character	Ctrl+Shift+Q, then type character

*For this keyboard shortcut to work, in Preferences > Application > Undo, the Redo Key setting must be Cmd-Shift-Z/Ctrl-Shift-Z.

Baseline shift

Baseline Shift-upward 1 point	Cmd-Option-Shift-+ (plus)	Ctrl+Alt+Shift+)
Baseline Shift-downward 1 point	Cmd-Option-Shift-– (minus)	Ctrl+Alt+Shift+(

Style text

Character Attributes dialog box	Cmd-Shift-D	Ctrl+Shift+D

Text style toggles:

Plain text	Cmd-Shift-P	Ctrl+Shift+P
Bold	Cmd-Shift-B	Ctrl+Shift+B
Italic	Cmd-Shift-I	Ctrl+Shift+I
Underline	Cmd-Shift-U	Ctrl+Shift+U
Word Underline	Cmd-Shift-W	Ctrl+Shift+W
Outline	Cmd-Shift-O	Ctrl+Shift+O
Shadow	Cmd-Shift-S	Ctrl+Shift+S
All Caps	Cmd-Shift-K	Ctrl+Shift+K
Small Caps	Cmd-Shift-H	Ctrl+Shift+H
Strike Thru	Cmd-Shift-/	Ctrl+Shift+/
Superscript	Cmd-Shift-+ (plus)	Ctrl+Shift+0 (zero)

	Mac OS X	**Windows**
Subscript	Cmd-Shift- – (minus)	Ctrl+Shift+9
Superior	Cmd-Shift-V	Ctrl+Shift+V

Horizontal alignment of text

Left alignment	Cmd-Shift-L	Ctrl+Shift+L
Right alignment	Cmd-Shift-R	Ctrl+Shift+R
Center alignment	Cmd-Shift-C	Ctrl+Shift+C
Justified alignment	Cmd-Shift-J	Ctrl+Shift+J
Forced justify	Cmd-Option-Shift-J	Ctrl+Alt+Shift+J

Tracking and kerning

Increase Kerning/Tracking 10 units	Cmd-Shift-]	Ctrl+Shift+]
Decrease Kerning/Tracking 10 units	Cmd-Shift-[	Ctrl+Shift+[
Increase Kerning/Tracking 1 unit	Cmd-Option-Shift-]	Ctrl+Alt+Shift+]
Decrease Kerning/Tracking 1 unit	Cmd-Option-Shift-[	Ctrl+Alt+Shift+[

Horizontal/vertical type scale

Decrease scale 5%	Cmd-[	Ctrl+2
Increase scale 5%	Cmd-]	Ctrl+1
Decrease scale 1%	Cmd-Option-[	Ctrl+Alt+2
Increase scale 1%	Cmd-Option-]	Ctrl+Alt+1

Word space tracking

Increase Word Space 10 units	Cmd-Shift-Control]	Ctrl+Shift+2
Decrease Word Space 10 units	Cmd-Shift-Control [	Ctrl+Shift+1
Increase Word Space 1 unit	Cmd-Option-Shift-Control]	Ctrl+Alt+Shift+2
Decrease Word Space 1 unit	Cmd-Option-Shift-Control [	Ctrl+Alt+Shift+1

Special text characters

New paragraph	Return	Enter
New line	Shift-Return	Shift+Enter
Indent here	Cmd-\	Ctrl+\
Discretionary new line	Cmd-Return	Ctrl+Enter
Discretionary hyphen	Cmd-- (hyphen)	Ctrl+- (hyphen)
Nonbreaking standard hyphen	Cmd-=	Ctrl+=
Nonbreaking standard space	Cmd-Space bar *or* Cmd-5	Ctrl+5
Breaking en space	Option-Space bar	Ctrl+Shift+6
Nonbreaking en space	Cmd-Option-Space bar *or* Cmd-Option-5	Ctrl+Alt+Shift+6
Breaking flex space	Option-Shift-Space bar	Ctrl+Shift+5
Nonbreaking flex space	Cmd-Option-Shift-Space bar	Ctrl+Alt+Shift+5
Nonbreaking en dash	Option-- (hyphen)	Ctrl+Alt+Shift+- (hyphen)

	Mac OS X	**Windows**
Break at discretionary hyphen only	Cmd-- (hyphen) before first character in word	Ctrl+-(hyphen) before first character in word
Nonbreaking em dash	Cmd-Option-=	Ctrl+Alt+Shift+=
Breaking em dash	Option-Shift-- (hyphen)	Ctrl+Shift+=
Breaking punctuation space	Shift-Space bar	Shift+Space
Nonbreaking punctuation space	Cmd-Shift-Space bar	Ctrl+Shift+Space

For quotation marks, see page 130

Resize tables

Resize table, rows, and columns (not content) proportionally	Option-Shift-drag	Alt+Shift+drag
Resize table, rows, columns, and content non-proportionally	Cmd-drag	Ctrl+drag
Resize table to a square; content doesn't resize	Shift-drag	Shift+drag
Resize table, rows, columns, and content proportionally	Cmd-Option-Shift-drag	Ctrl+Alt+Shift+drag
Resize table, rows, and columns (not content) non-proportionally	No modifier keys	

Jump between table cells *(non-linked cells only)*

Jump from one cell to the right or from the end of a row to the beginning of the next row	Control-Tab	Ctrl+Tab
Jump back to previous cell	Control-Shift-Tab	Ctrl+Shift+Tab
Jump one character at a time within a cell or from the end of one cell to the beginning of the next cell	Right arrow	Right arrow

Import a picture

Get Picture dialog box (Item or Content tool)	Cmd-E	Ctrl+E
Grayscale to black-and-white, or color to grayscale	Cmd-Open	Ctrl+Open

Pictures and picture boxes or Béziers

Center picture in box	Cmd-Shift-M	Ctrl+Shift+M
Move picture in box 1 point	Arrow keys (Content tool)	Arrow keys (Content tool)
Move picture in box ¹⁄₁₀ point	Option-arrow keys (Content tool)	Alt+arrow keys (Content tool)
Fit picture to box	Cmd-Shift-F	Ctrl+Shift+F
Fit picture to box (maintain aspect ratio)	Cmd-Option-Shift-F	Ctrl+Alt+Shift+F
Enlarge picture in 5% increments	Cmd-Option-Shift->	Ctrl+Alt+Shift+>

	Mac OS X	**Windows**
Reduce picture in 5% increments	Cmd-Option-Shift-<	Ctrl+Alt+Shift+<
Constrain item or bounding box to square or circle	Shift-drag	Shift+drag
Resize box proportionally	Option-Shift-drag	Alt+Shift+drag
Resize picture and box (Item > Edit > Shape off for Béziers)	Cmd-drag	Ctrl+drag
Resize picture and box (constrain proportions of box, not picture)	Cmd-Shift-drag	Ctrl+Shift+drag
Resize picture and box (maintain aspect ratio)	Cmd-Option-Shift-drag	Ctrl+Alt+Shift+drag

Picture styling *(grayscale)*

Picture Contrast dialog box	Cmd-Shift-C	Ctrl+Shift+C
Negative	Cmd-Shift--(hyphen)	Ctrl+Shift+- (hyphen)
Halftone (grayscale, line art only)	Cmd-Shift-H	Ctrl+Shift+H

Runaround/clipping

Modify dialog box, Runaround pane	Cmd-T	Ctrl+T
Edit runaround path (Non-White Areasor Picture Bounds Type)	Option-F4	Ctrl+F10
Modify dialog box, Clipping pane	Cmd-Option-T	Ctrl+Alt+T
Edit clipping path	Option-Shift-F4	Ctrl+Shift+F10

Lines

Increase width to preset size	Cmd-Shift->	Ctrl+Shift+>
Increase width by 1 point	Cmd-Option-Shift->	Ctrl+Alt+Shift+>
Decrease width to preset size	Cmd-Shift-<	Ctrl+Shift+<
Decrease width by 1 point	Cmd-Option-Shift-<	Ctrl+Alt+Shift+<
Line Width field, Modify dialog box	Cmd-Shift-\	Ctrl+Shift+\
Constrain angle to increment of 45°	Shift-drag	Shift+drag
Constrain to current angle	Option-Shift-drag	Alt+Shift+drag

Bézier box or line (or clipping path)

Item > Edit > Shape toggle on/off	Shift-F4	F10
Add a point*	Option-click line segment	Alt+click line segment
Delete a point*	Option-click point	Alt+click point
Constrain movement of line, point, or handle to increment of 45°*	Shift-drag	Shift+drag
Temporarily suspend text reflow	Space bar	Space bar
Retract one curve handle	Option-click handle	Alt+click handle

*With Edit > Shape checked

	Mac OS X	**Windows**
Retract both curve handles	Control-Shift-click point**	Ctrl+Shift+click point
Expose/create curve handle	Control-Shift-drag point**	Ctrl+Shift+drag point
Select all points in active item (combined items)	Cmd-Shift-A *or* triple-click point	Ctrl+Shift+A *or* triple-click point
Select all points in active item (single path)	Double-click point *or* Cmd-Shift-A	Ctrl+Shift+A *or* double-click point
Convert Bézier line to filled-center Bézier box	Option-Item menu > Shape > ⬭	Alt+item menu > Shape >

*If Zoom (instead of Contextual Menu) is the current Control Key Activates setting in Preferences > Application > Interactive, omit the Shift key.

As Bézier is being drawn

Move point or adjust handle	Cmd	Ctrl
Convert corner point to smooth point	Cmd-Option-Ctrl-drag from corner point	Ctrl+click, press Ctrl-F2, then drag from corner point
Convert smooth point to corner point	Cmd-Option-Ctrl-click smooth point	Ctrl+Alt+click smooth point
Retract one curve handle	Cmd-Option click curve handle	Ctrl+Alt+click curve handle
Delete selected Bézier point while drawing shape	Delete	Backspace

Convert Bézier point

To a corner point	Option-F1	Ctrl+F1
To a smooth point	Option-F2	Ctrl+F2
To a symmetrical point	Option-F3	Ctrl+F3
Corner to smooth	Cmd-Option-Ctrl-drag from point	Ctrl+Shift+drag from point
Smooth to corner	Cmd-Option-Ctrl-click point	Ctrl+Alt+Shift+click point

Convert Bézier segment

Curved to a straight segment	Option-Shift-F1	Ctrl+Shift+F1
Straight to a curved segment	Option-Shift-F2	Ctrl+Shift+F2

Style sheets

Open Style Sheets dialog box	Shift-F11	Shift+F11
Open Edit Style Sheet dialog box	Cmd-click style sheet with Content tool	Ctrl+click style sheet with Content tool
Display Edit Style Sheet menu	Ctrl-click style sheet name	Right+click style sheet name
Apply No Style, then style sheet	Option-click style name on Style Sheets palette	Alt+click style name on Style Sheets palette

Note: If an F key is chosen as a Keyboard Equivalent for a style sheet, it will override that F key's default command.

Keyboard Shortcuts

	Mac OS X	**Windows**
Color		
Open Colors dialog box	Cmd-click color on Colors palette *or* Shift-F12	Ctrl+click color on Color palette *or* Shift+F12
Apply color to multiple items via Colors palette	Select one item, then Cmd-drag swatch over each item	Select one item, then Ctrl+drag swatch over each item
Anchored boxes		
Text to box (anchor box and delete text)	Option-choose Style menu > Text to Box	Alt+choose Style menu > Text to Box
Check spelling		
Check Spelling > Word	Cmd-L	Ctrl+W
Check Spelling > Story	Cmd-Option-L	Ctrl+Alt+W
Check Spelling > Layout	Cmd-Option-Shift-L	Ctrl+Alt+Shift+W
In the Check Spelling dialog box:		
Lookup	Cmd-L	Alt+L
Skip	Cmd-S	Alt+S
Add current suspect word to open auxiliary dictionary	Cmd-A	Alt+A
Add all suspect words to current auxiliary dictionary	Option-Shift-click Done button	Alt+Shift+click Close button
Find/Change		
Find/Change palette	Cmd-F	Ctrl-F
Change Find Next button to Find First in Find/Change	Hold down Option	Hold down Alt
Close Find/Change palette	Cmd-Option-F	Ctrl+Alt+F
Wild card (Find what)	Cmd-?	Ctrl+?
Space	Space bar	Space bar
Tab	\t	\t *or* Ctrl+Tab
New paragraph	Cmd-Return *or* \p	Ctrl+Enter *or* \p
New line	Cmd-Shift-Return *or* \n	Ctrl+Shift+Enter *or* \n
New column	Cmd-Enter *or* \c	\c
New box	Cmd-Shift-Enter *or* \b	\b
Punctuation space	Cmd-. (period) *or* \.	Ctrl+. (period) *or* \.
Flex space	Cmd-Shift-F *or* \f	Ctrl+Shift+F *or* \f
Backslash	Cmd-\ *or* \\	Ctrl+\ *or* \\
Previous box page number character	Cmd-2 *or* \2	Ctrl+2 *or* \2
Current box page number character	Cmd-3 *or* \3	Ctrl+3 *or* \3
Next box page number character	Cmd-4 *or* \4	Ctrl+4 *or* \4

	Mac OS X	**Windows**
Utilities > Line Check command, jump to next instance	Cmd-;	Ctrl+;

Indexing

Add highlighted entry	Cmd-Option-Shift-I	Ctrl+Alt+Shift+I
Edit highlighted index entry *(Mac OS X only)*	Double-click	

Compare components

Compare two style sheets, colors, lists, H&Js, dashes & stripes, or print styles	Open dialog box from Edit menu, Cmd-click two components, then Option-click Append (Import button in Print Styles)	Open dialog box from Edit menu, Ctrl+click two components, then Alt+click Append (Import button in Print Styles)

Web

Page Properties dialog box *(Web layouts only)*	Cmd-Option-Shift-A	Ctrl+Alt+Shift+A
New XML dialog box	Cmd-Shift-X	Ctrl+Shift+X

Preferences

Preferences dialog box, last displayed pane	Cmd-Option-Shift-Y	Ctrl+Alt+Shift+Y
Preferences dialog box, Paragraph pane	Cmd-Option-Y	Ctrl+Alt+Y
Preferences dialog box, Trapping pane	Option-Shift-F12	Ctrl+Shift+F12
Preferences dialog box, Tools pane	Double-click item creation *or* Zoom tool	Double-click item creation *or* Zoom tool

Output

Print dialog box, Setup pane	Cmd-Option-P	Ctrl+Alt+P
Print	Cmd-P	Ctrl+P
Save Page as EPS	Cmd-Option-Shift-S	Ctrl+Alt+Shift+S
Usage dialog box, Font Usage	F13	F2
Usage dialog box, Picture Usage	Option-F13	

Index

Index

L

Index

Index